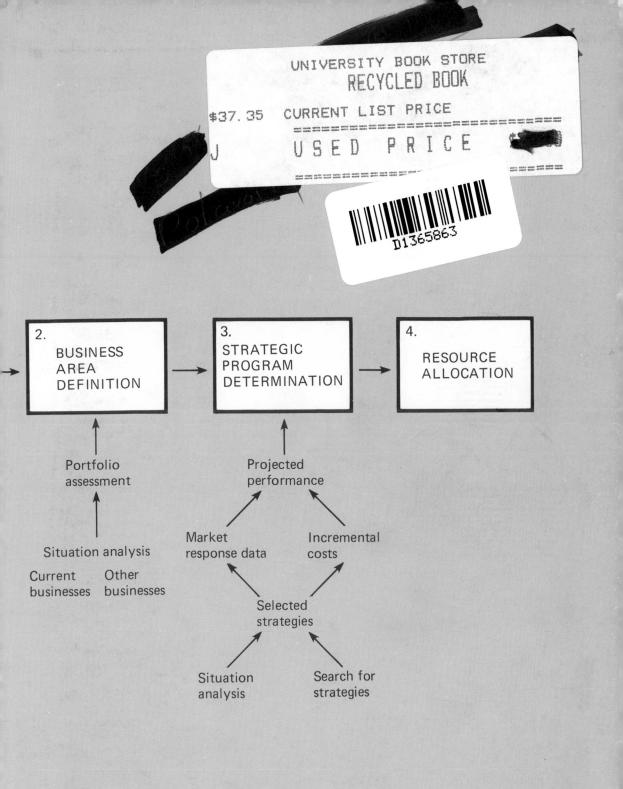

second edition

MARKETING STRATEGY AND PLANS

David J. Luck
University of Delaware

O. C. Ferrell
Texas A & M University

Prentice-Hall, Inc., Englewood Cliffs, New Jersey 07632

Library of Congress Cataloging in Publication Data

LUCK, DAVID JOHNSTON.
   Marketing strategy and plans.

   Bibliography: p.
   Includes index.
   1. Marketing–United States–Management.
2. Marketing–United States–Management–Case
studies. I. Ferrell, O. C. II. Title.
HF5415.13.L75 1985   658.8   84-18038
ISBN 0-13-558362-4

Editorial/production supervision and
  interior design: *Eve Mossman*
Cover design: *Diane Saxe*
Manufacturing buyer: *Ed O'Dougherty*

Printed in the United States of America

10 9 8 7 6 5 4 3 2 1

ISBN 0-13-558362-4 01

Prentice-Hall International, Inc., *London*
Prentice-Hall of Australia Pty. Limited, *Sydney*
Editora Prentice-Hall do Brasil, Ltda., *Rio de Janeiro*
Prentice-Hall Canada Inc., *Toronto*
Prentice-Hall Hispanoamericana, S.A., *Mexico*
Prentice-Hall of India Private Limited, *New Delhi*
Prentice-Hall of Japan, Inc., *Tokyo*
Prentice-Hall of Southeast Asia Pte. Ltd., *Singapore*
Whitehall Books Limited, *Wellington, New Zealand*

Contents

PART TWO *STRATEGIC DECISIONS AND THEIR INTEGRATION* *30*

Preface

In *Marketing Strategy and Plans* we have sought to write a textbook that will inform and attract a reader by its realism, its clear statement of principles and methods, and its enabling of reader participation. We trust that teachers will find it quite teachable and that its illustrations, charts, and cases are ample.

Our primary focus is a course that integrates marketing's functions and variables into a cohesive plan. At an undergraduate level this should be the last course in the marketing program. The student would minimally have had introductory courses in marketing and in management and also marketing research. There is no absolute dichotomy between graduate and undergraduate textbooks, in our view. Instead the criterion of choice is how fully a book converges with the teaching techniques of an adopter. For the purpose of utilizing this book in a graduate-level marketing management course, the three long cases located at the end of the book offer greater depth and complexity. Those cases are referenced after the briefer end-of-chapter cases, to indicate where they should be used.

The learning objectives in *Marketing Strategy and Plans* are stated early, and the structure is mentioned frequently to keep the reader oriented to the text's progress. For each phase of strategy making there is graphic explanation followed by real-world applications. The review questions following each chapter summary provide a self-test of comprehension of the major ideas presented in the chapter. The one to three cases after a chapter permit application. We have included fairly brief cases at that point to minimize disruption of the concepts' logical flow.

One device to instill some personal interest in strategic decisions is to introduce, at the outset, a young and actual marketing strategist. This individual and others surface at other times to personalize the text. Various industries and types of jobs are included in the text and cases.

The first chapter is a substantial one, in order to implant perspectives, key terms, and the basic decision model. We include there also an essential organization structure for making strategic decisions. That organization knowledge is expanded in Part II at the four levels of decision makers. The four chapters in that part provide a broad foundation of structure and models at those four levels—and between them. Part II also provides some tools, with analytical methods.

On that foundation, Part III considers the environmental variables that are vitally important in strategy choices. Then in Part IV we go to the creation of strategic programs in product/market units. We trace the changing strategic options over the cycle of product life and renewal. Our focus then narrows to the marketing elements, in chapters dealing with each of the traditional four functional areas. Then the whole strategy is integrated again by a chapter on the marketing plan (which has been written with some thought to guiding students assigned to write such a plan). Finally, implementation and control bring the subject matter full cycle.

Let us stress one caveat: There is no single method or model that is ideal for strategic decision making. Space restricts us to offering a single process in most stages of a strategy's development, but we hope that the readers will carry away no misconception that, in actual practice, these tasks must proceed "by the book" (i.e., *this* book). Most managers may be successful in using variants that they find more congenial. Also we should acknowledge what may be apparent: that we could not present every detail in the decision-making processes. That would be futile, even if space were no consideration, because the marvelous central idea in a strategy tends to occur in an intuitive flash that defies description. Students should be well aware of the importance of that art and encouraged to gain it as their marketing careers blossom.

Two current situations bode well for a marketing-strategy book: (1) in practice, business executives are very concerned with this subject; and (2) in academe, its courses are proliferating. The subject also is a young one, academically, so that novel approaches should be given full consideration. However, there are also some negative aspects that include (1) a current trend of corporations to shrink planning staffs (a trend related to depression impacts) and to place strategic decisions under the control of line managers, (2) the disenchantment with analytical methods that have been much in vogue, and (3) the amorphous state of management concepts that, in absence of consensus, are difficult to select for a textbook.

Given the pioneering stage of strategic writings, we earnestly hope that we have chosen our concepts and illustrative material wisely. And we hope that the reader will find that we have written them lucidly and will experience reading with some of the enjoyment that has been ours as authors.

David J. Luck

O. C. Ferrell

Acknowledgments

Authors must be aware of their dependence on the extant literature and the accumulated knowledge of their subject fields, particularly when writing textbooks. We are much indebted to a great many who have published their concepts and findings. They are identified largely in the footnotes citing their works.

Some fellow academicians have more directly contributed with suggestions and stimulating ideas, among whom are Robert Linneman, Richard Merner, and Pradeep Rau. Our debt is large to outside reviewers who were retained by the publisher, namely to Prof. John McDonald, Wayne State University; Prof. Forrest S. Carter, Michigan State University; Prof. R. Viswanathan, Southern Illinois University; Prof. Dipankar Chakravarti, University of Florida, Gainesville; and Prof. Edward T. Popper, Northeastern University. We want to thank a number of academicians who have contributed teaching cases that form important attractions of the book and who include: Thomas

Bertsch, Bruce Gunn, H. Michael Hayes, A. H. Kizilbash, Peter J. LaPlaca, Fred Miller, Phillip Niffeneger, and Lawrence Ring.

From the business world we have enjoyed the assistance of a number who are engaged in marketing and corporate planning activities. They probably cannot all be recalled, as the creation of this book extended over a number of years. We will specifically mention those who expended efforts to make our cases on their firms accurate and readable. The companies and individuals are: Abbott Laboratories (Thomas Craig), American Safety Razor Company (Joseph Mills), BIC Corporation (Leah Colihan), Continental Group (George Linkletter), and Gillette Company (Janice Marnell). We appreciate the insights that were given to us by George Johnston and William Rhyne in their planning system in Armstrong World Industries.

The support furnished at Prentice-Hall must be described as ideal, particularly on the part of Elizabeth Classon (editor-marketing) and of Eve Mossman (production editor). A remarkably thorough and intelligent copy editing by Marie Lines has greatly improved the manuscript. Notable improvements as well as skillful typing were contributed by Rita Beasley.

The book's virtues are partially attributable to the above, but any faults or errors have been our own. We will be grateful to readers who inform us about the latter.

1

Basic Concepts and Systems

Business management is undergoing drastic changes now in order to meet challenges from various directions. American businesses face particular challenges from overseas competitors, and one of the principal aspects of this was highlighted by John Naisbitt in his sensational best seller on trends in American society. Here are some excerpts from his statements:

> There is unprecedented criticism of American business management throughout the world today. A great deal is because of [its] short-term orientation. . . . In America today "the numbers" are pervasive. . . . And the numbers are short-term.
>
> Japanese managers, by contrast, pursue long-term strategies *despite short-term costs*. . . . There are many signs, however, that American managers are beginning to change. Long-term planning has become a familiar theme. . . .[1]

The change in business planning toward a long-range perspective is one way in which management is definitely becoming strategic. *Strategy* is a magic word in today's business vocabulary, a real "hot button"—and therefore a vital emphasis in education for business management. Strategy requires systematic methods and discipline too, and those subjects are what this book is about. It

---

[1]John Naisbitt, *Megatrends* (New York: Warner Books, 1982), pp. 79–83. Italics are Naisbitt's.

also requires ingenuity and decisiveness—a book cannot really teach those qualities but may encourage students to develop them.

Marketers are becoming integral members of strategic-planning activities, which explains why strategy is now a common subject in marketing curricula. Marketers contribute in two dimensions: to corporatewide plans, which should be market based, and to the creation of marketing strategies and their coordination with a firm's overall effort. Part II of this book is concerned mainly with corporatewide plans; the balance deals chiefly with marketing's strategies. This first chapter, like all beginnings, lays the groundwork, which consists of providing terms, definitions, and orientation that will speed later learning and relate our subjects to the economy and future vocations.

THE MEANING AND QUALITY OF STRATEGY

Strategy has various meanings, but we must select and adhere to a single definition, which is:

A scheme or principal idea through which an objective would be achieved.

For instance, the early producers of computers leased their equipment, rather than sell it. By this means they were able to hold on to their customers and to replace an existing machine with a more-advanced one at will. Leasing was a core strategy in the plans of those companies during that era.

That scheme or key idea, however, would be useless standing alone and must be created in context with several important determinations. The aggregate of the initial idea, together with these other main decisions, constitutes the "strategic plans" that guide the organization. Both terms are concerns of this book, but *strategic planning* describes most of the content. What strategic planning includes will be explained later.

A few qualifications of our definition of strategy are in order. One concerns the length of time that a given scheme or plan should be in effect. There are many who would not consider a decision that covered a period of less than three years to be a strategy, and some would make the period even longer. Naisbitt, in the quotations above, was implying periods of such length because Japanese managers tend to set and pursue such long-term goals. Three years should be the minimum-length criterion in our definition of strategy. That is, decisions on major investments and campaigns commit the firm to living with their market consequences for three to five years (sometimes longer). During that period there will be changes externally and internally whose impacts demand that the firm replan its strategy at least an annual interval. The plans governing specific operations are conventionally annual in length, and they should be integral parts of the strategic-planning process. When referring to the annual-planning segments, we will refer to them as "periodic" plans.

Another point to be made here relates to the origin of the word *strategy* in military thought. It is unfortunate that many businesspeople fail to recognize that military strategy is quite different from strategy in the business world. In business, one's competitors are not "enemies," nor do strategies aim to annihilate competitors and thus end a war. A danger of a military attitude is to become so obsessed with vanquishing one's rivals that the needs of buyers, the forces of the environment, and the economics of long-term prosperity are all ignored.[2]

Another question should be addressed here: What is the difference between *tactics* and *strategy?* Many decisions must be made during the course of executing a strategic plan. Some arise due to contingencies that cannot be foreseen. Others relate to details of implementation (which are probably delegated to the line people who carry out the work and which need not be resolved until they occur). There will be a few references to tactics, but this is a book on strategy.

Examples clarify definitions, and so we are going to look at a few actual strategies that businesses have adopted. The first two are famous moves in the petroleum industry:

> In March 1982 a major oil company, ARCO (Atlantic Richfield Company), suddenly announced a program that sharply departed from the marketing practice of all the major oil companies. It was a two-pronged strategy: (1) all sales at filling stations would be for *cash* (no more credit cards would be accepted); and (2) ARCO prices would be cut deeply. The result was a rapid shift of business to ARCO.
>
> Shell was a leading competitor and retaliated within a few months. Shell had a contrary strategy. It announced that its stations would accept *any* credit card (especially ARCO ones). Then when a customer had bought Shell products with another firm's credit card, Shell would open an account for that customer, charge his or her purchase to it, and send that buyer the new Shell card. (This would be accomplished without changing prices.)

These key schemes with which two large firms sought to attract the retail gasoline market have several qualities to be noted. They were ingenious and were so sudden that they caught the rivals by surprise. Two perhaps less-obvious qualities are the ones we want to emphasize: (1) each strategy held a *differential advantage* whereby the strategist would be unlike rival firms in some attractive way (or, as one soft drink used to call itself, "deliciously different"); and (2) each was well timed, coming when the *strategic window* was open. The term *strategic window* was coined by Abell and refers to the ideal timing or opportunity for using a particular strategy. In our gasoline example, the "window" was open for a successful price-cutting strategy at the point where oil companies were keeping prices up to the high-petroleum-crisis level when consumers were suffering from a depression and were avid for lower prices. When ARCO capitalized on the situation by halting credit sales, it opened a

---

[2]This problem was described by Jean D. Jackson, "Abandon Restrictive Wartime, Strategy, Competition Language," *Marketing News*, March 18, 1983, p. 7.

different window that Shell perceived—to lure away the dedicated credit card buyers among ARCO's clientele. Most strategic windows are fleeting opportunities that can be seized only by firms that are alert and can mobilize the right resources.

Good strategies are difficult to devise—especially for a firm or product in a weak situation. Something of the difficulty can be seen in the following actual case, in which we are disguising the name of the decision maker:

> Chester Trimble worked for the drug firm of Abbott Laboratories, Inc. in its central offices north of Chicago. He was located in marketing and had a title of product manager. His responsibility was the planning and monitoring of several products. Being newest of the product managers, he was assigned some of the lesser products.
>
> One of his products was a penicillin, an antibiotic brand. We are going to refer to it as "Product C." It was one of Abbott's penicillin products at that time, which formerly had sold well. Abbott had been generating new antibiotics, stengthening its product line, particularly with "Product E." As Product E had much better potentials, it was given much stronger marketing support and had eclipsed Product C.
>
> Product C clearly was doomed to early termination unless Trimble quickly found a new, winning strategy that would revive its sales. Product C's market share had been eroding rapidly, for it had to compete with most major firms in addition to Abbott's other brands. It was a tough challenge to Trimble's ability to think strategically.
>
> It was evident that with its lean budget Product C should not try to go head-to-head against the major antibiotic brands that sought sales across the whole market. One requirement of its strategy would be that of identifying some segment that it could exploit. Trimble searched medical literature to find it, and he did.
>
> Pediatricians, he noticed, were troubled in treating children with strep throats, because the parents would stop administering the antibiotic when the soreness disappeared—although actually the disease was not cured.
>
> Having found and defined the market or business to be targeted, some strategic program that would attract it was required. Trimble did conceive of a promotional campaign that seemed likely to appeal to pediatricians. One item in the program was this ingenious gimmick that would encourage parents and children to complete the full prescribed dosage. The doctors were provided with sets of colored blocks, each numbered for one of the doses. The idea was that a child would look forward to and demand the next block (and dose) from the parent. The device actually worked very well. The program revived the brand for a few more years of profitable sales (although eventually Abbott did terminate it).[3]

Trimble's experience suggests the aims and the efforts of the search for the right strategy. This can be very intriguing and rewarding, but recognize how it requires creativity and work. It shows the difficulties involved in finding a real differential advantage and the importance of perceiving the strategic window.

An immense variety of strategies might be considered or invented, but only certain ones are appropriate for a given market and time. Also the choice

---

[3]Printed with permission of Abbott Laboratories.

varies with the particular brand's situation. Again let us go back to Abbott Laboratories for an example:

> The firm's leading antibiotic, Erythrocin, was managed by another person, whom we will call Dave Fine (not his real name). This product manager had quite a different situation. The firm was giving his brand strong support, and it was being sold as a broad spectrum drug to the general market. Fine would not be looking for some market segment to promote since he could attract purchases from the medical profession in general. With much larger funds he could consider using a variety of promotional means and on a much bigger scale. The right strategy for Fine's product would be quite different from Trimble's.

The great variety of potential strategies and the grave risks in deciding on which to adopt make it essential to be *systematic* in reaching strategic decisions. Our next section describes a decision model for achieving such a system.

MAJOR STRATEGY DECISIONS

There must be an established method of reaching repetitive decisions. By use of a consistent, appropriate method, a decision maker can be efficient and become proficient. When such a method is expressed in writing, it helps to ensure comparability among both present and past decisions about the same problem. The decision-making method should further indicate the data needs and how they should be analyzed. Since strategies are reconsidered or initiated at least annually and are the most significant of management decisions, these remarks apply especially to them.

This section introduces the strategic-planning process with an overall view and a description of its basic elements. The elements will then be elaborated upon with a description of the underlying analyses and information needs. The process described here is not the only one that may logically be used in strategic planning, but it does represent a common ground among the variations one finds in the literature.

Strategic planning consists of *four* major decision steps. It is imperative that all four steps be completed, although some managers might alter the order. Most managers shuttle back and forth or recycle as they proceed. These four steps are as follows:

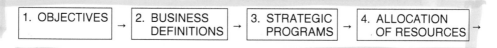

1. OBJECTIVES → 2. BUSINESS DEFINITIONS → 3. STRATEGIC PROGRAMS → 4. ALLOCATION OF RESOURCES →

Some reflections about these four decision stages indicate that none could possibly be omitted:

1. A plan must head in some direction, toward some clear goals. Although goals may be modified later because of what is learned during planning, some definite objectives must provide the starting point.

2. No one can plan accurately for a business without a clear definition of what that business is: What markets will form one's area of marketing? What products? In what industry or against what competitors? Even if these areas will remain the same as in the firm's present business, they should be accurately defined. Obviously, any contemplated changes here will radically affect strategy.
3. The strategic program contains the steps or schemes that must be implemented in order to accomplish objectives. Part of this is the marketing mix to be employed. The knowledge and ingenuity of the people who formulate this program are immensely important.
4. The strategic program would only be a dream unless there were resources to carry it out. Allocation of funds is an essential step. There may also be scarce resources such as physical facilities and special personnel that need to be earmarked for particular programs.

The arrow to the extreme right of our four-stage diagram represents the implementation of the strategic program (or strategy). Our discussion of that phase, since it follows the strategy decisions, will not take place until the last few chapters of this book. Until then we will focus on the four-stage strategy process and its applications.

PLANNING MODEL ANALYSES AND DECISIONS

Many lesser decisions are made in the process that leads up to each of the four major decisions in strategic planning. Each of these is decided after numerous analyses of data and consideration of the views of those involved in the decisions. Who takes part in these decisions? The answer to that question will be deferred until later in this chapter because it is unnecessary at this point. Here we are going to discuss general methods involved in making these decisions. These methods would apply to anyone making strategic decisions. Relevant people and their locations in a firm's organization will be described in the following section.

This section is divided into four subsections, each dealing with one of the four major decisions. Within each section is a diagram—a fragment of our simple four-stage one—which depicts the detailed steps surrounding the major decision (the one found in a box).

1. Objectives:

Setting objectives is the primary step in planning, because everything that is decided should be aimed at the accomplishment of goals. Initially, the planner should assume that the strategies now being pursued will not change.

In a later stage, however, the planner may find that new strategies are needed, and he or she may decide to revise the initial objective in view of whatever is feasible.

Three words are often used for these aims, sometimes interchangeably: objectives, goals, and missions. For our purpose, *goal* may be considered as having the same meaning as *objective*. A *mission,* however, is considered as something else: a broad statement of the kind of firm that those directing it want it to be. Thus a mission tends to be a broader and longer-range concept than is an objective. Naturally, a firm should define its mission, but with our concern for a more definite and disciplined sort of planning, we will concentrate on objectives.

Our fragmentary diagram shows the three forces that shape the objectives (the arrows entering the box) and the substage that follows, the future planning gap:

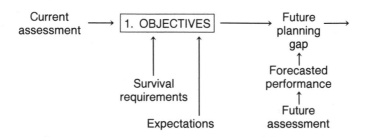

Current assessment is the opening phase of formal planning. During this phase one finds what has been happening to the strategic unit (the firm or some part of it) for which strategy is being decided. In addition it is vital to determine *why* this unit has behaved as it has and to obtain details on its current situation and trends.

A logical beginning is to examine the objectives that had been set for this current period and to compare them with actual performance. (By *actual* we mean the projected performance based on that realized to date, because the assessment must take place some time before the current period ends—one cannot make plans for 1986 on the night of December 31, 1985!) Actual performance is compared with the objectives and any difference or differences are noted (e.g., a sales objective of $800,000 for 1985 with actual sales of $778,000). The difference is the *current planning gap.* (In the example there is a negative gap of $22,000 in sales. If sales had been $831,000 there would have been a positive planning gap.) For longer-range plans, such as one spanning a six-year interval, short yearly intervals would also be assigned individual goals that cumulate to the distant objective.

Merely to compare the firm's own performance with its planned level does not suffice. A *situation analysis* of what underlies those figures should be made. (Some authors would describe the first decision stage as a situation analysis. However, we do not, since one may make a situation analysis at other stages also.) One aspect of this analysis may be a *marketing audit,* an extensive determination of the firm's marketing strengths and weaknesses.[4]

Sample questions that should be answered in such a situation analysis are these:

What is the firm's current market position? How has this changed over a past period?

How has the firm's share of market changed, in comparison with that of its principal rivals? How have their strategies differed from ours?

How do our firm and product stand in the images and interest of buyers? Of distributors? How much support are the latter giving us? Why?

What general environmental changes have occurred that might explain our performance?

These questions are specific to the marketing realm, but of course the situation analysis should deal with all the functional areas.

This stage and those that follow will be illustrated with the story of an actual small manufacturing firm in a very lively industry:

Systel Computers, Inc. is located in San Jose (in California's "Silicon Valley"). In 1981 it entered the fiercely competitive although fast-growing computer industry. Its founders were three people who had substantial experience with other computer manufacturers.

Systel's objectives for that first year are unknown to us. It would have introduced to the market its sole product, a small computer for businesses named "Report/80." Perhaps a modest loss for the first year of 1981 was expected. If so, Systel's managers faced a shock: a loss of $1,500,000—a deep negative planning gap. Moreover, market position was poor because the hoped-for wide distribution of Report/80 had not been obtained. The feature that was expected to make Systel's machine uniquely attractive to business buyers "also made it unattractive to the retailer."[5]

The trends and situation identified in the current assessment should carry heavy weight in deciding objectives, but there are also personal (and probably more subjective) goals to be considered. One is the managers' views of the firm's *survival requirements.* There would be some minimum level of market position and of cash resources that the firm must have to stay in existence as a robust competitor, and objectives should not fall below that. In addition there are the *expectations* of those who have power over the organization. These are usually the owners and the top executives. In firms that have to raise capital, however, the expectations of key people in the financial community may also exert much influence. These three factors—current assessment, survival requirements, and expectations—will have to be resolved and melded into one set of objectives, expressed in specific numbers.

There will likely be more than one vital aspect for which some targets or

---

[4]For an excellent discussion of marketing audits, see Philip Kotler, *Marketing Management,* 4th ed. (Englewood Cliffs, N.J.: Prentice-Hall, 1980), pp. 650–58.

[5]John A. Byrne, "The Shotgun Approach," *Forbes,* March 29, 1982, pp. 62–64.

objectives should be posited in strategic planning. There should not be many, as that would be confusing. One objective should be made the dominant one whose attainment is the overriding consideration.

The strategic objectives should be related to the mission or missions of the firm, and the firm's peculiar circumstances may dictate the type of objective to choose. The traditional form of objective for annual planning has been some aspect of net profit—e.g., return on assets (ROA) or return on investment (ROI). That would be unsuitable for many firms whose growth opportunities require considerable cash. For them, cash flow is of more importance than net profits. Some of the most dynamic companies, such as Teledyne, make cash flow the sole corporate objective and also require such an objective of the subsidiary units.

Decisions at this stage include both the type of factors (e.g., dollar sales, cash flow, etc.) and the level at which to target each objective. These always are critical decisions and in many cases difficult. Look back at our example of Systel Computers, Inc., the small firm that had a disastrous first year with its small computer. It could hardly face another great net loss, and what it desperately needed was money. Let us consider the picture faced by Systel when plans were being decided for its second year of existence:

> When Systel's managers were deciding objectives for 1982, the huge negative planning gap suffered in 1981 provided no practical guidance. Survival was the main motive, which meant that cash flow was the most critical aspect. A bedrock minimum of cash was needed to cover the 1982 operating expenses. Beyond that, Systel's president had persuaded others to put some $700,000 into the business recently to finance its introduction of a different product, so cash flow for interest on that was imperative. Working capital was also needed to replenish the firm's coffers. The cash flow needs would be somewhat contingent on the timing of the new product venture and size of its marketing campaign in 1982.

The objectives we have been describing for Systel were those applying to the total firm. Marketing, one of the departments for which objectives should also be set, would need different kinds of objectives (e.g., number of units sold, number of new customers, inventory turnover, etc.). Such functional objectives, however, are subordinate to and would be decided later than the objectives of the firm as a whole.

Beyond the decision on objectives, as shown in the above diagram, lies the *future planning gap* determination. This assumes continuation of the current business and strategy. It is calculated as simply the forecasted performance minus the objective (in the criterion that was chosen for the objective). Here are two examples:

Forecasted performance	13.2%	ROI
Objective	−15.0	ROI
Future planning gap (negative)	(1.8%)	ROI

Forecasted performance	$3,900,000	sales
Objective	−3,500,000	
Future planning gap (positive)	$ 400,000	sales

In the first instance above, the organization is going to fall short of its objective, and so it must seek some strategic means of avoiding that shortfall. The second instance presents a much happier prospect, and management might tend to be complacent about strategies. It is likely, however, that the powers-that-be in the firm will raise the objective to at least the forecasted level—perhaps to a still higher level in order to stimulate the search for even better strategies.

The *future assessment* that is shown feeding into the performance forecast is another situation analysis. This one, though, involves analyzing the variables that are likely to affect the firm's or unit's future performance abilities. It is an evaluation of three factors that seriously affect the firm, projected for the relevant planning period, and then synthesized into a net effect on performance. (We of course mean the performance measured by the objective criteria.) These three factors are

Threat analysis
Opportunity analysis
Differential advantage analysis

Threat analysis is an evaluation of the external threats (environmental ones) that are likely to affect the planning unit significantly during the planned horizon. Such a threat was defined by Kotler in this fashion:

> . . . a challenge posed by an unfavorable trend or specific disturbance in the environment that would lead, in the absence of purposeful marketing action, to the stagnation or demise of a company, product, or brand.[6]

Competitive threats are a constant concern. Typically they come from domestic rivals, but increasingly from foreign firms, such as Japanese firms in the semiconductor markets (both U.S. and worldwide) and soon in computer markets (at the time of this writing). Banking has faced in the past five years and will continue to face threats from various quarters. Few threats have come from banks in other nations, but many have come from major city banks and holding companies spreading into smaller cities. Outside of the once clearly defined banking industry, savings institutions were empowered to do virtually everything a bank does. Then came huge nonbanking firms like Sears, American Express, and Merrill Lynch either buying up banks or offering hitherto exclusively banking services. Banks have become very earnest strategic planners, with much of their attention focused on the competition.

Environmental threats also come from other directions, which we will explore later. An example is surely the atomic power industry, which has been stunted by such factors as rising equipment costs, public scares of accidents, government restrictions, and renewed abundance of fossil fuels. The largest

---

[6]Philip Kotler, *Marketing Management: Analysis, Planning, and Control*, 4th Ed., © 1980, p. 99. Reprinted by permission of Prentice-Hall, Inc., Englewood Cliffs, N.J.

tobacco firms, with growth stopped by environmental changes, sharply changed their development strategies. That long-time staple, salt, has come under siege with rising concern for low-sodium diets, with drastic effects on its firms' strategies.

Opportunity analysis, the other side of the coin, anticipates favorable situations within the scope of the firm's present business. Like the proverbial "ill wind" that does nobody good, one firm's threat may be another firm's golden opportunity. The stifling of atomic power's growth brought opportunities for coal and oil and for the manufacturers of equipment that burns the fossil fuels. That a firm's threat in one of its markets may also be an opportunity for a new product is shown in this case:

> The sodium scare has been having a serious effect on the Morton Salt Company. The company is said to have lost 10 percent of its sales in 1981 in the table salt market. However, Morton had introduced a new sodium-free salt that rapidly became popular and added 12 percent to the company's table market sales—more than balancing the loss in regular salt sales.[7]

The third element in a performance forecast is the *differential advantage,* one of the salient qualities of a good strategy mentioned early in this chapter. The question here is the degree (if any) to which the firm's existing strategy is of superior effectiveness as compared with that of its competitors. There are both advantages and disadvantages, and they may vary among the markets sought. The *net* differential should be judged, it is hoped, in an objective manner despite a human tendency to overvalue one's own strategy. Reference at this stage is only to the differentials of the currently used strategy. Differentials may lie in many facets of product, production, distribution, powerful resources, technology, and adaptiveness of the firm. Whatever facts and opinions can be gathered from the field or from experts within the firm should be used in making these assessments.

When all three aspects have been analyzed (threats, opportunities, and differential advantages), the results should be brought together and synthesized into their joint effect on the kind of performance that has been set as the objective. For an example, let us return to the small firm of Systel and consider some factors (some actual and others fictitious for sake of example).

When Systel Computers, Inc., pondered its forecast of performance in its current business area, small computers for business use, these might have been some of the factors taken into account:

Threats:
    A stagnant economy
    Very high interest rates
    Rapid emergence of new technologies in computers
    Drastic changes in software and applications

---

[7]*Time,* March 15, 1982, p. 71.

Opportunities:
  Continued strong growth in demand for computers, especially person-
    al ones
  Special needs of minor market segments by no means all satisfied
Differential advantages:
  Systel's young and ambitious management
  Flexibility of a small firm to move fast in exploiting opportunities
  Low overhead: small volume lines could be profitable
Differential disadvantages:
  Firm's shortage of capital and credit standing
  Lack of dealer support
  Stigma of an unsuccessful product launch
  Relatively puny abilities to develop, make, and market equipment, es-
    pecially the complete systems that were the demand trend
  Limited reputation compared with the big and established manufac-
    turers

In Systel's example, we would hardly need any precise analysis to arrive at a dismal performance forecast if the firm keeps to its present course. The unpopularity of its current product was gross enough, alone, to foreshadow that. For a more-established firm, even one with a limited product line, a complicated analysis is involved. Such an analysis should chart and quantify the various threats and opportunities and the relative differentials against competitors. Only when translated into numbers can these factors be combined into an index of future performance and a future planning gap be accurately defined.

The future planning gap serves as an intermediate step between the setting of objectives and the definition of the business areas in which the firm (or planning unit) will contend in the future. If there is a positive gap, perhaps only minor work is needed in defining the business area. *Business area* is the scope of markets, products, and technologies in which the firm participates. When faced with a large negative planning gap, a firm will probably have to modify at least one of these elements. There are surely few industries in which an honest look into the future would not alter the performance forecast substantially. Also, any ambitious and strong firm would place its objectives high enough that a revamping of the business would have to be considered. Now that we have set the stage for entering the business definition, let us do so.

2. Business Area Definition:

If the firm or strategic unit is forecasted to have a negative future planning gap, managers may either adopt a more effective strategy or change the firm's business—or take both types of action. We have been discussing the process that leads up to such decisions. The logical first step would be that of the definition of the business, so that when a search is made for strategic programs it will be related to the entirety of the targeted business areas.

Our using the word *area* does not refer to geographical areas, which would rarely be the basis for defining any portion of a firm's business strategically. When the firm's management is considering the directions in which it might go for developing new areas, these may be described in terms of one of three types of dimensions (or a combination of them): (1) the technologies by which products are created or distributed; (2) the customer segments of certain characteristics (demographic, lifestyles, industry, etc.); and (3) the function or use made by the customers. Many alternatives might be considered in choosing a specific strategy along these dimensions. A determination of the firm's future businesses is not confined to such expansions into new areas, however, as there are three general options: (1) deleting some current business area that is unprofitable, (2) continuing in current areas with expansion or contraction in them, and (3) entering areas new to the firm.

The importance of these decisions cannot be denied. Notorious errors have been made in failing to enter a new business area of great promise (such as Eastman Kodak and others turning down what became the Xerox business)—and the contrary (such as Xerox's costly error of entering the computer business by acquiring a firm incapable of surviving in that industry). Great care should be exercised in redefining areas in which the business will contend. The process of reaching such decisions should include these steps:

1. Defining the firm's existing business
2. Identifying and defining other business areas, with particular efforts to find recently opened and unexploited ones
3. Interpreting what those areas demand, and estimating their volumes of purchases
4. Judging whether one's firm is well constituted to enter any new business and to maintain a sustainable competitive advantage in it

Two other aspects must be considered about any new business area before a final decision is reached. One is timing, that is, whether a *strategic window* (described above) is really open at that time. The other is feasibility, that is, whether a strategic program is practicable. There must be millions of throats in China, for instance, that need cough drops, but who has a strategy for marketing to them? And a small candy company may see huge demand in the chewing gum market, but how can it squeeze in against Wrigley *et al.?* Although the decision process has not yet reached the third stage of finding a strategy, often it is apparent in this second stage that the search would be futile. (We can diagram the process of a business area definition on p. 14.)

Portfolio assessment examines the current businesses of the firm, or, we might say, its existing set of strategic units. A number of analytical methods have been developed and are widely used for this process. We will defer discussion of these to Chapter 3. The need to assess the current businesses before

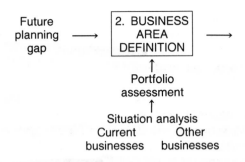

Future
planning
gap ⟶ 2. BUSINESS
AREA
DEFINITION ⟶

↑
Portfolio
assessment
↑
Situation analysis
Current   Other
businesses   businesses

proceeding to new ones would be a complex task in such diversified firms as Westinghouse, ITT, or General Mills. The process is much simpler and more readily examined in a small firm like Systel, which will be described at the end of this section. Similar analyses should be made of any new alternative businesses in which the firm may become involved.

At this stage a *situation analysis* again provides the data needed for a portfolio assessment. This analysis should be guided by preset objectives or policies regarding a desirable mix of businesses: in growth, profit rates, stability, risk, or whatever are the key criteria.

There is always the possibility that retention of the firm's existing business units may be the ideal strategy. For example, Anheuser-Busch, predominantly a brewing company, was supposedly concerned for many years about how to reinvest its large cash flow. Portfolio assessment, however, kept indicating that nothing could be better than expanding in brewing. Minor redefinitions like entering the light-beer area were then adopted.

Let us now visualize possible choices among strategies as arranged along vectors in two dimensions—technologies and markets. On such a grid, firms may decide on broad or on narrow strategies. With respect to markets, the wise choice often is broadly covering a number of markets and maximizing volume. The contrary choice is "niching"—which consists of taking a narrow focus on a particular market, popularly called *market segmentation*. In Anheuser Busch we spoke of a company that covers virtually all markets in its industry (brewing), whereas the following retailing example is of a firm that has stayed with a more-limiting strategy concentrating on a market niche:

Dollar General Stores is a retail firm that was founded in 1939 in Scottsville, Kentucky, the site of its first store. By 1982 Dollar became a large chain, still headquartered in Scottsville and still in the business in which it began. As *Forbes* described it: "The growth formula is simple: DG's 850 stores are located in small rural communities ranging from Atoka, Okla. to Pocomoke, Md. The company strives to be a no-frills discounter of everything from clothing to housewares to shoes."

The Turner family, who control and manage Dollar General Stores, have held to the same merchandising strategy, and their firm's profits have steadily risen. Again quoting from *Forbes:* "Part of the reason [for its stock's all-time high price] is that investors like the way the Turners run things, and they aren't expecting any surprise diversification. 'All of Pennsylvania has just 21 Dollar General Stores, so there's plenty of room for expansion doing just what we do now,' says Cal [Turner] Jr. with a smile. 'We're going to stay right in our niche.' "[8]

Anheuser-Busch and Dollar General are attractive examples, but they are among a minority in the ideal situation of being in businesses to which they are well adapted and in which they have growth potential. We might notice also that their markets differ: Dollar General deals with a market segment, whereas Anheuser-Busch broadly covers its market/technology area (it produces a variety of brands and promotes to the general public).

Most firms must instead seek expanded or different business areas in order to fulfill their growth objectives—or even to stay afloat. It takes courage to expand into new products or markets, and it takes objectivity to drop those that can no longer offer a worthwhile return. Also required is thorough situation analyses. In the business area decision, emphasis should be placed on the differential advantages of the firm in relation to those of its competitors. By maximizing its position as probably the greatest sales organization and distribution system to supermarkets, Procter & Gamble has selected almost wholly new product fields. By contrast, Xerox underwent a loss of around $185 million in 1975 when it prematurely entered the computer industry, for which it proved to be ill prepared.

> Diebold, Inc. is a striking example of redefining one's business. Diebold was an old company (begun in the 1860s) and the leader in its business area in 1970. Its business market was banks, and its product line included safes, security systems, and drive-in teller windows. Banks' branch networks had been expanding rapidly, which meant excellent demand for Diebold's product line, but Diebold foresaw that this growth was going to slow as branches became saturated.
>
> The firm of Docutel earlier had introduced automated teller machines for banks, and it had a commanding lead in that line. Two electronic giants were entering with their automated teller machines in 1970, IBM and NCR. It was a rapidly expanding business area, however, and would be an excellent fit with Diebold's existing reputation, clientele, and product line. Despite all the obstacles, Diebold's analysis led it to choose automated teller machines as the most logical redefinition of its business. It next needed to create strategies to penetrate that business, to which we return later.[9]

The steps taken in defining the business areas in which the firm is to engage are obviously more complicated in multiproduct firms than in single-product firms. We will therefore describe the essence of such a decision in a single-product firm. We now resume the story of Systel in this second key strategy decision area:

> It was all too clear to Systel's managers that there was no way for its existing product of 1981, Report/80, to succeed in the office market for small computers. Nor could Systel come up with another small computer for that market so quickly.

---

[8]Jeff Blyskal, "Renegade Retailers," *Forbes*, May 24, 1982, pp. 63–66.
[9]"Diebold's Shift to Automated Tellers Works," *Wall Street Journal*, July 15, 1982, p. 33.

Alternative needs for electronic equipment in offices were then considered, and two very significant points were noted:

1. Even though the major computer makers were pushing hard for rapid automation of offices, Systel suspected that there would remain a large market segment that preferred to move very gradually in office automation. This view had been expressed by a consultant who said, "A lot of office managers are frightened to death over all the hoopla about office automation."
2. Another point, in the words of Systel's president, was: "While everyone had gone crazy trying to build small computers, what had gone neglected was a simple device that could turn an electronic typewriter into a high-quality, inexpensive word processor."[10]

Systel management considered that the new market niche just described was not only unexploited but appropriate for its differential advantages. It hoped to find the answer for that market need and redefined its business to be that of word processing.

3. Strategic Program Determination:

One step toward accomplishing the objectives was to define or redefine the firm's business. Business definition is only part of the means of reaching goals, however. Specific ways of succeeding in the business must be found. These "ways" usually constitute one or more core schemes supported by some underlying ideas. Together the schemes make up a program of strategies, and so we speak of a *strategic program*. Finding or conceiving these strategic ideas tends to be the most creative act in strategic planning. Following is another diagram, this one a process for developing a strategic program:

The steps in the above process would be followed in a deliberate effort to find or conceive a successful strategy in an already defined market. It often

***

[10]*Forbes*, May 29, 1982, p. 64.

happens instead that some great idea or invention has been found somewhat by chance. In that case, the task is to search for a market. However, we are considering here an orderly planning process. That is, the market or need is decided before seeking the best strategic program to exploit it, a market focus that avoids wasted effort.

Again the *situation analysis* underlies a key decision. Here the market focus leads to concentration on factors relevant to that market. The strategist needs an analysis that yields insights into the situation and possibilities, in definite terms. Subjects to be dealt with include

Specific characteristics and unmet needs of buyers and users

Competitive products already contending in that market and their reasons for success or failure

Technology and product or package features already available in this and in comparable product fields

Images of and loyalty to brands and product types now sold to that market

Product history and position of existing products

Differential advantages (and disadvantages) that this firm has in relation to others in this market

This knowledge prepares the strategic planner to search for and think creatively about strategic ideas. The right idea may already exist in another market, such as liquid soap being used in washrooms and institutions. The small firm of Minnetonka, Inc., recognized the potential for a consumer toilet soap product and created a strategic program for "Softsoap," which became a market sensation. Perhaps an idea or a technology that is already known in (or even patented by) the firm's laboratories will fit the market opportunity. Having such "off-the-shelf" technology is of course a major advantage.

When a basic strategic idea has been found, a number of other strategic ideas will be required for its implementation—details of the marketing mix and of production. When this whole set is put together, one has a strategic program:

Systel Computers, Inc., was under pressure to design a word processor unit that would be suitable for its targeted market. Also strategic marketing ideas must be generated. Another firm had just launched a product that would meet the need that Systel had identified, so speed and finding differential advantages were vital.

Systel rapidly designed and tested a device that would sit alongside an electronic typewriter on a secretary's desk. It also devised ways to produce and market the machine so that it could be priced substantially under the other firm's product—a price that also would be only half of what the major manufacturers were asking for their word-processing units. Beyond that, Systel had two distribution ideas for the strategic program:

1. On its own brand Systel would offer office equipment dealers an unusually high markup, affordable because of the production costs.

2. Systel would go ahead with "a private-labelling deal with Olympia USA, whose brand was on 30 percent of the electronic typewriters sold in the U.S."[11] [This should mean over 5,000 units being sold through Olympia's dealer network.]

What Systel did strategically has some interesting angles. First, it recognized a strategic window. It then created a differential advantage in new technology that might give it a sufficiently strong position to succeed in this redefined business. That advantage gave Systel leverage to add a pricing advantage and to establish an additional distribution channel. The sales increment through the new channel probably reduced Systel's production costs, which added a further advantage. What remained to be seen was whether that strategy would prove sustainable against the larger rivals.

A longer period than that described in this example may elapse before a contemplated strategic program has been elaborated and tested. Such a situation often occurs when an actual market test is going to be included. Haste is hazardous when the proposed strategy is very novel or expensive. Also the market-leading firms can often afford to be deliberate. Procter & Gamble, again mentioning a conspicuous example, spends months or even years in testing and perfecting its new products or marketing programs—although it can move quickly. Sometimes a strategic program must evolve over a long period, which is one reason why long-range strategic planning is essential. Our example of Diebold, Inc., is a case in point:

> "Its move into the teller-machine business was neither quick nor painless. Diebold raided its competitors for electronics expertise and built a research center, but seven years and $20 million later, just when banks were beginning to buy teller machines, the 1974 recession hit. 'It brought the whole thing to a screeching halt,' Earl F. Wearstler, president, says. . . . A few years later, though, Diebold's luck changed. When the banks were ready to buy again, some of its competitors faltered."[12]
>
> Diebold found the right strategic moves by working closely with banks to develop programming and incorporating flexibility in its machines, and also by making service convenient and quick. It had waited, too, until the "strategic window" was open. This strategic program has been so effective that a 1982 survey found Diebold selling 47 percent of the automated teller machines in 1982, when its earnings advanced 37 percent over those of the previous year during a recession.

The fourteen years that Diebold spent in evolving its strategic plan is abnormally long but not unique. When several years are required for a strategic plan, it is also evaluated in annual segments so that its development can periodically be tracked.

In the process of strategic program determination a number of strategic ideas should have been found. More than one of these ideas may have sufficient promise to be considered further. The evaluation of whether to pursue a

---

[11]*Forbes*, May 29, 1982, p. 66.
[12]*Wall Street Journal*, July 15, 1982, pp. 33, 45.

specific strategic idea should include (1) the market response or purchases that may be expected from buyers during the planned periods and (2) the additional costs that the program will incur. An important question is, Would the gained revenues exceed the incremental costs by a margin great enough to meet the firm's objectives? Estimation of market response is the tougher determination. Records of past experience and buyer research would aid in making an accurate judgment. Actual market testing may be conducted to obtain a fairly reliable indication of the program's effects.

The last step in this stage is to determine whether the proposed program meets the objectives. If not, there are three options: (1) search for a more effective strategic program, (2) return to the second step and redetermine in which markets the firm should contend, or (3) return to the first step and change the level of objectives to one that seems feasible. For the annual plans, it may be too late in the year to go through the whole process again, so there would be no strategy change for the coming year. The managers would continue to search for a longer-run, goal-satisfying program.

4. Resource Allocation:

Resource allocation is the final stage of strategic planning. The resource of most concern is money, of course, although staff and facilities may also be assigned to specific programs. The analyses to be made at this point are largely financial ones. The main criteria in deciding allocations are (1) the size of investment, (2) the rate of return to be earned, and (3) the risks faced. The length of time for payback is a concern, as is the amount of funds available.

In large organizations like Diebold, the planning units or strategy centers stand below the corporate management, which decides the allocation between the units. A number of products with their individual strategic programs have been submitted. Rarely is the available capital enough to fund all the programs, and so hard choices may have to be made by top management. Therefore it is possible that a strategic program, which planners considered worthwhile relative to the firm's objectives, may have to be shrunk due to restricted funds. In that case, its unhappy planner must return to the third stage and decide how much of that program can be retained.

Questions arise in deciding resource allocations even when there is a single program, as in Systel:

> Despite having a single product and program, Systel's resource allocation was not easy. The $700,000 capital infusion of 1981 would not fund the program that had been outlined. It was ambitious in that (1) production would have to be expanded sixfold, (2) employment would have to be expanded fivefold, and (3) a sales force would have to sign up three hundred dealers by the late summer of 1982. The program was so logical that the executives did not want to retrench it, and they believed that it would prove to be appealing to funding sources. That proved to be right, for they found venture capital firms willing to put up $2.5 million, which would carry the strategic plan through 1982.

The completion of the strategic plan also ends our current discussion of it. The work would then move into the much more laborious tasks of preparing detailed plans for its implementation.

ORGANIZATION FOR STRATEGIC PLANNING

Strategic planning's rapid rise has occurred largely within the past decade. Its managerial tools of accounting and budgeting systems, economic forecasting, and data processing have been long available, but obstacles remained in *organization.* When corporations began strategic planning, it was confined to the corporate level. The planning at that level was often remote from operations and markets. It was therefore "gross" in two senses of that word: "lacking fine distinction or specific details; lacking perceptions." The need was an underlying organization, or infrastructure, down in the corporation to work with corporate planners. A structure like the one we will discuss took form.

This structure brings three types of planning participants into the process, at two lower levels. On one level would be the managers of the functions (production, marketing, etc.), each becoming the strategic planner for that function. On the same level, if the firm was rather large and had diverse products, a separate manager would be assigned to each product. This would be a product or brand manager. Both of these planners would be in *middle management.*[13]

Still larger firms may have groups of related products. Each group or division would be placed under a general executive, who would have authority over all functions (and therefore full profit responsibility). This brings an intermediate level into strategic planning. These groups are called *strategic business units,* or SBUs.

Here are the three planning levels and their managers:

Corporate: The chief executive officer (CEO) and assisting
                          executives. Staff corporate planners may help

---

[13]We should mention a recently reported trend in U.S. corporations relative to (1) who makes the strategic decisions and (2) middle management and planning staffs' importance and role. The recession of the early 1980s had placed pressure on corporations to reduce their management personnel. Two trends connected to this were reported:

> "Corporate structure is changing to accommodate broader information gathering and to let data flow from shop floor to executive suite without the editing, monitoring, and second-guessing that had been the middle manager's function . . . [and] . . . Market place and manufacturing decisions are made by the first-line managers, whose power had been eroded by staff." (*Business Week*, April 25, 1983)

This restructuring would increase the work of the CEO's planning aides and would shift more of the strategy-making tasks below the corporate level onto line executives. This would not affect strategic planning's need or basic nature. The load placed on line managers would heighten the value of systems with which they would make these decisions, with models like those we are presenting.

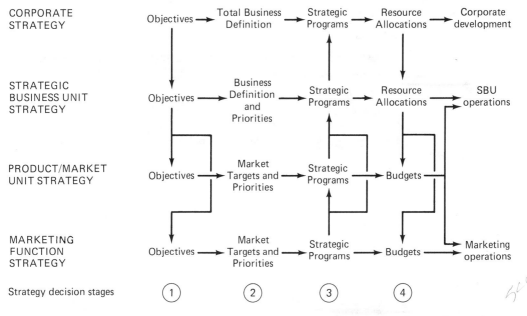

create corporate strategies and coordinate lower levels.

Strategic business units: Under a general executive who is subordinate to the CEO but practically stands alone in SBU strategies. (In Chapter 4 we will explain why complex corporations should have SBUs, and we will discuss their features, roles, and strategic decision processes.)

Middle management: Product/market units (PMUs) in which a product or brand manager concentrates on a single product or line, planning broadly across all functions.

Marketing functions (and nonmarketing ones too) that concentrate on a certain function, for which they plan broadly across all products.

These four types of planning units should be coordinated into an integrated planning system.

The interactions of the four kinds of planners as they progress through the four key decisions are charted in Figure 1-1. The four decisions are sequenced across the figure, left to right. The vertical arrows indicate how a decision made on one level serves to guide or inform a decision at the next level. Figure 1-1 should be seen as a road map for the entire strategy process. As with a road map, you would not try to memorize it. However, you would re-member where it is so that it can serve as a frame of reference.

The CEO and corporate planning staff initiate two decisions: objectives and resource allocations. These serve as directives to the SBUs, who decide what their individual objectives are and how to allocate the resources that have been earmarked for each of them (which become budgets governing the lower levels). The top-down chain of decisions then divides into two branches at the SBU level as the objectives are communicated to the PMUs and to each functional department (those in marketing areas and in other functions not in-dicated here). Both middle-management levels are similarly allocated their portion of resources by the SBU.

In reverse, the decisions about strategic programs form a bottom-up chain. Managers of marketing functions and of each product (or market) have concentrated on defining their markets, potentials, and priorities. They then create and propose its program. The functions' proposals relate to what the PMUs plan and are therefore shown as flowing into that level, as well as to the SBU management to which the functions report. The problems faced by the SBU management are complicated by having to reconcile these two flows of somewhat independent plans. Corporate executives finally decide whether, given the corporation's overall programs and goals, all the SBUs' proposals are meritorious and can be afforded.

The strategic program proposals include financial projections so that the SBU and corporate planners can consider expected profits and resource needs. When the allocations have been made, modifications of those proposals will probably be necessary. After all this is agreed on, budgets are issued that will govern every unit during the period ahead. Each functional manager can then proceed with detailed plans and schedules for the next operating period. The PMU managers, who have no operations to oversee, do have continuous work in coordinating and keeping on top of implementation. Further comments about Figure 1-1 will be made at appropriate points later on.

A PREVIEW

The plan of this book follows a logical sequence. Understanding the rationale of this sequence will help you assimilate and think about these subjects. This opening chapter has given you some fundamentals and now concludes with a preview of the following chapters.

Two basic premises have guided the design of this book. First, marketing strategy is actually determined and implemented in conjunction with all of a firm's functions. *Integration* is a significant term in the approach being taken and is a principle that one marketing executive of an industrial equipment manufacturer expressed in these words:

> We have an integrated planning effort. It starts with the business strategy, and is then supported by the marketing plan, manufacturing plan, technological plan,

FIGURE 1-2. An outline of this book's subject matter.

			Chapter number
PART II	The internal situation: A systematic decision process that integrates planning; and the principal decisions made at each level	Corporate decisions	2
		Analytical methods	3
		Business unit decisions	4
		Marketing function decisions and product/market unit decisions	5
PART III	The external situation: Markets, competitive, and other environments that present opportunities and threats, to be solved with strategies	Markets	6
		Competition	7
		Technology and other environments	8
PART IV	The basic strategy level: Optional strategies over the lives of products, and the situations with which they must cope	Developing products	9
		Young products	10
		Mature products	11
PART V	The marketing mix: Optional strategies for each of the marketing functions, and the situations in which they are appropriate	Product	12
		Price	13
		Promotion	14
		Distribution	15
PART VI	Applying the strategic process	Plans	16
		Implementation and control	17

and human resource plan. Therefore the marketing plan has to be considered in this context and is not designed to stand alone. It is intended as an action document to respond to both corporate and divisional (SBU) strategy and objectives.[14]

Second, our discussion focuses on the determining of strategic programs, which is the most vital and creative act. In this the two main goals are to (1) know and diagnose the situation and (2) select or create an appropriate strategy that is distinct from—and superior to—that of one's competitors.

The remainder of the book is divided into five parts. Their subject scope and chapters are summarized in Figure 1-2.

This completes your introduction to marketing strategy.

---

[14]David S. Hopkins, *The Marketing Plan*, Report No. 801 (New York: The Conference Board, 1981), p. 33.

SUMMARY

This opening chapter has provided the foundation for reading this book: some central concepts, the organization structure and system assumed in the balance of the material, and the sequence of treatment coupled with its rationale.

We discussed, first, the dramatic need for a strategic perspective in today's American business. Then we explained the meanings of *strategy* and of *strategic planning*, emphasizing that the latter is our main concern. What strategy means was also illustrated by citing the experiences of an actual strategist in the marketing department of a drug manufacturer.

The heart of strategic planning was then explained in a four-stage decision process that consists of determining objectives, business definitions, strategic programs, and allocation of resources. Those four steps were then amplified by a description of the method for determining each of these decisions. The decision process began with a current assessment of the situation, serving as a baseline from which to plan ahead. A diagram of that prior stage was given, and the small firm of Systel, Inc., was introduced as our running example. The stage ended by determining the *current planning gap.*

After the deciding of objectives, another interim stage was presented, the *future planning gap.* Underlying that determination was a situation analysis. The conduct of such analysis was discussed with the three major types of factors involved: threats, opportunities, and differential advantages. This brought us to the second major decision: the business area definition, in which a firm decides in which markets and product lines it is going to contend. Examples of firms that have concentrated on the same market repeatedly, as well as examples of those that have diversified, were cited.

Strategic program determination was discussed, again with a diagram of steps to be taken. Examples were of both short-range and long-range programs. This section concluded with a description of the fourth stage of allocating resources.

The organization structure was described on three levels: corporate, strategic business units (SBUs), and middle management. The last includes both functional departments and product/market units (PMUs). We then diagramed and discussed the sequence of decisions made at each level in a coordinated manner. Finally, we explained how the book is structured relative to the basic principles given in Chapter 1.

REVIEW QUESTIONS _____

1. *Is strategy a military concept or one of enterprise management like business administration—or both? Does it make any real difference which viewpoint one takes?*

2. *Sales representative John X is scheduled to call on the Peerless organization this afternoon. He has worked out an idea for inducing Peerless to*

switch to his products instead of using those of a rival supplier. He calls this idea his "strategy." Would you call that a strategy or a tactic? Why?

3. What was John Naisbitt's basic point in comparing Japanese and U.S. companies' strategic planning? Is that significant enough to be highlighted, as he did, as one of the main trends in the United States?

4. In evaluating the strategies of companies in the same industry (e.g., Ford versus Toyota versus VW), what specific qualities of their strategies would you consider?

5. Review the episode in which Chester Trimble decides on a periodic strategy for a "Product C" penicillin. What aspects of his behavior made him successful?

6. For each of the four major decision steps in strategic planning, state briefly what should be accomplished.

7. If a firm's objectives are set too low in strategic planning, what are likely to be the long-range effects on the firm? If set too high? If defined wrong qualitatively, in terms of the wrong factor?

8. Explain the meaning of future planning gap. How does its determination affect the rest of the strategic-planning process?

9. Select one firm with which you are somewhat acquainted or one that does business in your area and is not a top firm, in either the brewing or soft-drink business. Do a "threat analysis" for it, listing and explaining the various threats that it probably faces. Select two as the most serious threats.

10. For that same firm, what kinds of differential advantages could be used effectively in its marketing?

11. Again for that firm, define its present "business" or "industry" clearly enough so that its markets and competition can be identified. What might be another business that would be beneficial for it to enter if expansion is needed?

12. Do you believe that diversification is generally good for a healthy firm? If so, why does the stock of Dollar General Stores, a firm that does not diversify, sell high?

13. What strategic principles or lessons could you draw from the story of Systel or of Diebold?

14. Resource allocation is one of the main tasks of a CEO. Explain why a strategic-planning system is practically essential for such decisions.

15. For each of the four levels of decisions shown in Figure 1-1, state one or more of the strategic decisions made there.

Mrs. Merkt's Shoo-fly Pies

There is, if you can imagine it, such a thing as a product's selling too successfully—and the proprietor of the Old Dutch was facing such a problem with one of the products it sold. Let us see how the problem arose.

The Old Dutch was primarily a restaurant and gift operation, including the sale of baked goods, located on one of the most heavily traveled highways of southeastern Pennsylvania. This is the picturesque Pennsylvania Dutch region that is frequented by tourists, drawn mainly to see its Amish people and their farms and to savor their cooking. The Old Dutch was the most successful of several such establishments in its area. Its style of food was "the real thing," and its pies, advertised as genuine products of Amish homes, fully met this claim. Strict ethics were observed in the area about such representations, for violation would have risked ostracism.

The most popular dish of that country is shoo-fly pie, a simple but unique Pennsylvania Dutch dessert. Its nature and qualities have been described in this way:

> Its crust is composed of unbleached white flour. Its filling is a molasses/brown sugar blend, with added spices. Its rich, pleasing taste is not too difficult to obtain. However, to get the moist ("slippy") filling and still have a perfect, flaky crust absolutely requires the exact proportions and spices of the old recipe that is the secret of some Pennsylvania Dutch housewives.

This brings us to the producer of the pies featured by the Old Dutch. She was Gretchen Merkt, who, with her husband Otto, had a prosperous farm that had been in the Merkt family since the first members migrated to the region from Germany in the late 1700s. Gretchen and Otto had raised four girls and four boys, of whom all but one still lived on or adjacent to the family farm and helped to operate it and sell its products in the city Farmers' Market.

Gretchen had long been famous for her pies and used to bake an extra quantity to be sold at the family stand in the Farmers' Market. When Otto and the boys were reconstructing some of the farm buildings, Gretchen realized that if a baking facility were installed in one of the smaller outbuildings, she could make and sell more pies. Otto found some used but serviceable commercial baking ovens, and when they were installed, Gretchen and the girls began baking in large quantities. Soon they were baking six dozen pies in a 3½-hour morning, six days a week. They sold well at the Farmers' Market, but she and Otto believed they could find an outlet that would bring a better price.

At that time, the Old Dutch was selling pies baked in its own kitchen that could not compare with the real Amish pies. While its proprietor was seeking a farmwife to bake them, a relative of the Merkts referred him to Gretchen. An arrangement was reached whereby a truck would deliver the bulk ingredients to the Merkt farm daily and pick up the finished pies. Gretchen insisted on procuring the spices herself, though, since this was the vital secret in her recipe.

Note: Case A, "Bloomington Bank and Trust Company," also focuses on formal strategic-planning systems. It is much more detailed than Case 1-1 (see pp. 525–539).

For material in this case we are indebted to George A. Reinhart. Names are fictitious, because the participants were willing to have the facts published provided that the names were not revealed.

Gretchen soon recognized that the family's production could be increased if they specialized in one kind of pie. Because of its popularity, shoo-fly was the natural choice, and soon they reached a steady production rate of 300 per day, six days a week. The Old Dutch was well able to sell this quantity at $2.50 for a 9-inch and $3.25 for a 12-inch size. It widely promoted the "Genuine Mrs. Merkt's Shoo-Fly Pie"; it was plainly the best in the area, and Gretchen was the most efficient baker. The Old Dutch was willing to pay her the greater part of the margin earned on the pies because it was a fine attraction. Here were sold about 60 percent of the shoo-fly pie that was sold along the highway, and this stimulated volume in meals, gift, and curios. Within a year, though, the proprietor complained that he was running out of shoo-fly pie too often; he estimated that he could sell at least 50 percent more on a busy day.

The obvious solution would be for Mrs. Merkt to increase her production. But she refused, because 300 pies was the maximum her family could produce in an 8-hour day, and she and Otto were not pressed for more income. She would not permit anyone outside the family to work with her secret process in her kitchen, and, like other Amish cooks, she would have found a proposal to share her recipe with any other household repulsive, so it would have been unwise to raise the idea. Meanwhile, the proprietor of the Old Dutch yearned for the additional business that would accrue from offering more genuine shoo-fly pies.

DISCUSSION

1. Apply the strategic decision process to the situation faced by the Old Dutch's proprietor. Following the method given in Chapter 1, reach each of the four key decisions, insofar as the facts given in this case permit you.
2. Your analysis should have found more than one strategy that might be chosen. Which of the options would you prefer? Why?
3. How might a small firm like the Old Dutch benefit from using a formal planning process? What would be some differences between a process suitable for it and a formal process in a large corporation?

CASE 1-2

Downtown YWCA

Center City, U.S.A. is a community of 160,000 persons located in central Iowa. It is primarily an industrial town with more than 100 medium and large manufacturers of machinery, tools, and chemicals. Center City's downtown, like many others, is suffering with industrial

---

Names of the organizations and the executives are disguised to protect their identity. This case was prepared by Professor A. H. Kizilbash, Northern Illinois University, as a basis for class discussion.

blight and decay. Most large retailers and other businesses have moved out of the down-town.

A YWCA located in the downtown of Center City has found itself in a difficult situa-tion. Its membership has dropped by 28% in the past 5 years and the revenues from vari-ous recreational and athletic programs have been halved. The Managing Director believes that the "Y" is no longer reaching many persons of middle- and upper-income back-grounds. Out of 2,050 paid members, the Director believes approximately 1,800 have blue-collar jobs and are in the lower middle class.

Center City has a very successful YMCA with large and modern facilities. It is be-lieved that this YMCA is a "poor man's country club." It attracts a large number of persons from middle- and upper-income backgrounds. Center City also has 3 country clubs which offer health and recreational facilities. The local park district is considered to be one of the most successful in the state. It offers a full range of recreational and athletic programs. There are 2 junior colleges located in town and they also offer many recreational facilities. For instance, if a person is looking for swimming or aerobic dance lessons, she can choose from those offered by YWCA, YMCA, Park District, Country Clubs, or Junior Col-leges.

While YWCA membership is restricted to women and children, YMCA is open to both sexes. YMCA only offers physical fitness and recreational programs and facilities. YWCA, in contrast, provides certain needed community services, such as a temporary home for women in transition, in addition to recreational programs and facilities. In providing athletic and recreational services, YWCA is in direct competition with YMCA and the Park District. Both YMCA and the Park District are thought to be more successful than the YWCA. The Director has been quoted as saying that the primary purpose of Center City YWCA is to meet the needs of women in the community. In this regard it is interesting to note that the YMCA has more female participants in its athletic and recreational programs than the YWCA.

The Director of Center City YWCA recruited the services of a local marketing consul-tant to look at their situation and to make recommendations. Excerpts from the consul-tant's report are presented in the remainder of this case.

EXHIBIT 1
Goals and Objectives (Survey Results)

There is considerable disagreement among staff, board, and members as to the objectives and goals of the Center City YWCA.

- Serving the needs of women.*
- Serving the needs of underprivileged.*
- Meeting the needs of handicapped.*
- Continued survival.*
- Eliminate racism.*
- Fighting for women's causes.*
- Serve leisure time needs of the community.
- Helping unwed mothers.
- Providing assistance to abused women.
- Providing help to women in transition.
- Financial independence.*
- Provide programs for physical fitness.*
- Work with minority women.*

---

*Indicates frequently mentioned items.

EXHIBIT 2
Problems Facing Center City YWCA (Survey Results)

- YW has no direction.
- Has poor location (downtown).
- Organization is in limbo.
- Don't know which programs are successful.
- YW has a poor image in the community.
- Facilities are in terrible shape.
- Has the image of an unsuccessful organization.
- YW is trying to be something for everybody.
- Lack of appropriate balance between revenue and non-revenue producing programs.
- Not enough members.
- YWCA programs do not get adequate publicity.
- YWCA is not up with the trends.
- Organization lacks vitality.
- Failure to actively engage in long-range planning.
- Lack of agreement among staff members as to what should be the goals and objectives of YWCA. Some want it to be primarily a physical fitness and recreational agency; others want to make it a social change agency.
- Poor location in a high crime area.
- Money-making programs do not get necessary support of funds.
- Too much powerful competition from YMCA, health clubs, and others.
- Going in all directions.
- Unwilling to change.
- Don't drop programs as fast as they are added.

EXHIBIT 3
Strengths of Center City YWCA
(Survey Results)

- Children's market (ages 2–12) well served with athletic and recreational programs.
- Good dance program.
- Good swimming program.
- Special service programs for women (e.g., Battered Women's Program).
- Aerobics dance for adult women.
- Special programs for the mentally handicapped.
- Personal touch in instruction.
- Lower cost of lessons.
- Good instruction.

EXHIBIT 4
Overall Image (Survey Results)

Most respondents indicated that YWCA has a dual image. On the one hand it is recognized for its physical fitness programs for children, and on the other hand it is known as an institution that offers some social services for women. The overall image is not very strong and is neither very positive nor negative. It can be best described as that "other institution, other than YMCA." The image is quite fuzzy. YW does not have the image of an alive, contemporary, and successful organization. Its name is often associated with the decade of the 1950's and with the militant women's movement.

DISCUSSION

1. Develop a marketing program (including strategy) for the Center City YWCA.
2. How can the Center City YWCA segment the market, differentiate itself from the other institutions, and develop a unique market position?

Must do
2. before 1.

PART TWO

STRATEGIC DECISIONS AND THEIR INTEGRATION

2

Corporate Decisions

We approach the study of marketing strategies by first dealing with the corporate strategies. The latter are broader than the scope of marketing and concern the whole spectrum of functions managed in the entire enterprise or its major units (SBUs). Therefore this chapter focuses on the chief executives' strategic decisions. We first explain their roles and then describe the corporate planning system, with a decision model and an overview of top-level strategic problems. We then discuss several of the chief options and the factors relevant in choosing them. Finally, we illustrate the decision tasks involved in allocating resources to strategic programs.

LEADERSHIP OF PLANNING

In large firms, the corporate level includes the chief executive officer (CEO) and the supporting executives and staff. With ultimate power at the top, its decisions affect or constrain all decisions at lower levels. The top level plays a vital role in strategic planning. Lorange has described the CEO's role in these terms:

> The CEO is the person ultimately responsible for strategic decision-making in the firm. Although he might have delegated larger or smaller parts of this task, he is still responsible. Given that a strategic planning system is intended to facilitate

better strategic decision-making, it is clear that the system must be designed to suit the needs of and the decision-making style of the CEO. Unless the CEO is able to understand and feel comfortable with the rationale for the particular design, he will probably not make much use of the strategic planning system as an integrated part of his decision making.[1]

Lorange's statement contains two notable points: (1) there would be no strategic-planning system without the CEO's determination to have it, and (2) the system's nature depends on the CEO's decision style.

Beyond leadership, the CEO and assistants exercise such functions as the following, which profoundly affect the plans created by those lower in the corporation:

1. Directions come from the top (but not rigid directives that would stifle creative thinking below). The *mission* of the firm (the long-range vision of what the firm intends to become) and the specific *objectives* that the lower managers are expected to meet are decided at and communicated from the top level. That the rewards of those managers are normally keyed to meeting objectives adds weight to this.
2. All significant strategic actions proposed by the various management units in the firm will require *approval* at the top level. Every plan developed by those managers will be conceived with an eye to what the top executives appear to strive for.
3. All of the *funds are allocated* from the top. This function alone would ensure strong influence by the corporate level over strategic planning.

Planning is a very personal thing. How and whether it is done and whether it is effective in directing actual operations depend on the attitudes of various managers at all levels. Those attitudes toward planning tend to be positive—and compliance with plans is high—when the CEO has a strong conviction about the need for planning, exerts leadership in the plans' formulation, and follows through to ensure adherence to them.

CORPORATE DECISION PROCESS

The four-stage planning that was charted in Figure 1-1 and explained in Chapter 1 applies to each level of strategic decision making. Some adaptations must be made, however, for its use at each level. The corporate level is distinguished by having a dual concern with (1) strategies determined for the entire firm and formulated at this level and (2) strategies that lower-level units initiate for their own management, which the corporate level approves or modifies or rejects.

---

[1]Peter Lorange, *Corporate Planning: An Executive Viewpoint*, © 1980, p. 257. Reprinted by permission of Prentice-Hall, Inc., Englewood Cliffs, N.J.

FIGURE 2-1. Major decisions made in corporate strategic planning. The four major decisions are listed across the top of the figure.

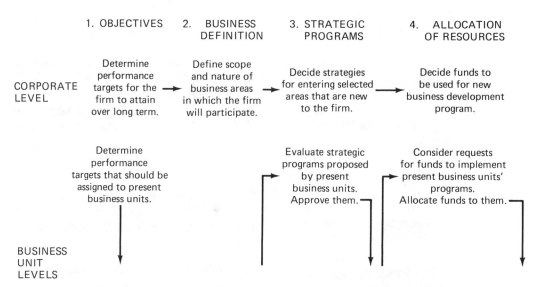

Figure 2-1 is our basic model from Chapter 1, with the same four major decisions, but it includes the two-level concern of corporate management. Corporate planning differs from that of the underlying business units in the firm in having (1) the maximum breadth, spanning all the units, and (2) the longest-range horizon. For us, *long range* means a planning interval of a three years' minimum, although five years is customary and ten years or longer may be appropriate for major projects. The corporate level is equally concerned with annual plans and will indicate down the line what is expected during the coming year. Each unit's executive should be allowed to suggest a fair level for its goals.

Modern CEOs tend to evolve their objectives gradually and in consultation with fellow executives. These exchanges not only elicit helpful insights but also prepare everyone to accept the finally determined objectives. Indeed, frank and informal discussions between managerial levels are important in creating a good planning environment.

Bear in mind that our discussion will concentrate on strategic planning for very large firms. Small firms typify our economy, in which a proprietor or manager does whatever planning exists. Such a person is unlikely to use any systematic model. Somewhat larger firms have managers for each function. These managers may have a planning relationship similar to that depicted in Figure 2-1, on a single level under the CEO. All strategic decisions would probably be formulated by that CEO. It is in major and diversified companies that SBUs and PMUs are organized. We will concentrate on them to study modern strategic management, although our principles should be useful in smaller firms.

OBJECTIVES

Before deciding on objectives, top executives should have decided on some other important aspects. For example, the long-run mission of the firm is usually expressed only in words, whereas objectives should also be specified in numbers (for levels of performance) and dates (responsibilities for completing performance). Besides the broad missions, both the top executives' expectations and the performance levels required for survival should be considered.

The kinds of objectives must be defined early also, consistent with the firm's mission. What we mean by *kinds* may be evident in the following three common objectives, which are related to a situation in which they would be appropriate:

- When the primary consideration is to make the firm's securities more attractive: maximize net profits (perhaps in terms of return on the stockholders' equity [ROE])
- When the firm is in mortal combat with strong competitors in consumer-packaged goods, and it is vital to stand well with distributors and to maintain sales-force morale: a market performance goal (perhaps share of market [SOM] in units sold)
- When the firm has fine growth opportunities or is under pressure to accomplish growth (from stockholders or financial firms): set objectives for growth of available funds (that is, cash flow)

In determining the level of objectives, it is necessary to consider: (1) the firm's current assessment (discussed in Chapter 1), and (2) changes in the environment that are foreseen during the period being planned. As any review of recent business history reveals, enterprises are increasingly facing radical and rapid change. As far as changes can be anticipated, strategies should endeavor to cope with them.

Several "scenarios," or descriptions of the future, should be developed. Such scenarios become the basis of both long- and short-range planning. Just a single scenario is hardly sufficient for planning, since different environments may be plausible. A growing practice is *multiple scenario analysis* (MSA). One procedure for MSA follows these steps:

1. Isolate assumptions about the future which seem sure to occur during the planning time frame.
2. Identify key "impact variables" that are expected to have the most significant effect.
3. Specify other environmental variables which might affect the way that the impact variables will behave.

4. Construct at least two scenarios (descriptions of possible futures) that depict a range of behavior of the impact variables.[2]

With these scenarios in hand, planners can proceed further into strategic planning. They may choose to develop strategies to fit each scenario or may first choose one scenario and develop strategy for it.

Thus the long-range objectives for the whole firm are set. These are then translated into interim objectives for each year so that the periodic plans will converge toward the longer-range goals. The CEO should take part in these determinations and, as the leader of planning, inform other corporate and lower-level executives about what is expected in the future. A specific figure summarizing the objectives of the whole organization will probably be given so that lower-level managers and decision makers can seek strategic means whereby their business units can contribute appropriately.

DEFINING THE CORPORATE BUSINESS

When the planning activities begin for a particular future period, the firm should already have a clear statement of its overall business scope and that of each planning unit. Such a statement is a prerequisite to planning, because each strategic decision should deal with a homogeneous product and market, for a uniquely suitable strategy.

Definition of the total business scope for each planning unit is crucial. These definitions, however, must eventually change with the environment and with the changing character of the firm. How one firm redefined its focus over its history can be illustrated by summarizing the experience of the Continental Group, Inc., which has evolved over more than eighty years from a relatively simple business to a complex set of businesses:

> Continental Can Company was formed in Syracuse, New York in 1904, with an initial investment of $500,000. It incorporated in 1913 and was listed on the New York Stock Exchange the next year. The company quickly expanded can manufacturing technology, products, and marketplace coverage.
>
> Continental Can acquired several other can manufacturers over the next fifteen years in the United States, entered the Canadian market, and later acquired other can companies in Mexico and Europe. If it had defined itself initially as a manufacturer of cans serving the United States, it would then redefine itself as "international."
>
> Continental Can made greater changes in its business focus in 1942 when it acquired four makers of paper and fiber cans. More change ensued over the next fourteen years as Continental not only increased its product offering in metal, paper, and fiber cans but also acquired other firms that made paper cups and plates, crown caps, fiber drums, stoppers, paper bags, corrugated boxes, collapsible tub-

---

[2]R. E. Linneman and Harold E. Klein, "The Use of Multiple Scenarios by U.S. Industrial Companies," *Long Range Planning*, February 1979, p. 83.

ing, glass bottles and jars, paper milk containers, and other packaging products. In this era, Continental Can was outgrowing its title and might have defined itself as an international and comprehensive packaging manufacturer.

Also over its first seventy years, Continental Can had acquired firms that made a variety of products outside packaging: e.g., lamps and home furnishings, tools, auto stampings, aircraft maintenance, sausage casings, and plastic pipe fittings. These clearly would fall outside a definition of "packaging," which was the core business. Perhaps because it could neither plan nor operate efficiently such a conglomerate, Continental sooner or later disposed of most of those businesses.

Meanwhile, in 1947 Continental made a backward integration to obtain its own source of raw material and acquired two timber companies. Subsequently more timber firms and lumber manufacturers were added. Much of their output was sold to users outside of Continental's own plants and for varied purposes; this added to the redefinition of Continental's business area outside of packaging.

The firm's name was changed to reflect its growing diversity, in 1977, to The Continental Group, Inc. In that year a wholly different type of business entered Continental's fold when it acquired an insurance holding company. Thereby it moved from a manufacturing into a service business, one with no affinity to packaging or forest products. Since 1977 the company has invested to broaden its insurance franchise. This includes the $86 million acquisition of a mortgage insurance company and recently (1983) of a life insurance agency system.

In 1979 Continental Group entered another industry when it purchased Florida Gas Company for $351 million, which operates an interstate gas pipeline in the southeast. This began diversification into energy. The energy business in turn expanded with additional ventures in pipeline operations, hydrocarbon extraction, and particularly oil and gas exploration and development. A significant expansion in energy occurred when Continental bought a half-ownership of Supron, a gas and oil exploration and development firm. Its energy sector was increasing further in 1983, when it received long-awaited Federal approval to begin carrying petroleum products also through its pipelines.

When a firm makes so many changes, how can one define it? The company did that in broad terms in 1983:

... Continental Group has become a diversified international corporation active in packaging, forest products, insurance, and energy.[3]

Its mission was indicated in the report quoted above with statements like these: "manage each of these businesses for superior performance"; "concentrate our efforts in attractive segments"; and "build a portfolio of businesses that combined have a sustained growth rate exceeding that of the gross national product." We assume that the company was also being directed toward some more specific objectives that top executives were privately assigning to its various divisions in quantified terms.

To orient ourselves to the level of strategies that are under discussion, we show an organization structure of the Continental Group's businesses in Figure 2-2. This is a complex firm. And like the 3M Company whose sectors are listed in Chapter 4, it has a strategic decision level between the corporate and

---

[3]*Annual Report to Shareowners* (Stamford, Conn.: Continental Group, Inc., 1983).

FIGURE 2-2. Strategic-planning levels in the Continental Group, Inc. in 1982. This chart does not include all the strategic-planning centers in the Forest Products group, nor does it fully adhere to the titles given to them in the firm.

Source: *Continental Group at a Glance* (Stamford, Conn.: Continental Group, Inc.).

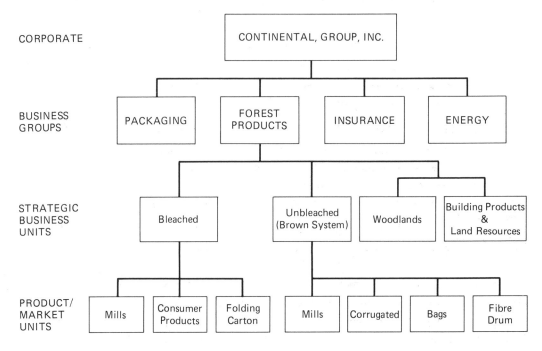

SBU sectors, which are labeled as "groups" of similar businesses. For one of these groups, Forest Products, its SBUs and some of its PMUs also are shown.

By internal analysis, existing businesses may discover how to improve their efficiency and realize their potentials. *External* analysis of each industry and market in which the firm contends is often even more beneficial. Porter asserts that

> understanding industry structure must be the starting point for strategic analysis.[4]

As he describes structural analysis, it concerns

> the basic, underlying characteristics of an industry rooted in its economics and technology that shape the arena in which competitive strategy must be set.[5]

Market potentials and the share that the firm is likely to capture should be anticipated in order to arrive at a sales forecast and projected profits for each planning unit.

---

[4]Michael Porter, *Competitive Strategy* (New York: Free Press, 1980), p. 7
[5]Ibid., p. 6.

If the performance required by the objectives could not be attained within the firm's present product/market scope, some diversification should be considered (unless it is preferable to divest some weak present business to bring results up to that level). Since the number of possible options for diversification may be overwhelming, a systematic way of identifying the more worthwhile options is desirable. Diversification decisions involve two steps: (1) selecting the businesses to consider and (2) deciding whether there is a strategic program that is feasible for the firm and has a good chance for successful entry. These steps are tightly linked.

Preceding studies of the firm and its competitive ability would have highlighted its differential advantages and weaknesses as compared with rivals. With these criteria for deciding on appropriate businesses, the analysis can proceed. Some of the analytical methods applicable to this type of problem will be covered in Chapter 3. The best among the alternatives can serve as a tentative redefinition of the firm's business, pending decisions on available resources for such ventures.

STRATEGIC PROGRAMS

The third major stage in corporate strategy decisions consists of finding the means or programs for entering them. This is the second part of the business development decision (selecting the possible areas having been the first). Let us describe the interrelations of these two decisions with a hypothetical decision that might have been considered in a company like the Continental Group, Inc. (not an actual incident):

1. Should Continental Group redefine its business—and, if so, into what industry?
   a. It has been falling short of its objectives and needs performance improvement unlikely to be obtained in its present business.
   b. The firm has capability in metal containers, of which one product line that it has not entered is steel drums. It has various functional strengths that would make it competitive in that line.
2. How—with what strategy—would Continental Group enter the metal drum business? Would such a strategic program enhance the firm's performance and make that a desirable area for new development?
   a. To enter this business, Continental Group should install its own production equipment rather than acquire any of the existing firms. An innovative marketing program that should succeed has been planned, but no ways to differentiate its drums from those of competitors are envisioned.
   b. Considering the competition and that the market for drums shows only meager growth over the next five years, as well as entry costs, profit potentials for Continental Group would fall below its target level. This option is discarded.

Deciding on new fields of business and formulating strategies to enter them should be deliberated long and hard. The alternatives considered in one year, say in 1985, may have first been considered years earlier, say in 1979, when the situation was not ripe (the strategic window was not open). Perhaps an area first considered in 1983 was rejected because of questionable prospects. Again in 1984 the firm was not yet ready with a superior product; but by 1985 these obstacles were gone, and the firm had the marketing capabilities. Therefore the determinations on what area to enter and on the strategic programs may be the culmination of years of thought and research.

Alternative strategic programs will be described shortly in another section. A number of programs may be conceived and analyzed. Two or more of the better programs should be detailed in writing. Then their costs and revenue projections should be estimated over a long-term period, together with investments. This analysis ends with comparative projections that enable the firm to choose the program best fulfilling the objectives.

RESOURCE ALLOCATIONS

A program can be executed, of course, only when the necessary funds are provided. The ultimate decision is whether—or how much of—the funds sought for a program will be approved. And approval for any large sum is the responsibility of the CEO or board of directors. The fourth decision in the strategic-planning process, resource allocations, is often the most difficult for corporate management because there are so many contenders for available funds. Probably no corporation will have a flow of funds that will satisfy all requests made in the planning process. Some corporate planners say that their work largely involves taking funds from someone and giving them to someone else. Although true in one sense, that statement masks the immense amount of fact digging and analysis that underlies intelligent allocations.

The corporation makes three types of strategic allocations of funds:

- Existing business units' products, whose market positions should be maintained and whose features or quality should be improved.
- Extensions of existing product lines into a greater variety to serve new or segmented markets or into innovative designs that would replace them.
- New businesses and products, lying outside the defined focus of the existing units, that will be developed with the corporation's strategies.

It may be apparent that deciding how to cut the corporate pie into the right-sized pieces (to maximize performance) for those three types of claimants is hard to determine. The decision is rendered more complex because there are numerous markets and product lines—both existing and projected, as well as short- and long-range objectives. An example of resource allocation will be given later in this chapter.

This decision stage ends the corporate strategic-planning cycle. The work of the planners is continuous, however. They must monitor or assist the new corporate expansion projects that have been authorized, study the performance of the various SBUs, scan the outside environment, and look at prospects.

STRATEGIC OPTIONS

Finding or creating strategies has been discussed without stating the types of alternatives that might be considered. Actually there is a myriad of conceivable strategies, but our discussion can be limited by describing the categories or kinds of expansion strategies.

As a first step in categorization, consider two general dimensions in which a business may be redefined: (1) remaining within the scope of its existing product market areas or (2) moving into other areas. Each of these two dimensions contains three types of general strategies:

— Redefining within present areas of business:
    Lateral integration
    Backward integration
    Forward integration
— Expanding into business areas new to the firm:
    Concentration
    Diversification
    Conglomeration

Those strategic options are shown graphically in Figure 2-3. The business area in which a firm is participating at the time of planning is in the left portion of Figure 2-3. For its customers in that area, the firm is currently performing certain functions (e.g., a bank is carrying on certain services for consumers' savings while a paper company is manufacturing certain types of papers). With no change in strategy, the firm would continue in the same technologies to produce products for the same markets. The firm may expand its business while remaining in the *same* technologies in these three ways:

— *Lateral integration:* The firm penetrates its markets further, on its own or by merging with or acquiring another firm in the same business. The result should be selling a greater quantity of the product because more customers are acquired from the merged firm. For example, when American Stores (a supermarket chain) in the East acquired Alpha Beta Stores in the Far West, the former firm became larger with more customers served.

— *Backward integration:* The firm can also expand its business by creating or acquiring its source of supply. When Continental Group, Inc., acquired some timber companies as raw material sources for its paper containers, it was integrating backward.

FIGURE 2-3. Vectors for corporate expansion strategies.

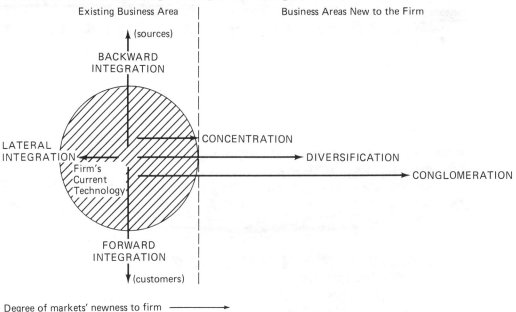

Degree of markets' newness to firm ——————▶

Forward integration: In the opposite direction, a firm may expand by acquiring its own customers or replacing them in a distribution channel. Or it may move into a stage of manufacturing beyond its current stage, and thereby benefit from greater value added to its original product. Continental Group exemplified this by moving into a byproduct manufactured from its own natural gas. The automotive field has many examples of manufacturers taking over or building their own wholesale and retail outlets: tires, gasoline, mufflers, and other items.

Integration is an option that firms usually consider among their strategies for growth. It may involve limited risk, since the firm is already familiar with the markets in that business (and in backward integration can ensure a market with its own purchases). Unfamiliar technology, however, may be a serious risk (as in moving backward to product parts or materials), as may be unfamiliar managerial tasks (as in directing a distribution network of stores when integrating forward). Integration may also be precluded by overcrowding of competition, by cyclical or flat sales in that business, or by inability to acquire a viable firm without paying an exorbitant price.

In Figure 2-3, there are three other strategies, whose arrows run outside the circle of the firm's existing technology. Let us describe them:

Concentration includes going into business areas that are on the periphery of the firm's existing technology, but in which it is selling to markets it already serves.

Diversification goes further into different technologies (and, usually, markets), but it is still in the same general industry.

Conglomeration represents a radical change of business, with basic changes of technology as it moves into new businesses (and usually different marketing techniques).

Trying to depict corporate strategies with the single dimension of technology presents an incomplete picture. Moving into new markets also carries a firm into new businesses. Both the technology and the market dimensions are charted in Figure 2-4, which should clarify the meanings given for these three options.

The first, or northwestern, square in Figure 2-4 (number 0,0) involves lit-

FIGURE 2-4. Technology and market vectors for classifying strategies.

Source: Adapted from H. Igor Ansoff, "Strategies for Diversification," *Harvard Business Review,* September–October 1957, pp. 113–124. Copyright © 1957 by the President and Fellows of Harvard College; all rights reserved.

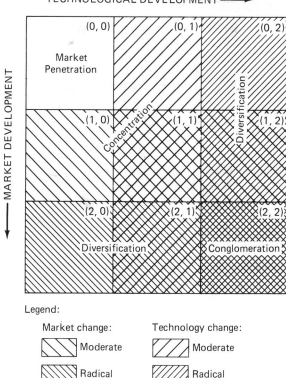

tle change, which is why it is not shaded. Often firms expand while keeping within that cell when its full demand has not been exploited.

— *Concentration* is the most typical expansion strategy route. If a firm's position is well established in its present markets, it may take advantage of this by moving to cell 1,0. If its strength lies more in technical abilities and efficiency, it may do better in cell 0,1. Somewhat more venturesome is moving slightly from its established base by doing both (to cell 1,1).

> Lubrizol Company early in its existence (in the 1920s) determined to concentrate on oil additives. This meant dropping most of its product line and sales force to funnel resources into developing additives. Since then it has obtained 600 patents in the business and added a variety of related products.
>
> The results are hardly surprising: Lubrizol holds a strong grip now as leader of the oil additive business. It has been a very profitable strategy. The firm has averaged the highest return on equity (almost 26 percent) of any U.S. chemical company during the five years through 1981.[6]

Concentration was clearly the best corporate strategy for Lubrizol to choose, capitalizing on its R & D and production experience. It is attractive, however, only when the markets that the firm is serving are growing ones and not excessively crowded. Of course managerial abilities are essential to tap opportunities and to use resources in them.

Diversification, in our restricted sense of the word, refers to strategies that take the firm into radically new technology or new markets (not both). By *new* we mean new in the firm's experience. We cannot draw a precise boundary to distinguish diversification from concentration and conglomeration. Our criterion is that the firm faces different markets, competition, or technology in such expansion. One major benefit of entering the new business is that a different set of demands is being marketed to. General Motors moved into diesel locomotives' manufacturing long ago, which meant taking its familiar technology into a radically different market. That was a fortunate decision in 1980–81 when the railroad's demands for motive power held up while the demand for automobiles declined.

Conglomeration occupies the extreme cell (2,2) of Figure 2-4. A firm that conglomerates is willing to compete in businesses that are heterogeneous both in markets served and in products offered. This option moves furthest from an existing base in markets and product lines. Managements of corporations that adopt this type of strategy must be versatile and able to absorb risk. Strong finances and management skill are needed.

Conglomeration can bring about the fastest rate of expansion because it encompasses the widest variety of opportunities. This strategy had its heyday during the 1970s when it was very popular—particularly to investors and other financial interests—but it is less popular now. The troubles to which it can lead are like those being encountered by the largest of conglomerates, Inter-

---

[6]*Forbes,* January 4, 1982, p. 116.

national Telephone & Telegraph (ITT). With its earnings dropping sharply and a number of its 250 units being unprofitable, ITT is now striving to divest.[7]

METHODS OF IMPLEMENTATION

Beyond the selection of a general kind of strategy are two stages: (1) searching for *opportunities* for expansion (such a specific task in each case that we will not discuss it here) and (2) choosing the method of *implementing* the general expansion strategy. There are four general routes for implementing expansion:

Development
Acquisition
Joint Venture
Licensing

Development and acquisition are usually more common than joint venture and licensing.

Development means newly creating or implementing the business expansion through the work done within the organization, an internal route. With respect to moving into new markets, the firm would create its own selling and distributing facilities and move in under its own power. In new-product expansion or innovation, the firm would do so through its own design and development capabilities. (Sometimes outside expertise is used, but it is a company-managed expansion.)

The advantages involved in developing a new product are that (1) the firm may exclusively offer it if features can be patented or processes kept secret; (2) even though the firm may not retain exclusivity, it will have a long lead time over competitors' entries; and (3) what is created tends to be more innovative or appropriate to the firm. *Dis*advantages include (1) risks that the development efforts will fail; (2) a lack of the needed expertise or other resources within the firm; (3) the frequently long period required for development, which may be ten years or much more for really innovative products (and sometimes a long period for developing a new market); and (4) the risk of competitive "scoops" that beat the firm to the market.

Acquisition is the purchase and owning of what has been developed by another firm. The acquirer may take over or merge with another firm in its entirety. (Thus DuPont purchased New England Nuclear in order to bring electronics skills and products into its great chemical empire.) The acquisition may involve taking over only one business or division of the selling firm. (For instance, ConAgra purchased Banquet Foods from RCA, which enabled ConAgra to diversify quickly into frozen prepared foods.) Sometimes a single product is acquired, usually along with the facilities to make or serve it.

---

[7]"ITT: Groping for a New Strategy," *Business Week*, December 15, 1980.

There are strong advantages to the acquisition route: (1) the relative speed of its accomplishment, (2) the fact that what would be acquired is already established and can be evaluated concretely before the expanding firm decides to take it over, and (3) specialized personnel and facilities can be brought over with the acquisition to ensure continued operation without draining the staff of the acquiring firm. The wisdom of using acquisition depends on whether there are businesses that can be acquired. A model of this strategy is the building of the James River Corporation in the paper business. Its entrepreneurs started by purchasing small paper mills that could be bought at rather low prices, simply because they could not contend against the large and more modern paper corporations. Their strategy was that they could build a large business composed of small mills, with low capitalization, which would grow to a large base over which to spread their overhead costs. With this approach James River has become a large and profitable member of the paper industry.

In many cases, the following disadvantages rule out acquisitions: (1) too high a price may be demanded for an existing business that is a proven success or has rosy potentials; (2) it may strain the acquirer's finances and managerial capacity; (3) the potential profits of the added business may prove to be illusions; (4) the transfer of management and technical personnel from the acquired business may be disappointing; and (5) the acquired business may turn out to be too incompatible. The problem of depending on key people in the acquired firm can be illustrated by General Foods' troubles in acquiring Burger Chef, of which GF eventually had to dispose. And because of incompatibility RCA eventually had to sell Banquet Foods, mentioned above, which it had acquired earlier:

> Banquet never fit into RCA's high technology, show business world. "They were thinking of Skylab when Banquet was talking chicken pot pies," says A. H. Rosenfeld . . . "It's the old story that the shoemaker should stick to his last." Banquet officers agree: "The electronics and food worlds are miles apart. . . ."[8]

Some conglomerates have been able to acquire a wide heterogeneity of businesses and manage them profitably. But firms like RCA that have traditionally concentrated in one industry tend not to have that versatility.

Joint ventures offer a route that is short of assuming full ownership of an acquired firm or a newly created one. As the term indicates, ownership is shared with one or more other firms. Two situations in which this is logical occur (1) when the new business is partially based on the special competence of an expanding firm in one technical field but also requires such competence in an utterly different field; and (2) when, in the case of ventures in foreign countries, nationals often better understand how to deal in their own country and legal restrictions sometimes require that foreign investors share ownership with nationals.

---

[8]"New Owner Rejuvenates Banquet Foods," *Wall Street Journal*, February 8, 1982, p. 29.

Both situations are found in the Dow Corning Corporation. The business area in which it operates is based partly in chemicals (in which Dow is one of the top companies) and in specialty glass products (in which Corning Glass Works is world leader). These two firms went together in joint ownership of Dow Corning. In turn, to deal with the Japanese market, Dow Corning holds half ownership in a joint venture with Iwaki Glass, a Japanese manufacturer.

The joint venture method may be the right choice when a partner firm is needed for supplying technology or resources or for risk sharing. Also, of course, foreign nations' laws or market-entry difficulties make this route favorable for overseas expansion. On the other hand, it obviously reduces potential profits and raises questions of whether the partner firm will prove to be compatible.

Licensing means the obtaining of rights (to a product, a component, or a technology) from the firm that owns the patents or has other means of exclusivity. Licensing is commonly used to gain access to certain processes or some part or component. "Cross-licensing" is sometimes found, in which firm A licenses use of its patents to firm B, which, in turn, licenses its patents to firm A. Licensing and the three other routes just described should be considered as possibilities.

DECISION FACTORS

The corporate planners should have found or conceived of a number of alternative strategies for the expansion of the firm's business. They will have to make very painstaking appraisals of each alternative's relative merits. These should of course be judged in terms of the corporate objectives. There also are judgments regarding which of the four routes of expansion (development, acquisition, joint ventures, or licensing) would be best, given the situation. An equally important question will be whether or not the programs are within the firm's practical capabilities. None of this is general or theoretical. Specific markets, products, and firms must be considered.

To expand or diversify is a risky and complicated decision. Underlying it should be the evaluation of numerous factors specific to the firm's situation and to the expansion area being studied. We cannot discuss all those factors in depth, but we can list several categories:

1. Market situation
   Characteristics of the given market
   Size of potential purchases
   Needs of buyers for the selected product
   Growth projections
   Location of market clusters or of key accounts
2. Competitive situation
   The firms that now offer such products or that are likely to develop
   products that would rival the product being considered

Strengths and competitive practices of those firms
Degree of sales concentration among strong competitors
Market-share forecasts for competitors
3. Differential advantages of this firm over competitors
Product superiorities and breadth of assortment
Market position: Image and reputation
Customer loyalty
Established distribution channels
Sales organization
Technology: Production
Product development
Facilities
Financial strength
Management and other personnel
Natural resources
4. Convergence of proposed diversification to the firm
Management experience, style, and attitudes
Product-line compatibility
Marketing organization and abilities
Technical competence

A heavy stress should be placed on the firm's differential advantages. A brief statement that well expresses a strategy based on such advantages is found in an advertisement of Gould, Inc. (a very large electrical firm):

Over the last five years, sales of Gould's electronic products have grown from $230 million to almost $700 million. That's a compound annual growth rate of 32 percent. Pretax earnings have tripled, and the recent divestiture of our industrial group means that almost 70 percent of pretax earnings now come from electronics.

This growth will be further stimulated through expanded research and development efforts and by small selective acquisitions to increase our product offerings within targeted market segments.

With this new corporate strategy, we are building on our proven technological capabilities to give us the strongest competitive advantage. This positions Gould for market growth to provide above average returns for our shareholders.[9]

The future payoffs for each strategy given serious consideration should be projected in relationship to objectives. Long-term plans projections may have to reach far into the future. The results that should be expected from a given strategy are, of course, hazardous to estimate, but this is necessary. Forecasting the effects of a strategic plan will be discussed later, when our scope is narrowed to a single planning unit.

---

[9]From an advertisement by Gould, Inc., in the *Wall Street Journal*, February 3, 1982, p. 3. Quoted with permission.

ALLOCATION OF RESOURCES

The resources of money and other facilities are like lifeblood for the corporation's various units. How to share them among those claimants is one of the most significant decisions for a CEO. It falls on the corporate-level management to evaluate each unit's request, to appraise the merits of its proposed programs, and to decide what it should be allocated.

Envision this in terms of cash flows: Whatever are the firm's salient objectives, the provision and use of funds is vital. Besides the various operating SBUs' needs, corporate programs such as those described in this chapter need funds. Like other determinations, these should be in two time frames: the long-range and the short-range or periodic (annual) plan. Key factors to be weighed for every SBU are (1) its profitability, (2) its ability to generate funds, and (3) the amount of funds that it will consume. Cash flow determinations are one stage in resource planning, in a series of tasks that culminates in detailed plans and budgets.

Decisions on resources can be illustrated by describing an imaginary firm:

Beaver-Western Industries (or BWI) is a moderately diversified producer of machinery and its components. Most sales are to industrial customers, and products are shipped directly from BWI factories. BWI began as a merger of two makers of propulsion equipment: Beaver in gasoline propulsion and Western in steam. When the steam market dwindled, the Western division was disposed of, but Beaver is much alive and serves gasoline- and diesel-powered vehicle and equipment manufacturers. BWI has expanded beyond that business and now has four SBUs: Able division, Beaver division, Coda division, and Dare division. Our story begins in 1983 when BWI's corporate planning staff was working on plans for 1984 through 1988.

As BWI's cash flows were being analyzed, its planning people took due note of how the company had performed, by division, during the current year of 1983 (as estimated for the full year on the completed portion).

1983 Estimated performance

Division	Cash flow (millions)			Net profit (percentage of equity
	Generated	Used	Net flow	
Able	$19	$30	$(11)	10.5%
Beaver	25	10	15	15.7
Coda	8	7	1	5.2
Dare	2	6	(4)	2.8
Total from operations	$54	$53	$ 1	
Corporate programs	0	2	(2)	
Total	$54	$55	$ (1)	12.4%

Taking the above situations into consideration as well as the proposals coming up from the SBUs and the prospects of those units and of the corporate development program, the planners' assessments would deal with such points as the following:

Able Division is in the fastest-growth market now and will be for several years to come. It has proposed an expansion in its product line and will have further needs for cash to keep up with expanding demand. It will generate about 50 percent more cash in 1984, but its needs will increase nearly as fast, so that a negative flow should be expected in that SBU—well justified to hold market share and enjoy growing profits in that business.

Beaver Division should increase its profit rate in 1984, but it is so well established in mature markets that its cash needs will actually not increase while sales rise moderately. A greater cash flow in 1984 is a reasonable expectation, which will fortunately balance the negative flow of Able Division.

Coda Division is in unstable markets and has been a problem in the past. Prospects for 1984 are for somewhat better profit, but looking further ahead one sees such dangers that the division does not merit more investment. Less cash should be put into it next year, so that it will be a better cash contributor.

Dare Division was newly created a few years ago for expansion of BWI into new markets, including a few really innovative products. Its prosperity still lies in the future, for real market growth has not yet materialized. This division will be kept on a cash diet until that growth is imminent, so it will be given less cash and will presumably break even in 1984 cash flow.

The corporate development programs are three: (1) a new product to be developed that is really in Beaver Division's area and has been assigned to it; (2) longer-range development of a new-product line that may someday constitute a new business; and (3) completion of laboratory work on a product already being evolved, whose placement in an SBU cannot be decided yet. These will jump corporate expenditures to result in $5 million negative cash flow.

The foregoing ideas would be adopted for allocations, provided that they would produce the targeted corporate objectives and that the financial section ensures that the funds will be available.

The foregoing discussion has centered on two principal strategic problems decided at the corporate level: (1) defining the business and determining if and how it should be developed in new directions, and (2) allocating resources to the various strategic units. Those are continuing decisions for corporate managers, but other strategic questions will arise for top-level decision too. Here are some examples of what we mean:

An electrical manufacturer has traditionally sold its appliances only under its one brand name. The question arises of breaking that tradition when a leading mass retailer asks this firm to make similar appliances under this retailer's own label.

A health and beauty-care products manufacturer considers whether to begin marketing also by direct selling to homes.

A chemicals manufacturer has been making plastic pipe in three plants. It has been proposed that a big Texas plant be built that would consolidate all that manufacturing in one place.

A corporation has enjoyed abnormally large cash inflows, giving it large surplus funds. Meanwhile its common stock is selling at an absurdly low price. Should those funds be used to buy up about 15 percent of the outstanding stock (increasing the remainder's value)?

You will notice that those decisions differ in character from the two types we have dwelt on, as they are not comprehensive (across the firm). They are indicative of the more narrow but serious issues—of strategic import—that top management must occasionally decide.

SUMMARY

In this chapter we first explained why we have elected to study corporate strategy decisions as the starting point for a book on marketing strategies. We discussed the leadership role of the CEO.

We then unveiled the decision process for corporate strategies. This process is a modification of the basic model in Chapter 1 because the planning on that level is two-faceted: guiding and approving the plans made at all the lower levels and also conducting the master plan for the total firm. We then elaborated on that by explaining the decisions at each phase: determining objectives, defining the corporate business (illustrated by the evolution of the Continental Group, Inc.), finding strategic programs to accomplish the desired redefinition of the firm's business, and deciding on resource allocations.

We then went into some detail regarding the six broad options for changing the firm's business, which were also shown graphically. Besides the negative option of retrenching or deleting existing business areas of the firm, there are six positive options for its expansion:

Redefining within present areas of business:
    Lateral integration
    Backward integration
    Forward integration
Expanding into new business areas:
    Concentration
    Diversification
    Conglomeration

In the next section we further discussed changing a firm's business by dealing with the four methods of implementing expansion: development, acquisition, joint venture, and licensing.

Such strategic decisions are important ones and are difficult to make. We outlined the chief factors on which such decisions would tend to rely. And, finally, we briefly described the culminating decision regarding allocating the firm's resources among the programs for both its existing businesses or products and its development (redefinition of businesses). By depicting those decisions in a hypothetical manufacturer of machinery (BWI), we set forth a number of the considerations faced. In closing we reminded readers that the corporate development strategies discussed in Chapter 2 do not constitute all the major problems on which corporate management must decide—although they would tend to be the salient ones. We mentioned various strategic problems that are also part of corporate long-range planning and of top-level strategizing.

REVIEW QUESTIONS

1. *Describe the chief strategic-planning tasks that CEOs perform that make them the key persons in the process.*
2. *At the corporate-executive level, the planning process works in two directions. What are these directions?*
3. *Distinguish between corporate planning and planning conducted at lower levels, in terms of having somewhat different concerns.*
4. *Is any* one *kind of objective superior to* all *other kinds? Explain.*
5. *How might you use a "scenario" to make planning more thorough and realistic? Why would it be better to create more than one scenario?*
6. *Recall (or reread) the stages of the Continental Group's development over its approximately eighty-year life. How did its main objectives seem to change over that time? Its defined business? How did those changes affect what strategic programs would be appropriate for the Continental Group? Or the uses of its resources?*
7. *For the allocating of resources, this textbook speaks of three general strategic decisions. What are they?*
8. *Six options for corporate strategy are grouped into two categories. Among those various options, which one tends to be the most risky? The least risky? Which one is likely to involve the most radical changes, for the firm, in technology and in markets?*
9. *If your firm was a rather small one that specialized in making shoelaces, a business area without growth potential, and had excellent relations with its customers (shoe manufacturers), which of the six vectors for expansion would appear to be the most logical? Explain.*
10. *For the Continental Group, conglomeration was the* last *corporate strategy undertaken. Can you suggest why this would tend to be the last one?*
11. *The K Company wishes to diversify into another specific business field, an industry that is characterized by numerous competitors. The K Company has strong financial resources but needs a rapid boost in its profits at this time (that is, within several months) and in its growth outlook. Which*

method of implementing its diversification would be the most logical in this situation?

12. *The K Company is considering merging with the L Company. To induce the present L Company owners to do this, K Company would have to offer them somewhat over $20 million of its stock in exchange. Name several important factors about L Company that the K Company decision makers should analyze before making such a large commitment.*

Teledyne, Inc.

Teledyne, the Los Angeles-based conglomerate, has been an outstanding success story. Most striking in its history is probably the character and role of its founder and—to date—only chief executive officer, Henry E. Singleton. This was described and commented on by Forbes *magazine in the article quoted below. All of the article pertinent to our purposes is included, and omissions are indicated by ellipsis points.*

When the business history of this era is written, Dr. Henry E. Singleton will probably be one of its towering figures, the equal in accomplishment, if not in fame, of great corporate entrepreneurs like Alfred P. Sloan Jr., Gerard Swope, David Sarnoff, Royal Little. This aloof son of a well-to-do Texas rancher is noteworthy in two respects: for the name and quality of the company, Teledyne, Inc., that he built from scratch; and for his almost arrogant scorn for most conventional business practices. Henry Singleton has always marched to his own drummer—and to a music that most of his peers could not even hear.

His record speaks for itself. Until 1960 Teledyne did not even exist. Five years ago, when it was barely 14 years old, it ranked 202nd among major U.S. corporations listed in *Forbes'* profits 500. Year by year it has climbed in the *Forbes* lists and last year stood number 68, an upstart that had climbed over the heads of great American corporations like International Paper, Avon Products, Texas Instruments, Ingersoll-Rand. . . .

But what really distinguishes Teledyne beyond its position on various lists is that during a period when inflation has been eroding most corporate profit margins, a period when corporations have been selling more and enjoying less, Teledyne's profitability has been growing, not shrinking. Its return on equity, nearly 33% last year, was matched among multibillion-dollar (sales) companies only by American Home Products and Avon Products. After taxes, its return on manufacturing sales was a fat 7.2% *vs.* 5.4% for industry as a whole.

Has Teledyne had setbacks? Indeed it has, but look how it has pulled out of them:

Its Packard Bell division couldn't make it in home TV sets and quit the market. By emphasizing the profitable remainder, Packard Bell is larger and more profitable than ever today.

During the medical malpractice fiasco, Teledyne's Argonaut Insurance had to withdraw from writing such policies and TDY's casualty business took a $104 million writeoff. But by pushing its conventional workman's compensation and other casualty businesses, Argonaut rebuilt its profits and last year they set a new record—$56.7 million.

Who is this business genius Henry Singleton, who turns setbacks into successes, who rarely appears at the Business Round Table or rubs shoulders with his corporate peers? How does he do it? Can he keep it up?

First the "who." He is a ramrod-erect, austerely handsome man of 62 who spent three years at Annapolis, then switched to the Massachusetts Institute of Technology, where he earned a bachelor's, master's and doctorate of science, all in electrical engineering. Educated as a scientist not as a businessman, he did not leap into entrepreneurship

From Robert J. Flaherty, "The Singular Henry Singleton," *Forbes,* July 9, 1979, pp. 45–51. Printed with permission.

but trained for it over several decades at the best schools of practical management in the U.S.—first as a scientist at General Electric, then as a management man at Hughes Aircraft, then in the early days at Litton Industries when founder Charles "Tex" Thornton and Roy L. Ash were building one of the first truly "hot" companies of the post–World War II era. Not until 1960, when he was 43, did Singleton found Teledyne. He did so in company with two of the best brains of the modern business world: George Kozmetsky, now dean of the College of Business Administration at the University of Texas, and Arthur Rock, perhaps the U.S.' most imaginative venture capitalist.

· · · · ·

Maybe because of his unusual background, Singleton has an almost uncanny ability to resist being caught up in the fads and fancies of the moment. Like most great innovators, Henry Singleton is supremely indifferent to criticism. During the early Seventies, when investors and brokers alike lost their original enthusiasm and deserted Teledyne, Singleton had Teledyne buy up its own stock. As each tender offer was oversubscribed by investors of little faith, Singleton took every share they offered. When Wall Street—indeed, even his own directors—urged him to ease up, he kept right on buying. Between October 1972 and February 1976 he reduced Teledyne's outstanding common 64% from 32 million shares to 11.4 million.

Normally a serious man, Singleton allows himself to laugh when he recounts how his stubbornness prevailed. "In October 1972 we tendered for 1 million shares and 8.9 million came in. We took them all at $20 and figured that was a fluke and that we couldn't do it again. But instead of going up, our stock went down. So we kept tendering, first at $14 and then doing two bonds-for-stock swaps. Every time one tender was over the stock would go down and we'd tender again and we'd get a new deluge. Then two more tenders at $18 and $40."

Shareholders who tendered happily at $14 or $40 watched in dismay as, only a few years later, the shares soared to $130. Henry Singleton had been right. The rest of the world—including some of his directors—had been wrong. "I don't believe all this nonsense about market timing," Singleton says. "Just buy very good value and when the market is ready that value will be recognized."

What is most impressive is that Teledyne's capital shrinkage was not achieved at the expense of growth, or by partially liquidating the company. All during these years, Teledyne kept growing. Where in its early days it had grown through acquisitions—145 in all—in its capitalization-shrinking days Teledyne grew from within, and steadily. In 1970, when acquisitions had ceased, revenues were $1.2 billion; in 1974, $1.7 billion; in 1976, $1.9 billion; and so on. This year Teledyne will do $2.6 billion. Yet in the years when sales were more than doubling from the $1.2 billion level, Teledyne made only one minor acquisition. Nor did Teledyne get deeply into debt. In the early stages of his stock-buying program, Singleton did have Teledyne borrow rather heavily but he paid the debt down again out of cash flow. In the process he wiped out all of Teledyne's convertibles and warrants. *Dilution?* Singleton virtually *dehydrated* Teledyne's capital structure. Growing the business while shrinking its capital. Quite a trick. Certainly unique in recent business history.

When investors, disillusioned with growth, again began to be dividend conscious, Teledyne continued to refuse to pay a cash dividend. The second-highest-priced stock on the Big Board (after Superior Oil), Teledyne's cash yield is zero.

But there were other rewards for investors. With revenues growing, profit margins thickening and capitalization shrinking, Teledyne's remaining stockholders enjoyed fantastic upward leverage. During the years 1969 to 1978 revenues increased by 89%, net profits rose 315%. But look at earnings per share! They soared 1,226%. With all those profits being plowed back, Teledyne's equity per share jumped from $11.38 to $68 between 1969 and the end of 1978. All through the early Seventies Wall Street ignored the stock. It was a conglomerate. It had four bad years. It wouldn't pay a dividend. It kept buying its stock against all rhyme and reason. Ugh! Scarcely an analyst bothered with it. For years Teledyne was stuck in a narrow range, rarely getting above 20. But finally Wall Street caught on. After selling as low as 7 7/8 in late 1974, Teledyne stock leaped to over 69 in 1976 and, in 1978, finally passed the 100 mark. Teledyne, which broke all the rules, was one of America's best-performing stocks.

So far, we have not even mentioned what Teledyne makes or sells. That's because what Teledyne makes or sells is less important than the style of the man who runs it. The fact is that Singleton unashamedly runs a conglomerate. What are the products and services upon which Singleton has put his stamp? Offshore drilling units, auto parts, specialty metals, machine tools, electronic components, engines, high fidelity speakers, unmanned aircraft and Water Pik home appliances.

A conglomerate, of course, but Singleton is not even slightly disturbed by the label "conglomerate." Says he: "Today, being a conglomerate is neither a plus nor a minus. While not many companies are called conglomerates, most are." He ticks off some names: GE, Westinghouse and RCA.

This diffuse company is actually quite tightly run. Its board of directors consists of only six people, not the usual dozen or more, and all of them close friends and associates. . . .

Teledyne's management team is a seasoned one. Of the 150 principal executives who worked there in 1976, most are still with the company. They have grown with the organization. Rarely has Teledyne had to reach outside for a turnaround man in a bad situation.

Singleton works closely with his president, George Roberts, who has his doctorate from Carnegie-Mellon in metallurgy. Roberts is the chief operating officer, and an extremely effective one. This is not the kind of conglomerate where headquarters staff only loosely supervises a number of good-size, semi-independent operations. Taking a leaf from Harold Geneen's book, Teledyne has supertight financial controls. Taking a leaf from 3M's corporate books, it breaks up a huge business into a cornucopia of small profit centers—129 in Teledyne's case.

The largest of Teledyne's 129 companies, TDY Continental Motors, is under $300 million in annual sales. It is one of nine companies created out of Teledyne's Continental Motors acquisition. Some of the really small TDY companies are only a few million in annual sales—for example, TDY Engineering Services. "We go to an extreme in splitting businesses up so we can see problems which would be passed over in companies where the units are larger," says Roberts. "By our plan no one business, all by itself, will become momentous." This means the survivability of the entire company will never be jeopardized by failure of one single operation.

What matters is this: So far in 1979, all 129 are profitable. For the last two years only one, semiconductors, was in the red, and that by just a few million.

By setting up computer controls, by training each manager to do what is expected of him, Roberts can handle as many as five company annual profit reviews in a single day. Nor does he waste time and energy in airports and limousines. The heads of the 129 companies take turns coming to him and Singleton in their modern, clean but lean Century City offices on L.A.'s Avenue of the Stars.

Forbes interviews over a thousand company managements every year and we turn instantly skeptical when they tell us: "We're profit-oriented not product-oriented." The fact is that few companies really are that way. Teledyne is a rare exception. "Forget products," Roberts begins, "here's the key: We create an attitude toward having high margins. In our system a company can grow rapidly and its manager be rewarded richly for that growth if he has high margins. If he has low margins, it's hard to get capital from Henry and me. So our people look and understand. Having high margins gets to be the thing to do. No one likes to have trouble getting new money."

Roberts is saying nothing exceptional. What *is* exceptional is the way Teledyne practices what it preaches. There are very few companies of any size, and certainly none of the billion-dollar class, that are as tight with a capital dollar as Teledyne. This year its capital spending will exceed $100 million for the second straight year, but this is a rather miserly sum in relation to Teledyne's cash flow of more than $300 million. Texas Instruments, a company of equal size and technological orientation, will spend more than three times as much. Many companies normally spend more for capital projects than they take in as cash. Not so with Teledyne. This is the real secret of Teledyne's ability to grow.

The key, then, is discipline: no ego trips, only new investments that will quickly pay off in the form of enhanced cash flow. Says George Roberts: "The only way you can make money in some businesses is by not entering them.

"Internally we hold up high-margin companies as examples. Our margin on sales is now over 7% after taxes, vs. a national average for manufacturing of 5.4%. Since we run a broad cross section of businesses, it is clear the rest of American industry can improve, too.

"Take any big old giant company like U.S. Steel. If they really accounted for their business conservatively and line by line in detail as we do, they might conclude they didn't have any margins at all. We make the point that the margin of every product, every project, is important. We preach that our average and the company average is only the average of all their individual moves."

Risk too, is carefully rationed. A coolly rational man, Singleton despises surprises. It is company policy that divisions which are defense contractors will remain relatively small. "We don't want any big prime contracts," says Roberts. "We prefer to be important, technically oriented subcontractors who serve those who want to be prime contractors." That way, if a large contract is aborted TDY will not be hurt.

The effect of all this emphasis on restricting risk and insisting on high returns, Roberts says, is that he's been able to stop preaching. "Now everyone understands that all new projects should return at least 20% on total assets. When leveraged up return on equity can be 30% to 50%. This is so ingrained that few lower-returning proposals are even presented anymore. We hardly ever discuss one."

"Our attitude toward cash generation and asset management came out of our own thought process," says Singleton. "It is not copied. After we acquired a number of businesses we reflected on aspects of business. Our own conclusion was that the key was cash flow."

Singleton may be a scientist and an intellectual but he has an old-fashioned respect for cash. You can't pay bills with bookkeeping profits. He knows that companies have gone broke after reporting big profits for years—Penn Central, for example, and W. T. Grant. He wants to see the color of some of that money in his companies' reports. He wants each company to throw off cash over and above its reinvestment needs, cash that can be utilized for overall corporate purposes. This kind of real, hard cash flow enabled Singleton to buy up his company's stock when it was lying on the bargain counter. It has enabled Teledyne to reduce debt to the point where it amounts to only about 22% of total capital as against 32% and 52% for conglomerates like ITT and Gulf & Western.

Of course, every management wants—or says it wants—a high return on its capital. Henry Singleton wants something more: a *cash* return. Singleton won't pay cash dividends to his own shareholders but he expects them from his company presidents—all 129 of them—over the long run. Roberts says: "Net income without cash is not necessarily net income. We build cash generation into the system of paying our managers. Bonuses can be 100% of base salary."

If it is curious that a man who started as a scientist and became an operating man should finally make his greatest mark in finance, Singleton has nevertheless done just that. American business is still gripped with a mania for bigness. Companies whose stocks sell for five times earnings will think nothing of going out and paying 10 or 15 times earnings for a nice big acquisition when they could tender for their own stock at half the price. Shrinking—a la Teledyne—still isn't done except by a handful of shrewd entrepreneurial companies.

You can explain quite simply what Singleton did financially. When stocks like Teledyne sold for 40, 50 or 60 times earnings he used his high-priced stock as currency to buy other companies relatively cheaply. Then, when his own stock became relatively cheap after the conglomerate crash of 1969, he went in and bought enough of it to shrink the capitalization back to where it was when Teledyne had been a much smaller company. He did so not by selling off assets . . . but first by borrowing, then by husbanding cash from operations.

More recently, Singleton has been turning his hand to the stock market . . . In choosing stocks, he projected Wall Street dogma and relied on his own experience. Teledyne had a below-average multiple he was sure would rise in time. Many other conglomerates were in the same situation. Singleton decided to buy those he felt were well run and undervalued.

· · · · ·

Singleton's biggest move was to put over $130 million . . . into Litton. TDY now holds 27% of Litton, 9.3 million shares, at an average cost of about $14. . . . TDY's Litton holdings are worth $270 million, and still 25% of its insurance company's equity portfolio.

"A fabulous [$140 million] gain," says Chairman Fred R. Sullivan of Walter Kidde & Co., "but when Henry first put all that in one stock I thought he'd gone crazy." Fellow Litton alumnus Sullivan didn't think Singleton crazy, however, when he bought 19% of Walter Kidde.

"I felt Litton was a sound investment," Singleton says. "It's good to buy a large company with fine businesses when the price is beaten down over worry about one problem." (He refers to Litton's costly and protracted shipbuilding fracas with the U.S. Navy.) He adds: "Litton's problem was not a general one but an isolated problem—as ours was with Argonaut Insurance. To me it was hard to believe the heads of a $3 billion or $4 billion business would not be able to handle *one* business problem."

· · · · ·

Singleton may not have to wait forever to be taken out of some of these companies at a good profit. Last year Teledyne bought a block of 450,000 shares of its own stock—$40.1 million worth at the then-going price of $90—from American Financial Corp., a Cincinnati-based financial holding company. Having studied Singleton, American Financial's bosses knew he would be a logical buyer for the shares when he had the cash. And so we have the clue to what may be Singleton's trump card with his stock portfolio. He may simply be waiting until the managements come to the same conclusion he came to: A company's own stock is its best investment. When that day comes he'll be happy to sell their own stock to them. At a nice profit, of course. But potential raiders, beware. Singleton says he wouldn't sell any of his blocks to would-be acquisitors.

Liquid as Teledyne is, why does Henry Singleton still flatly refuse to disburse any cash to his own stockholders—except in exchange for their shares? A few years ago, when Teledyne stock was selling around 10, one of his closest associates begged him to pay at least a token dividend. Singleton refused. He still refuses. To begin with, he asks, what would the stockholder do with the money? Spend it? Teledyne is not an income stock. Reinvest it? Since Teledyne earns 33% on equity, he argues, he can reinvest it better for them than they could for themselves. Besides, the profits have already been taxed; paid out as dividends they get taxed a second time. Why subject the stockholders' money to double taxation?

· · · · ·

If there is a serious weakness in this otherwise brilliant picture, it is this: Teledyne is not so much a system as it is the reflection of one man's singular discipline and his contrary style of thinking and acting. Henry Singleton is trim and healthy at 62 and has no interest in retiring, but man is not immortal. "George Roberts could run this company without me," Singleton replies when asked about Teledyne-without-Singleton. Time will tell.

At any rate, Singleton has found a way to run a multibillion-dollar company in an entrepreneurial, innovative way. Only a handful of giant companies have succeeded in doing that. General Electric, General Motors, IBM, 3M, Dow Chemical perhaps. It may sound farfetched but Teledyne has a fair chance of ending up in that league.

1. Evaluate Henry Singleton's skills as a corporate strategist. What specific qualities and what types of actions have contributed to his success?

2. The Teledyne strategies are rare among large business corporations—and among conglomerates generally. Should and can most corporations adopt and implement similar strategies? Explain.

3. There is *no* mention of *marketing* at any point in the above article from *Forbes*. Nor is much said about any other function. Why? Does its absence from the article mean that marketing plays little part in Teledyne's success? Explain how marketing may help to make possible its success and through whose decisions.

CASE 2-2

Continental Group, Inc.

From its world headquarters in Stamford, Connecticut, the officers of The Continental Group administered, in 1983, worldwide packaging operations and a diversity of businesses in North America. The Continental Group (CG) was now among the very large enterprises, employing nearly 48,000 persons and obtaining revenues exceeding 5.5 billion. We described steps in its history on pages 34 and 35 of Chapter 2. That growth will be summarized under "Background" below. Next its era of diversification since 1976 will be described, leading to a major strategic proposal. CG's financial picture in 1983 then is displayed in exhibits, including performance data of its major business segments. Last are some data on external yardsticks.

BACKGROUND

The firm came into existence in 1904 as the Continental Can Company. With aggressive marketing, it surpassed its perennial rival's can volume by 1950, becoming the leader in its industry. Any management would be proud of such an achievement. Since can manufacturing is one of the most standardized of processes and its markets are stable, a natural tendency would be to concentrate complacently on can markets and production efficiency. Continental Can's management had greater ambitions and took the company into varied other types of packaging. This included lines of paper and paperboard packages as well as acquiring its own large resources in forest industries.

CG's management also was willing to risk experimenting with operations in quite diverse businesses, as was related in Chapter 2. Being relatively small acquisitions compared with CG's size, the commitments were not irreversible. In fact CG divested most ventures outside of packaging and forest products that had been initiated before 1976. Development policy changed sharply in that year, symbolized by a name change to The Continental Group.

RECENT DEVELOPMENT

With a new name and strategy, CG's management began steps to diversify radically. Its main actions are told year by year below. Related data on the corporation and its business groups, at the end of the case, should also be considered. Review Figure 2-2 also, in which the four levels involved in strategic management at CG are charted (the corporation, its four broad segments, the SBUs within them, and their PMUs). Our attention here relates to the top two levels.

1977: CG stepped outside its established businesses to acquire Richmond Corporation for $372 million. This brought with it Life Insurance Company of Virginia, a major and growing underwriter of various life policies; and the Lawyer's Title Insurance Company, one of the nation's largest title companies. Also acquired was Western Employees Insurance Company, whose business emphasized workmen's compensation insurance in the far west. Thus was started the Insurance segment.

During this year CG's packaging segment made important product improvements and launched new ones, while the forest products segment enlarged its holdings and plant and stepped up efficiency. Such strengthening of existing businesses was occurring each year, but we will omit such details.

1979: Major acquisitions in another very different business took place, mainly Florida Gas Company, which operated a 4,200-mile natural gas pipeline from oil country in the southeast to the Florida market. This included extensive gas-producing fields and a subsidiary that extracted hydrocarbons from the gas stream. Florida Exploration Company was another important part of this acquisition and was primarily engaged in ownership and exploration of Louisiana oil fields.

This diversification led CG to reorganizing into its present four business groups: (1) Packaging; (2) Forest Products; (3) Insurance; and (4) Energy, divided into transmission and exploration and production.

1980: No significant diversification took place in this year, a time to consolidate CG's new businesses. At this time its most extensive development was of the Forest Products segment, in which CG's cumulative investment rose to $907 million—to expand timberlands and increase the volume and efficiency of paper and paperboard manufacturing. Over the past five years, CG's revenues had risen by 66 percent and its earnings by 100 percent.

1981: Investors Mortgage Insurance Company was acquired this year, to broaden the company's offerings in the realty insurance field. Florida Exploration Company took a major step by obtaining leases on 333,000 acres of oil and gas lands and launched a large-scale exploration effort.

1982: Again a big step was made in the energy segment, by investing $393 million in Supron Energy Corporation, which owned over 400,000 acres and added 180 percent to CG's oil and gas reserves plus many producing wells. CG took 50 percent ownership, and Allied Corporation took the other half. Also Florida Exploration continued its ongoing partnership with Shell Oil Company for both land and offshore production in areas new to CG. That segment set a record in oil drilling this year when 107 out of 142 wells drilled proved successful.

The insurance segment was notable in launching an innovative type of life insurance policy that resulted in a 40 percent increase in its life policy sales. Also the western-oriented subsidiaries began to market in eastern regions and headed for possible national coverage.

CG's capital expenditures were allocated as follows in 1982 among its producing groups:

Packaging	$ 95 million
Forest products	112
Energy:	
Transmission	12
Exploration & producing	214
	$433 million

The company expected that for 1983 nearly half of capital expenditures ($400 million) would be in oil and gas exploration and development. Also CG received government approval to convert a portion of its natural gas pipeline to begin carrying light petroleum products like gasoline and jet fuel. Called the Transgulf Pipeline, this project was slated for completion in 1986 at an ultimate cost of more than $400 million.

Also during 1983 significant changes were completed in the management structure to decentralize operating divisions. This enabled the corporate staff to focus on strategic planning and capital resource allocation.

AN IMPORTANT DECISION

Beginning in 1981 the corporate management of CG had been involved in a series of decisions that was drastically revamping its portfolio of businesses. This was known as an "asset redeployment program" in which a realignment of assets amounting to $400 to $500 million had been anticipated. By the summer of 1983 even larger scale redeployment was being considered. This included the sale of its remaining businesses in Canada (but retaining an equity in the firm acquiring CG's packaging operations there) and lesser actions. A more dramatic action was then under consideration: the sale of the Forest Products' Brown System.

The Brown System was strong in corrugated containers, fiber drums, bags, and sacks—virtually a complete line in all forms of containers. The Brown System since acquisition had been well maintained by CG and was quite salable in 1983. If CG did decide to part with that segment, it should be only after long and careful analysis.

Some arguments in favor of keeping the Brown System would include its value in offering a wide product line. Its facilities had been steadily improved to keep a competitive edge in efficiency. Indeed CG has just finished spending $74 million on modernizing the Hodge, Louisiana complex (part of the Brown System and one of CG's largest), which expanded its capacity by 21 percent. The Brown System's 23 plants and mills were major users of the company's enormous timber acreage. Also, some of CG's outstanding managers and staff were in the Brown System. It was likely that such a divestment—losing those people, facilities, and products—would be a shock to the remaining packaging and forest product segments.

Arguments favoring the sale of the Brown System were imposing too. It was pointed out that the divested units were in very cyclical and competitive markets where profit margins were generally low despite substantial investment requirements. CG would still retain a few of its largest mills that would be well located relative to its southern timberland base. The remaining production units of the Forest Products group would stress products made more to specialty requirements than the commodity-like products of the divested plants.

With regard to the effect on CG's timberlands, that could have positive aspects. It would release about one million acres from supporting the company's manufacturing functions. It was suggested that those properties would become a sort of corporate endowment offering a number of options for future income. One might be creating a management services company which also would manage timberland for other companies or for corporate pension funds. Meanwhile, the thinking ran, this would be an appreciating asset aiding CG's overall financial strength.

The effect on CG's current finances was something else to consider. One firm offer from a leader in the paperboard industry was around $525 million for the Brown System. That could enable substantial changes in CG's financial position. It could be used to reduce its large debts or to redeem a portion of CG's outstanding stock, making the remainder worth proportionately more. It could increase the company's future ability to strengthen its position in more promising fields of business. The investment of CG in the Brown System at that time was nearly $450 mllion.

Such a major decision also would need to be related to the company's mission. It was stated around that time as:

> Continental Group will seek to be known as a superior competitor in mainstream industries on which society depends, and for excellence in all it undertakes.[1]

Comments that elaborated on that mission statement, in the same source, included these: "We consider this unifying statement essential to a diversified company, such as ours, that has no single focus on technology, industry or market. It guides us in setting objectives and

---

[1] *1983 Annual Report,* The Continental Group, p. 13.

EXHIBIT 1   **Statement of consolidated earnings, Continental Group, Inc. and subsidiaries for years ended December 1**

(in millions, except per share amounts)	1982	1981	1980
Revenues	$4,979.0	$5,194.4	$5,119.5
Other Income	77.1	104.7	51.8
	5,056.1	5,299.1	5,171.3
Costs and Expenses			
Cost of goods sold and operating charges	4,394.3	4,544.2	4,470.8
Selling and administrative	322.5	379.8	370.6
Research and development	28.2	41.0	36.9
Interest	135.2	122.8	117.0
Interest capitalized	(41.3)	(25.5)	(25.0)
Gain on debt retirements	—	(24.8)	—
	4,838.9	5,037.5	4,970.3
Earnings Before Income Taxes and Insurance Operations	217.2	261.6	201.0
Provision for Income Taxes	87.4	68.5	46.0
Earnings Before Insurance Operations	129.8	193.1	155.0
Equity Earnings of Insurance Operations	50.4	49.1	45.2
Net Earnings	180.2	242.2	200.2
Dividends on preferred and preference stocks	23.6	24.9	25.1
Net earnings applicable to common shares	$ 156.6	$ 217.3	$ 175.1
Net Earnings Per Common Share	$ 4.80	$ 6.61	$ 5.35

Source: Annual Report of The Continental Group, 1982. Reprinted by permission of the company.

EXHIBIT 2   Consolidated balance sheet, December 31, Continental Group, Inc. and subsidiaries

(in millions)	*1982*	*1981*
Assets		
Current Assets		
Cash	$ 65.7	$ 220.8
Receivables	547.1	542.2
Inventories, at LIFO cost		
Current cost	756.4	826.5
Excess over LIFO cost	(384.6)	(425.7)
	371.8	400.8
Deferred income taxes and other assets	67.4	85.0
	1,052.0	1,248.8
Investments and Advances		
Insurance Operations	547.6	544.7
Unicon Producing Company	154.3	—
Other	166.3	182.7
	868.2	727.4
Property, Plant and Equipment, at cost		
Buildings and equipment	2,716.2	2,665.6
Accumulated depreciation	(1,422.2)	(1,363.2)
	1,294.0	1,302.4
Oil and gas properties, net	623.8	464.9
Timberlands, net of timber harvested	114.3	95.0
Construction in progress	71.7	87.8
Land	20.1	20.9
	2,123.9	1,971.0
Other Assets	162.3	187.7
Liabilities and Equity	$4,206.4	$4,134.9
Current Liabilities		
Accounts payable	$ 302.6	$ 372.0
Short-term debt and current portion of long-term debt	31.5	63.1
Taxes payable	74.5	59.3
Accrued payrolls and employee benefits	137.0	181.0
Other	239.2	159.6
	784.8	835.0
Long-Term Debt, less current portion	1,005.9	960.6
Other Liabilities		
Retirement benefits	258.2	214.4
Deferred income taxes	161.9	185.3
Other	91.0	85.7
	511.1	485.4
Redeemable Preference Stocks	275.3	281.3

EXHIBIT 2 (*continued*)

(in millions)	1982	1981
Preferred and Common Stockholders' Equity		
$4.25 cumulative preferred stock	**5.1**	5.1
Common stock (issued 1982—32,627,000 shares;		
1981—33,093,000 shares)	**32.6**	33.1
Paid-in surplus	**347.4**	351.7
Common stock in treasury	**—**	(10.1)
Net unrealized investment gains	**40.0**	21.9
Foreign currency adjustments	**47.5**	76.3
Retained earnings	**1,156.7**	1,094.6
	$4,206.4	$4,134.9

EXHIBIT 3   Continental Group, Inc., corporate performance, 1977–82
(dollar figures in millions; index based on 1977)

Year	*Revenues*		*Operating earnings*		*Earnings per share*	
	Current	*Index*	*Current*	*Index*	*Current*	*Index*
1977	$3,661	100	$257	100	$4.45	100
1978	3,944	108	292	114	3.47	78
1979	4,511	123	368	143	5.27	118
1980	5,119	140	410	160	6.11	137
1981	5,795	158	420	163	6.61	149
1982	5,564	152	339	132	4.80	108

EXHIBIT 4 Continental Group, Inc., segments' contributions to earnings (in million dollars)

Year	Packaging			Forest industries	Insurance	Energy			Corp. total
	Cans	Diversified	Total			Trans-mission	Exploration & production	Total	
1977	*	*	$203	54	—	—	—	—	$257
1978	*	*	191	48	54	—	—	—	292
1979	*	*	185	77	85	20†	—	20	368
1980	119	68	187	77	69	63	14	77	410
1981	72	66	138	103	84	67	28	95	420
1982	93	51	144	24	60	92	19	111	339
Assets of each segment, December 31, 1982	$993	331	1,324	973	547	285	844	1,129	3,973

*Not shown separately for indicated years.
† Three months' results only.
Source: Calculated from Annual Reports of the Continental Group for the above years. Used by permission of the company.

EXHIBIT 5 Continental Group, Inc., proportions of revenues and earnings by segment

Year	Packaging	Forest products	Insurance	Energy	Total
Revenues					
1977	73%	22%	—	—	100%
1978	70	20	10%	—	100
1979	66	21	11	3*	100
1980	62	19	9	9	100
1981	59	19	10	11	100
1982	58	18	11	14	100
Operating earnings					
1977	84	16	—	—	
1978	58	8	33	—	100%
1979	47	19	28	6*	100
1980	40	18	18	24	100
1981	31	25	21	23	100
1982	42	10	18	30	100

*Three months' results only.

Source: Calculated from Annual Reports of the Continental Group for the above years. Used by permission of the company.

EXHIBIT 6 Gross national product of the U.S., 1977–82
(current value dollar figures in billions)

Year	Dollar GNP	Percentage of 1977
1977	$1,918	100
1978	2,164	113
1979	2,418	126
1980	2,633	137
1981	2,938	153
1982	3,073	159

Source: Statistical Abstract of the U.S.

EXHIBIT 7 Net profits of U.S. manufacturing corporations
(current value dollar figures in billions)

Year	Total net profits	Percentage of 1977
1977	$70	100
1978	81	116
1979	99	141
1980	92	131
1981	101	144
1982	71	101

Source: Survey of Current Business, various issues.

priorities and in making operating and strategic decisions. . . . Since none of us has the time or talent to achieve excellence in more than a few select endeavors, our philosophy helps us in narrowing choices. . . . We have built on the competitive strengths Continental Group has developed during its 80 years of operation . . ."

DISCUSSION

1. Identify the arguments that favor and oppose the sale of the Brown System. Analyze the relevant data, including the exhibits, and decide which of the arguments are substantiated.
2. Would your decision be to divest the Brown System or to retain it? Why?
3. Consider the entire sweep of CG development strategy since 1976. Would you describe it as conservative or venturesome? Has the perspective tended to be long-range or near-future?
4. Reread the three objectives of CG that were quoted in this chapter on page 35 and also the mission statement above. Does the evidence indicate that the company has been able to accomplish them—up to 1983? Explain.
5. On April 15, 1984, the closing price of CG's common stock on the New York Stock Exchange was 33 1/4. Its price/earnings ratio was 9 times. Look up its current quotation. What does this imply regarding investors' evaluation of CG's strategies and performance?

CASE 2-3

Bic Corporation

In the autumn of 1980, executives of BIC Corporation were absorbed in completing their plans for the calendar year of 1981. The firm dated back to 1958, when the French firm, Société BIC, acquired the Waterman Pen Company in Seymour, Connecticut, naming the new firm the Waterman-BIC Corporation. In 1963, the growing company moved into larger and more modern facilities in Milford, Connecticut where it is headquartered today. By 1980, the company had established itself as an aggressive marketer of consumer goods in the United States and compiled a history of growth, but there were problems to consider for the next year and longer term.*

HISTORY

The BIC organization may be credited largely to the enterprise and genius of Marcel Bich. He was a salesman of office supplies in France who entered the manufacture of ink wells.

---

*The material quoted in the early part of the case largely is reprinted from the February 28, 1977 issue of *Business Week,* copyrighted © 1977 by McGraw-Hill, Inc., 1221 Avenue of the Americas, New York, NY 10020. The case itself is published with the permission of BIC Corporation.

M. Bich had an inspiration regarding opportunities to make and sell mass disposable products, and in 1953 he acted by launching his firm and developing the European market. Certain key ideas guided him:

> "Marcel Bich came up with the fantastic idea of disposable, cheap consumer goods," says Jean Plé, president of Gillette France. "With each new product he simply pursues that basic philosophy a bit further. So far he hasn't made a mistake."
>
> Bich does agree that he does seem to have uncanny marketing insight, but he also maintains that even disposable products cannot sell unless their quality is high. "My personal marketing strategy has been never to promote a product until it is equivalent in quality to the No. 1 product on the market. I continue to finance development of the product until I know that we can outdo the competition."
>
> M. Bich directs his business with one central philosophy, which is this: Manufacture and sell only products that can be made cheaply, used relatively briefly, and then thrown away.

Adhering to those principles, the BIC organization established first its French factory and then others in Italy, Greece, and the United States. M. Bich did not attempt to innovate his products, but rather relied on improving existing products and gearing his factories for their mass production.

The United States firm was founded to invade the country with BIC's inexpensive throwaway pen. In 1958, companies were selling ball point pens in the United States, but they proved to be no match for BIC in product quality or marketing savvy. Nor could they match BIC's economies of scale which subsequently brought the pen's price down to 19 cents. Indeed, BIC had most of the market for nearly ten years until Gillette's Paper Mate division introduced its line of cheap pens. Gillette proved unable to outflank BIC, although it remained a viable competitor in the stick pen business.

Gillette had been the first major marketer of disposable lighters in the United States, when its Cricket brand was launched in 1972. As it had done with its pens, BIC first developed its lighter business in Europe and in Canada, and when it entered the United States in 1973, Gillette already enjoyed 40 percent of that market. When BIC entered, demand grew rapidly at first, and it gained ground fast on Gillette after its flashy "Flick Your BIC" campaign was launched. Until 1977 the two brands' sales were running about even, when BIC decided that it should go after greater market share, as is discussed later.

Disposable shavers had long been used in hospitals, but it was Marcel Bich who recognized their potential in consumer markets and introduced them in Europe in 1975. In 1976, BIC Shavers moved into Canada, and Gillette correctly anticipated that the U.S. invasion would soon follow. Gillette put its Trac II twin-blade head on a plastic handle and marketed it as a disposable under the name of "Good News!" In late 1976, BIC invaded the United States with its single-edge shaver, priced at only 55 percent of Good News! Although well known for its pens and lighters, BIC faced some serious obstacles: (1) Gillette's virtually complete distribution of shavers; (2) Gillette's prominence in reputation and its domination of the U.S. blade market; and (3) the need to convince consumers that BIC's single blade shaver, with its price advantage, was as attractive as Gillette's twin-bladed entries. BIC began a heavy advertising campaign that gradually gained market share although continuing to sustain losses.

RECENT TRENDS AND DEVELOPMENTS

A review of operating results over five years (1976 through 1980) follows.[1]

The sales and income (before tax) figures follow for each of the three main product segments, in terms of percentage share of the whole. Sales and losses for pantyhose

---

[1]The operating data on BIC Corporation have been obtained with permission from its annual reports for the indicated years.

BIC Corporation annual results (in millions)

	Sales	Profit before income tax	Net profit after income tax
1976	$122.8	$20.0	$10.0
1977	134.8	12.9	6.9
1978	153.6	16.0	8.5
1979	179.0	16.4	8.8
1980	192.0	24.8	12.3

	Percentage of net sales			% of profit (before tax)		
	Pens	Lighters	Shavers	Pens	Lighters	Shavers
1976	51%	43%	6%	80%	32%	(12)%
1977	46	45	9	120	39	(59)
1978	42	46	12	92	58	(50)
1979	41	47	12	76	70	(46)
1980	41	44	15	64	62	(26)

Pens:	BIC's percentages of units sales		Pen industry
	Ball point pens	Total of all pens	Approximate total units (in billions)
1976	66%	42%	2.2
1977	64	42	2.3
1978	60	40	2.7
1979	62	40	3.0
1980	61	40	2.9

Disposable lighters:	BIC's percentages of total sales	Approximate total unit sales (in millions)
1976	41%	215
1977	52	262
1978	50	310
1979	53	370
1980	52	400

(which were discontinued in 1977) are included with shavers for two years, but were too minor to affect the picture.

BIC's penetration of markets for each of its three product lines also provides important information. BIC market shares for both the product category (e.g. disposable shavers) and the total industry (e.g. total shaving market in the United States) are given.

Relationship of disposables to U.S. domestic blade market (in shaver units)

	Disposables % of wet shave market	BIC % of wet shave market	BIC % of disposable shavers
1976	7%	.2%	3%
1977	15	4.5	30
1978	20	8.0	40
1979	25	11.0	44
1980	29	13.0	45

In writing instruments, Gillette had copied BIC's approach in the pen business in 1975 by reducing its prices sharply to obtain market share in the commercial or office business (which is said to account for about one-third of BIC's pen volume). By cutting prices on its Write Brothers disposable ball point pens, Gillette began pressures that caused margins on that business to slip by almost ten percentage points. Buoyed by successful penetration, Gillette then aimed at the retail business and is reputed to have raised its share from 13 to 20 percent between 1977 and 1978. BIC responded vigorously with a television budget that is said to have doubled its expenditures.

In disposable lighters, BIC in 1976 could see that supply was catching up with demand and that they faced two options: (1) maintain or lower spending on lighters, thereby earning substantial short-term profits or (2) vigorously go after market share. They chose the latter course and in 1977 slashed wholesale prices by 32 percent. Because BIC had lower production costs and was the more daring, Gillette held off retaliation. When they did cut price, BIC cut further, and a price war ensued. By the end of 1978 BIC's "big play" had won about 50 percent of the market while Gillette's share had eroded to 30 percent. Later, in 1979, Gillette again started pricing hostilities by selling its Cricket at 10 percent under BIC's price.

With its shaver, BIC found that its costs of production, promotion, and overhead were excessively high (relative to prices) while it struggled to make inroads on Gillette's market dominance. After years of losses, the product was nearing a breakeven level in 1980.

CURRENT OUTLOOK

BIC executives entered the current scene with a winning record: three highly successful invasions of long-established U.S. markets, in terms of sales penetration. Profits from its writing instruments and lighters enabled BIC to subsidize the costly introduction and promotion of its new line of shavers.

In 1980, BIC launched a new writing instrument, the BIC Roller. Roller-type pens were the fastest growing segment of the pen industry at that time, growing at a rate of about 40 percent in 1978 and another 60 percent in 1979. Pentel was said to be the market leader in this line with its 98-cent "Rolling Writer" holding a 60 percent share. It was believed that Pilot was second (an 89-cent pen) and Gillette third with its "Quick-silver" (at 89 cents). BIC already had gained market leadership with the pen in Canada since its introduction there in 1979. Its U.S. volume was said to have gained about a 20 percent share by fall, 1980, and very large promotional outlays might be considered for 1981. As the total pen market grew by only 1.2 percent in units from 1979 to 1980, obviously BIC could achieve growth only by taking market share away from others.

In lighters, BIC's current situation remained favorable. Despite Gillette's price discounting started in 1979, BIC's market share in 1980 kept growing, although its wholesale price remained above the competition. The whole lighter field had done well in 1980, too, with sales rising 11 percent or more—faster than the gross national product. BIC's performance was in spite of an inventory loss (due to fire) that temporarily hampered filling orders.

Aside from continuing losses, BIC was successful in shavers during 1980 on other counts. Sales and market share were rising well. BIC was also nearing its goal of saturating retail outlets. It had begun manufacturing the BIC shaver in Milford in April 1978, which avoided the 25 percent import duties that they had incurred when the shavers were imported from BIC's plant in Greece.

On the other hand, competition in shavers remained severe. The BIC "Lady Shaver," introduced in December, 1977, was slogging along with a small share of women's shavers. It was said to lag behind Schick's "Personal Touch," ASR's "Flicker," and Gillette's "Daisy."

In the general environment, observers were encouragingly pointing out that there was a strong overall rise in demand for disposables. Consumers also were showing a greater consciousness of prices and value. To some degree that was caused by a generally softening economy in the United States. What was progressively developing in negative economic trends was indicated in these newspaper headlines:

August 1979: "Mild Recession for 18 Months," *Fortune* magazine
December 1979: "Prudential Insurance: Moderately Severe
            Recession"
March 1980: "Size of Recession Proliferates"
September 1980: "Predictions and Inflation Point to a Prolonged Recession"

As BIC executives resolved their plans for 1981, the October 4, 1980 issue of *Business Week* magazine reported that its economic index stood at 138.6. That contrasted with an index of 150.6 in early October 1979. There had been a slight rise over the past month from an index standing of 137.6 in early September.[2]

DISCUSSION QUESTIONS

Describe a general strategic plan that BIC Corporation executives should have pursued during the period 1981 to 1985. Also describe a specific periodic plan that you would have recommended for 1981.

1. Looking ahead through 1981, consider what long-range opportunities and threats might have been perceived at BIC in 1980. Given those premises, what general program seems most logical? Be explicit about both assumptions and proposals.
2. Outline a *specific* corporate plan for BIC Corporation for 1981. This plan should be consistent with your determination for 1981. Your analysis should arrive at selecting one or more of the corporate strategy options and justifying it. Following the strategic planning model (Figure 2-2), your analysis would include the following stages:
   a. What current planning gap did BIC seem to have in 1980? This may be guessed only if you first set some current objectives for them in sales and profits for 1980. In setting them, ignore the actual 1980 data and study trends of 1976-79.
   b. What objectives would you set for 1981 in sales and profits? Describe the way that you arrived at them.
   c. Consider the current situation and future trends and indicators that the case men-

---

[2]*Business Week,* October 27, 1980, p. 2.

tions for 1980. Given that, estimate the likely sales volume that BIC seems likely to reach in 1981, if present corporate strategy is maintained.

d. Does that indicate a future planning gap or not? Negative or positive?

e. Would you or would you not recommend that the business areas of BIC Corporation be redefined in order to achieve the 1981 objectives?

f. Describe strategic actions you recommend for BIC in 1981.

g. What impact would your proposal probably have on the amount of funds to allocate for 1981 compared with 1980?

3

Analytical Methods for Strategic Decisions

The availability of data for strategic planning has grown dramatically during the information age—not only in its magnitude but in the capacities of computers and in the communications links with data sources. These aids to decisions are of limited use, however, unless the managers also have analytical methods and models to process and interpret the data. This area of knowledge is becoming a requisite for marketing planners, as indicated by its early location in this book.

PURPOSES OF ANALYTICAL METHODS

The general need of strategic planners is to match (1) the firm's resources and market strengths with (2) the opportunities and threats that will be found in the market environment. A large and complex firm, on which our discussion focuses, has a number of heterogeneous product/market units, which complicates that matching task. These various products at any time constitute a set that is called the firm's "product portfolio." The general purpose of the analytical methods that we will cover is to optimize the profits yielded by making the right investments in the portfolio's various strategic programs. Each PMU in the portfolio requires evaluation and comparison with the others, so that the funds allocated to it—and to the other PMUs—constitute the optimal aggregate for the firm.

The three main stages of strategic decisions are diagnosis, prognosis, and prescription:

1. In the *diagnosis* one examines the current situation by asking the following kinds of questions: Where is this strategic unit (such as an SBU or a PMU) situated at present, in significant aspects? Has it performed as well as planned? What have been its trends? Can any causal factors be identified?
2. In the *prognosis* one looks ahead at the changing situation over the planning period: How are the influential variables likely to change? How would that affect the performance of the strategic unit?
3. The *prescription* determines the actions to be taken: How can one capitalize on any advantages that were found in the diagnosis while coping with the various changes that have been anticipated in the prognosis?

Only a portion of the questions asked in those three stages can be answered by the three analytical methods examined below. These methods particularly stress the market position of the various PMUs in the portfolio and competitive relationships.

GROWTH/SHARE MATRIX

The growth/share matrix method is frequently called *portfolio analysis,* which is rather confusing because all the major analytical methods for strategy also analyze a portfolio to some degree. Therefore we prefer the designation *growth/share matrix* method because that literally describes the graph on which it is displayed. The graph has two dimensions that represent two factors, respectively: the growth rate of the total industry sales of the particular product category and the share of business that our firm holds. Share of business (sales) is expressed as a ratio between our sales volume and that of the leading seller (or if we happily stand at the top, the next-largest seller).

The growth/share method stemmed from a discovery by the Boston Consulting Group (BCG) regarding the experience curve, or learning curve. We will oversimplify its description, since only its basic idea is important here.

The experience curve is a long-known tendency for the labor-hours spent in producing each unit of a product to decline at a steady and predictable rate relative to the cumulated number of units produced. In its studies the BCG discovered that this behavior was not peculiar to production costs alone but to total cost behavior and for a wide variety of products. This tendency is represented in Figure 3-1. You may observe in its curve that when the cumulated product doubled, from 50,000 to 100,000 units, the cost per unit fell by 20 percent. This rate of decline would be repeated with each successive doubling of cumulated production.

From this the BCG inferred that if a firm could produce the most units of a certain product (more than any rival), it would enjoy a powerful cost advantage competitively. Market share thus became one dimension of the BCG's

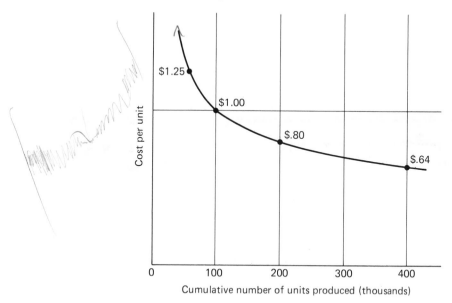

FIGURE 3-1. A cost experience curve. Costs shown are declining on a 20 percent experience curve, with each doubling of cumulated production.

y-axis: Cost per unit

$1.25

$1.00

$.80

$.64

0   100   200   300   400

Cumulative number of units produced (thousands)

portfolio analysis grid. The logic of the other dimension is rather evident, since doing business in a fast-growing market would accentuate the experience curve advantage as well as accelerate the garnering of the profits.

A growth/share matrix is shown in Figure 3-2. This matrix indicates, for each of four products, the following:

1. Its volume of dollar sales (represented by the diameter of the circle)
2. The growth rate of the market in which the product is competing
3. The market share that the firm's product holds, in comparison with the share held by the competitor that has the largest share

Growth rate is simply the percentage by which the sales volume of all firms has changed over the most recent period for which such information is available. *Market share* is a ratio of one's own share to that of the leading firm in this market. We give two examples below, in each of which our brand is Brand B.

Brand	Dollar sales	Percent of total sales	Relative market share
A	$30,000,000	60%	2.0
B	15,000,000	30	0.5
C	5,000,000	10	0.17
	$50,000,000		

In this case, our brand has only half the market share held by Brand A, or a 0.5 ratio.

In the second example, the two top-selling brands have equal shares:

Brand	Dollar sales	Percent of total sales	Relative market share
A	$20,000,000	40%	1.0
B	20,000,000	40	1.0
C	10,000,000	20	0.5
	$50,000,000		

It is apparent that a relative market share around 1.0 is a strong competitive situation.

In a growth/share matrix such as that in Figure 3-2, the values of a and b must be determined by the analyst, for they are arbitrary. If a were given a

FIGURE 3-2. Market growth/market share matrix. Positions of four products are indicated by circles, whose diameters represent their sales volumes.

Source: Adapted from *The Product Portfolio,* Perspectives No. 66 (Boston: Boston Consulting Group, 1970); and from D. F. Abell and J. S. Hammond, *Strategic Market Planning* (Englewood Cliffs, N.J.: Prentice-Hall, 1979), p. 178. Reprinted by permission of Prentice-Hall, Inc., Englewood Cliffs, N.J., and Boston Consulting Group.

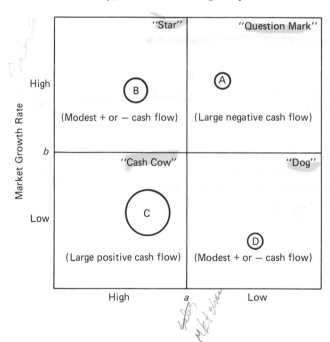

value of 1.0 then only when our product's share is above that of any rival would it stand in the left half of the matrix. Often a somewhat lower relative market share (e.g., 0.8) would be in a sufficiently strong position to compete successfully. The growth rate criterion (b) must also be stipulated, and an appropriate rate would vary among industries. In a dynamic electronic product a rate of something above 25 percent annual growth might be normal, but in the farm equipment industry that would be fantastic. It is strategically important to set the right values for a and b, as they would serve as cutoff points in management's assessment of the portfolio (those lying on the left side having preferential treatment).

Two perspectives enter the setting of these cutoff points. Internally, management wants to put investment emphasis on the products that relatively are best in its portfolio. Externally, there is the important aspect of how each product compares with its competitors, because a few leaders are likely to dominate the also-rans. Internal versus external comparisons are also of concern in demand growth. Viewing from both angles enables one to divide the matrix regarding (1) how low (or high) a product's share of market should be in order to be a viable competitor and (2) what "par" growth rate the overall portfolio should maintain.

Another consideration is the variation among competitive situations faced by different products. Here are two hypothetical examples: Brand J is in a product category that is quite fragmented in the market, as eight brands each hold between 8 and 11 percent market share and there are also some very low-selling brands. In Brand K's category, in contrast, there are only three brands, whose shares are 41 percent, 40 percent, and 19 percent. Since no one or two brands dominate, Brand J might succeed with share ranging anywhere from 7 to above 11 percent, whereas for Brand K any market share position below 0.95 would be perilous.

Let us now discuss the positions of the four products shown in Figure 3-2.

Product A would be considered a Question Mark because, while there is a fine opportunity for it in a growing market, it has apparently been an "also-ran" against competing products so far. Its cash flow might look like this:

Cash revenues	$400,000
Cash expenses and investment	700,000
Net cash flow	($300,000)

Product B is a bright Star because it is exploiting its growing market well and holds a superior market share. It brings in large cash flow, but so much has to be spent to keep its competitive place and expand its operations that there may be little or no net cash balance left—like this:

Cash revenues	$1,235,000
Cash expenses and investment	1,240,000
Net cash flow	($5,000)

Product C can throw off cash as easily as a productive Cow gives milk. This is because it is earning large revenues, but its mature market does not need lavish development expenditures, yielding a cash flow like this:

Cash revenues	$2,750,000
Cash expenses and investment	1,900,000
Net cash flow	$ 850,000

Product D is considered a Dog because it has neither prospects of good market growth nor a leading market share from which to obtain what market still exists. If the company is still reaping some cash flow from it, or if it fills an essential place in the product line, it may be nursed along on a subsistence diet. Otherwise it is likely to be terminated:

Cash revenues	$300,000
Cash expenses and investment	280,000
Net cash flow	$ 20,000

The product life cycle (PLC) also relates to the growth/share matrix theory. Let us reexamine the four products (A, B, C, D) described above to see how they tend to be connected with the stages of product life. For reference purposes we are showing those four life stages in the conventional PLC curve in Figure 3-3. Let us begin with Product A, as it was located in Figure 3-2:

It is likely that Product A is a fairly new one for the firm and is still in the *introductory* stage. The firm may be one among many that perceived the opportunity to enter such a product, which means that market share is fragmented among them. The demand for the product is still small, although rising, so it has not reached a real growth condition. The Question Mark relates to doubts about whether Product A is going to capture a viable market share and whether the total market will ever rise to a growth stage.

Product B is in a category that is enjoying a real *growth* stage. It is a Star whose rapid growth is repaying the heavy initial investment, a state that was accomplished by a competent marketing program that has lifted it to a leading market share.

Product C is in the *maturity* stage, well-entrenched competitively and doing a stable volume of business.

Product D is probably in the *decline* stage, since the total volume in that business is on the way down.

The four matrix quadrants may not perfectly match the four PLC stages. One example would be a brand in a stable volume category that is in the sad state of holding a low market share. This would be a Dog in the mature stage of the PLC. It should also be mentioned that when the matrix represents only the most recent period's performance, either total category volume or one brand's share may have taken a temporary fluctuation up or down, putting it briefly across one of the dividing lines. For products that fall close to those lines, there should be careful consideration of whether one is looking at a short-run aberration and whether it may still hold some attractive strategic possibilities.

In Figure 3-2 we have only seen how these products and their markets are performing currently. The strategist is concerned about decisions for a

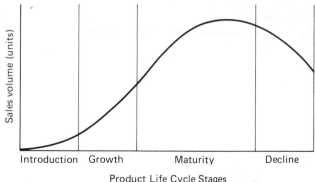

long-range future. Projections could be made for the growth/share matrix by predicting each of the three elements in Figure 3-2 although such projections entail effort and risk (in contrast to the ease and factual certainty in using current data).

Future positioning and sales volume are given in Figure 3-4 in which the

FIGURE 3-4. Projected positions on a market
share/market growth matrix. These are the
four hypothetical products shown in
Figure 3-2. The arrow represents the
desirable direction of cash flow.

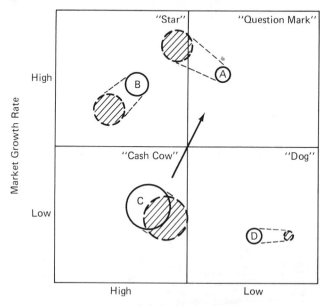

shaded circles represent the future data three years or so hence. This matrix also includes an arrow to indicate the desirable direction of cash flow, which is pumped from the Cash Cows (which are presumed not to need it) to new opportunities, which are to better the competitive positions of the Question Marks and to develop and acquire other new products. Note that specific boundary line criteria have also been shown (merely as an example, since these properly differ in various industries).

In Figure 3-4, Product A is expected to gain markedly and to become a Star. Product B would strengthen its grip in share of market, one whose growth rate was slackening but would still be attractive. Product C would still be one of the leaders in its category, contending for a stabilizing market but still looking like a staunch cash supplier. Product D would slip badly in market share, but it seems highly doubtful that its no-growth market would justify more support. On balance, this product portfolio is in a fair situation, but new products are needed to keep it healthy.

MARKET ATTRACTIVENESS/BUSINESS ASSESSMENT ANALYSIS:

This second method of assessing a portfolio, like the first one, uses two terms in its name as labels for the two axes of the matrix. Again the strategic units that are being evaluated are positioned in the matrix. Rather than using a single factor along each matrix, however, this technique combines a number of factors into a composite value for market attractiveness (of the market to which that unit caters) and of the position of the business in it. The method gained fame after its initiation at General Electric and promotion by the major consulting firm of McKinsey & Company.

The matrix is presented in Figure 3-5. Each dimension is divided into thirds (not halves) because the findings are better indicated with nine cells. Note that those cells are placed in three zones. When a unit is in a strong business position and the market is highly attractive, there is the greatest overall attractiveness. And the opposite is true when business position is weak in a market of low attractiveness. Three businesses (X, Y, and Z) have been placed in Figure 3-5. How were their positions determined? Following is an explanation.

Such determinations should be unique for each firm and market because the significant values in deciding strategies of Company A in the shoe industry would vary greatly from Company B in the container industry. The steps, though, would be the same:

1. Decide which particular factors make a market attractive and which would gauge the firm's important strengths and weaknesses. Obtain data measuring these factors.
2. Decide which criteria would be fair boundary points between the three

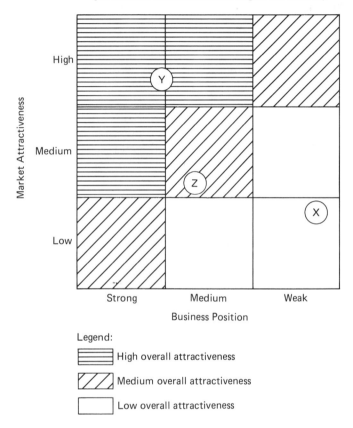

FIGURE 3-5. Market attractiveness/business position matrix. Three business units are displayed according to their composite ratings on the two dimensions.

Source: Adapted from Derek F. Abell and John S. Hammond, *Strategic Market Planning: Problems and Analytical Approaches,* © 1979, p. 272. Reprinted by permission of Prentice-Hall, Inc., Englewood Cliffs, N.J.

Legend:

High overall attractiveness

Medium overall attractiveness

Low overall attractiveness

zones for a factor (e.g., what rate of market growth would be considered "high" rather than "medium").

3. Place these factors under major groupings, such as financial and marketing.

4. Assign within each grouping weights for each factor, and also assign weights to place on each group—according to the perceived importance of each.

5. Multiply the weights by the measured values of each factor. Then repeat this for each grouping under *market attractiveness* to arrive at the composite score for that dimension.

6. Repeat the fifth step for the *business position* factors, arriving at a composite score.

7. Place each business that is to be compared on the matrix, for its two composite scores.

Table 3-1 lists some factors that the particular business firm might consider relevant to the market.

The selection of the factors and their weighting involve a high degree of judgment. Some of the factors, such as barriers to entry of new competitors, also defy any definite measurement, and the criteria for assigning them to high, medium, and low involve some degree of opinion.

These steps will be illustrated for a hypothetical firm, Otsego Mills, which is primarily a grain milling company with some diversification in foods. The criteria that Otsego Mills established for various market factors are shown in Table 3-2.

To guide planning decisions, criteria such as those shown in Table 3-2 will be used to screen various business units. In addition to the criteria and to the measurements or estimates for each factor, we need values to score for each of the three cells along each dimension. A simple scoring, used here for example, is assigning 1.0 to a high or strong level, 0.5 to medium, and 0.0 to low or weak. Let us say that Otsego Mills was assessing three of its businesses on market attractiveness and business position factors. We will use only three factors on

TABLE 3-1   Factors that relate to market attractiveness and to business position

Market attractiveness factors	*Business position factors*

Market factors:
  Size of market (dollars or units)
  Growth rate (over a specified period)
  Diversity of market segments
  Sensitivity to price and promotional
    activities
	Market factors:
	  Our firm's share of market
	  Our growth rate
	  Our participation in diverse segments
	  Our influence on the market with price
	    and promotion

Competition:
  Types of competitors
  Degree of concentration of business in few
    competitors
  Levels and types of integration
	Competition:
	  How we compare with competitors in
	    marketing and other strengths
	  Our own level of integration

Financial and economic:
  Contribution margins earned
  Leveraging through experience and
    economies of scale
  Barriers to entry of new competitors
	Financial and economic:
	  Our contribution margins
	  Our experience and scale
	  Barriers to our entry

Technological:
  Maturity and volatility
  Patents and copyrights
  Manufacturing process technology
    required
	Technological:
	  Our ability to cope with changing
	    technology
	  Our own patent protection
	  Our own manufacturing technology

Source: Excerpted from Abell and Hammond, *Strategic Market Planning,* p. 214, with permission of Prentice-Hall, Inc.

TABLE 3-2 Criteria used by Otsego Mills to screen its businesses. (Example is hypothetical.)

	Market attractiveness factors		
Factor	*High*	*Medium*	*Low*
Size of market (annual dollar sales)	Over $100 million	$30 million–$100 million	Under $30 million
Growth rate per year	Over 6%	3%–6%	Less than 3%
Diversity of market segments	8 or more large segments	3–7 large segments	Virtually one homogeneous market

	Business position factors		
	Strong	*Medium*	*Weak*
Our share of market	Over 30%	20%–30%	Under 20%
Our growth rate per year	Over 6%	3%–6%	Less than 3%
Our participation in market segments	Are now in over 75% of market segments	Are in 40% to 75% of segments	Are in less than 40% of segments

Source: Adapted from Abell and Hammond, *Strategic Market Planning*, p. 218, with permission of Prentice-Hall, Inc.

each dimension, those shown in Table 3-2. Our illustration will be of three product lines or businesses of this firm, which are fictitious but will be identified as follows: Business X—pie crust shells; Business Y—frozen bread loaves; and Business Z—granola bars.

The selected factors are likely to have varying impacts or importance relative to the overall dimension. Therefore weights need to be estimated for the relative impact of each factor. These are assigned as shown in Table 3-3, where this stage is illustrated for only a single product line, Business Z.

The rated factors are more numerous than those in Table 3-3 in practice and would be unique to the particular firm and to the particular industry. The basic method, however, has been presented.

The composite scores for market attractiveness and for business position would now be displayed on the nine-cell matrix, for each of the business units that are undergoing strategic planning. That is done to show them graphically, although the analysis could be made with the statistics themselves. This matrix is our Figure 3-6. On it are plotted just three business units, one of them being business Z which has been scored in Table 3-3.

A larger number of business units would usually be found in a corporation making such an assessment, but for ease of illustration a portfolio of only three units has been included in Figure 3-6. The following seems evident:

> Business Y is in the "high overall attractiveness" zone, which suggests that it should be given heavy support. Since our firm is in only a medium business position in a high-growth market, serious analysis is needed to find the factors that are relatively weak for our firm and their impact.

TABLE 3-3 Scoring of Otsego Mill's hypothetical "Business Z" on market attractiveness and business position factors

| Factor | Market attractiveness factors | | |
	Score	Weights	Weighted score
1. Size of market	0.5	35	17.5
2. Growth rate of market	0.5	40	20.0
3. Diversity of market segments	1.0	25	25.0
Overall market attractiveness		*100*	62.5

| | Business position factors | | |
	Score	Weights	Weighted score
1. Our share of market	0.5	40	20.0
2. Our growth rate	1.0	40	40.0
3. Our participation in diverse segments	0.0	20	0.0
Overall business position		*100*	60.0

Source: Adapted from Abell and Hammond, *Strategic Market Planning*, p. 219, with permission of Prentice-Hall, Inc.

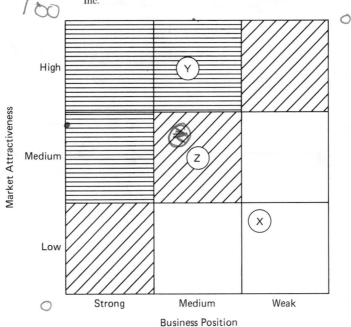

FIGURE 3-6. Market attractiveness/business position assessment. Composite scores are plotted for three business units. Data are hypothetical.

Source: Adapted from Abell and Hammond, *Strategic Market Planning*, p. 219, with permission of Prentice-Hall, Inc.

Business Z, for which we did the calculations, is in a "medium overall attractiveness" situation. In this neutral position, it is possible that no substantial changes in strategy will be warranted.

Business X, with its "low overall attractiveness," should cause much concern. The size of its circle indicates that it has the largest business volume of the three units, but it is in a weak position in a market that does not appear to offer a good opportunity.

POOLED BUSINESS EXPERIENCE

The two methods that have been described offer portfolio classifications based on two variables (growth/share) or several variables summed on two axes (business attractiveness). These have a special convenience of showing products' positions displayed on a grid chart. We will now discuss a quite different method that is based on analysis of past business experience. Within the General Electric Company planning studies of this nature were conducted in the early 1970s, in which the actual experience of many of its products could be combined or pooled. This activity was then moved to Harvard University, where this team of analysts was able to enlist the cooperation of many firms and thus obtained a wide spectrum of business experience on which to determine strategic principles.

The Strategic Planning Institute (SPI) was formed to conduct these studies, and the project was given the name Profit Impact of Marketing Strategy (PIMS). Today this important work tends to be known simply as PIMS. The SPI is composed of participating companies (of which there were around 150 by 1977) that report on a number of SBUs within them. Each member company contributes approximately one hundred items of information about each of the SBUs for which the PIMS service is desired (with substantially over one thousand SBUs now included). At first the SPI tested a large number of regression models on computers to find the ideal set of factors that relate to profitability. Eventually it identified thirty-seven factors that accounted for around 80 percent of the net profit variation in its sample of SBUs. Also, cash flow was found to be a function of nineteen factors. The selection and weighting of these factors was accomplished empirically through computations of the model.

The PIMS data are intended to address a number of the questions faced in business strategy decisions. Abell and Hammond have identified four major questions:

1. What factors explain differences in typical levels of return on investment (ROI) and cash flow among various kinds of business?
2. What rate of ROI and cash flow is "normal" or "PAR" in a given type of business, under given market conditions, and using a given strategy?
3. How will ROI and other measures of performance, in a specified business, be affected by a change in the strategy employed?
4. What are promising directions to explore to improve the performance of a given business?[1]

Most of the over one hundred items of data reported by member firms are quantitative facts (e.g., the value of finished goods inventory). Others are judgments (e.g., the relative quality level of the product versus competitors' quality). Member companies receive a great many findings from PIMS for which they pay large fees, but most of these data are not made public. A number of interesting findings have been published by the SBI, however, and we will describe two of them. These will indicate the nature of the many PIMS findings that are aiding strategic planners in the member corporations.

Possibly the most famous findings have concerned the effects of market share on business performance. The relationship between market share and profit (expressed as return on investment, or ROI) is shown in Figure 3-7. The higher ROI levels earned by the firms that lead in market share (in their SBUs' respective businesses) are impressive.

---

[1]D. F. Abell and J. S. Hammond, *Strategic Market Planning* (Englewood Cliffs, N.J.: Prentice-Hall, 1979), p. 272.

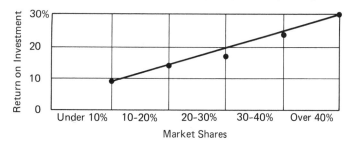

FIGURE 3-7. Relationship of pretax return on investment to market share. Data are from a PIMS study.

Source: Robert D. Buzzell, Bradley T. Gale, and Ralph G. M. Sultan, "Market Share—A Key to Profitability," *Harvard Business Review*, January–February 1975, p. 98.

Market share is again analyzed for its effects in Figure 3-8. This is a different format, another grid. And the relationship shown here is to the annual market growth of the SBU's business category. The variable or, possibly, dependent factor in this grid is cash flow, which is given by the numbers in each of the nine cells. This is a ratio determined by the following fraction:

$$\frac{\text{Cash flow}}{\text{Average investment}}$$

These have been calculated for the average of the particular PIMS reporting SBUs that happened to fall within each of the market growth/market share cells. Since the format is similar to that of the BCG growth/share matrix, the same labels (e.g., "Star") are placed in the four corners. The numbers show a clear pattern, with high cash flow ratios for Cash Cows and the lowest for Question Marks. This tends to confirm the basic thesis of the BCG.

The data in the above example are just broad averages of U.S. corporations, but they are a rough yardstick for comparing and diagnosing any firm's performance. Actually the PIMS service has made such analyses of groups of firms that are similar to a particular member firm and offer more realistic standards of comparison.

Some other PIMS findings are also useful for prescriptive purposes and deal specifically with certain functions and with the effects of certain strategies. Our next example is of that nature, but it is presented in the form of a table. Table 3-4 contains a PIMS analysis of firms according to their changes in promotional budgets for their sales forces, for advertising, and for sales promotion. In general it shows that market share falls when promotional funds are reduced, and the contrary result when they are increased (which is hardly surprising). There is a common tendency between consumer products and industrial products. Yet a much higher sensitivity is indicated for sales-force expen-

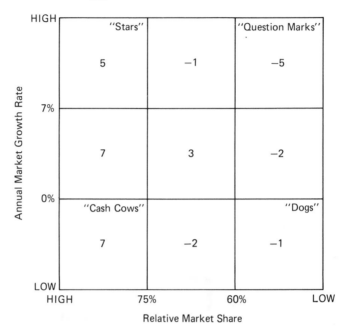

FIGURE 3-8. The impact of relative market share on cash flow. Figures inside each cell are the ratios of cash flow to average investment.

Source: Abell and Hammond, *Strategic Market Planning,* p. 283. With permission of Prentice-Hall, Inc.

ditures in the consumer goods firms than for those in industrial products. Such data should be interpreted with great care and with due consideration of factors peculiar to one's industry, but they illustrate how marketing strategists might use pooled business data in order to increase market share.

The foregoing are examples of PIMS findings that have been published. Far more is furnished confidentially to the participating firms (for substantial fees). They now receive findings in three report series:

1. "PAR" reports, which show normal cash flow and ROI for given situations. These enable managers to consider what would be reasonable expectations for their business and to set control standards.
2. Strategy sensitivity reports, which predict what would happen if certain strategy changes were made.
3. Optimum strategy reports, which predict which combination of strategic moves results in optimal results in income or cash flow.[2]

---

[2]Condensed from Abell and Hammond, *Strategic Market Planning,* pp. 277–78.

TABLE 3-4 Influence of marketing budgets, for promotion, on market share obtained

	Rate of change in market share					
	Consumer products firms			Industrial products firms		
Change in budget:	Sales force	Advertising	Sales promotion	Sales force	Advertising	Sales promotion
Cut by 5% or more	−3.0%	−0.0%	−0.2%	−2.8%	+0.8%	+0.4%
Steady (± 5% or less)	−0.6	+1.9	−0.5	−0.5	+0.9	+2.7
Increase over 5%	+6.6	+3.0	+3.7	+3.7	+1.9	+4.2

Source: Robert D. Buzzell and Frederick E. Wiersma, "Successful Share Building Strategies," *Harvard Business Review*, January–February 1981, pp. 141–42.

APPLICATION AND EVALUATION

Several other strategy analysis methods have been devised and used, although the three we chose are representative. Among the formal methods are the A. D. Little model and Shell International model. Both of these are multiple-factor methods with some similarity to the business attractiveness method. There are different methods, including the use of future scenarios and models incorporating risk factors, but they have been less popular. We should also mention that "pooled business experience" is conducted within a number of industries by planning institutes, research associations, or trade associations—among banks and among department stores, for instance, but these are narrow-spectrum samples compared with PIMS.

A recent survey of corporations indicates that they frequently use these methods. In Table 3-5, Coe's reported findings include data from a sample of 209 firms. Since Coe's survey included only manufacturers of industrial equipment, we can only surmise that satisfactory use is also being made by consumer goods and services marketers. We omitted from her table the A. D. Little method, which forty firms reported using—with results comparable with those of the methods shown.

The development of formal analytical methods has undoubtedly benefited strategic planning, and it may be one reason why such planning is becoming more pervasive. By and large, the described methods are attractive, and their methods and implications are quite comprehensible to upper management. Nevertheless, some critics have been pointing out serious shortcomings in these methods and the pitfalls involved in relying on them too heavily. Let us start our evaluation with the growth/share method.

The use of merely two factors as well as direct indications for cash flow make the growth/share matrix appealing. However, less weight is now being placed on the growth/share matrix because of recent recognition that (1) it can exaggerate the value of gaining high market share and (2) a number of products do not necessarily behave that way in terms of cost. A more current view follows:

> The news for the 1980s isn't that the experience curve has been proved wrong. Indeed, its logic has been refined, its implications plumbed for new ideas such as shared costs and the life cycles of technologies. What's happening now, though, is that the curve is being consigned to a much reduced place in the firmament of strategic concepts. With it is going a good bit of the importance originally attached to market share.[3]

The market attractiveness/business assessment matrix is appealing because it combines a number of factors and tailors the factors used and their weights to the particular type of business and the firm in which strategy is be-

---

[3]Walter Kiechel III, "The Decline of the Experience Curve," *Fortune*, October 5, 1981, p. 139. © Time Inc. All rights reserved.

TABLE 3-5 Numbers of companies reporting their satisfaction with strategic planning analysis methods

	Degree of satisfaction with analytical approaches			
	Very satisfied or satisfied	*Generally satisfied*	*Very or somewhat dissatisfied*	*Total*
Product portfolio	26	5	5	36
PIMS	24	7	8	39
Market attractiveness	21	10	6	37
Shell International	14	6	4	24

Source: Barbara J. Coe, "Use of Strategic Planning Concepts by Industrial Marketers," in *The Changing Marketing Environment: New Theories and Applications,* 1981 Educators' Conference Proceedings (Chicago: American Marketing Association, 1981), pp. 13–16.

ing planned. Of course much more effort is involved in the analysis, and implications are unclear when compared with the growth/share method. Also subjectivity and more estimation enter, which mar accuracy and may diminish confidence. It is difficult to select "correct" factors and to weight them fairly. Often the set of factors that is logical for one business under consideration differs from those logically affecting another business that the firm wants to show in the same matrix. Our example of this method was only diagnostic (looking at the current situation). The various factors could also be forecasted for a prognosis, but much more effort would be required.

Either of these portfolio assessment methods can aid a strategic planner in the initial steps of major decisions. Beyond these approximations, however, one must look for critical factors and unique aspects of the particular situation. Depending solely on these assessments might lead to serious error. An example might be the implication of Figure 3-4 that cash should be taken from Product C to support growth in Products A and B. If that were overdone and if Product C were very vulnerable to competitive attacks, it might lose share and cash flow irretrievably.

Besides the two methods described, the following methods can be used to assess portfolios:

Industry maturity/Competitive position matrix
Sector profitability/Competitive capabilities matrix
Risk versus reward
Strategic position/Operating performance
Cash generated/Cash used

These other methods have been described and criticized in a number of articles.[4]

---

[4]Yoram Wind and Vijay Mahajan, in "Design Considerations in Portfolio Analysis," *Harvard Business Review,* January–February 1981, pp. 155–65, discuss several optional methods.

Pooled business experience offers an information base for deciding strategies that is much better than depending on the firm's own experience. The PIMS reports especially have been a major advance in pooling. Besides providing comparisons with other firms, the PIMS model has empirically demonstrated the effects of various strategic moves.

Nevertheless, any user should be aware of the limitations in PIMS. For some industries the sample of contributing firms may be too small for reliability, a notable case being service industries. Emphasis on current earnings can be detrimental to a long-range perspective in planning. Considerable doubts have been raised about the effects of variables not used in the PIMS model. And there are doubts about whether the induced variables still actually account for 80 percent of profit variability. In these or any comparisons there is the question of how one's own business compares with the averages.[5]

A strategy planner should realize that analytical tools only aid and do not determine courses of action. Their proper role has been defined as follows:

> Strategy analysis methods are no substitute for insightful strategic thinking. Indeed, their greatest weakness is that the superficial appeal of the general prescriptions may over-ride the careful analysis of the fundamentals that are the basis for competitive advantages in the particular situation. The details of the situation invariably dominate the generalizations of the methods.[6]

Erroneous interpretation of these analyses can easily occur. An example is placing blind faith in the experience curve, which has been found to be inoperable in many industries. The experience curve also gives an allure to market-share goals that can lead to destructive price cutting among firms struggling to gain market leadership. Another danger of that curve consists of ignoring the possibility that firms late entering into a product field may have observed and profited by the pioneer's experience—and may also have improved technology lacking in the pioneer's plant. Other naive misjudgments may stem from relying on the PLC or the growth/share matrix. Basic errors may include wrong definitions of the markets actually sold to, or of who the competition really is.

Some of the premises of strategy analysis that should be questioned were described by Day as follows:

> Two strategic premises deserve especially careful handling: (a) that profitability is strongly related to market share, and (b) that high growth markets are more attractive than low growth markets. Not only do these premises occupy a central position in any strategy assessment—but they often yield grossly misleading strategic signals. The problem is that both premises are valid in general but often false in particular.[7]

---

[5]These are among a number of critical points raised by George S. Day in "Analytical Approaches to Strategic Planning," *Review of Marketing 1981*, ed. Ben M. Ennis and Kenneth J. Roering (Chicago: American Marketing Association, 1981), pp. 89–105.

[6]George S. Day, "Better Insights from Strategy Analysis Methods." Reprinted by permission from the Journal of Business Strategy, Summer 1983, Vol. 4, No. 1, Copyright © 1983, Warren, Gorham & Lamont Inc., 210 South St., Boston, Mass. All Rights Reserved.

[7]Day, "Better Insights from Strategy Analysis Methods," p. 7.

The particulars in a given situation, as indicated by Day, are important. Peculiar factors in a situation must be recognized. Also the analytical tools should merely be regarded as aids. Used wisely, they are vital to the strategic process.

Analytical tools are just a means to an end—the end being good strategic decisions. The interpretations of the date and the kinds of strategies they call for are what is most interesting to study. Later, as we deal with specific decisions, we will discuss and illustrate the applications of several of these methods.

SUMMARY

In this chapter we first established the important needs served by analytical methods to accomplish the "matching task" of strategists—to attain an optimal match-up between a firm's resources and its opportunities. We then pointed out that there are three stages in this task: diagnosis, prognosis, and prescription. Present and future market positions can be identified through analytical methods, which are also essential for prescribing the right strategy.

The market growth/market share matrix was the first method discussed. The experience curve theory that underlies this method was then described. Examples of the growth/share method followed, with data and charts. We explained the significance of positioning in the four quadrants of the matrix, which are popularly called "Question Mark," "Star," "Cash Cow," and "Dog." These positions were related to the four stages of the product life cycle, with which they tend to be (but are not invariably) connected.

We then considered the market attractiveness/business position method of analyzing a portfolio. It combines multiple factors on each of the two dimensions of its matrix (these being *business assessment* and *market attractiveness*). Positions of the PMUs or SBUs being analyzed are then placed in a nine-cell matrix. These positions indicate their relative attractiveness for the firm. We listed numerous factors that might be included. We also explained the setting of criteria (for high, medium, and low levels in either dimension), as well as the remaining steps.

Pooled business experience is an approach based on actual past records of firms that pool their data with others. The PIMS project of the Strategic Business Institute conducted massive regression analyses of pooled business data to find the set of factors that accounted for most of profit variation. Hundreds of corporations now participate in pooling their data in PIMS, and they in turn receive reports and special studies regarding strategic actions. Several examples were presented.

Finally, we examined some data on the usage of the foregoing analytical methods and gave a brief critique of their limitations.

1. *You are going to make a diagnosis with regard to starting strategic planning for the next three years, in a beverage company whose main product is a prominent cola soft drink. Suggest some kinds of data useful in the diagnosis. When you proceed to make a prognosis, would any different data be suitable? How would analysis of those stages assist in the prescription stage?*

2. *Define the two variables used in the growth/share matrix. Why are these particular variables so often of interest to managers?*

3. *As part of the training program in a corporation, a recent college graduate was required to read literature on subjects that included portfolio analysis. The trainee then took a quiz whose suggestions sought to probe whether the readings had been well understood. One of the questions dealt with portfolio analysis, in which three assertions were made about the growth/share matrix. The trainee was asked to decide if each was fully correct and, if not, to rewrite the statement, to qualify or correct it. Here are the three assertions:*

   A product that is a "Dog" would be incurring a negative cash flow and would have a low profit as a percentage of sales (low relative to the firm's average).

   A product that is a "Star" would have a cash flow that was marginal: either slightly positive or slightly negative. Its profit rate (percentage of sales) nevertheless would be positive and substantial.

   A product that is a "Question Mark" would have a negative cash flow, negative profit, and poor future prospects.

   What should the trainee have answered?

4. *Draw a graph like the one in Figure 3-4, using the same values along its two axes. Then draw circles that position the following six PMUs according to these data:*

	Relative market share	*Market growth*		*Relative market share*	*Market growth*
PMU 1	0.3	+ 2%	PMU 4	0.6	+28%
PMU 2	0.8	+22%	PMU 5	0.4	+17%
PMU 3	0.4	+31%	PMU 6	0.9	+14%

   The above represent the product portfolio of the Ergo Company. How would you consider the company's current position, as shown by that analysis, as an overall judgment: a sound competitive position or a rather shaky one? What specific situations lead you to that judgment?

5. *The Ergo Company's planner is going to work on strategies for two years ahead, and the following positions are forecasted for the existing portfolio at the end of that period. The planner has assumed that present strategies*

will continue over that time, and effects of environmental forces have been taken into consideration. Also enter these positions on your graph in some contrasting color or shading. Now, looking into the future, is your

	Relative market share	Market growth		Relative market share	Market growth
PMU 1	0.2	− 9%	PMU 4	0.9	+16%
PMU 2	0.6	+27%	PMU 5	0.3	+25%
PMU 3	0.4	+14%	PMU 6	0.8	+ 4%

assessment of Ergo Company's position the same or has it changed? Explain. Let us suppose that each of these six PMUs has around the same sales revenues. What major changes seem to be needed in the company's marketing strategy?

6. *What factors of major importance to the future of a firm does the growth-share analysis omit? Use the Ergo Company as an example for discussion.*

7. *Answer the following three questions with regard to the market attractiveness/business position analysis (the second one discussed) in comparison with the growth/share analysis:*
   a. *In which of these methods is less subjectivity or guesswork involved?*
   b. *Which of these two methods would an average business manager more readily understand and apply?*
   c. *If the problem you are dealing with is that of determining which markets, in which the firm has not done business, would offer it the better opportunities, which of the two methods would be superior? Why?*

8. *Explain the connection between an industry's having a steep cost experience curve and the applicability of the growth/share matrix.*

9. *In what ways have the PIMS findings benefited the marketing strategists in firms that participate in PIMS?*

10. *One of the SBUs in your corporation is earning a 21 percent return on investment and is yielding a cash flow that is three and one-half times its rate of investment. Its industry is growing a steady 5 percent annually, and its share of market is about 45 percent. How would you rate its performance: rather good or rather poor? (Consult the data in Figures 3-7 and 3-8.)*

11. *King Robotics, Inc., makes industrial equipment and is in the midst of planning for next year, when sales are forecasted to rise very little. You as a consultant are present in a budget-setting meeting, where an executive proposes cutting back sales-force expense by 10 percent and sales promotion by 20 percent. If you had the data in Table 3-2 and considered them reliable, how would you respond to that proposal?*

12. *The personnel manager is examining the merits of applicants who want the new job of assistant in corporate planning. Should a demonstrated ability in statistics or high college scores in that subject be given any weight? Explain.*

Lynch and Reynolds, Inc. (A)

David Hutchinson entered his office and removed his papers from his briefcase. It was January 10, 1974 and as he sat down he reflected on the previous afternoon's meeting. His presentation on the mobile machinery industry had been reasonably well received.

David's report had considered general industry characteristics, growth trends, and the future outlook. He had divided the industry into three basic product/market segments —industrial trucks, construction equipment, and agricultural equipment. In addition he had been able to further refine construction equipment into a number of subsegments. Against this background he had reported on eight major industry participants—Allis-Chalmers, Caterpillar, Clark, Deere, Eaton, Hyster, International Harvester, and Tenneco's J. I. Case.

Using the information compiled by his research assistant, Dave had tried to assess the positions and business strategies of the eight companies. In doing so, he had highlighted certain financial figures (see Exhibit 1), drawn market growth/relative share portfolio charts for each company, and had calculated and drawn charts showing industry growth versus company growth for each business unit within a company. Dave had presented his report before his boss, Gene Laisne, and two other officers of Lynch and Reynolds; all had appeared very interested and had asked a number of questions during his presentation.

Dave was pleased that his project was progressing so well. What remained, though, was to focus on Allis-Chalmers. Following the presentation, Mr. Laisne took Dave aside, "One of our clients is very interested in Allis and now that you've completed this general phase, concentrate on them. You seem to have a good understanding of the environment Allis faces, the factors likely to impact their future performance, and the competitors with whom they must deal. The competitive situation is critical. Are there any special opportunities that Allis can take advantage of? Go into detail on what they should do for the next, say, five years. What strategy ought they to follow?"

Dave had known careful analysis of Allis would follow the general industry analysis. At Dave's request, Mark, a research assistant, had just finished gathering some more information about Allis-Chalmers (see Exhibit 1).

Dave poured himself a cup of coffee. A great deal of work was still left to be done. What strategy would Allis follow in the future?

Exhibit 1

MEMORANDUM
TO: Mr. David Hutchinson
FROM: Mr. Mark Osborn, Research Assistant
RE: Further Information on Allis-Chalmers

When David Scott, formerly of Colt Industries, Inc., arrived to take over as president and chairman of the board of Allis-Chalmers, he found "a centralized company in the classic sense, seemingly wedged in a rut of fat payrolls and low productivity. He consolidated plants, pared off unprofitable products, and cut operating costs and payrolls."[1]

Unfortunately, despite great expectations, by late 1970 and 1971 it became obvious that the turnaround would not be smooth. For Scott, late 1970 proved "a doubly bitter pill. Not only did he fall short of his much-publicized earnings goals, but he also encountered trouble in the two big businesses that he sees as major producers of Allis profits in the future: construction machinery and electrical equipment."[2]

According to the March 13, 1971 issue of *Business Week*, "When Scott first arrived at Allis, he was so dissatisfied with the management of the construction equipment division that he stepped in and ran it personally for three months. He replaced five of its six top executives and consolidated its operations, which were spread over five plants, into two in Springfield and Deerfield, Ill.

"Production of motor graders, tractor scrapers, and crawler tractors was moved to the Springfield plant. The company began production of improved models of the two-crawler tractors, HD-16 and HD-21, as well as a new five-ton model HD-41, the 'largest in the world.' As these changes took place, the company experienced a surge in sales that they had not anticipated and, according to Scott, the effect was 'a manufacturing problem of huge magnitude.'

"As many as four or five carloads of parts from two of the shutdown plants were arriving weekly at Springfield and had to be stored along side assembly lines. As new orders flooded in, the plant went to seven-day 24-hour operations, costing $2.5 million in overtime alone for 1970. Parts delivery from suppliers had to be accelerated, costing another $2.5 million."[3]

The agricultural division is also not doing well. In 1971, Scott was denying rumors that Allis would sell the division. To achieve consolidation, he closed three plants and effectively phased out some farm lines simply by raising prices.[4] Recently a stock market analyst noted that Allis had been "a tough ship to turn around. I think the problems were greater in magnitude, to start with, than Dave Scott and the people he brought in anticipated. And this coupled with the fact that despite their size, they really aren't dominant in any market they serve, except perhaps for some of their process systems and outdoor equipment lines. It makes it a tough company to get a handle on.

"But in Ag, of course, they made some very critical mistakes in 1970 and 1971. Before the market was starting to heat up a little bit, they played the game that J. I. Case played back in the '60s and loaded up their dealers with inventory during a slack period and really weren't able to work off those inventories when strength appeared in the Ag equipment market, although they started to show some signs of life in the second half of 1972, and are going to have a decent year in 1973. They are not going to have an exceptional year, it appears. Their big problem is that their dealer organization is not too strong. Their dealers are just not in it with the Deeres, for instance, and probably for that matter with Harvester. I think in the long run this is probably going to cause them a great many problems. I think that Scott, for some time has wanted to get out of that business, but there haven't been any takers. Another problem with Allis is they haven't been introducing new products as the cycles indicated they should—primarily in their tractor line. Therefore, they were losing market share in the larger horsepower sizes. Now they are introducing with it a large horsepower line but it is going to be expensive and it may be too little too late."[5]

Non-mobile Machinery Groups

Given below is some more information about the products manufactured by Allis-Chalmers by its various groups other than the groups manufacturing mobile machinery.

The Process Systems Group is divided into five divisions: Minerals Systems, Hydraulic, Aggregate Processing, Commonwealth Divisions, and Naval Nuclear Components.

---

[1]*International Management,* May 1970, p. 51.
[2]*Business Week,* March 13, 1971, p. 96.
[3]*Ibid.,* pp. 96–97.
[4]*Ibid.*
[5]Wall Street Transcript, March 26, 1973, p. 32327.

The Minerals Systems manufactures cement making equipment, smelter equipment for copper ore processing, iron ore pelletizing plants, paper making machinery. The Hydraulic Division manufactures hydraulic power and control equipment such as hydraulic turbines for generating electricity, large-volume water pumps (with applications including water supply, waste treatment), industrial pumps, valves (with applications such as water supply, waste treatment). The Aggregate Processing Division supplies to the aggregate, mining, and asphalt equipment markets. Its products include crushing and screening equipment with applications that include manufacture of sand and grinding of ores, shredder mills used in refuse processing, asphalt mixing plants. The Commonwealth Divisions are so named because, in addition to the Compressor Division in the U.S., they are made up of operations which are headquartered in Canada, Great Britain, and Australia. The Compressor Division produces compressors for various industrial applications. The Canadian and British operations manufacture pumps, compressors, processing equipment, and mining equipment.

The Industrial Electrical Group consists of several divisions manufacturing electric motors of a wide range of capacities, large generators of electricity, industrial control equipment, switchgears, and several electric and electronic devices.

The Power Generation and Delivery Groups consist of several divisions supplying a broad line of equipment to the electric utility industry. Its products include power breakers, overhead distribution transformers, power transformers, residential underground transformers, power regulators, and power switching equipment.

EXHIBIT 2 1973 Summary financial data

	Allis-Chalmers	Caterpillar Tractor	Clark Equipment	Deere & Co.	Eaton Corp.	Hyster	Internat'l Harvester	Tenneco
4 Year Sales Growth	8.5%	12.3%	15.0%	17.9%	9.6%	6.8%	12.1%	19.8%
Return on sales	0.9	8.2	4.8	8.9	5.7	5.5	2.8	5.9
Return on assets	2.6	14.9	11.8	15.1	11.9	6.2	6.6	9.0
Debt/Equity	.45	.24	.27	.24	.37	.34	.36	—
Return on equity	3.7	18.5	15.0	18.5	16.5	11.7	9.0	17.0
Retention rate	70	65	62	77	64	71	64	42
Sustainable growth	2.6	12.0	9.3	14.2	10.6	8.3	5.8	7.1
Market/Book value	.40	2.81	1.72	1.56	1.21	—	.75	1.55
Cash flow	$35M	355M	70.7M	214.2M	123.9M	23M	191.1M	386M

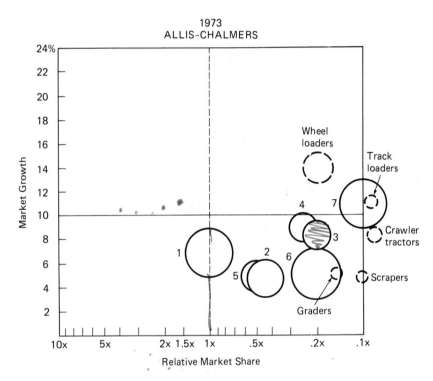

1973
ALLIS-CHALMERS

Market Growth (y-axis): 24%, 22, 20, 18, 16, 14, 12, 10, 8, 6, 4, 2

Relative Market Share (x-axis): 10x, 5x, 2x, 1.5x, 1x, .5x, .2x, .1x

Wheel loaders
Track loaders
Crawler tractors
Scrapers
Graders

1 Process Systems
2 Power Generation & Delivery
3 Lift trucks
4 Industrial-Electrical
5 Industrial-Consumer tractor
6 Agriculture
7 Construction Equipment

NOTES:
Broken circles represent breakout of
Construction Equipment Group
19/32" circle = $100 million in sales;
e.g., 3, 4, 5.

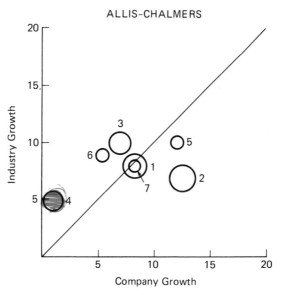

ALLIS-CHALMERS

1 Agriculture
2 Process Systems
3 Construction Machinery
4 Power Generation
5 Material Handling
6 Industrial-Electric
7 Industrial-Consumer Tractor

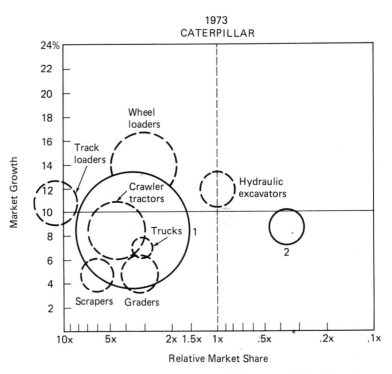

1973
CATERPILLAR

Market Growth

Relative Market Share

1 Construction Equipment   19/32″ circle = $100 million in sales
2 Lift trucks

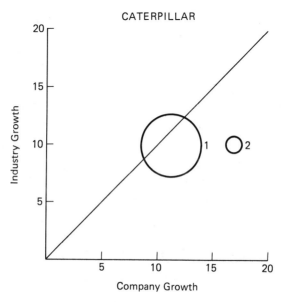

CATERPILLAR

1 Construction Equipment
2 Materials Handling

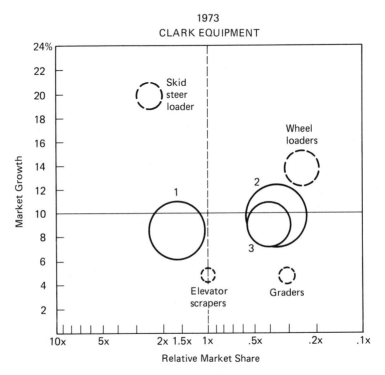

1973
CLARK EQUIPMENT

1 Lift trucks
2 Construction Equipment
3 Axle & Transmission

NOTES:
Broken circles represent breakout
of Construction Equipment Group
19/32'' circle = $100 million in sales

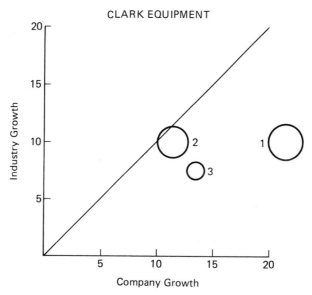

CLARK EQUIPMENT

1 Construction Machinery
2 Material Handling
3 Axle & Trans., Truck

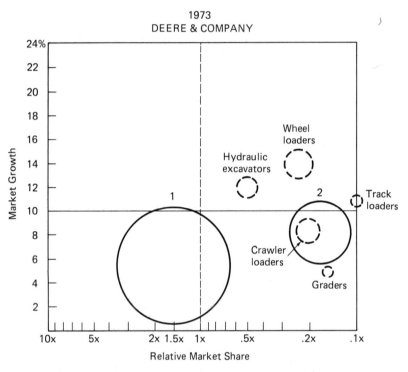

1973
DEERE & COMPANY

1 Agricultural Equipment
2 Construction Equipment

19/32" circle = $100 million in sales
e.g., Wheel loaders

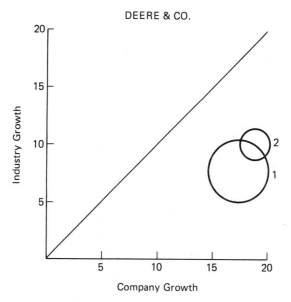

DEERE & CO.

1 Agricultural Equipment
2 Construction Equipment

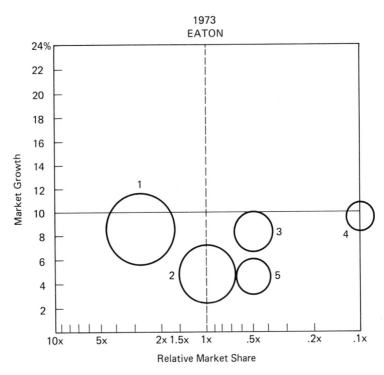

1973
EATON

1 Truck & Off-highway components
2 Automobile components
3 Lift trucks
4 Construction Equipment
5 Industrial Power Transmission

19/32″ circle = $100 million in sales

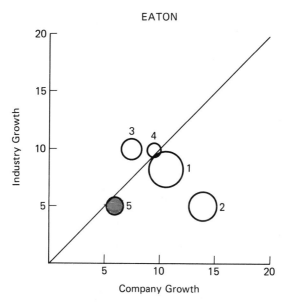

EATON

1 Axle & Trans., Truck
2 Axle & Trans., Auto
3 Materials Handling
4 Construction Equipment
5 Power Generation

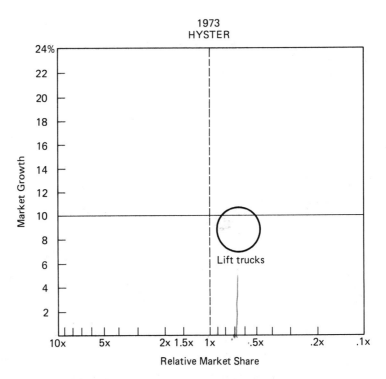

1973
HYSTER

Lift trucks

19/32″ circle = $100 million in sales

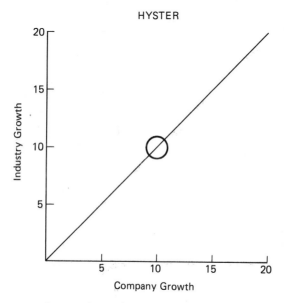

HYSTER

Construction equipment

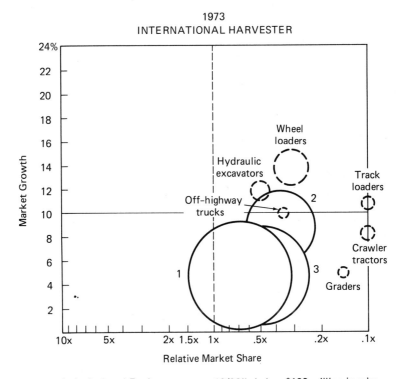

1973
INTERNATIONAL HARVESTER

Market Growth

Relative Market Share

1 Agricultural Equipment   19/32" circle = $100 million in sales
2 Construction Equipment
3 Trucks

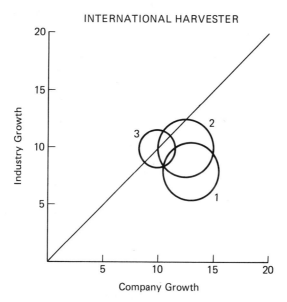

INTERNATIONAL HARVESTER

1 Agricultural Equipment
2 Construction Equipment
3 Trucks

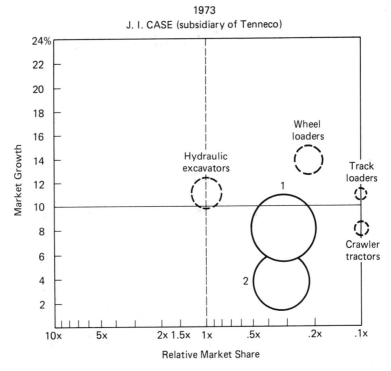

1973
J. I. CASE (subsidiary of Tenneco)

1 Construction Equipment   19/32" circle = $100 million in sales
2 Agriculture   e.g., Hydraulic excavators, Wheel loaders

DISCUSSION

Analyze each of the eight companies and its product line. Use any methods that you find suitable, in order to provide the basis for answering the questions raised by Mr. Laisne. These would come under the following three categories:

1. The competition with which Allis would contend
2. The competitive market positions or strengths of each firm
3. Your opinion of the relative strengths of the firms competitively—totally and by market segment.

The question raised on the specific strategy that Allis ought to follow in the future should *not* be answered yet. That is postponed for Case 4-3, Lynch and Reynolds (B), which will be preceded by our chapter on strategic business units.

4

Business Unit Decisions

This chapter covers four major aspects of business unit decisions:

1. Establishing the strategic business units (SBUs) and defining their scope so that they can plan efficiently
2. Creating an organization with an SBU for strategic planning
3. Establishing a flow-model decision system tailored to the SBU's situation
4. Selecting the strategies from the available options (some of which will be illustrated)

Our focus moves down from the corporate-planning level to the strategic business units (SBUs). Bear in mind that SBUs would be found only in diversified firms that deal with a variety of markets (which is one reason why the BIC Corporation in Case 2-3 was not divided into SBUs). We should approach this level's strategy by pointing out how the situation here differs from the corporate one. In an *intermediate* position, the SBU must accommodate to the corporate plans above, as well as guide and approve the planning of the PMUs below. Also, the SBU tends more toward *short-term orientation* (to periodic plans) than does corporate development strategy. And the SBU managers are much involved in the *operations* that carry out the plans and in supervising the several functional departments—including marketing.

ESTABLISHING BUSINESS UNITS

Determining the strategic units is much simpler in a new firm than in an existing one. When dealing with an existing organization that has evolved with scant regard for strategic planning, there are normally struggles with the status quo. This emphasizes the need for clear and logical definitions of each unit's sphere.

First one must fully grasp the characteristics needed in an SBU. It should meet four criteria:

1. An SBU should be largely self-contained and should include technical, production, and marketing operations. An SBU should have authority, control, and accountability for its own strategic plans and results.
2. An SBU should serve a distinct and clearly defined set of markets that have significant characteristics in common.
3. An SBU should contend against a distinct set of competitors or within a distinct industry.
4. An SBU should be in a position to decide and to implement its own strategies. This results when the three preceding criteria have been met.

The markets and products that an SBU deals with should be fairly homogeneous, with key factors in common. When this is true, an SBU can develop suitable broad strategies to guide all of its underlying PMUs. In some lines of business, of course, the business volume may be insufficient to justify the administrative costs of a separate SBU. In this case, there may be more than one such group in the SBU. However, putting together ill-matched PMUs under one SBU's management would necessitate the creation and implementation of heterogeneous and inefficient plans.

When determining the organization structure for planning in a corporation, the approach may be a "top-down" sequence that begins at the top of the organization or a "bottom-up" sequence that starts with the underlying units.

In a "bottom-up" approach, the product/market units first need to be defined. Abell developed from earlier management theory the use of three dimensions in defining PMUs.[1] We will borrow Day's description of these three dimensions:

1. Customer *functions* performed by the good or service.
2. The *technologies* or alternative ways that the function can be performed.
3. Customer *segments,* which are groups with similar needs and characteristics which are strategically relevant.[2]

---

[1]Derek F. Abell, *Defining the Business: The Starting Point of Strategic Planning* (Englewood Cliffs, N.J.: Prentice-Hall, 1980).

[2]Condensed from George S. Day, *Strategic Market Analysis: Top-down and Bottom-up Approaches* (Cambridge, Mass.: Marketing Science Institute, 1980), pp. 2–3.

We will illustrate those three dimensions with the following hypothetical example:

Ideal Cabinets, Inc., has manufactured a great variety of cabinets for fifty years, but it has never tried to organize these products into logical groups to rationalize planning. A new sales manager was assigned to divide the business into product/market units. He listed many optional categories along the three dimensions, a few being:

Function: A cabinet may hold tools, medicine, clothing, kitchen wares, bulk materials, etc. And it may have a decorative function or merely such utility functions as easy access and preservation.

Technology: A cabinet may be made of wood, metal, or plastic. It may be suspended on a wall or be free-standing. It may be portable or built-in, etc.

Segments: Customers may be distinguished by varying uses and preferences. Military barracks have needs and buying methods that differ from those of hotels/motels. Builders of low-price tract homes differ from custom home builders. The do-it-yourself consumer is still another category.

The *bottom-up* sequence examines all the existing products and markets in which the firm does business, breaking them down into finer units related to the chosen dimensions. Ideal Cabinets might consider this unit, for instance: wooden tool display cabinets for hardware and home-building retailers. This process might reveal not only numerous units but also gaps in the product line.

Many such identified units would be too small to support separate managers: The wooden retail tool cabinet volume might be one such unit. Smaller units could be combined with reasonably similar units. For example, wooden cabinets (same technology) or retail cabinets (same segment) or those that store similar items (same function) might be merged under a single responsible manager.

Once the PMUs have been defined, the various SBUs' scope could be considered. This, of course, assumes the firm is large enough to have the intermediate business unit level. Because Ideal Cabinets is "all cabinets," it probably has neither the size nor the heterogeneity to justify the management overhead of SBUs.

A *top-down* approach may be chosen instead, in which the first step is to determine whether the whole firm is large and diverse enough to justify organizing it into separate SBUs. Economically, in order to have its own factory, laboratory, and marketing organization, each SBU must generate a rather large profit.

The top executives of some very large corporations have found, as Du-Pont did, that their diverse products and markets demand too many SBUs to be dealt with directly from the top. The SBUs are therefore placed in groups, reducing the span of supervision at the top. The desirable number of groups may be small, as seen in Minnesota Mining & Manufacturing (3M Company). In 1980, 3M with sales above $6 billion had placed its many SBUs in ten groups. The following table lists their types of business and sales (note that each SBU comprised a large business).

Product groups	1980 Sales (millions)
Abrasives, adhesives, building service, and chemicals	$ 866
Business products	1,076
Consumer products	396
Decorative and protective products	284
Electrical products	543
Health care products and services	499
Photo and graphic arts	706
Recording materials	533
Tape and allied products	777
Traffic control, safety systems and advertising services	376

Source: 3M Company, *1980 Annual Report.*

Each of these large businesses had a number of SBUs, which in turn had various PMUs. The surgical sector of health-care products, for instance, included plastic casts for orthopedists, skin staplers for surgery, and eye transplant lenses for ophthalmologists among just its new products in 1980.

Ten groups, however, were too many, and 3M had other reasons for wanting to combine them into a smaller number. In 1981, 3M merged them into these four groups:

Electronic and information technologies sector

Life sciences sector

Graphic technologies sector

Industrial and consumer sector

We have gone into these details about one corporation's organization structure between its corporate and SBU level partially because it illustrates the benefits of attaining some homogeneity in each unit for strategy advantages. At 3M the following comments were made by its CEO regarding the above action:

> If you look at our Industrial and Consumer Sector . . . you will find many of 3M's longer-established—and still very fruitful—technologies, such as coating and bonding, fluorochemistry and film. In the other three sectors, there are many of 3M's newer technologies, such as in electronics, health care and photography. By combining operating units in this way, we expect greater synergism in research and development, both within and among business sectors.[3]

That statement, in effect, was saying that there was an important "strategy" in restructuring the company's strategic management units (at that level) in or-

---

[3]"3M's New Organization Structure," a message to stockholders from the chief executive officer (St. Paul, Minn.: 3M Company, 1981), p. 2.

der to position each for long-term growth through homogeneous technological strategies and synergies in each of the four groups. This would in turn enable the subgroups and SBUs in each group to determine and to implement better strategies in marketing and in market development.

The organizing task would then proceed below the "group" level (in a huge firm like 3M) to define the SBUs and then the PMUs that compose each SBU. Or the firm could build up its units beginning with the basic PMUs, which it would group into homogeneous SBUs, and so forth. The build-up approach is intuitively appealing, but we have little basis for declaring that either approach is better. Obviously, organizing for strategy making is difficult in large and diversified organizations. But it is also a critical task in smaller ones.

ORGANIZATION WITHIN BUSINESS UNITS

The principal concern of an SBU is not its planning but its *operations*, which its top managers must oversee. One is the chief marketing executive (CME) of the SBU. Many more people are engaged in the operations of marketing and other functions than in planning, but the latter is recognized as an essential activity. The chief planning responsibility consists of creating strategies for the total SBU and later includes gaining acceptance of them at the top of the corporation and monitoring their implementation.

We will briefly examine the relationship between an SBU and the two types of underlying units: the PMUs and the functional units (see Figure 4-1).

The product managers' major role is that of planning, for which they are in frequent contact with the SBU managers. Marketing, however, is primarily concerned with its operations, as are the other functional departments. We independently connect marketing with the SBU level in Figure 4-1 because it prepares and submits its own plans. Since Figure 4-1 shows only the routing of the plans, it has no connection between functional departments and PMUs. In fact there is much communication between these units, as they must agree on actions to be taken and keep informed during implementation.

FIGURE 4-1. Planning relationships between an SBU and its constituent units

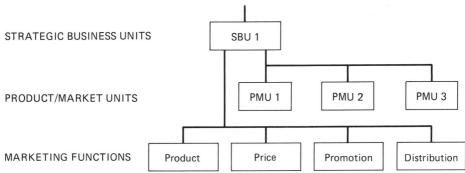

STRATEGIC DECISION SYSTEM

You will recall the decision model for corporate planning that was presented in Chapter 2. An SBU likewise needs a decision system, which should of course be different from that of the corporate model. The four basic planning decisions (objectives, defining the business, strategic programs, and resource allocations) have been retained in the SBU model shown in Figure 4-2.

Note that the SBU ties into corporate decisions above and into the PMUs' and functions' decisions below. Although this chart omits some of the details found in Figure 2-2 for corporations, it has the same essentials. Again we explain the decision system step by step, using as an example one division of BWI, the hypothetical firm that we followed in Chapter 2. And again the discussion begins with the first decision, setting the objectives.

1. Objectives:

All planning should begin with a current assessment or audit of the environment and of the organization's performance in it. Our chart in Figure 4-2 identifies the three main aspects on which this assessment focuses: (1) condi-

FIGURE 4-2. Systematic process for strategic planning in a strategic business unit

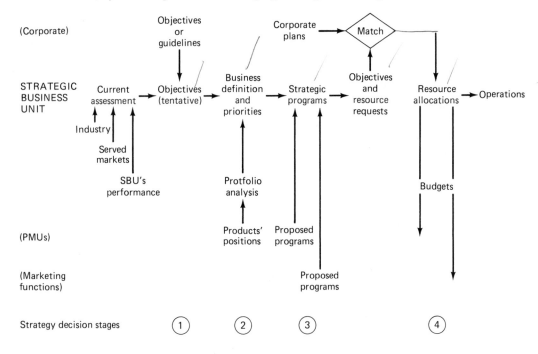

tions in the *industry* in which the SBU is competing, including competitive activities and one's own competitive position; (2) changes in the *markets* that this firm is serving (or should serve); and (3) this SBU's *performance*, including the effectiveness of current strategies and the ability to meet current objectives. This situation analysis indicates also where the unit seems to be headed and reveals some problems and strengths.

Able Division was one of the four SBUs in BWI. This division was composed of six PMUs that engaged in some of the most dynamic industrial markets in which BWI competed. Its planners assessed the current situation and found the following:

  a. The industry had maintained in 1983 the same excellent growth rate as in 1982.
  b. It had attracted five other firms to its markets, of which two offered broad product lines that practically duplicated Able's.
  c. The newcomers had already captured about 10 percent of the market and had caused selective price weakening.
  d. Able had held its number-two place in the market close to the leader, although that had eroded from a 27 to a 25 percent share.
  e. Buyer surveys were showing that Able's quality image had stayed high, but its product was being considered high priced and hard to repair.
  f. Relative to objectives that had been set for 1983, Able slightly exceeded those for sales but was a half point below its ROI objective of 11 percent. Its cash flow was more negative than expected, resulting in over a $2 million deficit.

A current assessment, such as that above, is one determinant of an SBU's objectives. It should be blended with the expectations of the corporate executives and those of the SBU itself. An SBU should have a counterpart objective for each objective of the corporation: For example, if asset turnover is a corporation goal, the SBU should also set a specific asset turnover objective. The corporation's CEO may arbitrarily dictate the objectives for the SBUs, but it is wiser to give SBUs some latitude to propose the level of performance they consider feasible. In the latter case, a CEO should inform the SBU heads of the performance levels that the whole corporation intends to reach, which would then serve as guidelines for SBU planning.

On the basis of existing strategies, Able Division's prognosis for 1984 was keeping a 24 percent share of the market. With that and a market growth forecast, it projected a 10.8 percent ROI (which was good) and a negative cash flow of $3.9 million (which was bad).

The CEO of BWI had informed the head of Able Division that for the whole corporation an ROI of 13 percent was expected for 1984 and that he expected Able Division to "reach a breakeven cash flow." Thus challenged, the Able Division staff searched for economies and came up with these modified objectives for 1984: an ROI of 11.3 percent and a negative cash flow of $1.9 million. But these were only tentative figures until there was final decision on the strategies to adopt.

2. Business Definition:

Like the total corporation, an SBU should reconsider its area of business—the markets it wants to serve and products to offer. Its range of choices is much narrower, though, because any venture into technologies and markets that would be radically new ones (for that firm) should be corporate-level determinations.

In addition to deciding whether to expand into any new areas (or to withdraw from any current ones), the SBU faces decisions on the priorities in dividing resources among its PMUs. The SBU executives should indicate these levels or priorities to the PMU and functional managers, to enable the latter to be realistic as they consider their own plans.

> Able Division in 1983 was composed of six PMUs, each headed by a product manager, and of seven products (as a few did not afford separate managers). Also it had several functional departments, five of them in marketing functions.
>
> In the SBU's views, all seven products were sufficiently healthy to continue, but their attractiveness for allocating funds varied. New-product development had scheduled no product introductions for 1984, but two would be test-marketed by the new-products manager (not considered to be a PMU). At the SBU level a divisionwide venture for marketing spare parts was being contemplated for 1984.

3. Determining Strategic Programs:

Having the business areas defined and the priorities for resources considered, the SBU planners are prepared to examine whatever strategies will be proposed. SBU executives may develop some proposals to deal with overall programs. The proposals from the various functional departments tend to be more numerous and involve most of the expenditures. There will also be the proposals from each PMU, which are likely to contain the more interesting strategy ideas, since each PMU manager is basically a strategist for that product and market area. All of these underlying plans must be melded and must be matched with the SBU overall strategies. The whole must then be made acceptable at the corporate level.

This planning involves a large portion of executives' time and normally extends over a long period—three months or more. Many meetings and many more casual conversations between planners and executives will take place while these strategies are evolving. The lower-level managers (functional and PMU) will be sounding out the attitudes of higher-level executives who will ultimately have the power to approve whatever plans are submitted. A well-managed corporation has prepared forms on which the planners down the line will place and analyze specified data and descriptions of their current audits, their prognoses, and their strategies. The amount of time, effort, and thought that goes into this process would surprise anyone who has not participated in it.

As has already been mentioned, the SBU has to reconcile proposals from the various planning units below and has to produce a total plan. There will of course be conflicts: For example, the sales promotion department has an excellent idea for a huge coupon campaign that would divert funds from advertising, whose manager—allied with some of the product managers—finds it very repulsive. Meanwhile, the sales manager seeks to reproportion regional expenditures in ways that conflict with the SBU's intentions. Negotiations take place, and it is hoped that the compromises will still be near optimal in their results.

At Able division, tension mounted as the date approached for presenting plans. Each functional and product manager appeared before the four executives who were the approving committee and made a pitch for his or her plan. The committee had some difficult decisions to make. For instance, there was this choice: For Product D a brilliant strategy was proposed, but it faced a declining market; whereas Product F's market was rising, but its manager had only a vague strategy statement. And so the plans bounced back and forth and were extensively reworked. After four hectic weeks, the plans were approved to the committee's satisfaction (but not to everyone's).

4. Resource Allocations:

How a firm allocates its resources is critical, and these decisions must finally be determined at the top. Each SBU will have done its utmost to make a persuasive case for what it wants in order to implement its proposed programs. When it learns what has been allocated from the top, the SBU has the task of parceling that out among its functional units and—simultaneously—among its PMUs. Both of these allocations are shown in Figure 4-2.

Given the allocations decisions and with information obtained while the planning process was under way, an SBU may cycle back to change some earlier decisions. Objectives may be raised or lowered. Plans for expansion or diversification may or may not appear logical or feasible now. When an SBU has finished all of this financial-balancing act, it can issue line-by-line budgets to each underlying unit so that the managers can complete planning and prepare for implementation when the next period begins.

Able Division now reconsidered its objectives and found the 20 percent sales increase goal to be justified. By strenuous efforts, though, its expenditures could be held to only a 14 percent rise. This would improve its negative cash flow, so that it would only be $1.3 million.

These revised goals were taken to the top corporate executives for approval. The executives found the sales projections to be sound but the cash flow unacceptable. After some give-and-take, the Able executives agreed to postpone some outlays while the top executives yielded somewhat on the cash flow. They reached agreement on a negative $800,000 goal, and the SBU's budgets were then prepared.

DECIDING SBU STRATEGIES

The SBU executives must decide on strategies for two levels in the organization: those for the underlying functions and PMUs, and those on their level that concern the whole SBU. In the case of a PMU's or a function's strategy, the task is one of approving or asking for changes in the program that has been submitted by the subordinate manager. In its evaluation of those proposals, the SBU management must consider the effects of any SBU-wide strategic changes on the underlying units. Thus these SBU decisions are complicated.

Our discussion will concentrate on the third among the four main decisions in strategic planning—conceiving or choosing the strategy. Bear in mind that either of the two previous decisions (objectives and defining the business) may be altered when the available strategic actions have been considered. We will first describe some of the general types of options available to strategists. We will then deal with the analysis that may be followed to reach conclusions.

Options:

An SBU should have been created, as we earlier pointed out, so that its underlying units (products and markets) have substantial homogeneity and so that common overall strategies of the SBU will be applicable to all the PMUs. It is in regard to such common factors as the following that the SBU planners are responsible for strategy:

Common technologies among all the units
Use of common production or distribution facilities
Use of some natural resources in common
A common brand name on all the products
Joint use of a single sales force

The foregoing tend to be very important to the entire SBU, and so the strategic plans are major decisions. Changes in any of them often require large expenditures and long development periods. In these respects the planning orientation is therefore rather long term (although often shorter than the corporate view, for the factors dealt with at the top level are on an even broader scale).

The strategic options related to these broad factors cannot be placed into neat categories. Instead there is an immense variety specific to various situations. The alternative new positions that one might seek for a brand name (in buyers' minds) and the various ways of achieving that are one example. The alternatives in new technologies are altogether different for paper manufacturers than for data transmission services.

The options regarding the treatment of the PMUs, however, can be stated clearly and related to the division of the SBU's resources. The options can be placed into four broad categories:

1. *Build market share.* This calls for putting relatively heavy investment into a PMU because greater share would reap profit gains and future larger cash flows.
2. *Maintain market share.* Such a PMU would be yielding good returns and must be defended with substantial investment. However, efforts to expand its market position would lead to diminishing returns.
3. *Harvest.* Growth possibilities are very dim for a PMU that is still quite profitable. Funds devoted to this unit should be diminished so that there will be a larger earnings margin to be harvested over much of the remaining product life.
4. *Divest.* All support would be withdrawn from a unit that is in this condition. The divestment might be gradual for a unit still yielding a positive cash flow. Otherwise the withdrawal would be rapid.

Deciding on which option is best for each PMU would be based on its projected earnings position, on the amount of resources available for the SBU, and on projections of how the SBU will perform relative to this objective. Note that the projected earnings for each PMU should consider the strategy that it wishes to adopt, since the presence or absence of an effective strategy can make a world of difference. Recall the case of Product C, the antibiotic product in Chapter 1, for which a clever strategy saved a brand from divestment.

Analysis and decision:

An SBU is composed of its parts, let us repeat, and therefore its planners must analyze and decide on whether to approve the strategic plans of those parts (functions and PMUs), as well as the possible strategies that they must create for the overall SBU. There are important interactions between the strategies at these levels. (For instance, if the SBU planned to purchase a large block of network television time for 1985, all of its PMUs would necessarily reckon with this in their advertising plans.) Bear in mind that the two levels should keep each other informed.

Regarding the decision making on the SBU strategies (those that comprehensively affect all of the business unit), only general statements may be made. There are two main phases. The first phase consists of identifying where new strategy is needed (in technology, improved image, etc.) and the nature of the problem faced. Analyses of performance, of threats, and of opportunities all contribute to isolating and evaluating the strategy needs. The second phase consists of creating or selecting the specific strategy to solve the problem. Since strategic changes across a whole SBU tend to be major projects, these decisions usually require longer deliberation, greater analysis of various op-

TABLE 4-1 Projected cash flows of product/market units in the Able Division.
(These are forecasts determined prior to any changes from existing strategies. This example is hypothetical.)

Product/market units	Cash flows							Total SBU
	A	B	C	D	E	F	G	
Revenues	$5,000,000	$7,100,000	$14,000,000	$3,700,000	$1,800,000	$ 8,200,000	$2,000,000	$41,800,000
Expenditures and investments	8,500,000	7,300,000	10,900,000	3,400,000	2,500,000	10,400,000	2,700,000	45,700,000
Net cash flow	(3,500,000)	(200,000)	3,100,000	300,000	(700,000)	(2,200,000)	(700,000)	(3,900,000)

tions, and more managers participating than do the lesser and shorter-run strategies predominant at the PMU level.

With regard to the tasks of the SBU relative to the underlying units' planning, we can follow a more specific example. One of the early steps would be analysis of the projected performance of those units without changing any of the current strategies. Our example returns to the Able Division, which has seven products within its six PMUs. One of the key objectives, again, is cash flow, whose projection for the seven products is given in Table 4-1, assuming present strategies continue. (Other objectives could be illustrated as well.)

The prognosis in Table 4-1 looks sad for this SBU, which we earlier said projects a positive ROI but needs a heavy investment of funds in dynamic markets. Together with these financial data, the strategist can study a portfolio assessment like the growth/share matrix, although we are omitting that for this stage of analysis. As already mentioned, top management at BWI refused to consider such a cash drain by the Able Division. This meant that new strategies must be found for some of these products and perhaps for the overall SBU to avoid this cash outflow.

FIGURE 4-3. Market growth/market share matrix portfolio analysis. The seven product/market units currently being sold by Able Division are indicated by circles. Shaded circles are the projected positions, and diameters are proportional to sales volumes. Some future products are also indicated on the upper right.

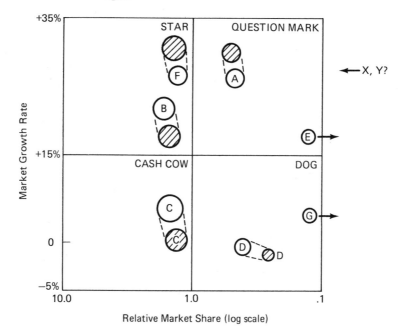

We will skip all the creative and analytical toil that would have ensued while the various units sought better strategies (in terms of satisfying the imposed objectives). Let us return to their planning at a point where they have produced strategies that are expected to be satisfactory—and maybe optimal. New projections are made on that basis, whose data can also be positioned on a portfolio matrix. We do that in Figure 4-3. The circles in this matrix for predicted sales volume (the shaded ones) are smaller than they would have been in such a chart based on the figures in Table 4-1. That is because Able Division has had to cut back heavily on its expenditures and therefore expects to obtain lower sales volumes. Figure 4-3 also indicates that two weak products, which had been draining cash, are going to be eliminated. Two new products are needed, in the SBU's assessment, and they are designated as X and Y—but they lie outside the market at this time.

Other forms of analysis probably would be used, including the market attractiveness/business position assessment described in Chapter 3. Let us say that the SBU planners had selected appropriate analytical factors and criteria, with which they scored the seven existing products. These values are given in Table 4-2. The seven products' positions are shown in Figure 4-4. This approach has also found Products E and G to be very unattractive for this firm. Three are highly attractive while Product C is problematical—the top sales producer that is in a mediocre position on both axes. Its opportunities and possible strategies should be given the deepest consideration.

The search for possible strategies in such situations should be wide and deep. Great ideas may be found in the firm's or the individual's own experience or observations. Pooled experience like the PIMS analyses may prove to be applicable in giving direction to the search. The literature on strategy may offer guidance. Among the authors who have created hypotheses on strategic decisions in given situations is Charles Hofer. Here is one of his:

> When the degree of product differentiation is high, the nature of the buyer's needs primarily noneconomic, the degree of market segmentation moderate to high, the product complexity high, the purchase frequency low, and there are barriers to entry in the distribution or technological area, businesses should:
>
> (a) Focus their R & D funds first on modifying and upgrading their existing product line, second on developing new products, and last on process innovations.
> (b) Allocate substantial funds to the maintenance and enhancement of their distinct competences, especially those in the marketing area.
> (c) Develop a strong service capability in their distribution systems.
> (d) Seek to expand the geographic scope of their operations if possible.[4]

An experienced strategist should, as Hofer has, create guidelines for determining the appropriate actions in given situations. Those quoted above would be applicable to a corporation or to an SBU. Smaller planning units like PMUs would have a more-limited range of options.

---

[4]Charles W. Hofer, "Toward a Contingency Theory of Business Strategy," *Academy of Management Journal*, December 1975, p. 805.

TABLE 4-2   Scores of Able Division's product/market units on a market attractiveness/business position portfolio assessment. Data are hypothetical.

Product/market unit	Market attractiveness	Business position
A	87	29
B	72	65
C	56	50
D	20	63
E	60	9
F	86	83
G	14	12

A strategist should not place too much weight on a PMU's position on a portfolio assessment chart. That may be obvious, although such assessments have been the chief method discussed. A strategist, however, should place much weight on the dollar figures on a product's performance and potentials, some of which we have shown in Table 4-1. Also—and this cannot be overemphasized—the specific strategic actions proposed for each unit are key considerations. What will be the effects on the strategic program? A great strategy may make an average product position into a strong one (and vice versa). For

FIGURE 4-4.   Display of Able Division's product/market units on the market attractiveness/business position matrix.

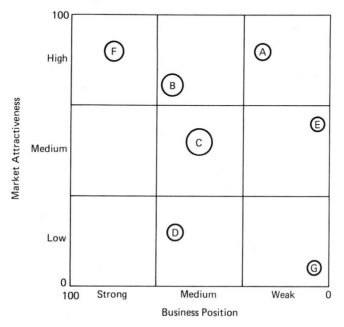

this concern we return to Product C, the Cash Cow that is critically important to the Able Division.

Let us say that three strategic approaches are being considered for Product C:

1. An *investment* strategy in which a strong promotional program and a cosmetic product improvement would be launched for Product C during the period ahead—hoping that a stronger market position would raise profits and cash flow.
2. A *divest* strategy, which would pull back on promotional and service outlays for Product C. If this would not dent sales volume much, it could reap a large cash flow for other opportunities.
3. A *no change* approach, continuing the present strategy and level of support.

Careful study of each of the proposed strategies would be required in order to project its outcome with tolerable accuracy. On the surface, option 1 would seem to be the most appealing to marketers, but financial projections must also be considered. Let us say that the proposed increase of $450,000 in promotion is projected to yield a $1,400,000 increase in sales volume. After analysis of the incremental costs involved, a $300,000 increase in cash flow is projected, as well as increased net profits. Suppose that option 2 would produce a smaller cash flow and option 3 a diminished cash flow. If the key criterion were effect on cash flow, option 1 would be a clear choice. In real life, however, such projections may be hazy, and the proper choice may be more doubtful.

This simplified discussion ignored alternative investments. Since Product C is only one of a family of PMUs, there might even be more attractive investments with regard to achieving the desired objective (e.g., better cash flow). All the alternatives should be considered (after the strategies for each have been formulated) before reaching a conclusion on Product C.

The ultimate forecasted financial results, in cash flow, for the Able Division product line are given in Table 4-3. There are several notable changes from Table 4-1:

a. The larger outlays for Product C.
b. Cutbacks in planned outlays for Product A
c. Terminating Products E and G

The third step would have the greatest effect in curbing the negative cash flow. (As stated earlier, the Able Division has a good net profit but is in such growing markets that its cash drain is serious.)

These decisions would be more complicated than our description of them. One factor is that the SBU has its own expenditures that have not been shown separately in Table 4-3 (e.g., its administrative overhead and its research and development activity). Furthermore, it is unrealistic to expect *no*

TABLE 4-3 Projected adjusted cash flows of product/market units in the Able Division.
(These forecasts given in Table 4-1 have been altered to reflect new strategies.)

Product/market units	Cash flows							
	A	B	C	D	E	F	G	Total SBU
Revenues	$4,800,000	$7,700,000	$15,400,000	$3,700,000	0	$ 8,300,000	0	$39,900,000
Expenditures and investments	8,000,000	7,400,000	11,500,000	3,400,000	0	10,400,000	0	40,700,000
Net cash flow	(3,200,000)	300,000	3,900,000	300,000	0	(2,100,000)	0	(800,000)

costs of terminating a product, for these actions really entail large costs. Then there are the "inescapable" fixed costs, a portion of which have been absorbed by Products E and G, that would be loaded on the remaining products.

And still another complication is found in real life, in that strategy making is "contingency planning." That is, its decisions are attempts to adapt to events that may lie ahead. Even though some contingencies cannot be precisely visualized or their probability of occurring be stated with accuracy, the strategist should deal with them. Some of the contingencies in market and competitive aspects may have entered some of the above decisions. What the strategists should do is a "scenario analysis" in which alternative future situations are imagined for the most significant variables in the environment. Then appropriate strategy adjustments may be related to them, giving consideration to their probabilities.

We might consider two scenarios for Product C, as follows:

1. Scenario 1: An innovation that is superior to Product C in a vital attribute enters the market. In fact, laboratories of our company have almost perfected such a product, which would quickly overtake Product C. The questions are when it would be ready to market and also whether any competitor would beat us to market with a similar innovation.
2. Scenario 2: A federal agency has been investigating whether Product C is dangerous in a particular use. If it becomes banned from this use, a market segment that has accounted for 15 percent of sales would disappear.

Without going further to explore their strategic implications, it should be evident that these scenario analyses are important.

We have been viewing some techniques for strategy decisions at the SBU level. Our attention has particularly been on cash flow analysis, which is only one of the objectives that strategy may be directed to attain. The assessment methods described are useful, especially in avoiding overenthusiasm about some brilliant strategy that unfortunately has low market potentials or for which the firm is ill positioned. On the other hand, the quality of a proposed strategy is critical too. Contrast these two examples that are classics of good and poor strategies:

1. Despite a flat market for filter cigarettes in the 1965–75 period, Philip Morris launched an excellent and costly strategy to reposition its Marlboro brand in the public's image. Result: Marlboro catapulted ahead of Winstons and stayed there, much to its profit.
2. In the rapidly growing and IBM-dominated computer market, RCA and General Electric attempted to penetrate with a contrary strategy, emphasizing lower prices rather than service. Result: dismal failure, which led to both firms' exiting from computers.

These examples show how a powerful strategy may be worthwhile even in lackluster markets—and the opposite. The quality of the strategy is an important aspect, and it should be considered alongside the formal analysis systems like those we have presented.

SUMMARY

Our attention shifted in this chapter to one level lower in a large corporation's organization—to its strategic business units (SBUs). We first dealt with setting up SBUs and noted that these should meet four criteria:

1. An SBU should be largely self-contained and accountable for its strategic plans and results.
2. It should serve a distinct set of markets that have common characteristics.
3. It should contend against a distinct set of competitors.
4. It should be in a position to decide and implement its own strategies.

Determining the SBUs through a top-down sequence versus a bottom-up sequence was discussed. Three dimensions were suggested for definitions: customer functions performed by the product, alternative ways of performing that function, and customer segments. How the number of units varies with size was shown by examples. Also discussed was the fact that some very diverse corporations place SBUs in a few groups to form another decision level above the SBU.

Next our concern was within the SBUs and their organization for planning. We mentioned that the SBU managements are more involved in operations than in planning. Their planning decisions were described in three dimensions: coordination with corporate plans, coordination of the underlying PMU and functional plans, and the overall plan of the SBU itself. The discussion included the chief marketing executives who direct that function within an SBU.

Our third subject was an SBU strategic decision model. It was constructed on the same four basic stages as the general model in Chapter 1, modified because of relationships with the levels above (corporate) and below (PMU and functional). This was charted in Figure 4-2. An example was used from the hypothetical BWI firm described earlier, but now we dealt with only one of its SBUs. For this "Able Division" we described tasks in setting objectives, defining its business, determining its strategies, and allocating resources among its PMUs.

Having covered the strategic decision process, we returned to the decision on strategies to look more closely at the general options: (1) build market share, (2) maintain market share, (3) harvest, or (4) divest. The analysis was illustrated with data on our hypothetical Able Division with the aim of optimizing cash flow. Both the growth/share and the market attractiveness/business position analyses were illustrated. Some options for one of the PMUs were considered and their effects were diagramed; this led up to a strategic decision. Contingency consideration in the planning was the final subject.

1. *Define* strategic business unit, *naming its main characteristics. What are the chief benefits gained by having SBUs in the organization?*

2. *Look at the BIC Corporation case (2-3) and try to determine why that company apparently did not find it logical to be organized into SBUs.*

3. *Name an advantage of taking a "top-down" approach in organizing a corporation for strategic management. Also an advantage of the "bottom-up" approach. Why do the authors of this book believe that both approaches should be considered?*

4. *For a CME, or director of marketing, in an SBU, point out several of this executive's planning tasks. In what respects would the PMU managers depend on this executive? In the other direction, what should the CME expect from the PMU managers?*

5. *In what ways has the strategic-planning process (Figure 2-1) at the corporate level been modified in Figure 4-2 for the SBU management? Why were these changes necessary?*

6. *In our example of the Able Division, point out how its objectives for 1984 posed challenges for its management. Trace the effects of these objectives on the subsequent strategic decisions.*

7. *In the product portfolio projections shown in Table 4-3, Product E has been deleted but Product A continued. This is in spite of what is shown for their projected cash flows in Table 4-1, in which product A is forecasted to have a much larger cash flow deficit than product E. What may be some of the considerations for continuing product A?*

8. *Describe why "contingency planning" should lead to more realistic strategic decisions.*

Honeywell Information Systems

Honeywell, Incorporated, was a major industrial firm in 1983. Its headquarters were in Minneapolis, but its manufacturing and marketing were located worldwide through its over 125 subsidiaries. The corporation, originally a maker of thermostats, had expanded and now produced a broad line of instruments and equipment for industrial and governmental clients. During the previous twenty years, its dollar sales volume had grown ninefold and its profits per share more than threefold.

Honeywell was organized into the following four principal divisions, each of which was in turn composed of a number of strategic business units:

>   Environmental Systems and Controls
>   Aerospace and Defense
>   Information Systems
>   Industrial Systems and Controls

The company participated in the computer industry partially through a number of computer components manufactured by the last-named division. Its computer business was to a greater extent in its Honeywell Information Systems division (HIS). HIS manufactured complete computers, whose prices ranged from minicomputers that ran below $30,000 to systems that might run over $7 million. It also offered a broad line of software. HIS manufactured in nine plants domestically (in Massachusetts and Arizona), and its sales volume in early 1983 comprised nearly 31 percent of the total for all of Honeywell.

Honeywell faced some difficult strategic problems with HIS in the spring of 1983. These were described in the following article from *Business Week.*

Honeywell's Survival Plan in Computers

Honeywell Inc. tacitly acknowledged it had big trouble in computers last fall when it abruptly brought in its biggest management gun, James J. Renier, to take over as president of Honeywell Information Systems Inc. (HIS), its ailing computer subsidiary. Renier, a hardnosed, 27 year company veteran, had an unblemished record of success in managing a wide array of Honeywell operations. After six months on the job, he has begun to implement his own strategies for overhauling the Minneapolis computer company.

Reprinted from the May 23, 1983 issue of *Business Week* by special permission, © 1983 by McGraw-Hill, Inc., pp. 108–115.

The 53-year-old Renier, widely regarded as heir apparent to Honeywell Chairman Edson W. Spencer, is gambling his reputation that he can turn around HIS. Long-standing problems at the subsidiary became apparent two years ago, when operating earnings started falling. Last year they plunged an excruciating 46% to just $79.8 million as sales fell 5% to $1.7 billion. For Honeywell, which has keyed its overall strategy to growth in energy conservation, productivity enhancement, and other products tied closely to computer technology, Renier's success is crucial. "I firmly believe these strategies cannot develop without the company being in the computer business," he says.

PICKING OFF CUSTOMERS

If Renier fails, the company could well be knocked out of the marketplace for powerful mainframe computers. Along with Burroughs, Sperry, and NCR, Honeywell faces stiff competition from industry leader International Business Machines Corp. Industry experts have been predicting the demise of one of IBM's traditional mainframe competitors by mid-decade. Says David L.R. Stein, executive vice-president of the Gartner Group Inc., a Stamford (Conn.) market-research firm: "It looks entirely likely that more than one company might have to exit the [mainframe] business by the end of the decade."

For more than five years now, Honeywell and the other mainframe manufacturers have been under increasing competitive pressure as lower-priced minicomputers and micro-computers have become powerful enough to take over tasks normally performed by the larger mainframes. However, while IBM succeeded in diversifying into faster-growing information processing markets, its competitors failed to move quickly into such high-growth areas as office and factory automation.

Honeywell has built an impressive number of customers, which it hopes to tap for sales of new products. International Data Corp. estimates that the company has an installed base of 17,943 mainframes worth $7.6 billion world-wide. But the mainframe market is slowing drastically, and such competitors as IBM and the Japanese are starting to pick off some of Honeywell's customers.

One of the biggest users of Honeywell mainframes, General Electric Information Services Co. (GEISCO), is holding a runoff between Honeywell's new top-end mainframe and a competing model from NEC Corp. The two computers are "running stride for stride," says Raymond W. Marshall, a GEISCO senior vice-president. A loss for Honeywell not only would cost it between $50 million and $100 million in sales over five years but also would be an embarrassing black eye. The company acquired General Electric Co.'s computer operation 13 years ago and until last year owned 16% of GEISCO.

At the same time that competition is eating into Honeywell's sales, its future presence in Europe is threatened by the nationalistic French government. Last year, when the government moved to take greater control of CII-Honeywell Bull, Honeywell dropped its share from 47% to 19.9%. The French company markets HIS products in much of Europe. It was also responsible for developing Honeywell's DPS 7 medium-size business computer, a model it still produces for the U.S. company.

Renier contends that Honeywell and the French company are too dependent on one another for the relationship to be disrupted. Indeed, under an agreement worked out with the government, Honeywell and the French company will maintain some marketing and technical ties for at least nine more years. Honeywell's ownership, however, is likely to be reduced even further as the French government pours money into CII-Honeywell Bull, and the U.S. company's often testy relationship with the French could become even more tenuous. The possibility that Honeywell may form a joint venture with a Japanese company has French officials worried about Honeywell's long-term future in the computer business.

SQUELCHED SPIRIT

Such problems in markets at home and abroad will be major challenges for Renier, but in many respects his biggest challenge will be shaking off the torpor that has settled over HIS in recent years. Honeywell makes an effort to foster strong esprit de corps in executive ranks. Former executives, for example, keep in touch through an informal group known as Honeywell Organization Graduates, or HOGs. But a number of departees say this spirit was squelched under Renier's predecessor, Stephen G. Jerritts, who was president between 1979 and 1982.

Management ranks were decimated as executives fled the slow-moving bureaucracy and infighting that characterized Jerritts' tenure, according to former HIS executives. In the past year, two of HIS's seven regional sales managers have left the organization, and former executives estimate that about 25 vice-presidents have departed in the past five years.

'HORSE SENSE'

"They killed the entrepreneurial spirit in HIS, because it was such a political environment," says one former executive. "Unless Renier can solve that problem, he's going to have a very hard time competing in today's market." Honeywell also lost touch with its markets under Jerritts, that former executive adds, because executives often made decisions that would do more to protect their power bases than meet market demands. "The troubles we're seeing now have been developing for years, and Renier knows that," says another former executive who has maintained close touch with the company.

Renier has already moved quickly to get expenses in line with lower earnings at HIS. Within weeks of taking over the operation, he slashed 1,750 employees from the payroll, mainly staff and middle managers. This brought to 2,900 the number of layoffs in the past year by Renier and Jerritts. Renier contends that such tough "horse sense" measures are half the battle in turning around HIS. "[HIS's problems] are from the book of familiar quotations as far as I'm concerned," Renier says. "Your competitors become more aggressive, you underestimate the recession, you have management inefficiencies in the organization, and your expenses get out of line with revenue. [Then] your operation's in trouble."

But Renier will have to do more than just make internal changes. Honeywell will have to make it big in the new growth markets if the company is to survive in the computer business, industry experts agree. In the booming micro-computer market, Honeywell is far behind competitors. It finally introduced its first microcomputer, the Microsystem 610, in April, more than a year behind schedule and significantly behind its mainframe and minicomputer competitors. Nonetheless, Renier believes that because its software will work with Honeywell's larger computers, the new model will have strong appeal to existing customers for use in distributed processing. Customers such as Deloitte Haskins & Sells, the accounting firm, already are placing large orders.

At the same time, its main diversification into nonmainframe computers, a foray into minicomputers that enjoyed strong growth until 1980, has gone sour. By the time that Jerritts was shunted aside last fall—he remains a senior vice-president—orders had plummeted 40% and HIS was suffering widening losses from the operation.

TARGETING INDUSTRIES

The slump in minicomputers is due, in part, to the failure of Honeywell's "niche" marketing strategy. The company has for several years been trying to boost hardware sales and improve margins by selling complete systems—combining hardware and software—to address the specific problems of customers in targeted industries. For example, its successful Compass system, using the Honeywell DPS 6 minicomputer, offers a program for managing accounts in pharmacies.

Renier contends that this strategy has faltered largely because of organizational problems. Under Jerritts, the niche-oriented systems businesses were lumped with Honeywell's general hardware business into one big profit-and-loss center. In the process, Honeywell's dominant "mainframe culture" stifled their development, he says. In March, Renier reorganized HIS to separate the systems businesses and hardware sales. Three systems divisions were set up to attack the office, manufacturing, and applications markets.

'ONE BIG BLOB'

Now, each of these divisions will be a separate profit-and-loss center and have marketing responsibilities for its own products, although each will still rely on Honeywell's general sales force to sell them. In the past, the systems businesses were limited to using Honeywell hardware. Now, however, they will be allowed to use whatever equipment best suits the purpose—including, if need be, IBM hardware.

Renier believes that these measures will encourage entrepreneurial activity in HIS to develop and market new systems without the bureaucratic interference that has often slowed Honeywell in the past. "Now we're going to have a standard products [hardware] business that runs like one and a systems business that runs like one," Renier says. "They may be supportive, but we're not going to force those two cultures together into one big blob." The niche business can expand significantly by selling to existing customers alone, Renier contends. "We could look outside our base of customers, but why do it?" he asks. "I don't think you build your base by looking for a new one."

To reduce his research and development costs, Renier is now actively seeking cooperative agreements and joint ventures with other companies. He recently encouraged Sperry Corp. to join the peripheral products company that Honeywell and Control Data Corp. jointly owned. And now Honeywell is in talks with NEC, he says, "to see whether there isn't some ground for cooperation."

Neither Renier nor NEC will discuss the content of their talks, but some former Honeywell executives believe that the company is trying to forge a major cooperative agreement with the Japanese computer maker, which for years licensed Honeywell computer technology. Now NEC has its own strongly competitive mainframe computer, and at least one former executive speculates that Renier may try to reverse that relationship. "I wouldn't be surprised to see Honeywell end up manufacturing an NEC computer [under a license agreement] and use it as a follow-on to its new large-scale computer," the former executive says.

POOR SELLING JOB

Renier also will have to juice up Honeywell's marketing efforts, which languished under Jerritts. Honeywell draws high marks from customers for its field-service organization, but the same customers say the company does a poor job of selling new products. "I don't think Honeywell has ever sold us anything," complains one user. "We've sold ourselves and then gone and told them what we wanted." Adds Ronald J. Smith, vice-president for administration at Gelco Corp.'s Gelco Courier Services unit and president of the Honeywell Large Systems Users Assn.: "The fact that there has been no visible marketing effort [over the last three years] has caused some of them to migrate to other companies' equipment."

Few who know Renier are ready to say he will fail. He commands enormous respect within Honeywell's organization, and his reorganization of HIS is crafted from his recent experience as president of Honeywell's successful Control Systems business, which accounts for nearly two-thirds of the company's $5.5 billion in sales. He built morale and productivity there with programs to improve the quality of the workplace and is out to do the same at HIS with cooperative management techniques.

"After the layoffs, morale was extremely low," says one staffer who lost his job. "But friends tell me it has improved a lot." Meanwhile, Renier's cost-cutting is taking effect: HIS, which had a small operating loss in the first quarter of 1982, had a "modest" operating profit during the same period this year.

But whether this improvement will blossom into a full-fledged turnaround is an open question. "I think it's going to take more than reorganization to salvage the thing," says the Gartner Group's Stein. Most former executives respect Renier's abilities but remain skeptical about whether he can return HIS to long-term real growth. "They picked the right guy, and if anyone can do it, he can," says one. "But it's a herculean task."

DISCUSSION

Consider HIS, which as a division is a sort of super-SBU in the Honeywell organization, in the light of the brief information given in the above article.

1. Identify and state the key problems that HIS faced (internal and external).
2. Conceive of three strategic options that would have merited consideration by Renier, the new head of HIS. Which one would you prefer? Why?
3. If the four divisions of Honeywell were being evaluated with the matrix in Figure 4-3, in which quadrant would you place HIS?
4. What factors would you have chosen for Honeywell to use in a market attractiveness/business position analysis? Based on those factors, in which of the cells in Figure 4-4 would that analysis probably place HIS?
5. If HIS stood second to IBM among the five top manufacturers of computer mainframes in 1983, what is your guess on where it would rank in 1988? Considering the answers you have given above, if you had been a director of Honeywell in 1983, how would you have ranked HIS among Honeywell's four divisions as to favoring them in allocating the corporation's resources.

CASE 4-2

Gillette Company

The corporate history of the Gillette Company will be described briefly, emphasizing the products it has marketed and their fortunes. Closer attention will be paid to events as perceived in 1982 and to the outlook at that time. The company's several strategic business units (or "business segments" in its terms) will be the focus of analysis.

A SHARP OPERATION

The razor business is "one of the most profitable large businesses in the world," and Gillette Company seemed to have a permanent lock on it into the 1950s, as *Forbes* magazine has pointed out.[1] This all goes back to King C. Gillette, who created the safety razor, with which he built one of the first great multinational organizations and a marvel of marketing effectiveness.

Only four years after founding the firm, in Boston, King Gillette opened a branch office in London and rapidly obtained sales and profits through western Europe. About twenty years later, he said this of his safety razor:

> There is no other article for individual use so universally known or widely distributed. In my travels, I have found it in the most northern town in Norway and in the heart of the Sahara Desert.[2]

Gillette set for himself this goal: to offer consumers high quality shaving products which would satisfy basic grooming needs at a fair price. Having gained more than half of the entire razor and blades market, Gillette's manufacturing efficiency enabled marketing programs on a large scale that propelled the company forward in profits and in market leadership. It surely was, if a pun may be overlooked, a sharp operation.

The company easily weathered World War II and emerged in a very healthy condition, in both finances and shavers' preferences. Its profits rose to a net of $6.80 per share in 1948. That was a record that it has not even approached since that year.

That also was the year of its first major acquisition, the Toni Company. Toni was the fabulous creation of Richard ("Wishbone") Nelson, inventor of the do-it-yourself home permanent kit, which was having high popularity with American women. Unfortunately, their love affair with home permanents did not last, and sales ceased to grow, at least in U.S. markets. A second large acquisition came in 1955, the Paper Mate Company, a leader in the ball-point pen business. It too was prosperous, but soon Bic's stick pens at low prices came over from France and cut into that business. During this era, Gillette was slowly losing its edge, and its net profit per share slumped to $1.33 in 1964.

DIVERSIFICATION

Into this crisis stepped a new Gillette CEO, Vincent Ziegler, who was aggressive, marketing-oriented, and ambitious for the company. As he took over, Wilkinson Sword (an English firm) had introduced the stainless steel blade in the U.S. and was taking substantial sales away from Gillette in the razor business. Ziegler was able to cope with this attack and revive Gillette's own stainless blades. The financial revival was aided by recent introduction of Gillette's first notable innovation outside the shaving market: Right Guard deodorant in its new aerosol spray can.

Ziegler evidently believed in diversification through acquiring other companies, in various product lines. He acquired all of the following within the next several years:

Braun AG (a German manufacturer of small appliances)
S.T. Dupont (French maker of luxury lighters)
Eve of Roma (high-fashion perfume)
Buxton Leather goods

---

[1]Robert J. Flaherty, "The Patient Honing of Gillette," *Forbes*, February 16, 1981, p. 83.
[2]Gillette Company, *1980 Annual Report.*

Welcome Wagon, Inc.
Sterilon hospital razors
Jaffra Cosmetics (home sales)

Four of those acquisitions proved unprofitable or unsuitable and were divested, and the other three yielded low profits by Gillette standards. Ziegler also pushed internal development of new products, which included these:

Earthborn shampoos[3]
Nine Flag colognes
Purr, an electric hair untangler
Toni hair coloring products
Digital watches
Smoke alarms
Fire extinguishers
Hand-held calculators

Those products had this in common: they all failed. Ziegler also drove the international operation into razor and toiletries distribution into far corners of the world at excessive expense.

This era did have its successes. Cricket lighters were brought out through the Dupont firm and did well. Soft & Dry antiperspirant joined Right Guard as expansion in that market. However, the scare about aerosols destroying the ozone layer caused the spray versions of those deodorant products to drop suddenly, presenting a crisis. Meanwhile Gillette's Trac II razor came out as a great success, and so the razor segment stayed in its dominance. Earnings per share did rise to $2.83 in 1974 but began to slip again.

The various acquisitions made under Ziegler added $100 million in debt and $10 million in annual interest costs. The result has been described as follows:

> As corporate margins shrank, Ziegler took a chance and cut back on the advertising budget to bolster profits. This did not hurt the Paper Mate pen operation, which was stagnating from a lack of new ideas rather than ad dollars. The razor blade operation . . . adapted by putting all its ad chips behind one product, its new Trac II twin-blade shaving system, with dramatic success. But toiletries, full of new products and lacking the overwhelming consumer franchise that blades enjoyed, became a disaster area.[4]

Other troubles came from the French manufacturer, Bic, which was excelling in disposable products.[5] Its 19 cent throwaway stick pens particularly impacted Gillette's Paper Mate line of refillable pens and drove Paper Mate's share of the retail ballpoint pen market from over 50% down to 13%.[6] Gillette had retaliated with its new Write Brothers line of disposable pens, which failed on the first effort in 1972 but succeeded in building share when returned to the market with heavy price promotion in 1975. Bic also was threatening with two products that it was marketing with great success in Europe and elsewhere, its disposable razors and lighters.

At this juncture, Ziegler retired from active direction of the company and sought his successor. His first choice did not remain in office long, and then he chose Colman Mockler, who took over in 1976. We now proceed to strategies under Mockler.

---

[3]Later Earthborn shampoos were remarketed and are now part of the Gillette product line.
[4]*Forbes*, February 16, 1981, p. 84.
[5]See Case 2-3, "BIC Corporation," for an account of its marketing in the United States.
[6]Linda A. Hayes, "Gillette Takes the Wraps Off," *Fortune*, February 25, 1980, pp. 148–50.

STEERING A NEW COURSE

Forbes described Mockler's immediate program as follows:

> The centerpiece of Mockler's strategy was to cut costs dramatically and pour the money saved into ad and product development budgets. It meant a shift of $70 million dollars.[7] His cost-cutting crusade has remained in force to the date of writing, with the ultimate aim of reducing direct costs overall by 40 percent.
>
> As Mockler took office, the company's profit per share had slipped to $2.54. A number of product changes were taking place that year that had been in development. An important one was in packaging of its deodorants, which had lost about one-third of their market share with the scare about ozone effects of aerosol propellants. Gillette, which had not foreseen this and used only aerosol spray cans, brought out roll-on, pump-spray and stick forms by late 1976. The next year it would introduce new aerosol propellants that would be environmentally acceptable.
>
> Also in 1977 Gillette added to its already-leading Trac II shaving system a novel swivel razor, the Atra. This soon took its place alongside Trac II as the two most popular razors in the world, and a market share of over 50 percent in the U.S. was maintained. The previous year, Gillette sought to preempt the U.S. market for disposable shavers, from Bic, by bringing out its Good News! for men and its Daisy for women. (The latter was also a response to American Safety Razor's Flicker.) With such product innovations, Gillette not only held a majority of the U.S. shaving market (including the leading shaving cream), but up to 75 percent shares in countries around the world. (The large share of its sales on other continents is seen in Table 3.)
>
> During this period Gillette's main marketing war was in disposable lighters. When its Cricket was launched in 1972, it had been an instant success. Then Bic entered the U.S. and enticed smokers to "Flick Your Bic." A long-term price war ensued, in which Bic succeeded in outselling the Cricket by a small margin, but Gillette was persistent.
>
> Another notable product addition was in the deodorant/anti-persipirant line. This was named "Dry Idea," and its main feature was that it contained no water, goes on dry.
>
> Mockler succeeded in saving cash and shifting it into advertising and product development, and in maintaining the company's commitment to quality production. Dollar sales had risen by about 20 percent in 1978, but profit per share was up only to $2.65. The firm was poised for a number of new developments in the current period (in the timing of this case), which we define as 1980–81.

THE CURRENT SCENE

A principal aim of the Mockler management in 1980–81 was recovery of the company's former earning levels. Substantial progress was obtained, with earnings per share rising to $4.11 in both years. This was realized in part through the economy measures that were being pursued vigorously, but also through a number of other steps. Two outside acquisitions should be noted, that of Liquid Paper Company, which was the leading maker of typewriter correction fluid, and a small maker of skin care products, Aapri.

In 1980 two novel products were introduced that had been created in Gillette laboratories. One was Silkience self-adjusting shampoo, which automatically adjusted its action to hair roots' needs. The other was Eraser Mate pens, which wrote with erasable ink, in refillable cartridges.

Now let us review the 1981 situation of the several strategic business units. In Blades and Razors, Atra was keeping its place as top brand in the U.S. in dollar share of market, as well as gaining in all markets it had entered in other countries. A

---

[7]*Forbes*, February 16, 1981, p. 86.

new razor for women, with the Atra swivel head feature, was introduced. Good News! also kept top place in disposable razors in the U.S.

Among Toiletries and Personal Care lines, shampoo sales were growing fastest. Silkience self-adjusting shampoo was accelerating in sales, and a companion product was introduced: Silkience deep conditioner, which also had unique benefits. Aapri apricot facial scrub was another new product being pushed. Gillette also now had a subsidiary for direct sale to homes of skin care products, Jafra. As it was expanding its network of consultants who sold it, Jafra also was gaining.

In the writing instruments SBU, a disposable Eraser Mate pen had been introduced. Its rising sales offset declines in the original refillable Eraser Mate. Also a plastic tipped Flair pen was brought out, and Write Brothers stick pens were reported to be making some progress against Bic.

Braun, the appliance SBU in Europe, was enjoying higher sales in its electric razor and home appliance lines. It was negatively affected by currency exchange rates and by cutting back in the lines it was divesting: photography and hi-fi products.

The "Other" category shown in Tables 1 and 2 and in Figure 1 comprised mainly the Buxton leather goods (purses, key chains), the Dupont de luxe lighters of that French subsidiary, and its Cricket lighters (which had the majority of "Other" sales). The problem with the disposable lighters was hardly a lack of business, because worldwide sales of disposable lighters, in total, had risen from 45 million in 1971 to 800 million in 1980.[8] The trouble lay in the price war of attrition being waged against Bic.

As Gillette's management looked forward from 1981, it was from a prosperous situation. The company stood second (just behind Avon Products) in profitability in the whole cosmetics and toiletries industry. Some interesting possibilities in existing products that might be noted, included that of marketing the Braun electric razors in the United States. An old consent decree with the government would expire in 1984 that had forbidden Gillette to engage in electric razor business in the U.S. Interesting too was a Cricket Junior lighter that was ready to come out, which would cut the manufacturing costs of the lighter by 38 percent.

Also a weighty factor was the greatly rising costs of introducing new products in the cosmetics and toiletries industry. It had cost Gillette a cool $18 million to launch Dry Idea. And then for launching Silkience shampoo, the company laid out a record $30 million. Gillette executives probably were watching closely the relationships of promotion costs to profits, which are presented for its North American business segments in Figure 1.

Views of Standard & Poor's industry surveys on cosmetic and personal care products are pertinent to Gillette's prospects. We now quote a portion of them below:

Shipments again rose 4.7% in 1978, but tumbled 4.4% in 1979, and were virtually unchanged in 1980. Several theories could be advanced to explain the recent leveling-off of shipments. Although some personal care products are perceived as necessities . . . the aura of luxury that surrounds many products makes them susceptible to attack by consumers nervous about inflation and recession. The bulge in the teenage markets that fanned growth in earlier years has begun to decline, and the number of women entering careers is levelling off.

On the surface, the rising number of households expected in coming years would appear to benefit the cosmetics industry. . . . The other side of the demographic picture, however, points to the rising number of aging Americans . . . a decline in the number of persons per household, and a growing ethnic market.

These demographic trends suggest that marketing appeals in the future will attempt to

---

[8] *Forbes,* February 16, 1981, p. 87.

garner sales in a maturing population and exploit the ethnic and affluent singles markets. The market for male cosmetics has done well in recent years and will continue to be developed ... One of the most dynamic markets in recent years has been that of skin care products ... RICHARDSON–VICK'S Oil of Olay is the leading skin care product and accounts for a substantial portion of the total market. Two recent introductions—GILLETTE'S *Apricot Facial Scrub* and REVLON'S *European Collagen Complex*—may well provide still more competition for existing products that aim to preserve the youthful look.[9]

---

[9]*Standard & Poor's Industry Surveys,* Health Care, May 20, 1982, p. H-26.

TABLE 1 The Gillette Company—sales and operating profits of business segments (in millions of dollars)

Year	Blades and razors		Toiletries and cosmetics		Writing instruments		Braun products		Other (including disposable lighters)	
	Sales	Operating profits	Sales	Operating profits	Sales	Operating profits	Sales	Operating profits	Sales	Operating profits
1978	$557.7	$160.8	$433.7	$30.0	$141.0	$12.7	$370.5	$26.7	$207.6	($6.7)
1979	636.6	179.8	501.5	35.2	193.4	20.3	445.3	31.6	207.9	(12.9)
1980	743.0	204.6	597.1	49.6	289.3	31.9	496.1	23.6	189.8	(12.9)
1981	775.6	234.7	661.4	57.9	303.5	26.7	451.4	22.8	142.5	(10.9)

Source: Annual reports of The Gillette Company.

143

TABLE 2 The Gillette Company—sales and operating profits of business segments (in percentages of consolidated corporate totals)

Year	Blades and razors		Toiletries and cosmetics		Writing instruments		Braun products		Other (including disposable lighters)	
	Sales	Operating profits	Sales	Operating profits	Sales	Operating profits	Sales	Operating profits	Sales	Operating profits
1976	29%	71%	28%	15%	7%	6%	21%	10%	15%	(2)%
1977	31%	75%	26%	13%	8%	6%	21%	12%	14%	(6)%
1978	33%	72%	25%	13%	8%	6%	22%	12%	12%	(3)%
1979	32%	71%	25%	14%	10%	8%	22%	12%	11%	(5)%
1980	32%	69%	26%	17%	13%	11%	21%	8%	8%	(5)%
1981	33%	71%	28%	17%	13%	8%	20%	7%	6%	(3)%

Source: Annual reports of The Gillette Company.

TABLE 3 The Gillette Company—business segments profits as percent of investment

| Year | Operating profits as percent of identifiable assets of each segment | | | | | Total of all segments |
	Blades and razors	Toiletries and cosmetics	Writing instruments	Braun	Other	
1978	48%	14%	11%	9%	(4)%	19%
1979	44%	14%	9%	9%	(7)%	18%
1980	42%	19%	11%	6%	(7)%	18%
1981	50%	20%	8%	7%	(7)%	21%

Source: Calculated from Gillette Company annual reports.

TABLE 4 The Gillette Company—sales and operating profits by geographic area (in millions of dollars)

Year	Europe		Latin America		U.S. and Canada		Other		Total*	
	Sales	Operating profits	Sales	Operating profits	Sales	Operating profits	Sales	Operating profits	Sales	Operating profits
1978	$682.9	$65.7	$187.6	$30.4	$723.6	$110.7	$116.4	$16.7	$1,710.5	$210.4
1979	829.1	82.7	229.2	30.6	790.8	120.8	135.6	19.9	1,984.7	238.2
1980	938.7	79.8	294.1	39.3	914.5	146.5	168.0	31.2	2,315.3	277.6
1981	820.4	63.8	313.6	50.9	996.9	173.3	203.5	43.2	2,334.4	312.0

Source: The Gillette Company annual reports.

*Total includes corporate expenses charged against profit from operations as follows:

	(millions)
1978	$13.1
1979	15.8
1980	19.2
1981	19.2
1982	20.6
1983	22.7

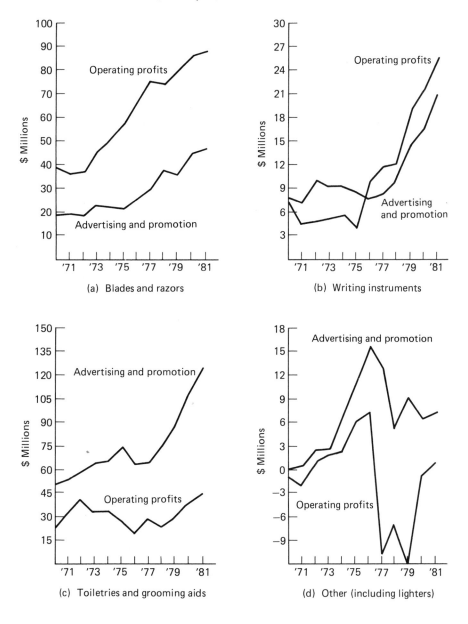

FIGURE 1. Gillette North America, promotion dollars versus operating profits, 1970–1981, by business segments. Promotion breakdowns are estimates.

Source: *Forbes,* February 16, 1981, p. 85. Sources of estimates were noted by *Forbes* to be Drexel Burnham, Merrill Lynch, Forbes.

(a) Blades and razors

(b) Writing instruments

(c) Toiletries and grooming aids

(d) Other (including lighters)

DISCUSSION

1. Evaluate Gillette management's direction of its strategic business units. Which of the following adjectives seem to describe its strategies?

venturesome	ingenious
conservative	rational
erratic	grandiose
aggressive	unimaginative
reckless	

Explain why you selected your particular adjectives.

2. If the intention, beginning with Ziegler, was to diversify Gillette out of the razor and blade business into a broad balance of product lines, has such an objective been realized? If not, should that have been a dominant objective?

3. Identify the environmental variables (market, competition, government, technology) that have impacted Gillette over its life. Which had the greatest positive and negative impacts? At the present time, what do you perceive to be the chief environmental forces with which Gillette should cope or exploit?

4. If you had been Gillette's CEO in 1981 and were viewing strategies for 1982 and beyond, which SBU would have appeared to merit the greatest increase in resources? The smallest? Why?

5. What changes in strategy should Gillette have been considering for 1982–85? Justify their importance.

Note: Tables 1–4 and Figure 1 should be included in your analysis. Also note that there is relevant information in some other cases: Bic Corporation, American Safety Razor, and Abbott Laboratories.

CASE 4-3

Lynch and Reynolds, Inc. (B)

In January 1974 David Hutchinson had been analyzing the mobile machinery industry. This analysis was the subject of Case 3-1, "Lynch and Reynolds, Inc. (A)." After Hutchinson had completed this analysis, his superior, Gene Laisne, had instructed him to make a more-focused analysis of one of the eight companies, Allis-Chalmers (Allis). This would be based on the data given in Case 3-2 and its exhibits.

Some of the critical problems that had faced the new management at Allis were described in the earlier case. It also told about that company's SBUs in Exhibit 1. Financial data about the eight competitors' conditions and performance were shown in Exhibit 2. Charts relating to each of the companies showed both (1) growth/share portfolio analysis (including specific product lines in the construction equipment business) and (2) growth trends of the company versus the overall mobile machinery industry.

The items listed below should be discussed after referring to the data in Case 3-1.

DISCUSSION

1. Assess Allis's situation and the alternative corporate strategies that the Allis management might consider.
2. Examine each SBU or business within Allis and each of the product lines it has in construction equipment.
3. Compare Allis with (a) all the seven other companies that are competing in each business and (b) each of them as total companies.
4. Recommend the strategy that Allis ought to follow for the next five years or so. This should specifically include each business in Allis's portfolio.

    Express your answers and underlying reasoning in a memorandum to Gene Laisne.

5

Marketing Decisions

The strategic decisions reached at the corporate and SBU levels tend to dominate the decisions of marketing and other middle-management units. We discussed corporate decisions first; with that background, we can now devote the rest of this book to marketing strategies.

In this chapter we set the stage for marketing's strategic planning. We will examine (1) the fundamental topic of marketing's role in strategic planning; (2) the organization of marketing managers for planning, a process complicated by the participation of *three* types of managers; and (3) the sequence and flow of decisions between marketing and other levels. In each of the remaining sections we will describe decisions made by one of the three types of managers: the chief marketing executive (CME), function managers, and product/market unit managers. In this chapter we confine ourselves to the identification of decisions and a description of the processes involved in making them. The following chapters will focus on alternative strategies and their selection.

MARKETING'S ROLE IN STRATEGIC PLANNING

The expectations for marketing's performance and contribution to the firm should be made explicit—which is also true of the other functional domains.

Given an explicit overall goal, marketing managers can proceed to set appropriate objectives and to create and implement strategies. The need for all sectors of the firm to integrate their plans and to function in unison cannot be overstated. We therefore begin with marketing's role and major tasks.

In his theorizing about marketing and strategic planning, Anderson states that marketing's chief contribution should be an optimal market position. That is, marketing should develop strategies that will best position the firm's offerings to attract buyers in the markets it intends to serve.[1] (This is subject to constraints of costs, profit goals, and other functions' capabilities.) He proceeds from this to identify three chief roles for marketing in strategic planning:

1. Determine optimal long-term positioning desired in target markets.
2. Develop strategies to capture those positions.
3. Negotiate with top management and other functional areas for support of marketing strategies.

To accomplish those three roles, marketing managers must make a number of decisions, which can be categorized as follows:

1. Identify the various markets that the firm is serving or would desire to serve; then select those that will be its targets.
2. Forecast potential demand in each of those markets.
3. Interpret the needs and wants of buyers in those markets.
4. Evaluate the competitive situation in those markets, including the firm's differential advantages and weaknesses.
5. Define the positions that the firm will need to obtain with buyers in order to win their patronage.
6. Set objectives for marketing performance to attain those positions.
7. Conceive or select strategies for achieving objectives.
8. Spell out the specific plans with which marketing would implement the strategies.
9. Determine marketing financial needs; then negotiate to win approval of both the strategies and the needed resources.

Note that in performing these tasks marketing is aiding the strategic planning at higher levels while it is also anticipating and providing for its own operations. The first five of the above decisions particularly are contributions to the broader planning at higher levels (but essential too for marketing's own work). The last four are more oriented to marketing's own benefit. These nine decisions in turn necessitate numerous marketing activities. It may be evident, for instance, that the marketing research and information system tasks entailed by those decisions are enormous.

---

[1]Paul F. Anderson, "Marketing, Strategic Planning, and the Theory of the Firm," *Journal of Marketing*, Spring 1982, p. 17.

Much effort is also required to create an organization that can make those decisions efficiently. Staffing, procedures, and training are also required. With such an organization in place, the strategic options can be identified, evaluated, and chosen—subjects dealt with in Parts III and IV of this book. The formulation of a proper mix of marketing activities is dealt with in Part V.

ORGANIZING FOR MARKETING PLANNING

The efficiency and job satisfaction of a firm's management personnel are affected by how well these individuals are organized and understand their responsibilities and relationships. We are considering here the organization structure for the three types of marketing managers that were mentioned earlier as taking part in strategic decisions, shown in Figure 5-1 on two levels.

Look first at the middle-management level in Figure 5-1. Each marketing function manager prepares plans for that functional area (e.g., distribution) and submits these plans to managers on higher levels. Each product manager (the typical title for the manager of a PMU) has a similar planning task for the assigned products. Coordination between these two types of planners is important. The chief marketing executive stands on the level above and conducts or oversees both the planning and the operations of marketing.

Wide variation exists, and the arrangement just described—which will be assumed in this discussion—is only one possibility. Another arrangement would have a top marketing executive also on the corporate level; this would alter the tasks described for a chief marketing executive of an SBU. Another variation is to have two heads of marketing—one a marketing services executive whose domain normally includes planning, and the other a sales executive who deals with operations. Less-diversified large companies would have no SBU level, so their CMEs would be on the corporate level. A small firm may have no marketing executive; its owner-manager will assume all planning tasks. The type of organization structure used in this book is that shown in Figure 5-1, which for a large firm is the easiest to understand.

We now have a structure for strategic marketing planning. As it has two levels, in addition to the corporate level above it, we next describe how strategy decisions would flow between these levels.

FIGURE 5-1. Organization of strategic planners in marketing. Solid line represents channel of responsibility and of reporting; broken line represents coordination.

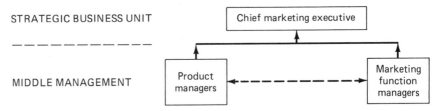

SEQUENCE OF STRATEGY DECISIONS

Systems must be devised and followed for efficient planning. The entire organization must take its actions in accordance with schedules and plans, or chaos will result. We will consider both the sequencing between decision levels and the timing of decisions (and underlying tasks).

Sequence between Levels:

The ways in which the three decision levels (corporate, SBU, and middle management) coordinate their flow of decisions up and down are complex. A great deal of communication goes on during the planning process, and it would be difficult to either discover or chart these various flows and interactions. We will not attempt to do so, but we will present a sequence of when determinations should be reached on each level relative to the other levels. That is, a particular step should be finished on one level before the next step is completed at the succeeding level. The planning steps are initiated on the top, or corporate, level. The strategic steps may be described as consisting of three cycles, which are charted in Figure 5-2.

The steps and their description in Figure 5-2 are presented—with some minor changes—in the terms used by Lorange and Vancil, the creators of that chart. These are not identical to our models and terms, but such differences should be ignored because the principles remain the same. What we should learn from Figure 5-2, a so-called snake chart, is the interrelationships and sequence of determinations between the three organization levels.

Schedules:

An important requirement of any strategic planner is, *Finish your plans on time.* The importance of schedules cannot be overstated: specifically what is to be accomplished at specific times. We will present a few more exhibits that relate to the timing of steps in strategic planning.

Broadly speaking, there should be more than one type of plan in nature and in timing under way at any given time. The two general types are program (or long-range) plans and periodic (or annual) plans (see Figure 5-3). Their relative phasing can be clarified by giving some dates. During the fourth quarter of 1984, for instance, a planner determines targets for the 1986 strategies. Then the strategic plan for 1986 will be finished and submitted during the first half of 1985. The operating plan for its implementation will be finished and approved later in 1985 so that it can be ready for action as 1986 opens. Then this planner continues to measure and monitor that plan's performance as 1986 progresses. Simultaneously the more-demanding work of creating plans for 1987 would be under way.

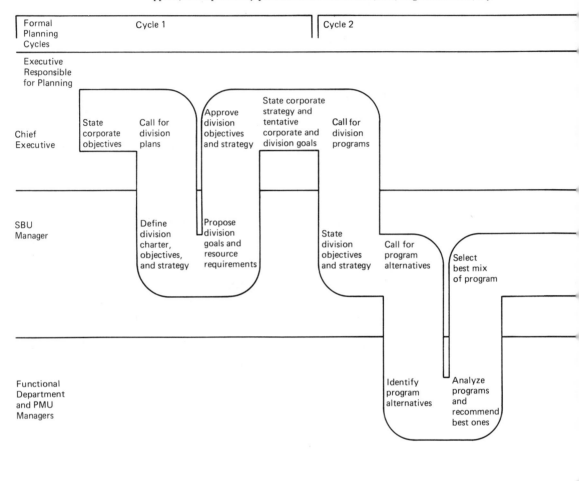

FIGURE 5-2. Steps in the strategic-planning process, showing the route of decisions between the three planning levels of a diversified firm.

Adapted from Peter Lorange and Richard F. Vancil, *Strategic Planning Systems*, © 1977, pp. 26, 27. Reprinted by permission of Prentice-Hall, Inc., Englewood Cliffs, N.J.

CHIEF MARKETING EXECUTIVE

The nature of the chief marketing executive's job is described in Figure 5-4, which contains excerpts from an actual position description and happens to conform to the arrangement assumed in this discussion.

How important strategy is in the chief marketing executive's work is indicated in Figure 5-4 as follows:

> The director of marketing reports to and acts for the head of the SBU with regard to all marketing decisions.

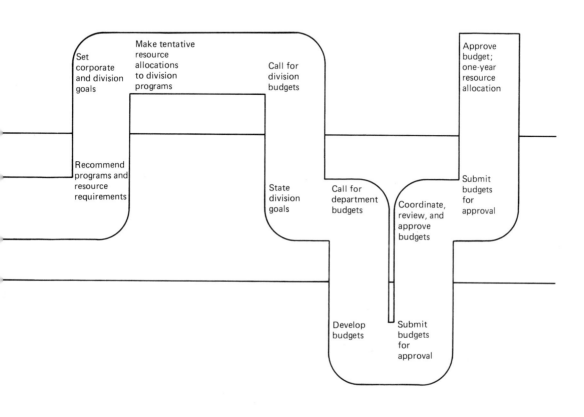

One of the two stated "basic functions" of this person is strategic planning. The other basic function is also tied in with the plans and is geared to them.

There were twelve items given in the actual job description as "functions and responsibilities," with strategy listed first. This also suggests its importance.

Another role the CME performs consists of presenting marketing plans and budgets for approval. A CME also serves as the marketing adviser to the top

FIGURE 5-3. The timing of long-range and periodic plans in IBM

Courtesy of International Business Machines Corporation.

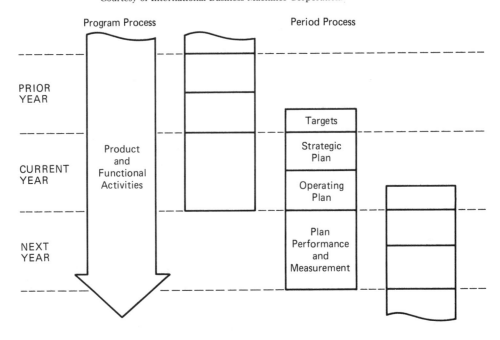

executive of the SBU or of the corporation and coordinates marketing with such other functions as production.

The CME is the leader and responsible executive for marketing. Much of the CME's time must be devoted to marketing operations and tactical decisions. He or she is also responsible for marketing planning. One planning role is as a "buffer" between (1) the expectations of and allocations by top management and (2) the concepts, hopes, and requests of middle-management planners. Another planning role is as a "blender" who reconciles the various proposals originating from the various middle managers with a coherent and effective *single* plan for marketing.

The stages in a CME's strategic decision process are shown in Figure 5-5. Let us follow the decision paths in the figure, beginning with the objectives established for the corporation. Once corporate objectives have been set, the particular SBU's head sets objectives, which brings us to the CME. Along with other managers in the corporation, a CME would have been thinking about the budgetary prospects lying ahead: How much funding is the unit likely to receive next year? Perhaps higher management has given some inkling of the financial picture as a guideline for planners. If not, there would undoubtedly be rumors. Given these objectives and anticipations, the CME can start to work on planning strategy.

Although goals of profit or cash flow are suitable down to the level of an SBU executive (who is profit-responsible), holding marketing directly responsi-

FIGURE 5-4. Excerpts from a job description of a chief marketing executive. This was quoted from a drug manufacturing company's organization manual.

Source: David S. Hopkins and Earl L. Bailey, *The Chief Marketing Executive, A Profile* (New York: The Conference Board, Inc., 1971), p. 57.

TITLE
Director of Marketing—Domestic Pharmaceutical Division

REPORTS TO
Senior Vice President/General Manager—Domestic Pharmaceutical Division

BASIC FUNCTION
Plan, direct, and evaluate all domestic pharmaceutical marketing of ethical and O.T.C. pharmaceutical products in accordance with approved profit plans.

Review and coordinate marketing plans with activities of the corporation and industry to assure maximum sales results.

FUNCTIONS AND RESPONSIBILITIES
1.   Devise and implement long-term as well as short-term marketing strategies to achieve optimum profit. . . .

---

ble for profit would be wrong as it only contributes to profit performance. Marketing goals, as seen in Figure 5-5, should be in terms of both market objectives and financial objectives. Both types are described in this example:

> *Market objectives* are what the firm intends to achieve in its markets—with buyers and against competitors—and marketing is responsible for them. They may be such detailed aims as the following:
>
> Expand the selling of our products in certain markets or become the number-two seller in the toothbrush industry in 1986.
>
> Expand our customer base by X percent; get our brand Z into two-thirds of the drugstores; successfully introduce four new cosmetics in 1987; and so forth.
>
> Those would be specific items that might be listed among objectives, but broader and more quantified market objectives are the concern here. The most popular aim would be market share (the product's sales as percentage of total sales in that category). Each product would have its own status. For instance, Product 1 would have a 22 percent share of market (SOM); Product 2, 16 percent SOM; Product 3, 35 percent SOM; and Product 4, 19 percent SOM. These would have to be combined into a composite for the SBU, and the weighted average for those four products might be 25 percent SOM in the current year of 1984. Marketing's planning objectives would be for the future, however, and might be 26.5 percent SOM for 1985.

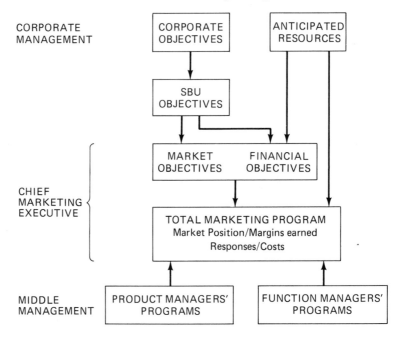

FIGURE 5-5. Marketing strategy process of the chief marketing executive relative to higher organization levels.

Financial objectives would refer to the earnings side of accomplishments planned. Marketing is not responsible for net profit (since so many nonmarketing actions and conditions affect profits). It is easy to set cost objectives that would constrain marketing's expense, but this accomplishes very little in guiding the CME to an optimal strategy. Some measure that reflects profitability is what strategy needs.

A compromise is to set marketing's goals for a gross margin earnings figure that embraces only what can fairly be assessed against marketing, such as the "net marketing contribution" shown below:

	1984 *Actual**	1985 *Objective*
Sales	$5,200,000	(See discussion)
Less: Marketing expenses	900,000	
Cost of goods sold (manufacturing)	3,000,000	
Total costs charged against marketing	3,900,000	
Net marketing contribution	$1,300,000	$1,450,000

*Projected at time of planning 1985.

Although manufacturing and inventory fluctuation costs that are charged to cost of goods sold are outside of marketing's domain, it is in marketing's power to affect the mix of products sold. Therefore, like marketing expenses, this is a variable somewhat controllable by the CME. With the above objective to meet, the CME is challenged to come up with a feasible plan in which the *combination* of sales revenues, marketing expenses, and cost of goods sold can reach the net marketing contribution objective. (Note that marketing is not charged for costs of financing, taxes, administration, and other overhead that its plans could not affect.) The CME has much latitude in devising such a plan.

Now turn to the "total marketing program," which is in the box under "objectives" in Figure 5-5. However specific the marketing objectives may be initially, the CME must spell them out in more detail in the marketing program. The market position will be stated in more specific accomplishments. On the financial side, specific costs will be broken down. The relative margins yielded by various products and customer categories will then be examined so that a richer mix of products and markets can be planned for the period ahead.

FUNCTION MANAGERS:

Marketing is composed of a number of functions that basically differ in their nature and in the skills and background required for competence. Students are usually told early in marketing studies that the "4 P's" make up the "marketing mix." The functional divisions in marketing are not that simple or few. The following functions come directly under the control of a majority of chief marketing executives:

Field sales management
National accounts
Merchandising
Sales training
Sales research and reporting
Customer service
Sales promotion
Advertising
Distributor/dealer relations
Product pricing
Product service
Marketing research
Physical distribution and warehousing[2]

These functions are listed according to the frequency with which they are under that control. The number of function managers who report to a CME would be fewer than the number of items above and would be grouped so that maybe five or six would report directly. A sales manager, for example, would probably oversee at least four of the activities listed above, but there may be specific plans drawn up by each subfunction manager.

---

[2]Hopkins and Bailey, *Chief Marketing Executive*, p. 15.

What are the planning tasks of a function manager in marketing? We would place them into two categories:

1. Plans for the specific functional area. An advertising manager, for instance, has primary responsibility for all advertising. If someone named Mary Malloy were in this position she would be responsible for initiating decisions on advertising policies and objectives, on conducting advertising research, on approving proposed campaigns and expenditures, and for relationships with advertising agencies and media. Malloy would also be responsible for implementing or monitoring advertising. Those would tend to be annual or periodic decisions, but she also should be involved in longer-range strategies that advertising should accomplish cumulatively over several years.

2. Plans initiated by the product managers, whom she would advise. To some degree an advertising manager may have power to veto or modify a product manager's advertising plans. The CME tends to give much weight to each function manager's views on activities in that function. Normally function managers are allies of product managers but sometimes take contrary positions. The CME would mediate any disputes.

In simpler forms of organizations that have no product managers, a CME would rely on function managers' advice on strategies and plans from the viewpoint of that marketing area.

A flow model that describes a marketing function's decision process is shown in Figure 5-6. A function manager may receive several types of data that will serve as bases for deciding what activities are to be performed and how extensively. Note that five specific kinds of inputs are indicated in the program formulation in Figure 5-6:

Sales objectives may indicate how much effort or activity will be compared with that of the current period. If unit sales are to grow by 3 per-

FIGURE 5-6. Systematic planning process for a marketing function.

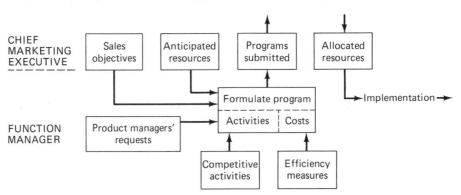

cent, for instance, then the distribution manager may figure on that much more work for that function. The sales department may calculate whether more people are needed in the field or in office work to gain that sales growth.

Anticipated resources provide clues on how much expenditure growth, if any, is likely to be acceptable when budget requests are up for approval.

Product managers incorporate certain expectations of effort by functional departments. When they pass this word along to the appropriate function's manager, the latter may reckon with that in the plan.

Competitive activities may have been observed that will affect what the function manager may want to do during the next period. If the sales manager learns that the two chief competitors have expanded their sales forces in the Southwest, this may be a good reason to ask for a comparable increase.

Efficiency measures should always be sought, and a bright manager would probably have been discovering new ways to make the department cost efficient. These too would affect both the activities to be programmed and the expenses predicted.

A functional manager should consolidate these various information inputs and decide what program should be presented to the chief marketing executive for approval at that level. We already have described the CME's work beyond that point. Later, when resources have been allocated, the function manager issues specific instructions for subordinates, and the plan is implemented.

This process may seem more lifelike when we observe a function manager going through it, and so we return to the advertising manager, Malloy. She had to consider such diverse information inputs as the following:

The increase in sales objectives of the SBU, which also meant higher market-share goals for most of the products. As this was being sought in a stagnant economy, advertising in the coming year of 1985 would need to accomplish more than in 1984. A step-up in advertising would be constrained, however, by word that top management intended to hold expenses down to only an inflation price increase plus a few percentage points. This suggested a +9 percent limit, but she would hope for a +10 percent maximum.

Within those overall parameters, Malloy considered a number of specific tasks for advertising. A notable piece of news was word from the manager of new products that two important new brands would be launched in March and April, about whose advertising he had conferred with her. Individual product managers had also come in to discuss their advertising hopes, such as Wise's request for a 15 percent rise in ad outlays and Trimble's for a 30 percent rise in view of the novel promotion strategy he had devised.

Thanks to what had been learned in some recent advertising experiments, Malloy also considered ways that would gain more results per advertising dollar. She also knew that the three chief competitors had raised their advertising programs faster than had her company in 1984, about 4 percent. And one top marketer had said that his company intended to have the biggest ad budget in the industry in 1985.

After long analysis of all this information and after writing a statement of advertising objectives for 1985, Malloy arrived at the following budget request:

Item	1984 Actual	1985 Proposal
Media cost (including agency commissions)		
Brand A	$ 750,000	$ 770,000
Brand B	150,000	0
Brand C	200,000	210,000
Brand D	1,120,000	1,250,000
Brand E	900,000	1,005,000
Brand F	640,000	600,000
Brand G	580,000	400,000
Brand H	335,000	310,000
Brand I	*	320,000
Brand J	*	215,000
Other brands	208,000	240,000
Other agency fees	175,000	185,000
Direct-mail printing and mailing	2,019,000	2,300,000
Artwork, etc.	65,000	70,000
Advertising research	50,000	65,000
Communication and travel	70,000	75,000
Salaries		
Administrative	90,000	100,000
Other	117,000	130,000
Overhead (20% of salaries)	42,000	46,000
Total	$7,511,000	$8,291,000

*To be introduced in 1985.

Overall, Malloy held the 1985 increase to a shade over 10 percent, which might be acceptable. Her decision should have been reached through a serious effort to identify the tasks that advertising must accomplish in 1985 relative to the expected environment. Whether $8 million is an "ideal" amount to spend on advertising relative to marginal profitability is a good theoretical question but is difficult to answer.

Malloy's media expenses are for specific products, among which she has discriminated. Brand B would lose its advertising because the CME decided to phase out the brand that was in a fading market. Malloy is generous with Brand E (which was Wise's) because the competitive task and the brand's growth momentum indicated that it should be a profitable use of advertising. She is instead stingy with Brand C (Trimble's) and would have cut its budget except for its new strategy.

PRODUCT/MARKET UNIT MANAGERS

The manager of a product/market unit is typically called a *product manager* or, if he or she is responsible for only a single brand, *brand manager*. A different organization might have a *market manager* who develops specified markets (for all products that the firm sells) rather than specific products. A basic question in organizing PMUs is whether to define their scope in terms of products or of markets. A matrix of market groups and product groups in PPG Industries is shown in Table 5-1, which indicates the options for that company in defining its PMUs. Our discussion will refer only to product managers, but it should be understood that the same principles apply to market managers and brand managers.

The greatest benefit of a product manager organization may be that a single person becomes specialized in the assigned product or products. He or she then concentrates on that area for devising strategies, preparing plans, and controlling results. A good product manager is able to analyze markets and competitors, search for strategies, and position the product in the market. Higher-level executives, however, must approve of all of the product manager's decisions and strategies, and their implementation is the responsibility of the various functional departments. As shown in Figure 5-7, a product manager stands in a horizontal relationship to functional departments in marketing, manufacturing, and other operations. Product managers have no authority over these operations and must rely on their managers' cooperation or, lacking that, the support of the CME who approved the strategic plans.

You may recall the two product managers, Trimble and Wise, who were described in our opening pages. As in that situation, there would be a high po-

TABLE 5-1 Categories of customers and product groups marketed to them by PPG Industries, Inc., as of 1984

Major Customer Groups	Product groups, by divisions			
	Chemicals	Coatings and resins	Fiber glass	Glass
Agriculture	X	X		
Aircraft manufacturers			X	X
Appliance manufacturers		X		X
Auto manufacturers		X	X	X
Building construction	X	X	X	X
Chemical manufacturers				
Container manufacturers		X		
Furniture manufacturers		X		
Industrial equipment	X	X		
Textile weavers	X		X	

Source: Communication from the company.

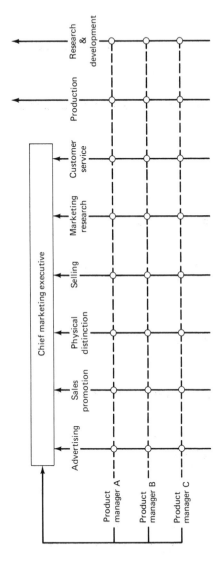

FIGURE 5-7. Planning relationship matrix in an organization with product managers. Solid lines represent responsibilities; broken lines represent coordination.

tential for conflict between product managers, as each desires a larger share of the resources allocated to marketing and its functions. Something of this was indicated in the discussion of function managers above, where the advertising manager, Malloy, was rationing advertising funds among the various products. It is preferable, of course, to avoid heated disagreements by working out differences in strategic concepts and in requested expenditures long in advance of final decisions. Product managers and function managers normally learn how to plan and operate with harmony and negotiation, but potentials for conflicts are always there.

Note that in Figure 5-7 the concern of a product manager extends across all functions in his or her strategic plans and is not confined to marketing. In a sense, these people are "general managers" for their products. Nevertheless, it is usual and proper to place them in the marketing part of a corporation. The key problems in their planning and their main expertise are within the marketing area. Also this location aids in attaining a distinct market base in planning.

A PMU's strategic plans serve as building blocks for, and thus should be completed before, those of its SBU. Strategic planning for a PMU is more complicated than that for a marketing function, which in turn means that the PMU's planning process is also more complicated. A model for that process is shown in Figure 5-8.

Product Manager:

The development of strategic plans is an almost continuous task. When specific determinations begin, the product manager must be armed with substantial information. As shown on the left side of Figure 5-8, the planning follows three routes. Consider the first step:

> The total demand for the type of product and market now served by the PMU is stated first. This may be termed *industry sales* of the defined product category. The maximum opportunity lying ahead is then given in the projected industry sales (preferably for both the next year and for a longer term). The product manager bases this on whatever information is available, including the corporation's forecasts of sales and market conditions.
>
> The next item is calculating the share of sales that this PMU's product or brand has currently captured. Product managers tend to watch this factor carefully, and so this fact should already be known.
>
> An extensive situation analysis should contribute the third and most important level of analysis. All information that seems relevant to the market and product should be applied here. The product manager is seeking to identify the unmet needs of buyers, competitive differentials, strengths of his or her own product, and vulnerability of competitors. Current performance is also compared with objectives to find any cur-

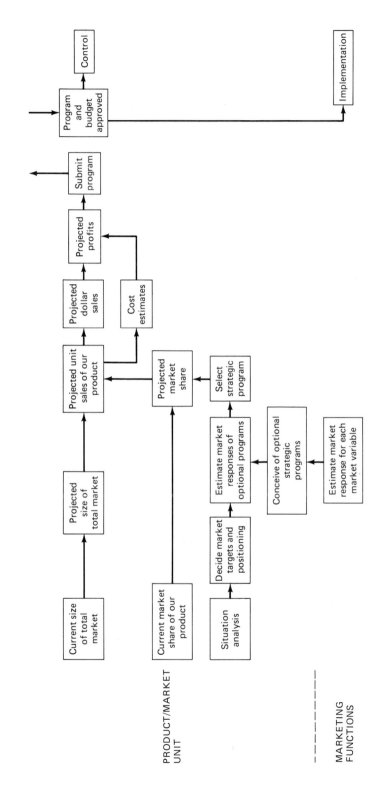

PRODUCT/MARKET
UNIT

- - - - - - - -

MARKETING
FUNCTIONS

FIGURE 5-8. Systematic process for strategic planning by a product/market unit.

rent planning gaps. And, also similar to higher-level planning, continued present strategy should be projected to see if the probable results would be a significant future planning gap.

The situation analysis prepares the planner to make such key decisions as the following:

Evaluate existing markets to determine whether the identical markets should be the aim of the next strategic program. The decision may be to narrow the markets on which efforts will focus or to attempt penetration into other unserved (or unpromoted) markets. Thus the market targets are selected.

Decide how the product or brand ought to be "positioned" in the target markets. For instance, what are buyers' perceptions of the product versus rivals' products now? What different perceptions (positions), if any, should the strategic program seek to accomplish? Perhaps the brand is not carried by a sufficient number of retailers or is receiving poor support by many. Again, what positions in retail stores and in retailers' images should be sought? When the desirable positions have been identified, goals can be set for strategies.

Next the planning work enters its most creative phase, that of the strategic program. The task of formulating an effective *marketing mix*, which blends the numerous marketing functions as well as such nonmarketing activities as production, is highly challenging. The search for strategic programs should always keep the market targets and positions (already defined) clear. The planner should consider various ways to use each function and should emerge with more than one program to consider. A human tendency is to "satisfice" with only one conceived program. However, when two or more options have been conceived, their comparisons will lead to a better strategic decision. Figure 5-8 shows this phase beginning at the bottom level in the marketing functions, where specialists have been offering their expertise to the product manager.

Next consider the matter of market response. When the product manager is facing a decision about whether to include a certain action in the plan, he or she must determine the expected payoff. If the proposed action was to offer a 20-cent price-off to consumers with a coupon, the question is, How much would sales increase and what profit would result? The planner hopes that the function manager, in the department that specializes in implementing such actions (in this case, the sales promotion department), can aid in predicting the market response. Sometimes empirical research may have demonstrated the degree of market response to a similar action. Or the function specialist's longtime casual observation of effects may supply a fairly good guess.

If only one variable is changed in the current program, in a proposed future one the market response determination is clear-cut. If there are several new features in the proposed program, the interactions and synergies among them present a very tough estimation problem. Nevertheless, the explicit decision maker must come up with some specific estimate of a program's effects on sales volume.

The planning at this stage has moved up to the box of estimating market responses of the optional programs under consideration. Of course the option with the highest response is chosen. Its effect on current market share is then assessed, arriving at the projected share. This in turn is multiplied by the whole market's size, which determines the sales forecast for the product. If that has been made in units (as Figure 5-8 assumes), the costs of production and shipping of that physical quantity will be analyzed. Simultaneously, using the expected price level, the dollar sales are forecasted. And these combined indicate the projected profits.

The product manager has now completed all the decisions and prepares them for the chief marketing officer and other officers of the SBU for their approval. Typically these PMU plans go with the SBU's plan up to the corporate level for approval also. If approved, the top level would presumably also approve resources for implementation as part of the SBU's budget. When the approvals are complete, the detail actions are delegated to the functional departments for implementation. The PMU will continue while implementation proceeds, as Figure 5-8 shows, to monitor the actions and results. If results or actions are at variance with the plans, the product manager will seek to exert controls and to meet contingencies with tactical actions.

The planning system that has been described should be efficient, although other processes might be used. Also, the planner will often recycle back to earlier steps, will have many communications around the organization, and will have many more information inputs than are found in our simple model. Planning is never cut and dried. There should be contingency plans too—alternative actions that management can substitute when conditions turn out to be seriously different from those anticipated.

We are now going to illustrate the PMU planning by following our product manager of the antibiotic product, Chester Trimble:

> Trimble began to plan for the year ahead by noting that the entire penicillin sales of the industry for oral administration (by mouth rather than injection) was just above $180 million. That was the arena in which Brand C was contending. After much calculating and consultation with the company's sales forecasters, he projected industry sales at $190 million for the year ahead. (He also did longer-range planning on a three-year basis.) The forecast was also translated into physical units in pounds.
>
> The current market share of Brand C was a mere 2 percent of market (or dollar sales of $3.6 million). Over the past three years it had eroded from over 4 percent. For the present year's plans the hope was to hold 2.3 percent of market, so this present year had an actual planning gap of −0.3 percent. The prognosis for the product, if the same strategy continued, was poor. Evidently some new strategy was needed.
>
> Analysis of the situation began with the general observation that unless something drastic happened to revive the brand, it would soon be terminated. Its prof-

it rate was only 3.1 percent of sales. Since the SBU management wanted three times that profit rate and a husky share of market too, Brand C seemed doomed to extinction. Given that threat, Trimble looked closely at the markets now served by Brand C. The company retained a service that reported on prescriptions of drugs, by brands. In these figures he found that Brand C's best results were with pediatricians: Over 10 percent of the twenty-four thousand pediatricians sometimes prescribed this brand, more than double that of any other type of physician. Since this was the most favorable market segment, he looked for some means whereby Brand C might be positioned as the drug of choice among pediatricians, for at least some illnesses. As mentioned at the beginning of this book, he found such a situation in strep throats. Therefore he expected that any doctor who began to use it for a strep throat would also prescribe Brand C more generally.

Trimble soon conceived of the idea that has been described earlier, a gimmick in which the doctor would give ten numbered toys to a parent to ensure that all ten doses would be given to the child. He had other sales promotional and advertising ideas (gathered from a number of sources). With the sales promotion manager's advice, that promotion was described in specifics. More sales calls on pediatricians would be necessary. He worked with the sales department in deciding how much greater coverage and cost would be entailed. He also collaborated with the advertising agency on a suitable new theme and weight of the next campaign.

Putting together all of that marketing mix, Trimble came up with a sales response estimate: Sales to pediatricians would rise from $1.6 million to $2.8 million while sales to other physicians would stay at the current level of $2.0 million.

With that program and an optional one designed, Trimble considered their effects on market share. For the program described, the projection was a 2.6 percent market share, with all the gain coming in the pediatrician sector and other physician segments holding their own. The alternative program was judged to raise market share to only 2.2 percent and was discarded. Now the 2.6 percent figure could be multiplied by the industry sales forecast of $190 million for the dollar projection. Likewise the unit sales were forecast, which enabled costs of production and distribution to be figured. The projected profit was then calculated. As the profit would be more than triple the present year's and be up to 7 percent of sales, Trimble felt that higher management would probably approve his program and its budget.

Beyond the plan for the next year, there is the more distant future to consider. Trimble's SBU and the overall corporation are interested in his brand in a longer perspective. The extended effort needed to achieve long-range goals calls for current decisions and actions. The role of Trimble's brand in reaching those goals must be projected and planned for.

The strategic plan that we have discussed so far should be followed by an *operating* plan. This would specify exactly what is to be done, by whom, and with what budgets.

SUMMARY

This chapter will serve as a background for the study of marketing strategies. It has introduced their organization and decision flows, and it has identified them before describing their decision processes.

First we discussed the role that marketing plays with regard to strategy —both as a participant in corporate strategy and in conducting its own planning. Then we listed its nine chief duties in planning.

We described the organization for marketing strategy as being a trio of managers: the chief marketing executive, the function managers, and the managers of the PMUs (whom we have lumped together under the title of product managers). In the next section we dealt with the flow of decisions between levels and with the timing of long- versus short-range plans.

Each of the three types of managers was then discussed separately. We explained the tasks and position of each in planning, and we identified their strategic decisions. A decision process suitable to each type of manager was charted and discussed stage by stage. That was illustrated by some calculations. An advertising manager was introduced as an example of functional planning. For product management, we returned to the manager who first appeared in Chapter 1. With this knowledge, a reader should be able not only to visualize what takes place during our chapters on marketing strategies but understand why it operates that way.

REVIEW QUESTIONS

1. *You have been asked to develop an organization plan for the marketing activities of a large corporation. You begin this with a job description of the chief marketing executive. What would you give as the main roles that this executive would perform for strategic planning?*

2. *Later in this work, you laid out a sequence of steps that a unit should follow in developing a marketing plan (in general, for any strategic unit). What is the first and key determination that such a planner would have to decide? What should be the final decision?*

3. *What are the three main strategy-making units (the three types) in a marketing organization, according to this chapter? Why would all three be needed in any large firm (i.e., what is the essential role of each)? Could any other arrangement possibly work effectively?*

4. *In a three-level planning organization (of an entire corporation): (a) Where does the planning cycle begin? (b) What information or determinations would have to be communicated from that level to the next one in planning sequence? (c) What information or determinations would have to flow in the other direction?*

5. *Why is it logical that the original creative decision making in strategic planning begin in the PMUs and the functional departments?*

6. *Describe how long-range and short-range plans should be coordinated. Which (long or short range) should be the dominant ones, in your opinion? Which tend to dominate in the real business world?*

7. *Explain in your own terms what we mean by a CME's acting as a "blend-*

er" in planning. As a "buffer?" Identify how this is indicated in Figure 5-5.

8. Distinguish between the meanings of market objectives *and* financial objectives *that a CME should have set before the marketing plans. How do these two tend to conflict? What compromise should be sought?*

9. *Describe the relationship between the marketing functions' managers (e.g., sales manager) and the PMU managers in the strategic planning process. How are disagreements between these two types likely to arise? Would this tend to happen in a healthy organization?*

10. *When function managers such as Mary Malloy are determining their department's plans, what kinds of information should they have on which to decide? What—or who—would be the main sources?*

11. *In what ways does a PMU manager have authority and power over his or her assigned product/market sector? What does this manager significantly lack? Why would you suppose that despite these serious limitations, the jobs of brand and product manager attract some of the best young marketing talents?*

12. *Explain how the following enter importantly into the planning work at the PMU level: (a) market response estimates, (b) creativity, (c) marketing research, and (d) market-share estimates.*

American Safety Razor Company (A)

American Safety Razor Company's fight for survival was one of Virginia's biggest business news stories in 1977. Philip Morris, the parent company of American Safety Razor (ASR), had been seeking a buyer for the troubled subsidiary. However, sale was not easy, because profits of ASR had declined each of the previous three years (see Exhibit 1). Philip Morris also insisted that prospective buyers guarantee to retain all 870 ASR employees. The Bic Pen Company had agreed to buy ASR; however, the Federal Trade Commission blocked the sale and claimed that such an agreement would be in restraint of competition.

Since no other purchase offers were considered acceptable, Philip Morris decided to close ASR. Manpower was reduced drastically as part of Philip Morris' liquidation plan. In operations alone, one-third of the work force was laid off. The national sales force was cut from eighty people to thirty. Then, in September of 1977, ASR's president, John R. Baker, and eight other company executives finalized an agreement to purchase ASR from Philip Morris. The executives paid $600,000 of their own money and $15 million which they had borrowed from two banks and a federal aid program.

COMPANY STRATEGY

Baker's initial marketing strategy after acquisition of ASR was to offer lower prices than Gillette and Schick and to expand ASR's share of the existing female market with the unique women's razor, *Flicker*. From 1960 to 1976, ASR had focused on increased advertising expenditures, expansion of the sales force, greater consistency in product quality, competitive pricing, and development of new products. However, the new owners could not afford expensive, high risk marketing strategies because of the financial strain of purchase and the need to pay off company debts that amounted to over $1 million a year in interest alone.

Baker expected ASR to "bounce back" and grow. He believed that ASR had an advantage over competition because the new owners were the company's managers and the existing work force was determined to succeed. However, management continued to search for ways to speed the improvement of company profits and market share.

COMPANY SALES COMPOSITION

As indicated in Exhibit 1, ASR's sales were approximately $28 million for the year prior to management purchase of the firm. Seventy percent of company sales were in the "wet shave" consumer market. Its own brands provided more than three-fourths of the dollars obtained by ASR from that market segment.

This case was prepared by Joseph R. Mills, Customer Service Manager of American Safety Razor Company, and Thomas M. Bertsch, Associate Professor of Marketing at James Madison University. Confidential information has been disguised. Reproduced with specific permission.

Industrial products provided the next largest portion of ASR sales revenue. Twenty-seven percent of company business was in the industrial market segment. Sales growth since 1967 was attributed largely to the efforts of ASR to serve industrial consumers, regardless of how unique the product might be.

The surgical blade market segment accounted for less than 5 percent of ASR's sales. Although the demand was not large, surgical blade sales were consistent in volume.

The remainder of company sales revenue came from foreign markets. By 1977 ASR's international sales had almost reached $2.0 million. Shaving blade products accounted for approximately sixty percent of the sales dollars from exports and industrial products accounted for the rest.

BLADE MARKETS

Domestic Consumer Market

In 1977 the United States' "wet shave" market was estimated by the health and beauty aid industry to be $400 million per year at the retail level. That year, Gillette was holding 55 percent of the shaving blade market. Schick claimed 22 percent, and ASR held 11 percent. The remainder of the "wet shave" market was divided between Bic and Wilkinson.

Little market growth was expected for at least the next ten years, because of the slow rate of population growth. Opportunities were increasing in the women's market segment, because teen-age girls were shaving at an earlier age and more frequently than they did during the early 1970's. However, males were shaving less frequently. Beards were more widely accepted in the late 1970's than they were in the early 1970's, and the popularity of the "bearded" look had increased. Very few electric razor users switch to blades, so that market segment did not represent a significant area of possible growth for ASR. Firms in the blade industry expected most new domestic consumer business to come from either increasing market share of their company or opening up new markets.

Industrial Blade Market

The industrial blade market in the United States was estimated by industry leaders to be in the $40 to $50 million range. ASR held about 20 percent of that market, which made it one of the largest manufacturers of industrial blades in the United States. Ardell Industries, Crescent Manufacturing, and Winsor Manufacturing had 10 percent, 5 percent, and 2 percent, respectively, of the industrial blade market. Exacto and Durham, which offered a limited product line, each had gross sales in the $5 to $6 million range. Of the four major producers of shaving blades, only ASR competed in the industrial market.

Surgical Market

The surgical blade market was estimated at only $6 million. Bard-Parker was the sales leader with a 59 percent share of the market, ASR was a distant second with 29 percent, followed by Beaver with 8 percent. Proper, a foreign company that imports large quantities of blades to the United States, was next with 2 percent of the market. The surgical blade market was very small compared to the "wet shave" consumer market.

International Market

The sales potential of foreign "wet shaving" markets was estimated by one industry leader to be ten times the actual dollar sales to the United States' market. In 1977 Gillette accounted for between 80 and 90 percent of the foreign sales of United States' blades.

Shick, Wilkinson, and ASR also competed in the overseas market, but Gillette had taken the lead in teaching people to shave.

ASR has mixed results from its efforts to penetrate foreign markets. The company had approximately half of the shaving blade market in Puerto Rico. However, high labor costs forced closing of its production facility in Scotland, and its efforts in Brazil to provide technical assistance for blade manufacturing did not meet expectations. Even though setbacks were encountered in several foreign markets, the new owners of ASR still believed that some international markets could be highly profitable for ASR.

PRODUCT STRATEGY

ASR offers over 500 different versions of packaged shaving, industrial, and surgical blade products. See Exhibit II for a list of product line changes made by ASR.

Products by Gillette have become the industry standard for comparison. Therefore, ASR's shaving blade products are judged against Gillette's products and designed to meet those standards. However, ASR's shaving systems, such as Flicker and Double II, are designed to be distinctive in appearance.

Typically, major competitors in the blade industry denied that they develop products in response to the introduction of a new product by a competitor. Company representatives usually stressed that they were responding to consumer needs, not actions of competitors. The industry practice, though, was for major producers to quickly follow a competitor's innovative product with a competing product. When Wilkinson introduced its stainless steel blade in the early 1960's, all major competitors followed with similar products. In 1969, Gillette introduced its Platinum Plus blade and competitors followed with versions of the platinum-chromium blades. Eighteen months after ASR introduced Flicker to the women's "wet shaving" market, Gillette introduced Daisy. The time between introduction of a new type of product and introduction of a similar product by a major competitor is now only 10 to 12 months.

New product introductions are one way for a firm to increase market share. However, a new, better shaving blade product may not gain much market share. This fact became painfully clear to ASR soon after the introduction of twin blade systems in 1971. Gillette's introduction into this product category was the Trac II. Schick called its introduction Super II. ASR decided that they had one of three choices: make no introduction, make the same design as Gillette and offer it under a different name, or make a slightly different product. ASR's management decided they had to make an introduction because of the large market potential involved. The ASR version came out eight months later and was called Double II.

Since ASR was late in entering this new consumer market segment, management chose to try a modified twin blade system. The new version was a double edge bonded blade system, which offered twice as many shaves as the Trac II and Super II. The shaving system uniquely featured a gap between the bonded blades that permitted the cut hair to be washed away. With discounts offered, the consumer could buy the ASR system at the same price as Trac II. ASR's new product was a good one, according to consumer tests, but Double II did not pick up the 16 percent market share expected (See Exhibit III).

The major marketing emphasis in the industry since the middle 1960's has been directed towards the marketing of "shaving systems" versus razors and blades. One of the newest systems to be introduced is the disposable razor. Some market analysts estimated that the disposable razor category could build into a twenty percent segment of the estimated $400 million blade market. By 1978, Wilkinson and Schick had followed Bic and Gillette into the low priced disposable razor market with their own versions of a disposable razor.

ASR offered industrial blades for the carpet industry, utility knife blades, and specialty blades for the food, textile and electronic industries. There was also an industrial line of injector, single edge, and double edge blades. The company had been able to convince its industrial customers that disposable blades mean a quality product and a reduction of machine downtime. The strategy of ASR was to find new industrial users for disposable blades, but the market is specialized, so customized orders were common.

ASR offers a full line of surgical blades and handles. Since competitors have not made any recent introduction of new products for this market, ASR has devoted its efforts to technological and quality improvements. Consistent processing effort is expended to improve sharpness and durability of their surgical blades.

Although standard branded shaving blade products and industrial blades were sold in the international market, many products were especially prepared for each market. For instance, in South America, many double edge blades are sold one at a time; therefore, ASR individually wrapped and packaged each blade for that market. Package labels for Europe were printed in four languages: English, French, Portuguese, and German. In the Far East, a single edge blade with an extra thick back for easier handling was sold instead of the standard single edge blade. Customized orders were accepted in the hope of building repeat business.

DISTRIBUTION STRATEGY

Most razors and razor blades in the United States were sold in retail grocery and drug stores. New retail accounts were solicited directly on the basis of their expected volume. ASR had decided to concentrate on large accounts. Therefore, it used distributors to serve small accounts, but it sold direct to large accounts. Much of the industry was dominated by large accounts, such as chain drug stores and supermarkets.

The company was hesitant to reject requests for dealer labels. Management felt that ASR could not compete unless its product offerings were in a dominant position on the shelf. This was particularly true of wholesalers and retailers, who were willing to push their own brand considerably more than a manufacturer's brand.

In general, demand for manufacturer's brands of blades was not growing significantly. However, ASR saw an opportunity to increase their market share in the dealer brand segment of the market. A product was considered eligible for dealer labels if it had at least 8 to 10 percent of the branded market. All dealer label accounts were handled by a small corporate department which performed the necessary marketing functions. ASR held 75 percent of this growing market segment.

ASR sold its surgical blades through a national hospital supply company, which acted as exclusive distributor for the blades. The distributor was permitted by contract to ship to any location in the world. The 1976 contract between the two firms also included renewal clauses.

ASR's industrial products were sold to both users and distributors. Brokers were used to sell less than 20 percent of the products. ASR's industrial sales force concentrated its efforts on the large volume customers and distributors. Many of the direct customers were manufacturers in the electronics, textile, and food industries.

The International Marketing Division utilized distributors in most countries, because ASR did not employ an international sales force. ASR preferred to sell to many distributors within a country in order to obtain wide distribution and to avoid dependence on a single distributor; however, many foreign distributors had exclusive selling rights in their country. The most active accounts were in Latin America, Canada, and Japan.

PRICING STRATEGY

ASR's prices for unique products, such as Flicker and single edge blades, were competitive with other shaving products in the market. If a retailer did any local promotion of ASR's brands of products, then cooperative advertising was arranged. ASR's double edge, injector and Double II products were priced less to retailers than similar items offered by competitors.

ASR was the price leader for industrial blades. Since dealer promotions and national advertising were not used for industrial blades, this market segment was a consistent contributor to profitability.

The company's surgical products were priced low in relation to competition. The national distributor established the resale prices, and the wholesale prices were renegotiated annually.

ASR's products were sold in foreign wholesale markets for approximately one-third less than they were in the United States. Price quotes on export orders did not include shipping costs, although domestic prices included shipping charges.

PROMOTION STRATEGY

The amount spent by ASR on national advertising varied according to the newness of the product. Established products, such as single edge blades, were not advertised. However, a product such as Flicker did receive attention. Flicker was both a relatively new product and one which was dominant in the market. Therefore, ASR allocated $1 million for promotion of their Flicker ladies shaving system in 1977.

Razors and razor blades were typically marketed with large expenditures for promotion. Gillette, for example, spent $6 million on promoting its new "Good News" shaver in 1977. Gillette also planned to support its new "Atra" (automatic tracking razor) with a $7.7 million advertising campaign in 1977. Major competitors of ASR had spent large sums of money on consumer-directed advertising and promotion to maintain strong national brand preference.

The Bic Pen Company, which had been blocked from buying ASR, decided in 1976 to compete in the American branded blade market. It planned a large and expensive introductory marketing program for 1977. Nine million dollars was budgeted for sales and promotion of its single blade, lightweight razor that is completely disposable. Part of the promotional strategy was to give away a disposable razor and blade to 40 percent of the United States' households.

Promotional methods used by major producers of blades included give-aways, rebates, cents-off programs, couponing, cooperative advertising with retailers, special displays, and volume discounts. The industry relied heavily on the use of TV advertising. However, several other advertising media were used, including full-page magazine ads and Sunday newspaper supplement ads.

MARKETING ORGANIZATION

Prior to the planned liquidation of ASR by Philip Morris, the marketing group consisted of brand managers, assistant brand managers, a market administrator, a single marketing researcher and an assistant researcher. By 1978 the group had been reduced to the Vice President of Marketing, the Director of Product Management, and the Director of International Marketing (see Exhibit IV). ASR's top management felt that the smaller marketing team could handle the reduced advertising budget and target market segments.

Both the sales group and the marketing group were based in Staunton, Virginia. The Vice President of Sales reported to the company President. The Directors of Field Sales, Industrial Products, and National Accounts reported to the Vice President of Sales. Three Field Sales Managers reported to the Director of Field Sales. Twenty-four Regional Managers reported to the Field Sales Managers. ASR had four selling divisions: Branded Products, Private Label Products, Industrial and Surgical Products, and International Marketing.

The sales force represented the only link between the company and large retail accounts, such as chain drug stores and supermarkets. Chain stores were very important since they represented the key strategic approach of the ASR shaving blade business. Each regional sales manager was expected to spend much of his time in developing sales to the big chains.

Until late 1974, ASR's field sales people received a compensation package composed of straight salary plus fringe benefits. Then, in 1975, an incentive system was introduced which included a monthly commission, a semi-annual incentive for participation in company promotional programs, plus annual compensation opportunities related to regional profitability. The new compensation package was introduced to help both the sales managers and the salespersons. By 1978 the sales managers felt that ASR was attracting better quality, experienced salespersons and that the sales personnel liked the new incentive rewards.

EXHIBIT I Five-year comparative income statement for ASR*

Item	Year				
	1973	1974	1975	1976	1977[†]
Net sales	$22,909	$26,089	$28,008	$27,917	$30,286
Royalties and other revenues	24	27	94	75	51
Total operating revenues	22,933	26,116	28,102	27,992	30,337
Variable cost	8,768	9,692	9,924	9,965	11,225
Shipping expense	630	618	579	653	794
Fixed manufacturing	4,001	4,602	4,767	4,086	4,278
Available contribution margin	9,534	11,204	12,832	13,288	14,040
Advertising	1,616	1,601	1,744	1,882	1,324
Sales force and promotion	4,503	5,571	7,451	8,070	8,462
Mkt. research/mkt. adm.	379	449	453	417	346
General and administrative	1,290	1,320	1,720	1,397	1,479
Research and development	506	547	599	702	627
Total operating expenses	8,294	9,488	11,967	12,468	12,238
Operating profit	1,240	1,716	865	820	1,802
Interest expense	0	0	0	0	0
Other expenses	245	432	24	118	723
Profit before taxes	$ 995	$ 1,284	$ 841	$ 702	$ 1,079

*In thousands of dollars.
[†]Amounts projected prior to management purchase in September.

EXHIBIT II   Product line changes of ASR

Year introduced	Major products	Status as of 1977
1875	Star Safety Razor	Replaced with Gem Razor
1889	Gem Safety Razor	Continued, with modification
1915	Ever-Ready Shaving Brush	Continued
1919	Gem, Star, and Ever-Ready shaving blades	Continued
1933	Lightfoot Soap	Discontinued in 1973
1934	Electric shaver	Discontinued in 1934
1935	Pile Wire-Carpet	Discontinued in 1977
1935	Surgical blades and handles	Continued
1947	Double edge shaving blade	Continued
1948	Injector shaving blade	Continued
1963	Stainless steel coated blade	Continued
1969	Face Guard shaving blade	Continued
1970	Personna Tungsten Steel blades	Continued
1971	Flicker	Continued
1973	Personna Double II shaving system	Continued
1974	Perrsonna Injector II blade	Continued
1975	Double Edge II	Discontinued in 1976
1975	Lady	Continued
1977	Single II shaving system	Continued

EXHIBIT III   Market performance of twin blade systems

Product	Date of introduction	1971–1973 advertising dollars	Jan. 1974 share of total razor blade market	1973 Sales
Track II (Gillette)	1971	$117 million	23.2 percent	$10.9 million
Super II (Schick)	1972	$ 4 million	6.3 percent	$ 2.5 million
Double II (ASR)	1973	$ 3 million	1.3 percent	$ .6 million

EXHIBIT IV Marketing—Sales organization

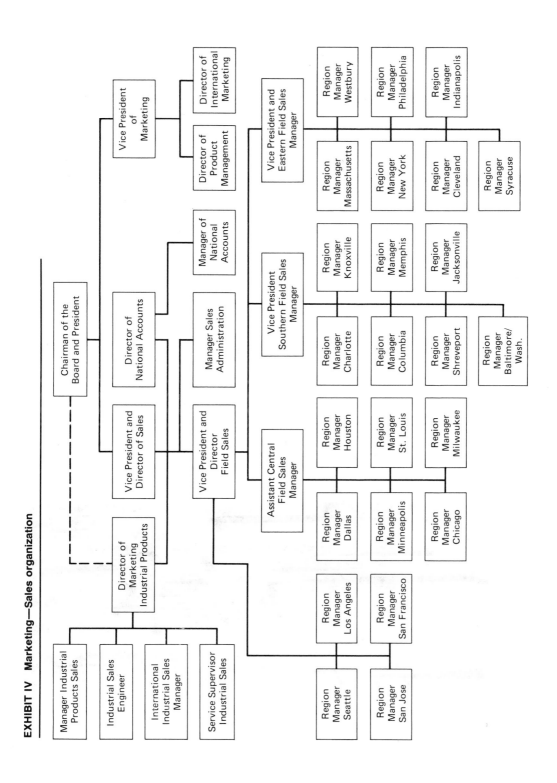

DISCUSSION

1. Identify the key problem areas of American Safety Razor at the time that it was being converted into a separate and independent company in 1977.
2. Describe the various markets in which ASR was competing in 1977. What was ASR's competitive position in each of them? What strategic position did ASR apparently take in each of those markets?
3. What would be the tasks for marketing in renovating ASR as a strong factor in the razor and allied industries? What would be ASR's greatest strategic needs?
4. Study the marketing organization chart in Exhibit IV. Given that structure, who would be the logical individuals or groups to decide ASR's marketing strategies? How well would all the aspects of marketing be represented in formulating strategy? Do you see any changes in the marketing organization that seem necessary in order to reach effective strategies in marketing? Any changes for implementing—going into action with—the adopted strategies?

CASE 5-2
RCA Corporation, Mobile Communication Systems Division (A)

The course of developing and launching technical products may be long and tortuous. That describes the history of one new product of the RCA Corporation, as it was vividly told in Fortune *magazine.[1] This case was drawn from that article.*

Twenty-five miles southwest of Pittsburgh . . . sits one fief of the far-flung RCA Corporation. The mobile communications systems division, which manufactures two-way radios, is a small sliver in the corporate scheme of things. [In 1976] it took in only $40 million in revenues—not much for RCA, a $5-billion colossus. But the success of the business is of consummate concern to a lot of people whose hopes and futures hinge on it. . . .

For years the business was an ignominious loser. It was kept in the fold in part because several of RCA's top line executives had dabbled in the operation during their careers and were emotionally attached to it. But by the early Seventies, after the death of David Sarnoff, the corporate patriarch, change had seeped through management, and sentiment was no longer sufficient reason to hang on to a failing business . . .

The drama that has been unfolding since then involves a division fighting for survival. It tells something, in microcosm, about corporation men under pressure and their relationships with one another. . . . It also tells something about the process of developing a product, for in the case of RCA's division, the introduction of a successful new mobile radio was seen as the path to survival. As usually happens in real life, the path wandered from the one mapped in management textbooks.

---

[1]Aimee L. Morner, "A Product Is Born," *Fortune*, February 1977, pp. 125–33. All rights reserved.
This case is reproduced with permission of the RCA Corporation.

A JOB FOR SUPERMANAGER

In 1970, Irvin Kessler, an executive vice-president, became an important personage at Meadow Lands when RCA widened his domain from five to six divisions—the new one containing the mobile-radio business. Kessler knew he would find plenty of action at Meadow Lands, and though the division's affairs represented but a small part of his total responsibilities, he became deeply engrossed in them.

In a previous job, Kessler had overseen RCA's work in space electronics—including the lunar module—and was appalled that the mobile radio division had failed to incorporate advanced technology developed in the space business. He prodded the division into using large-scale integrated circuits in a two-way, hand-held portable radio—christened the Tactec—that was developed to replace a clumsy Japanese import RCA had been selling. With its miniaturized components, the Tactec was conveniently compact, a classy item. But by 1973, the operation was still beset by start-up problems, and component deliveries were lagging. Losses mounted to an eye-popping $3.3 million that year—the worst in a decade.

NOT ANOTHER BATH, THANK YOU

The head of the division in those days was a marketing whiz and twenty-five-year veteran of Motorola. He was trying to beef up RCA's market share by sending forth products to compete on all fronts with his former employer, which had far and away the lion's share of the domestic land-mobile-radio business—about 60 percent. He had the division strung out in all directions, probing a potpourri of new products, including computer-aided dispatch systems and paging devices with which RCA had no experience. For all that floundering, RCA—with less than 7 percent of the market—still placed a poor third, behind General Electric, which had over 20 percent.

The general thinking at the top was that the business required a large market share and economies of scale—neither of which the mobile division enjoyed. Anthony Conrad, who was then president of RCA, considered selling the operation or shutting it down, but feared a distasteful write-off. Only two years earlier, RCA had written off an epochal $400 million on its ill-fated computer venture; Conrad and many other top executives thought that, as one of them puts it, the mobile business might represent "a miniature version of the computer play."

THE LITMUS OF POPULARITY

Kessler took a different view. Of course, the division had to make money, but he thought that his peers . . . failed to realize that volume and market share weren't everything. "If you offset the lack of volume by designing a product for a profit, and if you are selective in the market, you can be highly profitable," he says. With a limited infusion of capital and "tender, loving care," Kessler thought, he could turn the mobile business around.

Early in 1974, Kessler headed for Manhattan from his office in Moorestown, New Jersey, to make a pitch for the mobile business to Conrad. Despite the gush of red ink in 1973 . . . , the fourth quarter had been profitable, as efforts to stamp out inefficiencies in both manufacturing and marketing had begun to pay off. Though Conrad was only mildly impressed, Kessler finally persuaded him that he could keep things running in the black. Better still, he said, by the end of the year he would mastermind a strategy that would enable the division to funnel cash back to headquarters.

A PHILOSOPHER IN THE BOONDOCKS

In doing that, Kessler knew they had to abandon the policy of proliferation followed by the division head, who had quit after repeated disagreements. To replace him, Kessler brought in a leader to take Meadow Lands "out of the wilderness"—Jack Underwood, who had worked for Kessler in the aerospace business. Underwood, forty-nine, had joined RCA back in 1948, and had proved himself a skilled engineer and a cost-conscious manager. In the Fifties, Underwood fathered RCA's automatic electronic test equipment and since the mid-Sixties had been managing that product line. Now eager to move up, he asked Kessler to find him a new job.

Underwood took the post at Meadow Lands even though the prospect of running the mobile business was hardly enticing. Though he thought that he had a "fighting chance" of meeting Kessler's commitment to Conrad, he says, "it was the furthest thing from being a piece of cake."

[Underwood and Andrew Inglis, head of the communications and systems business, met at night to lay out a narrowly focused strategy to replace the me-too approach. RCA had a substantial foothold in only one segment of the business:] mobile radios for vehicular use. Not to be confused with Citizens Band radios. . . . RCA's technically sophisticated FM models are of the type used in police cars and utility trucks.

The total market for land-mobile radios in the U.S. was running at some $600 million a year in 1974. About one-third of that market was accounted for by vehicular mobiles in the mid-range in both performance and price ($800 to $1,000 for what the trade calls a "plain vanilla" radio—i.e., one without options). In an exhaustive study, the division's marketing staff concluded that the company could in five years bring its share of this middle tier of the market up to 15 percent. Underwood and Inglis decided to winnow down the number of new products being developed to just one well-targeted radio.

They soon faced a problem that rears its head in a lot of product-development programs. Because the lead time for the new product was about three years, development in technology could render the new radio obsolete even before it hit the market. "We believed," Inglis says, "that as technology advanced, the medium-priced mobile of the future would have the performance of the high-priced mobile today." So they set as their objective creating a radio that carried a mid-range price tag, but whose performance equaled that of the best then on the market—Motorola and G.E. products that sold (in plain vanilla) for $1,000 to $1,500.

THE JOYS OF BEING PRETTY GOOD

In order for such a product to turn a profit, Inglis had to set forth precise cost goals. Searching for a reasonable target, he took a look at Motorola's gross margins, which were substantially wider than RCA's. The old line of RCA mobiles, which had a high labor content, was eating up money. "We found," Inglis says, "that practically all of the differential between our product cost and Motorola's could be explained by the difference in volume and the relative cost-effectiveness of our design." Inglis knew that RCA could never make up the difference in volume; even with 15 percent of the market, the company would be churning out only about a quarter of Motorola's production. But he figured that, by concentrating on a cost-effective design, he could substantially improve RCA's current gross margin.

In the fall of 1974, Underwood set out to sell the same idea to Conrad in New York. During the meeting, he told the boss that the plant was now efficiently meeting delivery schedules. Tactec was starting to take off, and the division had been in the black for four quarters. Though Underwood harbored his own secret doubts about whether the new strategy would boost profits in Meadow Lands enough to please New York, Conrad liked the idea. Recalls Underwood: "There was no time for anxiety. We had to move ahead with an act of faith."

To try to assure that the engineers were attuned to the thinking at the top, Underwood gingerly introduced "matrix management," a concept that he had employed in his aerospace work but that no one in the mobile business had ever used. Under this system, a program manager coordinates simultaneous efforts in design and engineering, and in the preparation for manufacturing, rather than having these functions proceed sequentially, as they had in the past. The critical link in matrix management is obviously the program manager, and Underwood recruited what he calls a "gung-ho guy"—George Mitchell, thirty-six . . .

Mitchell had done a stint as a systems engineer at Motorola, but left for RCA in 1965 because, he says, the trek up the corporate ladder was painfully slow. . . . He was the product manager for the TACTEC, which captured 15 percent of the $60-million market for top-of-the-line portables, in less than three years. When attention shifted to the vehicular mobile, he felt that another successful product would give his career a big boost. . . .

WHERE LESS IS MORE

[The engineers], in planning the product, carefully examined the specifications of two top-of-the-line models—Motorola's Micor and General Electric's Mastr II. They figured that they could outclass the Micor—in looks, if not in performance—by trimming the size of the transmitter/receiver unit, a critical selling point, since it had to be kept small in order to slide easily beneath the seat of a truck. The design team pegged the new unit at three inches, which was about three-eighths of an inch lower than the Micor's.

On a few occasions, Mitchell shared doubts about the competitive merits of the RCA design with the soft-spoken and unflappable chief of the engineering team, Lee Crowley. He liked the looks of G.E.'s Mastr II, whose transceiver was one-half inch lower than the RCA design and smaller than any other unit then available.

But both Mitchell and Crowley knew that if they proposed to chop another half inch from the height—a 34 percent overall reduction in size—it would mean throwing out hundreds of drawings, jacking up the cost, and adding three months to the production schedule. And since Underwood had just come aboard as the boss, Mitchell and Crowley didn't want to inaugurate their relationship with him by petitioning for more time and money.

At a full-fledged program review in October 1974, some twenty-five engineers, marketing men, manufacturing representatives, and managers from the field were mustered . . . at Meadow Lands to take a look at a preliminary mockup. No one liked what he saw, least of all Underwood and the people who would have had to sell it. Fresh in their minds was the handsome Mastr II. Though it had been kicking around the marketplace nearly two years, Underwood, still learning the business, had stumbled across it only a month earlier at a convention of police chiefs in Washington. "By God," he recalls thinking when he saw it, "that was a fine design. I wanted to hire G.E.'s designer."

But even more than that, Underwood wanted his own engineers to upstage G.E., and he knew that Kessler would be aghast at RCA's clunky mockup. Underwood told his men: "Stop giving me a comparison of how we're doing against Motorola. The guy to compete with technically is G.E." In translation that meant shooting for top-of-the-line performance and lopping an additional one-half inch from the height.

After the meeting, some twenty engineers shuffled back to the drawing boards to rethink the new mobile. They took a second look at the Mastr II to see how G.E. had done things, and at the Micor to pinpoint wasted space. One thing became clear: The quickest way to reduce height was to use hybrid modules in which integrated circuits are bonded to a ceramic substrate with gold and platinum leads.

The radio already had three hybrids, which were borrowed from the Tactec, and though Crowley felt strongly that using more of them would save "real estate," his proposal would have added about 3 percent to the production cost. When he reluctantly asked for some relief on the budget, Underwood's response was—. . . "no way." [He] had repeatedly admonished the engineers to abandon their natural proclivity to use technology for technology's sake, and he said the hybrid modules could not be justified as cost-effective. . . .

TIME TO WEAR TIN PANTS

A bit miffed, Crowley felt that the rejection was "unreasonable," because, as he puts it, the "rules changed, but not the goals." But Crowley did get three extra months tacked on to the schedule, enough time for the engineers to plug a few of the modules into a vertical rather than horizontal position, and to painstakingly redesign a few critical components. When the next engineering review rolled around in the spring, they proudly showed off a handsome-looking radio, one-half inch lower than the first prototype.

Though the new design met with unanimous approval that day, the engineers winced a bit as they awaited a crucial item on the agenda. In spite of a loud protest from Crowley, Mitchell—under pressure from Underwood—had scheduled a discussion of costs. Says Crowley: "You always have to wear tin pants if a cost review is held in the early stages. I knew we were high on costs, but I considered costs a non-problem then."

A heated debate about the numbers soon broke out. According to estimates by the financial-management group, costs were racing ahead of target by a staggering 31 percent. Not so, said Crowley. His best guess was that costs were off by a mere 8 percent. At the end of the presentations, Underwood slowly rose and incisively handed the engineers a verbal report card: an "A" for technical achievement, an "F" for costs. Crowley hotly defended his calculations. A bit swayed, Underwood changed the "F" to an "incomplete."

With his own success as a program manager on the line, Mitchell took charge of a new committee that sought, as he says, "to squeeze pennies out of dollars." They focused on the 100 most expensive components, which account for just one-tenth of the total number, but more than three-quarters of the production cost.

The buyers, who had repeatedly solicited bids for parts ranging from a $20 transistor down to a 10-cent capacitor, again canvassed vendors to strike better deals. Mitchell had told them to buy no more than a three-month supply of any part, in order to keep inventories down and minimize the risk of design changes. But in the case of one component, a crystal filter, the engineers had developed the specifications with a supplier and were confident about its performance. Together with the buyers, they convinced Mitchell that by placing a two-year order with staggered delivery dates, and by shrewdly coupling the order with one for Tactec, they could save $81,000.

As Kessler breezed through the plant one day, he came across one of the prototypes and stopped in his tracks. "Why that ghastly gray?" he asked. He didn't really care what the color was, but he wanted something "with pizzazz, like blue and cream." The designers spent seven months dreaming up alternatives. Finally, they presented him with the recommendation of a Pittsburgh consulting firm, a modest "sand-drift beige" and "royal brown," which to their surprise and relief met with Kessler's approval.

Because they had to slash labor costs by 40 percent in order for the radio to be cost-effective, managers in manufacturing worked closely with the engineers early on, suggesting features that should be incorporated to make the radio economical to produce and test. The engineers designed modules that, by simply plugging into the transceiver, eliminate not only 150 feet of wire in each model—a total saving of 237 miles this year alone—but also a lot of errors by assembly workers. In addition, each plug-in module has three custom-designed pins that fit easily into automatic test equipment.

THE PERSISTENT HURDLER

Trying to nail down a commitment from corporate headquarters for necessary new equipment was a nerve-racking process. During 1974 and 1975, the purse strings tightened at RCA as corporate profits sagged. The commercial-electronics group—of which the mobile business is a part—lost nearly $56 million in those two years. Underwood had to do a bang-up selling job in New York to get any equipment with a price tag of more than $250,000, the amount needing approval at headquarters.

With each lap Underwood took around the track, Kessler was on hand to coach. One of his key roles, he says, is "to inculcate an awareness in people of what's acceptable at the corporate level." For any division manager seeking capital, what's acceptable is a healthy return on investment, say 10 percent. At Meadow Lands, the return was running a slim 2 percent when Underwood set out to make his sales pitch. But Underwood was deftly chipping away at the investment, with the hope that he could boost the return enough to get the needed capital.

THE BILL COLLECTOR'S REWARD

Though he had started reducing the lofty level of receivables almost as soon as he arrived at Meadow Lands, Underwood felt New York breathing down his neck on this subject in late 1975. By the end of 1975, partly because of the efforts to trim receivables, the division's negative cash flow turned to a positive $5 million.

To cut back the level of investment in inventory, the engineers designed the new radio so that it could be warehoused more efficiently. Under the old system, a mobile was tuned to a certain frequency range, tested, and put on the shelf until it was plucked to fill an order—a procedure that mightily increased the number of models that had to be stocked and inflated the value of the inventory. With the new design, a finished radio is built to a customer's specifications by putting together previously manufactured modules only after the order is received at the plant. At the last moment, the heart of the radio—a temperature-compensated crystal oscillator—is slipped into place to determine proper frequency.

Underwood estimated that this new approach would reduce inventories by 15 percent. But a cornerstone of the scheme was the purchase of some advanced, computer-controlled equipment to test the crystal oscillators—a facility that had to be approved by New York.

After four months of review, the request landed on Conrad's desk. The supporting data stressed that the equipment would reduce labor costs by $1 million during its first five years in operation. "Something got lost in translation," Underwood recalls. "Conrad thought that he was being asked to get RCA into the crystal-manufacturing business, which was something the company had decided not to do a few years ago." Conrad's answer was a resounding no. "Inglis and I called Conrad's staff and suggested that somebody tell the boss—diplomatically—what we were really talking about." Several weeks later, Conrad relented and picked up the tab.

As Underwood slashed the budget of the engineers, whose ranks had been thinned by layoffs, he found himself on the defensive. "It was the old Army game," he says. "They were bound and determined to tell me that every tremor on their budget would mean a six-month delay." But as things turned out, they rallied and met most of the remaining milestones in the schedule. They built four models of varied frequency and power levels, and by last fall, says Crowley with a sigh of relief, they had "beaten the cost bogey" on three of them. Their success is a significant step in the pursuit of the golden gross margin.

Suggestions for a name for the new radio had filtered in to Meadow Lands from the engineers, factory workers, field force, and advertising agency. Kessler, ever the individualist, did not like any of them. Eager to cement in the customer's mind the technological link between the new product and the successful Tactec, he borrowed from the Tactec name itself. The result—Veetac, which stands (loosely) for "vehicular, totally advanced communications technology."

Tantalizing a skeptical sales force with a product not yet in production is a procedure not to be coveted. By mid-November only nine engineering models had been built, production equipment was still filtering into the factory, and materials were in dismayingly short supply. The automatic test facility for the crystal oscillators was clicking away—but in a temporary home in the accounting department.

"YOU NEED FAITH"

"If we had Utopia, we would never have introduced the Veetac until we had preproduction models and were building for inventory," admits Mitchell. "But sometimes you just can't wait. You worry that the competition is going to come out with something. At that point you need faith that the designs are good. In this case, the timing was right. Veetac has the margins that can make 1977 comfortable for us, and by announcing it early, we got a flying start."

As the first Veetacs roll out of the plant for delivery this month, the division awaits the verdict of the marketplace. On the basis of performance, the Veetac is, without doubt, a top-of-the-line radio. But the results on pricing are a bit off the intended mark. Though the flurry of propaganda bills the Veetac as a mid-priced mobile radio, a trip through the maze of numbers indicates otherwise on most comparisons. Says one disgruntled field manager: "We have a high-priced mobile. That's all there is to it."

Back at Meadow Lands, the team that spawned the Veetac is pleased with its offspring. Says Kessler, who optimistically thinks that the issue of survival has been put to rest: "We have to learn to manage our success." Mitchell seems destined to move up in the hierarchy after a session in the fall at Harvard's advanced-management school. For the engineers, it's back to the drawing boards to conjure up some auxiliary equipment to offer as options.

Underwood has again asked Kessler to find him a new home. But wherever he goes, he says, he will periodically check up on the Veetac's progress. "It's a lot like having a child," says Underwood. "You always care how it turns out."

DISCUSSION

1. Trace the sequence of decisions in this case. Then answer these questions: (a) Who determined the objectives? (b) Who determined the alternative strategies that were given serious consideration? (c) Who decided which strategic program would be selected? (You will notice some natural shuttling back and forth between decisions, which adds complication.)

2. As was mentioned in the case, "the path wandered from the one mapped in management textbooks." Point out where the path in this case wandered from that recommended in this book. Did such divergency appear to have any ill effects on the decision's results (in terms of the objectives)?

3. Identify the decisions or advisory inputs made by marketing people in this case. What faults, if any, do you find in their roles? What additional contributions ought

they to have made? How would such inputs be likely to improve the decision's outcome or efficiency?

4. Suppose that you were determining a better system to be followed in the Mobile Communications Systems Division for deciding new-product strategies. What changes would you make, particularly with regard to marketing?

PART THREE

*ENVIRONMENTAL VARIABLES
IN STRATEGY DECISIONS*

6

Market Decisions

Defining and analyzing markets and measuring their potential are early decisions in developing a marketing strategy. This chapter provides a framework for making these market decisions.

First we cover ways of finding, defining, and analyzing categories of potential customers (target markets). Then we will be concerned with measuring and projecting market and sales potentials for the target markets. Since the marketing strategy should be designed to satisfy a defined target market, it is logical that finding a market and estimating its size and characteristics are among the first steps in strategic-planning decisions. Marketing intelligence is most helpful in this initial stage of formulating the marketing strategy.

American Express Company's "Do you know me?" advertising campaign has been one of the country's most popular campaigns in recent years. The number of its cardholders quadrupled between 1974, when the ads were first aired, and 1982. The company eventually discovered that it had neglected a significant market, however—women. American Express estimated that the 2.5 million women who held its card in 1983 represented only 20 percent of the potential women's market.

To make a dent in this lucrative market, American Express conducted a campaign aimed at women in sixteen national women's magazines and on TV in seven cities constituting about one-fourth of the U.S. population. The campaign featured "confident, independent women using their American Express cards" and tripled women's interest in the card in those cities where the new commercials were shown.[1]

TYPES OF MARKETS

A *market* is defined as individuals and organizations with purchasing power, desire, and authority to buy products. In a developed country it is often the desire or willingness to buy that receives the most attention in determining consumer demand. For major purchases, such as homes and automobiles, purchasing power (wealth, money, or credit) is an important determinant of the ability to purchase. Authority (acknowledged by law or social custom) is an important consideration for products not available to all members of society. For example, it may be illegal for some segments of society—minors and people with criminal records—to purchase explosives.

[The first step in finding a market is to delineate the type of market that is to be served] Consumer markets consist of individuals purchasing products for personal, household, or family wants. America's marketing giants usually aim their multimillion-dollar ad campaigns at strongly defined consumer markets because the consumer goods are generally purchased on a repeat basis]

> Gerber Products Company is a name that has long been associated with baby food, which is a consumer good. Thus Gerber's market type is the consumer market, and its target market is parents of infants. The company is experimenting with opening up a new market, however—teenagers. A Gerber executive says, "We know there are closet users out there." In fact, late in 1979 Gerber anonymously conducted a "Secret Snack Sweepstakes" using advertisements in Glamour, Seventeen, and other "teen" magazines. Thirty thousand readers responded and received free jars of Gerber's Dutch Apple Dessert and another free coupon. Half of the respondents cashed in their coupons for more Gerber's. While Gerber is still in the consumer market, it may have broadened its target market.[2]

— *Producer markets* include organizations, governments, and private businesses that purchase goods, ideas, and services for use in producing, and/or operating, to serve the public and/or customers. *Reseller markets* include wholesalers, retailers, and other marketing intermediaries that buy products to sell to producers, other resellers, or consumers. Reseller markets usually buy finished goods, provide facilitating services, and then sell them for the purpose of making a profit.

Some organizations have diverse operations and may be vertically integrated. Therefore, they may sell to producer, reseller, and consumer markets. On the other hand, the organization itself can be part of another firm's pro-

---

[1]Bill Abrams, "American Express Is Gearing New Ad Campaign to Women," *Wall Street Journal*, August 4, 1983, p. 21.

[2]Gail Bronson, "Baby Food It Is, but Gerber Wants Teenagers to Think of It as Dessert," *Wall Street Journal*, July 9, 1981, p. 21

ducer market or reseller market. An organization, profit or nonprofit, that sells products or otherwise makes them available is never considered a part of the consumer market.

Of course, classifying types of markets into three categories is an oversimplification of the diversity of markets that exist. But the three markets we identify are mutually exclusive and are useful in identifying customers with similar characteristics.

SELECTING MARKET TARGETS

Market Targeting

[Market targeting consists of the decision processes and activities conducted to find a market to serve]. Targeting can be a complex task. It is difficult to develop appropriate customer profiles with much accuracy, and a rapidly changing industry may be expanding into new markets continually.

When a market has enjoyed steady growth for a period of time, less-profitable market segments may have been neglected. Such is the case in the cruise industry, which had enjoyed a 20 percent annual growth in the late 1970s. Most of the major cruise operators were much more interested in maintaining good relations with their steady, current customers than in attracting budget-conscious, first-time voyagers. Growth stalled in the industry in the early 1980s, and most lines entered into a war over the stagnant repeat cruising market.

Certainly, with competition so fierce, no one would expect a new firm to enter the market. But that is just what Miami-based Carnival Cruises did. Carnival, owning only one ship, promoted inexpensive fares to first-timers. It did so well in its first year that it contracted for three new ships at $170 million each to be built and put into service between 1985 and 1989. As Robert Dickson, vice-president of marketing at Carnival, said, "In tough times you have to go after one segment of the market." [Concentration on a single market segment allows the pursuit of the optimal opportunity. In this case, the segment that Carnival went after was not being adequately served and proved to be extremely profitable even in "tough times."[3]

The ultimate test of the usefulness of attempts to isolate markets is whether they help shape and refine the marketing strategy to make the offering compatible with the market. It is sometimes difficult to match products to market opportunities. One reason for this is that markets and external environmental forces are dynamic, and the needs and wants of the market change. AMF monitored the environment in the 1980s and decided to stick with premium-quality, premium-priced sports and leisure equipment. It estimated that upscale leisure products would dramatically increase in the future.

---

[3]"The Market for Cruises Is Listing," *Business Week*, October 4, 1982, p. 123.

Targeting Decisions

Early attempts to define and describe the market require a general targeting approach. This decision is usually based on marketing intelligence, information gathered about potential buyers. Since markets differ in their heterogeneity, different targeting strategies must be used.

Marketers can approach the total market as an aggregation, or one of several segmentation approaches may be used. Let us review these targeting strategies in more detail.

Market Aggregation. This approach (also called *undifferentiated marketing*) results in one offering aimed at the total market. Market aggregation does not recognize market segments. Instead it tries to satisfy the greatest number of buyers with a single product. Figure 6-1 illustrates a market-aggregation approach for Premium Saltine crackers, aimed at the total consumer market. Note that a single offering, developed from a single marketing strategy, is used to appeal to the total market. It is assumed that purchasers of this type of crackers do not significantly differ, so one basic offering can be used to appeal to everyone.

When a market-aggregation approach is taken, a product-differentiation strategy is frequently used. [*Product differentiation,* used most ofen when the product is physically similar to other brands, is a strategy attempting to distinguish it from the field of competing products] This is accomplished most often through promoting some element of the offering, such as price, availability, packaging, or some characteristic that can be made to seem "different." For example, Premium Saltine crackers have been promoted and labeled as "the cracker with CRUNCH." It is hard to tell if competing crackers have the same degree of crunch, or if crunch is an exclusive attribute of Premium. Premium also lets the buyer know that the crackers are packaged in "4 Keep Fresh Recloseable Bags" (this is stated right on the box). This attribute is supposed to differentiate Premium from other crackers.

Market Segmentation. This approach is an attempt to develop an offering that appeals to some part of the aggregate market. For market segmentation to be effective, the following conditions should exist:

1. It is necessary to identify and categorize actual or potential buyers into mutually exclusive groups (segments) that have relatively homogeneous responses to marketing-mix variables.

FIGURE 6-1. Market-aggregation approach for Saltine Crackers

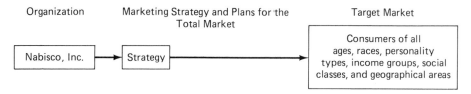

2. It must be possible to identify characteristics of the mutually exclusive groups that can be used as a basis for directing specialized marketing efforts to the different groups, recognizing the heterogeneity of the groups.[4]

The isolation of those behavioral and demographic variables unique to Chevrolet buyers (rather than Cadillac buyers) illustrates an attempt to use differences in buyers to formulate a marketing strategy. Even if the detailed information were available on Chevrolet buyers, it would be hard to obtain measures of marginal response to marketing variables for individuals and groups of people. This limitation, however, does not negate the usefulness of the fundamental concept—that knowledge of different reactions to marketing inputs is essential to the structuring of efficient marketing plans. In one of our examples in Chapter 1, we described how ARCO used marketing research to determine that there was a large market segment willing to pay cash for discounts on gasoline. Therefore ARCO eliminated its credit card and developed a cash-only marketing strategy. The result was improved profits resulting from increased market share.[5]

Multisegment Approach. Figure 6-2 illustrates a multisegment approach for an auto importer such as Mazda. A multisegment approach is that used by an organization in trying to provide multiple offerings to appeal to two or more market segments. For example, Mazda offers a piston as well as the rotary engine, for consumers who want conventionally powered subcompact automobiles. The rotary is used in the Mazda RX–7 sports car.

The multisegment strategy allows the enterprise to increase its share of the market by recognizing the heterogeneous wants and desires of submarkets. Although there may be additional costs of planning, organizing, and con-

---

[4]Harper W. Boyd, Jr., and William F. Massey, *Marketing Management* (New York: Harcourt Brace Jovanovich, 1972), p. 89.
[5]"How ARCO Used Marketing Research to Go 'Cash Only' in a Plastic Society," *Marketing News*, January 6, 1984, p. 1.

FIGURE 6-2. Multisegment approach to markets

trolling the multiple offerings designed for different markets, these increases can be offset by developing better convergence between the offerings and the various submarkets.

Market-Concentration Strategy. This targeting strategy focuses on efforts to serve one market segment. Many companies have found it efficient to gain a large share of a segment of the market. For many years, Timex has concentrated on the segment of the watch market that looks for economy, ignoring the segments that view watches as jewelry or chronometers. Timex was successful because it recognized the huge dimensions of an ill-served segment of the watch market. Bulova, Hamilton, and Benrus, in fact, were actually reaching only a segment too; perhaps they thought they were appealing to the aggregate market and that the economy segment was too small to serve.

In contrast to General Motors, which uses a multisegment approach in trying to appeal to all market segments, Mercedes-Benz of North America concentrates its efforts on the luxury segment of the automobile market. The average price of its automobiles is significantly higher than that of American cars. Only one out of every two hundred cars purchased is a Mercedes. Figure 6-3 illustrates the market-concentration strategy used by Mercedes-Benz. Note that the luxury market is a small portion of the total market. Over the years, changes in the Mercedes marketing strategy (with emphasis on luxury and distinctiveness) have helped to develop a luxury-sports offering.

Through a market-concentration strategy, the enterprise can achieve a strong market position because of its greater knowledge of the desires and wants of a specific submarket. Furthermore, many operating economies can result because of specialization in production, distribution, and promotion. It is widely believed that vast social and economic changes have broken traditional mass markets into smaller segments. Companies have discovered that the key to profits lies in pinpointing and delivering what these new consumer groups want.[6]

---

[6]"Marketing the New Priority," *Business Week*, November 21, 1983, pp. 96–106.

FIGURE 6-3. Market concentration

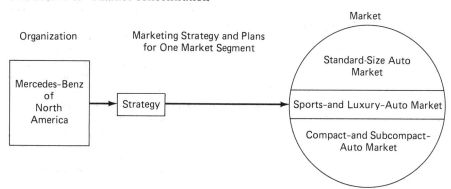

WAYS OF SEGMENTING MARKETS

When a multisegment or concentration approach is used in targeting, a method of identifying some subpart of the aggregate market must be found. The primary ways of segmenting markets include geographic location, demographics, psychographics, and benefit analysis. Table 6-1 provides examples of breakdowns of these major variables used in segmentation strategy. Each breakdown could relate to a market segment. The breakdown method helps to shape the development of marketing strategy.

Geographic Segmentation

Segmentation by region, county size, city, population density, or climate is the most obvious way of identifying subparts of the aggregate market. For example, the market for snow tires can be linked to climate. More auto air conditioners are sold in Texas than in Maine, and more cars are rustproofed in Illinois than in Arizona. Many firms use a geographic-segmentation strategy because it is easy to apply and relates directly to the distribution decisions about where to make products available.

For many products, geographic segmentation does not provide insights about the uniqueness of the subparts of the market. For example, variables other than geographic location are more important in determining which movies or records will be successful in the marketplace. Often, product usage rate or some other segmentation factor is identified by geographic area when the variation in demand is really linked to some other segmentation variable, such as ethnic group.

TABLE 6-1   Major segmentation variables

Stage I *Variables useful in diagnosing* *why buyers want products*	*Stage II* *Variables useful in guiding* *the marketing strategy to a* *specific target*
Psychographic Segmentation:	*Demographic Segmentation:*
Personality	Age, sex, nationality
Lifestyle	Education, religion, race
Self-concept	Occupation, income, social class
Attitudes	Marital status, birthrate, family size, and family life cycle
Benefit Segmentation:	*Geographic Segmentation:*
Economy	Region
Convenience	Urban, suburban, or rural
Service	Climate
Prestige	State, county, or city

Demographic Segmentation

Demographics is one of the most popular methods of segmentation. It permits the marketing strategist to classify purchasers in a very direct and efficient manner. Variables that can be distinguished as states of existence—sex, family size, education, income, race, age, and so forth—are used in demographic segmentation. Relating consumption to one or more of these can be useful in targeting a marketing strategy. For example, the Neiman-Marcus stores focus on the 25- to 45-year-old middle-income and middle-to-upper-income population group, career women, and single-person households.

Although demographic segmentation may explain the existence of a phenomenon, *why* an ethnic group, for example, exhibits certain behavorial traits may be difficult to determine. But demographic segmentation has practical significance. After significant market differences (psychological reasons for buying for example) have been determined, demographics can be used, often combined with geographic variables, to target the marketing strategy to the market with the greatest potential.

Segmentation by using several variables usually provides a clearer picture of the market to be served. Figure 6-4 illustrates segmentation of the market for a packaged dessert mix. In this case, the heavy-usage market is middle-income families that have two or more children.

Demographic studies are useful in describing and measuring population size, composition, and distribution changes. Discovering the consequences of these variables and their variations and plotting their connections are even more useful.[7]

The baby boom generation has grown up, and it should change the way marketers promote many goods: Yesterday's "babies" are now at the age when they should do most of their spending.

> Levi Strauss & Company formed its Levis for Men Division in 1976 for the consumer over 25 years of age. The reason—there are fewer teenagers on the horizon, and the 60 million or so people of the baby boom generation who grew up in jeans made a very appealing, and at the time untapped, market. Levis is now looking at the age-50-and-over market.

A measure of changing labor-force participation and structure has been helpful in evaluating marketing strategies and making decisions to communicate with selected groups. As more women (approximately 50 percent of them) have taken jobs outside the home, Procter & Gamble has increased its advertising expenditures on evening television.

These examples illustrate that demographics can be useful in those narrow decisions that are important in beaming parts of the marketing strategy, such as communication, to the right market. Demographics is not as useful in

---

[7]Kenneth C. Land and Seymour Spilerman, *Social Indicator Models* (New York: Russell Sage Foundation, 1975), p. 305.

FIGURE 6-4. Multivariable segmentation

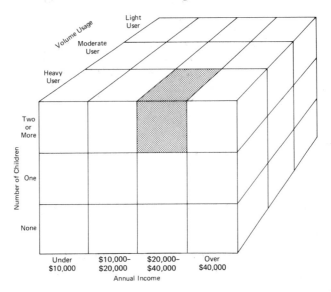

diagnosing *why* variation in consumption is occurring. Psychographic segmentation, discussed next, is useful in the broader and more general parts of the marketing strategy that deal with why the product is purchased.

Psychographic Segmentation

Personality, lifestyle, and buying motives are typical psychographic variables used to subdivide markets. Psychographic segmentation usually provides more in-depth explanations about buyer behavior than does geographic or demographic segmentation. Its usefulness, however, varies according to the abilities of marketing strategies to devise specific applications.

Self-concept and lifestyle have been two of the most popular psychographic areas for studies in recent years. Analyses of how products relate to a person's lifestyle and individual self-concept are made in terms of psychological attitudes. Something lacking in a person's lifestyle, for instance, might produce a desire to buy a product.[8] As marketers become more analytical in selecting markets, the use of psychographics will increase.

A leading advertising agency, Needham, Harper and Steers, has used lifestyle research to determine the right marketing strategies for specific lifestyle segments.[9] Table 6-2 shows the kind of lifestyle data used in market targeting. The people's descriptions in Table 6-2 are an oversimplification of the diverse

---

[8]Emanuel H. Demly, "Over-the-Counter Life-Style," *Psychology Today,* 5 (April 1972), 76.
[9]William D. Wells, "Film of Findings Shows Uses of Lifestyle Research," *Marketing News,* published by the American Marketing Association, June 17, 1977, p. 9

TABLE 6-2 Male and female adult lifestyle profiles

Female lifestyles	Male lifestyles
Thelma, who is old-fashioned, wishes the world would be the way she fondly remembers it, lives by rules that she hates to see change, and wouldn't like a trip to Paris where she wouldn't even understand the language.	*Fred,* the frustrated factory worker, married early, had children, and now has trouble making ends meet. He'd rather lead a glamorous life and he needs fantasy to make his current life bearable. He wants a sports car, likes products that are endorsed by show business personalities, and doesn't think there is too much sex and violence on TV.
Candice, the chic suburbanite, who supports women's liberation, has many activities, and buys only whole-grain cereal for her children.	*Scott,* the educated cosmopolite, buys foreign-made products if they are of high quality. He is concerned with consumer issues and the ecology, and won't drive his car if he can take public transportation. He lives a fast-paced life, shares home responsibilities, and believes men should dress fashionably.
Mildred, the militant mother, married early, had children, and now wishes the women's liberation movement had happened in time to help her. She likes soap opera and lottery tickets because they help her escape into a fantasy world.	
Cathy, the contented mother, married early, had a big family, and likes it that way. She thinks women's liberation opposes Biblical teachings, is trusting and relaxed, and buys only the cereals her children demand.	*Dale,* the devoted family man, married early, fathered a family and is happy. A blue-collar worker with a high school education, who likes to put down roots in his community, he is more interested in knowing what a product can do for him than what star endorses it and worries about excessive sex and violence on TV.
Elsa, the elegant socialite, says women's liberation is unnecessary if a woman has a man to take care of her. She spends little time preparing meals, but spends a lot of time and money on cosmetics and high-fashion clothes, thinks face creams are better if they cost more, and plans a trip to Paris.	*Ben,* the self-made businessman, believes you get what you pay for, values his time, eats bacon and eggs despite his doctor's disapproval because "there's no substitute," and thinks the government should keep its nose out of private industry.

Source: Reprinted from William D. Wells, "Film of Findings Shows Uses of Lifestyle Research," *Marketing News,* published by the American Marketing Association, June 17, 1977, p. 9.

lifestyles that exist, but some of these oversimplifications may be useful in aiming a marketing strategy at a specific lifestyle.

It is suggested that, if given a $500 bonus, Dale would pay bills and buy a new household appliance; Scott would indulge a boyhood dream by buying an HO train set; Fred would vacation in a Minnesota cabin; and Ben would buy 12-year-old Chivas Regal.

Thelma and Mildred both buy nail polish, but they don't respond to the same marketing strategy. Fred and Dale may need insurance, but Dale will buy from the agent who sold insurance to his father, and Fred will go where he is made to feel like a person with some status.[10]

---

[10]Ibid.

Although people in the United States like to be thought of as individuals, we often mimic the current trends or fads that are in vogue in our society. A popular way of describing lifestyles is to determine what fads are "in" and what ones are on the way out. Certain preferences in food, drink, clothing, and entertainment are always apparent on both a national and a regional basis. Although most people do not become that involved with these fads, knowing what is current and what is outdated can have great marketing significance.

From the marketer's perspective, psychographics is useful in diagnosing markets and deciding what actions to take. In the initial stage of marketing-strategy planning, psychographics is especially useful in finding significant reasons why consumers buy. Correlative demographic and geographical variables can then be determined for aiming the strategy at a specific market target.

The practical consequence of studying psychographics is that it provides insights into consumer response to stimuli. For example, package designs, new products, and the consideration of alternative advertising copy involve consumer reaction to stimuli. Marketing research procedures used to measure psychological variables include attitude measurement and scaling procedures.

One of the problems in using psychographics is finding the practical usefulness of the psychological variables analyzed. For example, discovering that consumers who purchase the most beer are politically conservative is not as useful in formulating a marketing strategy as is analyzing psychological reaction to colors used in packaging, or measuring attitudes about the product created by the use of advertising copy.

Benefit Segmentation

Benefit segmentation focuses on those benefits that are associated with the product. It is used to determine what benefits or problems exist and what importance they have in a purchase decision. For example, consumers may look for different benefits from the same product. Some of the different benefits desired in toothpaste include decay prevention, bright or white teeth, a good taste, fresh breath, and economy. A demographic breakdown of categories of people who desire these benefits indicates that those interested in bright teeth are tobacco users or single; consumers concerned with decay prevention have larger families.[11] Table 6-3 illustrates the relationship between the various product benefit segments and demographic, personality, and lifestyle factors.

The benefits that can be identified and used in market segmentation relate to any measurable variable. Economy, service, convenience, prestige, or product configuration could provide the desired benefit. For example, the drug Isordil, prescribed to heart patients to reduce severe chest pains, entered the market in 1959 and now claims a whopping 46 percent of its market. Ives

---

[11]Russell J. Haley, "Benefit Segmentation: A Decision-Oriented Research Tool," *Journal of Marketing*, published by the American Marketing Association, July 1968, p. 33. Reprinted by permission.

TABLE 6-3 Description of toothpaste–market segments

Segment	The sensory segment	The sociables	The worriers	The independent segment
Principal benefit sought	Flavor, product appearance	Brightness of teeth	Decay prevention	Price
Demographic strengths	Children	Teens, young people	Large families	Men
Special behavioral characteristics	Users of spearmint flavored tooth paste	Smokers	Heavy users	Heavy users
Brands disproportionately favored	Colgate, Stripe	Macleans, Plus White, Ultra Brite	Crest	Brands on sale
Personality characteristics	High self-involvement	High sociability	High hypochondriasis	High autonomy
Lifestyle characteristics	Hedonistic	Active	Conservative	Value-oriented

Source: Russell Haley, "Benefit Segmentation: A Decision-Oriented Research Tool," *Journal of Marketing,* July 1968, p. 33. Reprinted by permission.

Laboratories, maker of the drug, claims that it lasts longer than competitors' products and is better at relieving certain types of pain. Thus the drug is obviously quite beneficial to the patient.[12]

Benefit analysis is useful in the diagnosis of markets and determination of a direction for the marketing strategy. It is often used to pinpoint *why* consumers are purchasing. Demographic or geographic variables are then used to direct the marketing strategy to the target market.

MARKET POTENTIAL, SALES POTENTIAL, AND SALES FORECAST

There are three different determinations involved in the analysis and projections of markets: market potential, sales potential, and sales forecast. To clearly distinguish them, we will give a definition and an example of each of these.

Market potential is defined as the capacity of a market to assimilate a product or product line of an industry. This usually refers to the amount of the product that the market can purchase in either the current period or the next period that is under planning.

Example:

It may be estimated, based mainly on economic variables and consumer attitudes, that the automobile industry has a market potential of selling 9 million units in the United States in the year 19–.

Sales potential is defined as the maximum share of market potential that an individual firm within the industry can expect to obtain for a specific product or product line.[13] This also is typically for the current period or that under planning.

Example:

Based on its current share of the market, marketing efforts, production capacity, and other considerations, General Motors may expect to obtain a 55 percent market share in 19–. In other words, its sales potential would be 4.95 million units.

Sales forecast is a prediction of the dollar or unit sales for a product or product line that an individual company anticipates in a future period under a given marketing plan.

Example:

The Chevrolet Division of General Motors may forecast sales of 300,000 Cavalier units for the model year 19–. This might translate to a $2.8 billion sales volume.

---

[12]Michael Waldhole, "Marketing Often Is the Key to Success of Prescription Drugs," *Wall Street Journal,* December 12, 1981, p. 1.

[13]Francis E. Hummel, *Market and Sales Potentials* (New York: Ronald Press, 1961), p. 8.

This sales forecast would be based on expected actions by competitors, other environmental variables, and allocation of marketing resources for Cavalier and competing products within the General Motors product mix—applied against a total industry forecast.

Figure 6-5 illustrates how market potentials, sales potentials, and sales forecasts are used in formulating market strategy. An understanding of general economic and social conditions is the first systematic step in developing a sales forecast. Economic indicators such as gross national product (GNP), new housing starts, employment, and capital investments can sometimes be used to predict industry market potential. Industry market potential will also depend on other environmental trends and changes in buyer preference. The measurement of market potential is necessary to determine an upper limit on the sales or unit volume for an industry. A company that achieved this level would be a monopoly. Some utilities, such as telephone, gas, and electric companies,

FIGURE 6-5.   Steps in developing and revising market potentials, sales potentials, and sales forecasts.

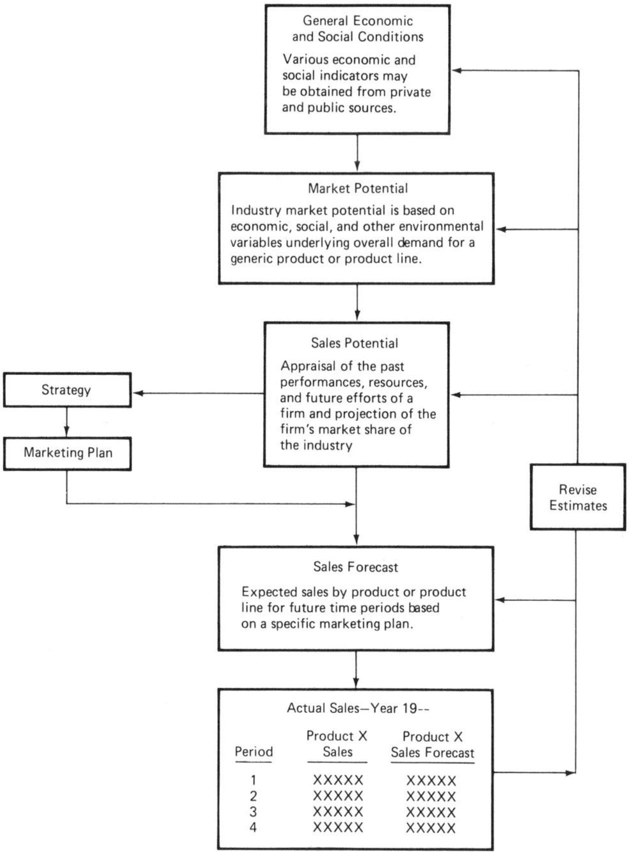

are effective monopolies. Therefore their market potential would be the same as sales potential. But most companies expect their sales potential to be some fraction of the market potential.

The sales potential of the firm is based on past sales performance (if any), expected changes in competitive structure, and projections of events favorable or unfavorable to the firm. A sales forecast is the final step; it is used to finalize the marketing plan and allocate marketing efforts. The sales forecast does not necessarily predict a sales outcome; it is usually used to estimate an outcome under a given marketing plan. After the forecast, the plan may be revised, or sometimes products may be deleted if the sales forecast indicates profit levels that are not satisfactory to the firm.

DATA SOURCES

Market potentials are based on an analysis of the underlying causation of aggregate demand for a product or product line. Therefore its measurement is most often generated from social and economic variables that are linked to aggregate demand. The government and many nongovernment organizations supply secondary data helpful in estimating market potential.

The Survey Research Center, Institute for Social Research, University of Michigan, distributes information on buying intention and consumer finances. The data contain, for example, survey results that provide insights concerning the number of consumers that plan to purchase durables such as automobiles, refrigerators, or television sets.

The Yankelovich Social Monitor (private, for-profit research service) traces major social trends and attitudes toward lifestyles on a longitudinal basis. Firms such as Ford Motor Company and Northwestern Mutual Life Insurance receive information about general attitudes toward marriage, children, work, recreation, and government regulation of business.

The F. W. Dodge Corporation compiles data on new construction starts. Since new construction is an excellent indicator of general economic conditions, this indicator is used by many firms in estimating market potential. The demand for household appliances, carpeting, construction materials, furniture, financing, home moving services, and insurance could be partially derived from new housing starts.

The *Survey of Current Business* is a widely used source of information about the GNP. It provides a forecast of GNP by four purchasing groups: consumer, business (also nonprofit organizations), foreign, and government sectors.

The *Federal Reserve Bulletin* gives statistical series regarding those parts of the economy most sensitive to market potential. The *Index of Industrial Production* is classified by industrial groupings (products) and by market groupings (industries and submarkets). Additional data helpful in estimating market potential are provided by the Bureau of Labor Statistics, *Economic Indicators* (Council of Economic Advisers), and *Business Cycle Developments*, published through the Department of Commerce.

Standard Industrial Classification (SIC)

The *Standard Industrial Classification System of the United States Economy* is one of the most useful and convenient methods of organizing market-potential data.[14]

The Standard Industrial Classification (SIC) is a uniform numerical system for classifying establishments engaged in economic activity in the United States. The purpose of the system is to promote uniformity and comparability of information for manufacturers, resellers, and all other economically productive establishments. The classification system has obvious value for those firms that sell to producers and resellers, because SIC numbers are keyed to secondary data available from government and nongovernment sources.

Figure 6-6 traces the subdivision of electrical machinery (major group 36) to the group classification of electric transmission equipment (361), down to a

---

[14]*Standard Industrial Classification Manual,* 1967.

FIGURE 6-6.   SIC classification.

Source: Patrick J. Robinson, Charles L. Hinkle, and Edward Bloom, *Standard Industrial Classification for Marketing Analysis* (Cambridge, Mass.: Marketing Science Institute), p. 10.

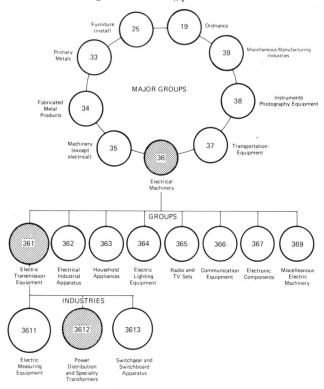

specific industry (3612), the industry of power distribution and specialty transformers.

Sales and Marketing Management's Survey of Buying Power

The *Survey of Buying Power* is among the most widely used of secondary data bases for market potential. It is especially useful in estimating demand for consumer products. It is published annually by *Sales and Marketing Management* and provides estimates of population, income, and retail sales for all standard metropolitan statistical areas (SMSAs) in the United States. In addition, data are provided by counties, major metropolitan areas, and states, as well as for the entire country. Retail sales are broken down further by various categories such as food, automotive, apparel, and eating and drinking establishments.

The Buying Power Index component of the *Survey* provides the percentage of total national sales that could be expected in a trade area. For example, if the Denver-Boulder metropolitan trade area has a buying-power index of .7335, then that area would have .73 percent of the total national market potential. Therefore the *Buying Power Index* is a ready-made market-potential index for industries and generic products included in the survey.

The *Buying Power Index* should be used only as a market-potential guide in estimating sales potential. This index is only one data source. Other considerations, including population, number of households, market structure, and the firm's resources, must be analyzed to better pinpoint sales potential. The sales forecast for a firm may vary significantly from a direct correlation to the *Buying Power Index.* In some cases, a marketer could devise a weighting system for systematically adjusting the index to expected company sales.

Internal Data Sources

Data for estimating market and sales potentials or forecasting can also be developed internally to reflect more accurately the different variables that can influence sales. The market-survey method, which can be based on interviews with knowledgeable persons inside the firm, will be discussed in the next section. The firm's own marketing information system may supply insights about market strengths and weaknesses, and current sales trends. Other functional areas in the firm, such as accounting, finance, and corporate planning, may provide data about a firm's internal operations and indicate resources that relate to sales potentials and forecasts.

The sales and cost data collected by the accounting function are among the most overlooked source data for sales forecasting. These data do not necessarily flow directly to marketers who are forecasting sales, but a well-organized marketing information system would allow the marketing function to gather from all over the firm data that could be useful in forecasting.

It should be obvious that a voluminous amount of data is available to the firm to use in estimating potentials and developing forecasts. It is also evident that the information is worthless unless it can be organized by a method or procedure to provide an estimate for management. In the next section, we will describe such methods.

METHODS USED IN MARKET
MEASUREMENT AND FORECASTING

An understanding of methods of measurement is helpful to the marketing strategist for several reasons. First, it should provide insights into evaluating the accuracy of various methods. The more complex the technique, the more important it is that the marketer understand its assumptions, possible shortcomings, or advantages. Second, when the marketer must help decide what measurement technique should be applied, he or she must have some knowledge about the appropriate use of alternative methods. We will examine major methods of measurement, including judgmental forecasting, sales-force estimates, buyer expectations, time series analysis, and regression, and illustrate the application of each.

Judgmental Forecasting

A common approach relies on a jury of executive opinion to obtain sounder forecasts than might be made by a single estimator.[15] To put the results in better perspective, the jury members are usually given background information on past sales. Then their estimates are sometimes weighted in proportion to their convictions about the likelihood of specific sales levels being realized. In other cases, decision trees help to harness executive judgment in transforming preliminary estimates into more realistic forecasts.

For some longer-range market forecasts, a number of companies now employ modified Delphi techniques, in which the opinions of experts are converted into an informed consensus by means of highly structured, multistage polling.

A large company that has several divisions, which manufacture and market toiletries and cosmetic products bearing well-known brand names, used the following forecasting approach:

> Each branded product is assigned to a brand manager, who is responsible for the brand's marketing strategy and support. Twice a year, the brand manager is interviewed regarding prospective sales volume in the next calendar year. The first such interview takes place at the beginning of the current year; the second, about midway through it. The interviewing is conducted by an outside specialist in order to encourage frankness and realism on the part of those being interviewed.

---

[15]This section has been adapted from David L. Hurwood, Elliot S. Grossman, and Earl L. Bailey, *Sales Forecasting*, Report No. 730, The Conference Board, 1978.

The brand manager's supervisor is also interviewed at the same time and is asked to supply separate estimates for all the brands in his or her charge.

Each round of interviews takes two or three days. The executive being interviewed is asked a series of questions, which, by the end of the interview, elicit the executive's most realistic forecast for a brand in terms of its "most likely, minimum and maximum" sales.

The minimum forecast is the volume the respondent sees being achieved if a number of unfavorable things should occur—for example, inadequate promotional support, strong competitive countermoves, perhaps even an unfavorable ruling by some regulatory agency affecting the product. The maximum sales forecast is the highest figure that could realistically be expected if everything turned out well. The most likely sales figure is one fixed somewhere between these two extremes.

Insistent probing forces the respondent to "back up" these estimates with sound reasons. All of the brand executives' assumptions and explanations are made explicit. The interviewer plays the role of a skeptic, challenging the defense of every judgment or estimate. (For example: "Last year this brand sold much less than you're forecasting. How come your forecast for next year is so high?") No wild speculations or casual estimates are accepted by the interviewer, who presses tactfully to uncover the basis of all judgments.

Sales-Force Estimates

The sales personnel of some firms—field representatives, managers, or distributors—are considered better positioned than anyone else to estimate the short-term outlook for sales in their assigned areas.[16] To eliminate the obvious possibilities for bias, companies generally try to divorce such estimating procedures from the setting of quotas that will determine the participants' compensation. Also, they often supply the participants with measures of past sales and forecast results; and they may arrange later to adjust the results on the basis of undue optimism or pessimism exhibited in the past. Sales-force estimates are usually subject to revision at successively higher review points along the way.

> Ex-Cell-O manufactures diversified industrial items, including machinery, precision parts and assemblies, aerospace and electronic products, and expendable tools and accessories.
>
> Ex-Cell-O's "new order" forecast is based on four major inputs: (1) forecasting of economic trends; (2) forecasting of industrial demand for products of the kind made by the company; (3) field sales-force forecasts; and (4) Ex-Cell-O historical performance data. Sales analysts, armed with their computer storage and retrieval systems, supply the first two of these inputs. The headquarters marketing staff, aided by information from distributors and the company's own sales personnel, is primarily responsible for the last two. The foundation of the forecasting process, however, is the third input, which rests on the intimate market knowledge and the estimating talents of the sales personnel, in the field—both the company's own sales force and its distributor network.
>
> Each field sales manager, salesman, and distributor is familiar with the chief cus-

---

[16]Ibid.

tomers and potential customers in his area. Each is supplied by the group's staff with historical data concerning past orders, by customer, and machine-tool category. Each sounds out his customers and prospective customers periodically regarding probable purchases, during the next year and a half or so, of machinery of the type Ex-Cell-O offers. And each consults with the product sales managers in his region, and benefits from their specialized knowledge regarding technical and market developments.

Users' Expectations

Although the number or dispersion of product users in many markets—or the cost of reaching them—would make such an approach impractical, some manufacturers serving industrial markets find it possible to poll product users about their future plans.[17] They then use this information in developing their own forecasts. The findings from a survey of buyer intentions can be conducted most efficiently when (1) the cost of contacting buyers is low; (2) buyers are willing and able to disclose their intentions; (3) secondary information or other indirect information sources are not adequate.

Firms in very concentrated markets have sometimes been able to capitalize on the buyers' own interests in the making of good forecasts. An example is the division of one diversified firm, which sells its products, mainly OEM (Original Equipment Manufacturers) items, to major automobile companies. Its need is for forecasts for the period two to three years away when these items would actually be sold and made. The principal prospects in this case are willing to give the supplier some advance indication of the total product volume they will purchase if their own plans work out.

General-purpose surveys conducted by outside organizations are valued by a number of forecasters for the indirect clues they are sometimes able to give of future market demand in their own industries. Besides some company-sponsored projects of this kind, such surveys include the McGraw-Hill survey of capital expenditures and the Conference Board's survey of capital appropriations. They also include surveys of consumer sentiment and buying intentions made by such organizations as the Survey Research Center of the University of Michigan and again by the Conference Board.

While the findings of such surveys often are not translatable directly into forecasts of demand, they serve as economic intelligence for the guidance of forecasters—possibly in "fine-tuning" their final forecasts—or, occasionally, as input variables for regression models used in forecasting.

Time Series Method

Time series forecasting is a statistical forecasting tool that is used to extrapolate past sales or market potentials into the future. This may be done by mere inspection of a series of sales points plotted on a graph, or by other methods. For example, the average rate of change may be projected visually or by using statistical smoothing techniques, trend lines, and graphs. Changing

---

[17]Ibid.

patterns of demand for individual products, geographical territories, customers, and particular product characteristics may be extrapolated in this manner.[18]

The rationale underlying this technique is that the original data of a series are composed of a secular trend, a cyclical component, a seasonal component, and an irregular component. Functional equations (multiplicative and additive models) can be used to represent relationships between components. The mechanics underlying any time series procedure is to predict future behavior once a model to describe past behavior has been delineated.[19]

Regression Analysis

Time series analysis does not deal with the underlying variables that may be linked to demand (forecasts are a function of time). On the other hand, various statistical methods can be applied to mathematically predict sales or market potential. Variables such as advertising expenditures, prices, population, income, and new housing starts are often treated as independent variables, whereas sales is assumed to be the dependent variable.

The basic approach is to assume that sales, Y, is a function of various independent variables:

$$Y = f(x_1, x_2, x_3, \ldots, x_n)$$

Simple Linear Regression. We will first illustrate simple linear regression. The assumption is that one independent variable, such as the *Sales and Marketing Management Buying Power Index* described earlier in this chapter, is a straight-line function with sales for some specific product. The relationship can be illustrated as

$$Y = a + bx + e$$

where

Y = dependent variable (sales)

x = values of the *Sales and Marketing Management Buying Power Index*

a = value of y when $x = 0$

b = change in y per unit change in x

e = error in estimating sales Y

---

[18]Walter Gross, "An Analytical Approach to Market Forecasting," *Georgia Business*, 30 (November 1970), 4.

[19]Paul E. Green and Donald S. Tull, *Research for Marketing Decisions*, 3rd ed. (Englewood Cliffs, N.J.: Prentice-Hall, 1975), pp. 665–66.

Multiple Linear Regression.   The addition of other independent variables can, of course, increase the accuracy of prediction. When they are added the equation becomes

$$Y = a + b_1 x_1 + b_2 x_2 + b_3 x_3 + e$$

The use of regression models forces the forecaster to consider major variables influencing sales. It also makes it necessary to objectively quantify relationships and estimate the degree of reliability that can be attached to the model. On the other hand, not only does this method require the technical skill of developing the model, but much experience and judgment may be necessary to select variables and understand how the forecast can be used by marketers. Overreliance on regression can result in forecasting errors when the nonstatistical assumptions underlying the basic relationships are no longer valid.

PRACTICAL ASPECTS
OF FORECASTING METHODS

Few companies rely nowadays on a single, all-purpose method of forecasting. An important reason, usually, is that experience has shown certain methods to be inherently more feasible and appropriate for certain purposes or certain product or market situations than for others. Also, there is frequent insistence on having more than one set of independent predictions for the sales series, as a check for reasonableness.

Here are the characteristics that experienced practitioners consider to be hallmarks of a superior forecasting system:

1. The system encourages an open-minded weighing and testing of alternatives.
2. Its predictive power and cost are well matched to its purposes.
3. Its input data are appropriate, consistent, and reliable; and they are protected from contamination and misuse.
4. Its procedures discourage aimless intervention and tinkering while encouraging the adjustment of first approximations in light of new facts.
5. It has adequate provisions for tracking, updating, and self-correction.
6. Its management users are alert to the possibilities of forecast error; they understand the underlying assumptions; they are familiar with and accept the forecasting methodology; and their own contribution and involvement at critical points is ensured.

More than anything else, a sound sales forecast still rests on sound judgment—whatever the specific techniques employed along the way. Forecasts obtained by other means are still usually tempered by management judgment before their "official" adoption.

For many companies, flexibility is now emerging as perhaps the most distinguishing feature of their forecasting programs. For example, there is a much greater willingness than in the past to consider and to evaluate a variety of forecasting techniques. And, more than ever before, the primary mission has become that of finding and applying the right combination of methods for the particular forecasting job at hand.[20]

The techniques and approaches used in practice to estimate future sales do not have to be perfectly accurate to be useful to marketers. Although accuracy is important, it is apparent that no method can take into account all unpredictable variables, such as the actions of competitors or buyers' attitudes. Therefore the method used in market measurement and forecasting should allow the marketer to systematically project sales by using scientific approaches as well as judgments and experience. If the limitations of the methods are understood, adjustments can quickly be made when the basic assumptions underlying the technique change.

Market measurement and forecasting are part of marketing intelligence and should be viewed as important in the development of marketing strategies.

SUMMARY

In this chapter we reviewed the fundamental marketing concepts that structure decisions, keeping in mind that one of the first steps in marketing—strategy development—is to analyze and define markets.

We considered different types of markets (consumer, producer, reseller), discussed alternative methods of targeting markets (aggregation, segmentation), and looked at several segmentation strategies (geographic, demographic, psychographic, benefit). Next we examined the topics of market potential and sales potential. These estimates are generated with the help of information found either through such sources as SIC codes and the *Buying Power Index* or within the firm. Finally, we described some basic processes, both qualitative and quantitative, used in the development of sales forecasts.

REVIEW QUESTIONS

1. How does the type of market (consumer, reseller, producer) affect the formulation of strategy?

2. Discuss some of the factors that should be considered in defining the market for a totally new product.

---

[20]The section adapted from Hurwood, Grossman, and Bailey, *Sales Forecasting.*

3. Why is product differentiation helpful when market aggregation (undifferentiated marketing) is used?

4. How does the decision maker decide to use either a multisegment approach or a market-concentration approach when a market segmentation strategy is selected?

5. Why did your text suggest that psychographic and benefit segmentation are useful in diagnosing why buyers want products, while demographic and geographic segmentation are useful in guiding marketing strategy to a specific target?

6. What is the relationship between marketing objectives, generic markets, and sales targets?

7. Select a brand and describe the generic, specific, and brand markets of which the brand is a part.

8. Compare and contrast the merits of forecasting using survey (judgemental, sales-force, and user expectations) methods versus statistical forecasting methods.

9. Select a brand and describe that brand's generic, specific, and brand markets.

Susie's Warehouse

In early 1979, Susie Benson, owner of Susie's Warehouse, was meeting with Lance McDougle, a local management consultant who specialized in working with restaurants and cocktail lounges. She was concerned with the lack of profitability of her business and with the decline in sales that she had experienced since 1977. She also was concerned with the cash flow of the operations since her cash balances were approaching a precarious level.

"Lance, I called you last week because I have some problems with my operations that have begun to bother me and I am not sure which way to go in solving them. My friend, George Simpson, the owner of the Oak Lounge, recommended you and said that you may be able to help me. I have been in this business for a long time, and it is a rough one, but I feel that it is time for me to seek some new ideas."

"Susie, I may be able to help you, but it would be helpful if you would fill me in on the background of Susie's Warehouse and tell me a little about your current operations."

"Well, I opened Susie's Warehouse in late 1967. For years I had wanted to open a restaurant/cocktail lounge because I believed it would be profitable, exciting and recession-proof. Since this place was the culmination of my dreams, I planned to call it Susie's End, but this name caused so much kidding from my friends that I changed it. The building was leased under a five year lease with options to renew. I have considered moving to a new location, but the expense of such a move would be prohibitive (due to leasehold improvements) and I have not been able to locate a lending institution willing to finance a move. In addition, I have a large place here, and to find a suitable building of comparable size would result in my rent being increased about four times from the present level.

"Unfortunately, Susie's has had a history of losing money. I was profitable from 1968–1973, but since then I have had consistent, but small deficits. This is, of course, after my salary of $18,000 per year. I do have some thought on why my sales have been declining. Although the population in this area has increased, the number of eating and drinking establishments has increased faster than the population. This has spread the entertainment dollar thin in my market area. Since I usually have to pay all bills within two weeks of delivery, I have been having a problem with cash flows.

"Until the end of 1978, the entertainment in Susie's was live bands. I changed to disco in January 1979 for several reasons. The first was the increasing popularity of the disco concept and the ability of disco bars to draw the high-spending young clientele. The second concerned the cost relationship between disco and live bands. Once the initial investment is made in the disco set-up, the day-by-day operating costs are much lower than live bands.

"Another area that I have changed was my meal policy. Until November of 1978 I offered a full lunch menu in the front section of the building and offered a full dinner menu at night until 11:00 p.m. The lunch business is profitable and I have no plans to change it. However, the full dinner service was losing money so I decided to drop it. The cost of the food service was not being offset by the profits from increased liquor sales."

COMPETITION

Susie's Warehouse is located in the northeast section of town (Exhibit I). This location is not an ideal one. Most of the development of new night clubs and restaurants is taking place in the southwest section of town and Susie's may not count on drop-in business from customers traveling from one night spot to another. In addition, the residents living in the area surrounding Susie's have a lower average income than the town as a whole.

Susie does believe that she has certain competitive advantages over her rivals in the disco business. The first is that several professional buildings are located in an office complex that has just opened nearby and she hopes to draw some business from this source. The Warehouse only charges 75¢ for a well drink while the other discos charge $1.50 to $1.75 per drink. She has the largest disco in town, both in terms of the size of the dance floor and the square footage of the entire complex. Since Susie's is located on the edge of a shopping center, customer parking is abundant and close.

ADVERTISING

Susie's Warehouse is advertised on the four most popular local radio stations. These stations reach 70% of the relevant target market, 21 to 35 year olds. Approximately 80% of this advertising is paid by trade-outs, that is, the stations are given vouchers that may be used for food and drink. In the past the stations have used these trade-outs in the proportion: 80% liquor, 20% food. Since these vouchers are issued at retail value, Susie is able to save considerably on her radio advertising costs. The local newspapers have refused to accept trade-outs so Susie does not use newspaper advertising. Susie has not used any sort of special promotions or featured mixed drinks.

SALES ANALYSIS

Susie's Warehouse's sales consist of two components, food and liquor. To be profitable it must maintain sufficient sales volume in both parts of the business.

The food sales are, at present, carrying the business; this was not always the case. Food sales have been growing consistently since July of 1976 when they were at the $32,000 per month level. In 1976 and 1977 the growth rate was rather slow. The growth rate accelerated in the last six months of 1978. During this period, sales have averaged $46,000 per month.

The sales increase of 44% is partly attributed to a 32% increase in food prices. The rest of the increase is directly related to the growth of real volume. Some of this growth was accomplished during the same period that menu dinners were eliminated. Lunch volume has increased enough to cover the loss of menu volume.

Liquor sales were very high at one time, especially in the beginning of 1977. Since that time, there has been a steady decline in liquor sales. This decline in liquor sales coincided with the development of increased competitive pressures. Two new discos offered alternative drinking spots within a short distance of the Warehouse. Another contributing factor to the decline was the opening of four new discos in the southwest section of town. This has shifted crowds from the northeast areas.

Approximately 65% of the total liquor sales are generated on the weekend (Friday, Saturday and Sunday nights). The rest of the sales are spread out over the other four days. Susie feels that she now has the capacity to support a doubling of sales volume of liquor, even on her busiest nights.

Susie has found it difficult to pinpoint the particular causes of the decliine in liquor sales due to the vast number of changes that have occurred in the last two and one half years. One change was the switch from live entertainment to disco. Dropping live entertainment caused a reduction in food and liquor sales. It also allowed for a significant reduction in costs. The menu dining was dropped in November of 1978. The recent (late December) introduction of the 75¢ well drink was instituted to build up sagging liquor sales.

Lance interrupted at this point. "Susie, you have given me sufficient data for me to begin work. Let me digest what I have and meet with you next week. By that time I will have worked on a cash flow forecast, looked at your pricing and food policies, and come up with some suggestions on advertising and promotion. I believe that we can come up with some dynamite ideas and make Susie's Warehouse profitable again!"

INDUSTRY NOTE

Well managed cocktail lounges are often very profitable and recession-proof. But the industry also has high risks. Regulators from all levels of government are always examining your operations. Infractions of the law may cause the loss of your liquor license, resulting in the loss of the major portion of your investment. Of greater concern is the fact that bar customers are fickle and are quick to patronize competitive operations when your bar is no longer considered to be an "in place."

A crucial element of success is the selection of a bartender. A bartender is often responsible for the day-by-day inventory control, ensuring that the waiters and waitresses provide a high level of customer service and, in general, keeps the customers happy through a congenial attitude. It is not unusual for customers to follow a favorite bartender from bar to bar.

Above all, the bartender must be honest and efficient in mixing drinks. Most of the business is conducted in cash and tight cash controls must be maintained. A poorly mixed drink will cause customer dissatisfaction and lost business. It is also important that the proper amount of liquor is poured in each drink. An excerpt from a report on bars and discos illustrates this point. (*Entrepreneur,* July, 1980, p. 22)

> If you're selling drinks for $1.50 each, and use 1 ounce of liquor, a quart bottle could generate $48 revenue. Assuming you bought the liquor for $7, that would be a $41 gross profit. Taking off another $10 for labor and other overhead, you could clear $31—if your bar were managed right.
>
> But what if instead of pouring accurate 1-ounce shots, your bartender pours 1½ ounces? (It happens, since it's a great way to increase tips.) Your number of drinks has been cut from 32 to 21, and your gross profit has gone from $48 to $31.50. Say your bartender gives away four free drinks out of that same bottle. Now your gross is down to $25.50
>
> Liquor control puts more dollars in your pocket. Many owners order special shot glasses with the 1-ounce mark etched at ¾ or ⅞ of an ounce. Then they pour the ounce the customer ordered by going over the etched line. This looks like you're giving the customer a bargain. And if you wanted to keep the liquor at the actual ⅞-ounce serving, your profits would be even greater. A 32-ounce quart would yield 36.5 drinks, for a gross of $54.50

Another point to consider is the types of drinks that your customers order. "Well" drinks (lower priced liquor served when a customer fails to specify a brand) will be the lowest priced mixed drinks and provide the lowest gross margin; higher priced "call" drinks (the premium brands which customers order by name) will provide a higher margin. But the highest margins come from exotic mixed drinks, such as Margaritas, Bloody Marys, Harvey Wallbangers, tropical and other theme drinks. These drinks, which sell for a $.50 to $1.50 premium, may actually cost *less* to prepare than a well drink. The reason for this is that, because of the mixes, they may be prepared with less than an ounce of liquor, while still retaining full flavor. The mixes will cost a few cents per drink. Thus, using the data from Exhibit V as a guide, the following chart may be developed:

Type of drink	Size of shot	Cost of liquor	Cost of mix	Drink price	Gross margin $	Gross margin %
Well	1 ounce	$.156	- 0 -	$1.00	$.844	84.4
Call	1 ounce	.219	- 0 -	1.50	1.281	85.4
Tropical	¾ oz.	.164	.05	2.00	1.786	89.3
Tropical	1 ounce	.219	.05	2.00	1.731	86.6

If it is possible to induce the customer to "trade up" from a well drink to a tropical drink, the gross margin on sales is increased from 84.4% to 89.3% but more importantly, the dollar profit per drink is increased by (1.786 – .844) $.942.

EXHIBIT I Susie's Warehouse location analysis

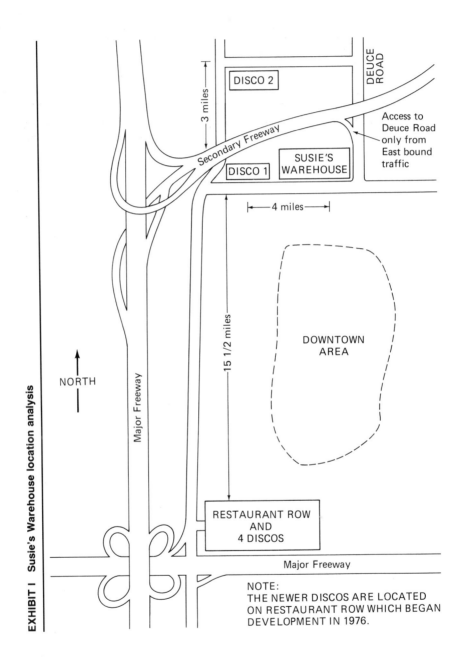

NORTH

DISCO 2

3 miles

Secondary Freeway

DEUCE ROAD

Access to
Deuce Road
only from
East bound
traffic

DISCO 1

SUSIE'S
WAREHOUSE

4 miles

15 1/2 miles

Major Freeway

DOWNTOWN
AREA

RESTAURANT ROW
AND
4 DISCOS

Major Freeway

NOTE:
THE NEWER DISCOS ARE LOCATED
ON RESTAURANT ROW WHICH BEGAN
DEVELOPMENT IN 1976.

EXHIBIT II Susie's Warehouse selected operating data

Sales in
000s of $s
Gross Profit
in % of sales

	Jul	Aug	Sep	Oct	Nov	Dec	Jan	Feb	Mar	Apr	May	Jun	Total
1976–1977													
Liquor	10	10	15	18	17	25	22	26	25	28	21	16	233
Gross Profit	79	78	71	82	77	68	89	79	81	80	81	80	79
Food	32	32	28	32	29	35	33	30	32	33	38	33	387
Gross Profit	58	54	50	55	52	51	54	54	55	57	52	58	54
1977–1978													
Liquor	16	12	11	12	13	19	7	5	9	10	10	13	137
Gross Profit	79	79	77	81	75	84	78	81	81	82	84	81	80
Food	37	40	39	43	46	45	39	37	41	40	43	42	492
Gross Profit	60	48	57	52	53	52	59	59	55	51	61	54	55
1978–1979													
Liquor	12	11	8	8	7	12	7	—	—	—	—	—	63
Gross Profit	82	79	79	81	78	78	79	—	—	—	—	—	79
Food	45	45	43	50	47	52	41	—	—	—	—	—	323
Gross Profit	54	53	53	55	59	56	56	—	—	—	—	—	55

EXHIBIT III   Susie's Warehouse
1978–1979 Operating results
First seven months

Sales:		
Food	$323,412	
Liquor	65,823	
		$389,235
Cost of Goods Sold:		
Food	$145,535	
Liquor	13,823	
		159,358
Gross Profit		$229,877
Expenses:		
Rent & Taxes	$ 28,512	
Wages	129,596	_wages too high_
Advertising	15,125	_3.8_
Utilities	18,660	
Administrative	14,829	
Repair & Maintenance	8,349	
Miscellaneous	17,804	
Total Expenses		$232,875
Net Profit (Loss)		($2,998)

EXHIBIT IV Operating expense ratios
Typical ranges for bars with annual gross
sales $150,000–$200,000

Item	Ratios as a % of sales	
Sales	100	100
Cost of Goods Sold	27	33
Wages	18	21
Entertainment	–0–	5
Utilities, Taxes, Licenses	8	9
Depreciation	2	3
Administrative	1	2
Advertising	1	2
Repairs and Maintenance	2	3
Bar Supplies	1	2
Miscellaneous	3	4
TOTAL	63	84
NET PROFIT	37	16

Source: Industry Publications.

EXHIBIT V Drink measurements and costs

Size of shot (ounces)	Number of shots			Cost per shot if 1 quart costs $5.00 (cost in $s)
	Fifth	Quart	Liter	
$3/4$	34.1	42.6	45.1	$.117
$7/8$	29.2	36.6	38.6	.137
1	25.6	32.0	33.8	.156
$1 1/4$	20.5	25.6	27.0	.195
$1 1/2$	17.1	21.3	22.5	.235
$1 3/4$	14.6	18.3	19.3	.273
2	12.8	16.0	16.9	.313

DISCUSSION

1. Define the target market that Susie's Warehouse (SW) was currently intending to serve. What other local market segments do you believe would also be worth Susie's serious considerations?

2. How is SW positioned to serve its target market, in product offered and in other attributes that would be of some importance to consumers in that market segment? How does SW compare with competitors?

3. What is your opinion of SW's positioning to attract the other market segments you have suggested?

4. Name one or more short-term objectives (implemented in three months or less) that might help to "turn around" SW for its survival? What might be some specific actions to reach that or those objectives?

5. What would be your main long-term objectives for SW, in terms of operating results (in numbers) and in terms of the firm's quality? In view of those objectives, how would you want to reposition SW in terms of its markets and of successfully serving them? After thinking about SW's resources and limitations, can you see ways to make those feasible?

7

Competition and Marketing Strategy

Competition is in many cases the most significant environmental factor influencing and shaping the firm's marketing strategies. To survive and be successful, a firm uses available competitive tools after evaluating its competitive environment. For example, Bic produces disposable products that are similar to competing products but less expensive. Therefore price is a key competitive technique used by Bic. It would be difficult for most firms to match or beat Bic's price and still make a profit. Therefore superior distribution, product quality, or manipulation of some other feature may be necessary to compete with Bic.

This chapter focuses on the impact of competition on marketing strategy and suggests strategies for coping with various competitive situations. Pure competition or anything resembling it is the bane of the marketer. One of marketing's main functions is to enhance the buyer's perception of the value that the offering or product provides. By achieving that goal, marketing takes the firm's offering out of the ruck of pure competition and puts it into a monopolistic competition or an oligopoly situation (more likely the former). The rival firms try to achieve this too, but usually only a few of the competing firms develop a winning strategy. Several firms then emerge as the profitable ones that serve the consumer well, thus achieving profitable prices and higher volume. Net profit is maximized, the consumer is satisfied, and there is social gain. Competitors that produce on a commodity basis may remain, as in the pharmaceutical industry, where private brands are often provided for consumers who prefer low price to brand-name products.

Our discussion begins with a definition of competition. We then examine the competitive environment and the evaluation of competitive relationships. Next, we analyze competitive positions and describe various competitive strategies.

COMPETITION DEFINED

Competition relates to rivalry, attempts to gain advantage in the marketplace. The term usually denotes two or more sellers and two or more buyers exchanging a product, with buyers and sellers acting independently.

Competition is an important factor in formulating marketing strategy. A firm usually has limited control over market structure: Therefore, strategies are developed to cope with the situation and surpass competitors. For example, consider the various competitive situations for selected Eastman Kodak Company products, illustrated in Table 7-1. In overall planning and strategy

TABLE 7-1 The competitive environment for selected Eastman Kodak Company products

Kodak's products	Major competition	Market position	Kodak's core strategy
Instant cameras and instant film	Polaroid Corp. and other new competitors	Kodak is a challenger to the well-established leader in a low-profit declining market	New feature to allow users to peel photo from bulky chemical backing
Photographic paper	Fuji Photo Film Co. and other foreign companies	Kodak's dominance of this market has declined from 92% to 50% market share	Maintain share of market by stressing the quality image of Kodak paper and discounting products in Japan to combat Fuji
Office copier (Ektaprint copier)	Xerox, IBM, 3M, and others	Serious inroads made on Xerox's dominance in a highly competitive market	Top end of the copier business, emphasizing quality and reliability
Disk camera	Fuji and GAF	Leader in the pocket instamatic snapshot market	New camera format using tiny disk negatives

Source: Adapted from Thomas Moore, "Embattled Kodak Enters the Electronic Age," *Fortune,* August 22, 1983, pp. 120–28.

formulation, the costs and long-range profits from penetrating new markets in disk cameras and office copiers must be weighed against sustaining and defending the company's position as a leader in the processing-paper field. Kodak had to accept the challenger's role in trying to compete with Polaroid in the instant-camera/film market and in trying to compete with Xerox in the office-copier market. These firms are entrenched, well-established leaders in their respective markets.

On the other hand, Kodak still occupies but is fighting to maintain the dominant position in the processing-paper field and the inexpensive consumer–camera/film market. Competitive forces and new technology are Kodak's major environmental inputs in strategic planning. The pressures of rivalry force Kodak to develop products that have a unique niche in the marketplace.

COMPETITIVE ENVIRONMENT

The strength of a marketing strategy depends on key ideas that give the strategist the ability to exploit the weaknesses of competition or defend itself against competitive threats. Customers, suppliers, potential entrants, and substitute products are all competitors that may be prominent, depending on the industry.[1] The state of competition in an industry depends on five basic forces, as illustrated in Figure 7-1. The collective strength of these forces ranges from intense in such industries as meat packing, air transportation, tires, steel, and fast food, where only a very few firms earn high returns on investment, to mild in such industries as oil field equipment, soft drinks, beer, and office equipment unless there is room for high returns on investment.[2] The weaker the forces outlined in Figure 7-1, the greater the opportunity for high profits.

Regardless of the state of competition in an industry, the success of any marketing strategy depends on the strength of a competitive analysis.[3] The analysis of competition focuses on an understanding of the specific competitive forces (in Figure 7-1) that act as constraints.

Evaluating Competitive Relationships

Market share, patents, trademarks, financial standing, consumer goodwill, marketing-strategy effectiveness, and most internal or external resources are all variables that are used in competitive evaluations. For example, mar-

---

[1] Michael E. Porter, "How Competitive Forces Shape Strategy," *Harvard Business Review*, March–April 1979.
[2] Ibid.
[3] Bruce D. Henderson, "The Anatomy of Competition," *Journal of Marketing*, 47 (Spring 1983), 7–11.

FIGURE 7-1. Forces governing competition in an industry.

Source: Michael E. Porter, "How Competitive Forces Shape Strategy," *Harvard Business Review*, March–April 1979.

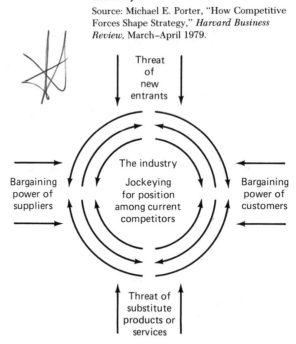

keting-strategy effectiveness in competitive struggles is illustrated by the fact that Procter & Gamble says its product is as effective as Listerine but tastes better. However, Warner-Lambert has done a very good job in promotion—actually emphasizing that Listerine doesn't taste good.

Table 7-2 illustrates an assessment of competition for an industrial product. In this example, the Northwest Lathe Company has developed a rating of itself compared with three major competitors. This rating, if objective, should permit Northwest to better understand its position relative to competition. In the planning and strategy search, Northwest should use this information to determine differential advantages as well as factors to improve. Table 7-3 illustrates an assessment of competition for a consumer packaged goods product. Note the emphasis on marketing mix considerations through brand comparisons.

Increasing market share, obtaining leadership, or achieving high rank in an industry is usually associated with competitive evaluation of a firm's success. Note that a firm's profits are determined by a combination of factors, and some firms maintain satisfactory rates of return with small market shares. For example, Jack Daniels Distillery in Lynchburg, Tennessee, has a small share of the whiskey market, but its basic product, "Sour Mash Whiskey," provides a satisfactory return on investment. The goals of the firm must determine the approach to competition and specific marketing strategy that will succeed.

TABLE 7-2 Assessment of competitors for an industrial product

Important buying factors	Northwest Lathe Co.	Competitor		
		x	*y*	*z*
Advertising/Sales promotion	Good	Good	Fair	Good
Customer service	Good	Fair	Poor	Good
Market identity	Poor	Ex.	Good	Fair
Performance against delivery promise	Good	Fair	Poor	Poor
Price	Equal	Equal	Equal	Equal
Conformance to specifications	Good	Good	Good	Ex.
Product design—Functional	Ex.	Fair	Good	Ex.
Product literature	Good	Ex.	Fair	Good
Salesperson/agent caliber	Fair	Good	Fair	Fair
Salesperson customer coverage	Fair	Ex.	Good	Fair
Salesperson product knowledge/experience	Poor	Ex.	Good	Fair
Technical assistance in product use	Good	Ex.	Good	Good
Completeness of product line	Fair	Ex.	Ex.	Ex.

Note: Classification of factors as excellent (Ex.), good, fair, or poor should be based on systematic marketing intelligence, including the perceptions of current and potential buyers.

The following situations would suggest the need for new strategy in relation to competition:

1. Market share must be increased or maintained to improve profitability.
2. The competitor's products are launched head-on against existing products.
3. The competition has advantages due to environmental considerations —i.e., new technology, government regulation, customer attitudes, etc.
4. New opportunities develop when competition becomes vulnerable—for instance, in product shortages, financial difficulties, strikes, or changes in customer attitudes.

Terms of sale, research and development, service, sales force, distribution network, and advertising are typical marketing variables that are used to develop competitive strategy. It is difficult to determine when a sudden shift in demand will restructure competition and set the stage for alteration of the existing marketing mix. Consider the plight of Canadian publisher Harlequin Enterprises Ltd.:

> Harlequin has long been the leading name in romance novels, holding about 90 percent of this female-dominated market and marketing exclusively to women. In 1980 the firm earned $26 million on sales of $265 million, much to the envy of competitors. Then Harlequin made a series of marketing blunders that changed the industry.
>
> Harlequin began diversifying into new businesses. It bought a mail-order business, a school supplies retailer, a textbook publisher, and several magazines. It

TABLE 7-3   Assessment of competitors for a consumer packaged product

For Review	Your product	Brand A	Brand B	Brand C
Marketing considerations				
Store analyses:				
Distribution levels				
Retail prices				
Shelf facings				
Inventory/sales ratio				
Promotions				
Market trends by type				
"Your" brands' trends, size, etc.				
"Recession" brands				
Media planning				
Allocation, effectiveness, spending:				
Media choice				
Media effectiveness				
Expenditures				
Geography				
Usage				
Sales management				
Sales force deployment:				
Geographic coverage				
Efficiency (time costs)				
Potential				
Time allocation:				
Customer potential				
Store work				
Time for service				
Time for problems				
Sales reports:				
Correct information				
Meaningful information				
Testing				
Existing brands:				
Marketing plans				
Line extensions				
Advertising copy, etc.				
New brands:				
Product appeal				
Marketing strategy				

Source: 1979 Nielsen Brand Marketing Analyzer, *Nielsen Researcher*, A. C. Nielsen Company, Corporate Communications, Northbrook, Ill.

also dumped its U.S. distributor of its romance novels, Simon & Schuster. Within two years the only new venture that did not have to be discarded as a miserable failure was the mail-order company. More serious, though, Simon & Schuster started its own Silhouette line of romance novels and gained a 30 percent market share by mid-1983. Perceiving this opportunity, several other publishers also jumped into the market, dramatically increasing competition.

Despite the fact that the retail market for romance novels increased by 60 percent between 1981 and 1983, Harlequin did very poorly. Harlequin, which had once had a stranglehold on the market, saw its share plummet to 45 percent, half of what it had been only twenty-four months earlier.[4]

This example illustrates the need to reevaluate competitive relationships during the strategic-planning process. Changes in the demand for products should also be anticipated, and business area definition must maintain strategic determination. Harlequin probably forced competition upon itself when it dropped its powerful distributor. The Canadian firm failed to realize that its romance novels constituted a large part of Simon & Schuster's business. Since Simon & Schuster was a large firm with many resources available (it is a subsidiary of Gulf & Western Industries), it jumped at the chance to produce romance novels on its own. Normally, the industry leader would do quite well in a fast-growing market, but this example proves that a firm's competitive strategy, and its marketing strategy, have a great deal to do with its success.

ANALYSIS OF COMPETITIVE POSITIONS

A firm's marketing strategy depends on its size and position in the market.[5] A firm with the largest market share is known as the *market leader,* while firms with a low market share are called *market nichers.* Between these two types of firms are firms that are called *market challengers* and *market followers.*

Market share can be measured in several ways. When all the competitors in a market sell a single type of product, beer for example, their share of total volume can be calculated in physical units. If the strategic business unit markets several different types of products or services and its competitors do likewise, the market share is simply the firm's dollar sales divided by the estimated total sales in its served markets.[6]

A common strategic goal of firms is to increase market share.[7] Market leaders, such as Anheuser-Busch and General Motors, try to hold on to their existing market shares. The number-two and number-three competitors, such as Ford and Miller Brewing, aggressively try to catch the leaders. In this sec-

---

[4]Peggy Berkowitz, "Harlequin's Formula Romance Books Face Stiff Battle in Newly Competitive Industry," *Wall Street Journal,* July 21, 1983, p. 22.

[5]Adapted from Philip Kotler, *Marketing Management: Analysis, Planning, and Control,* 5th ed. (Englewood Cliffs, N.J.: Prentice-Hall, 1984), pp. 273–86.

[6]Robert D. Buzzell and Frederick D. Wiersema, "Successful Sharebuilding Strategies," *Harvard Business Review,* January–February 1981, pp. 136–37.

[7]Ibid.

TABLE 7-4 Market shares for leading U.S. automakers

	%
General Motors Corp.	44.1
Ford Motor Co.	16.8
Chrysler Corp.	9.3
American Motors Corp.	2.1
Volkswagen of America, Inc.	0.9
American Honda Motor Co., Inc.	0.3
Japanese Imports	21.5
European Imports	5.0

Source: Ward's Automotive Reports, 1983 Market Share.

tion we discuss how marketing strategy depends on an analysis of competitive positions. Table 7-4 lists the relative competitive positions of U.S. automakers. Examples from this table will be used to illustrate concepts.

Market Leader

Within an industry, a single company will usually dominate its competitors and hold the largest market share. The dominant firm tends to be a leader in providing new products, distribution networks, promotional coverage, and price adjustments. The leader is recognized by competitors, suppliers, and sometimes regulators as being dominant in the industry. As Table 7-4 indicates, General Motors is the market leader in the automobile industry. The competitors' strategy may involve confronting, ignoring, or copying the leader; whereas the dominant firm attempts to maintain its leadership position. This position may be defended by increasing the size of the total market, maintaining the current market share, or expanding the current market share.

Total market size can be expanded by locating new users, such as Diet Coke did with its ad campaign, "Just for the taste of it." This implied that even someone who was not a regular diet cola consumer could enjoy Diet Coke. This approach helped Coca-Cola make Diet Coke the number-one diet soft drink in less than six months. Finding new users for a product can also increase market share. For example, Arm & Hammer has touted expanded use of baking soda, such as air freshening (in refrigerators) and as a substitute for toothpaste. Market share can also be enlarged by increasing the number of times that individuals use the product. Listerine attempted to increase market share of its mouthwash by suggesting that individuals rinse twice per day—once in the morning and again before going out at night.

Market Challenger

The firms that follow the market leader can be considered market challengers if they decide to confront the leader and others to increase market share or market followers if they maintain their current market share. These companies tend to be smaller in scale than the market leader. A market challenger can increase share by attacking its competitors directly (Pepsi vs. Coke), emphasizing areas where competitors are weak (Walmart did not take on K-Mart directly but instead sought to position its stores in smaller communities, knowing K-Mart had a stronghold on the larger cities), or taking market share from smaller competitors.

Strategies that a challenger can utilize include cutting the price, offering less-expensive and poorer-quality products, offering higher-quality products, enlarging the product line, improving the product, reducing the cost, expanding the promotion, increasing the services, and improving the distribution.

To succeed, a challenger must usually develop more than one strategy. A complete strategy formulated successively will generally be more successful than relying on a single strategy element. Ford Motor Company has confronted General Motors by emphasizing product quality, design, economy, and value.

Market Follower

While some companies following the market leader attempt to increase market share, not all choose this strategy. Some companies may feel that there is more to be lost than gained by attacking competitors who are stronger and will last longer in battle. Unless new-product developments or distribution breakthroughs occur, a follower strategy may be adopted. The market follower must maintain current customers and capture its share of new ones. Costs must be kept low while product quality is high. Market followers may be as profitable as or more profitable than the leaders. Chrysler Corporation has been forced into more of a follower role instead of acting as a direct challenger to the much larger and financially superior General Motors. But Chrysler ranks higher than General Motors in the area of innovativeness.

In industries with minimal product differentiation, similar service provision, and high-price consciousness, the price battles may occur at any time. Therefore a longer-term perspective is often taken, and short-term customer grabbing through price drops is ignored. These companies choose instead to parallel the leader in price and service offerings, which tends to stabilize market share over time.

Market Nicher

Niche strategies are now being used in a broad cross section of industries. Evidently market niching is increasingly becoming the primary strategy of many successful firms.[8] Niching is a promising option for companies that are

---

[8]David W. Cravens, "Strategic Marketing's New Challenge," *Business Horizons*, March–April 1983, p. 20; and "Marketing: The New Priority," *Business Week*, November 21, 1983, p. 96.

not market leaders. Serving a niche or segment of a product market is a feasible way for many smaller firms to gain and hold market share. The ultimate market niche is large enough in size and purchasing power to provide acceptable profits, show potential in terms of expansion, and be ignored by market leaders and significant competitors. Unique efficiency and effectiveness exist to service the market niche, and goodwill developed with customers allows defense of that position against major competitors. The goal is to cater to a specific market's needs to the best of the firm's abilities. American Motors' emphasis on four-wheel drive in its Jeep and AMC Eagle product lines illustrates this point. American Motors is emphasizing the advantages of a unique two-wheel/four-wheel drive system to develop a unique niche in the automobile market.

The firm may choose to serve one category of customer, develop expertise in vertical integration, cater to a specific volume of purchase (i.e., small, medium, or large), sell to a large commercial account, specialize in a given geographic region, maintain a single product line, develop a made-to-order business, offer only extremely high or low priced products, or provide services superior to those of competitors. Consider how an enterprising entrepreneur has found a niche for his product in the competitive and heavily promoted toothpaste market:

> Jerome Milton Schulman is the president and sole employee of Jerome Milton, Inc. Schulman, a 70-year-old chemist, has been successful in marketing Shane toothpaste, which he developed to help bleeding gums and sensitive teeth. He originally blended the toothpaste to combat his own problems with canker sores and fever blisters, but he also gave some to friends with similar dental problems. The toothpaste got such good reviews from his friends that Schulman hired a company to manufacture 200,000 tubes of his toothpaste.
>
> Schulman then took his toothpaste and several testimonial letters from his "customers" to Chicago wholesalers and retailers. At first skeptical, the merchants soon agreed to sell his product after Schulman began advertising Shane and promised to buy back any unsold tubes. Seven hundred Chicago stores decided to carry Shane and collectively ordered over 150,000 tubes. In 1983, soon after Shane was well entrenched in Chicago, Schulman gathered up his samples and his testimonial letters and developed plans to have Shane introduced in eleven eastern cities.[9]

Successful low-market-share firms invariably have some common characteristics. They compete only in areas where their particular strengths are most highly valued. They make efficient use of their limited R&D budgets. They specialize rather than diversify and emphasize profits rather than sales growth or market share.[10]

---

[9]Bill Abrams, "A New Toothpaste Takes Off, Promoted by Single Employee," *Wall Street Journal,* May 26, 1983, p. 29.

[10]R. G. Hamermesh, M. J. Anderson, Jr., and J. E. Harris, "Strategies for Low Market Share Businesses," *Harvard Business Review,* May–June 1978, pp. 95, 100.

COMPETITIVE STRATEGIES

Many firms compete by recognizing a few strategic factors important to success. For example, concentrating their resources on a small segment of the market, Fisher-Price competes by providing wooden toys for the preschool child. This market comprises 10 percent of the toy market, and Fisher-Price has distinguished its line from competing products.

Although the success formula may be difficult to determine, strategic planning should consider such factors in finding some way to develop a competitive advantage. For example, branding and packaging are popular techniques for distinguishing consumer products that are too homogeneous to differentiate physically. Therefore, sellers of milk, sugar, and eggs emphasize brand names and unique packaging.

> 7-Up has been innovative in promotion to survive in the face of heavy competition from Coke and Pepsi. It has concentrated on the lemon-lime market, offering its beverage as an alternative to colas. When many soft-drink manufacturers ventured into new markets, 7-Up began distributing its cola, "Like," and has fought hard to improve the market share of its flagship brand. The company has further differentiated 7-Up with a $60 million advertising blitz, telling consumers that its drink is caffeine free and has no artificial colors or artificial flavors, which most other soft drinks have. The company hopes that such a campaign will swing some of the health-conscious soft-drink market over to its brand.[11]

Based on its resources and the competitive situation, 7-Up has positioned itself as the quality lemon-lime product. Firms must take offensive or defensive action to create a defendable position in an industry. "Firms have discovered many different approaches to this end, and the best strategy for a given firm is ultimately a unique construction reflecting its particular circumstances."[12] Outlined below are strategies relating to (1) overall cost leadership, (2) differentiation, (3) market segmentation, and (4) positioning.[13]

Overall Cost Leadership Strategy

The overall cost leadership strategy can be achieved by aggressive construction of efficient-scale facilities, vigorous pursuit of cost reduction from experience, tight cost and overhead control, avoidance of marginal customer accounts, and cost minimization in such areas as research and development, product, promotion, distribution, and pricing. While quality and service cannot be ignored, low cost relative to competition is the core strategy. R. J.

---

[11]Richard Morgan, "Critics Charge Seven-Up with 'Scare Tactics,' " *Adweek*, May 30, 1983, p. 16.

[12]Michael E. Porter, *Competitive Strategy* (New York: Free Press, 1980), p. 37.

[13]Adapted from Porter, *Competitive Strategy*, pp. 35–46.

Reynolds, Whirlpool, Goodyear, and Inland Steel have all achieved a low-cost position. Caterpillar has also achieved a low-cost position and significant differentiation.

> It has been said by a consumer electronics expert during a period when the U.S. was experiencing spiraling inflation, "Electronics is the only product group in existence that has undergone reverse inflation." As competition increased, both at the manufacturing and retail levels, and technological advances came along, prices of home electronics products have fallen.
>
> For instance, in 1977 a Technics cassette deck sold for about $350. The deck required its owner to manually push a button to rewind the tape, and recording levels were metered by a now outdated needle. The matching 50-watt receiver cost $500. By 1981 a comparable Technics complete with advanced soft-touch controls, fluorescent metering lights, and dbx noise eliminator still sold for about $350 even though prices on nearly every other consumer good in the country had risen greatly. The receiver, complete with a much more accurate tuning mechanism, also sold for $350.
>
> Technics was able to offer such advanced products because technological advances had helped it cut costs on the manufacturing end, and these same advances were viewed as a premium by the market, thus allowing increased production and providing further economies of scale.[14]

Understanding how costs fall or units produced rise is important in developing overall cost leadership. A low-cost position requires high market share, favorable access to raw materials, or other similar advantages. To achieve a low-cost position capital expenditures, aggressive pricing, and early losses to build market share may be required.

Differentiation Strategy

Creating something that is perceived industrywide as being unique can take many forms. Approaches to differentiating can include unique features, distribution, innovation, or other dimensions.

> There is an old saying which says, "If you build a better mousetrap the world will beat a path to your door." Well, occasionally bigger is synonymous with better as is the case with Prince Manufacturing Inc.'s larger tennis racket design.
>
> Prince developed the big racket in the mid-1970's, but it was slow to catch on despite claiming to provide more powerful shots and a "sweet spot" three and one half times larger than a conventional racket. Pros shunned the new racket (only three players used the Prince rackets in the 1978 U.S. Open) but by 1982 many top players were using big rackets.
>
> The larger racket is considered to come under the "high-priced racket" category in which sales had been slipping until Prince revolutionized the industry. Prince, which is the only large racket with a patent on its design, owns between 30 and 40% of the market. AMF Head is second with about a 22% market share (AMF Head was able to increase its share by 8 points in one year after introducing its

---

[14]Laura Landro, "Technology, Competition Cut Prices of Electronics Gear as Quality Rises," *Wall Street Journal*, December 1, 1981, p. 25.

own larger racket in the Spring of 1982). Other sporting goods manufacturers like Wilson and Dunlop have also gotten into the big racket business, but probably too late to wrestle much of the market away from Prince.[15]

Differentiation provides insulation against competitive rivalry because of brand loyalty and less concern about price. The customer loyalty and need for a competitor to overcome uniqueness provide entry barriers. Interestingly, achieving differentiation may sometimes preclude gaining a high market share due to the perception of exclusivity, which is incompatible with high market share.

Market Segmentation Strategy

Market segmentation strategy rests on the premise that the firm is better off serving a narrow segment of customers than it would be by competing more broadly. All the factors discussed in Chapter 6 on market segmentation are appropriate here. The market segmentation strategy achieves low cost or differentiation or both in its narrow target market. The segment of the market served could relate to buyer groups, geographic areas, product lines, or any other significant way to segment markets (see Chapter 6).

Many markets today can be characterized as hypersegmented, consisting of increasingly smaller market segments that have been identified and targeted. The late 1970s and the early 1980s have brought about soaring costs of production and some changes in the lifestyles, values, and attitudes of many consumers. In return for a lower price, some individuals are becoming increasingly willing to buy a product or service that is not as precisely tailored to their desires as it would have been in an era of stable prices and plenty. For many marketers, this trend offers the opportunity for a new strategy called countersegmentation.[16] Countersegmentation is an aggregation or clustering of market segments instead of segregating them. This can be achieved by pruning back on existing product lines and thus eliminating market segments, or by fusing market segments—that is, by attracting consumers from existing segments to fewer and larger segments. The choice of approach depends on the firm's current market position and its resource base.

The first approach should be reserved for large companies with broad product lines that appeal to various market segments with numerous product sizes and brands. The market share can thus remain intact, although fewer product variations are offered. Small and unprofitable segments can be dropped. Food manufacturers like Campbell Soup, Heinz, General Mills, and Del Monte are offering fewer product variations and products with longer shelf lives. The fusion approach is suitable for both small and large producers. It can mean offering a no-frills, standardized product and capitalizing on con-

---

[15]Claudia Ricci, "Oversize Tennis Rackets Gain, Stirring Rivalry among Firms," *Wall Street Journal*, June 2, 1983, p. 27.
[16]Alan J. Resnik, Peter B. B. Turney, and J. Barry Mason, "Marketers Turn to Countersegmentation," *Harvard Business Review*, September–October 1979, pp. 100, 103.

FIGURE 7-2. Three competitive strategies

Source: Adapted from Michael E. Porter, *Competitive Strategy* (New York: Free Press, 1980), p. 39.

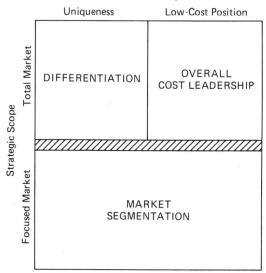

sumer willingness to trade reduced satisfaction for lower prices. Japanese automakers have fewer models and styles from which the potential buyer can select as compared with their U.S. competitors. The Japanese automakers tend to make optional equipment as standard and thereby reduce production cost, resulting in more value to the consumer. Although countersegmentation exists, most firms view the mass market as splintered. They are therefore targeting their products for specific segments.

The position of differentiation, overall cost leadership, and market segmentation is depicted in Figure 7-2. The strategies differ in dimension other than the functional difference. Efforts for implementing them involve different skill and resource requirements as well as organizational requirements. Table 7-5 summarizes observations about these requirements.

Positioning Strategy

Positioning strategy consists of an integrated combination of product or service, distribution, price, and promotion strategies. It establishes how a product or brand is intended to be perceived by the target market relative to competitors' offerings.[17]

---

[17]David W. Cravens, "Strategic Marketing's New Challenge," *Business Horizons*, March–April 1983, p. 21.

TABLE 7-5 Requirements of the three competitive strategies

Strategy	Task and resource requirements	Organizational requirements
Overall Cost Leadership	Access to capital Engineering expertise Control of labor Ease of manufacture Efficient distribution	Cost control Control reports Incentives based on meeting objectives
Differentiation	Marketing Engineering Creativity Technology	Coordination of R&D and marketing Measurement and evaluation Personnel
Market Segmentation	Concentrating on a particular target market through a combination of the above requirements	A combination of the above requirements

Source: Adapted from Porter, *Competitive Strategy,* pp. 40–41.

⟶ In competitive positioning, the firm attempts to determine the difference between competing products and determine an ideal marketing mix to exploit differences. Efforts to position or reposition a product should be part of the current-assessment and future-assessment stages of strategic planning. Several elements of strategic positioning should be considered:

1. Developing a competitive position means recognizing the element of limitation. It sets parameters around creating a marketing mix for a specific target market.
2. The position determines the correct competitive milieu—that we have correctly defined the product category in terms of those products that consumers feel are close substitutes for each other.
3. A position policy determines relationships with customers. Do we want to bring in new users to the product category, to increase existing customers' frequency of use, or to attract specified users of competitive brands?[18]

The pressure of rival companies creates the need for competitive positioning to maintain and increase market share. Competitive positioning requires a systematic analysis of competitors.

In most positioning strategies, an explicit or implicit frame of reference is the competition. In other words, as well-established competitor's image can be

---

[18]Alvin A. Achenbaum, "Who Says You Need Research to Position a Brand?" *Journal of Advertising,* 3 (July 1974), 21–24.

exploited to help communicate another image referenced to it. Second, by doing so, customers are made to believe that the firm using this strategy is better than or as good as a named competitor. Avis used the campaign "We're number two, so we try harder," to position itself as a major car rental agency along with Hertz and away from National, which was a close third to Avis. Positioning explicitly with respect to a competitor can be an excellent way to create a position with respect to an attribute, especially price/quality. Products that are difficult to evaluate, such as liquor products, are often compared with those of an established competitor to help the positioning task. The selection of a positioning strategy involves identifying competitors, relevant attributes, competitor positions, and market segments. Research-based approaches can help in identifying the above. The positioning decision is often the crucial strategic decision for a company or brand because the position can be central to customers' perception and choice decisions.[19]

These strategies are alternative or viable approaches for dealing with the competition. A firm that does not have a competitive strategy usually becomes ineffective and almost always has low earnings on investment.

> In the mid-1970s U-Haul International, Inc., abandoned a thirty-year strategy of relying on commissioned dealerships (mainly service stations). It began to focus on a company-owned chain of moving centers that offered truck and trailer rentals as well as other services. U-Haul's commissioned dealership networks dropped from a peak of 14,000 in 1974 to 5,600 in 1981.[20] Jartran Inc., founded by James A. Ryder in 1978, decided to aim its distribution strategy at the service stations U-Haul had abandoned. The result of all this was that Jartran's sales increased rapidly. U-Haul has now reversed its marketing strategy and is attempting to regain its service stations and other independent dealers.

SUMMARY

Competition refers to two or more sellers and two or more buyers exchanging a product, with buyers and sellers acting independently. Competition is influenced by five basic forces: threat of new entrants, bargaining power of customers, threat of substitute products or services, bargaining power of suppliers, and the industry (struggle for position among competitors).

Competitive evaluation of a firm's success can involve assessing market share, leadership, or rank within an industry. To develop a competitive strategy, marketing variables such as terms of sale, products, service, sales force, distribution network, and advertising are manipulated. To maintain success, competitive position must be reevaluated during the strategic-planning process.

Marketing strategy depends on a firm's size and position in the market. Market leaders have the largest market share and usually dominate their competitors. The dominant firm tends to be a leader in providing new products,

---

[19]David A. Aaker and J. Gary Shansby, "Positioning Your Product," *Business Horizons,* May–June 1982, pp. 56, 58, 62.

[20]"U-Haul: A Strategy Reversal Moves It Back to Gas Stations," *Business Week,* May 4, 1981, pp. 162–64.

distribution networks, promotional coverage, and price adjustments. Competitors may react by confronting, ignoring, or copying the leader. Market challengers confront the market leader and others to increase market share. Market share can be increased by attacking competitors directly, emphasizing areas where competitors are weak, or taking market share from smaller competitors. Market followers do not attack competitors and are content to maintain current customers and capture their share of the new ones. Market nichers service a niche or segment of a product market and are not considered market leaders. Unique efficiency and effectiveness exist to service the market niche that is ignored by market leaders and significant competitors.

Four competitive strategies were presented in the chapter. The first, overall cost leadership, involves construction of efficient-scale facilities, cost reduction tactics, overhead control, avoidance of marginal customer accounts, and cost minimization in all areas of operation in general. Second is differentiation, which deals with creating something perceived as unique in terms of features, distribution, innovation, and so forth. Third is market segmentation, which presumes that a firm is benefited by serving a narrow segment of customers rather than competing more broadly. Fourth is positioning, which consists of an integrated combination of product or service, distribution, price, and promotion strategies. A firm must recognize its limitations and target a specific market, develop substitute products or services, and determine whether it wishes to bring in new users, increase frequency of use, or attract customers of competitive brands. A firm lacking a competitive strategy generally becomes ineffective and receives a low return on investment.

REVIEW QUESTIONS

1. *What specific forces govern competition in an industry and how do they influence a firm's marketing strategy?*
2. *How do firms assess their competitive position?*
3. *How do size and position in the market influence a firm's marketing strategy?*
4. *Distinguish between market segmentation and countersegmentation, giving examples of each.*
5. *Is it possible for a firm's offering to position itself? Justify your answer.*
6. *Under what circumstances may it be impossible to break up a market into niches? What are the dangers of using an incorrect niche formation strategy?*
7. *Is it possible for competition to arise from a totally different industry? Give an example. How can firms prepare for this?*
8. *Suggest an approach that can be used by a local family restaurant to determine the business's strengths over its competitors.*
9. *Discuss the importance of finding a competitive advantage.*

Colgate–Palmolive Company

NEW YORK—After much hard work, Keith Crane, the chairman of Colgate–Palmolive Co., and his household-products lieutenants have restored the company to just about where it was 10 years ago.

Regression may seem a peculiar goal. However, Mr. Crane took over in 1979 a company hobbled by misfit acquisitions and sparse top management. His predecessor, David Foster, had tried, unsuccessfully, to propel Colgate out from under the shadow of the industry's giant, Procter & Gamble, through additions such as sports, food and apparel companies.

In that shopping spree, Colgate managed to buy a lot of trouble. It was turned into a company sapping the profits of its traditional lines to acquire other businesses already past their peak profitability. Moreover, Mr. Foster, a flamboyant man renowned for his dictatorial style, was unable—by his own admission—to delegate authority. A further complication was rumors about his personal problems.

. . . . .

"For the past five years, it has not been much fun to own Colgate stock, follow the company or work there," says Daniel J. Meade, a securities analyst at First Boston Corp. "After half a decade of milking the heart of its business—by cutting back advertising, underfunding research and limiting new-product moves—Colgate decided to support its operations and run its business for the long term."

SEARING RETRENCHMENT

Mr. Crane imposed a searing retrenchment. He severed most of Mr. Foster's $935 million of acquisitions—at a cost of at least $96.5 million in reported write-offs. The 60-year-old Mr. Crane terms the divestitures the first steps toward his goal of a minimum 14% return on capital, compared with 10.6% last year and 7.5% in 1979. He also reorganized management, revised advertising budgets and moved to strengthen basic product lines with a new emphasis on production and profitability.

The benefits of these maneuvers haven't been immediately apparent, partly because the company's results in the first nine months of this year were hurt by foreign-currency translations. Nine-month net income declined 4.9% to $131.9 million even though the year-earlier earnings had been reduced by a $16.1 million loss on discontinued operations. Sales rose only 3.1%. In all 1980, earnings from continuing operations edged up about 5% to $196.3 million, or $2.40 a share, on a 14% gain in volume to $5.13 billion.

Mr. Crane still faces the same business problems that confronted Mr. Foster when the latter took charge of Colgate in 1971: the brutal competition in the soap, detergent and toothpaste markets and Procter & Gamble's dominant position. He also can fall back on the same strength: Colgate's ability to ferry its products through well-entrenched marketing channels in some 54 countries.

Reprinted from *Wall Street Journal*, November 23, 1981, pp. 1, 8.

Beyond clinging to that advantage, Mr. Foster had taken a quite different approach.

. . . . .

Mr. Foster had emphasized marketing rather than developing new products. His strategy was to try to outflank P & G with noncompetitive products that could be dressed up with jazzy advertising. So he began an ambitious diversification plan to move Colgate out of its traditional household and personal-care products.

EARLIER OPTIMISM

"One of the most exciting and productive aspects of our company's new direction," he told shareholders in the 1972 annual report, "is the increasing emphasis on developing new product categories distinct from our traditional product lines, in which market growth is generally limited to the growth of the population."

But Mr. Foster's strategy backfired. After he acquired sports companies, sales of golf and tennis equipment hit a plateau. Riviana, an acquisition known for Carolina rice, was hurt by a decline in rice prices. Lums restaurants and Pangburn candy suffered widening losses. And the biggest blot on Mr. Foster's portfolio was Helena Rubenstein, the cosmetics company, which quickly fell into red ink.

"They were all vanity acquisitions," says an advertising executive who handled Colgate accounts during the Foster years. "After Kendall (a medical-supplies company) and Riviana, the rest was junkola."

Moreover, Colgate's efforts to introduce new products generally foundered during the Foster regime. Frequently, the company took a short cut in rolling out new merchandise: it acted as a mere distributor rather than developing its own products. For example, it sold Alpen, one of the first "natural" breakfast cereals, for Weetabix Co. of Britain. In its first year, 1973, the product's American sales reached about $17 million—a 1% market share, which was considered remarkable in the industry. But as competitors entered the natural-cereals field, Colgate fled rather than spend money on marketing, says Jack Salzman, an analyst at Smith Barney, Harris Upham & Co.

Also introduced in 1973 was Pritt Glue-Stick, which Colgate sold under the license from Henkel Co. of West Germany. This product also was dropped after a few years.

In other cases, Colgate's marketing magic failed to stir consumer interest. For example, a detergent laced with blue dye colored all the laundry in test marketing. And a dishwashing detergent packaged in waxy cartons similar to those used for orange juice was rejected by test-market mothers in Buffalo; they feared a hazard to children, who might think that the containers held juice.

"These are mistakes that P & G would never make," a former consultant to Colgate says. "You learn in this market to make simple and functional products. Colgate went for additives."

SOME SUCCESSES

The company has scored some successes, of course, Irish Spring soap, introduced in 1972, was one in the Foster years. Fresh Start, a powdered laundry detergent, was Mr. Foster's last project, although it went into national distribution in April 1980, after Mr. Crane had taken over. The detergent, cleverly packaged in a clear plastic bottle, has been a boffo success, with sales in the final seven months of last year topping $70 million. The product commands a 5% market share and could pull in sales of more than $100 million this year, says Hercules Segalas, an analyst at Drexel Burnham Lambert Inc.

But not everyone is impressed. "Fresh Start is another example of Colgate's effort to keep up a bold front that something's happening," a Colgate consultant says. "Colgate has yet to rectify its 'me-too products' syndrome. I can't think of a single technological innovation from that company domestically."

In swinging Colgate back to its basic businesses—toothpaste and soap—Mr. Crane is reaching back into its history. Founded in 1802 as a soap and candle maker, Colgate began making toothpaste, which initially was sold in jars, in 1877. In 1928, the company merged into Palmolive-Peet Co., whose Palmolive soap was then the world's top-selling brand.

ADVERTISING PRIORITIES

One way observers gauge Mr. Crane's new emphasis on the company's basic businesses is through his advertising priorities. He has publicly proclaimed a reduction, "where appropriate," in the number of brands that Colgate will support with advertising.

While some marginal products were stripped of media budgets altogether this year, Fresh Start and toothpastes were among the few designated for heavy outlays. In the first half, Fresh Start marketers spent $13 million, compared with about $11.8 million all last year, according to Leading National Advertisers Inc., which tracks ad spending.

Colgate is polishing its toothpaste image with about $17.9 million in television and magazine promotions for Colgate Dental Cream and $3.9 million for Ultra Brite this year. Observers say the company can't afford to let its market share drop further than its current 24%, which compares with a 1977 share of 26.5%. P & G, with its Crest and Gleem brands, accounts for 40% of the $675 million annual market.

CHANGE IN STRATEGY

Both companies recently launched gel-type toothpastes to stalk some of the market controlled by Beech-Nut's Aqua-Fresh and Lever Brothers' Close-Up. Ad expenditures are expected to be revved up for the contest. "Crane believes this product should've been out there five years ago," an outside marketing consultant says. "He said we have to be first. We're on a bomber run."

The underlying change in strategy is noted by John Czepiel, a professor of marketing at New York University. "Colgate always poured more money into coupons, trade dealing and other short-term promotions rather than basic consumer advertising designed to build consumer franchise," he says. "Now they're trying to support brands to maintain a share of the consumer's mind."

Such long-range strategy contrasts sharply with the policies of Mr. Foster, who had a reputation for restraining outlays on marketing to puff up short-term earnings. An example of the Foster approach involves Mersene, a denture cleaner introduced three years ago to compete with Warner-Lambert's Efferdent. "Foster jammed Mersene into national markets without checking out repeat purchase of the product on a test basis," says an advertising executive involved at the time. That way, the executive adds, Mr. Foster could book orders without much spending on marketing and thus could bolster quarterly earnings. Mersene retains a small share of the market, with no advertising since the 1980 third quarter.

Colgate watchers say Mr. Crane already shows signs of fulfilling his promise to improve product innovation. Last year, he increased research spending 15% to $46.3 million. "Colgate has significantly underspent over the past 10 years on R & D," Mr. Segalas of Drexel Burnham says. "The company's efforts have been stop and go."

Although as a percentage of sales, research remains a meager 0.9%, the same since 1975, Mr. Salzman of Smith Barney says, "At least they're being more aggressive in absolute numbers. But," he adds, "compared with P & G, which spends six times as much, Colgate isn't funded to have an even shot at making major technological breakthroughs."

1. Identify the marketing strategies—both good and bad—that are mentioned for Colgate-Palmolive Company.
2. Compare the strategies of Mr. Foster and Mr. Crane. How does the company's situation render one man's strategies more appropriate or effective?
3. Did Colgate-Palmolive copy the strategies of Procter & Gamble, the industry leader? Should it have?
4. The writer of the Colgate-Palmolive article said at one point, "Mr. Foster had emphasized marketing rather than developing new products." Would you either (a) disagree with the writer or (b) disagree with the limited definition placed on "marketing"?

CASE 7-2

Abbott Laboratories

In 1967 Abbott Laboratories was 79 years old, and the small firm that began as the Abbott Alkaloidal Company had grown to be one of the ten largest in the pharmaceutical and medical supplies industry. Its sales were now $303 million, on which it earned net profits of 9.3 percent. Abbott's main product lines were in prescription pharmaceuticals, intravenous solutions, infant nutrition, vitamins, and sugar substitutes. Further growth potentials appeared to lie in the fast-growing consumer cosmetics business.

A step in that direction, then under way, was acquisition of the Murine Company, with its famous brand of eyewashes. Another way could be converting one of its prescription drugs into an over-the-counter (OTC) product.

Abbott selected for this strategy a product that it had introduced about 15 years earlier, named Selsun. This was a $2\frac{1}{2}$ percent selenium sulfide formulation that was widely prescribed by physicians for treating serious dandruff and other scalp disorders. Selsun had steady demand, but marketers foresaw a much larger volume, if it could be sold as a consumer OTC good. A 1 percent formulation was created that was determined by the Food and Drug Administration (FDA), after Abbott had tested it, to be acceptable in 1970.

PRODUCT'S BACKGROUND

The new product was a 1 percent selenium sulfide solution, colored blue to make it distinct. The logical name for it was Selsun Blue. The president of Abbott's consumer product division, Harry Upton, later said this about it:

> The product was designed as an OTC product, but . . . with some elegance in terms of other qualities as a shampoo. The original $2\frac{1}{2}$% was designed as a doctor's therapeutic product, and

there wasn't a lot of thought given to hair care benefits. They didn't try to find the best combination of detergents or whatever other things went into a shampoo to make it an elegant product. With Selsun Blue a lot of thought was given to these characteristics . . . to satisfy as much as possible the cosmetic benefits that were needed along with the anti-dandruff benefits.[1]

The new product's market entry was soon implemented, and its distribution was national late in 1970.

Selsun Blue was planned to enter the anti-dandruff category of the shampoo business. An estimated half of the U.S. population has dandruff problems, and a growing awareness was prompting usage of dandruff products. In that category, Selsun Blue would face stiffest competition from Tegrin and from Head & Shoulders, a Procter & Gamble product that was the best-seller of all shampoos. Its competitive strategy was essentially that of emphasizing it superior dandruff control.

Abbott had established a strong anti-dandruff image for Selsun, and so it was decided to position the new brand on the therapeutic side of Head & Shoulders. As Upton also was quoted:

Selsun Blue was specifically targeted as a consumer-marketed, television-advertised product, but it was targeted at a segment of the audience that wanted a more effective dandruff product. We recognized that this would be a smaller portion of the market than Head & Shoulders had, but where were you going to attack them—on the cosmetic side? No. Head & Shoulders had already preempted that position. That was what indicated a more therapeutic positioning for our Selsun Blue in the first place. The story was definitely based as an appeal to people who had a dandruff problem.[2]

The new product's television advertisements received full-scale test marketing from October, 1972 through April, 1973, in one midwest and one west coast region. This exposed 20 percent of the country to that advertising, and sales quickly rose to a satisfactory level. Soon Selsun Blue passed its original goal of 2 percent of the total shampoo market. During its first ten months sales passed $10 million, and a 12 percent share of the anti-dandruff category was gained in 1974, when it became the second-largest anti-dandruff brand. In 1976 it reached 18 percent share of that category market. This was gratifying although far below Head & Shoulders' more than 50 percent share of that market.

POSITIONING STRATEGY

Abbott is said to have aimed Selsun Blue at an 18–49 year age range. Its commercials had little glamour and were straightforward. The one featured in the 1975–76 dandruff season (January–April) showed an older authoritative man who gave the following message:

Audio: VOICE OVER: Do you have persistent dandruff itching? Flaking? These are the leading anti-dandruff shampoos. Yet only . . .
Visual: Fatherly figure closer up. Message at his upper right: "Contains The Anti-Dandruff Ingredient Most Widely Prescribed by Doctors."
Audio: . . . one contains the anti-dandruff ingredient most widely prescribed by doctors. Selsun Blue. Yes, only . . .
Visual: Father figure still closer up.

---

[1]Harry Upton as quoted in Arthur H. Rotstein, "Selsun Blue: How a Prescription Product Made It as a Consumer Product," *Product Marketing,* March 1977, pp. 37–41.
[2]Rotstein, "Selsun Blue," p. 153.

Audio: . . . Selsun Blue contains the anti-dandruff ingredient most widely prescribed by doctors. Maybe that's why . . .

Visual: Zoom in on Selsun Blue bottle and box.

Audio: . . . Selsun Blue is one of America's fastest growing shampoos. Do you have dandruff? Selsun Blue . . . helps to really control dandruff with regular use.[3]

About this time, Abbott decided to shift its emphasis to position the brand so as to win over more of the under-35 years market segment. As Upton also said, "We are light as a product line among younger people, and the greater degree to which we can extend our appeal to a more youth-oriented user, the greater we'll be able to expand our market share."[4] The next campaign's commercial featured an attractive young woman with beautiful hair as the spokesperson, although the modified commercial's emphasis was on the brand's dandruff-fighting properties, plus cosmetic benefits.

LATER POSITIONING

After a slight rise in market share going into 1977, Selsun Blue began to be impacted with greater competition. Part came from Helene Curtis' new Suave shampoo, whose strategy was price-oriented: a double refund offer and a lower price. This made a sizable dent in the market—especially, it was said into Head & Shoulders, which lost 4 or 5 share points in the anti-dandruff category.[5]

During this period, Selsun Blue's share of the anti-dandruff category rose to nearly 20 percent and then slid to around 15 percent in 1980. One reason may have been that the shampoo business' dormancy in new products ended and a number of new brands entered. Abbott is said also to have felt there were deficiencies in the brand's promotional program. They changed advertising agencies, and promotion then was aimed at *proven clinical* effectiveness. For 1981, the main objective was to maximize market share and to reach it by emphasizing product effectiveness, aiming at Head & Shoulders. The new copy for that year would be:

There's good,
There's better,
There's blue,
and then there's SELSUN BLUE.
Best dandruff shampoo money can buy.
Compare dandruff shampoos.
Clinical tests have proved SELSUN BLUE has the most complete dandruff control.

SELSUN BLUE contains the anti-dandruff ingredient that doctors prescribe the most.
Remember:

There's good,
There's better,
There's blue.
SELSUN BLUE
SELSUN BLUE works the best.[6]

---

[3]Copyright by Abbott Laboratories, Inc. Used by permission.

[4]Rotstein, "Selsun Blue," p. 40.

[5]Nancy F. Millman, "Dandruff Shampoo Area Picks Up," *Advertising Age,* February 6, 1978, p. 8.

[6]Copyright by Abbott Laboratories Inc Used by permission.

COMPETITIVE AND MARKET SITUATION

Overall Abbott Laboratories was a strong performer as it went into 1981. Its annual sales growth over a five-year period had been 21 percent, the second highest in the prosperous pharmaceutical and health supplies industry. Its net profit rate, as return on equity, ranked fifth among the 42 largest firms in that industry. Abbott's sales volume lay mainly in two divisions: 50 percent in its professional and nutritional division and 41 percent in its hospital and laboratory division. The consumer division, in which Selsun Blue was located, was one of three relatively small divisions that together produced 9 percent of sales. Its notable products were the Murine line, Selsun Blue, and a promising new product to treat hemorrhoids that was an Abbott exclusive.

The growth of the shampoo business, in total, was superior to consumer products generally. Its dollar volume rose by 55 percent from 1977 to 1980, about 15 percent faster than its prices. During this period a rash of new products appeared, although Head & Shoulders kept leadership, with a bit over 10 percent market share of the total shampoo industry (equal to 55 percent of its anti-dandruff segment). Second in sales rank was Revlon's Flex with almost a 10 percent share.

S. C. Johnson, the leading company in wax and polish household products, had expanded into hair care products. Hair conditioners were coming into vogue, and Johnson first established its new Agree brand of conditioner. Then it followed with Agree shampoo, which was introduced with record high marketing investment (for that industry). Its promotional theme was "Stop the Greasies"—a cosmetic appeal. Then in 1980 a new record was over $10 million spent by Procter & Gamble to launch its new Pert shampoo, featured for "bouncin' and behavin' hair."

The most striking innovation also came in 1980 when Gillette launched its Silkience brand. It was presented as "scientifically formulated to clean the hair's roots without damaging or drying the ends." Its companion hair conditioner was claimed to differentiate between hair that needs conditioning and that which does not. It was evident that "science" was entering the shampoo industry. Retailers were said to have pointed out that, in this competitive onslaught, the brands that were holding their own were advertising heavily or were promotionally priced. (Gillette too had invested over $10 million in the introduction of Silkience.) Also stronger sales were seen through beauty salons.[7]

During this period, Abbott made some modifications in Selsun Blue. One was proliferating with three types so that different needs might be served: (1) regular, the original formulation, (2) for dry hair, and (3) for oily hair. A more pleasant scent was added too. The brand continued in the same style of white plastic bottle and the same label.

When considering in 1981 its strategic program for Selsun Blue, Abbott marketers would have recognized these factors:

- Consumers' concern with personal grooming was rising.
- The total shampoo market was growing fast relative to total consumer demand.
- Its sales in 1981 likely would surpass $1.2 billion.

These factors might have had particular bearing on the objectives for Selsun Blue and on the level of financing its marketing expense. In the marketing area, a key decision would be whether to continue hammering on the brand's anti-dandruff properties or whether some other positioning should be sought in consumers' images. Related to this was the choice of target markets in future strategy. There might also be effective options among the following dimensions:

New labels or packaging
New varieties

---

[7]Pat Sloan, "Shampoo Market Is in Lather," *Advertising Age,* October 10, 1980, p. 52.

A different brand name
Entering the baby shampoo segment
Basic reformulation of the product
Employ a very famous spokeswoman (e.g., a model or star actress)

Selsun Blue offered a history of effective marketing and was yielding good profits for Abbott Laboratories. Could its future be a rosy one too?

DISCUSSION

1. In the marketing planning for Selsun Blue's next few years, what positioning should be sought by its advertising? Among what market segment?
2. Should there also be some strategic actions taken in nonpromotional aspects of this brand's marketing? Or in nonmarketing aspects?
3. How would the competitive situation be likely to affect the future of Selsun Blue? How would it affect the company's decisions on increasing—or retrenching—its expenditures on this brand? Would you favor Abbott's raising marketing budgets for this brand (relative to the total marketing outlays) or not? State your reasoning.

CASE 7-3

Kelso Products, Inc.

One Monday in mid-October, 1982, Adele Laval returned to her office at Kelso Products. She had gone on vacation directly after attending the annual meeting of the Pet Foods Institute (PFI) in Kansas City. Kelso Products did not make pet foods, but it supplied ingredients to pet food manufacturers which justified membership in the PFI.

Adele had scarcely gone through her stack of mail when Will Braun popped in and said:

"I'm glad you're back and looking marvelous. Also hope you learned a lot at the PFI. Talk about timing! Yesterday Anson looked in for you and asked if you could do another of your 7-day wonder studies on (would you believe it?) pet foods. Seems that Lessing and Black have gotten turned on too about us going into that business."

Regarding who was who, Adele was assistant marketing manager of Kelso, whose work included planning, research, and keeping on top of the firm's competitive and marketing situations. Will was her superior, the vice president–marketing manager. Anson Buckley was the firm's president, and Lessing and Black were its most influential directors.

Source: John C. Maxwell, Jr., in *Advertising Age,* May 10, 1982, p. 35. Reprinted with permission from the May 10, 1982 issue of *Advertising Age.* Copyright 1982 by Crain Communications, Inc.

BACKGROUND

The firm's name was Kelso-Mix Company when it was founded in 1924. Then it produced only cattle feeds in its single mill located in central Kansas. Forty years later it still was a one-plant cattle feed firm, with 1965 sales of almost $6 million. For the next ten years a more ambitious president expanded the animal feeds lines, extended Kelso's selling into most U.S. cattle producing areas, got into the Pacific export trade, and built new mills in South Dakota and eastern Washington. These steps raised Kelso's volume by 1975 to over $19 million.

Buckley had greater aspirations for Kelso when he took over. To signal the broadening of the firm, its name changed to Kelso Products. He brought new efficiencies by rebuilding the Kansas plant and instituting modern controls. He improved capabilities with the hiring of excellent laboratory scientists and doubling the sales force. He hoped to end Kelso's complete reliance on low-margin commodity products by finding and entering specialty products. Several had been put on the market by 1982 in human diet supplements and special feeds for zoos and medical laboratories.

Buckley did succeed in nearly tripling sales volume to over $50 million projected for 1982. Profits pleasingly nearly doubled. Still, Kelso remained mainly a commodities maker, as they still comprised over 90 percent of dollar volume. As he looked around for other fields to penetrate, pet foods were appealing.

INFORMATION

Adele first confirmed with Buckley what he needed and the timing. She was to present a brief report at the next meeting of the directors, ten days away. This would be a general picture of the pet foods industry. If that view was inviting enough, she would later direct a depth study on Kelso's potentialities.

Actually she had been eyeing the pet food industry for a long time and had a file of information. Some of that will be shown below. Annual articles from *Advertising Age* on pet food sales were a main source. She chose data for 1977, 1980, and 1981 to show both current and longer-range trends. She had also notes and hand-outs from the PFI meetings and found items in the latest issue of *Feedstuffs,* a leading industry paper.

The pet food business, as shown in Table 1, divides into dog food and cat food (other animals and bird feed excluded). On the whole, the total pet food volume in current dollars had risen nearly 45 percent in four years but barely 10 percent between 1980 and 1981. In that year physical volume was up by a bit over 1 percent.

Looking at the pet food sales of leading manufacturers, Adele noticed that sales were substantially concentrated in such firms, although there were numerous contenders. The volumes of the leading firms in each category are found in Table 2.

Ralston Purina was already a giant rival of Kelso's in cattle feeds, part of Ralston's $2.5 billion sales to agricultural buyers in 1981. Pet foods constituted 23 percent of that company's sales and contributed about 30 percent of its profits. Its pet food leadership was entrenched in 1956 when it introduced a novel extruded dry food, Purina Dog Chow. Dry dog foods overtook canned six years later and remained the most popular form, as their price was lower. Ralston's volume had tapered lately, partly because of Quaker's new soft-dry food. Ralston was fighting back with its soft-dry "Moist & Chunky" and four other new brands launched in 1981. Ralston had demonstrated how to segment the market, first with its takeoff from Dog Chow with Puppy Chow for puppies and later with "Hero" for big dogs, which comprised less than 30 percent of the canine market but consumed an estimated 60 percent of dog food.

Carnation was a diversified food company that had long been near the top of canned dog foods and was participating in both cat and dog markets. It had succeeded in "brand extension" strategy with entries of its "Friskies" in several categories.

General Foods also was a long-standing dog food maker that innovated moist dog food in 1962. Its "Gainesburgers" brand had been extended to several to dominate the moist category, which lately had been hurt by price resistance. GF had been making a game try for a good position in the canned category with its "Cycle" brand for twelve years, which one trade paper recently had described as a "sad quest."

Quaker Oats was another veteran in canned dog food that also had gotten established in cat food. Its recent main success had been initiating a "soft-dry" type of dog food with its brand "Tender Chunks." That was dry but soft like meat and less expensive than canned dog food. Quaker was believed to have captured 10 percent of the dry dog food market before Ralston could retaliate with its "Moist & Chunky" version.

H.J. Heinz, the venerable firm that evolved from pickles, had gotten into cat food through its Star-Kist division's fish, which delights cats. Although Heinz had been in pet foods for only eight years, its "9-Lives" led the canned cat food business, and they had entries in dry and moist cat food too.

The competitive positions of those firms may be analyzed in Table 3, which shows the figures Adele tabulated of leading brands in each of the eight categories.

In a particularly interesting session at the PFI meetings, Selling Areas–Marketing (SAMI) had shown the most recent pet food figures from its national retail sales data service. These dealt with the latest 28-day reporting period ended June 25, 1982.[1]

In comparison with the same period in June, 1981, these changes were reported:

	Changes 1981 to 1982 in	
	Tonnage	Dollar volume
Dry dog food	+3.7%	+ 9.4%
Wet (canned) dog food	−2.2	+ 4.2
Moist dog food	−9.6	− 5.1
Dog food snacks	+1.6	+14.3
Wet cat food	+6.2	+15.0
Moist cat food	+2.3	+ 6.3

Total dollar volume of dog food was reported as a 7.2% gain from June, 1981, a slowdown from the growth rate of the two previous years. Cat food data was more favorable, in the SAMI people's view as it reflected a steady increase in the number of U.S. households owning a cat.

A continuing growth in generic (unbranded) labels was a striking trend, which were reported as follows:

	Change 1981 to 1982 in	
	Dollar volume	Market share
Wet dog food	+50.6%	+0.8 share points
Dry dog food	+99.6	+2.1
Wet cat food	+93.8	+1.2
Dry cat food	+26.3	+1.1

Another SAMI subject was the growth in number of pet food brands over the past 10 years. The percentage change in brands on the market between 1972 and 1982 was as follows:

---

[1]Also reported in *Feedstuffs,* October 4, 1982, pp. 5, 42

	Change in number of brands
Wet dog food	− 32%
Dry dog food	+100
Moist dog food	+ 82
Dog food snacks	+ 65
Wet cat food	− 25
Dry cat food	+209

The current number of brands ran as high as 154 in dry dog food and 105 in wet dog food. Only 31 brands were in moist dog foods and 73 in dog snacks.

Adele had been watching Heinz because that relative newcomer to pet foods had been aggressive. They obviously were trying their possibilities in dog foods. Last fall Heinz began to market test its new "Meaty Meal" in six upper midwest states, including adjoining Nebraska. This product differed from existing dry foods by having a coating of meat. This was the main appeal in its test campaign that was costing a national equivalent of $25 million in ad media. The brand seemed to be selling well, but it was questionable whether it would support that level of advertising outlay. Rumors were around that Heinz was looking to acquire another dog food company. Another rumor was that the British owners of Liggett Group were seeking to sell its pet food division.

Advertising of manufacturers' brands in this industry seemed quite high. The best estimate seemed to be around $300 millions expenditure in 1982. In its main medium of TV about $179 million had been spent in 1981.

Adele also noted an item that had appeared in the trade paper, *Feedstuffs,* about Quaker Oats pet foods, from which we excerpt:

> Quaker pet feeds division increased sales to $319.2 million in 1982 compared with $297.9 million in 1981 and $252.8 million in 1980.

> Quaker attributed the increase in overall physical volume of sales in the pet food division to the introduction of the dry dog food Kibbles 'n Bits. . . . Quaker closed a canned pet food plant in Pascagoula, Miss., in response to a steady decline of canned pet foods in the industry in recent years. Quaker blamed consumer price consciousness for the shift away from canned pet foods.[2]

A related factor might have been the stagnant consumer income in 1981 when, according to Federal government reports, per capita income rose by 10.2 percent, offset by price rises of 10.2 percent. As the nation went deeper into depression in 1982, real consumer income fell.

Finally, Adele brought out some data on cattle and their feeding for comparative purposes. They were these three series:

	Index of meat production (1967 = 100)	Number of cattle fed (in million)	Cattle feed purchased (in billion)
1970	108	112.4	$ 8.0
1977	105	122.8	14.0
1978	104	116.4	14.5
1979	106	110.9	17.8
1980	111	111.2	18.6
1981	112	114.3	18.9

Her prediction of the average number of cattle fed during 1982 was 115.7 million head. The cattle feed purchase data were in current dollars, unadjusted for price changes.

---

[2]*Feedstuffs,* October 4, 1982, p. 7. The Quaker Oats data relate to its fiscal years that end on June 30 of the indicated years.

TABLE 1 Pet food sales, by type of product (sales in million dollars)

| Type | 1977 | 1980 | 1981 | Percentage changes | |
				1977–1981	1980–1981
Dry dog food	$ 975	$1,388	$1,521	+ 42.4%	+ 9.5%
Canned dog food	703	759	790	+ 11.2	+ 4.1
Moist dog food	317	317	281	(11.4)	(9.6)
Whole biscuit snacks	90	192	214	+137.8	+11.5
Soft-dry dog food	20	140	130	+650.0	(7.4)
Total dog	2,105	2,796	2,936	39.5	5.2
Canned cat food	505	602	730	+ 44.6	+21.3
Dry cat food	295	425	524	+ 77.6	+23.3
Moist cat food	138	165	188	+ 36.2	+21.0
Total cat	938	1,192	1,442	+ 53.7	+21.0
Total both	3,043	3,988	4,378	+ 43.7%	+ 9.9%

TABLE 2 Pet food sales, by manufacturer (sales in million dollars)

| | 1977 | | 1980 | | 1981 | |
	Sales	Market share	Sales	Market share	Sales	Market share
Ralston Purina	$ 996	32.7%	$1,163	29.2%	$1,246	28.5%
Carnation	353	11.6	495	12.5	482	11.0
General Foods	333	10.9	354	8.9	387	8.8
Quaker Oats	287	9.4	351	8.8	340	7.8
Liggett Group	201	6.6	224	5.6	241	5.5
Heinz	139	4.5	247	6.2	277	6.3
All others	740	24.3	1,147	28.8	1,404	32.1
Total	3,049	100.0	3,982	100.0	4,378	100.0

TABLE 3 Pet food sales by brand (in million dollars)

Type and Brand	Company	1980	1981
Canned dog food:			
Alpo	Liggett Group	$166.0	$178.0
KalKan	KalKan	98.	102
Ken-L Ration	Quaker Oats	78.	76.
Mighty Dog	Carnation	70.	73.
Friskies	Carnation	58.	60.
Cycle	General Foods	54.	52.
Ken-L Ration Tender Chunks	Quaker Oats	24.	32.
Recipe	Campbell	15.	19.5
Skippy Premium	C.H.B. Foods	13.	19.
Vets	C.H.B. Foods	19.	19.
Cadillac	Cadillac	16.	17.5
Skippy, Dr. Ross	C.H.B. Foods	15.	15.
M.I.S.	KalKan	—	11.
Strongheart	Swift	11.5	10.0
All others		121.5	106.
Total		$759.0	$790.0

Type and Brand	Company	1980	1981
Moist dog food:			
Gainesburgers	General Foods	$75.	$73.
Ken-L Ration Burgers	Quaker Oats	67.	61.
Top Choice	General Foods	50.	50.
Ken-L Ration Spec. Cuts	Quaker Oats	32.	30.
Gaines Variety Complete	General Foods	25.	27.
All others		62.	42.
Total		$311.	$281.
Soft-dry dog food:			
Tender Chunks	Quaker Oats	$95.	$85.
Moist 'n Chunky	Ralston Purina	40.	35.
All others		5.	9.6
Total		$140.	$129.6
Whole-Bisquit Dog Snacks			
Milk-Bone Snacks	Nabisco Brands	$95.	$106.
Bonz	Ralston Purina	41.	45.
Jerky Treats	Heinz	21.3	23.
All others		35.0	40.
Total		$192.	$214.

Dry dog food:			
Dog Chow	Ralston Purina	$330.	$300.
Puppy Chow	Ralston Purina	120.	140.
Gravy Train	General Foods	66.	92.
Dog Meal	Ralston Purina	73.	85.
High Protein Cycle	General Foods	60.	76.
Chuck Wagon	Ralston Purina	65.	60.
Meal Time	KalKan	52.	60.
Alpo Beef Flavored	Liggett Group	50.	53.
Come 'N Get It	Carnation	23.	50.
Hero	Ralston Purina	22.	36.
Friskies Dinner & Cubes	Carnation	45.	34.
Mainstay	Ralston Purina	50.	30.
Fit & Trim	Ralston Purina	18.5	19.
Alamo	Liggett Group	22.	13.
Kasco	ConAgra	12.	12.
Jim Dandy Chunk	Jim Dandy	11.5	12.
All others		363.3	449.
Total		$1,388.	$1,521.

Canned cat food:			
9-Lives	Heinz	$185.	$205.
Friskies Buffet	Carnation	126.	135.
KalKan	KalKan	88.	116.
Purina 100	Ralston Purina	37.5	57.
Puss 'n Boots	Quaker Oats	24.	23.
All others		139.5	194.
Total		$600.	$730.

Dry cat food:			
Cat Chow	Ralston Purina	$112.	$150.
Meow Mix	Ralston Purina	73.	84.
Friskies	Carnation	82.5	52.
Special Dinners	Ralston Purina	36.	45.
9-Lives	Heinz	37.5	42.
All others		84.	151.
Total		$425.	524.

Moist cat food:			
Tender Vittles	Ralston Purina	$100.	$125.
9-Lives Square Meal	Heinz	25.	30.
Moist Meals	Quaker Oats	17.	18.
All others		17.	15.
Total		$159.	$188.

Source: John C. Maxwell, Jr., *Advertising Age,* May 10, 1982, p. 35.

DISCUSSION

1. If you were writing the report for the Kelso board of directors, how would you describe the following items?
   a. The significant features of the pet food market and its segments
   b. Demand changes among the product categories and what might account for them
   c. The makeup and intensity of competition and whether it varies among product categories
   d. Expectations over the near future in pet foods markets and competition
2. In view of your analysis, answer the following questions as well as you can without knowledge of Kelso Products' capabilities:
   a. Does the pet foods business, in general, seem attractive for Kelso?
   b. What segment of the industry would you suggest that Kelso enter? Or would you prefer entering with a broad line and appealing to dog and/or cat owners generally?
   Support your views with data and reasoning.

8

Technological and Environmental Decisions

The environment of a firm provides many opportunities and constraints. The freedom to make decisions and the flexibility of marketing actions are functions of external-environment factors. The environment is dynamic, sometimes rendering what is successful today as a failure in a future time period.

The thrust of this book—marketing decision making from the standpoint of the executives who develop strategy—is an internal point of view, a view within the firm. The external environment, however, includes competitive forces, which we view as being basically uncontrollable. It so vitally affects the fate of a marketing strategy that it must be considered an input in planning.

Of course, the firm may have to cope with a myriad of external elements or factors. Discussing them within a single chapter requires that they be reduced to few specific categories. We have already discussed competition in Chapter 7. The following groups are of strategic importance to marketers and are not mutually exclusive or exhaustive: (1) technology, (2) the economy, (3) social forces, and (4) the government (legal and regulatory forces).

TECHNOLOGY

Few forces have more visibility in marketing than technology. For example, millions of dollars were spent to introduce videotape recorders, turbo engines, and desktop copiers. Technology is developed from the attempts of organizations and individuals to find new ways or approaches for accomplishing tasks.

In marketing, technology relates most directly to improving existing products and discovering new products. It encompasses the processes by which ideas are conceived, nurtured, developed, and finally introduced into the market as new products and techniques.[1] The major considerations in the development of new technology are organizational goals and marketing objectives directly related to new methods of production, plant and equipment, and other task-oriented parts of the organization.[2] A technological improvement, or technological improvement by a competitor, usually requires a corresponding adjustment in marketing strategy.

For example, NCR Corporation lost its number-one standing in the cash register business when it failed to switch quickly enough from electromechanical models to electronic point-of-sale terminals in the early 1970s. To counter this decline in market dominance, the company has recently introduced personal computers, word processors, semiconductors, telephone communications networks, and transaction-processing equipment—handling payments, withdrawals, and so forth, at the time of occurrence. Broadening its product offering represents a significant change in strategy.[3]

The Importance of Technology in Marketing Strategy

Fast-changing technology can restructure an industry and quickly alter consumption patterns. The microprocessor that revolutionized the computer industry in the early 1970s by dramatically improving computing at a smaller cost is one example of how a technological breakthrough can have a significant effect on an industry.

Rapidly advancing technology in this minicomputer industry requires dynamic and aggressive marketing effort to survive the competitive forces. It is becoming increasingly necessary to understand a client's business, and to provide software and other special services. For instance, consider the many home computer advertisements that are now shown on television and in other media. In the late 1970s there were no such campaigns. The computer is generally thought of as a tool for improving the quality of human life, but recently the computer has been called on to improve itself.

Computers are now being used to create new "super chips," which will give military electronics systems ten times their current computing power. Hughes Air-

---

[1] Robert J. Holloway and Robert S. Hancock, *Marketing in a Changing Environment* (New York: John Wiley, 1973), p. 155.

[2] Robert C. Shirley, "A Model for Analysis of Organizational Change," *MSU Business Topics*, 22 (Spring 1974), 109.

[3] "NCR: Trying to Expand Its Consumer Base with a Batch of New Products," *Business Week*, December 19, 1983, p. 68.

craft Company is using the computer to design Very High Speed Integrated Circuits. The computer is being used because of the high degree of complexity involved in developing these chips. These chips are said to be "as complex as 100 Los Angeles street maps printed on a thumb tack."

Technology seems to go hand in hand with a dynamic industry like today's computer industry. But technology is also the friend of firms competing in a mature or even declining market.

> Through the 1970s, medical imaging systems based on high-frequency sound waves (ultrasound) became commonplace. Ultrasound was found to be less risky than X-rays and is therefore often used to diagnose abnormalities in unborn children. The market grew rapidly between 1975 and 1982, with sales reaching $600 million in 1982. By this time the market had reached the saturation point and sales were down substantially in 1983.
>
> A new firm, Acuson, hit the market with a technologically advanced system later that year and sales began to come back. The Acuson machine produces pictures up to four times clearer than older models. One ultrasound specialist said, "People will always buy state-of-the-art equipment," and Acuson was able to develop just that.[4]

Firms should become involved in the innovation process and be prepared to exploit any new opportunities that turn up, just as Acuson did in the above example. Acuson was able to apply technology advances from many areas (scanning, computer control, signal processing) to develop its innovation, whereas advances in the computer industry, for example, have been generated entirely within that industry. Where do these advances come from? Typically through research and development (R&D).

The 776 companies that are charted by *Business Week* spent approximately $36 billion on R&D in 1982. This figure represented an 11.5 percent increase over the previous year's expenditures and was up from the $16 billion spent in 1976.

Financial resources are a key factor in using R&D as an integral part of a firm's strategy. For example, the top four spenders—General Motors, AT&T, IBM, and Ford—accounted for over 22 percent of all R&D expenditures (see Table 8-1). Some industries, such as office equipment and instruments, may allocate as much as 5 percent of sales to R&D, while service industries may allocate less than 1 percent.[5]

A firm does not have to put large financial resources into R&D to compete, although the entire planning process, including strategy search, will be influenced by the R&D efforts of competitors. Since R&D can result in improved products that could create or destroy a firm's differential advantage, technological developments must be a strategy consideration, and some ap-

---

[4]"Ultrasound Is Probing New Markets," *Business Week*, May 2, 1983, pp. 35–37.
[5]"The U.S. Still Leads the World in R&D Spending," *Business Week*, June 20, 1983, pp. 122–24.

TABLE 8-1   Top 15 U.S. companies in R&D expenditures

In total dollars (millions)

1.	General Motors	$2,175
2.	AT&T	2,126
3.	IBM	2,053
4.	Ford Motor	1,764
5.	Du Pont	879
6.	United Technologies.............	834
7.	General Electric	781
8.	Eastman Kodak	710
9.	Exxon	707
10.	Boeing	691
11.	Xerox	565
12.	ITT	519
13.	Dow Chemical	460
14.	Hewlett-Packard	424
15.	Sperry..........................	398

Reprinted from the June 20, 1983 issue of *Business Week* by special permission, © 1983 by McGraw-Hill, Inc.

proach to forecasting technological changes is helpful in the planning process. A firm should recognize that rapid technological development within an industry will shorten the product life cycle.

Patents, a Strategic Factor

The fundamental marketing-strategy consideration resulting from the patent system is idea identification and protection in the differentiation or standardization of products.[6] The legal significance of the patent relates to the doctrine of natural rights to ideas as property. Its economic significance relates to a guarantee of profits as a reward and motivation for innovation. If the patent turns out to be commercially worthless, the failure must be evaluated in relation to marketing capabilities as well as the nature of the invention.

Active involvement in R&D is one way to obtain new patents to provide the firm with opportunities to differentiate products and enter new markets. In the generation of new business based on invention, patents serve to encourage the inventor by providing a chance to launch a product without interference from competition.[7]

One problem the firm may have with patents is great uncertainty relating to court decisions on what constitutes authentic "invention." The federal

---

[6]Wroe Alderson, "A Marketing View of the Patent System," in *Patents and Progress*, ed. Wroe Alderson, Vern Terpstra, and Stanley J. Shapiro (Homewood, Ill.: Richard D. Irwin, 1965), p. 228.

[7]David Smith, "Technological Innovation and Patents," in *Patents and Progress*, ed. Alderson et al., p. 247.

courts of appeal have invalidated a certain percentage of the patents examined. It is up to the firm to develop a sound logical defense to protect patent rights. For example, the familiar rabbit logo of Playboy Enterprises, Inc., has to be protected against infringers all over the world. It is impossible, however, for Playboy to know about every infringement, and in some cases the cost of protecting the logo is greater than the damages.

Firms must also recognize that merely holding a patent with some degree of protection from competition does not automatically result in success. Most R&D that leads to a new product requires marketing expertise and resources to develop the product commercially. Many firms have patents for useful products but fail to develop a marketing strategy to launch their products successfully. Still other firms develop good marketing strategies but fail to gain the financial resources or venture capital necessary to implement a marketing program. Most inventors want to see a good marketing plan based on sound marketing research before supporting a new technology. Larger, financially successful firms have the advantage of obtaining new patents and rushing to the market before the patent is obsolete. Sometimes this advantage backfires, as we shall see later with RCA's videodisk.

Forecasting Technological Changes

An organization's planning department should include technological forecasting.[8] A technological forecast can provide the firm with an estimate of the probability and significance of environmental developments important to the planning process. A company's technology-forecasting methods should include, first, changes in the task processes or technical aspects of the product; and second, forecasts of social, economic, and political trends that may be integrated with technological events. The technological forecasting activity must then be linked to the firm's strategy search. Many corporations are responding to accelerating change by inclusion of technological forecasts, environmental scanning, and the sociopolitical consequences of technology as inputs in their strategic planning for new and existing products.[9]

Specific approaches that firms may use for technological forecasting include the following:

1. *Delphi probes.* The researcher uses repeated surveys with informed respondents, providing each survey's results as feedback to their next response.
2. *Scenarios.* Many different kinds of scenarios, or stories of the future, have been utilized. There have been many scenarios of future developments

---

[8]William L. Swager, "Technological Forecasting in Planning," *Business Horizons,* 66 (February 1973), 37.

[9]Gene R. Laczniak and Robert F. Lusch, "Futures Research: New Perspectives for Marketing and Corporate Planning," Midwest Marketing Meeting, St. Louis, April 1977, pp. 1–2.

in automobile transportation, drugs, space travel, and aviation. Scenarios can be systematic and logical efforts to forecast changes in technology.

3. *Trend extrapolation.* This is a very popular technological-forecasting method. An event or key variable, such as the number of automobiles in a city, is plotted against time. Also, more-advanced mathematical models can be used to forecast trends.[10]

It is most important in the strategic development of technology that the firm be oriented toward a generic market or have some basic goal in its R&D efforts. Consider the following situation:

> Many firms hit on hard times in the ever-changing, fast-paced home computer market. Texas Instruments reported a $183 million loss on home computers during the second quarter of 1983 and withdrew from the home computer market in the third quarter of 1983. Atari lost over $300 million during the same time, and Mattel lost another $100 million. Why did all these companies and others do so poorly in what was supposed to be one of the best growth markets of the decade?
>
> Many would argue that they did not properly market their new technology. These companies overestimated demand and underestimated the speed with which competitors would introduce more-advanced, more-cost-effective systems. Texas Instruments and Atari, in particular, waited too long before introducing their lower-cost machines and were then unable to differentiate their models from the competition—with disastrous results.[11]

Even though the firm cannot control with certainty its own technological development or its competitors' technological breakthrough, it can be prepared to act quickly and adjust marketing strategy to deal with new technological environments. Marketing intelligence activities, such as technological forecasting, give the firm the best insights on when to act, what decisions to make, and how to direct its own technological development program toward the goal of profitable products.

THE ECONOMY

An economy is a total system within which products are produced, distributed, and exchanged. Macroeconomic variables, which are virtually always beyond a firm's power to control, constrain or stimulate both potential sales volume and costs. Therefore, forecasts of macroeconomic changes are an input in the strategic-planning process.

---

[10]Robert Holloway, "Marketing and Futuristic Methods," in *Public Policy Issues in Marketing*, ed. O. C. Ferrell and Raymond LaGarce (Lexington, Mass: D. C. Heath, 1975), p. 175.

[11]"Home Computer Field Baffles Manufacturers and Many Buyers, Too," *Wall Street Journal,* July 26, 1983, pp. 1ff.

Macroeconomic Variables and Their Significance in Strategic Decisions

An exhaustive list of the macroeconomic variables that could be used as an input in strategic planning would be very long indeed. A few typical ones are shown in Table 8-2. These variables relate to a firm's supply, demand, and price levels for its products. Interest rates, employment, and productivity should be monitored in planning because of their impact on strategy.

Economic factors should weigh heavily in the strategy search. Probable demand magnitudes resulting from macroeconomic changes are factors of fundamental effect on strategy formulation. In the strategic-planning process, the decision maker may take into consideration levels and trends of income and prices; shortages or surpluses of resources, labor, and capital; economic weapons that governments are likely to use to correct such serious problems as excessive inflation or deflation; levels of employment or idleness; and the diseconomies of pollution, congestion, and various social ills.

Fluctuations in the Economy

Demand is one of the most critical variables; its expansion or contraction can throw a product plan far off course. Industrial products whose demand fluctuates much more widely than the general economy—goods like machinery or cement—should be managed with a vigilant regard for demand, but even staples like coffee are considerably affected.

Supply, the other side of the economic coin from demand, is also important in strategic planning. The relative abundance or scarcity of materials has often been a fundamental factor in determining what to produce or how to design and produce it, to take advantage of what will be available.

Price levels form another economic factor that critically affects the management of products. Sharp short-run price changes, for instance, can cause serious inventory losses or windfall profits and thus are factors in production-rate

TABLE 8-2 Selected macroeconomic variables used in strategic planning

Production in units	Distribution exchange	Prices	Finance
Steel	Rail freight traffic	Metals	Prime commercial-
Automobiles	Intercity truck tonnage	Consumer price	paper rate
Oil/Gasoline	Inland waterways	index	Money supply
Coal	freight	Wholesale price	Corporate-bond yields
Paper	Retail sales	index	Consumer installment
Lumber	Wholesale inventories	Cost-of-living	loans
New housing	Automobile sales	index	Stock prices
starts	Soft-goods sales	Farm commodities	Savings-and-loan
			deposits

plans. The more worrisome price-level phenomenon has been general inflation. Costs, expected selling prices, and buying power of the market all hinge on the rate of inflation, which has fluctuated in the 1980s. Accelerated inflation is also dangerous in heightening the possibility of sudden deflation and economic collapse.

Another resource that has been greatly affected by shortages recently is *money and credit.* Rising interest rates have resulted, for both consumer and business borrowers, in diverting the allocation of funds and boosting costs. Nonavailability of funds has delayed or prevented many new R&D programs, promotional campaigns, and other marketing activities. Selectivity and prudent cost controls, in response to tightening funds, have become vital in product decisions.

Influence on Strategy Search by Forecasts of the Economy

From the standpoint of any firm's management, the economy is uncontrollable. The internal actions that a firm may take, then, are those of anticipation and intelligent adaptation through strategy selection.

The magnitude of economic problems and the challenges of dealing with them should be appreciated as the basis for understanding requisites of the strategic-planning process. This was illustrated by the fluctuation of oil supplies between 1973 and 1983.

> The sudden scarcity of oil in 1973 was an economic blow to U.S. consumers. The steep climb in prices of gasoline and other petroleum products caused consumer demand to drop, which was fortunate in one sense because it allowed the country to keep adequate stocks of fuel and fuel oils on hand. As prices continued to rise, however, there was a large decline in the market for large cars, severely hurting U.S. automakers. As gasoline price increases declined, consumers became accustomed to the higher prices, and large cars were again in demand. Another oil crisis in 1979 sent prices of oil to an all-time high, and consumers moved back to smaller cars. By the mid-1980s prices had decreased and stabilized, and large cars were again in demand.

The foregoing series of events highlights one very important marketing requisite for dealing with economic change: a competent intelligence system. The petroleum marketers may have had very frequent and rapid information with which to monitor petroleum supplies (despite some corporations' contention that they did not have such information for government agencies). The automotive industry, however, apparently lacked this information, and the impact of the petroleum crisis on that industry demonstrates how vital such intelligence would have been to those manufacturers' product planning.

A second competence needed relative to economic factors for the marketing of products is that of readiness to react. If one automobile company, for example, had been speedier than its rivals in the interpretation of intelligence received on the petroleum situation and could have altered its programs faster, it might have shifted into compact-car promotion and production earlier. Thus, at least one of the Big Three manufacturers could have gained considerably in market share, in early 1973, over rivals in compact models. Given such an ability, American Motors, which fortunately happened to be mainly a small-car maker, could expand its efforts to exploit the situation (although it was hampered by limited facilities). A few years later, American Motors lost market share when consumers again demanded large domestic cars and small imports. In the 1983–84 period some General Motors divisions continued to produce some large full-sized models that had been scheduled for deletion in 1982. For example, Pontiac imported its full-sized Parisian from Canada because this car had already been phased out in the United States.

Readiness and flexibility alone are insufficient to make adaptation to economic changes profitable. Those who manage products must also interpret the received intelligence correctly. Most of the U.S. petroleum industry seems to have done this regarding probable long-run supply trends, for they curtailed expansion of refineries for several years before the crisis and were not sitting with idle plants then.

Finally and importantly, the manager needs to have a repertoire of strategies or contingency plans that may be implemented in advance of the change, and this calls for accurate economic forecasting. Forecasting is a task better entrusted to specialists, whose predictions should be vital determinants of marketing plans. It was all too apparent that the automotive industry had not given even long-range petroleum supply trends due weight in planning the future product mix. Most recreational-vehicle manufacturers were even more lacking in optional strategies: They had no other present or potential products to which they could turn and partially recoup their market losses.

SOCIAL FORCES   *The issues of concern in society*

Social forces include the structure and dynamics of members of society and their issues of concern. Especially in the last two decades, matters of vital concern that relate to strategy formulation have been identified.

Figure 8-1 illustrates the social impact of marketing actions on society. Marketing actions, which are based on strategy, are judged and evaluated by members of society involved in and concerned about exchange transactions. The consequences of these judgments or evaluations are social issues that should influence strategy formulation.

Social Issues Important in Strategic Planning

Some of the issues that could be considered in strategic planning include poverty, equal opportunity, quality of life, environmental deterioration, and the consumer movement. If some aspect of the marketing strategy involves an issue of concern, the consequences must be taken into account in the planning

FIGURE 8-1. Consequences of the marketing and society interface.

MARKETING ACTIONS	MARKETING/SOCIETY INTERFACE	CONSEQUENCES
(based on strategy and plans)	(perceptions and behavior of social units involved in or concerned about exchange transactions)	(Manifest and latent reaction to marketing actions, including issues and areas of concern)

process. Let us examine some existing social issues that are of increasing concern in strategic planning.

The changing roles of women in society are definitely on the minds of marketers. In the past women were typically portrayed as "happy homemakers." Recently, however, women have more often been portrayed as busy executives rather than as housewives or secretaries. Studies conducted by the advertising agency of Altschiller, Reitzfeld, Solvin reveal that women are unhappy with ads portraying the stereotyped housewife and the equally stereotyped executive. Because of these findings, the trend for the 1980s appears to be the use of the "fully dimensional woman," a woman who avoids being stereotyped in one of the above categories.[12]

Environmental and ecological concerns are of increasing importance to marketers. "An affluent society, with life-style choices calling for heterogeneous consumption patterns with materialistic acquisitions as the focal point of self-esteem, has found that material disposition becomes a necessary prerequisite for basic maintenance and pollution control."[13] With the advent of environmental/ecological groups, the design, function, and perceived use of products as reflected in marketing strategies must take into account resource depletion, waste, and pollution.[14] The impact of environmental lobby groups in influencing public opinion is growing.

Changing values of the general public, sometimes reflected in feelings of confusion, powerlessness, and frustration, have resulted in the support of social causes and welfare organizations.[15] Public issues such as poverty, equal employment opportunities, malnutrition, disease, and social injustice are reflected in activities of social-cause organizations, human-rights groups, and welfare and poverty groups.

The role of marketers in promoting *social justice* has increased. If the public first accepts the activities of marketers in solving social problems, it subsequently expects participation and ultimately demands participation.[16]

Another explanation of consumer discontent focuses on *product prolifer-*

---

[12]Mary Bralowe, "Advertising World's Portrayal of Women Is Starting to Shift," *Wall Street Journal,* October 28, 1982, p. 31.

[13]Donald L. Perry, *Social Marketing Strategies: Conservation Issues and Analysis* (Pacific Palisades, Calif.: Goodyear, 1976), p. 35.

[14]Ibid., pp. 30, 35.

[15]Gerald F. Cavanagh, *American Business Values in Transition* (Englewood Cliffs, N.J.: Prectice-Hall, 1976), p. 145.

[16]Phillip I. Blumberg, *The Megacorporation in American Society* (Englewood Cliffs, N.J.: Prentice-Hall, 1975), p. 3.

ation and *technical complexity.* The social and ecological impact of products and marketing actions is becoming more important in the purchase decision.

Consumer issues are increasingly being resolved by trained specialists. The professionalization of consumer affairs in the federal government is very much in evidence. Significant research and investigations are being performed by congressional aides, regulatory-agency staffs, and administration professionals.

Marketers are often characterized as "the problem" or as uninterested in the consumer's problems. But many firms are now taking a more active role in meeting the concerns of the consumer before they become public issues. The shift is toward the identification of consumer issues and inclusion of creative solutions to problems in the strategic-planning process.

The Public-Policy Process

Public policy refers to widely shared and generally acknowledged principles guiding behavior for society as a whole. These are made explicit in law and formal units of government, but a narrow legislative interpretation should be avoided.[17] Implicit public policies guiding the action of marketing executives stem from the recognition of general societal commitments and shared values of the public.

The public-policy process involves members of society—individuals, organizations, and special-interest groups—identifying issues of concern, explaining conflicting viewpoints, negotiating and compromising to reach a solution and establishing some means to attain social and economic objectives.[18] There has been a trend toward the blurring of the public and private roles in society. Therefore, marketers should be more familiar with both the explicit (legal regulatory forces) and the implicit (general public and social sanctions) components of public policy.

GOVERNMENT

As political and social objectives of the society crystallize and a consensus emerges, pressures develop for leadership. When the pressures become more intense, they provide the necessary base that makes government response politically feasible. Executive or administrative action and legislation follow.

Consideration of social issues and participation in the solution of problems are also essential in the formulation of strategy. Thus, as government leads, pressures develop on business to move in the same direction. The history of the struggle to achieve environmental protection, create equal employ-

---

[17]Lee Preston and James J. Post, *Private Management and Public Policy* (Englewood Cliffs, N.J.: Prentice-Hall, 1975), pp. 11, 52.
[18]Ibid., p. 56.

ment opportunities, and solve consumer problems reflects the interface between business and government.

Legal and regulatory forces at the federal, state, and local levels pose constraints and sometimes opportunities in the formulation of marketing strategy. Evaluating government reaction to existing and proposed strategy is important in the planning process. Organizations striving to be competitive and innovative in marketing sometimes do not stop to consider the ramifications of government regulation. For example, the manufacturer of Personna razor blades was once issued a Federal Trade Commission complaint when the company sent out samples enclosed in home-delivered newspapers. The FTC thought the promotion could be harmful to children in the homes receiving those papers. This shows how the government seriously constrained an ill-planned marketing strategy. The government also has the authority to force a company to take false or misleading advertisements off the air if it cannot substantiate them.

> In July 1983, the FTC ordered Bristol-Myers Company and Sterling Drug Inc. to discontinue ads which say their products (Excedrin, Bufferin, Bayer) are superior to competitive pain relievers unless they have two chemical studies to back up their claims.[19]

An interesting sidenote to this example is that although the FTC has the power to keep advertisers in line, it is apparently not using this power as much as in the past—in fact the FTC has relaxed its policies concerning advertisers' claims. Many companies that were forced to live up to more stringent rules in the past have asked the FTC to review their cases in the hope of getting more favorable treatment. Even the sentence handed down to Bristol-Myers and Sterling Drug in the preceding example represents a more generous stand by the FTC because it erased a tougher ruling issued two years earlier.

In general, the scope of legislation, regulation, and administrative actions focuses on the prevention of anticompetitive trade practices and the direct protection of consumers against injury. It is no longer necessary to associate physical harm with a product to obtain government intervention. There is a growing trend toward passing laws that foster rational purchase decisions and the economic well-being of the buyer. Misrepresentation or material omissions in advertising, labeling, or packaging have been major areas of legislative concern. In the areas of credit policies, warranties, and service, glaring examples exist of customer dissatisfaction and government interest.

Federal Regulatory Agencies and Legislation

The Federal Trade Commission, Food and Drug Administration, and Consumer Product Safety Commission have the broadest authority over marketing actions. Many laws specify standards for textiles, toys, automobiles, and

---

[19]Jeanne Saddler, "FTC Easing Roles Requiring Firms to Support Ad Claims," *Wall Street Journal*, July 21, 1983, p. 29.

other products: One of these three agencies is often responsible for monitoring or enforcing compliance with these laws.

Here is a brief description of these agencies and their primary function:

Federal Trade Commission. The FTC, consisting of five commissioners and their staff, exists to prevent anticompetitive trade practices and to provide direct protection of consumers from unfair and deceptive marketing practices. This agency is responsible for the enforcement of most marketing and consumer legislation. In many areas, investigations are made on a case-by-case basis. Therefore, new-product and marketing strategy must be evaluated when there is reason to believe that the FTC will interpret the action as anticompetitive, unfair, deceptive, or dangerous to consumers.

When the FTC determines that a violation has occurred, it issues a cease and desist order to the business to stop the practice. The firm can appeal to have the FTC order rescinded, but until it is rescinded, the FTC is empowered, by a provision of the Trans-Alaska Pipeline Act of 1973, amending the FTC Act, to fine the firm $10,000 a day for each violation.

Consumer Product Safety Commission. The commission has powers to prescribe mandatory safety standards for virtually all consumer products except those for which specific legislation already exists. Excluded are products such as tobacco, motor vehicles, economic poisons, firearms, aircraft, boats, drugs, cosmetics, and foods. Manufacturers are required to conduct a "reasonable testing program" to make sure their products conform to established safety standards, and they are accountable for knowledge of all safety criteria applicable to the product. The commission can ban products from the market if they are hazardous and product standards would not offer protection to the public. Firms found in violation of the standards may be issued penalties ranging from $2,000 to $500,000 per violation. Top executives may be subjected to criminal penalties of up to $50,000 and one year in prison.

Food and Drug Administration. The Food and Drug Administration (FDA) is responsible for the safety of consumers in the following product areas: food, medical devices, cosmetics, veterinary products, and related hazardous consumer products. The FDA conducts research and develops standards to encourage safe, pure, and wholesome foods, drugs, and cosmetics. It has the authority to require truthful packaging and labeling and proper disclosure of important information. The main objective is to protect consumers by enforcing laws and regulations to prevent distribution of adulterated or misbranded products.

Other federal, state, and local agencies may also need to be considered in planning; those above are only examples of the type of government units that regulate marketing actions. These agencies not only have a legislative mandate to operate but are also keenly aware of issues important to the public and sanctions favored by the administration.

These agencies have guidelines to determine what marketing actions violate the law. But since their staff members and resources are limited, subjective decisions are made to rank the most important issues or areas of concern. The FTC has broad powers to determine when laws and regulatory guidelines are being violated.

A firm that does not consider the consequences of its marketing actions may have its marketing strategy changed by a regulatory agency. Sometimes the regulatory measure relates to all products in the industry rather than to the evaluation of one firm's marketing strategy and actions. For example, the Consumer Product Safety Commission established the requirements for child-safe closures on prescription drugs, and for improved reflectors and braking systems on bicycles.

To cope with the regulatory environment, the firm should determine what agencies evaluate its actions and comply with their guidelines and orders. Also, in the strategic-planning cycle, probable government reactions to proposed strategies and actions should be forecasted.

The development of a marketing strategy requires a comprehensive understanding of the legal aspects of decisions. Some of the landmark federal acts affecting marketing are these:

Sherman Antitrust Act (1890). Motivated by the great growth of monopolies, the government instituted legislation to control collusion and conspiracies in restraint of trade. The Sherman Antitrust Act declared illegal any contracts, conspiracies, or other attempts to monopolize a market.

Federal Trade Commission Act (1914). This act was adopted to help strengthen the broad scope of the Sherman Act. It stated that unfair methods of competition in commerce were illegal. It also set up the Federal Trade Commission to enforce legislation and stop unlawful methods of competition.

Clayton Act (1914). This act strengthened the Sherman Act by naming specific activities that tend to lessen competition. These activities include (1) price discrimination, (2) excessive dealings, (3) tying arrangements, (4) refusals to deal, and (5) the acquisition of another corporation by which competition may be lessened substantially.

Robinson Patman Act (1936). This act prohibits discriminatory pricing. The central provision of the act prevents price discrimination between different purchasers of commodities of like grade and quality. Under the act, discounts may be granted to purchasers only if they are based on actual cost differences or economies of scale, or to meet the lower prices of competitors. The act has important ramifications for all areas of marketing practice.

Consumer Goods Pricing Act (1975). This act prohibits the use of price-maintenance agreements between manufacturers and resellers. Fair-trade laws had permitted the manufacturer to set a resale price at which dealers within a state were supposed to sell the firm's product.

Legal Considerations in Strategic Planning

The marketer should approach legal and regulatory problems logically, with a view toward the economics and advantages of compliance with the law. On the other hand, it is the task of marketers to assist in the development of appropriate public policy by pointing out, where it is appropriate, any weaknesses in proposed or existing legislation.

Understanding of the latest interpretation of laws and marketing regulations is necessary if the marketer is to comply with legislation. But compliance with all the legal and governmental forces is complicated, owing to the vagueness of some laws and changing interpretations. For most firms, professional legal guidance is a vital service. A large firm should receive routine legal counsel from its own staff. Small firms may have to rely on attorneys outside the firm.

Marketing managers can assist in the effort to decrease legal problems by trying to keep posted on legislation that could have an impact on the marketing strategy. And this includes legislation involving issues of concern to various interest groups as well as those of concern to regulators. Issues relating to environmental pollution, equal opportunity, and consumer safety present real-world problems for the strategist to consider. Once a decision is made or a stand is taken, some special-interest group may question the firm's position. This is the nature of our pluralistic political system, and the strategist must be prepared to defend decisions. Also, flexibility is essential so that strategy may be changed or problems corrected if marketing actions are illegal or ethically unsound.

SUMMARY

The firm's external environment exerts forces that are for the greater part uncontrollable. Rather than just describing what the external environment is, we analyzed chief factors of concern and briefly discussed actions marketers can take to integrate environmental issues into strategy decisions. Although they have limited control over environmental factors, they usually have some degree of freedom in deciding how to respond to the environmental situation.

The environmental variables that we examined include technology, the economy, social forces, and the government. Although we discussed these factors in separate sections, they do interact to form a specific issue, a unique problem, or an opportunity for marketers. Marketing planning and strategy development should take into account the impact of these forces, and the marketing strategy should be planned with flexibility to adjust for possible changes in these variables. External environmental forces structure the buyer response and directly influence the ability of marketers to implement strategies.

We have provided an overview to show how the external environment should be a consideration in marketing-strategy decisions. The environment is dynamic; major issues develop opportunities or threats and then fade without warning. In developing marketing strategy, it is important to act but not over-act on the current situation.

REVIEW QUESTIONS

1. *How do technological and environmental forces differ in their impact on strategic planning from internal factors?*
2. *Is the external environment really uncontrollable?*
3. *How can a firm ensure that research and development relating to new technology will be directed toward opportunities in the marketplace?*
4. *How does a firm determine which macroeconomic variables are important in strategic planning?*
5. *How do the consequences of marketing actions create social issues of concern?*
6. *How does the firm determine which social issues should be a consideration in strategic planning?*
7. *Is there any way to forecast possible government intervention in marketing actions of the firm?*
8. *How should the firm deal with regulation in strategic planning?*
9. *Could a marketing strategy be based on a future environmental event? Give an example.*

RCA Corporation, Mobile Communication Systems Division (B)

The Mobile Communications Systems Division (MCSD) of RCA created a new product during 1974–76. This was a mobile radio for vehicular use that was eventually branded with the name "Veetac." Details of its development were related in Case 5-2, whose rereading is essential for this continuation of that case.

The MCSD (A) case in Chapter 5 presented an unfolding account that primarily dealt with the engineering or technical personnel's problems and behavior during the product's development. You have just read about technological variables and their effects on strategy in this chapter, Chapter 8. It is timely, then, to reconsider the MCSD (A) case from a technological viewpoint, as our questions on the (A) case addressed it from the marketing viewpoint.

In so doing, you should be aware that in practice the marketing and the research and development (technical) branches of a firm have many problems that should be shared mutually, with inputs from both sides. The marketability and the technical specifications and design of a developing product are highly interdependent, but an adequate interface (or communication) between decision makers of both areas is difficult to achieve—or to implement with enough frequency.

DISCUSSION

1. Find and describe the technological forces that were affecting the course of and the success of the Veetac's design.

2. What objectives of the technical work were the engineers apparently trying to accomplish? Do you believe that those were harmonious with the marketing objectives or the market needs of the product?

3. What were the engineers' apparent sources of information or the assumptions on the basis of which their decisions were made?

4. How did the behavior and decisions of the SBU head (Kessler) and of the CEO affect the progress and quality of the design work? Those of Underwood?

5. Use a two-column format for the following: In one column, briefly outline the series of decisions made on the Veetac as it progressed. In the other column, outline the series as it should ideally have proceeded to arrive at the best strategy.

6. List several recommendations that a consultant would probably make to Kessler for the more efficient development of new products and their strategies in the MCSD.

Rival Manufacturing Company

Was it just a glorious fluke? The winning ticket on a never-again, 90-to-1 combination? From 1972 to 1976 little Rival Manufacturing Co. of Kansas City, Mo. averaged a 49% return on equity. (This with scarcely any leverage: Debt was a low 13% of capitalization.) In the fiercely competitive, low-margin, pots-and-pans business, Rival had come up with a better pot. Rival looked like a real up-and-comer (*Forbes,* August 15, 1975).

But that was yesterday.

The dust has settled now at Rival. Isidore (Hack) Miller, 73, is still president. His hair is still chocolate brown and he vows he'll die in the saddle. He claims his squat little Crock-Pots once again have 80% to 90% of the U.S. slow-cooker market and are still his biggest, most profitable product line. But Rival's net income has dropped steadily from $23.5 million in 1975 to $4.6 million last year. Sales have shrunk from $126 million to $73 million. And return on equity has plunged from 77% to 9.1%.

"I think we did one helluva good job," says Miller defiantly through a bluish haze of cigar smoke. "Last year was the worse we've ever had and we still netted 6.3% on sales—that's better than most of our competitors do in a good year."

"Most companies that have gone as far up the mountain as we did have come back down in a loss position," adds Executive Vice President Charles W. Rootes with a marked Missouri twang.

"Let me tell you, survival isn't all that bad," he goes on, chronicling the short life of most products in the small-appliance business: "There were about 30 companies that copied General Electric's electric knife and most of those copiers got cut up real bad. In the evolution of hair dryers we've watched companies damned near go out of existence. That made quite an impression on us."

"We knew the Crock-Pot wouldn't last," says Miller after a pause, "That was reasonable."

So Hack Miller maintains that the Crock-Pot was simply a bonanza to be enjoyed while it lasted. But was it? Was the Crock-Pot the golden opportunity that could have launched the little company into the ranks of great U.S. corporations? Was it what sandpaper was to 3M, or rock drills for Ingersoll Rand? That's a fair question, but so is this: Would a man, fresh out of some prestige business school, have spotted the enormous potential in an obscure mail-order bean cooker? Miller did (thanks in part to years of experience as a housewares buyer for New York's Macy's department store). Would such a man also have sidestepped as adroitly as Miller most of the pitfalls spawned by the Crock-Pot's overnight success?

Those problems began to pour in right along with the first delighted letters from the newly Crock-Potted. First there was a production bottle neck. The Crock-Pot—basically a heating element in a steel can lined with covered stoneware—required absolutely round and level liners so steam won't drip back onto the cooking food, basting it. An imperfect liner that allows steam to escape could cause inadequately cooked food—possibly even botulism. But achieving such uniformity of shape in an ancient handicraft like pottery proved surprisingly difficult. The reject rate in the early stages reached as much as 80%. Many potteries refused to manufacture for Rival.

From *Forbes,* June 11, 1979.

"I debated for a long time whether we should make the liners out of glass, which would have been a lot easier to manufacture uniformly," says Miller. He decided against it because, he says, glass didn't produce quite as nice a taste, lacked the nostalgic appeal of stoneware, and—the clincher—was too easy for competitors to copy. "We'd have opened up the situation to competition much quicker if we'd used glass," says Miller.

To improve production quality and ensure supply, Miller took Rival full steam into the difficult pottery business (to be economic, kilns must be run round the clock). He also licensed a Japanese assembler to provide additional production for the U.S. market. "This was a calculated risk," says Miller, who concedes that it backfired, spawning future competitors: "He opened up probably more outside pottery sources than he needed." By borrowing more money, Miller could have opened up his plants at a faster pace instead—but he's glad he didn't. "Going from $126 million in sales to $75 million in just two years, we'd have gone under if we'd had more debt leverage," says finance man Rootes.

There were unexpected problems as well, problems a small manufacturer doesn't normally encounter, like watching to see that credit lines to wholesaler customers didn't get out of hand: "A set of distributors would have a line of credit with us to support $400,000 worth of business and all of a sudden they'd be buying $3 million from us annually," says Rootes. "But we couldn't just expand their credit. The credit-worthiness of their business hadn't really changed." So Rival demanded cash in advance. Strangely that hurt their other lines of business. "They'd buy Crock-Pots up to the limit from us and then say 'the hell with your can openers,' " says Miller.

Was it a mistake to set such rigid credit limits? "We went far beyond what any reasonable credit analysis would dictate with all of these people," says Rootes. "With unlimited credit we'd have made more gross profit on more volume, but instead of losing $60,000 when General Wholesale (a New England wholesaler) went down the tubes we might have lost $6 million. And instead of losing $250,000 when W. T. Grant went under, we could have lost $4 million on them."

· · · · ·

Then Miller got a bad break. There was a fire at Rival's largest supplier. Miller was distracted by the urgent need to replace that production. Says Rootes: "In retrospect the peaking of the market was that Christmas selling season. Our replacement efforts were overdone." Rival ended up awash in Crock-Pot inventory.

As order backlogs began to dwindle, Miller responded aggressively by trying to introduce a much broader product line. "We tried to blanket the competition, to run away from them instead of doing it with price," he says. "We developed a full line so that we had more models than the rest of the industry put together. But we tried to ram too many models through manufacturing at the same time. Each model had to be engineered separately. So we did not produce them according to our schedule that year. As a result, we lost placement in all those catalog showrooms in February where you're either in or out depending on what the committee selects."

By 1976, sales volume was nose-diving. "When those sales turned down . . . well, then it's too late," Rootes says. "You can't turn that inventory down as fast as you'd like. So we went on for a year and a half with way too much inventory for the sales we were doing."

· · · · ·

As the spiraling downturn gathered speed, Miller desperately tried to capitalize on the still-valuable Crock-Pot name, introducing the Crock-Plate and the Crock-Oven. But he was rushing now, and he made mistakes. Neither product has done well. "The control dials weren't good. And we didn't learn how to sell them. We said the Crock-Plate would do the work of ten appliances. That was overblowing the damned thing."

Meanwhile Rival's dividend payout, always generous, soared from 34% of earnings in 1975 to 135% two years later; Rival was paying out more than it was earning. This was not to line the pockets of Miller and Rootes, who between them own just 2.4% of the stock. Why then? Miller concedes that there "might" have been some pressure to maintain such lavish payouts from the controlling (28.9% of the common) interests.

. . . . .

Should some of that money have been used for purposes other than dividends?

"What would we have done with the money?" Miller asks. "Just acquiring companies isn't by itself the whole answer." That's a curious response since the Crock-Pot and indeed much of Rival's product line came to the company by acquisition. But Rootes makes the same response: "We certainly didn't pay out too much. We have almost $20 million in cash now and no well-defined plans as to what to do with it."

Listen to Miller: "My tongue was hanging out when I saw this Cuisinart food processor come out for about $200. We studied it, we tried it, and we very regretfully said, 'It's not for us. We don't think we can make money against all the people we know are in or are coming in.' Now our stockholders can say to us, 'What's the matter with you fellows? Here's one of the greatest items to come along and you don't have it. You're asleep.' But that was a decision on our part.

"Now, coffeemakers," he goes on. "We muffed the situation there. We could have been about three or four years ahead of Mr. Coffee. We had an arrangement with Siemens (the German electrical products giant), who had six or seven models and could have had any of them for a 2% royalty. But our sales department figured that the price they'd have to sell it at was too damned high." Says Rootes: "We thought it had to sell at $29 to be a volume item. There were a lot of percolators around at $19, but we overlooked the fact that the price break had moved up with inflation. When North America Systems came out with Mr. Coffee, they sold it in volume at $40."

Today the brightly lit design rooms of Rival Manufacturing are full of plans for a simple folding snack table ("We bought the tooling for this line of Versa-Tables for a pittance," says Miller).

Rival Manufacturing is going to stay around, thanks to Hack Miller. But an up-and-comer? No. That Crock-Pot was a fluke.

DISCUSSION

1. What technological forces were affecting Rival Manufacturing Company during the period covered by the above article (1972–79)? How well did Rival cope with or anticipate those forces?

2. Miller is quoted as saying, "I think we did one helluva good job." Do you agree? If you disagree to any extent, in what ways would you fault the company or its leadership?

3. Outline a program on which you would embark, if you were in Miller's place, with which Rival could capitalize on technological change.

PART FOUR
PRODUCT/MARKET UNIT STRATEGIES

Developing Products' Strategies

9

Marketing programs are actually formulated in the individual product/market units (PMUs). In Chapter 3 we discussed several aspects of products, including the product life cycle (PLC). This theory usually describes a product's life in terms of demand or sales volume, which begins when the product is being introduced or commercialized. Our view differs by considering that a product's life begins when it is being created and developed.

Different situations call for different strategies. Because product strategies change over the life of a product, the PLC theory provides a convenient means of classifying marketing strategies. Our discussion of strategies, therefore, is based on the five major PLC stages:

Evolution or development (from idea to commercialization)
Introduction
Growth
Maturity
Decline

New products are those in the first stage of evolution. Table 9-1 shows the relationship between decisions about new products and decisions that precede and follow.

The five sections of this chapter will (1) explain the nature and scope of

TABLE 9-1   Relationship between new-product strategies and other strategies

Corporate strategies	Determining the firm's scope: (a) the customers to be served, (b) the technologies to be applied, and (c) the products to be offered
New-product strategies	Discovering and selecting the customers' functional needs that are to be satisfied
	Conceiving and selecting product ideas that will fulfill those needs
	Giving direction and specification in the development work
	Testing performance and market acceptance of the proposed product
	Planning the new product's market introduction
Introduction strategies	Devising marketing plans that would establish the new product in the target markets

product strategies, (2) describe how product strategy decisions may be placed in the organization, (3) discuss the overall decision process, (4) describe optional strategies, and (5) explain briefly how decisions on strategies may be made.

NATURE AND SCOPE

New products have become one of the greatest business concerns. Maintaining competitive product offerings is essential to a firm's survival. For manufacturers this means taking large risks and making large investments. New-product strategies should obviously be made very carefully.

A new product typically incurs losses early in its market introduction. Nevertheless, corporations are tending to rely on young products for much of their profits. For example, in a recent policy statement by the CEO, the 3M Company required all of its divisions to obtain at least 25 percent of profits from products introduced during the previous five years. The prevalence of this policy is shown by findings in Booz, Allen & Hamilton's more recent comprehensive study of new products: Between 1976 and 1981 corporations obtained 22 percent of their profits from products introduced during the previous five years, and they planned to increase this percentage to 32 during 1982–87.[1]

Despite its popularity and importance, the term *new product* has evidently not been defined to general satisfaction. We all are aware of how the word *new* has been abused in advertising and means something different to a seller than it does to a buyer. Rather than getting bogged down with defini-

---

[1] *New Products Management for the 1980s* (New York: Booz, Allen & Hamilton, 1982), p. 4.

tions, we prefer to indicate our meaning by listing categories of new products, borrowing those of the Booz, Allen & Hamilton study mentioned above:

New-to-the-world products: New products that create an entirely new market. (These made up 10 percent of the new introductions observed during the study.)

New product lines: New products that for the first time allow a company to enter an established market. (20 percent of total)

Additions to existing product lines: New products that supplement a company's established product lines. (26 percent of total)

Improvements in or revisions to existing products: New products that provide improved performance or greater perceived value, and replace existing products. (26 percent of total)

Repositionings: Existing products that are targeted to new markets or market segments. (7 percent of total)

Cost reductions: New products that provide similar performance at lower cost. (11 percent of total)[2]

The above six categories are listed in order of risk involved. In the quoted study (which observed some thirteen thousand products launched by over seven hundred companies), the first two—and most innovative—categories constituted 60 percent of new products that were most successful. Nevertheless the study found that over half the studied companies "introduced no new-to-the-world products over the last 5 years." This failure may reflect conservatism or pressures to gain immediate profits from minor product changes rather than face the wait and risks entailed in developing real innovations.

New products also involve many functions and specialists throughout a company, a subject we will treat shortly. New-product decisions are of the broadest scope and must take into account a great many variables; this will become evident as the decision process is being described. The vast number of possible courses of action or options relevant to new-product decisions also affects planning tasks. Our space limits us to describing the most common options of major decisions.

Let us now look at the organizational setting for these new-product decisions and set the stage for the strategic-planning process.

ORGANIZATION

The position of any decision maker and his or her relationship to others in the firm profoundly affect what decisions may be made and how they may be

---

[2] *New Products Management for the 1980s,* p. 4. Another set of categories of new products, from research by Calantone and Cooper, will be described on page 291.

reached. Complicating factors for new products are indicated below, where we list various matters that should be assigned to four chief functional areas of a manufacturing firm. All of these matters must be coordinated by strategic planning.

Research and Development:
1. Estimating the technical probabilities of finding or creating desired products to meet users' needs.
2. Determining the research methods and facilities to be employed.
3. Determining the design, specifications, and performance of the product.
4. Correcting product shortcomings and devising improvements on the basis of tests or usage.

Production and engineering:
1. Determining feasibility and requirements of producing the contemplated product.
2. Planning the production facilities and methods.
3. Establishing complete specifications for production and materials.
4. Establishing quality standards and control systems.

Finance:
1. Projecting revenues, costs, and investments for the product venture.
2. Determining budgets for all activities.

Marketing:
1. Identifying unsatisfied needs and competitive openings that offer competitive opportunity.
2. Projecting sales potentials in selected markets.
3. Gathering or conceiving product ideas that would fit needs.
4. Planning and conducting product and concept tests; and evaluating test results.
5. Establishing sales forecasts and market performance standards.[3]

Although generally descriptive, the above list covers only a fraction of the involvement of various functional departments during the course of a product's evolution. One requirement for organizational placement of new-product direction, then, is that it be pivotal and allow ample communication with and coordination of the involved departments. Such supervision should also be removed from the ongoing operations of the functional departments and from the product managers of existing products. The latter tend to be preoccupied with their present products and have little vision or time for new products.

---

[3]Adapted from David J. Luck, *Product Policy and Strategy,* © 1972, pp. 7–8. Reprinted by permission of Prentice-Hall, Inc., Englewood Cliffs, N.J.

Three logical forms of organizing management are these:

New-product committees
New-product managers
Venture groups

Committees contain representatives from the affected departments and thus encompass a variety of viewpoints. They tend, however, to suffer from a lack of direct responsibility and from the limited time and commitment of their members, who naturally are chiefly concerned with their regular jobs. Committees should properly serve as review boards for advising and for approving of new-product plans and progress, rather than as overall managers of new products.

A new-product manager is usually a specialist unattached to the units responsible for implementing the plans. A whole *department* of new-product management is clearly superfluous, for that would duplicate the existing organization and be resented. The new-product manager would have at most a small staff.

Venture groups or teams resemble committees in drawing members from the involved units. However, assignment to a venture group is full time and continues until work on the evolving product is finished. Venture groups also bear direct responsibility for their decisions and accomplishments. Such teams tend to be expensive and are the logical method only for very large and innovative new products or new-technology projects.

In very active corporations, a single manager for new products may not suffice. Extreme cases are the companies that were said to have the largest number of new products during 1981, Campbell Soup and Unilever (which includes Lipton and Lever Brothers). Each of these companies introduced twenty-one new products. Considering that a typical new product requires years to evolve, these companies must have had many projects under way at any given time.[4]

Small firms, of course, cannot afford to have specialized managers or groups for new products. The owner or manager may be the technical person who invents or develops new products. The inability of such a small firm to organize product planning efficiently may be a serious handicap.

The complexity of the relationships among the various functions involved in new-product development is indicated in Figure 9-1. Imagine a situation where no new-product management exists and where these specialities attempt to communicate and work with each other without some centralized co-

---

[4]In the only comprehensive study of product development time, the median period was about five years (from idea to commercialization). The range was from eight months (a ballpoint pen) to fifty-five years (television). Lee Adler, "Time Lag in New Product Development," *Journal of Marketing Research*, January 1966, pp. 17–21.

FIGURE 9-1. Interfaces of new-product management. The main series of strategic decisions is shown horizontally, and functional inputs vertically.

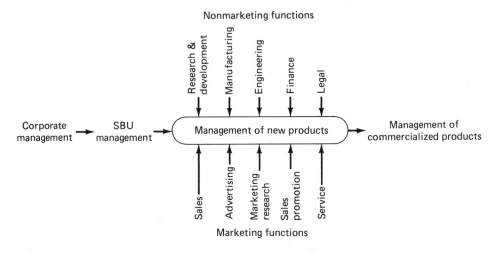

ordination. Under those conditions, new-product development is inefficient, if not chaotic.

DECISION PROCESS

A systematic model of the decisions to be made during a new product's evolution is needed to keep the work progressing and to make decisions in the right sequence. We will describe one logical sequence of such decisions, embellished with examples. The decisions will be of two types: (1) those that should be made prior to the planning and implementation of a specific product, which we will call *predevelopment decisions;* and (2) *development decisions* on a particular product.

Predevelopment Decisions

Three determinations must be made before making decisions for individual products:

Corporation goals, on which all planning is based.

Generic competitive strategy, which determines the firm's pattern of behavior relative to its rivals. (This is "generic" because these are the broad policy decisions regarding competition; specific ones would be made later.)

Generic development strategy, which determines the general approach to be taken in obtaining new products.

The path taken within the organization structure toward new-product development will vary according to the particular choices made during this predevelopment phase. Various paths are charted in Figure 9-2.

✶ *Corporate goals* serve to direct product development and to provide criteria for approving plans submitted to higher-level executives. As an example, Gould Incorporated set these criteria:

- The new product can be introduced within 5 years
- It has a market potential of at least $50 million and a 15 percent growth rate
- It will provide at least 30 percent return on sales and 40 percent on investment
- It will achieve technical or market leadership[5]

These are unusually high standards and would require a very active search for product ideas. However, Gould was in a fast-growth and high-return industry where such goals would be attainable. Most firms' objectives would be much lower.

---

[5]Philip Kotler, *Marketing Management: Analysis, Planning, and Control,* 4th Ed., © 1980, p. 313. Reprinted by permission of Prentice-Hall, Inc., Englewood Cliffs, N.J.

FIGURE 9-2. Four paths that may be taken in decisions that precede a new product's development. Letters refer to discussion in text.

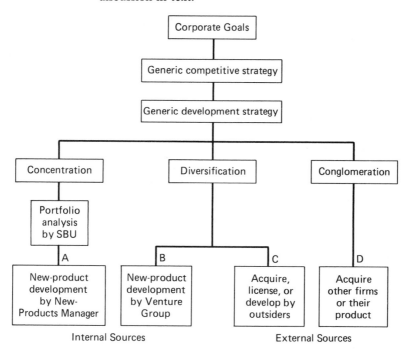

After establishing goals, the firm must set *competitive strategy*, which we discussed in Chapter 7 and Porter describes as

> . . . taking offensive or defensive actions to create a defendable position in an industry, to cope successfully with . . . competitive forces and thereby yield a superior return on investment for the firm.[6]

Porter has identified three generic types of competitive strategy: (1) overall cost leadership, in which volume and efficiency are the means of outperforming competitors; (2) differentiation of the firm's product or service offering, "creating something that is perceived industrywide as being unique"; and (3) focus, in which the firm concentrates on a certain market segment, geographical market, or segment of the product line. The significant effects of a competitive strategy on product choices may be evident. Overall cost leadership would tend to stress simplification of products, in contrast with the extensive redesigning, additional models, and special features that would be consistent with a differentiation policy.

Figure 9-2 shows *generic development strategies* above the three options that were discussed in Chapter 2, and four lettered paths leading from those options. If the decision is to concentrate within the firm's present business areas, one of the SBUs should be entrusted with creating the new product in path A, and the work is assigned to the new-products manager there. Diversification would tend to go too far outside the present business areas. If the preference is to develop products for that area using the firm's own personnel, a special venture group may be formed (or sometimes a venture department already exists), which is path B. Path C is the decision path for a firm to go outside in order to find products to enter the new business—this may involve developing new products or acquiring or licensing what others have created. For

---

[6]Michael Porter, *Competitive Strategy* (New York: Free Press, 1980), pp. 34–40.

TABLE 9-2 **Sales and profits of Beaver Division Products**

Product	Sales	1983 Projected results Gross profit (or loss)	Profit (loss) as % of sales	1982–83 Change in sales
A	$ 7,060,000	$(116,000)	(1.6)	−11%
B	8,438,000	314,000	3.7	− 1%
C	26,804,000	2,588,000	9.6	+ 8%
D	29,522,000	2,497,000	8.4	+13%
E	7,214,000	642,000	8.9	+21%
F	3,177,000	(606,000)	(19.1)	+10%
Total	$82,215,000	$5,319,000	6.4	+ 7.6%
1983 Objectives	$84,000,000	$5,250,000	6.2	+ 9.7%
Current planning gap	($1,785,000)	$69,000	0.08	− 2.1%

conglomerates entering technologies and markets that are strange to the firm, the surest route is D, to buy another firm already in that business.

Portfolio analysis can begin with an examination of the current product line's situation in the product life cycle. We will illustrate PLC usage with an example that we have used before, the Beaver Division, an SBU of the hypothetical BWI corporation. Current performance of its six commercialized products, as shown in Table 9-2, indicates their PLC status.

The data in Table 9-2 indicate that sales and profit performance by Beaver Division fell within 2 percent of the 1983 objectives. Two products, however, failed to make a profit: Demand for Product A had declined; and Product F had been introduced only recently and had not yet become profitable. As two products account for over 95 percent of profits, the division seemed to be vulnerable.

An analysis of the various products' PLC status is shown in Figure 9-3, with the individual items arrayed under the PLC curve. The six commercialized products are positioned along the curve, and five products under development are shown at their stages of evolution. Because none of the five new

FIGURE 9-3. **Beaver Division's products related to the product life cycle. Each product is located in its approximate life stage in 1983. Bars indicate the income earned or the outlays or loss incurred by each product.**
This style of analysis was initiated by Philip Marvin in *Machine Design*, January 8, 1959, pp. 107–11.

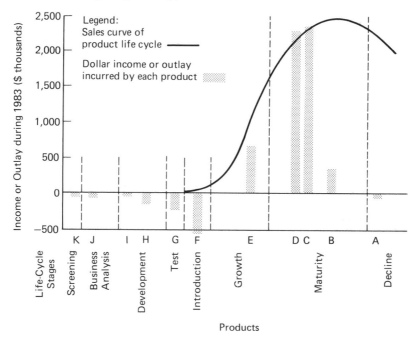

products has yet been marketed, the figure shows only the negative outlays for development work.

The PLC determinations deal only with current status and are preliminary to *portfolio analysis.* This stage of analysis should extend to the external environment (market, competitive, and other relevant factors). Portfolio analysis was presented in Chapter 3, and in Figure 9-4 we repeat its two-dimensional matrix. The six Beaver Division products are plotted showing the growth rate of their product category and their shares of market. Included are both current positions and three-year projections.

Figure 9-4 shows that there is only one "Cash Cow" in Beaver Division's portfolio, Product C, which stands below the division's growth norm for its product category but above its market-share criterion. There is only one "star" too, in Product D, which is above the norm for both growth and share. Table 9-3 shows that these are the only real profit makers. Projections are favorable in that four are expected to increase market share. The future position should be of concern, though, because the two weak products would worsen and only one would enjoy a market of accelerating growth.

FIGURE 9-4.   **Portfolio analysis of the Beaver Division's products on a market growth/market share matrix. Current (1983) positions are indicated by solid circles, whose area is proportional to sales volume. Forecasted position and volume (for 1986) are indicated by shaded circles.**

Source: Based on George S. Day,"Diagnosing the Product Portfolio," *Journal of Marketing,* April 1977, p. 34.

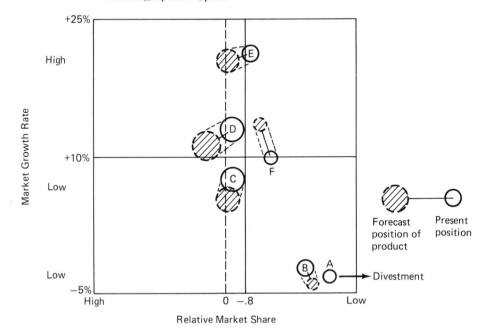

TABLE 9-3   Projected financial performance of Beaver Division Products

| Product | 1983 Actual results | | 1986 Projected results | |
	Sales	Gross profit or outlay	Sales	Gross profit or outlay
A	$7,060,000	$(116,000)	0	0
B	8,438,000	314,000	$ 6,000,000	$(200,000)
C	26,804,000	2,588,000	27,000,000	2,100,000
D	29,522,000	2,497,000	36,000,000	3,500,000
E	7,214,000	642,000	14,000,000	1,500,000
F	3,177,000	(606,000)	6,000,000	500,000
G	0	0	4,000,000	(100,000)
H	0	0	2,000,000	(400,000)
I	0	0	0	0
J	0	0	1,000,000	(300,000)
Total	$82,215,000	$5,391,000	$ 96,000,000	$6,600,000
1986 Objectives			$106,200,000	$7,100,000
Future Product-Planning Gaps			(10,200,000)	($500,000)

Planning should be explicit, arriving at figures with which the future planning gap can be calculated. This is done for Beaver Division in Table 9-3, which shows three-year changes that are expected and compares future results with goals. Beaver Division expects that only three of those products now being evolved will actually be marketed, and one will fail to survive the development cycle (I). The planners are not optimistic about any other new products emerging during those three years. The key data in Table 9-3 are on its bottom line. The division is not expected to meet its assigned objectives.

The environment must also be examined in making strategic decisions. Alternative solutions to the planning gap may be found not only in a stronger line of products but also in other marketing elements.

Strategic Development Decisions

Our discussion assumes that needs or opportunities for new products have been established. Decisions then proceed to strategies to create specific products. A *marketing strategy* will direct the work of evolving an actual product. Kotler divides marketing strategy into three parts:

1. The *target market.* Exactly for whom and for what uses is the product intended?
2. The *market position* that is desired for the new product. Where should it stand in buyers' perceptions in comparison with rival products (in features, quality, prestige, or other critical attributes)?
3. What *objectives* are sought in the new product? The type of objective

needs to be defined (e.g., cash flow, market share) and the level (e.g., $400,000 in its second year, or 25 percent share).[7]

Marketing-strategy decisions are shared by the SBU and PMU levels. The decisions should be consistent with corporate objectives and generic strategies. An explicit marketing-strategy statement will enable technical specialists to translate the concept into the eventual product.

Given the marketing strategy, the decision process for evolving the product proceeds. In Table 9-4 a decision flow for new products' evolution shows seven stages.

As each stage is completed, management should make the strategic or "kill" decision. A negative finding would kill the project unless the decision is instead to cycle back to an earlier stage. The phrase "back to the drawing board" may apply, especially when the proposed product is aimed at a great opportunity.

As a product's development proceeds through these stages, from a mere concept to an actual prototype and to final specifications and testing, the funds invested rise at an accelerating rate. Simultaneously, champions of the product may become increasingly desirous of completing and marketing it—and increasingly reluctant to halt the work. Many new-product fiascoes were due to stubborn faith in the product despite evidence that it would fail.

The particular sequence shown in Table 9-4 is only one of many that might be followed. A different sequence occurs when the new product has been invented or conceived first, before any determination of the markets and extent of demand. That is, it occurs when (1) a new product just happens to be invented, (2) one innovation in products or technology spawns the recognition of other products that these findings now make feasible, or (3) the firm had developed such a product earlier before there was enough market to justify finishing its development. In this sequence step 4 would precede step 3.

STRATEGIC OPTIONS

At each stage of the development process, there is choice among a number of options, and obviously there may be almost numberless implementation options. Our discussion will cover some of the outstanding alternatives for each of the principal strategic questions. We will start with broad strategic decisions and then move on to those relating to specific products.

Some key decisions in *research strategy* greatly concern the marketers. One deals with the timing of products' creation relative to competitors' innovations. If the firm or SBU desires to be *pro*active and beat all competitors to the market with new products, the appropriate marketing strategy will be

---

[7]Philip Kotler, *Marketing Management: Analysis, Planning, and Control*, 5th Ed., © 1984, pp. 287–88. Reprinted by permission of Prentice-Hall, Inc., Englewood Cliffs, N.J.

TABLE 9-4 New-product development decision sequence

Stage	Task	Basis of decision	Strategic question	Product's fate
1. Generating of ideas	Find ideas for products that might serve target markets	External search: Analysis of markets and of existing products' position. Internal search: Ideation and discovery	Does each idea have enough merit to study it.	NO→Drop YES *continue*
2. Screening of ideas	Assess the ability of the product to fit company and market needs.	Appraisal of each idea relative to criteria established for new products	Does idea satisfy criteria well enough for intensive consideration?	NO→Drop YES *continue*
3. Business analysis	Assess product's potentials, financially.	Projection of markets and revenue forecasts; analysis of costs and investments	Do projections satisfy our profit and investment objectives?	NO→Drop YES
4. Concept development	Prepare descriptions of optional forms of the product and means of obtaining reactions to them.	Reactions and suggestions of typical users to presented concepts	Does concept offer sufficient appeal to potential buyers?	NO→Drop YES *continue*
5. Prototype development	Construct actual models of product (full-sized and working).	Users' reactions and product performance in trial usage.	Does product perform adequately and appeal to potential buyers?	NO→Drop YES *continue*
6. Final development	Product specifications and design approval; production facilities readied; total marketing plan completed.	Test-marketing in limited areas; results in sales, in buyers' attitudes, and in distributors' support.	Does test experience indicate that company's objectives will be met?	NO→Drop YES *continue*
7. Market launching	Commercialize the product with large-scale market entry.	Sales and profit results in early selling periods.	Does early experience indicate that we have a successful product?	NO→Drop YES →Continue product program

285

sharply different from a policy of being *reactive*, awaiting competitive entry before venturing with the firm's own rival product.

The *scale* of development work is also a vital concern, with regard to both the overall research and development effort and to that devoted to each project. Allocation of funds is a key problem. The scale of work includes deciding how many new-product ideas should be put into development and passed through each stage in order to complete any given number of commercialized successes. The study by Booz, Allen & Hamilton, quoted earlier, examined the average number of product ideas or projects that passed each stage during the period of their observations. For their five stages, the numbers and percentages were as follows:

Stage of process	Pass ratio	Percentage of initial ideas surviving
Screening and evaluation	5 out of 7	70%
Business analysis	9 out of 10	63
Development	2 out of 3	42
Testing	2 out of 3	28
Commercialization	1 out of 2	14

Thus one out of seven ideas for new products in U.S. manufacturing firms culminated in a successful product. In our example, the Beaver Division would have had to find twenty-eight ideas for new products in a given year to succeed in adding four new products to its line. This success rate, we should point out, represents excellent progress for American industry. An earlier study for 1968 had found that fifty-eight new product ideas were needed for each successful product.[8]

There are *product line* strategic decisions to be made also. Because these decisions are broader in scope than those made for an individual product, they would lie at the SBU level of organization. One choice involves the degree of completeness of the firm's products. There are five options available:

Materials, the ingredients that are sold to other firms for inclusion in their products.

Parts, which are finished individual pieces that will be assembled by other firms into products.

Components, which are finished operable units that also enter into other products. An example is a motor whose manufacturer sells it to a firm making air conditioners, in which the motor becomes a component.

Complete products that can perform alone, such as a television set.

Systems, which constitute a set of complete products that perform together—usually a complex series of operations. The air conditioning of an

---

[8]*New Products Management for the 1980s*, p. 14. It is perhaps obvious that pass ratios should not be interpreted too literally. Many contingencies may arise that make a firm's new-product experience currently—or in the planned future period—vary widely from that of its past record.

entire building would require a system composed of machinery, wiring, ductwork, thermostats, vents, etc., and a single manufacturer might elect to offer all or most of these units as a product.

Manufacturers, generally speaking, would prefer to offer as complete a product as they are capable of making and marketing. Some, however, have limited capabilities or have special reasons for producing only parts, materials, or other less complete forms of products. Conditions may change drastically in an industry, bringing concomitant changes in strategies—the computer industry is a prime example:

> In the computer industry's early days, only one firm produced a complete product (or mainframe), IBM. IBM bought many of its parts and materials from other firms. Others entered the mainframe sector of the industry, but far more numerous were firms that made only parts or peripherals. IBM rapidly expanded its product line to develop ever-proliferating systems for complete installations, and systems became a way of life for industry leaders (such as Honeywell, DEC, Sperry, Burroughs, and CDC.).
>
> Nevertheless, various strategies can be viable for different firms. We earlier described little Systel and its word-processing peripheral, but large firms also are participating with only parts and materials (e.g., 3M Company and National Semiconductor). One growing member of the industry now offers only peripheral subsystems (Storage Technology, nearing a billion dollars annual sales volume).
>
> With the great dynamics of the computer industry, though, today's systems may become only subsystems to vaster networks of products, created in what have been distinct industries. Today the telephone, copy machine, and computer industries are beginning to invade each other's domains and to create supersystems that combine their various technologies. The strategic product decisions of that industry are truly mind-boggling.

Another product line decision is how many products or brands to offer in each specific product category. Multibrand strategies lead to some variety among the offered brands. Or, under the same brand, flanker products or varieties of size, taste, color, or other characteristics may be the chosen course of action, again calling for minor development.

Proceeding from these broader questions about product strategy, decision makers must then deal specifically with *one* particular prospective product. They must address the following questions:

1. How do the target buyers use the product? How do they buy it?
2. In what qualities or attributes are those buyers most interested? Which of those qualities are lacking in the products now available to them?
3. What specific qualities or attributes should be offered in the new product and at what price? At what level of value should it be positioned relative to existing products?

These important questions should be answered only after extensive search for possible product improvements and research into buyers' needs and practices. If the product is to enter a consumer market, it might do any of the following for consumers:

1. Provide protection from the elements
2. Improve living environment
3. Make work tasks easier
4. Provide entertainment
5. Be relaxing or stimulating

6. Reduce time necessary for completing tasks
7. Facilitate sport, competition, or challenge
8. Make movement more efficient (transport)
9. Cure illnesses and their symptoms and results
10. Provide safety from harm

11. Improve or extend the senses (sight, hearing, touch)
12. Facilitate creativity or self-expression
13. Reduce confusion or complexity
14. Provide knowledge, information, or insights
15. Contribute to order or organization

16. Extend memory (e.g., recordings)
17. Provide storage
18. Satisfy physical needs (hunger, thirst, exercise)
19. Enable or improve communication
20. Afford status/prestige[9]

When the target market is composed of business or institutional buyers, of course, different sets of motives apply. The following list contains some motives expressed by industrial purchasing agents:

1. Ease of use or operation
2. Technical specifications
3. Reliability
4. Technical service
5. Maintenance ease
6. Training required to use the product
7. Sales service after date of purchase
8. Flexibility in adjusting to needs
9. Training offered by the supplier[10]

---

[9]Reprinted from Edward M. Tauber, "Discovering New Product Opportunities with Problem Inventory Analysis," *Journal of Marketing,* published by the American Marketing Association, January 1975, pp. 67–74.

[10]Excerpted from Donald R. Lehmann and John O'Shaughnessy, "Difference in Attribute Importance For Different Industrial Products," *Journal of Marketing,* April 1974, pp. 36–42.

FIGURE 9-5. **Example of a creative strategy statement for advertising of a new product.**
Source: Thomas Hatch in Glen L. Urban and John R. Hauser, *Design and Marketing of New Products* (Englewood Cliffs, N.J.: Prentice-Hall, 1980), p. 70.

CREATIVE STRATEGY STATEMENT

Market target

Current users of chewable antacid tablets, primarily the O-T-C brands, Tums, Rolaids, and DiGel.

Symptom targets

Heartburn is the symptom target for three major reasons:
1. Heartburn as a symptom has not been preempted by another brand, Tums, Rolaids, or DiGel.
2. The major thrust of the product's difference and the creative strategy is speed of relief, the primary concern of heartburn sufferers.
3. Effervescent type products are not used in significant quantities in the treatment of heartburn, thus cannibalization of Alka-Seltzer will be minimized.

Core selling proposition

Gives the heartburn sufferer high speed relief.

Strategy definition

The only antacid tablet offering superior palatability and superior efficacy; i.e., speed of relief.
1. Support the efficacy claim, explaining that it disintegrates rapidly to get to work in your stomach fast.
2. Support the palatability by referring to its cool, creamy taste.
Subordinate to the texture support palatability by referring to cool and creamy taste.

Product features

The product is a chewable antacid tablet with a difference. It is formulated to disintegrate fast; i.e., "it's built to fall apart," therefore, it goes to work fast.
This superiority offers the consumer two distinct benefits to help relieve his heartburn.
1. Superior efficacy; i.e., it disintegrates fast to get to work on your heartburn fast.
2. Superior palatability; i.e., a smooth, finer-textured tablet that "chews fast."

Only a few of the broad categories listed above may be applicable in a particular instance. Some needs may be identified by coupling consumer data with creative insight and the firm's relevant experience. There are many other possible sources for ideas on these needs and how to meet them, a subject beyond the scope of this book. Through diligent and systematic effort numerous options should be gathered, screened, and made available to strategists.

Concepts on how to market the product should be evolving also. Marketing feasibility is an early consideration. How-to-design and how-to-market are interdependent determinations. Of special significance to product decisions is the promotion strategy. The key propositions in the selling and advertising appeals should be decided early so that the product can be designed to actually deliver the promised qualities.

Such a selling proposition is contained in Figure 9-5, along with other elements of the creative strategy for promoting a new antacid tablet. Given such a statement, the advertising people can begin to create copy while the laboratory people seek to formulate a product that offers the proposed consumer benefits.

For other types of products, creative strategy statements would differ from those in Figure 9-5. In some respects that antacid tablet was not difficult to describe, for it represented only improvements on brands already being sold. However, it had subjective qualities that might be hard to convey to the research and development people. A creative strategy statement for a new automobile would be much longer and would contain many specific details on what is required (e.g., fuel consumption, acceleration, seating room, exterior dimensions, weight).

The ultimate product's success (or failure) will be quite dependent on whether innovative and appropriate options have been found. Acquiring or conceiving them is an enormous challenge, but further decision steps remain, which will now be described.

MAKING AND ADMINISTERING
THE DECISIONS

At this stage strategists have defined and interpreted both the market and the competitive situation, have positioned the desired product, and have acquired the best available options. That they must now choose a course of action is rather apparent, but just saying that they "make" a decision gives an inadequate idea of what remains to be done.

The decision is not a single one, but rather a complex set of decisions on various aspects of the product as well as its anticipated marketing and production. All decisions must be compatible, and trade-offs will have to be made —some of them necessitated by financial constraints.

It would help management immensely, in making such decisions, to have a definition of the ingredients of new-product success, based on actual experience. Such principles would provide general directions for deciding specific strategies for a particular product venture. Research that would establish which factors have differentiated between successful and unsuccessful new products has been undertaken only recently. The outstanding study at this time (1984) is that by Calantone and Cooper on industrial products.[11] We are

---

[11] Roger Calantone and Robert C. Cooper, "New Product Scenarios: Prospects for Success," *Journal of Marketing*, Spring 1981, pp. 48–60.

summarizing some portions of their report that will suggest the value of such data. The researchers, in their words:

> hypothesize six blocks of variables to be determinants of new product ventures ... From these six blocks a total of 77 variables were identified ... [and] measured using a mailed questionnaire with scaled questions. Managers in ... randomly selected industrial firms were ... asked to supply data on two typical new product ventures: a commercial success and a commercial failure ... Data were collected on 195 new product cases.

By use of cluster analysis, nine groups or clusters of new-product types were chosen and given descriptive names. The three types that nearly tied for the highest success rate and that with the poorest rate were as follows:

	% of successes
The Synergistic "Close to Home" Product	72%
The Innovative Superior Product with No Synergy	70
The Old but Simple Money Saver	70
· · · · ·	
The Innovative Mousetrap That Wasn't Really Better	0%

Calantone and Cooper then prepared a scenario that described the factors characterizing each type. Here is an excerpt from the scenario for the Synergistic "Close to Home" Product:

> These products were most notable for their similarity to the company's existing products and markets. They scored low on the newness to the firm dimension, and kept the firm closest to home in terms of product class, production process, technology used, distribution and sales force, advertising and promotion, and competitors faced. Such products also featured a high degree of technical and production synergy and proficiency. The product was a high technology one and tended to be a defensive introduction.[12]

This study's findings must not be followed blindly. They are based solely on industrial products, and their validity may be somewhat time-dependent. Among industrial marketers they would often be inappropriate; for example, with a firm that must diversify out of its existing business area in order to grow and prosper—or with a firm that is oriented entirely to low-technology products.

Before proceeding to develop a product idea, one should carefully recheck whether the product would be an ideal solution to the buyers' problem. Failure to use such caution resulted in great losses for one company that had developed optical scanning devices because it misjudged its markets. That case is described below:

> You could have bought stock in the Recognition Equipment Company in 1966 for as little as $23 a share and resold it in 1968 for as much as twelve times your in-

---

[12]Calantone and Cooper, "New Product Scenarios," p. 59.

vestment—a wonderful profit. The company had been formed in 1961 to specialize in the development of optical scanning devices, and in 1968 there was great optimism about the future of those devices. But if you had held that stock until 1975, you would have seen it sink to only $2.25 a share. What happened? William Zarecor explained it as follows:

"... For some time, the capability of computers to read printed characters optically through pattern recognition has been technically feasible, and at a quick glance the commercial data-processing business seemed to suggest an obvious area in which to apply it. People were taking typewritten documents, keypunching cards from them, and then entering the data into computers via the cards. Obviously, if the original typewritten documents were to be read directly into the computer, redundancies would be eliminated. The market for this idea was the entire world of punch card users. . . .

"Could anything be simpler, more straightforward? Yet optical scanning has barely scratched the surface of that market over the past ten years, and . . . companies have come and gone in a futile attempt to do so, while others have struggled along. . . .

"Was there really no market at all? The answer is that the look at the market was superficial. Using punched cards to enter data into computers may be redundant, but the jump . . . to the conclusion that there was a need to read typewritten documents directly was incorrect. The real need was for lower costs . . . of original data entry . . . [to] make one act serve a dual function: create the data and enter it into the computer at the same time."[13]

Recognition Equipment Company was one of those that "struggled along." By 1975 it had sustained an accumulated deficit of over $20 million, but in that year it finally turned a profit and began to prosper. However, its marketing strategy had changed with a realization that its product was not needed in data processing but had other applications, such as sorting letters or reading documents (e.g., credit cards). Heavy research spending was involved (over 10 percent of sales revenue) to reengineer its product for those markets. Had the markets been targeted correctly in the first place, the product would have justified the great optimism of the 1960s.

After rechecking the market interpretation, one would proceed to choosing the product strategy options. This will be discussed in four stages:

1. Identify and maximize the differential advantages that can be incorporated into the product.

2. Hold strictly to the basic criteria of the marketing-strategy and product-positioning concepts.

3. Repeatedly determine whether environmental changes may have rendered the strategy obsolete.

4. At every stage of its evolution, test whether the product is satisfying the strategic criteria.

---

[13]Reprinted by permission of the *Harvard Business Review*. Excerpt from "High-Technology Product Planning" by William D. Zarecor (January–February 1975). Copyright © by the President and Fellows of Harvard College; all rights reserved.

Differential advantages are the special benefits or features in a product that make it more attractive (to buyers) than competing products. Utterly "me-too" products, which often appear in the market, are difficult to establish unless they carry a popular brand name or have other potent advantages over competitive products. It is obviously wise to research consumers before defining product concepts in order to identify all significant shortcomings of the products currently on the market and to decide which benefits or features would yield the greater advantages.

Therefore the development process should be preceded by a statement of the differential advantages to be sought during the design work. Some may be discarded at the outset as clearly not feasible; others may be discarded after design efforts fail. But it is best to start with a "dream list" of all the high-priority advantages that seem desirable. In choosing among the differentials, promotional potential should be a major consideration. For instance, if the product category is most effectively promoted by television, advantages that can best be communicated by that medium would be strongly preferred. This is a crucial phase of the decision process.

Adherence to the *marketing strategy* including the *positioning* defined for the product (in buyers' perceptions and in relationship to competition) is essential. The *criteria* that guide the many decisions during the creation of the product and its marketing plans should be *explicit* statements of what is desired. Many product failures can be traced to vague or fuzzy criteria that made the laboratory or design people guess what the specifications ought to be. The expression that seems adequate for marketing purposes is very likely to be ambiguous for the people who have to decide exact dimensions, materials, performance, and other actual characteristics.

Determining the particular options to be incorporated in the new product's specifications, then, is purely a matter of choosing those that best fulfill its concepts (as translated into the decision criteria.) At any stage of the process, it is vital that these criteria be *precise* and translatable into actual designs. The task is usually complicated because compromises or changes have to be accepted as the product evolves. That is, a desired quality seems either impossible or too costly, given price or investment constraints. (The first design for an automatic washing machine, for example, would have met most of the needs felt by homemakers. However, it would have been priced five times the maximum people would have paid for it.) Whenever the product concept has been compromised, planners should reconsider whether the product can still fulfill its objectives and whether the project should be continued.

In practical terms, a new-product manager can scarcely put in writing all the qualities desired in a product or state them in the technical terms that the research and development people need. Nor can all of the needed criteria be anticipated. This makes it highly desirable for key-marketing or new-product management people to be in frequent communication with key designers and technical researchers. The importance of this intercommunication is generally recognized now, although the problem of bringing it about remains. Many corporations are locating their new-product managers and their research and development managers conveniently close so that they may have a continuing dialogue.

The fourth rule is to *monitor the environment* into which the intended product would be launched. To ignore what is happening in the market, in newly emerging technologies and in competitors' offerings, would be sheer folly. A serious change may happen too quickly or subtly for prompt response, of course, so contingency plans should be ready.

> One of the most famous of product failures, the "Edsel" car, was partially caused by environmental change. The car's concept had been considered in the Ford organization for about a decade, and the Edsel would be positioned in the medium-price category of the industry. Demand in that category had been growing for many years. At the exact time of the Edsel's introduction, unfortunately, demand peaked and eroded fast—and so the project could not possibly have met its sales projections.

Firms pay special attention to competitors' actions or rumors of what they are doing or contemplating. News that a competitor has just ordered new tooling or is hiring certain technical staff can significantly affect a new-products program. It is equally important, though, to monitor buyers, despite the costs of market surveys and data services.

Testing to prove whether or not the product will satisfy the criteria set and meet favorable market reaction is mandatory, in whatever form is appropriate. Even in the first stage a product idea should be screened objectively against acceptance criteria by qualified internal people. Later when the project has been adopted and concepts of the product can be stated intelligibly, "concept tests" with users, dealers, or perhaps other impartial experts should be conducted. When actual prototypes have been made (if they are portable), "product tests" are needed. Such tests enable potential buyers to use or study or sense the proposed product (preferably a number of alternative variations, to help find the best combination).

The most decisive testing of many consumer products is a "market test." We need not discuss the methods here, since such discussion belongs with research techniques. Market tests are impractical with virtually all industrial products, with infrequently purchased consumer products, and with low-volume products. For mass-consumed packaged products, however, market testing is the culminating proof of whether or not a new item should be commercialized. Because such a test is so vital and expensive, objectives that must be met to indicate probable market success must be established. The following criteria were used by the Gillette Company in connection with the four-market testing of a new women's shaver:

> The Gillette Company staged a test market experiment of the "Daisy," a new shaver for women, in two pairs of markets: Dayton-Milwaukee and Memphis-Seattle. Some specific test market objectives were:
>
> 1. Achieve a 1.4 percent share of the entire blade market in Dayton-Milwaukee and 2.0 percent share in Memphis-Seattle.
> 2. Generate the equivalent of $686,268 in full revenue sales in Daisy's first year in the test markets.

3. Achieve a 9 to 11 percent trial rate among the potential women shavers in the test market areas.
4. Achieve an initial repurchase rate of 65 percent, followed by subsequent repurchase rates of 80 percent, then 90 percent.[14]

The objectives given for the Daisy were performance measurements, which allowed Gillette's management to judge whether that product should be introduced nationally. They do not uniquely measure consumer reception of the product alone, for all of the marketing strategy affected the results. If the company wanted consumers' evaluations of the product, it would have needed different data. As the company had previously obtained reactions to the product in use tests, it might have been satisfied about the product element in the strategy.

The dangers of slighting the five principles given in this section are grave. The "Edsel" stands as an example in several respects, besides that of a suddenly adverse change in market. The positioning of the new car was intended to appeal to young men "on the way up" who would trade for higher-priced cars. The designers, however, apparently had difficulty translating this concept into the actual car. There was scant testing of whether the car that they did design would fulfill the target market's desires. And it was quite apparent that the car lacked significant differential advantages over the already-established makes. The resulting fiasco naturally convinced the Ford management that the kind of principles discussed above should be closely adhered to in the future.

Our discussion has dealt primarily with the product variable in the development stage of the PLC, because that is of greatest concern to management. We have also dealt with the broader context of the marketing strategy for the launching of the product on the market. That strategy serves to direct the product's management during its next PLC stage, the introduction one—at least at its beginning. We will pick up the thread of the life cycle and strategic management during the introduction stage in Chapter 13.

SUMMARY

In this chapter we divided treatment of marketing strategies among five stages of the product life cycle. The first PLC stage, that of evolution or development, was treated in this chapter. This stage's decisions were oriented between the broad corporate and SBU plans and the introduction stage. The meaning of *new product* was indicated by listing six categories:

New-to-the-world
New (to the firm) product lines

---

[14]S. H. Starr, N. J. Davis, C. H. Lovelock, and B. P. Shapiro, *Problems in Marketing*, Fifth Edition (New York: McGraw-Hill, 1977), pp. 682–83. Copyright by the President and Fellows of Harvard College and reprinted by express permission.

Additions to existing product lines
Improvements in existing products
Repositionings
Cost reductions

On organization for new-product management, three alternatives were stressed: new-product committees, new-product managers, and venture groups. We described complications in this management's relating to and coordinating many other functions, each of which contributes to the planning process.

The decision process involves two major phases: (1) predevelopment decisions—corporate goals, generic competitive strategy, generic development strategy, portfolio analysis (traced with an example of a hypothetical product line); and (2) strategic development decisions—marketing strategy (target markets, market position, and objectives) and a seven-step series of development decisions. Strategic options were then described in terms of research strategy, scale of development work, and product-line strategy (in several degrees of completeness up to a full system). Options in product design were discussed, particularly with regard to the buyers' needs to be served. This was then related to creative promotional strategy for the new product.

Our final section described five principles that should be observed in deciding and implementing strategy: (1) redetermine whether the market opportunity is correctly interpreted; (2) maximize differential advantages in the product; (3) adhere strictly to the marketing strategy; (4) keep informed of changes in the environment during the period of development (which includes precision in design criteria and an ample dialogue between new-product management and the designers); and (5) test at every stage to ensure that the design is faithful to the product concepts and marketing strategy—and also to decide whether the product will succeed.

REVIEW QUESTIONS

1. *Consider the sequence of strategic planning, over time, of the interrelated plans. What do we call the major strategy whose determination should precede that of new-product strategies? What do we call those that would follow?*

2. *Is there a single product category or definition that would be termed* new-product *or are there several categories? If more than one, which is the most common category?*

3. *What four general functions in an enterprise usually cooperate in making their respective decisions and in actions related to new-product development? What is the* first *decision normally made? Which of the four functions makes that decision?*

4. What are three logical forms of new-product organization? Is it possible and reasonable for all three forms to be functioning within a single corporation simultaneously? Explain.

5. Does a new-product manager seem to have a simpler problem of interfacing with other managers for coordination of his or her responsibilities than other managers have? Or a more complex problem? Why is that the typical situation?

6. Before specific decisions are reached relative to a new product, what other decisions should have been reached earlier?

7. What is meant by generic development strategies? What are the broad types?

8. What is portfolio analysis intended to accomplish in new-product decisions? What did it reveal for the Beaver Division (as portrayed in Figures 9-3 and 9-4)?

9. Name the three major parts of the marketing strategy for new products and explain the purposes of each.

10. What strategic question is faced at each of the seven stages of a new product's development? What different sequence is frequently found? Does that change the questions to be faced?

11. What is a pass ratio? When a firm has the experience to determine such a ratio, what may be its value?

12. When the new-product decisions progress to their focus on the particular product, what are the chief questions that should be answered?

13. What is the purpose of a creative strategy statement? Should one be determined for every new product?

14. What general phase of decisions follows the market targeting and interpretation? For which of its steps is marketing responsible?

15. Do the form and extent of testing of new products vary much in practice? In what situations would different methods or degrees of elaborateness be justified?

Dev Industries

Rex Coppom, founder, president and chief researcher at DEV Industries, Inc. in Denver, is now marketing two models of a negative ion generator: the Biotron and Air-Care Systems. These solid-state electronic systems are defined by Coppom as "interior environmental improvement systems," and are designed to restore to the indoors the naturally balanced electrical forces that are found in the atmosphere on fair weather days. These devices emit an invisible "negative electron wind" that is purported by its manufacturers to alleviate a wide array of human ailments ranging from headaches and tension to fatigue and irritability.

Similar systems have been widely used in Germany and other countries abroad for more than 20 years, but in October 1962, the Federal Food and Drug Administration issued a press release listing seizure actions against several negative ion generator manufacturers. In the majority of the cases, legal actions were brought against manufacturers due to false and misleading labeling. Even though all of the manufacturers involved agreed to relabel their products, the FDA proceeded to launch a new enforcement drive against the claims that negative ion generator air purifiers were effective for treating or preventing diseases. Consumers were warned not to spend their money for such devices, and as a result, the popularity of negative ion generators declined.

Coppom formed Dev Industries in 1971 in eastern Wyoming and developed an improved system which combined the negative ion generator with an electrostatic field element. He continued to work on his idea in Wyoming until 1976, when he decided to move to Denver in order to be closer to a metropolitan center for marketing and distribution purposes. Now that the major technical problems have been resolved and a superior quality product has been developed, Coppom feels that Dev Industries needs to realign its priorities and focus more effort on its marketing program. The most formidable and challenging task facing his company, says Coppom, is to educate both the industrial and consumer publics about his product and inform them of its benefits while concurrently seeking to eradicate the negative attitudes which have built up towards the negative ion generator.

During a special meeting with Bill Emmerich, the recently-hired Chief of Marketing and Customer Services, Coppom discussed the situation facing Dev Industries. Emmerich was asked to redefine Dev Industries' marketing strategy to reflect the firm's shift from its previous production orientation to its current marketing emphasis and to design a comprehensive five-year marketing program focusing on the development of specific marketing opportunities in the commercial, industrial, and consumer segments. In order to accomplish this task, Emmerich first decided to gather as much information as he could find that was relevant to Dev Industries' target market, competitive situation, market potential, etc. He compiled the following information.

This case was prepared by Bruce Gunn, Professor of Marketing at The Florida State University, as a basis for class discussion rather than to illustrate either effective or ineffective handling of a marketing problem. Copyright © 1982 by Bruce Gunn. Used with permission.

HISTORICAL PERSPECTIVE

Much research concerning the biological effects of negative ions has been conducted since scientists discovered air ions over 75 years ago. Such experiments were difficult to perform, however, and much poorly-controlled work has been reported with the result that the subject carries a stigma of distrust. Both positive and negative ions are known to exist in the air around us at all times as a result of a natural electrical force field existing between the Earth, which is negatively charged, and the ionosphere, which is positively charged. This force field causes charged air ions to flow back and forth which cleanses the air of pollutants and helps to recharge our bodies. Indoors, however, humans cannot take advantage of this beneficial force field because the walls and roofs of buildings block out most of this ion flow. Meanwhile, air conditioners and heaters, cigarette smoke and other pollutants, and even some synthetic fabrics and carpets, either produce or attract positive ions. As a result, indoor air is flooded with positive ions, creating an electric field condition similar to that which exists just before a storm or weather front. As our bodies are bombarded by too many positive ions, a certain hormone is automatically secreted which reduces breathing by 30% in order to slow down our intake of positively charged pollutants. Unfortunately, this results in a decrease in the oxygen level of the blood, causing lethargic, depressed, or cranky feelings. The negative ions which are missing and causing the altered state of personality in such environments can be replenished by negative ion generator units, like the Biotron and Air-Care Systems.

Mr. Coppom first became interested in researching the effects of negative ions on humans while enrolled at the University of Munich in Germany during the 1960's. German research in this area had been going on since World War II when it was noticed that submarine crews were having trouble staying alert on long voyages. Few negative ions were detected in the air in submarines, as compared with positive ions, so the problem was solved with the installation of a negative ion generator to restore the balance. At the same time, German aircraft crews were having similar difficulties flying long-range missions, but this problem was solved by installing a "field unit" which replaced, inside the aircraft, the natural electrical field force for outdoors. Coppom worked with German engineers on such systems and then returned to the U.S. to continue his research in 1968. At that time, he decided to combine the generator and field units into one system.

The electric force field component was added to the system for two reasons. First, it serves to facilitate movement of charged matter and pollutants from the air into its field electrode elements where these pollutants are destroyed. Bacteria, virus and microbes are also drawn into these field elements and killed by the element's high electrical potential. Additionally, the field serves to distribute the beneficial negative ions more evenly throughout the room and to neutralize or override "stray" electric fields caused by charged plastics or synthetic materials. An examination of the two systems and their components follows.

PRODUCT INFORMATION

The Air-Care II is a room-sized unit, designed for areas up to 200 square feet. It consists of: 1) a Field Electrode, which attaches to the ceiling and creates the natural, fair-weather outdoor electrostatic field indoors; 2) a desk-top, multidirectional Negative Ion Generator, which contains the electronics to power ion and field generation, plus interconnecting cable connectors.

The Biotron Master System is designed for multiple room applications. This system consists of: 1) Electronic Control Module—to regulate and supply the necessary electric potential to remote Field Electrodes and Ion Generators; 2) Field Electrode—one unit per room or per 200 square feet; 3) Negative Ion Generator—available as hanging or desk-top model, 1 unit per room or area up to 200 square feet; 4) Interconnecting Cable, Connectors, etc.—to connect field electrodes and ion generator with the master control module.

Both systems carry a two-year limited warranty in components and workmanship. The Air-Care II includes simple do-it-yourself installation instructions. The Biotron also includes detailed installation instructions, but custom installation is available for either unit. It is necessary to analyze the target market of the two ion generator systems produced by Dev Industries.

DEV INDUSTRIES—TARGET MARKET

At the present time, Dev Industries views its target market as the industrial and commercial market segment. This broadly-defined market encompasses all types of business applications, including office buildings, retail stores, professional offices, and manufacturing plants. Systems have also been installed in hospitals, schools and in private consumers' homes; however, these markets are presently considered secondary segments which will be explored in a long-range program. This is because more preliminary research is needed for the hospital segment; for example, in order to substantiate the validity of the concept and scientifically prove the manufacturer's claims of more rapid healing, prevention of infection and removal of odor in patients' rooms. The general consumer, on the other hand, is considered the bottom market or the segment that Dev Industries is least concerned with at the present time. This is due to the massive, intensive education process that is deemed necessary prior to extensive coverage of this market, as well as the exaggerated expectations that the general public could probably build up regarding the negative ion generator. Although these devices are available to the consumer, no major effort is being made to develop this market segment.

PRESENT MARKETING PROGRAM

Currently, no funds are allocated in the budget for marketing, promotion or any type of advertising campaign. All publicity in the past has been derived from magazine, television, and newspaper stories which typically featured some users of the Biotron or Air-Care System. In general, emphatic support was given to the claims made by the manufacturer, and questions regarding the system were answered by these media. Although all of this free publicity created a favorable image for Dev Industries, no specific efforts were being channeled towards reaching and impacting its main target market: industrial and commercial users. A regional marketing effort for Denver had been tentatively planned, but problems had been encountered concerning which specific markets to seek out first. An examination of the present distribution process aimed at the existing target markets is presented below.

DISTRIBUTION NETWORK

Dev Industries has several dealers located in different parts of the U.S. who market the Biotron and Air-Care Systems regionally. A limited number of these dealers market these systems exclusively, with the majority of the dealers carrying an assortment of other related items, such as water distillers and purifiers, heating and air conditioning systems, and a variety of air filtering, purification, and sterilization devices. In addition to these outlets, both systems are also available to the public through periodic mail order advertisements in publications such as *The Wall Street Journal*.

However, there have been several negative impacts on the Ion Generator Industry. An example of this can be seen in the FDA statement published in 1978.

FOOD AND DRUG ADMINISTRATION STATEMENT

To date, the FDA has not made any specific claims against the use of negative ion generators. Because health claims have been made concerning the effects of using negative ion generators, these machines are classified as medical devices. In October of 1978, the Bureau of Medical Devices (BMD) stated its position regarding these devices as follows:

> "... to date, no valid scientific data which would lead the BMD's medical advisors to conclude that negative ion generators are effective for therapeutic use has been established. Although considerable scientific research has been conducted over the years to substantiate therapeutic claims for these devices, it is the opinion of our medical advisors that when research is of a controlled scientific nature, it has not demonstrated any beneficial effect. Furthermore, ion generation devices promoted as effective in the treatment or prevention of various diseases on allergic conditions through air filtration, purification or sterilization or germicidal actions are in violation of sections 502(a) and/or 502(f)(1) of the Food, Drug, and Cosmetic Act; that is adulteration or misbranding ... Negative ion generators may be marketed provided that the manufacturer makes no medical claims or representation for these devices ... Please be advised, however, in 1962, the Food and Drug Administration took action against several kinds of air purifying devices, including negative ion air purifiers. These products were seized on charges of false and misleading claims. Our view on devices termed air purifiers and negative ion generators has not changed to a great extent since then, as the evidence that has been presented in support of the effectiveness of such devices has not conclusively demonstrated that negative ions have significant therapeutic value."

Along with this nonsupportive statement by the FDA, this industry has additional problems of public acceptance.

PUBLIC ACCEPTANCE

As previously mentioned, education of the general public about the benefits and the concept underlying the effectiveness of negative ion generators still presents a substantial problem for Dev Industries. On one hand, most consumers do not have a clear perception of ions and what they are. Thus, since they cannot see, feel, hear or "touch" these particles, there is a tendency to believe that nothing is happening and that no visible difference in the environment results from the generators. Prerequisite to the development of a successful marketing program, then, it is imperative that the consuming public first be convinced of the scientific validity of the concept. After this is established, acceptance of the product will follow a cleverly designed promotion and advertising campaign. On the other hand, such statements as the aforementioned position issued by the FDA presents a serious threat to the development of an extensive target market.

Coppom does not feel, however, that statements made by the FDA have damaged the market for his product, nor does he feel that these statements pose a great threat to the growth in consumer acceptance in future periods. Rather, he fears that if a sudden increase in demand were to occur, Dev Industries would not have sufficient capacity to produce enough units to satisfy the demand. This would leave Coppom's firm vulnerable to a larger manufacturer who could meet the extra demand or seek to take over Dev Industries.

COMPETITIVE SITUATION

Although Dev Industries is a small operation compared to the many multi-million dollar firms in the U.S., it is the largest manufacturer of negative ion generators, and the only manufacturer of systems which combine the generator with the electric field element. It is also one of the few, if not the only firm, which is involved with ongoing research projects designed to further document areas of benefit for these machines. Most of its competitors' products are cheaply made and produce by-products, such as ozone, which presents a potential hazard to users of the devices. Dev Industries, on the other hand, prides itself on the superior quality products it produces, and expects to receive underwriter laboratory approval for its products in the near future.

In addition to its larger size, Dev Industries has another advantage over most of its competitors. Dev Industries manufactures only one product, as opposed to others in the industry that are involved in the production of a wide variety of product lines. Thus, more specialization, product knowledge, and concentrated research activities would tend to make the Biotron and Air-Care Systems superior in many ways to similar products made by competitors.

Their competitively superior position does not leave Dev Industries without problems. The following is a statement of one of the company's unresolved problems.

UNRESOLVED PROBLEM

One problem reported by several users is an accumulation of dirt on walls and carpets. This problem mainly exists in the more heavily polluted areas and occurs when the pollutants which radiate from the generator attach to the walls rather than the field electrode. In actuality, the field electrode collects a large portion of the pollution particles, but in areas with extremely heavy pollution problems, a significant enough portion of pollutants accumulate to present a problem to users. Coppom feels, however, that this problem can be turned into an asset for his company because it provides proof of the system's efficiency in cleansing pollutants from the air.

DISCUSSION

After Emmerich had collected and organized this information, he sat down and began to formulate a new marketing strategy. Describe the type of marketing program you would develop and present to Coppom, the CEO, if you were Emmerich.

CASE 9-2

RCA Corporation, Mobile Communication Systems Division (C)

A new product rarely evolves with an ideal and smooth progression of decisions. Nor can it often be based on wholly adequate data and on very accurate forecasts. Such deviations from the ideal are normal. To them add the foibles of human subjectivity that ensure that some failures will occur in every product development project.

Case 5-2 presented an unusually detailed account of how one product, a mobile radio, was developed. The questions for that case related to marketing's roles and organization for strategic decisions, which were discussed in Chapter 5. Case 5-2 actually dealt more with the process by which that product evolved and thus is relevant to Chapter 9. If you have not already read Case 5-2, you should read it now so that you will be able to discuss the questions in this case intelligently. Or, if you read it earlier, you should review it now. Besides that, some of the examples in Chapter 9 will provide some ideas and standards for your analysis of the case as directed by discussion questions below.

DISCUSSION

1. Using the terminology of Chapter 9, answer the following questions: (a) In which of the six categories of new products would you classify the Veetac? (b) In which, if any, of the given organization forms would you place the management of the Veetac project?
2. Compare the decision path followed in the Veetac's development with (a) Kotler's three parts of strategy making and (b) the sequence shown in Table 9-4. Were any omissions or deviations that you perceive in the Veetac project of potential danger to the product's success? Discuss your reasoning.
3. Try to write a brief "creative strategy statement" that would be useful in selling the Veetac. Is anything missing in the case or apparently in the division's product planning that you would need to write an adequate statement? Name some benefits that would have been realized if those people had prepared a creative strategy statement.
4. Write a brief list of changes that the division ought to make in its methods of identifying and developing a new product.

10

Introduction and Growth Strategies

Planning throughout an organization should be coordinated with the higher-level plans that are dominant. Those higher-level plans, however, are realized only through the strategies of the basic product/market units. This chapter discusses the marketing strategies of those units. New-product development, the subject of Chapter 9, is the responsibility of the new-product manager. When a product is "born" with its market introduction, it is placed in a specific product/market unit, and the PMU's strategies begin.

Clarification is needed of the timing of the introductory marketing decisions. *Work* on these decisions would begin long before the date of product introduction, perhaps originating during the earlier days of development. *Execution* would not take place, however, until the date of market launching. In this chapter we will first discuss strategies for product introduction. We will then cover the second PLC phase, the growth stage.

INTRODUCTION

An identical format will be used for each of the four product life stages covered in this chapter and Chapter 11. This format will comprise four parts: objectives, situation analysis, strategic needs, and strategy options. For the first three stages, an additional topic is the experience of that stage which provides a transition to the next stage.

Some worrisome questions must be asked in planning a new product's introduction:

Does our product have sufficient *differential advantages?* Will buyers consider it to be superior to whatever they now use?

Have we *good timing?* Is the strategic window really open at this time, with demand sufficient and the product market-ready? Can we preempt competitors from seizing the advantage?

Will our strategy prove to be *sustainable* against competitors who are in the market or who will soon invade it?

The planner has the greatest latitude of choices at this time, but also the greatest possibility for disastrous error.

Objectives:

Objectives set the requirements for the strategic program and also constrain what can be done. Three aspects must be considered:

1. Role of the product in the firm. It may be one of these:

A leader in *innovation* because of its uniqueness. (When RCA introduced its Selectavision videodisk player nothing like it was available. It was a very important venture, for RCA's CEO described it as "RCA's priority project for the decade."[1]

Entrant in a new market in which the firm has not yet participated. (When General Motors, long experienced with other diesel applications, began making diesel locomotives in 1939, it was newly entering the market to railroads.)

Entrant in a new-use category. (Liquid soap was used in hospitals and public washrooms but not in homes when Minnetonka saw an opportunity and brought out "Softsoap" for general consumer use.)

An improvement in an established product category. (When Procter & Gamble brought out its Pampers paper diaper in 1964, paper diapers were nothing new. P&G had developed features, however, that would make a more satisfactory diaper.)

An extension of the product line. This would include a product that actually is not much different from other brands already on the market. (Quaker Oats came out with its granola bar years after Nature Valley and other brands. Quaker was already strong in cereal products and merely extended its line.) This would also include "flanker products," such as the

---

[1]Edgar Griffiths, as quoted in the *Wall Street Journal,* July 6, 1981, p. 15.

addition by Oldsmobile of the Cutlass "Ciera" line to its established Cutlass line.[2]

2. Profit and volume goals.   Profit and volume goals have far-reaching effects on strategies. These objectives not only set the challenge but affect the level of funds available for the marketing campaign. If profit is the salient goal, prices may have to be high or expenditures low. If instead volume is mainly sought, a vigorous campaign strategy would be indicated.

> A classical example is the contrast between Hewlett-Packard and Texas Instruments in electronic products. H–P has stressed profits and higher margins by offering more-advanced technology at higher prices. As TI has stressed volume, its strategies have included cutting prices and maximizing production efficiency. These two companies have evidently defined their businesses differently, leading to divergent policies.

3. Investment payout period.   The firm must set some time limit on how long it will wait for a new product's profits to recoup its investments. The period's length should vary with the risks and life expectancy of the product.

> A long payout period like four or five years allows heavy initial outlays and an ambitious strategic program, as losses in the first year or so may be balanced out later. Short periods constrain the program and call for quickly effective marketing that may forgo maximum volume or a strong grip on the market. Many firms, though, cannot stand prolonged initial losses, or they need a fast payout to finance other projects.

Situation Analysis

The situation into which the product would be launched needs a very careful analysis before possible marketing programs can be considered. Of the many factors that should be taken into account, we will focus on some market and competitive ones. Four key aspects in a product's situation can be described as follows:

> *Degree of innovation.* The greater the similarity between a new product and others that have been marketed, the greater the reliance that can be placed on past experience. In such cases, sales potentials in the product category have also been proven. Such similarity does make it more difficult to impress buyers with significant differentiation from existing products. (Quaker Oats seems to have this problem with its granola bars.) A highly innovative product (like RCA's videodisk player) has more serious

---

[2]A *flanker product* can be described as a slight innovation in a firm's mature product "to defend the product against competition and to extend its life by adding product modifications or introducing slightly different brands to tap smaller market segments." Glen L. Urban and John R. Hauser, *Design and Marketing of New Products* (Englewood Cliffs, N.J.: Prentice-Hall, 1980), p. 495.

unknowns to face, more roadblocks to overcome, and a longer road to profitability.

Learning requirements. When buyers perceive high risk in trying a new product or find it complex and strange, the marketer faces the task of overcoming learning difficulties. Painstaking and repeated explanation may be needed when long habits are to be broken. (Railroad officials whose only experience was with steam found it hard to accept a diesel locomotive. And even a simple act of squeezing out liquid soap rather than reaching for a bar has apparently not been accepted by most American consumers.)

Market potentials. Obviously there is enormous difference in various products' potentials, in both life expectancy and quantity sold per year. Sales volume forecast is a key step in strategic planning. For frequently purchased mass-marketed consumer products (like soap or many foods), a market test would objectively gauge probable sales. Such a basis for estimation would not be feasible for industrial equipment (diesel locomotive) or appliances (videodisk players).

Competitive forces. Serious consideration of the competition is necessary before deciding whether to enter a market and with what entry strategy. After identifying the kinds of barriers, the strategist should examine relative advantages of incumbent firms in that market (such as their established distribution and reputation) as compared with the firm's own innovations.

Strategic Needs

The planner has determined the significant factors or problems through the situation analysis. Now a strategic program must be designed to market the new product successfully (that is, to reach the established objectives). In our basic four-step series of decisions, formulating the strategic program is the third. At this point, we are dividing that decision into two stages: (1) defining what *needs* to be accomplished and (2) formulating a marketing *program* that would succeed, by choosing the right strategic *options*. Here we will discuss the needs, and our next section concentrates on the options.

The analysis of needs should primarily cover those of buyers or consumers. As the majority of goods must reach a consumer through a channel of retailers and perhaps wholesalers, the needs of those distributors also must be satisfied in the product's introduction. (For services and for business or institutional goods sold directly to ultimate buyers, distributors' needs do not apply.) We will speak of five key needs of consumers and three of distributors.

Consumer or buyer needs:

Awareness of the new product. A buyer must be aware that the new product exists and must know about its uses or the needs that it is designed to satisfy. This awareness should include the brand name and label so that a buyer can differentiate the product from substitute products.

Information about the product and its merits is always needed by a buyer. The amount of information that a buyer needs may be minimal when only a small risk is entailed by a trial purchase. When high risk and high cost are perceived by buyers, much information, many messages, and a long period may be required to convince purchasers.

> Consider, at one extreme, a person who becomes aware of the new Quaker granola bar in a store, priced at 30 cents. A trial purchase is cheap, and since the product is basically similar to other granola bars, risk is minimal. In contrast, the person considering RCA's new videodisk player priced at around $500 needs much information and reassurance. Far greater were the information needs in 1950 of a railroad executive faced with decisions about spending many millions to replace steam locomotives with diesel power. A less-risky decision, but still one demanding an immense amount of information, would be that of airline executives now considering buying the new Boeing-757 or Airbus for their fleets.

Position of the firm's new offering, as perceived by the buyer. How does the buyer define what the firm is offering in terms of what the product does, its quality, and its value and relative advantages? Unless a superior position is gained in the buyer's mind, the new product will not be bought.

> For example, when General Foods was preparing to introduce its "Gainesburger," which was the first moist dog food in a patty, there were two main product types against which to compete: (1) the extruded dry dog food like Ralston's Dog Chow, which would be much lower priced and was the larger seller, or (2) canned dog food, which was higher priced and made up less of the market. Which should GF position its new product against? It elected to go against the canned products. And how could GF's product be positioned favorably against them? GF sought an image like that of hamburger patties, emphasizing ease of serving and storing.

Inducements to buy are typically needed, even if awareness, information, and positioning needs are being satisfied. Both hesitation in trying the new product and inertia in buying and using what one is accustomed to must be overcome.

> If the buyer is induced to try a consumer product, its advantages will often be perceived, and purchase will follow. We will discuss some of the options to accomplish this in the next section. These would contrast with suitable inducements for a very costly industrial product.

Availability is another vital requirement. The new product must be placed within a buyer's reach, as conveniently available as the products it hopes to supplant. Achieving this depends on distributors' willingness to carry and to promote the new product.

ibutor needs

Profitability. Retailers and wholesalers obviously are operating to earn profits. They are also reluctant initially to take on a new product (for they are offered several times as many as they are willing to stock). A retail buyer must perceive that the profit margin yielded by a new product and/or its turnover rate are equal to or exceed those of substitute products now being carried. Indeed, because of the risks involved, retailers tend to demand some special extra profit on their first orders.

Dependability. A distributor will have had both bad and good experiences with vendors and with manufacturers' brands. Can the firm marketing the new product be depended on to have a marketable design and good quality and a capable promotion program that will attract buyers? Will it fulfill its promises in maintaining quality, in deliveries, and in other support?

Physical handling. Several aspects of handling may prove to be critical. Size of containers and cartons, freedom from damage and breakage, ease of warehousing and of stocking shelves, ease of displaying the new product, and assortments available are some of the factors that must be planned right in marketing new products. No mere details, these are serious considerations of dealers as they examine new products.

The above discussion of the principal buyer and distributor needs will serve as a background for decisions on the options available in a marketing strategy.

Strategic Options

The second phase in determining a new product's strategies involves assembling the various options or alternatives and selecting the composite that best meets the (already determined) needs. This phase may in turn be divided between the general strategy for the product and its particular marketing strategy.

The *nature of the firm* strongly affects the *general strategy:*

Is the firm the *innovator* (first out) or a *follower* (a later entrant) with the new product? The innovator's strategies are affected by having to take the creative risks and having to judge the size and rate of exploiting the potential market. A follower is intent on taking away market share, determining whether the innovator's strategy can be improved on, and deciding how to render the innovator's product obsolete.

What *differential advantages* does the firm have for market entry? They may depend on these aspects:

> Quality or features of its version of the new product
> Costs and efficiencies

Effective field sales force and distribution systems that can move the product into and through the market

Advertising and promotion expenditures and expertise that can attract buyers

Brand name or firm's reputation that is already established

If a firm has such advantages and creates a strategy that maximizes them in the situation, its position as an innovator may be almost invulnerable or, as a follower, it may be able to gain a strong beachhead very quickly.

The *nature of the industry* and its *markets* constrain the alternatives:

The competitive nature of the industry is important. (In a high-technology industry, firms make product changes fast. Therefore a *technology-driven* strategy is needed that stresses product development and manufacturing. A consumer mass market instead calls for a *marketing-intensive* strategy.)[3]

Two general options for an entering firm are (1) to reduce competitive barriers by using the same competitive strategy as incumbent firms—and hoping to do this better, or (2) to avoid competitive barriers with a different strategy. In studies of hundreds of entering firms, Yip found that a majority of firms took the first approach of emulating, although they were in a poor position to do so (and none gained the market share held by top incumbents). It appears wiser to find and use a different strategy.[4]

The *scale of entry* in the product launch needs to be determined and will affect the strategic program. By "scale" we are referring to both the size of program and the phasing of the market entry:

1. The size of marketing campaign in market entry would depend on such factors as total potential sales, expected growth rate, and consumer resistance, as well as how quickly competitors are likely to follow. A follower would have to spend more lavishly when the innovator of the product already has a strong foothold.

2. In the phasing of the market entry, there are three general options:

   National introductions make the product immediately available to the whole nation at the announcement date. This approach can use a huge fanfare in national media and is logical when other firms are expected to enter soon. It is used, for instance, by automobile companies when they bring out a new line or model. Services and direct-marketed products

---

[3]Robert Stobaugh and Piero Telesio, "Match Manufacturing Policies and Product Strategy," *Harvard Business Review*, March–April 1983, p. 114.

[4]George S. Yip, "Gateways to Entry," *Harvard Business Review*, September–October 1982, p. 85.

Zone or *rollout* introduc̶t̶i̶o̶n̶s̶ ̶~~~
eas and then phase it into others. This is the com̶~~~
marketed packaged goods, where production startup, distribution, and
the sell-in to distributors are immense tasks. Also a gradual rollout permits the marketer to learn by trial and error while introduction proceeds.

Segmented introductions are especially suitable for industrial products
for which the manufacturer can identify prospects and their purchasing
likelihood. For instance, GM might have considered that the Santa Fe
was one of the more progressive railroads in technology and segmented it
among a few potential diesel locomotive buyers, to focus on selling to early adopters.

The *rate of adoption* anticipated for a new product has a strong effect on
the scale and nature of its introductory program. Five characteristics of a product innovation can importantly influence the adoption rate, as Kotler states
them:[5]

1. The innovation's *relative advantage,* which is the degree to which it appears to be superior to alternative products that the buyer would substitute for it.
2. The innovation's *compatibility* with an individual's values and experience.
3. The *complexity* of the innovation, or the degree to which it is relatively
   difficult to understand or use. Strange or intricate products, in their usage, tend to mean long learning periods for consumers before they are
   widely purchased.
4. *Divisibility* of the innovation, which refers to the extent that it can be
   tried on a limited basis. Cough drops are an example of a highly divisible
   item that may be tried for a trivial investment. (Or perhaps, as in the recent introduction of N'Ice brand, small samples may be offered to gain consumer trial free.) On the contrary, an innovative central air-conditioning
   system would not be divisible and would be a risky choice for adopters.
5. *Communicability* of the innovation. Innovations that can be shown and
   demonstrated tend to have a faster rate of adoption because the *rate of
   diffusion* of the concept and its advantages is relatively fast (whether by
   word-of-mouth or by the seller's publicity or advertising).

The strategist must consider these five characteristics when forecasting
the rate at which the new product will be adopted. Such forecasts should be of
greater accuracy when based on marketing research and observance of comparable innovations' adoption experience.

---

[5]Philip Kotler, *Marketing Management: Analysis, Planning, and Control,* 5th Ed. © 1984,
p. 349. Reprinted by permission of Prentice-Hall, Inc., Englewood Cliffs, N.J.

The choice among alternatives would include the possible "marketing mix" that will make up the marketing program. The decision maker has a complex variety of options for marketing action. We will now summarize and illustrate the uses of the four major functions in market introductions. (Each function will be discussed in greater detail in Chapters 12 through 15.)

Product itself is the primary factor underlying success or failure in the introductory stage. The value a buyer perceived when observing the product tends to be a main determinant of whether he or she will try it. Subsequent repurchase will then depend on the product's value in use. In our sense, product includes package, label, and brand name.

> Consumers in large numbers decided to try Softsoap, for instance, because they could see that it would be easy to use: a liquid with a pump dispenser on an unbreakable plastic bottle. Furthermore, the design and colors of that bottle would well suit bathroom decor. A quite different product factor influenced people to try General Foods' new pudding pops: They bore the "Jell-O" brand name, which automatically gave a favorable impression.

The product should be regarded as a fixed element in the entry marketing mix. In this stage, the firm cannot afford the cost of altering the product's design except for correcting production faults. Nor can it afford any interruption for product change in the strategic program. All the steps to maximize the product's quality and fit with buyers' needs should take place before it is launched.

Promotion is the second most critical functional area in probably all new products. In cosmetics it tends to be the most critical; this may be true of many products whose consumer image is more important than the product's reality. Promotion is the primary means of positioning the product, chiefly with advertising—among consumer products—and by personal selling of business and institutional products. Awareness and information are also obtained principally through these forms of promotion.

Inducements to buy also depend in large degree on *promotion.* Advertising may be sufficiently alluring, and sales presentation may be persuasive enough, to induce purchase or at least trial of something new. However, sales promotion in any of several forms is very often the main enticement. Free trial by potential buyers can be accomplished by *sampling* of small and inexpensive items or by *demonstrations* or loans of such costly items as automobiles, motorcycles, or computers. The possible importance of demonstration for even small items was recently illustrated by Minnesota Mining & Manufacturing's (3M's) then-new Post-it notes, pads of paper with a strip of adhesive on the back. Post-its became a fine success, but people were indifferent at first. 3M overcame this indifference, as described below:

> But office-supply vendors had doubts about the need for a sticky-back paper. "When we showed it to people, their attitude was, 'You're making a big deal out of a three-by-five note pad,'" says Jack P. Wilkins, a 3M marketing director. Nonetheless, 3M test marketed Post-it notes in 1977. Results were mixed until the

company blitzed offices with samples, a strategy that proved important. "Until secretaries actually use Post-it notes, they don't realize how convenient they are," Mr. Wilkins says.[6]

Trial may be made cheap by *coupons* that reduce the price of initial purchases, or by initial price reductions on all purchases during a period, or by containers marked with the introductory price reduction. A frequent combination is to hitchhike coupons in free samples so that if trial of the sample is satisfactory, the first purchase is cheap. In general, various forms of promotion are used, and they are a highly flexible tool of product introduction. A strong program may convince distributors to stock the new item and thus increase its availability.

Price may or may not be one of the keys in the introduction stage. If large immediate sales volume is important (perhaps to fend off potential competitors), temporary price inducements as mentioned above are logical. More-lasting *penetration* price strategy with continuous low pricing, relative to costs, may be needed to keep frightening off competitors or may be wise if the "experience curve" of cost decline with volume appears to apply (so that the firm's progressively lower costs would remain a big advantage). In contrast, in some markets the sales are bound to grow only gradually regardless of price; in others some segments are willing to pay premium-level prices; and in still others incipient new entrants are unlikely over a long introductory period. In all those cases, relatively high prices at a *skimming* level are logical, to gain fast payback and move into profitability.

An important question arises as to a trade-off between quality offered and price. This applies particularly to a follower in market entry who faces an innovator whose pricing seems rather steep.

> When RCA entered the computer mainframe business against the leader, IBM, it made a brave decision on pricing strategy and took an option different from that of the other contenders. IBM was widely considered to be charging high prices, but it was offering outstanding softwear and training services to buyers. RCA decided to be attractive with substantially lower prices, but with a much lower level of service. The gamble failed, as buyers were nervous about installing computers and turned out to want the high level of service, even at premium prices.

Wide *distribution* may be obtained by a remarkably attractive new product with a strong promotional strategy. But among mass-marketed consumer goods, distributors are expecting more than that. Sales promotion in the form of displays, demonstrations, or other suitable forms of point-of-purchase promotion is always desirable. Missionary salespeople or sales training may be warranted for technical products. The main inducement for carrying a consumer new product, however, is extra profit. This normally is offered through special price discounts with initial purchases or over an early period of the introduction (say, sixty or ninety days after the first announcement). Such special

---

[6] *Wall Street Journal*, March 31, 1983, p. 31.

prices may overcome fear of risks for taking on a new product and may induce "stocking up" with large quantities, which in itself will pressure a merchant to strongly support and move the new product.

Another strategic aspect is the extent and quality of distribution. In some cases, the new product's manufacturer may offer *exclusive* representation— either where no one would take on the product without that advantage or where the potential sales or very high dealer quality needed justifies having only one outlet (especially common in business equipment). *Selective* representation is indicated for products for which dealers' prestige, wide assortments, or superior service and parts departments will bear importantly on whether buyers will position the product well or will get adequate information. This strategy is important for services. *Intensive* distribution is desirable for all consumer convenience goods that should offer maximum availability. While the above are strategically logical choices, one should recognize that many products often lack strong appeal. Or they are offered by minor firms and are unable to obtain the desired ideal distribution.

Examples

The selection of particular options with relationship to various situations, market needs, and products may be appreciated by reading some actual cases. In this section we list short statements about some contrasting examples—in a few instances merely dealing with one aspect of market entry strategy, but in some others presenting a fuller scope.

> When *Softsoap* was created by Minnetonka, Inc., it was a rather simple product— which used, as one observer put it, just "bathtub chemistry." Since competitors could readily enter the product category, time was short, and a rapid national introduction was the logical choice.
>
> General Foods' new product *Gainesburgers* was the result of many years' research and creation of technology that no competitor could soon emulate. Not only could market entry be gradual, but there was time for careful market testing. The "position" of the product was significant, and the product was entered in test markets with the "hamburger patty" image mentioned above. Sales in test markets were discouragingly low. Yet GF was assured by earlier consumer research that the product itself was right. Marketers suspected that the positioning was at fault, as dog owners were thinking of it as a snack rather than a meal. They went to work to redefine Gainesburgers as the substitute for a full can. Advertising (showing someone feeding two patties to a dog) was created to convey this image. Result of the test market this time showed very good sales. Thus repositioning and taking the pains to test-market produced a product success that remains the leader in its category.
>
> *Pampers* represents an enormous success reached through painstaking marketing effort. From various reports, this history is put together:
>
> Virtually all the diapers used were of cloth when Procter & Gamble began developing its paper diaper, although some other firms were selling paper types in small volume. The problems of designing machinery to make paper diapers turned out to be the most complex process. P&G executives could be confident

that no rival could soon reproduce their machines. Since it had time then, P&G had consumers test thousands of diapers in Dallas (hand produced). The test found the diaper too hot for babies, so it was redesigned. Test marketing of the improved variety was held in Peoria—fifteen months later—and these were machine manufactured. The product was offered at 10 cents per diaper, based on production costs for 400 million diapers per year. This test failed; resulting sales were under half the volume needed. But consumers were wild about the product.

Long analysis led P&G to believe that cutting the price to 6 cents per diaper would generate the volume required to cut unit costs and be profitable. Another market test held in Sacramento proved this analysis correct. Therefore in 1966 P&G proceeded with a rollout introduction into additional markets in the West.

P&G continued the rollout in markets and proceeded toward the East as it expanded production lines from one to eight. During this time lag (it was 1970 before Pampers could reach the Northeast), rival Kimberly-Clark had entered the eastern markets with its Kimbies and rolled out toward the West. However, Pampers' quality and marketing strategy proved to be superior so that it gained dominant market share in every area.

GM diesel locomotives had been in planning for several years before they were introduced in 1939. Until that time the only diesel use had been in small switching engines and a few passenger streamliners, but no one used them for heavy hauling. Railroad officials were extremely skeptical that diesel could replace steam. Mere selling efforts would get no place.

The only way would be to prove how a diesel could perform, and so GM built its demonstrator engine #103, a three-unit monster for its day. One by one GM had major railroads test it extensively, which proved GM's claim—the diesel engine would haul twice as much as a big steam locomotive at half cost and require only light maintenance. Seeing was believing, and diesel engines proceeded to make all the steam ones obsolete in twenty years. Despite the entry of rivals (only one of them having lasting success), GM still held a 75 percent market share forty-three years later.

RCA's SelectaVision videodisk player was not the kind of low-cost product that can be sampled or test marketed, and RCA was under pressure from rival firms (Magnavox and Pioneer) that had their laser-beam players already on the market (different from RCA's Capacitance electronic disk system). So the product had to be introduced nationally in March 1981, assuming that "with its superb technology and low price . . . it could become the huge communications corporation's premier product during the 1980s."[7]

The initial sales goal for the SelectaVision was 200,000 player units in 1981. By midyear only 28,000 units had been sold, and SelectaVision was not making a dent into the $8 billion that consumers were expected to spend on home entertainment products annually. Distributor support was proving to be a weak variable. This in turn stemmed from pricing; the product was becoming a price football, with retailers discounting it far below the announced retail price of $499—as low as $419. This pricing, though, resulted from low consumer interest in the product itself. RCA and many distributors expected sales to pick up soon, but as of mid-1981 the company faced big questions. Was it priced too high? Would consumers come to like the product? What was wrong?

---

[7] *Wall Street Journal,* July 6, 1981, p. 15.

Tracking the Introduction Stage

When the new product is introduced in the market, the task of tracking its degree of acceptance begins. Whoever is responsible for the product's marketing should watch vigilantly for signs of success or failure and for the factors responsible. Tactical decisions will probably be necessary to adjust the introduction strategy as problems arise. The strategic program and its implementation should still be viewed experimentally, and any changes are easiest to make during this period. Our discussion will not dwell on these tactical problems but rather on the ultimate questions during this stage: Is the introduction successful enough to continue marketing the product? When has the product (if successful) left this stage and begun its growth stage?

The variable commonly tracked for a product is its sales volume. In Figure 10-1 we have drawn three paths that a new product's sales may follow during this period. Introduction is shown to shift into the growth stage at a point of sharp and prolonged inflection of the sales curve upward.

In Figure 10-1 we show alternative paths of independent brands—*not competitors* but rather *different products*. (Conceivably all three patterns could happen among brands of the same product, but they could hardly all be launched at the same time as in our chart.) We now comment on these three:

Brand A would be one of the mass-marketed consumer products that is given a huge promotional effort immediately when launched. This would include potent special discounts to distributors, who would stock up at those prices and thus occasion very heavy sales from the factory. Since the new product would move at a slower rate out of stores, however, distributors would be working off their inventories for some time—during

FIGURE 10-1. Sales volume of new brands during the introduction stage. The three paths described here are meant to represent brands of different new products, not three competing with each other.

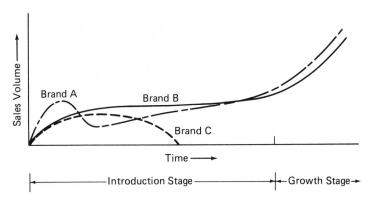

which factory orders would slump abnormally low. Possibly consumers too were given purchase inducements that led to their being temporarily overstocked. Eventually a normal growth curve sets in.

Brand B exhibits the steady but deliberate curve of growth while triers of the new brand are partially converted to repeat buyers. There is gradual growth until fairly suddenly the brand's popularity spreads and sales zoom upward.

Brand C represents failure, which is too common. About half of all new introductions fail ultimately to obtain enough demand to be kept on the market. A decision to terminate a new entry normally comes only after several months of trying and may be postponed for a few years.

We must make a number of qualifications about Figure 10-1. Sales figures do not actually occur in smooth curves but fluctuate in a jagged line. This means that three or more reporting periods must be monitored before a definite trend can be read. Sales of the new-product type should also be tracked. Sometimes the innovator's brand has no serious competitor for a long period and therefore has almost 100 percent of the market (e.g., GM's diesel locomotives or 3M's Post-its). In that case, that brand and product sales curves are practically identical. If new brands enter during that period (as Kimbies did while Pampers were being introduced), the original brand's sales curve inevitably falls below the rise of the total new-product type—although this phenomenon is more characteristic of the growth phase.

Profit objectives normally transcend sales objectives over a longer period. High costs and low volume of new-product sales usually mean negative profits during much or all of the introduction stage. (Exceptions can be products that are monopolizing their markets and can command skimming prices.) A firm should have projected and planned-for losses during this period. However, if losses are sustained too long or run too deep, the firm may withdraw the product.

The percentage of sales that are trial purchases ought to be determined —as against repeat purchases. Clearly an innovation that wins repeat buyers tends to gain a permanent market position. It is even more informative to learn buyers' intentions, if obtainable, in order to project sales changes (this subject will discussed in our last chapter). Pulling a product like Brand C off the market should not mean abandoning it forever, as a better opportunity may appear later on.

The Post Division of General Foods developed a ready-to-eat cereal innovation that contained dried fruit. Around 1965 it introduced "Fruit 'n Cereal" to the market and launched a national campaign. Despite its distinctiveness, after a year's campaign Fruit 'n Cereal failed to generate a profitable sales level and was withdrawn from the market. In 1982 Post Division introduced a similar product with the name "Fruit & Fiber," which became a success. Apparently consumers in 1965 did not feel a need for fiber in their diets, but they keenly sought it in 1982. Thus the *strategic window* had opened later and GF was able to recognize and exploit that opportunity.

Some new products and new brands never soar into a growth stage. They may, however, sustain a mediocre level of sales, be only marginally profitable, and be kept alive. This fourth possible path is not shown in Figure 10-1. For the sake of our covering other PLC stages, we assume that our product and brand do follow the upward-tilting growth curve. Before discussing the growth stage, we must point out that growth strategies should have been formulated very early in the product life in readiness for that growth—whenever and if it arrives.

GROWTH

For the fortunate firm, the gradual buyer acceptance of a new product becomes a surge of popularity, and sales turn sharply upward. This stage should make a PMU's manager rejoice and the firm anticipate good profits on the investment. The growth stage may be brief (less than a year for Softsoap) and normally does not exceed a few years, but these are exceptions (around ten years for paper diapers and fifteen years for diesel locomotives for instance).

An accelerated growth phase may be elusive or long awaited with some products. The RCA videodisk player was a case in point:

> The videodisk player fell substantially short of the 200,000 units that were RCA's sales goal for its second year on the market, 1981—failing to enjoy an expected "big surge at Christmas." Indeed, two years later in 1983, RCA's sales prediction was 300,000 units, a more sluggish growth than had been expected.

> The picture improved, however, toward the end of 1983, when the videodisk's sales growth quickened. Some RCA people were interpreting this as showing that the product had entered its growth stage. Perhaps it was not product shortcomings that were preventing consumer adoption but rather such factors as: it being a complex and novel product, prices having been kept too high, and depression psychology. These obstacles had disappeared, the reasoning went, and so sales accelerated.[8]

When a real growth stage is achieved, it may be perilous and—even when sales in the new product soar—it is the critical stage. This is the period of make-or-break, when the innovator has the only big chance of optimizing the realized market potentials and fending off new entrants. A game of "king of the castle" normally takes place, with the contestants playing for keeps. Marketing is the pivotal means of succeeding in this stage.

Objectives

Two major purposes are salient during a product's growth stage:

1. *Establish a defendable market position.*
2. *Earn an adequate return* to justify continuance after fast growth subsides.

---

[8] *Wall Street Journal*, July 2, 1981, p. 15; and February 4, 1983, p. 27.

Market position is of key importance because normally more competitors will enter the new product's category than can survive. There are several aspects of market position and the firm will have more than one option to pursue, as we will see. The market objective, however, must be balanced against the earnings objective. It would be quite desirable to obtain net profits from the product before the growth period ends. Otherwise the robust profit levels may never be reached. At a minimum, the new product should begin to earn a gross or trading margin (what is left after cost of goods sold is covered) that can more than amply pay the high marketing costs often required to defend market position. Actual cash flow is often negligible because of heavy investment during this period, but again there is wide variation among products.

The two general goals just stated call for quite different strategies, depending on the situation. Wide differences are particularly seen between (1) the innovator—or whoever emerges from the introduction in the lead—and (2) the followers who eventually attempt to drive a wedge in the new product's market.

Situation Analysis

The situation in this stage will be more evident when we examine graphically some alternative ways a product's sales may develop. Figure 10-2 defines the PLC in terms of the total sales volume of the particular new-product category.

The length of the growth stage is bounded at its beginning by a distinct upward inflection in the product category's sales. At some point the market starts to get saturated. Demand and the sales curve taper off—although usually some growth still continues.

Brand A in Figure 10-2 is assumed to be the original one, the innovator. The curve shown is not the only possible one, however, since innovators may be surpassed by stronger followers while the product is still in the introductory phase. Anyway, what was initially a 100 percent market share is whittled down as competitors enter the market. While the product category sales were soaring by 400 percent during the growth period, Brand A was able to push its volume upward by about 200 percent (a nice gain). It was still the leader with 50 percent market share as the stage ended.

Brand D had a much more rapid percentage sales gain, but as a follower it was starting from a base of zero. Its market share had risen to 30 percent by the end of the growth stage of the product category. Furthermore, it was still in something of a growth stage of its own at that time. Its sales were still growing substantially while those of Brand A had flattened.

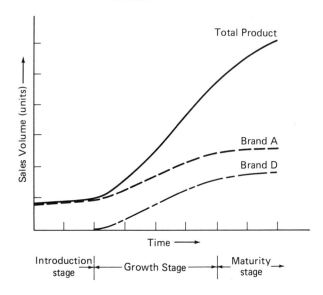

FIGURE 10-2. Sales of a new product during its growth stage. The total sales of the product category in each period are indicated by the solid line. Brand A was its originator. Brand D was an early follower that is a successful entrant.

Both Brand A and Brand D seem to have held on to large enough market shares to be successful contenders in the maturity stage. We have not shown any lesser brands that may have entered or left this market—and that in the aggregate had been taking share away from the two leaders. Some of them may also be able to continue successfully into the maturity stage.

The situation relative to the number of competitors at this stage varies widely. If the innovator has ironclad patents covering the product's essential features, no competitors may be able to create alternatives—and so there might be no rival. Bayer, a German originator of aspirin, held total sales of that product until its patents expired. Here are some contrasting cases where patents were not a key factor:

> In diesel locomotives, the entry barriers were enormous because of technological complexity. GM was supreme technically and furthermore held a big sales lead and scale of production. Only two real competitors came into the U.S. market, and only one (Alco/GE) survived the growth phase.
> Liquid toilet soap attracted a swarm of entrants quickly. Over forty firms are said to have entered the first year. The potential was high. Minnetonka was a small

firm, and technical difficulties were no problem. Entrants included such large firms as Clorox, Chesebrough-Pond's, and P&G.

The number of firms that can survive in such situations is limited. In consumer-packaged products not more than three or four competitors can find places on many retailers' shelves. Still fewer may develop enough volume to become profitable leaders. Meanwhile the character of the market changes, and the following may occur:

1. All the contenders will endeavor to find and effectively execute a strategy that will hold market share.
2. Buyers will have less need for information, because most of those who are going to buy in that product category either have tried it or have learned all they need to make purchase decisions. They may be, however, somewhat bewildered and uninformed about the various brands that are appearing.
3. Sales may rise so fast that the leaders may not have been prepared to handle the heavy pressure placed on production and distribution facilities. The problem is to meet demand without overbuilding plant while maintaining quality.

Far into the growth stage there may still be much doubt as to how large demand will grow and how much share a firm can take. This makes both marketing and financial planning very difficult.

The intensity of this situation may be as great as that in the early history of the paper diaper business:

> P&G was introducing Pampers on a zone basis, with some patent protection. They became so popular in each area that the growth stage quickly ensued, and production facilities were sorely taxed. Pampers were first launched on the West Coast and proceeded eastward, one region at a time. Meanwhile Kimberly-Clark had designed its version that skirted the patents and started the launch of Kimbies on the East Coast. Total sales volume more than doubled by 1976, and several other big firms had entered their paper diapers: Scott Paper, International Paper, Georgia-Pacific, Weyerhaeuser, and Johnson & Johnson.
>
> By 1976, however, all rival brands except Kimberly-Clark and J&J had dropped out. Pampers still held on to 65 percent of the market. The two other brands combined held over 20 percent, and the balance were stores' private labels (made by any of the above firms). J&J was in second place, and K-C had been forced to replace its Kimbies with a better-performing design under the name Huggies.

Thus the growth stage in paper diapers brought a great fortune to the innovator while losses were being incurred by firms that tried vainly to invade that lush market. In the midst of that stage (which continued past 1978) only two competitors remained, both giant firms but with just marginal market shares.

Strategic Needs

The needs that must be met through the growth stage are quite different from those during the introduction of the product. The main ones tend to be the following:

1. Define a defendable position that can be secured by the brand during this period. This should use whatever differential advantages the firm has already obtained or can create. Direct strategic actions toward occupying this position.
2. Establish a clear and conspicuous brand identity, apart from all rivals.
3. Create an image that will attract the desired market, and follow through to satisfy users.
4. Maximize availability of this brand to buyers.
5. Find the best balance between price level and demand, by establishing the product's value while also testing price elasticity.

The original marketer of the product should enter this field with all the advantages of an innovator, including market knowledge, technical skill, volume, and the reputation of the original or authentic brand. This firm's aim would then be to hold on to as large a market share as feasible—without sacrificing too much profit. Other brands that are followers face a different challenge. They must find any weaknesses in the innovator's product and strategic program. They may also find differential advantages that are relevant to the situation, which may include using more efficient recent technology. Assuming that the innovator's marketing strategy is successful in stimulating sales, the basic questions are these: Should a follower largely imitate that proven strategy? Or is it better to have a more distinctive program (perhaps better than the innovator's)?

> Many firms are successfully invading product categories in which the innovators have already become established.[9] A number of interesting examples have been occurring in the airlines industry, particularly since the federal government's deregulation. The most spectacular new entrant now is People Express Airlines, but the way was shown much earlier in Texas by Southwest Airlines. This firm began service in 1971 with just three planes. This upstart airline's shrewd strategies (in pricing, service, and promotion) stimulated traffic growth so much on the Dallas-Houston segment that in eighteen months it rose by 40 percent. And Southwest grabbed a 42 percent share of that market (just for starters!).

Strategic Options

The logical strategies in the growth stage are not constant, for as the product's demand moves through the stage, different requirements evolve and more options become available. At its start, the picture tends to be like that shown in Figure 10-2: There is a market leader, who is probably the inno-

---

[9]Yip, in "Gateways to Entry," describes optional strategies for such invasions.

vator, and a few followers who early try to penetrate the market. Early in this stage, the innovator is apt to stick with the original strategy. Not only has it worked, but rising demand keeps this firm too busy supplying product and expanding distribution to execute any changes in strategy. New entrants are more likely to try variations in marketing or product, but relative simplicity in programs is prevalent. As the stage proceeds, there is more jockeying for market position, by more contenders, and a variety of options are appropriate and adopted.

We will now review two general options in direction taken and will then describe some of the options for use of the marketing variables.

Build or hold share of market? For the leader or innovator of the product, a large proportion of the market may already be possessed. When Minnetonka held over 75 percent of the liquid soap market during its first year (1980) in this business (despite the efforts of new entrants) and GM held nearly all of the diesel locomotive business, neither would have worried about increasing market share, since each had such a vast margin of leadership. If the innovator has more than half the market, the question instead would be whether to attempt to keep such a large proportion or to let it decrease. Maintaining large market shares is costly, and a firm may opt to take a less-expensive route and harvest profits while allowing some erosion of market share. Others may have special reasons for wanting to hold market share.

> Texas Instruments typically seeks to hold market share in order to build sales volume fastest in its new-product categories. By drastic efforts, TI has been able to cut costs with growing volume faster than competitors, riding down the "experience curve" of efficiency—and thereby has stayed the leader in several electronics fields (e.g., transistors, calculators).[10]

A follower into the market has the more-complex problem of building market share, but conquering part of the innovator's share is costly and risky. Judgment must be made about how much market share is enough. No firm wants to be in a marginal share position, lacking the revenues and appeal to secure a defendable position before the growth phase ends.

How should the *target market* be defined? Some followers may choose to attack the leader in the entire market for the product category. Others may decide that they cannot succeed in wresting share away from the leader across the entire market, and instead they choose a segment or "niche" on which to focus their strategy. Among those who choose to invade the entire market, some will fail to gain a viable share—this is bound to happen if too many attempt it. On the other hand, followers who identify an actual market niche that the leader is not serving well may focus on that niche profitably. The re-

---

[10]Lately TI discovered that such a strategy is not failproof. TI entered the lushly growing personal computer market with that strategy, but unfortunately it suffered delays that made its entry too late and undermarketed. Already Apple and IBM had taken leadership in the higher-priced end of this computer market, while Commodore was far ahead at the low-priced end. TI underwent very heavy losses in this business and eventually abandoned it in the last quarter of 1983, which put the whole company into a deficit and was a serious setback for what has been one of the great marketers.

sult is the situation depicted in Figure 10-3. There we see at the right some large-volume/top-market-share firms that have become very successful in this product category. At the left of the figure are some smaller firms whose strategies can be profitable on smaller volumes sold to chosen niches. The firms not to be envied are those caught "in between," whose offerings have not gained enough share of the total market (which they tried to invade).

Figure 10-3 shows a *V* pattern or curve of the effects of the target market options. It clusters competing firms that have entered a new-product field into three outcomes. These are of course tendencies, and a fourth outcome is omitted: A firm that chooses to focus on a market niche may fail to penetrate due to a lack of sales potential or to erroneous strategy. Many cases of the *V* curve have been observed. For example:

> When the computer was in its introductory days innovators were few, notably Sperry and above all IBM, which strongly dominated. Among the numerous firms that entered was one with small resources that decided the best strategy was to find a market niche. It decided to direct its computer designs and marketing just to scientific uses. The result was the prosperous firm of Control Data, which established itself as leader in that market niche.
>
> Most other firms entering computers in that era chose instead to take on IBM

FIGURE 10-3. **The "V" pattern of competition. Dominant firms that cater to the whole market and "nichers" that successfully develop a certain segment are more profitable than those "caught in the middle."**

Adapted from Michael Porter, *Competitive Strategy: Techniques for Analyzing Industries and Competition* (New York: Free Press, 1980).

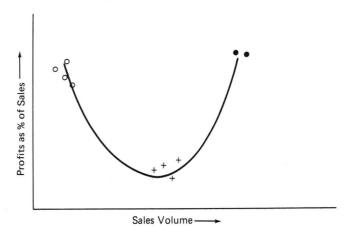

Legend:
● Firms that targeted the whole market and are dominant.
+ Firms that also targeted the whole market but won small shares of it.
○ Smaller firms that are focusing on market segments.

across the whole market. A few, including Honeywell and Burroughs, did obtain viable market shares. Some others, including the giants General Electric, RCA, and Xerox, failed to win profitable shares of market and pulled out of this business. (Later Xerox found ways to reenter some peripheries of this business, but that is another story.)

Competition not only is to be expected during the growth stage—and during introduction—but should be welcomed (up to a point of excessive contenders). When innovations emerge, the building of primary demand for the generic product is the key need. If other and vigorous marketers follow the innovator with rival offerings, the combined promotional efforts may penetrate buyers' awareness and induce purchase much more quickly than a single firm's efforts would.

> A manufacturer of health products came out with a novel packaging for a cold remedy, which was very convenient but expensive. On its own program, that firm did not gain enough sales to be profitable, and its management was niggardly in putting marketing dollars into it. Then news arrived that a major competitor was placing a similar product on the market. The first immediately doubled its efforts, and the combined campaigns produced fast growth in sales, a 500% increase.

We will now describe some of the strategic ways that marketing's functions can be used during the growth stage.

Product is a variable that has no drastic changes during the growth stage. The innovator would have no incentive to alter a product that has come into rising demand, at least during its early sales acceleration. Later changes that do not involve changing the basic product are likely to be made by a number of contenders. There will be proliferation of the variety of sizes, styles, or packages:

> One of the earlier entrants in liquid soap was Yardley (a famous brand in prestige bar soap), whose initial offering included three sizes of liquid containers and three varieties: old lavender (traditional Yardley scent), cocoa butter, and baby lotion. Obviously the third variety was an effort to win the infant-bathing market. Yardley evidently had a good strategy, as it early placed second to Softsoap with a reported 25 percent share of market.

As the growth period proceeds, even the leading brand has gained control over problems of supply and of product faults. Its management becomes able to widen the variety and, foreseeing a slackening of demand growth, seeks to open up additional uses or to exploit niches:

> Softsoap stayed with one size and design of container during the growth phase of liquid soap with one exception. A new container convenient for hanging in a shower broadened its use for bathing. A new name was given to this item—"Showermate"—and it too came in various colored containers.

Product change during the growth period may be radical in high-technology industries. The computer industry at the present time is in the midst of a rapid growth stage, particularly in microcomputers, but new products as well as proliferations are coming in a steady stream.

Price is likely to have an increasing frequency of change during this stage, although it is usually rather firm. Its volatility, of course, depends on the number of entrants and ferocity of competiton, as well as the growth rate of sales. When the innovator has been holding to skimming prices that are high relative to product cost, followers are very likely to shade those prices, and a downward trend sets in:

> The influx of new brands into the liquid soap market in 1980–81 was accompanied by a price-cutting epidemic. While the product was becoming a price football, Softsoap was able to keep its prices at a firmer level because of its better brand recognition. Nevertheless price cutting was making the product unprofitable in many areas.

The larger-selling brands also are better able to reduce price as production levels rise and costs decrease. Industrial product manufacturers sometimes lower prices one step at a time as they broaden their marketing efforts to additional segments that place less value on the product. Typically there is no price war during this stage, and managers of the stronger brands can decide price levels relative to more strategic goals. They would consider a trade-off between lowering prices and such alternatives as larger expenditures on promotion to stimulate sales, product proliferations, or strong selling campaigns to widen distribution.

Heavy pressure on price even during the growth stage is possible with few competitors in the market when there is extreme anxiety to capture market share and leadership:

> The innovator in freeze-dried instant coffee was General Foods' Maxwell House Division. Very popular, the product began fast growth within six months. Nestlé was a very early follower, however, and entered its brand at that time with vigorous marketing. Nestlé particularly featured large discounts to distributors, which touched off a virtual price war with Maxwell House. After a long battle, Nestlé emerged firmly as leader with its Taster's Choice. Prices have been relatively stable in that product category ever since.

Price cutting was not serious in paper diapers' growth period despite competition between several large manufacturers against P&G. Perhaps all recognized that the product was a good consumer value at P&G's price and that objectives of brand identification and consumer education were paramount.

Promotion tends to be the key variable while product demand is growing fast. Its role changes during this period and the market must be alert. The need to entice buyers to try the product is vanishing as they become familiar with it. Therefore sales promotion methods (coupons, samples, price-offs) should give way in consumer goods markets to emphasis on advertising that will carry timely messages—or to stepped-up personal selling in business and institutional markets. The role of these messages also changes, from a need to educate potential buyers about the product's merits and use to a need to engrain demand for a specific brand. (That is, the focus shifts from primary buying motives to selective motives.) Advertising may have its greatest effects during this period, when the product is still news and its features are of much interest to buyers. Much more will be said about the forms and uses of advertising in Chapter 14.

This also is a period of heavy expenditure on promotion—certainly relative to sales volume. The scramble to gain defendable market positions is most manifested in promotional activities. If users have high learning requirements to switch to the new product, promotion has a heavy task. Even with a product with low learning requirements, promotional outlays may be enormous:

> Minnetonka, Inc., plunged $6 million into its national advertising campaign for Softsoap in 1980, the introductory year. This was large indeed for a firm whose sales had totalled $25 million the year before. In the face of a rising market and competition for 1981, Minnetonka planned to raise advertising for 1981, it is said, to $15 million.[11]

Part of the promotional efforts, when the product is distributed indirectly through channels, should be aimed at retailers and wholesalers. The advent of a strong and massive campaign to consumers for a new product is in itself an inducement for retailers to stock it. The strategic program should also include adequate personal sales calls, point-of-purchase displays, trade show activities, and, particularly, special discounts to maximize distribution. As a result of these promotional programs aimed at buyers and distributors, each brand hopes to secure an adequate share of the market and be sharply differentiated in buyers' minds before the growth stage subsides.

Distribution may be second only to promotion as the key to sustained success. The innovator and early followers may have found it wise to distribute only selectively during the product introduction, perhaps to induce dealers to risk stocking it. That need disappears when strong demand becomes evident and every outlet would want to carry at least one brand of the new product. Intensive distribution normally becomes the goal: Get your brand within easy reach of the buyer. Furthermore, with the movement of the product growing, manufacturers want the distribution pipelines well stocked. Out-of-stocks at the retail level are naturally feared by a brand's managers lest buyers take substitute brands instead of the favorite.

An adequate physical distribution system connected with ample plant capacity is of prime importance during the growth period. Product managers may have nightmares about "backorder" situations in which they cannot restock dealers soon enough. This problem obviously runs outside of marketing and is a long-range problem in corporations. It is the crisis of sudden growth in new-product demand that gives marketers deep concern about production and distribution response. The problem is not one specifically connected with

---

[11]*New York Times,* June 10, 1981, p. 33.

any one strategic program, but the marketing strategist must anticipate these capabilities—and corporate strategies provide them.

The quality of retailers and of the services they provide after the sale are a greater concern than extent of distribution in a number of lines such as automotive, machinery, and electrical equipment. Where dealer quality is the greater factor, selecting and cultivating dealers during the growth phase is the strategic need. Entrenchment solidly with loyal and competent dealers can help a brand to fend off competition not only during the growth stage but long after:

> The leading Japanese producer of earth-moving equipment has been attempting to penetrate the U.S. market. The market leader in the United States (and in total world sales) is Caterpillar. Although this product field is now in its maturity, since its early days Caterpillar has stressed its dealer network. Now that Komatsu is attempting inroads in the United States, this is the great barrier: Caterpillar not only has twice as many U.S. dealers, but the dealers carry its products exclusively and are well capitalized. Komatsu instead must share with other brands more marginal dealers.[12]

All bonanzas must end sooner or later, and the growth in a new-product category's sales eventually tapers off because the number of potential buyers declines:

> Paper diapers maintained a sales growth rate of over 50 percent a year, on average, from 1968 to 1978. That surely constituted a growth stage. In the next two years, though, they settled down to a bit over 15 percent growth annually. That would be considered rapid growth in most industries, but it signaled the beginning of a more sedate upward trend in sales. The product had entered its maturity.

New prospects and quite different strategic opportunities lie ahead at this point. We will discuss them in Chapter 11.

SUMMARY

This chapter dealt with two of the product life cycle phases: introduction and growth. In these and in the two remaining phases described in Chapter 11, the discussion consists of four parts: the objectives, situation analysis, strategic needs, and the strategic options from which the planner may select the program.

Regarding the "introduction" objectives, three general aspects would have to be determined: role of the product (for which six alternatives were mentioned), profit and volume goals, and investment payout period. Following the objectives would be a situation analysis covering these aspects: the new product's degree of innovation, the learning requirements of buyers, the mar-

---

[12]Yip, "Gateways to Entry," p. 89.

ket potentials, and the competitive forces with which the product would contend.

The third phase of introduction was that of identifying the needs of buyers and of distributors. Those of *buyers* were detailed as awareness of the new product, information needed about it, positioning of the product in buyers' views, the inducements to buy, and what availability would be needed. Whether that availability is accomplished depends in turn on meeting *distributors'* needs, which include profitability, the manufacturer's dependability, and accommodating physical-handling requirements.

Several examples of products' introductory situations were then described. Different options logical for each situation were described. Then we discussed the tracking of developments during the introduction stage.

The *growth* stage was also covered with this format. After comments on its duration, the general objectives of the stage were explained (establishing a defendable position and adequate earnings). The situation analysis distinguished optional growth experiences of originators and followers, and examples were given. Next five strategic needs were enumerated, together with challenges faced in trying to accomplish them.

Strategic options were also found to differ for leaders and followers. Questions involved are: (a) whether to build or hold market share, (b) how to define target markets, and (c) how to respond to competition. The four general marketing functions were then each considered regarding their strategic use in the marketing mix for this stage.

REVIEW QUESTIONS

1. *In making the major decision of whether to introduce a new product, what are some key questions that should be raised?*

2. *Explain how the length of an investment payback period affects or constrains the other chief decisions that must be made about a new product.*

3. *A drug firm has discovered a novel substance that will cause people to sleep and to relax easily. To be effective, this new medicine would have to be used over a period of three weeks, along with certain diet limitations. Given these facts, what aspects of the market situation should this firm specifically analyze before deciding on whether to proceed with that project?*

4. *For the innovation's planning in question 3, what principal needs would have to be given careful consideration (outside the firm)?*

5. *Select some outstanding and rather new brand in any type of product that is familiar to you. Identify the differential advantages that seem to account for its market success. (These may be expressed in advertising or on labels.)*

6. *For the type of product described in question 3, which of the options would you prefer for the phasing of its market entry?*

7. In the introduction of that product, which one among the four general functions of marketing would be the most critical for a successful launch? Which would be the least critical? Why?

8. When does the introduction stage end? How would you recognize it?

9. Describe the course or nature of the PLC curve that you would expect for each of the following products (assuming that both are fairly successful): (a) for a very expensive and technical "robotics" product, a highly automated production machine; and (b) for a new mass-marketed detergent. How would you explain the differences between these two curves?

10. In what ways would the profit objective and pricing probably differ for the two products described in question 9?

11. What essential goals would a PMU manager hope to attain with a product while it is in its growth stage?

12. Your brand was one of the first two placed on the market, in an innovative product category. Demand was so good that this type of product moved into its growth stage, at which point you held a 40 percent market share. As marketing manager, what should you expect of the product during the next few years? What sort of actions should you be prepared to take?

13. What is a market niche? Why—and for whom—does it tend to be advantageous? What are the grave dangers in such a strategy?

14. What strategic needs in the growth stage can be contrasted with those to which a firm catered during a product's introduction stage?

15. What changes in emphasis occur between the four marketing mix functions (the four p's), as a product proceeds through its growth stage?

Perdue, Incorporated

Late in the sumer of 1976, Don Mabe, Executive Vice-President of Perdue, Incorporated, telephoned the assistant divisional controller, Mike Moriarty: "Mike, I want you to make this decision on whether or not we should get into chicken hot dogs," Mabe said. Moriarty, a young MBA who was rising in the company, eagerly undertook research to bring himself up to date on Perdue's possible first entry into the processed meat market. But a month later, Moriarty was still undecided. Although he was convinced that Perdue had developed a superior chicken hot dog, he was uncertain about demand for the product. It was possible that Perdue's supply of birds would not be sufficient to meet demand for the franks, so that outside purchases might be required. In addition, Perdue could do only preliminary processing of live chickens in its own plant; the company lacked final processing capability for hot dogs and therefore would have to depend on other meat processors to produce the franks.

Moriarty was also worried that advertising costs might make the entire project unprofitable if the advertising agency's projections were correct. In any event, he was unsure whether to advertise Perdue's new chicken product as a totally new product or to try to promote the product as an alternative to meat hot dogs. In addition, Moriarty wanted to protect Perdue's widely respected image and wondered if a line of hot dogs would damage that image of quality. Finally, consumer groups were pressuring the United States Department of Agriculture to halt use of mechanically deboned meat (MDM) in consumer products. They alleged that mechanically deboned meat was nutritionally inferior and contained possibly harmful bone bits. Moriarty was concerned that, at best, the planned use of MDM in Perdue's hot dog would cheapen its image. At worst, a USDA ban might force Perdue to rethink the whole hot dog idea.

COMPANY HISTORY

Perdue, Inc. was founded in 1920 by Arthur W. Perdue to sell hatching eggs to chicken farmers in and around Salisbury, Maryland. In 1933, the company began to sell live chickens—"broilers"—for human consumption. Five years later, Arthur's son, Frank, joined the business at the age of 19. He became president 10 years later.

Since the early 1940's, Perdue had been vertically integrating in an attempt to counter the cyclicality of the poultry industry. In 1941, the company became a commercial feed dealer to provide an internal source of chicken feed. In 1943, the first hatchery was added. Facilities for processing feed from soybeans and other ingredients were constructed between 1958 and 1961. In the late 1960's, Perdue executives noticed that prices were quite stable in the dressed poultry market and that prices were subject to great fluctuations

This case was prepared by Mark H. Johnson, and was revised by Gary Shaw, under the supervision of Assistant Professor Lawrence J. Ring, as the basis for class discussion and not to illustrate either the effective or ineffective handling of an administrative situation. Copyright © 1978 by the Sponsors of the Colgate Darden Graduate School of Business Administration of the University of Virginia. Used with permission.

in the live poultry market. Therefore, they decided that Perdue should get out of the live poultry market entirely. By 1971, dressed poultry from two new processing plants made up 100 percent of the company's products.

Perdue's backward integration was paralleled by a marketing strategy based on product differentiation and consumer pull. This strategy was unprecedented in the poultry industry. The company developed a physically differentiated chicken with a different color skin, more tender meat, and more meat per bird. The higher meat yield and different color skin were the result of Perdue's unique feed blend, a closely guarded recipe which was developed by company scientists. At the retailer's case, consumers could contrast the golden yellow color of the Perdue bird with the paler color of other processors' products. Perdue broilers were usually more tender because they were never frozen during processing or in shipment. Many consumers claimed that these features made the Perdue chicken a superior tasting bird. Perdue birds could also be distinguished by their wing tags, which said "Perdue" in large red letters and which offered a money-back guarantee if customers were unsatisfied.

Perdue executives had established strict quality standards, and this image of quality was carried to consumers through heavy television and radio advertising. The advertisements featured Frank Perdue, whose homespun message was his simple person-to-person concern for quality in chickens. Perdue's advertising-to-sales ratio was the highest in the poultry industry.

This marketing strategy enabled Perdue to command premium prices at the retail level and helped the company show a profit in every year since it was founded. (The company's sales and asset figures [for 1965–76] are shown in Exhibit 1.) According to industry observers, Perdue had shown growth and stability above average for the industry.

DISTRIBUTION

The company's marketing strategy, based on physical differentiation and quality, led the company to seek retail outlets where competition was not based on price, such as independent neighborhood grocers and butcher shops. Such outlets were most frequently found in the northeast section of the United States, in cities such as Boston and New York. In 1976, Perdue's sales were concentrated in those urban areas, channeled through between 40 and 50 independent distributors who handled poultry for several processors on a markup of about 3¢ per pound. But looking into the future, company executives wondered at the wisdom of limiting distribution to these outlets, which constrained growth, especially since the company's estimated 15 percent share of market in New York and Boston was close to maximum penetration through these channels in those two cities. Future growth would probably have to come through other channels, such as supermarkets.

Expansion into supermarkets, however, presented two problems for the company. First, supermarkets themselves were experiencing declining profits because of rapidly rising operating costs, intense competition within the industry,[1] and a consumer trend toward eating at restaurants and fast food chains. Supermarkets were reacting to this competitive challenge by expanding product lines and by offering non-food items and more further-processed food products requiring less home preparation time. Processed food items also carried higher margins to grocers than unprocessed items.

A second concern for Perdue executives with regard to supermarkets was Perdue's packaging. Perdue birds were shipped from processing plants in wooden or cardboard containers and were covered with ice. This method chilled but never froze the birds, a fact stressed in Perdue's advertisements. When shipments arrived at the grocer's meat department, the birds were removed from this "ice pack" and either packaged whole or cut up and packaged as chicken parts. Other chicken processors were selling pre-packaged

---

[1]*Wall Street Journal*, July 18, 1977, p.1.

chicken to grocers, thus saving the grocer the labor cost of cutting and packaging. Perdue was not equipped to do this pre-packaging at its plants on a large scale. Executives wondered how this lack of capacity might affect Perdue's ability to enter supermarkets in the future.

THE PERDUE HOT DOG

Perdue began to consider further-processed foods in response to an industry trend away from dependence on dressed fowl. A trade magazine stated in an editorial: "If one trend is emerging, it appears to be . . . product diversification and company diversification."[2] One of Perdue's largest competitors, Tyson's Inc., had established a large line of processed foods, and Bayshore and Longacre, nearby competitors, were already marketing chicken hot dogs. Another competitor, Holly Farms, had established its own chain of fast food chicken outlets. (Exhibit 2 shows the degrees of home preparation required by new food products introduced between 1971 and mid-1976).

In 1976, Frank Perdue approved a proposal to develop a Perdue hot dog, but said the final product would be subject to three conditions. First, the Perdue frank had to equal or surpass the quality of any hot dog on the market. Second, the new product line's revenues had to cover all costs, including overhead. Finally, the product had to be made of 100 percent Perdue meat. Frank Perdue was seriously concerned that the hot dog's image as a cheap and nutrition-poor food might tarnish the company's hard-earned and invaluable reputation as a producer of quality broilers. This concern was shared by all of Perdue's management.

No one at Perdue had any experience with hot dogs, so development was assigned to Don Poole, a laboratory manager. Poole worked with several different hot dog formulas, combining varying ratios of chicken and cockrel (rooster) meat with various spices. Each formula was tried out at the Perdue offices and then tested in the field with the help of the company's advertising agency. After some initial failures, Poole hit upon a formula that received favorable results in the product test, rating higher than what management defined as the best hot dog on the market, Oscar Mayer's.

Poole also conducted a test to measure the influence of the Perdue name on consumers' perceptions of the product. In that test, consumers were given two hot dogs, one labeled "Perdue" and the other labeled "Oscar Mayer." The sample of hot dogs labeled "Perdue" ranked higher than the sample labeled "Oscar Mayer," even though both samples were in fact identical Oscar Mayer hot dogs. Poole concluded that the Perdue name would be a significant marketing asset in the hot dog market. Poole felt confident that the final Perdue formula was superior in taste, color, and texture to any chicken or beef hot dog on the market.

PRODUCTION

Meat for chicken hot dogs came from broiler backs and necks, and from cockrels. Back and neck meat was most efficiently removed from the bone by mechanical deboning, a process which retrieved back and neck meat at a cost much lower than that of hand removal. Mechanical deboning was a relatively simple process.

However, processing cockrels posed several problems. Cockrels were more than twice as heavy as broilers, and Poole believed that the added weight would slow down the processing lines considerably. Because of their greater age, cockrels tended to be tougher birds, and the mechanical windpipe cutters at times could not cut the cockrels' throats.

---

[2]*Broiler Industry,* November 1976.

Perdue's present supply of cockrels required about 30 minutes of processing per week. However, the plant scheduled to process cockrels had little excess capacity. If hot dog demand was much greater than anticipated, Poole thought that these cockrel processing difficulties would force use of overtime or a second shift. On a straight shift, processing costs for broilers were $5,000 per hour.

The supply of cockrels was a concern to management, too. Perdue's internal supply of cockrel meat was enough for a maximum production of 67,000 pounds of hot dogs per week at the product-tested formula of 15 percent cockrel meat. However, Poole believed demand might be as high as 200,000 pounds per week. Since cockrel meat was necessary for the correct texture, Moriarty hesitated to reduce the percentage of cockrel meat without first testing the new formula. Also, the cockrel meat supply was steady throughout the year, while demand for hot dogs was seasonal.

The actual manufacturing of the hot dogs would have to be done within the leased facilities of a meat processing company, because Perdue had no machinery for making hot dogs. Poole had obtained an agreement with the Gwaltney Corporation of Smithfield, Virginia, that provided him with the use of Gwaltney's labor force and plant for a specified period each week. If demand exceeded this level, Perdue would then use the facilities of Briggs, Inc. of Maryland. Briggs had capacity for 300,000 pounds weekly. Bayshore, Inc. was already using Briggs' facilities to manufacture the Bayshore chicken hot dog.

Poole and Moriarty were concerned over control problems that might arise from possibly having to use two plants, neither belonging to Perdue. Poole found that the two plants produced hot dogs with slightly different colors and tastes, but he didn't know if consumers would be able to discern any difference once spices were added and the hot dogs were smoked. In fact, Poole thought that people would be unable to tell whether the hot dog was made from actual Perdue chicken once the meat was spiced and smoked. Poole was prepared to find a Perdue manager for the Briggs operation if the company started operations there.

In spite of these problems, Poole was encouraged by the successes competitors had had in introducing their chicken hot dogs. Longacre, a company with virtually no name awareness among consumers, was reportedly selling upwards of 100,000 pounds of hot dogs per week within six weeks of their introduction. Longacre spent much less on hot dog advertising than Perdue planned to spend and was also getting a price above that of beef hot dogs, even though "their hot dog was terrible," according to Poole. Longacre's sales were concentrated in upstate New York and Philadelphia. Weaver, another relatively unknown company, was selling a "fair amount" of chicken hot dogs, said Poole, with no advertising at all. Poole wondered how serious the production problems would be, especially if Perdue could achieve similar successes.

MARKETING

Moriarty gathered information on the hot dog market through the company's advertising agency. The agency divided sales figures according to two market areas. The first included only the metropolitan areas where Perdue broilers were already distributed. The second comprised these areas and the peripheral areas outside them. Table 1 shows the estimated hot dog volume in these two categories.

Moriarty also learned that the national hot dog market was composed of two segments, retail and institutional/concessionary. The advertising agency believed the national market was nearing $2 billion annually. Because of Perdue's strengths and experience in the retail sector, Moriarty thought it would be best for Perdue to remain in that segment with its hot dogs and ignore potential institutional/concessionary sales.

Within each geographical market were numerous competitors, most of them regional. (Exhibit 3 shows estimated total hot dog volume by geographic market.) One source showed that the largest share of the total Northeast market was held by Oscar Mayer with

TABLE 1   Estimated volume metropolitan areas (000)

	Pounds	Dollars
1976	118,414	144,364
1977	124,334	151,554

Estimated volume metropolitan areas and periphery

	Pounds	Dollars
1976	140,137	170,433
1977	147,143	178,928

a 25 percent market share. The top fifteen hot dog brands held 90 percent of the Northeast market, as shown in Exhibit 4.

Little advertising was done, most of it by regional spot television. Each market also had a significant number of lower-priced, unadvertised brands. Industry observers believed that the hot dog market was quite price sensitive and that consumers showed little brand loyalty. For example, the brand to which consumers were most loyal, Hebrew National, had only a 50 percent brand loyalty figure, and many of the brands had less than 30 percent brand loyalty. (See Exhibit 4.) Producers were also bothered by limited in-store space, for which there was strong competition. However, the fragmented nature of the industry also meant that no brand dominated more than one regional market.

Perdue executives segmented the hot dog market on the basis of an individual's annual consumption of hot dogs. They estimated that within Perdue's market, 26 percent of the total households were heavy hot dog users, 33 percent medium hot dog users, 29 percent light users, and 12 percent non-users. (Demographic characteristics of these segments are presented in Exhibit 5.)

Moriarty wondered if greater opportunities might exist in the light-user or non-user segments because he believed this group was probably less likely to buy on the basis of price and would be more influenced by chicken's nutritional advantages. (Chicken has less fat and more protein, pound for pound, than beef.) There also appeared to be a possible opportunity to increase primary demand by targeting light users and non-users who might have harbored some fears about the contents of hot dogs. These consumers especially would be influenced by the Perdue story of quality and nutrition. Moriarty estimated that Perdue's share of the hot dog market would be composed of new users of hot dogs as well as past light users of beef hot dogs.

Moriarty had talked to production and accounting people to estimate costs. He calculated that 1 package (1 pound) of hot dogs would cost 58.2¢ to process and package, based on a volume of 100,000 pounds weekly. This figure included 16.6¢ for broiler meat, 7.5¢ for deboning, 23.0¢ to Gwaltney for processing,[3] 4.2¢ for freight, 3.9¢ for labor, 2.5¢ for cockrel processing, and 0.5¢ for packaging. In addition, Perdue would have to invest $225,210 in equipment, $32,500 per year in salaried employees, and $15,600 in maintenance.[4] Moriarty also noted that, as of the end of August, Perdue had spent $219,000 on hot dog research and development. General and administrative costs were estimated at 4 percent of sales. Distributors' margins were 5¢ per pound, regardless of selling price, and retailers commonly took margins of 35 percent. The company could therefore expect to

---

[3]When and if Perdue had to use Briggs' facilities, this fee would increase to 28¢ to Briggs only. A Perdue foreman there would cost $12,500 per year.

[4]When volume increased to 200,000 pounds weekly, investment in equipment would total $345,210; salaried employees payroll would total $45,000; and maintenance would total $20,800 per year.

net 75¢ per pound from a selling price of $1.23 per pound, after distributors and retailers took their respective cuts. Longacre's chicken hot dog was selling for $1.19 per pound at retail; Oscar Mayer's beef hot dog, for $1.45 per pound.

To calculate cash flows, Moriarty used three time periods. Months 1–6 included the test market, to be done in Providence, R.I. Moriarty hoped to get a 5 percent market share in test, equalling 5,000 pounds per week. The second period, months 7–18, encompassed a move into Perdue's four largest markets: Boston/Providence, New York City, Philadelphia, and Baltimore. Again, Moriarty hoped to get 5 percent of the market. In the final period, months 19–30, Perdue planned to stay in the same four markets but wanted to increase share to 10 percent. Oscar Mayer, which was well established in Perdue's markets, had a market share of at least 10 percent in each market, and Moriarty wondered if it would be possible for Perdue to exceed this.

Since 1970, the Hygrade company had been introducing its beef hot dogs, Ball Park Franks, on a national market-by-market rollout. In 1975, Hygrade entered the New York City, Washington, D.C., Baltimore, and San Francisco markets with Ball Park and an estimated advertising budget of $2.5 million. A Hygrade spokesman said that in markets where Ball Park Franks had been introduced, the company had obtained no less than a 10 percent share of the market and as much as a 25 percent share, which placed it first or second in these markets.

The next question Moriarty faced was that of advertising and promotion. Perdue's advertising agency originally proposed a budget for advertising and promotion totalling $2.1 million. This budget included consumer and trade advertising, promotions, development of commercials, and a reserve. The total figure broke down into $304,150 for the 6 months in the Providence market and $1,814,000 for the 2 years (months 7–30) in the four-city market. But management executives, who thought that the budget was uncomfortably high, proposed an alternative budget totalling $189,000 for the test market and $1,205,000 for the four-city market. However, regardless of what dollar advertising level was set, Moriarty was still uncertain how to position the Perdue frank with the advertising. He couldn't decide whether the chicken hot dog should be promoted as something new or as something to compete with conventional meat hot dogs. (Exhibit 6 shows advertising expenditures [for 1975 and the first quarter of 1976] in major eastern cities for all further-processed meat products.)

NUTRITION

Poole was encouraged by the comments of some of Perdue's distributors: while on a tour of a Perdue plant, several distributors suggested to a company official that Perdue develop a line of chicken hot dogs, not knowing that the company was already doing just that. The distributors were confident a Perdue hot dog would be a big seller. Poole and others were very concerned about possible damage to Perdue's quality chicken image. Hot dog manufacturers had first come under fire in 1972 because of alleged nutritional shortcomings in their products. During that year, Consumers Union, publishers of *Consumer Reports* magazine, tested popular hot dog brands in their laboratories and found that their contents included an average of 28 percent fat, only 11.7 percent protein, and various extras. The article concluded:

> So it looks as though consumers are paying today's elevated prices for franks that are only 60% as nutritious as they were in the Depression. Besides the extra fat, modern consumers are getting an unpleasant bonus—a dismally high bacteria count, judging by most of the samples we tested for wholesomeness.[5]

---

[5]*Consumer Reports,* February 1972.

Consumer Reports added that two hot dogs contained 460 calories, but only 10 grams of protein. A comparable weight of poultry had 26 grams of protein; fresh or frozen fish had 25 grams; lean beef, veal, lamb or pork had 24 grams; and canned tuna had 17 grams. Regarding the bacteria problem, the article warned consumers to cook hot dogs to an internal temperature of 160° to kill most of the microorganisms. Boiling for 5 minutes or grilling for 20 minutes at 375° would bring the hot dogs up to this temperature. None of the test hot dogs were made from chicken.

Later in 1972, *Time* and *Life* magazines also printed articles critical of hot dog quality. By the end of 1972, annual growth in hot dog sales had dropped to 1 percent, down from the 1971 growth rate of 9 pecent. A spokesman for Oscar Mayer said that the decline was because of bad publicity. However, the American Meat Institute said that the decline was primarily owing to increasing prices for hot dogs.

Perdue's management was concerned that consumers still commonly held this negative image in 1976. Moreover, the use of mechanically deboned meat (MDM) in hot dog manufacture had the potential of further sullying this image. MDM was receiving an increasing amount of unfavorable publicity in the press and in regulatory agencies of the federal government.

MECHANICALLY DEBONED MEAT

Mechanical deboning of meat retrieved small bits of meat left on a carcass after retail cuts were removed by traditional hand methods. MDM was retrieved by crushing bones that had attached fragments of meat and straining the crushed material to remove most of the bone. The strained material contained mostly meat with a bone powder residue that could not be tasted or felt.

MDM had been in use in the fish and poultry industries in the U.S. since 1968, with an estimated annual production of 150 million pounds. In the mid-seventies, producers of red meat products began to use MDM for such products as bologna, pizza, canned meat balls, and frankfurters. MDM could not be used in such fresh meat products as hamburger. The attraction of MDM was its price. One producer said, "you're talking about a pretty cheap, edible product that would sell for 18 or 19 cents per pound. That would replace meat going into sausage production that sells for four times that much." Government and industry calculations showed that MDM could add a billion pounds per year to the United States food supply.

However, consumer groups and nutritionists were pressuring the United States Department of Agriculture to reverse its April 1976 policy allowing red meat processors to continue sale of products containing MDM. Critics charged that MDM products were potentially harmful because they contained finely pulverized bone. Such bone particles might cause allergic reactions, intestinal problems, or dietary complications in individuals who were on low-calcium diets. Consumer groups also claimed that bone particles were a contaminant, that end-products containing MDM should be labeled as such, and that the USDA should establish microbiological standards for MDM since the process generated heat.

In April 1976, the USDA issued standards for processing and using mechanically deboned red meat. Industry interpreted the standards as an official blessing of MDM, and its use spread. The USDA also ruled that bone particles were not a contaminant in meat products. The USDA's apparently favorable attitude toward MDM pleased industry but irke? some consumer groups.

Although MDM had been used in U.S. fish and poultry markets since 1968, sc European producers had been using MDM as early as 1964, and MDM chicken had / in some Japanese products since the late 1950's. One defender of MDM said in ? publication article that MDM contained twice the iron of manually deboned meat b of the presence of bone marrow in MDM. He also acknowledged that MDM contained more calcium than regular meat did, but pointed out that one pound of cheese contained six times the calcium of one pound of MDM. The possibility of non-food fragments in food was long accepted in pitting cherries, olives, peaches, and dates, all processes which used mechanical deboning equipment.[6]

Moriarty was concerned about the use of MDM in the Perdue frank. Mechanical deboning would be used to retrieve the broiler meat from broiler backs and ribs, which composed 85 percent of the Perdue frank. Although government regulations allowed up to 1 percent calcium in red meat MDM products, Poole had reduced the calcium level in the test-marketed hot dog to 1/10 of 1 percent. The proposed retail price for the Perdue frank was slightly above the market average, and inclusion of an inexpensive ingredient such as MDM might hurt the company's ability to obtain a premium price. Moriarty was also concerned that the MDM controversy might force Perdue to state "contains mechanically deboned meat" on the label or ultimately to reformulate the product with more expensive meat. Moriarty therefore worried that the image of MDM would contradict the proposed image of nutrition and superior quality for the Perdue frank.

Finally, Moriarty feared that an MDM hot dog would endanger the quality image that was an integral part of Perdue's broiler marketing strategy. In one advertisement, Frank Perdue reflected his emphasis on quality and natural ingredients:

> When people ask me about my chickens, two questions invariably come up. The first is, "Perdue, your chickens have such a great golden-yellow color it's almost unnatural. Do you dye them?" Honestly, there's absolutely nothing artificial about the color of my chickens. If you had a chicken and fed it good yellow corn, alfalfa, corn gluten, and marigold petals, it would just naturally be yellow. You can't go around dyeing chickens. They wouldn't stand for it.
>
> The other question is, "Perdue, your chickens are so plump and juicy, do you give them hormone injections?" This one really gets my hackles up. I do nothing of the kind. When chickens eat and live as well as mine do, you don't have to resort to artificial techniques. . . .

---

[6]*Quick Frozen Foods,* November 1976.

EXHIBIT 1   Perdue, Inc.—Sales and assets 1965–1976 (000)

Year	Sales	Total assets
1965	$ 31,624	n.a.
1966	35,558	n.a.
1967	37,956	n.a.
1968	38,096	n.a.
1969	47,507	n.a.
1970	56,670	$ 27,028
1971	63,031	40,923
1972	77,021	38,917
1973	88,592	51,572
1974	142,743	66,224
1975	179,196	99,998
1976	206,096	133,441

EXHIBIT 2 Perdue, Inc.—Food products introduced by 138 companies in 5 years (1971–1976)

		Degrees of required preparation*		
Food category	Total food items or units	Requires cooking	Heat & serve, mix & serve	Table ready, thaw & serve
Hors D'Oeuvres	192	22%	69%	9%
Salads	77	7	0	94
Entrees	2,037	32	68	1
Side Dishes	300	20	70	10
Dinners	271	22	58	20
Breads & Rolls	136	21	24	54
Cakes & Pastries	376	23	19	57
Dessert Pies	193	45	24	31
Snacks	108	4	14	82
Sauces & Gravies	188	25	63	12
Condiments	157	6	1	94
Bases & Mixes	254	30	64	6
Soups	108	35	63	2
All Others	902	38	40	22
Total	5,229	29%	52%	20%

Source: Broiler Industry.

*Percentages may not add to 100, due to rounding.

EXHIBIT 3 Perdue, Inc.—Hot dog volume by market (000)

	1975 actual	Estimated 1976	Estimated 1977
Boston/Providence			
Pounds	21,915	23,011	24,162
Dollars	26,517	27,842	29,234
New York			
Pounds	42,923	45,069	47,327
Dollars	55,143	57,900	60,795
Philadelphia			
Pounds	36,652	38,485	40,409
Dollars	42,150	44,258	46,471
Baltimore			
Pounds	11,285	11,849	12,441
Dollars	13,654	14,337	15,054
Periphery*			
Pounds	20,698	21,723	22,809
Dollars	24,828	26,069	27,374
Totals			
Pounds	132,286	140,137	147,143
Dollars	160,688	170,433	178,928

*Includes New Haven–Hartford, Springfield–Holyoke, Albany–Schenectady–Troy, Harrisburg–Lancaster, Wilkes Barre–Scranton, Portland.

EXHIBIT 4 Perdue, Inc.—1975 hot dog brand market shares and brand loyalty

Brand	Market share	Brand loyalty*
Oscar Mayer	25%	40%
Swifts Premium	12	24
Armour Star	11	29
Hormel	6	27
Ball Park	6	35
A&P	4	35
Eckrich	4	30
Wilson Certified	4	22
Morrell	3	19
Safeway	3	31
Farmer John	3	33
Hygrade	3	27
Hebrew National	2	50
Cudahy	2	24
Kahns	2	29
Other brands	10	
Total	100%	

*Brand loyalty is determined by dividing number of sole users by number of total users.

EXHIBIT 5 Perdue, Inc.—Demographic characteristics of hot dog user segments

Heavy Users (once a week or more)	26%
Medium Users (2 or 3 times a month)	33%
Light Users (once a month or less)	29%
Non-Users	12%

Usage level	Housewife age			
	18–24	*25–34*	*35–49*	*50 and up*
Heavy	25%	36%	31%	19%
Medium	33	31	30	28
Light	23	22	29	35
Non-User	19	11	10	18
	100%	100%	100%	100%

Usage level	Household income		
	$10K or less	*$10K–20K*	*$20K or more*
Heavy	25%	30%	26%
Medium	35	28	28
Light	24	28	35
Non-User	16	14	11
	100%	100%	100%

Usage level	Household size		
	1 or 2	*3 or 4*	*5 or more*
Heavy	16%	30%	39%
Medium	22	32	32
Light	36	26	19
Non-User	26	12	10
	100%	100%	100%

EXHIBIT 6   Perdue, Inc.
Further-processed meat industry
Advertising expenditures by market and by quarter (000)

| | 1975 | | | | | |
	1st qtr.	2nd qtr.	3rd qtr.	4th qtr.	Total 1975	1st qtr. 1976
New York	172.3	483.9	—	36.8	693.0	111.1
Philadelphia	17.6	150.2	—	—	167.8	—
Boston	155.2	110.0	41.0	32.2	338.5	144.6
Providence	13.8	8.0	4.3	6.4	32.5	56.1
Baltimore	18.5	77.5	52.0	13.5	143.0	74.1

DISCUSSION

1. Would you propose that Perdue ignore the institutional/concessionary market for hot dogs and confine sales to the retail consumer market? Why or why not?
2. In the retail sector, on which consumer segment would you concentrate? Explain.
3. What would you choose for the positioning of chicken hot dogs in advertising? What amount would you recommend for the two-year initial advertising budget?
4. In the phasing-in "market tests" that were described in the case, what levels of market share would you set as the minimum level, below which you would not advise going ahead further with the hot dog product? Roughly, what level of sales—in pounds and dollars—would you predict for the first two years of introductory marketing?
5. What would be your decision regarding the use of mechanically deboned meat (MDM)?
6. Assume that any of your choices above are included in Moriarty's marketing strategy for Perdue chicken hot dogs. Should Moriarty have decided in favor of Perdue's entering the chicken hot dog business? Support your answer with your key reasons or data.

11

Maturity and Decline Strategies

Demand for some products grows quickly and declines just as quickly. Such products are merely fads, or passing fashions. They experience no period of "maturity." The majority of products, however, do enjoy a growth stage and then settle into a long period with a "flat" sales curve—the maturity stage. Many such products have been around for a very long time. Individual brands may sometimes be more short lived than product types, but consider the longevity of the following brands:

Tide
Ivory soap
Saltine crackers
Clorox
Colgate toothpaste
Heinz catsup
Velveeta cheese
Ex-Lax
Three-in-One oil
Coca-Cola
 —and Pepsi, too!

These products seem to be immortal: Although they probably are not, they have been in a maturity stage for as long as most of us have lived.

A "normal" maturity stage is the longest of the PLC stages for most successful products, which means that more strategic decisions are made during this stage than in any other. In the first section of this chapter we discuss the maturity stage, again using the formula followed for the introduction and growth stages. From there, however, we will not move directly into a description of strategies for a product decline stage. Rather, our view is that declines are *not* inevitable—or at least may be long postponed. The means of rejuvenating a PMU form an intervening PLC stage and are covered in the second section of this chapter. Finally, we discuss the decline stage and the end of the PLC.

MATURITY

The upward curve of a product's sales starts to taper off eventually as potential new buyers become relatively few and rate of trial and use stabilizes. At that point different strategies—which farseeing marketers would have anticipated—become appropriate. Which strategies are applicable depends on the situation of the new product generically and of one's own brand specifically. Again, the strategist needs specific guidance in setting objectives.

Objectives

A firm seeks two general objectives for a product when it has entered the maturity stage:

1. *Cash flow.* The firm probably invested a great deal in the product during the earlier stages, far beyond the revenues the product has generated. First came the outlays to develop and launch the product, and then growing demand and increasing competition created additional financial pressures. By the time of maturity, the product can become a "Cash Cow" with a positive cash flow. A successful product will generate much more profit than the original investment.
2. *Maintain market share.* The dominant brands in a particular product category must hold their market positions in order to optimize profits: Strategies are aimed at entrenching these brands in the marketplace. Should market position deteriorate, the slide could become permanent. Other marginal brands must aim more desperately to strengthen their shares enough to survive, *if* survival is worth the cost.

We have not mentioned profit as a main objective, although all firms seek it. Profit tends to go hand in hand with cash flow but is less essential. In the maturity stage, strong cash flow tends to be the name of the game.

Market share and cash flow, however, tend to conflict, since the former often requires heavy expenditures. Thus managers need to strike a balance between these two objectives. If the expected product life is short, greater weight is given to cash flow. And the longer the product's life expectancy, the greater the logic of maintaining market share—or possibly expanding it—with short-run sacrifice of cash flow and profit. If competition or other factors are such that a negative cash flow is required to hold a viable market position during maturity, the product is probably not worth keeping.

Situations

Over the (probably) many years that a product, once established in the market, spends in the maturity stage, its situation will undergo a number of changes. Some understanding of these changes will be gained from viewing what happens to the product with regard to demand, that is, between the easing of the growth stage and the slipping into the decline stage. We are imagining something called Product Q, whose maturity stage continued for nine years and whose sales volume over that period is plotted in Figure 11-1.

The left side of Figure 11-1 shows that the product must have been an immediate success, as its sales were growing rapidly in its second half-year. That momentum subsided by the end of two years of product life, and the maturity stage was entered. Substantial growth continued until the peak—nearly 50 percent higher—in the eighth year. Generally, however, the sales curve was practically a plateau until a prolonged and sharp decrease in the eleventh year. During maturity the bumpy line represents reality.

Within the same product category of our Product Q, a number of brands would be contending for shares of total sales. These competitors tend to be

FIGURE 11-1.   **Maturity stage: curve of the sales volume of hypothetical Product Q.**

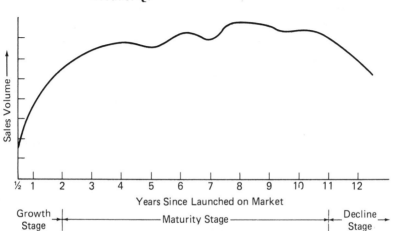

most numerous early in the maturity stage. Many flock to the market when they recognize the fast-growth bonanza, but there will surely be attrition in their numbers over time. When sales growth slows and maturity has evidently arrived, managers responsible for competing brands must answer the key question, How long will the maturity period last? Their decisions about how strong a marketing effort is justified and about whether to hold or expand market share will be partly predicated on their judgment about product life expectancy. As these managers watch the ups and downs of sales, they anxiously and continuously ask, Has the product peaked out in demand? Figure 11-1 shows three declines that proved to be false alarms. Some specific factors to monitor in order to predict or confirm such critical turning points will be discussed in Chapter 17. At this point we will describe only four of the general factors to be considered in situation analyses during this stage.

Market potential is one key factor. Long-range forecasts are prone to substantial error, especially late in the maturity stage, but the strategist should attempt them anyway. Short-range estimates of potential, on the contrary, are rather firm, since the current demand has been demonstrated by the product's sales history.

Demand elasticity, a related factor, is often unknown in spite of the recorded sales history because no firm really tested it. There might exist a high degree of price elasticity that could be exploited if a firm dared to make substantial price cuts. Or there may be high promotional elasticity that has not been demonstrated in the absence of any powerful promotion. If these or similar situations actually exist and are recognized, they would obviously have a major impact on marketing strategy.

Competitive factors inevitably loom up during this stage. They are important because from here on the set of competitors is well established, and all the competitors are going to be sparring for slices of a fairly constant market. Infighting is likely to be severe, and sizing up the chief competition is vital. The competitive aspects to be assessed include the following:

Market position of contenders. Not only how much market share does each have and what are the trends, but also in what areas and with which customer types is each strong? Furthermore, how is each positioned in buyer preference and images?

Distribution position. How extensively and favorably is each brand carried and featured by dealers? How does each stand in dealers' preferences?

Relative costs and facilities. How do rivals compare in cost levels? How extensive and efficient are their facilities, including sales and technical forces?

Economies of scale. Are costs radically lowered with increased scale or accumulated production volumes? How do rivals rank in this?

Competitive behavior. There are differences between industries in the policies adhered to in the treatment of competiton. Some compete with well-mannered respect, some vigorously but fairly, and some without scruple. The kind of competition that is expected affects both decisions about doing business and decisions about appropriate strategies. Also, how fast or how slow is competitors' response to our actions likely to be?

Demand segments are another key factor. The existence—or absence—of special types of buyers who are considerably dissatisfied with the goods and services now being offered is of strategic importance. Potential demand—its exact nature—and the firm's ability to target that market sector are also relevant factors.

The above factors generally need assessment as the maturity stage begins—and reassessment frequently. Other factors that we are omitting may be relevant, including those in the technological, government, and other environments.

Strategic Needs

Managers must correctly identify the needs of buyers and of distributors. While that is a fundamental truth for every strategic program, it is critical when a product's demand reaches maturity. Then competition becomes tougher, and rivals maneuver to win share points. The manager with greatest insight into those needs is the one most likely to succeed. We will now comment on five of the various types of needs.

User satisfaction and value become more critical, since in this stage a buyer becomes much more knowledgeable about competitors and the product's merits. Ways of making the product easier or more effective, more attractive, or more prestigious should be sought. There is always the possibility of improving designs, packaging, varieties, and services.

Availability was considered important during demand growth but is more so in the maturity stage as competitors struggle to gain or hold distribution channels. Inability to find a brand or to obtain its prompt delivery can quickly alienate past buyers.

Brand preference is sought by all the rival brands in order to build repeat buying or to lure away competitors' customers. This results partially from satisfaction and availability but is also a composite result of other marketing actions.

Market interpretation tends to be the crucial step in being creative and in tailoring the product and marketing mix correctly for the changing or special needs of buyers. To recognize the existence of certain segments with special needs and to anticipate what those buyers would respond to, as answers to their problems, demands intimate market knowledge. It demands also the power of transforming perceived needs into the goods or services that would be wanted. Although this strategic need pertains to all PLC stages, its payoff may be greatest during the maturity stage, when differential advantages over competitors are most needed.

Efficiency shows up as a principal need in the competitive battle. This includes efficient marketing action and organization as well as total efficiency of the firm. The efficient firms gain advantages in costs, resources, and ability to adapt to opportunities.

Strategic Options

In broad terms, management has three types of choices about continuing a product during its maturity;

1. *Hold* market share. This would entail strong marketing programs and large expenditures.
2. *Harvest* income from the product. The firm would reduce outlays and funnel revenues into cash reservoirs. Market share would gradually recede.
3. *Divest* from the product. The firm would wholly remove support and withdraw the product soon or perhaps immediately.

In the early part of maturity, those firms with dominant market shares tend to take the first option, although later on they may move to harvesting. Those with only marginal shares would consider whether their brand offered enough profitability for harvest; if unprofitable, divestment would be the logical choice.

> The paper diaper business offers a striking example of this choice. The second brand in market share, when growth tapered off in 1980, was that of Johnson & Johnson. This brand held about one-fourth of the market, and J&J's resources and marketing capabilities were comparable to those of P&G, whose Pampers had over half the market. Also, J&J had a longstanding reputation in products for infants. Despite those strengths, J&J abruptly announced that it was withdrawing from the paper diaper business.
>
> The videodisk player business, whose history we have also been following, proved to be unprofitable for RCA. Apparently, all home entertainment appliance manufacturers were experiencing losses in 1982. Facing much slower growth than expected and under pressures that had forced cutting prices by 40 percent since introduction, RCA had ample reason to divest it. On the contrary, RCA continued vigorous marketing efforts to build that business until early 1984 when it decided to withdraw the product from the market.

It may seem that both of those companies' decisions were wrong, but possibly each was logical. J&J develops many new products and has many opportunities to invest resources profitably. Although the market for paper diapers was over a billion dollars, the cost of winning a sustainable market position against P&G probably made competing on this front a relatively poor alternative. RCA, on the other hand, was developing technology and was trying to hold a long lead in market share for the videodisk player. However, RCA eventually decided that its long-range objectives could not be served by a strategy of staying with the videodisk player when confronted with competition from video cassette recorders. Although RCA had previously waited long, patiently, and successfully in other slowly developing markets, notably in color television, it decided to withdraw the product.

Once the general strategic decision has been made, managers must determine what marketing program to adopt. Each marketing variable should be assessed in its relationship to the particular situation and in combination with others. Managers must recognize possible synergies between actions in two or more variables. Some of the following options may be timely.

Product is often at the center of changing strategies for mature products. Rival brands are seeking to differentiate themselves within the market at large or to attract some other market segments to which new varieties would cater. A resourceful manager will find many proliferations for a basic product. We can readily find a few examples of how brands may gain some advantage over their rivals in a supermarket:

> Tuna fish may seem like virtually a commodity, with little means of differentiation. On the grocery shelves, however, we see that the top-selling brand (currently), Chicken of the Sea, has expanded beyond its basic offering. There is a fancy white variety for gourmets and a low-sodium one for people with dietary limitations. Also there is a "dinner size" for preparing the main dish. The number-two brand, Starkist, also offers a unique pack of three small cans, for the single person, as well as a "family size."
>
> In another section of the supermarket, Ragu spaghetti sauce, the top brand, tries to maintain its dominance by offering five varieties: traditional, homestyle (all-natural), marinara, with mushrooms, and with meat. Ragu also offers a variety of jar sizes. Taking advantage of this proliferation, Ragu induces the retailer to give more shelf space to its products, leaving less for rivals.
>
> Minnetonka packaged its liquid soap in a squeeze bottle that hangs in a shower. This moved Softsoap beyond the wash basin into the shower stall. This too increased the amount of retail shelf space devoted to Minnetonka products.

Computers have proliferated on a gigantic scale. Minicomputers and microcomputers have tapped enormous new markets and have also served as the strategies by which such new firms as Digital Equipment, Apple, Data General, and Wang have moved to dominant positions in their niches. The product changes in these newer computers, however, raise a question of whether we are speaking of extensions of an existing product (big computers) or the introduction of new products in the computer business. That is a matter of definition.

The product variable may also be the major element of a new strategy when the firm's brand has sagged during maturity because of buyers' dissatisfaction. That great marketer P&G, in the past few years, has faced a critical decision:

> Procter & Gamble Co. usually won't hesitate to kill a product that doesn't make the grade. But Pringle's potato chips, an engineering marvel that has produced losses nearly as great as the Edsel's, is one product P&G refuses to let die.[1]

---

[1] *Wall Street Journal*, October 7, 1981, p. 29.

Pringle's had been hailed as a triumph in innovation back in 1975 and threatened to lead the potato chip market, but by 1980 it held only a steady 4.5 percent of that market. However, P&G then claimed to have "learned how to deliver a delicious taste in Pringle's," and the improved product began to gain market share.

The intangible aspect of a product—the services offered by the seller—plays a more significant role as the maturity stage develops. When the product becomes a commodity (competing brands are observed to be pretty much alike—or sometimes actually are alike) rather than a specialty, there may be little opportunity to create sufficient differentiation. In this situation, the more competent firms may offer buyers superior service. In products of a highly technical nature, such as computers, the quality of service offered may be the core of marketing strategy.

Price is also a variable of increasing importance during the maturity stage. Some easing of price is normal, in competitive fields, because sales volume is still increasing but heavy expenditures in plant and promotion are decreasing. Price cutting among rival firms tends to grow, for although new entrants are unlikely, the marginal competitors are being squeezed. If such competitors cannot find a more-creative strategy, they resort to cutting prices in a hope for survival.

Price may be used for constructive purposes as well. A firm may expand revenues and perhaps sales by "trading up" buyers, by inducing them to buy a higher-priced line with more value or prestige:

> The paper diaper business again is illustrative. P&G was not content with the success of Pampers and domination of that market. It created a new design, with much better fluid containment, which it marketed under the name *Luvs*. With these improvements, P&G charged a 35 percent higher price and strengthened its grip on that industry—for Luvs quickly moved into second place in sales.

The example of Luvs was one of "trading up" buyers with an improved product. The contrary strategy may also be used:

> Dow was quite successful with its innovation in plastic food wrap, marketed under the name *Saran*. Saran became the dominant brand after competitors entered the market, but rival products were lower priced. Dow then brought out a somewhat lower quality product under another brand name—*Handi-Wrap*.

Dow thereby "traded down" and not only met competition—while maintaining the prestige of Saran—but greatly widened the product's use.

Temporary low-price inducements are widely used to attract consumers to a brand. They are also widely used in trade channels to encourage more outlets to carry the brand, to stock up and push the brand, or to move inventory gluts. These price inducements come mostly in the form of quantity discounts. In connection with some promotional campaigns, discounts may be offered to encourage dealer participation.

Promotion and promotional campaigns are used in a variety of ways during a product's maturity phase. General promotion usually involves advertising for consumer products and personal selling for business and institutional products. The aim is normally to maintain or improve the image and extent of brand identification in order to hold or to increase market share. Advertising may be used effectively in support of sales representatives and to gain selling leads, or it may magnify the success of sales promotional campaigns. So many kinds of media and promotion are used that we defer the subject to Chapter 15.

As a market becomes saturated, the payoff from advertising and selling tends to decline. If superior types of product appear, promotional effects may decline fast. When gimmicks (e.g., coupons, contests, special price deals) have to be used because advertising or selling is no longer worth the cost, it is time to harvest and divest the product. That is, when these special stimuli will not induce repeat buying, a brand's market share is about to slide.

Spending strategy—how much outlay for promotion would be profitable—is an important concern during this period. This decision is particularly hard in a volatile market—like that for liquid soap—as marketers attempt to penetrate a huge—over $900 million annual sales—market:

> Minnetonka had decided to raise its advertising outlay for Softsoap from $6 million in 1980 to $15 million in 1981. When that decision was made in 1980, it was said that Minnetonka's hope was to raise Softsoap sales from $40 to $67 million.[2]
>
> Apparently that goal was virtually reached (for if Softsoap represented the same proportion of the firm's sales in 1981 as in 1980, Minnetonka would have had $65 million in Softsoap in the latter year). Profit results were quite a different story. From 1980's net of $5.5 million, profits fell in 1981 to $1.5 million.

Minnetonka's hike in advertising outlays for this brand by 150 percent was quite open to question in view of the profit results. That was a tough decision, and we should recognize that such judgments seem much clearer in hindsight. Think about this matter: If *you* had to decide about advertising Softsoap, what factors in that situation would justify such a drastic expenditure? If Minnetonka did not choose this option, what risks were there for an even worse 1981?

The four major marketing functions have been discussed individually here, but in practice they do not have separate strategies. They (and subfunctions within them) must be melded into an effective marketing mix. Both the kinds of actions chosen and the amounts of resources allocated are combined into a composite program, one that takes advantage of the interactions and synergies between functions. And this marketing program must in turn be coordinated with the broader strategic decisions.

---

[2]*New York Times,* January 10, 1981, p. 33.

RENEWAL

Before we discuss *decline,* the last stage of the product life cycle, we will describe its alternative, *renewal.* The PLC curve implies that a product automatically slides downward from maturity into decline and eventual termination. Normally, however, optional strategies can postpone or avert decline, achieving *renewal* of demand.

Alert product managers and marketing directors recognize a number of possible ways to revive demand in a product or PMU long before action is necessary. Early in maturity, managers would anticipate that demand for the product type, or more particularly for their brand of it, would sag eventually. If such managers pay primary attention to the "market" aspect of a product-/market unit, they can easily detect conditions and marketing actions that will continue to win customers.

Too often have marketing managers and their superiors been near-sighted about the approach of a product's decline and about possibilities of renewal. This failure was highlighted by Theodore Levitt, who gave it the memorable name of "marketing myopia." Writing in terms of industries, he said:

> Every major industry was once a growth industry. But some that are now riding a wave of growth enthusiasm are very much in the shadow of decline. Others which are thought of as seasoned growth industries have actually stopped growing. In every case the reason growth is threatened, slowed, or stopped is *not* because the market is saturated. It is because there has been a failure of management.[3]

Marketers should take a dim view of such myopia, as has been well stated in the following, which uses product portfolio terminology:

> While an industry defined narrowly as a specific product-technology may ultimately become a "dog" and call for "withdrawal," extending that concept to a corporation's business unit should seem highly offensive to marketers. The business unit by all dictates of good marketing should indeed have been at the forefront of the new technology that obsoleted the old.[4]

Renewal is highly preferable to decline. In some situations this requires adopting a changed technology, as mentioned in the quotation above. However, in perhaps a majority of situations, marketing actions can avoid or postpone declining demand. And there are those situations in which no strategy can solve the problem in ways that are profitable or feasible for a firm.

One question should be addressed before considering the several renewal strategies, *When* should these strategies be adopted? Our placing this sub-

---

[3]Reprinted by permission of the Harvard Business Review. Excerpt from "Marketing Myopia" by Theodore Levitt (September–October 1975). Copyright © 1975 by the President and Fellows of Harvard College; all rights reserved.
[4]Ravi Singh Achrol and David L. Appel, "New Developments in Corporate Strategic Planning," *Proceedings of the 1983 Marketing Educators Conference* (Chicago: American Marketing Association, 1983), p. 507.

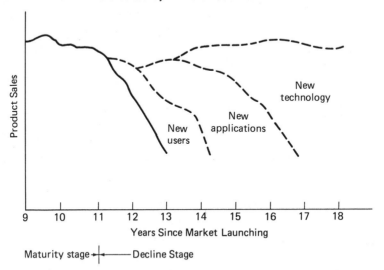

FIGURE 11-2.   Sales volume during a product's decline stage, showing possible effects of renewal. This diagram continues the sales history of hypothetical Product Q in Figure 11-1. How three renewal strategies may prolong the profitable life of the product is indicated by the broken lines.

ject immediately after discussion of the growth stage of the PLC may imply that renewal takes place at that point. It may, but other timing may be better in many cases. Renewal strategies are timely whenever (1) they would yield more profit than the present strategy, and (2) the strategic window is open. Their ideal timing is not tied to a product or brand's location in its PLC. However, their need becomes urgent when decline sets in.

The specific approaches for renewal of a PMU's demand are classified under four types: (1) new image, (2) new users, (3) new applications, and (4) new technology. These often are used in combination—for instance, a different technology may also create a new image for one's brand.

Effects of such strategies are charted in Figure 11-2, which continues the course of sales of Product Q. Our imaginary product would have suffered a steep decline in sales if it had not benefited from a renewal strategy, of which three types are shown. Without them, the product would have been withdrawn in less than two years. The adoption of new technology extended its life off the chart to the right. This chart is only illustrative, and optional strategies may be taken in any order or simultaneously. The illustration could as well have been for a single brand, and of course, a strategy may fail to save the product.

The four general categories of renewal strategies are described below:

New image. The demand for a brand—and possibly for a whole product class—may slide mainly because of buyers' perceptions. At one time the brand may have seemed to be the modern solution to consumers' needs, something really satisfying; but later it lost its appeal. Its image may have become bland and lusterless. The generic need that was served may be there—active or latent—and if an appealing new image can supplant the old one, the product's demand may revive.

New users. Buyers or users who refused to consume or use the product, or did so very lightly, may be attracted to it in one way or another (without changing the product substantially). For example, the product could be made more affordable, as in our example above of Dow's Handi-Wrap, a cheaper version of the premium-priced Saran. Many women became beer consumers when light beer was introduced because, presumably, they could drink it without worrying about calories. (The same strategy was not so successful when light wines were marketed, perhaps because wine had not been so perceived as being fattening.) Promotion alone, when beamed effectively at an additional target segment, may accomplish a great deal. Johnson & Johnson, foreseeing a declining number of babies, convinced many mothers that they too would benefit by using J&J's Baby Shampoo.

New applications. Most products can have more than one use, and frequently these alternatives hold substantial sales potential that has not been exploited for the product or brand. Sometimes these other uses are created by imaginative marketers. Usually, however, consumers have already discovered them, and perceptive marketing research may detect them. Some notable examples include putting Arm & Hammer baking soda into refrigerators to absorb odors and using A-1 steak sauce to make hamburger "taste like steak." Recall that Kleenex (the original brand of tissues) was first marketed as a means of removing cosmetics, and Scotch Tape was first used for mending book pages. These two are unusually versatile products, but they dramatize how this kind of strategy can accelerate demand.

New technologies. A product's demand often falls because new production methods, materials, or designs have made the firm's existing offering inferior to competitive products. This situation occurs most often when individual brands fail to make product improvements. "New" on a product's label is likely to mean some change the manufacturer has made in trying to increase the product's appeal. Tide detergent, for example, has been the dominant brand for about forty years and shows how one product can hold its own in maturity for many decades. What is less evident is that today's Tide embodies a much different formulation than that of the 1940s. Indeed P&G has changed its formulation many times to date, in efforts to ensure that the brand will retain the market leader position. There may have been slight if any change in some staple products like Domino sugar or Hershey chocolate bars, but most products must have undergone repeated improvements to stay alive.

A new technological strategy may well be coupled with one of the other strategies. New applications may result from a change in product. For example, the addition of a reflecting strip on Hartz flea collars made the product more valuable because it helped to protect a dog or a cat from automobiles. And speaking of automobiles, major product changes are customarily combined with a new image by putting a new name on the altered product. This strategy was required when Ford's Pinto acquired a bad reputation after fatal accidents related to the location of the fuel tank. When Ford replaced the Pinto with new models like the Escort, a new and attractive image could be built for the new brand name. A reader might ask whether this case should be considered as a new-product development rather than renewal. Perhaps, but to quibble about definitions does not aid our discussion. Our point is: Be it a new or an improved product, creating a new image can renew a PMU's hold on the established market.

The nature of renewal is illustrated below in three more-detailed examples. The first is a case of creating a new image for the venerable brand of Jell-O:

> Jell-O was born in 1897 and held on for 71 years before showing its age. Then the General Foods' dessert entered what looked like its sunset years. Sales volume began falling 2 percent to 4 percent yearly.... In 1970 the typical household bought 15.6 packages; last year, only 11.4.
>
> But General Foods decided against letting its octogenerian slip quietly away. [It] learned that brands once given up for dead can be revived with changes in advertising, packaging, pricing, formulation, and even names....
>
> In early 1979, General Foods decided to look at Jell-O as if it were a new product. Young & Rubicam, which had handled Jell-O advertising for 51 years, interviewed hundreds of consumers and found that Jell-O reminded them of pleasant family gatherings. Says Alexander Kroll, president of the agency, "There's an emotion about Jell-O."
>
> The previous Jell-O campaign, in contrast, was commonplace.... [The] new campaign ... doesn't mention recipes or Jell-O's low cost. The spots resemble soft-drink ads. Fast-paced shots show Jell-O fans of all ages shaking and eating their dessert as a chorus sings a snappy "Watch the wobble, see that wiggle, taste that jiggle ..." jingle.
>
> In addition, General Foods increased its TV outlay about 25 percent to $10 million. The added funds went for prime-time commercials as a way to influence Jell-O eaters. Previously, General Foods bought daytime TV to reach Jell-O's buyers, but not necessarily its ultimate consumers.[5]

That campaign stopped the erosion of Jell-O's sales and brought about a moderate improvement in both its sales and its market share.

Capitalizing on *new application* potentials for industrial products is likely to require more extensive work in product change or technical service, but this approach may be very profitable. DuPont provided a classical case of this in its nylon:

> First brought to market for use in circular knit yarns around 1940, nylon was used to make women's hosiery. It was an immense success, but there is a definite limit to how many stockings women can consume. Before that saturation was reached, DuPont had learned how to apply nylon to broadwoven fabrics, a much wider

---

[5] *Wall Street Journal*, September 11, 1981, p. 37.

market. Next it successfully applied nylon to warp knit yarns and, within a few years, made a breakthrough to use it in tire cords. By such new applications, the fiber's demand had been expanded over ten times in ten years.

DuPont did not halt its application work for nylon there, although most of those established markets were growing. When ways of using it in textured yarns were perfected, it went into many kinds of outerwear. Beyond that it was applied to carpet yarns in which it became the dominant fiber. These expanded its volume several times more.

Nylon's success eventually had to dim as it reached saturation and as better or more suitable fibers replaced it. DuPont kept leadership in synthetic fibers, though, in the development of dacron and other fibers for ever-widening applications of the synthetics. Nylon thus no longer has a rosy future, but its marketer has been an exemplary follower of Levitt's advice.

Another aspect of the nylon example should be noticed. Besides the right marketing information and strategies, the successful renewals of nylon depended on DuPont's technical strengths for product development and application. Marketing plans must coordinate and be supported by the rest of the organization. This point bears repetition because it may be overlooked.

Our third example illustrates that renewal in not easy to achieve. Even for the great electronics firm of RCA, a leader in American home entertainment manufacturing, technological changes were making viable product renewal very difficult. Besides videodisk players, RCA was marketing to the home-video market its videocassette recorders (VCRs) and color TV sets:

> Sales of VCRs last year rose to two million units. . . . But many consumers are holding back. Despite talk of standardization, buyers still have to choose between the incompatible VHS and Beta formats. The VHS version, which has about 70 percent of the market, is manufactured by Matsushita, which markets its VCRs under the brand names Panasonic and Quasar and makes the machines for RCA Corp. . . . [and others].
>
> As for color televisions, 11.4 million of them were sold in 1982. . . . Nearly every color-TV manufacturer is "either just breaking even or losing money on color sets." Because almost every home has a TV though, the industry doesn't expect large sales increases each year.
>
> That could change in a few years with the arrival of some of the new products the industry has been touting: flat-screen TVs, digital TVs, sets designed to accept teletext, and projection screens with higher resolution and better color. . . .[6]

The quotation above makes one appreciate how difficult it has been to keep abreast of competition in the home entertainment market. For the videodisk player, the strategic window opened on another market:

> It's a vision worthy of Salvador Dali or Steven Spielberg . . . this isn't a dream or a science-fiction movie, though. It's a demonstration of a new kind of coin-operated video game that could begin appearing in arcades this summer. A new company . . . called Laser Disc Computer Systems, Inc. produces the effects by combining

---

[6]Ibid., February 4, 1983, p. 227.

computer technology with optical videodisks. . . . The arcade business could certainly use such a boost . . . according to an estimate by the Yankee Group, a market research company in Boston [its revenues in 1983 will be] $400 million . . ., ending several years of spectacular growth. . . .

If such games catch on in the arcade, says the Yankee Group, home versions can be expected two years later. Pioneer Electronic Corp.'s U.S. subsidiary and North American Phillips Corp., through its Magnavox and Sylvania brands, already sell optical disk machines for the home, but the units are used mostly to show movies. They lack the computer power to play fast-paced video games. . . .[7]

RCA's videodisk machine, whose fortunes we have been tracing, had been experiencing growing sales in 1984, and the number in consumers' homes was estimated at around 500,000. Nevertheless, on April 5, 1984, the corporation announced that it would phase out that product during 1984.[8] A loss of over $500 million was cited that had accumulated during its five years' efforts to establish the product. A special charge of $95 million (after allowing for tax effects) would be required for phasing out the videodisk operation. RCA would continue to serve the product's owners for at least a few years by manufacturing disks for them.

The corporation itself was prospering and would make a substantial profits gain in 1984 despite the videodisk losses. The case is an interesting one, though: a product that was in early maturity with rising sales and yet was terminated. As we said earlier, it had been proclaimed by RCA's former CEO as its "Priority for the decade." What went wrong? RCA's current CEO called it a technical success but a commercial failure and pointed out that, with no other manufacturer promoting that technology (incompatible with others on the market), RCA could not afford the promotional costs of going it alone. The product was lacking, anyway, from a consumer viewpoint. It would play movies and other programs but not record off the TV set, as would videocassette recorders (which RCA also marketed). Thus sheer determination and leadership in its market could not suffice for RCA to succeed in making profits with the videodisk player.

DECLINE

The decline stage may be one in which the uses that the product served simply disappear. Although pastry is still in steady demand, consumer brands of baking powder have dwindled with the home-baking market. Two major food companies, however, continue to market their brands because sufficient demand lingers to this day. Other products' demand is lost to superior new products that serve that continuing purpose, and those old products' demand tends to evaporate, with short decline stages. Good market sense and timing are needed for decisions during this stage.

An example of astute strategic management in an extreme case is that of

---

[7]Ibid., April 19, 1983, p. 37.
[8]Ibid., April 5, 1984, p. 3.

the Garnet Mill and Lumber Company (the name is fictitious but the story is true):

> Garnet Mill and Lumber in the early 1960s looked good financially. Its profits had almost held at their peak level, sales were stable, its balance sheet looked clean, and it was one of the two leaders in its industry. However, the threats it faced became evident if you knew its industry: manufacturing wooden boxes. Other containers were much cheaper and lighter than wooden ones, especially corrugated paper boxes, and smaller wooden box manufacturers were failing.
>
> The largest stockholder in Garnet was a railroad, whose executives were so concerned that they had one of their financial experts appointed head of Garnet. He in turn had a top-drawer consulting firm come and study the firm to propose strategy. The consultants found the situation very grim. Garnet was virtually a single-product company. It was fully integrated from southern timber acreage to final distribution of its boxes from regional plants. It had a few oil wells on its lands, but exploration had found no more oil. It had tried to enter the corrugated box business by building one plant but found it could scarcely break even in that product. Garnet had technical and marketing abilities only in the wooden box industry, and only constant decline could be anticipated in that market.
>
> The consultants were expert in timber industries as well as marketing. Their recommendation: sell the timberlands to one of the large paper companies and dissolve the firm. This was adopted by Garnet's directors and stockholders. The time was ideal to sell timberland, and Garnet's brought such a large price that the stockholders were fully repaid their equities. For them the strategy was optimal.

Garnet's past management had been miserable, as it had milked the company's single business with no preparation for its decline. On the other hand, the final strategy was the best possible choice because the technologically strong paper manufacturer could utilize the timber profitably, which strategically sick Garnet Mills was unable to. And such decisiveness in execution is important when dealing with evaporating markets.

Garnet's situation was an extremely bleak one: Some of the more usual decline strategies are discussed below.

Objectives

Products or business units in a decline stage fall into only a few patterns, and so the alternative objectives also are normally few. They tend to be the following:

1. To divest the product or product line with minimum sacrifice of profit
2. To minimize damage to the firm's market position

These are somewhat conflicting objectives. When a market is fast disappearing, a product has to be terminated fast to avoid much loss. Abrupt action, however, is likely to offend buyers and distributors. If the firm intends to maintain a long-run position in the same market served by the sick product, priority has to be given to the second objective.

Situations

There are several factors involved when deciding on strategy during the decline phase:

Rate of market deterioration. When a product's sales are eroding gradually, a substantial marketing program may be worthwhile. All marketing support may be removed when demand is shrinking severely.

Market segments' potentials. Some buyers may insist on having the declining product, although most are deserting it. A product of this sort now is shaving soap: Some loyal shavers steadily brush it on their faces and make up a firm market.

Brand's market position. When a brand holds a strong competitive role in a declining product (like Calumet baking powder), its strategy should be quite different from one with a marginal position.

Financial situation. The price/cost relationship tends to be favorable for declining products if competition has diminished and if there is no longer any need to spend much on the product. If the investment is large and the product's revenues are high enough to generate some profit, these are further incentives to continue its production and marketing.

Interdependent products. A declining product may be used together with another profitable one, so that it should be kept in the line as long as the two of them together are profitable. There may be interdependence in distribution too (e.g., an appliance manufacturer would not offer an automatic washing machine without also offering a dryer because every dealer must have both).

Managers should be realistic in judging the importance of such situations, for there is a tendency to be sentimental about the good old product and to lack firmness about dropping it.

Strategic Needs

During a product's decline, the strategist should try to find strategies that would have these effects:

1. *Salvage investment and possibly profit.* The mood is one of austerity, looking for ways to operate with little outlay and yet to capitalize on whatever demand remains.
2. *Optimize timing.* The selected strategy must be effective and actionable within the remaining life of demand for the product. If that is likely to stretch out over years, a variety of strategies may successively be applied (for example, one program during gradual decline but also a contingency one to be quickly implemented when a final crisis is approaching).
3. *Retain goodwill.* Unless a firm intends to quit an industry completely, it does not want to undermine its market position for ongoing products

through insensitive actions taken while discontinuing a product. This need frequently overshadows the others.

During this stage a strategist requires information on possible renewal strategies, on costs and potential economies, and on the extent and nature of lingering demand for the old product.

Strategic Options

There are three general strategies to consider for adoption as the decline phase begins or as its situation changes:

1. *Harvest* the profits from the product while demand declines. The product continues to receive substantial market support as long as that will maximize profits.
2. *Spin off* the product or its strategic unit by either selling it to another firm or establishing it as a separate firm outside the organization. There is an assumption that the product or unit will have a healthy future under its new management.
3. *Divest* the product or unit, taking steps toward abandoning it entirely and withdrawing it from the market.

The first two strategies are the happier ones to take. The second, or *Spinning off*, may have very satisfactory results. Two recent decisions of the DuPont Company are illustrative:

> DuPont had built one of the better lines of products for maintaining the exteriors of automobiles, such as waxes and polishes. It included the very popular polish "Rain Dance," which was an admired marketing success. The company sold its whole SBU of those automotive products to Clorox, an aggressive marketer of consumer products. Shortly before that DuPont also spun off its large and long-established business in paints.
>
> Another example indicates that mutual benefits may result from a business being spun off from one corporation to another. Westinghouse marketed a full line of major appliances under its name, but it found that business unprofitable. White Consolidated Industries, something of a conglomerate, had earlier entered the appliance business when it purchased that SBU of American Motors Corporation. Succeeding with that, White Consolidated wanted to enlarge its share of the appliance market, and so it bought the Westinghouse brand. On the date that this transaction was announced, *both* White Consolidated and Westinghouse common stock rose in price. Investors perceived that both firms would profit by the spinoff.

Another example of a spinoff was the subject of our Case 5-1, "American Safety Razor Company," which Philip Morris had owned but decided to move outside the company under its own management. In these three cases, the SBUs were marketing to mature markets with limited growth potentials and probably had some declining products. Eliminating them from the corporate structure enabled the managements of DuPont, Westinghouse, and Philip Morris to concentrate on technologies and markets holding greater possibilities for their special competencies.

Harvesting seems like an attractive option when there will be years ahead to reap cash flow while demand subsides. Only firms with dominant market shares, however, should attempt harvesting. A firm with a marginal share (say, less than 25 percent share) will eventually be squeezed out by the leaders and should therefore divest promptly. A danger in harvesting consists of being lulled into sticking with a product too long while ignoring the hidden costs and the alternative better uses of the firm's resources.

Divestment can be taken rather promptly if the firm expects to have no future interest in the market that has been served. Actions must be timed, however, to avoid being left with considerable inventories of finished or unfinished products and materials. Usually the firm intends to participate in that market in the future, with other products or with replacements for the discontinued one. Then the firm must take pains (1) to give distributors ample time to get rid of the old product or else buy it back and (2) to allow for a smooth transition in launching a successor product. If parts and service will be needed by owners of discontinued products, the firm will have to ensure their availability.

During the harvesting phase, an appropriate marketing mix will differ from that during the maturity stage. Appropriate actions with the functions would include the following:

> Product would have little or no investment. It tends to be prudent to simplify the variety offered in the declining product. If only the better-selling items are retained, their volumes may still be profitable. Any changes would be superficial features or minor improvements in package and label.
>
> Prices tend to be upheld when only the leading brands remain; managers perceive nothing to gain in fighting over a shrinking market. This assumes that price warring had erupted during the growth or maturity stages that had forced out marginal competitors. In cases where a market segment continues to prefer the old product, prices may be raised because loyal consumers are willing to pay.
>
> Distribution is a function where economies are likely to lie. If the product has been sold through several channels, these may be simplified. The number of outlets may be pruned, to move the goods selectively through the better remaining market areas. This in turn means that the sales force sells selectively, so its efforts may be turned to stronger products. If this is the only line carried by the firm's sales force, it may instead be sold through agents whose costs would be lower per unit sold.
>
> Promotion by the sales force may also become more selective, which of course would be aided by simplifying distribution channels. If this product line is the only one sold to those markets, selling may be placed in the hands of agents, with substantial savings. Advertising would be targeted at the specific markets that still demand the product, using more-selective media.

While the outmoded product is declining, the firm's marketers are attracted to the more-modern products. Although the promise of profits in planning strategies for growing markets places them in the spotlight, old products need intelligent strategies too.

SUMMARY

In this chapter we described the objectives, situations, and optional strategies for the two latter stages of product life—maturity and decline. As the alternative to letting a strategic unit fail with a product's decline, we discussed renewal strategies.

In maturity, the main objectives are cash flow and maintaining market share, although the importance of these varies. How the situation tends to evolve during this period was diagramed, and some key factors affecting opportunities were given, including market potential, demand elasticity, competitive factors, and existence of market segments. Then needs that are particularly true of this stage were mentioned: user satisfaction, availability, brand preferences, market interpretation, and efficiency. Strategic options for this phase were organized under three categories: hold, harvest, and divest. Specific strategic use of the four types of marketing functions was also described.

The avoidance of "market myopia" that fails to anticipate the obsolescence of products and industries was the point made in beginning our discussion of renewal or rejuvenation of products (or if a particular product becomes obsolete, maintaining the life of the product/market unit). Renewal strategies were placed into four types: new image, new users, new applications, and new technology. Three extensive examples ended this subject.

The decline phase started with the sad account of a firm that failed totally as its markets evaporated. Then the key objectives were given: to divest the product with minimum loss of profit, and to minimize damage to the firm's market position. Five situation factors were described: the rate of market deterioration, the potentials of special market segments, the brand's market position, the financial situation, and any interdependencies among products. Three strategic needs were given: salvaging investment, optimizing timing, and retaining goodwill. The strategy options were also of three types: harvesting, spinning off, and divesting.

REVIEW QUESTIONS _____

1. *In a maturity stage situation, what aspects tend to be significant in determining marketing strategy? Which of these aspects changes materially during the decline stage?*

2. *What general objectives tend to be posed for a product's strategy during its maturity stage? Why is each important? What inconsistency between them needs to be compromised?*

3. *What main factors would you often have to reassess while a major product is in its maturity stage? Explain why such information is strategic.*

4. List the chief kinds of data that a PMU manager should request from marketing research when a product is in the maturity stage.

5. Give some of the common strategic alternatives for each of these marketing elements: price, product, promotion.

6. At the end of 1981 Minnetonka, Inc., the manufacturer of Softsoap (a product discussed in this chapter), had the following financial picture with respect to its current ratio:

Cash	$ 2,366*
Other current assets	29,385
Total	31,751
Current liabilities	$ 8,317

*000s are omitted.

During 1981 Minnetonka's total sales were $96 million versus $73 million in 1980 (in both years the majority of sales being in Softsoap). Its net income, however, fell to $1.2 million from $5.5 million in 1980. Consider both the strategic position of Softsoap during 1981 and the company's financial picture. Would you favor repeating the heavy advertising of Softsoap during 1982? If not, what other likely options would there be for the strategy of Softsoap and of the company.

7. What alternative is there to a product's going into a decline stage? If it does go into a serious decline, where does the blame usually lie?

8. In broad terms, what are the four approaches for renewing a declining product? These approaches might be synergistic, reinforcing each other. Give an example of this.

9. Compare this chapter's examples of GF's Jell-O and of DuPont's nylon, pointing out the contrast in their strategy choices. Was each choice appropriate to the product's market situation and technology?

10. For managers of declining firms, what moral might be drawn from the Garnet Mill and Lumber case?

11. What do you think would be the overriding strategic objective for a firm like the one mentioned in question 10?

12. In the product portfolio that you manage is one product whose sales have declined by more than 5 percent annually over the past three years. During that period the economy has been rather stable. What factors would you look into, in order to decide that product's strategy?

13. What would be the ideal time for staging the renewal of a product that will soon be suffering declining sales?

14. Which of the three chief options for the decline stage would be the ideal choice? What practical considerations often preclude taking that course of action?

Pittway Corporation

THE COMPANY

The Pittway Corporation was founded in 1950 as successor to the Pittsburgh Railways Company. The former company had operated the public transit lines in the Pittsburgh area, which may explain the name given to the new company. Pittway, however, did not engage in the transit business and instead began to develop itself as a diversified firm. By 1979 it operated in five industries and had eleven plants in the United States and Europe.

The first business acquired by Pittway was a firm in aerosol product packaging, and other packaging lines were later added. The second acquisition was the Alarm Device Manufacturing Company, and our interest is in that branch of Pittway. Subsequently Pittway acquired a valve business and publishing firms (and in 1979 had twenty-five specialized business publications). It also began to enter a number of large real estate development ventures that became its fifth business. Thus in the middle of 1979 Pittway was directing varied businesses from its Northbrook, Illinois, headquarters.

SMOKE DETECTOR HISTORY

In 1979 the alarm device business was one of the divisions of Pittway, in which smoke detectors were the most exciting product. An account of what had been happening in that product category was published by *Forbes* magazine. We quote below *Forbes'* succinct description of eight years of the smoke detector business.

"When they were first introduced on the market back in 1971, smoke detectors looked like the perfect business to get into. These small, plastic covered, screw-into-the-wall photoelectric and ion devices were simple to make, and since they offered home owners unprecedented on-site fire protection, the demand was sure to be there. And it was. From 50,000 units sold in 1971, the market quickly grew to a 10-million-unit-a-year business by 1978, worth more than $100 million.

"But that's only half the story. Because the business looked so good, dozens of producers flooded the market, cutting prices ferociously as they entered to gain market share. The average retail price for smoke detectors fell from $50 when they were first introduced to under $15 today. Then last year the market stopped growing. That convinced more than 20 companies, including Gillette, to call it quits, leaving only four major producers—Pittway Corp., General Electric, Honeywell and Wells Fargo. And none of them are making smoke detector profits worth talking about.

'What we have is a textbook case of an attractive product speeding through its normal life cycle,' says Nieson Harris, president of Pittway, the $255 million (sales) Chicago conglomerate which accounts for a third of all smoke detector sales. Executives like Harris realize that the industry has reached a saturation point where conservatively 25% to 30% of American households already own one or more smoke detectors. Harris does say, 'There are still a lot of smoke detector sales to be made.' Many states, for example, have made them mandatory in new housing and Boston will require them in all residences by 1981. Other manufacturers, however, are even less optimistic and are forecasting a falloff to 8 million unit sales a year fo 1983.

"Harris says Pittway is still making money on its smoke detectors and has no plans to quit the business. But it can't be making much, given that it is spending $8 million a year just to advertise its First Alert smoke detector. (In contrast, Pittway's biggest competitor, GE, says its advertising budget for smoke detectors has 'drifted downward' since 1976.) That may help explain why Pittway's net income fell to $23 million last year from $30 million in 1977.

"The best bet is that Harris is now using Pittway's smoke detectors as ice-breakers for a hopefully slower-growing but more profitable market in a new generation of home security devices—burglar alarms. The new intrusion devices, as the industry prefers to call them, should be in the department stores, discounters and hardware chains by the fall, with price tags ranging from $40 to $150. Says one eager executive, 'The smoke detector has led the consumer into home security awareness. Now he is ready to accept these new devices.'

"What's to prevent intrusion devices from succumbing to the same price-cutting fate that befell smoke detectors? Says Pittway's Harris: 'We're talking about an average $100 installation compared to a $30 installation. Intrusion devices won't be as easy to sell as smoke detectors, but at higher prices, if only 10% of the 75 million U.S. family dwellers respond, that means a $750 million market with lots of growing room.' "[1]

FINANCIAL SITUATION

For financial background relevant to this case, see the excerpts from consolidated income statements for the Pittway Corporation in Table 1.

---

[1]"Better Luck Next Time," *Forbes,* August 20, 1979, p. 113.

**TABLE 1   Consolidated income statement excerpts for the Pittway
Corporation ($000s are omitted, except in earnings per share)**

	1978	*1977*	*1976*
Total income	$257,668	$258,243	$166,056
Cost of sales	140,089	130,134	92,706
Selling, etc., expenses	64,252	62,454	34,829
Research & development	1,781	1,603	1,340
Federal income tax	20,600	27,400	15,390
Net income	23,400	30,015	17,434
Earnings per share	$4.75	$6.10	$3.56

Source: Moody's Industrial Manual, 1979.

To indicate the Pittway Corporation's financial liquidity, we are listing its current asset and liabilities as of December 31 in the given years:

	1978	1977	1976
Current assets	$122,823	$108,247	$71,413
Current liabilities	38,064	39,511	24,328

Note: In the above figures, 000s have been omitted.

In the summer of 1979, at the time of this case, Pittway's financial results were somewhat improved over 1978. Sales volume was more than 9 percent over the $255,609,000 volume of 1978. Net income was around 4 percent higher.

DISCUSSION

1. Judging by the actions taken by the Pittway management, in what stage of the product life cycle did Pittway's management seem to perceive the smoke detector? Where would they probably have located this product in the growth/share matrix? Does that agree with your own opinion?

2. According to *Forbes,* Pittway was spending $8 million in 1979 to advertise the First Alert smoke detector. What is a probable reason for its making that substantial expenditure? What would it have anticipated in that business? Would you also have made that decision?

3. As a firm that was well established in the alarm devices market, Pittway would have been plotting long-range plans for its participation in that industry. For five-year strategies, what would you suggest as the alternatives that it might have considered? Select one of these possible courses of action, and explain your choice.

12

Product

In this chapter we begin our discussion of the four major categories of controllable variables that the marketing planner utilizes. In the preceding two chapters, which oriented strategies to the progression of the product life cycle, these variables were spoken of in general terms. We will now look at each of the major categories in some depth to determine exactly how it may perform in a strategic program. This knowledge will also be relevant to the preparation of the specific marketing plan, which will be discussed in Chapter 16.

We chose product as the first variable because it tends to be the focal component of a strategy and of the marketing mix. In this chapter we (1) clarify the meaning of *product* and its significance, (2) describe its role as a variable in strategy, and (3) discuss the product variable as input in the stages of strategy formulation.

CONCEPTS AND SIGNIFICANCE
OF PRODUCT

The term *product* embraces more than physical goods, for a product may be intangible: Briggs and Stratton sells small engines for mowers, generators, and small industry equipment, which are goods: H&R Block sells income tax preparation and, more recently, legal advice, which are a service: Weight Watchers sells an idea—that of self-control in eating habits to get thin. The product that is offered may be in any of these three categories or an amalgam of all three, a good with connected services and ideas that together form "the product." The marketing of people (political candidates), places (New York City), and organizations all focus on a complexity of product benefits.

There are two main ways of conceiving of any given product: (1) the literally described product, which provides specifications for creating it, and (2) a broader concept that includes everything (both favorable and unfavorable) that a buyer receives in an exchange. A product is a bundle of satisfaction that buyers perceive that they will obtain if they enter into a transaction. When we buy an automobile, a book, or a ticket to a professional football game, we are looking at maximizing the benefits and minimizing the negative aspects of the transaction.

Lazer and Culley view a product as having three elements: attributes, benefits, and support system.[1] Figure 12-1 illustrates these elements of a product.

- Product attributes are associated with the core product itself and include such elements as ingredients, quality, style, brand, and package.
- Product benefits are what the consumer perceives as meeting his or her needs—the "bundle of potential satisfaction" that a product represents.

_____

[1]William Lazer and James Culley, *Marketing Management* (Boston: Houghton Mifflin, 1983), p. 444.

FIGURE 12-1. The three basic dimensions of a product
Source: William Lazer and James Culley, *Marketing Management* (Boston: Houghton Mifflin Company, 1983), p. 445.

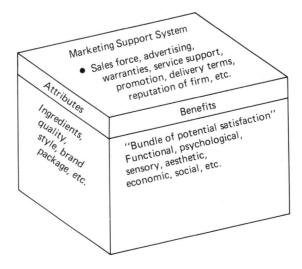

- The marketing support system includes all elements that the marketing organization provides in addition to the core product—for example, information, delivery, service support, warranties, and reputation.

In the eyes of the consumer, products are a mix of attributes, benefits, and a support system. For example, when a consumer buys a $150,000 Rolls-Royce, the economic and functional benefits are probably of less concern than such intangible attributes as style, brand, and quality. A Rolls dealer points out that for most buyers, who in the past have included Ernest Hemingway and Reggie Jackson, price is a secondary consideration.[2] Certainly a Rolls buyer expects a superb support system that includes warranties and parts inventories.

Product attributes are those properties or characteristics of a product that are intrinsic, or attached to the product, and are concrete, observable, objectively measurable, and relevant to consumer choice.[3] Packaging, brand, style, and ingredients are all examples of attributes. Attributes are not usually aggregated, or grouped together, in the consumer's decision-making process.

Product Mix and Product Line

A number of product/market opportunities may be available to the firm. Usually the product/market relates to a single SBU and supports the corporate mission. Product/market units (PMUs) relate to benefits, attributes, and support systems desired by specific target markets. The concepts of product mix and product line are important in relating the product/market to the SBU. Figure 12-2 illustrates the relationship between the corporate SBU, the product/market, and the development of product lines for General Mills. The General Mills cereal product items are similar in benefits, attributes, marketing systems, and production requirements. For example, there are only minor variations between Cheerios and Honey Nut Cheerios, whereas Total, a high-protein cereal, is very different from Cheerios and presweetened cereals such as Trix.

A *product mix* includes the composite or aggregate products a firm provides to the marketplace. A *product line* is an interrelated group of products based on benefits, attributes, support systems, or even production similarities. And a *product item* is a specific version of a product that can be designated by possible combinations or variations.

On the other hand, General Mills has many more product lines and in some cases numerous product lines in one SBU. For example, in General Mills' creative products SBU, there are both craft game and toy product lines. In the restaurant SBU, product lines exist with Red Lobster, Casa Gallardo, Good

[2]"Rolls-Royce Fire Sale," *Time*, April 25, 1983, p. 100.
[3]Tsung Wan Wu and Ralph L. Day, "An Approach to Conceptualizing Product Attributes and Benefits in Preference Research, *A Spectrum of Contemporary Marketing Ideas* (Proceedings of the Southern Marketing Association, ed. John H. Summey, Blaise J. Bergiel, and Carol H. Anderson, (November 1982), p. 132.

FIGURE 12-2. General Mills, Inc.: selected SBU's, product markets, product lines, and product items

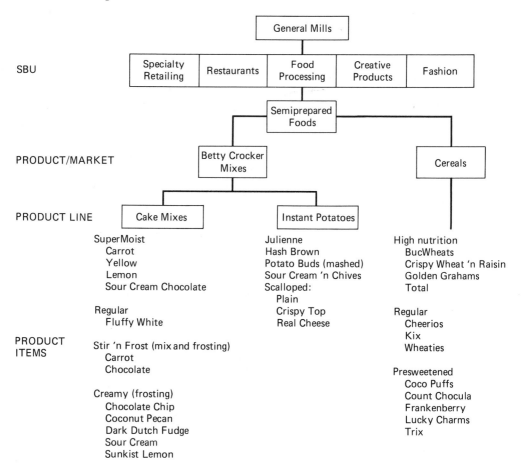

Earth, and Darryl's restaurants. Each of these restaurants offers a number of product (menu) items. The product mix, product line, and product item concepts are basic building tools in developing a product strategy as a part of the overall marketing strategy. A product strategy deals specifically with setting product objectives and positioning the product item, product line, and product mix to serve target markets.

PRODUCT AS A STRATEGIC VARIABLE

Having discussed the definition of *product* and its relationship to the firm, the question arises, of what value is product as a strategic variable in marketing? First let us consider products as being a controllable variable within the marketing mix. Product is a central variable, at the core of strategy. But this should not be exaggerated, for the weight of the product in strategy varies in different situations. Let us consider some alternatives.

Although price, promotion, and distribution can also be very effective, sometimes even overshadowing the product variable, it may be stated that since (1) better products are basic to winning and keeping patronage and (2) growth is a normal objective of enterprise, the product normally figures most importantly in strategy. How extensively the product variable will be changed at each occasion of strategy decision may be quite different in degree, depending on the outlook and objective. Here are three different degrees for the same firm, a cigar manufacturer:

1. The general market strategy may be to obtain gradual growth through inducing those who currently use the firm's product to use it at a greater rate. To accomplish this, this cigar maker might make only trivial changes in the product: for example, put the cigars in pocket-size packages so that they will always be available, or add a tip that would make smoking them neater and more socially acceptable (ideas that have of course been adopted).
2. The strategy may instead be to obtain growth through selling to those who would like to smoke cigars but, for one reason or another, do not find present cigars acceptable. These segments might be smokers who have colds, those wanting a shorter smoke, or those who are female and find that present cigars are lacking in femininity. These might be catered to by, respectively, mentholated cigars, light cigars, or perfumed cigars. These would be more substantial changes in the product than those suggested in the first strategy, yet nothing radical technologically for a cigar producer.
3. If the strategy instead calls for reaching consumers who would consume tobacco only in other forms than cigars or for serving other functions, radical change is needed in the product component. For the first group, pipe tobacco, chewing tobacco, snuff, and cigarettes are alternatives. Going outside tobacco uses but staying with frequently consumed, small-packaged items, there could be mints, chewing gum, breath sweeteners, and many others. The product answer may lie in developing some radically new product to fit these needs or emulating others already on the market. Thus, growth and changes in the product line are tied together.

How to make strategic use of the product is no easy question. The extent and specific character of innovation necessary are partially dependent on answers to these questions: (1) How dissatisfied is the (target) market with existing products—and in what ways? (2) How extensively must our firm alter or replace its current products to maintain whatever equality or superiority of attractiveness our offering needs to achieve objectives? In a firm that has been active in product-development work, there is another question: What product improvements or breakthroughs is our present technology capable of delivering now, or quickly? In this case, with better products virtually available, wisdom may advise introducing them whether necessary or not.

Time is a critical dimension of new products and is fundamental to their usefulness strategically. Let us distinguish long-range from short-range strategy: In the long range, if one uses a horizon of five to ten years, product can be a revolutionary variable in almost any industry. Even though there are limits to what can be developed, the very long range strategist has wide scope in utilizing product to effect corporate goals. In some industries (women's fashions for example), change is rapid. Two years or even six months may be "long" range, and product innovation is used flexibly.

In the short range, product is relatively static. Typical manufacturing industries require two to four years to develop and produce a substantially modified good. "Annual" models usually contain only minor design changes. Major changes occur less often. Products, particularly real innovations, thus tend not to be the chief implement of short-range marketing strategy.

For short-term strategy, there are variations in product that are feasible and flexible. It may not take long, for instance, to add new varieties (say, flavors or colors) to an existing product or to make cosmetic changes that may appeal to new markets. Various accessories, options, or combinations of products may add newness without long development. And there are always package and label changes that are quickly executed, of low risk, and not costly. On the whole, however, product tends to be the more difficult variable of marketing.

In 1981 Chrysler introduced the new K-cars, which were loaded with too many accessories and priced too high. Chrysler quickly responded with stripped-down versions:

> Chrysler's strategy in the mid-1980s was to have a $6.6 billion product development program to use the K-car engine, drive train, floorpan, suspension parts, and other components to produce a majority of the Chrysler product mix. The basic K-car has been extended to create the following product lines: Chrysler LeBaron/Dodge 400, Chrysler E class/Dodge 600, Chrysler New Yorker, Dodge Daytona, Chrysler Laser, and a seven-passenger Dodge Caravan/Plymouth Voyager minivan. This product-line extension cost savings tied to a wide product line of cars is the central part of Chrysler's strategy.

These product variations proved successful in helping Chrysler become highly profitable.[4]

Earlier we referred to product's being sometimes an uncontrollable marketing variable. Both *technological change* and *competitive action* lie mainly outside the firm's influence or the decision powers of its marketing executives.

---

[4]Ibid.

These often compel the firm to change products whether it wants to or not—"innovate or die!" Competitors, independent laboratories, and inventors—or some firm outside your industry that longs to enter it—are likely to keep striving to find product improvements or utterly new products to replace yours. This will affect even the strongest corporation.

When the Radio Corporation of America purchased the Victor Talking Machine Company in 1929, it acquired what seemed to be a very strong product. Hadn't Victor been not only profitable but also the dominant producer of phonographs and records here and abroad? These constituted the main home-entertainment medium until radio came along, and RCA already dominated that. Well, Victor was as sound as it looked for a while, but see what technology was going to bring:

1. Long-playing 33-rpm records, developed by a smaller firm (RCA Victor countered with its own 45-rpm records and players but eventually had to conform to the more popular 33-rpm.)

2. Television, which began to attract so much purchasing power that it squeezed both phonographs and radio to small shares of the home-entertainment field

3. High-fidelity records and players

4. Stereophonic sound, with its innovative records and players

5. Quadraphonic sound (better than stereo for the very discriminating)

6. Electronic tape recordings (starting to dislodge records)

7. Four-channel tape recorders and players

8. Eight-track stereo tapes and cassettes

9. Videodisks

10. Video cassettes

Today, phonograph and record operations occupy but a single line in the long enumeration of products in RCA's financial statements. The corporation remains one of the prominent labels in the tumultuous field of records and tapes, but with nothing approaching Victor's dominance of 1929. Was, then, Victor Talking Machine a wise acquisition? Financially, it apparently was, and perhaps both the reputation and the technical capacities of that firm served RCA well. As for products, surely change is "the name of the game" in management in the home-entertainment field. Although RCA may have strategically planned some of the changes mentioned, it is evident that it was *compelled* to do so by competitive innovation in its field of products. Here we have seen product as an *un*controlled variable.

No marketing variable should be considered in isolation from the others, as their interaction produces a conjoint impact on the market. In deciding strategy, particularly long-range strategy, it is well to begin the search with product, since, with the exceptions that we will meet later, that tends to be the primary variable that the other implements support. In the short run, there is a strong possibility that the primary implement should be promotion, distribution, or price, so these should be adequately considered.

THE ROLE OF NEW-PRODUCT DEVELOPMENT IN DEVELOPING MARKETING STRATEGY

The marketing literature has emphasized the management of new products rather than established ones, and indeed new products appear to be the creative side of products. However, it is difficult to draw a clear line of distinction between the concept of a new product and a mere modification of an existing one:

> Procter & Gamble markets "Pringle's New-Fangled Potato Chips," which closely resemble the traditional potato chips but are formed into a standard shape and stacked in cans. Those features, as well as the formulation, are not found in the traditional chips.

> The Mercury Division of Ford Motor Company introduces annual models in each Mercury line. The most recent model functions like last year's model and mainly comprises the same features, but it has some changes that are widely advertised.

> Spectrafoods markets a line of frozen fruits and vegetables. Some years ago the firm introduced frozen mushrooms and frozen strawberries to the market. It was the first to offer frozen mushrooms, but the strawberries were similar to those of other packers.

Which are new products? From their manufacturers' viewpoint, all of them are. From a technical viewpoint, perhaps all but the frozen strawberries contain elements of newness. But these viewpoints are of relative insignificance beside that of the market, since the significant criteria of being a *new* product are those relative to the buyer and user. These two criteria suggested by Wasson seem to be adequate:

1. That which offers a new level of value for some major product attribute; or
2. That which requires a significant degree of learning on the part of the user.

Analysis of the Product's Position

In Chapter 1 we listed some questions that would be raised in a "situation analysis" for the assessment of a firm's current and future position. Products are an important focus of situation analysis. The following three salient questions in this analysis may be answered by market feedback:

> How adequately is our product now satisfying identified demands?
> How adequate are competitive or substitute products.
> What is our product's current position in its life cycle?

Some of this feedback may exist in the routine marketing information system, but specific studies of buyers or distributors are commonly needed to furnish sufficient facts.

The answer to the first question is vital, for when inadequacies can be identified, they represent opportunities for improving the existing product or bringing out a new one. Users are frequently quite vocal about product faults, but more often the marketers must deliberately seek such information. Sometimes the need for product improvements that should be apparent is long overlooked:

> For many years, large families had wanted a compact station wagon that could carry seven passengers. When Chrysler introduced the Dodge Caravan/Plymouth Voyager in 1984, it became the only U.S. front-wheel wagon (minivan) that could seat seven passengers or carry more luggage than a conventional wagon, yet it offered the excellent visibility of and parked like a small passenger car.

There may also be deficiencies in products that do not matter to those currently using them but deter some other market segment from using them. These are much more subtle product problems, and it may be a long time before a manufacturer recognizes such an obstacle to usage or finds the solution.

> Chewing gum has always been sticky; that is surely common knowledge. The William Wrigley Company recognized that this product attribute precluded denture wearers from chewing it, for it would loosen their dentures. Wrigley went to work on this and came up with Freedent gum. Grateful denture wearers have responded, to Wrigley's profit.

The views and preferences of buyers or users of products are needed in concrete terms, on questions like these:

> How are existing products positioned in buyers' attitudes, with regard to each attribute considered?
>
> How frequently are such attitudes found? (That is, how widespread or numerous are these attitudes among potential buyers?)
>
> To what degree is each attitude a *determinant* of product or brand patronage?

The third question is very significant. The "attribute determinance," or weight that each demanded attribute would play in motivating buyers' choices, is a vital consideration in deciding what should be incorporated in a new or improved product.[5]

Obtaining consumers' images of competing brands or products with regard to important attributes (after ascertaining the chief attributes that tend to be determinant), on a quantifiable rating scale, is an approach to getting gen-

---

[5]This view was advanced in James H. Myers and Mark I. Alpert, "Determinant Buying Attitudes: Meaning and Measurement," *Journal of Marketing*, October 1968, pp. 13–20.

eral indications of needs for product improvement. Such comparative image ratings can then be treated with "item analysis," a method that indicates generally which attributes should be selected for enhancement in the marketing strategy."[6]

Packages are a part of the product offering on which consumers often voice their frustrations. The option of making the package more convenient or appealing is a way of changing the offering without modifying the product proper, at less cost. The marketer should approach this aspect of product positioning also with a list of user attributes, such as these:

Adequacy for protecting the product

Ease of opening, dispensing, and closing

Proper size and shape for storage

Disposability

Simplicity for use or preparation of the product

Eye appeal and quality connotation (including the label)

Value in reuse for other purposes

On the demand side, the needs in packaging would have been analyzed, as on the product side would be their degree of satisfying those needs. Another market is involved here also when the product is distributed through retailers, who may be highly interested in:

Ease of unpacking

Number of units per case

Ease of price marking and stacking on shelves

Protection from pilferage

Visibility on display

The reselling trades, wholesale and retail, are interested in all qualities of package and product that make the offering salable. Their approval and willingness to carry and promote it are needed for marketing success.

As discussed earlier, product positioning is the place a product occupies in a given market as perceived by a target segment of the market.[7] Projecting attributes and benefits that provide an image in the buyers' minds is crucial in positioning. Positioning is a natural progression when market segmentation is used. The term *product positioning* is used more specifically to connote three aspects of strategy:

- Positioning a product within its product line (internal organization)
- Positioning a product against competing products (external organizations)

[6]John R. Holmes, "Profitable Product Positioning," *MSU Business Topics*, Spring 1973, pp. 26–32.

[7]Yoram Wind, "New Trends for Some Old Tricks," *Wharton Magazine*, 4, No. 3 (1980).

• Positioning a product with regard to the markets needs (market segment oriented)[8]

Therefore the product's position actually refers to the buyers' (in a market segment) concept of the product (attributes and benefits) relative to their concept of competitive brands. 7-Up so successfully positioned itself as the Uncola with no caffeine that most competitors have responded by offering no-caffeine brands in their product lines. Rolls-Royce is positioned as the world's most elegant and expensive line of automobiles. The Corniche convertible was recently priced at $162,500. Ultra Brite is positioned as a whitening toothpaste that increases the users' sex appeal. Selsun Blue was positioned as a more effective dandruff shampoo. Head & Shoulders gained a broader position by appealing to both dandruff and cosmetic (beautiful hair) markets.

A product may virtually be positioned on a map that plots its perceived attributes and benefits against consumers' perceptions of competitive brands. Figure 12-3 illustrates the concept of perceptual mapping of benefits (psychological and economic) versus attributes (quality and style). The product could be automobiles, clothing, furniture, or housing. Note that Brand B appeals to the most economic benefit-oriented or quality-concerned market segment. On the other hand, Brand A appeals to a style-concerned market segment seeking psychological benefits. There are seven ways to position a product:[9]

1. Positioning a specific product feature. Synthetic motor oil is not mineral based and therefore protects your motor at hotter operating temperatures.
2. Positioning a benefit. The Volkswagen Rabbit Diesel is the cheapest car to buy and own in its class.
3. Positioning for a specific usage. Use Campbell's mushroom soup for gravies.

---

[8]Lazer and Culley, *Marketing Management,* p. 478.
[9]Wind, "New Trends," p. 37.

FIGURE 12-3. Perceptional mapping of product attributes and benefits to illustrate product positioning

4. Positioning for a user category. Crest toothpaste's "We want what you want, kids without cavities."
5. Positioning against another product. Ezra Brooks whiskey's "Move over Jack [Daniels], Ezra Brooks is here."
6. Product class dissociation. Use lead-free premium gasoline or something similar to introduce a product that differs from other products.
7. Hybrid bases. Use two bases for positioning, such as Head & Shoulders' appeal as antidandruff and cosmetic.

Product Innovation and Change

Product change or innovation should be guided particularly by the assessment that has been made of market feedback and of environmental changes, existing and predicted. The "repertoire" of alternative actions in the product variable should be a substantial one in any alert organization, because the many possibilities of new products—including features and services—would be a constant concern. The enterprise should have people specializing in searching for new-product ideas and creating alternative designs long before their adoption would be timely. And meanwhile, if market feedback indicates that something is wanted that those alternatives do not include, this would aid in pinpointing such discovery work, to create the solution to such a need.

Another angle from which the product and its needs may be studied is the competitive one. Each producer wants his product to have some feature or advantage with which it is singularly identified in a buyer's mind, as a differential in favor of that brand. Differential advantages are sought and exploited by service producers (such as banks, car rental agencies, and motels) as well as goods producers. When a new product is to be developed, the marketer tries to find differential advantages to incorporate in it. If instead one is dealing with an existing product, there is the quest to find some unique feature in it that would have market appeal.

Johnson & Johnson launched Affinity shampoo aimed at women over 40, freeing them from the tyranny of being young. (Most shampoo makers focus on the 18-to-34 age group.) A special shampoo was seen as being needed for hair that becomes brittle and coarse as it grays. Since by 1990 there will be 52.4 million women over 40 in the United States alone, there were compelling demographic reasons for a product with special appeal.[10]

The choice of a product attribute to feature may prove to be a wise one for Johnson & Johnson. But the big question is whether women over 40 will identify with a product made for women over 40.

In this instance, the marketer was fortunate enough to find a potentially attractive differentiating quality in the product. Where the problem is one of *creating* a new differential in the product, much development work may be

---

[10]"The Lather Wars Have Shampoo Makers Hunting for Niches," *Business Week*, January 9, 1984, p. 124.

entailed. When P&G created what became branded as Pringle's Potato Chips, it had to innovate in several ways: a new shape of product, in a new package, made with a radically different formula from that of the normal potato chip, utilizing a new process, and given a new brand name, which was displayed on a new label.

There are alternatives to finding a real differential in one's product. There are staple sorts of products that are uniform among various producers and that rarely have modification over the years (sugar, Portland cement, gasoline). In these cases, rivals may find differentials in their offerings through packaging, or some nonproduct components like physical distribution or unique promotion. For each product and its marketer, how extensively to differentiate is an individual problem each planning period.

Another weighty question needs to be answered prior to undertaking either new-product development or radical improvement: Can the organization develop such a product or improvement that will be feasible within its resources and other constraints?

The innovation project should be feasible on each of several counts, particularly these:

Creativity—the matter of whether the organization has the rare talents to conceive of the product or features that would have market attractiveness in the particular field.

Technology—once given the product concept, the ability to design a producible and satisfactory product, to work out its production methods, and to supply adequate quantities.

Time—whether the needed product can be designed and produced when strategically needed in the market. This can be a very tricky and dangerous variable.

Cost—a danger that might escalate fatally above what the firm planned or can afford. A subtle type of cost to reckon with is "opportunity cost," since funds invested in developing a product might have been applied more profitably elsewhere. A firm may starve the market needs of established products to nourish new ones' development, to its net loss.

To the foregoing factors should be added the very important one of marketing feasibility.

The feasibility aspects all affect the degree of *risk* faced when something innovative is sought through the firm's own resources. Many firms are unwilling to take these risks. Firms with very competent R&D laboratories or designers may run lesser risks, since they may already have discovered part of the technology that a desired type of innovation needs—that is to say, they have it already "on shelf." And with experience in the given product field, they can predict the feasibility of some desired innovation with some reliability. Procter & Gamble did this by launching a new chocolate chip cookie using two different doughs and an emulsifier technology that keeps the cookie moist. The new

Duncan Hines-brand cookie was successful in its first year, backed by a $100 million promotion budget.[11] This product was relatively low risk based on Procter & Gamble's experience and expertise in the food areas.

SUMMARY

In this chapter we introduced the first of the four controllable marketing variables. We also attempted to bring out the chief product inputs in strategy formulation.

We began with some definitions of *product* and then explained some ways in which it is a very significant variable in management's decisions—indeed, usually the most important one. Then we described the role that product plays in marketing (and corporate) decisions, as both a controllable and an uncontrollable variable.

We outlined the significance of the product mix and product line in examining and creating strategic business units and product markets. Product as a strategic variable received most of the focus of this chapter. Many examples were provided to illustrate adjustments to changing technological, social, and competitive environments.

Our discussion of the role of new-product development in devising marketing strategy complemented our previous discussions of new products. Considerable emphasis was placed on the impact of analysis of the product's position in maintaining a product offering that provides strategic differentiation. Finally, product innovation and change were examined to illustrate the need to continually adjust to the environment.

REVIEW QUESTIONS

1. *"The 'lifeblood' of a manufacturing firm is its new products, which therefore are the major concern of its product management." Comment.*

2. *What is the precise difference between a new product and an existing one? Can the distinction, practically speaking, be easily defined?*

3. *Is the product variable typically the most central or important in the determination of a marketing mix? If so, why? Is it because that variable is the one most readily controlled by the marketer?*

4. *Distinguish between a* product mix *and a* product line, *giving examples.*

5. *Compare a retail firm with a manufacturing firm in regard to the importance placed on the product variable. Would you say that it occupies a more central role in manufacturing firms because it is they (rather than the retailers) who design them?*

---

[11]"Products of the Year," *Fortune*, December 12, 1983, p. 76.

6. *What problems are involved when acquiring products as illustrated in the RCA–Victor example? Did the aftermath of that acquisition necessarily mean that RCA made a mistake in acquiring Victor Talking Machine? What particular variables were prominent in this case?*

7. *Where—at what stage or decision—would you prefer to begin your assessment of the need for a new product? Explain why.*

8. *What do the authors mean by speaking of "positioning" a product? How does that determination guide product strategy?*

9. *Describe the role of "differential advantage" in new-product decisions. Does this task impose much added effort in the decision process? Is it worthwhile?*

American Safety Razor Company (B)

American Safety Razor Company (ASR) began its life as an independent enterprise in the fall of 1977. Prior to that it had been a subsidiary of Philip Morris, but that company decided to spin off ASR if it could. When ASR's takeover by Bic Pen Corporation was blocked by the Federal Trade Commission, the company was sold to its executives and started out on its own.

Like any manufacturer, ASR's future depended substantially on its judgments in selecting its products, as well as their design, quality, and technological modernity. Products' success of course also depends on accurate perceptions of the markets to serve and of how to satisfy them. The market and product strategies that ASR had been following were described in the third and fourth sections of Case 5-1, American Safety Razor Company (A), which is required reading for this case. Data on ASR's product line were given in that case's Exhibits II and III.

ASR's product decisions and implementation depended in part on its own position and capabilities, but competitive actions and positions were also key considerations. Some information about two main competitors can also be found in earlier cases. One of these is Case 2-3, "Bic Corporation." The other is Case 4-2, "Gillette Company." Bear in mind that those cases encompass events after 1977, which were not known to ASR's president at the end of 1977. Use the later information only as hindsight judgments and ignore it when considering decisions made in 1977.

DISCUSSION

1. What does ASR's past history indicate about its philosophy in new-product strategy? In its technological resources? In being dynamic or venturesome? In those respects, how had ASR compared with its competitors?

2. What should be the products' role in ASR's future survival or prosperity? Does that role call for any change in product strategy or in the character of the firm?

3. Evaluate the products in the ASR line as of 1977. In what stage of product life does each seem to be? What markets do they seem to cater to? Which products would you expect to be the most promising? To which should the strongest support be given? Which should be phased out?

4. Write recommendations to John R. Baker, who was ASR's president, regarding the firm's general strategy for its product line in a long-range perspective. Be as specific as possible.

5. What short-term actions seem to be desirable for the year 1978? Consider both the expected profits and the impact on ASR's financial situation.

13

Price

Price is one of the most visible variables to the buyer, and besides being controllable, it is usually one of the more *flexible variables*. Price decisions are important, first, in creating a strategy. Along with product, price tends to be a key component of strategy and in some cases can be the most important component of the marketing mix. The ability of the marketing planner to achieve price flexibility means that price-oriented strategies can be efficiently executed. The price component of the marketing plan can usually be adjusted quickly and efficiently to fit current market conditions.

In today's fast-changing environment, it is not uncommon for an innovative product to enter the market and because of some new technical advantage gain instant success by underpricing the competition. Such is the case for Tandy Corporation's introduction of a pocket pager. The pager sold for about $100 plus a $4-per-month service charge while commercial pagers on the market were *leasing* for $100 to $150 annually plus an $8-per-month service charge.[1]

In this chapter we will first examine the significance of price and then explore price decisions in establishing a marketing strategy, marketing mix, and marketing plan. Price objectives will be analyzed, and some of the determinants of price (including supply, demand, and competitive considerations) will be related to strategic planning. The role of price policies in strategic plan-

---

[1]"Tandy Takes on the Telephone," *Business Week*, April 4, 1983, p. 68

ning, in creating a strategy, and in developing a marketing mix will also be covered. Finally, we will examine price setting in practice and the evaluation of price decisions in a dynamic environment.

CONCEPTS AND SIGNIFICANCE

Price is the exchange of something of value between parties involved in a transaction. Price setting involves the determination of some object that can be used to establish the value of the exchange to all parties involved in the transaction. Determining the values to base price is a strategic decision. The use of barter—the trading of products—is on the increase, because a dynamic economic environment (inflation, currency fluctuations, legal and tax implications) has resulted in increased payoffs from using barter in international trade and domestic marketing.[2] In fact, some companies have created barter agents to manage the bartering of their products for the products of other organizations.[3] In our economy, financial value (money, credit, or wealth) is most often used as the common denominator to establish value. Pricing as a strategic variable in marketing should be based on systematic decisions to assign a value to communicate the seller's estimated worth of the total offering.

Relationship between Price and Value

Price can add symbolic value to the marketing mix; witness the "snob appeal" created by the price of prestige automobiles, jewelry, and clothing that tends to increase demand for them. If the Cadillac Cimarron were priced as low as the Chevrolet Cavalier, it would lose its exclusive appeal; therefore, it would not be valued as highly by consumers who expect the Cadillac to maintain a luxury, "most expensive" image.

Strategic Importance of Price

Price is of unique strategic importance to marketing planners for a number of reasons. Not only is it an important consideration in matching firm resources and supply to buyer demand so that profit goals can be reached; price can be a powerful force in attracting attention and increasing sales. Unlike product, promotion, and distribution, price can be adjusted quickly and frequently to match supply or demand fluctuations, and usually at less cost.

The opportunities and constraints of using this variable are stated very succinctly by Martin L. Bell:

---

[2]"Many Companies Turn to Bartering as a Way to Get Vital Materials," *Wall Street Journal*, February 13, 1974, p. 125.
[3]Jack G. Kaikati, "The Reincarnation of Barter Trade as a Marketing Tool," *Journal of Marketing*, 40 (April 1976), 23–24.

The power of price to produce results in the marketplace is not equaled by any other element in the marketing mix. For this reason it is a dangerous and explosive marketing force. It must be used with caution. The damage done by improper pricing may completely destroy the effectiveness of the rest of a well-conceived marketing program. It may doom a good product to failure. Some pricing decisions, notably low pricing strategies, usually are irreversible; they must be used correctly from the outset. As a marketing weapon, pricing is the big gun. It should be triggered exclusively by those thoroughly familiar with its possibilities and dangers. But unlike most big weapons, pricing cannot be used only when the danger of its misuse is at a minimum. Every marketing plan involves a pricing decision. Therefore, all marketing planners should be equipped to make correct pricing decisions.[4]

The importance of price relative to other implements in the marketing strategy does in reality vary for different product categories. The statement by Bell effectively underscores the fact that marketers need to understand the impact of price decisions on the marketing strategy.

For firms in some industries, external determinants of price are so strong that the decision maker must build the marketing strategy around the price. For example, a firm that launches a new cigarette brand will usually have to design the marketing strategy with limited flexibility in price. All brands of cigarettes of the same size (king-size filter for example) are customarily sold in retail stores in the same city for about the same price.

Prices at well-known retailing establishments in upper Manhattan are often much higher than those at other stores in other parts of New York City. Merns, Inc., which is near the World Trade Center, sells silk ties with the Ted Lapidus label for $6.99 while the posh Ted Lapidus boutique on Fifth Avenue sells the same line for $55.00. Clearly, these two merchandisers have differing marketing strategies and sell to different target markets—each of which associates different things with the meaning of value.[5]

The importance that buyers place on price in relation to the value received means that product and price decisions are intertwined. Even though prices of competitive products may be the same, the buyer estimates the value received from the transaction. For most products, there is a real opportunity to enhance the product's acceptance with a good price decision.

SYSTEMATIC PRICE DECISIONS

As with all controllable variables we discuss in this section, price decisions must be coordinated with both organizational goals and marketing objectives. After marketing objectives have been determined, price objectives must be

---

[4]Martin L. Bell, *Marketing: Concepts and Strategy,* Third Edition, Copyright © 1979 by Houghton Mifflin Company. Used with permission.
[5]Jeffrey H. Birnbaum, "Location, Volume, Marketing Make Prices Vary Widely in New York City," *Wall Street Journal,* December 3, 1981, p. 27

established. Price objectives are not established in a vacuum; product, promotion, and distribution are alternatives and complements in creating a strategy, and the price objectives must be supportive, of other strategic-marketing decisions. If the firm has not made fundamental decisions about target markets and organization goals, it will be difficult to establish price objectives.

> After experiencing huge losses in the mid-1970s and being bailed out by the government while on the brink of bankruptcy in 1979, Chrysler Corporation rebounded by finding several ways to compete successfully in the auto industry. During the depths of its problems, Chrysler seemed to have trouble determining its pricing decisions. However, it experimented with various price rebates and discounts and eventually devised a price structure that compared favorably with that of the competition. In addition, Chrysler enhanced the value of its product by advertising its five-year, fifty-thousand-mile protection plan as the best in the car industry. Chrysler became profitable again by greatly reducing its production costs and avoiding expensive retooling by producing its entire line of cars from one basic chassis design.[6] This illustrates how price objectives must be coordinated with other business decisions.

After price objectives have been established, then supply, demand, competition, legal, and other constraints and opportunities must be appraised as determinants of price. This aspect of price setting varies because the nature of the product, size of the firm, competitive structure, government regulation, distribution structure, and other variables can be a major factor in determining the price that the firm should charge. For example, setting the prices for gasoline, a homogeneous product, is structured by local competition and supply and demand factors, as well as by government-regulated gasoline price ceilings. So the firm may have limited flexibility in varying the gasoline price set at the retail level. On the other hand, the firm that offers a new outboard motor with improved performance, greater efficiency, and lighter weight than the competition will have great latitude in setting the price. This product would offer benefits that could not be obtained from other producers, there would be less government regulation of price setting, and the product would be differentiated enough to restrict the competition—so boat owners who wanted this product would have to pay the price.

Figure 13-1 illustrates the systematic strategic decisions in establishing and evaluating price. As the figure indicates, policies are a contingent constraint on the range of acceptable alternatives. A price policy is a guideline or rule for setting prices, which should be consistent with price objectives and the external and internal determinants of price. Price policies should aid in attainment of the price objectives by stating guidelines for it; price policies can be established in planning the strategy and marketing mix, and they can be part of the marketing plan. We provide several examples of price policies later in this chapter.

---

[6]"Can Chrysler Keep the Comeback Rolling?" *Business Week*, February 14, 1983, pp. 132–36.

FIGURE 13-1. Systematic strategic price decisions

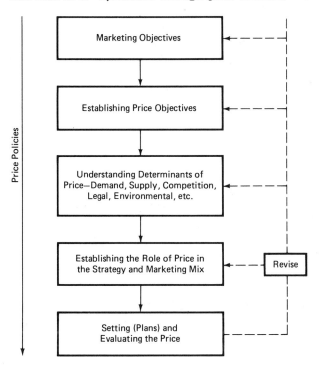

Establishing price in the marketing plan is an art as well as a science. Internal and external determinants of price are dynamic, so the marketing planner must adjust the price to the current situation. A price tactic by a competitor, a shortage, or a sudden increase or decrease in demand can mean that prices must be adjusted immediately. Also, the objectives, procedures, and policies used in setting prices do not always tell the marketer the exact price to charge; there is usually some degree of judgment involved. Therefore, continuously evaluating the price that has been set is an important part of pricing.

ESTABLISHING PRICE OBJECTIVES

The process of establishing objectives is structured by the firm's internal environment. As Figure 13-1 indicates, price objectives should be consistent with and contribute to marketing objectives.

A very large number of price objectives are available. The objective must be consistent with the organization's internal thrust and compatible with the external environment. We examine several price objectives that firms use in practice, including survival, target return on investment, market share, and others that are competition-oriented.

Survival

Survival is the most fundamental price objective. Most organizations will tolerate almost any difficulty (short-run losses, internal reorganization, reduction in size of operation) in order to continue in existence. Therefore, at least in the short run, some organizations price products with the objective of obtaining working capital for operations. Consider the following situation relating to Continental Airlines:

> Continental Airlines developed a survival pricing strategy in 1983–84. After large losses due to severe competition (low-load factors) and high costs of operations, the airline slashed its fares, salaries, and route system in half. After declaring Chapter 11 bankruptcy, superbargain prices ($49–$75 anywhere that Continental flew) helped convince the public that Continental was still in business. After short-term survival, Continental slowly increased fares to avoid price wars and to make the airline profitable.[7]

When Continental was faced with these problems, a survival pricing objective was the most logical objective. After Continental had survived, in the short run, pricing objectives shifted back to a target return. This example indicates that a survival price objective is a short-run, temporary objective that is used only when the firm faces a survival crisis.

Target Return on Investment

At one point in time, General Electric and General Motors stated that their pricing objective was to earn a 20 percent return on investment after taxes, and U.S. Steel's pricing objective was an 8 percent return on investment after taxes.[8] A target return on investment implies a unidimensional price objective, but most firms probably have several objectives (multidimensional) when setting price. General Motors, while stating its objectives as 20 percent ROI, also indicated that market share was a collateral price objective. A very popular collateral price objective for firms that desire a target return on investment is to also stabilize prices. Consider the Hewlett-Packard Company's well-known objective of pricing for profits:

> The fundamental tenet on which H–P is built—and the point they have strongly re-emphasized to their managers—is that rather than compete in price, H–P must concentrate on developing products so advanced that customers are willing to pay a premium for them. According to Hewlett, co-founder of the high-technology electronic firm, "After a few excursions in the opposite direction we've found that this philosophy fits our style of operation."

---

[7]Roy Rowan, "An Airline Boss Attacks Sky-High Wages," *Fortune*, January 9, 1984, p. 68.
[8]Robert F. Lanzillotti, "Pricing Objectives in Large Companies," *American Economic Review*, December 1958, pp. 921–40.

According to Packard, the other co-founder of the firm, "Somewhere we got the idea that market share was an objective. I hope that's straightened out; anyone can build market share, and if you set your prices low enough, you can get the whole damn market. But I'll tell you it won't get you anywhere around here."[9]

Most target-return-on-investment price objectives are achieved by intuitive decision making and trial and error, rather than by using a predictable model to generate a profit level. Also, as previously mentioned, when a target-return-on-investment objective is used, there are usually other, collateral price objectives, such as meeting competition and maintaining market share, or discouraging new entrants to the marketplace.

Limit-pricing theory suggests that established firms in an oligopolistic market are faced with the problem of choosing between (1) short-run profit maximization and (2) the limit price—the highest common price that the established sellers believe they can charge without attracting a single significant entrant to their market. Therefore, a limit pricing would compromise short-run return on investment to obtain "a higher level of discounted profits over the long-run planning horizon."[10]

Market Share

Market share is usually an important measure of the success of a firm's marketing strategy. A market-share price objective can be to maintain market share, or to increase it, or sometimes to decrease it.

> The U.S. auto market has been flooded with small cars during the past decade, and competition has become fierce in this market. Volkswagen's market share dwindled to 1 percent of the total U.S. Market high of 7.2 percent in 1970. Sales dropped 63 percent between 1981 and 1982 alone. The German firm, also recently unseated as that country's number-one automaker by Daimler-Benz, was forced to lay off one-third of its U.S. work force and negotiate a three-year wage freeze for the remaining work force.
>
> Perhaps Volkswagen could have done better if it had been able to hold the line on the price of its popular Rabbit. When the Rabbit was introduced in 1974 it cost $2,999. But as the German mark strengthened its position against the then inflation-plagued U.S. dollar, the price of a Rabbit spiraled upward. By the 1980s the Rabbit could easily cost more than $10,000 with options, typically much higher than comparable Japanese cars and domestic subcompacts.[11]

Price is typically one of the most important variables in improving or maintaining market share. But if market share is pursued without regard for

[9]Hewlett-Packard, "Where Slower Growth Is Smarter Management," *Business Week,* June 9, 1975, pp. 50–54.

[10]Lynn Phillips and Louis W. Stern, "Limit Pricing Theory as a Basis of Anti-Merger Policy," *Journal of Marketing*, April 1977, pp. 91–92.

[11]Robert Ball, "Volkswagen's Struggle to Restore Its Name," *Fortune,* June 27, 1983, pp. 100–104.

other objectives, it does not always achieve organizational goals. Price flexibility and, often, profits are linked to a firm's market-share position. As is the case with the target return on investment, collateral price objectives are usually needed with the market-share objective.

Other Price Objectives and Some Anticipated Problems

A more exhaustive (but not comprehensive) list of potential price objectives appears in Table 13-1. Note that objectives relating to target return on investment and market share constitute only a small part of this list. Only when a firm is explicit in defining its objectives can the marketer specifically evaluate obstacles and opportunities that structure price objectives.[12] Each firm must establish explicit price objectives to fit the existing internal and external environment. After examining the list of price objectives in Table 13-1, a firm might find, for example, that it faced one or more of these pricing problems in achieving price objectives:

---

[12]Alfred R. Oxenfeldt, "A Decision-Making Structure for Price Decision," *Journal of Marketing,* published by the American Marketing Association, January 1973, pp. 50–51.

TABLE 13-1 Potential pricing objectives

1. Maximum long-run profits
2. Maximum short-run profits
3. Growth
4. Stabilization of market
5. Desensitization of customers to price
6. Maintenance of price-leadership arrangement
7. Discouragement of entrants
8. Speedy exit of marginal firms
9. Avoidance of government investigation and control
10. Loyalty and sales support of middlemen
11. No demands for "more" from suppliers—labor in particular
12. Enhancement of image of firm and its offerings
13. Being regarded as "fair" by customers (ultimate)
14. Creation of interest and excitement about the item
15. Being considered trustworthy and reliable by rivals
16. Assistance in the sale of weak items in the line
17. "Visibility" of the product
18. "Market spoiling" to obtain high price for sale of business
19. Building of traffic

Source: Alfred R. Oxenfeldt, "A Decision-Making Structure for Price Decisions," *Journal of Marketing,* published by the American Marketing Association, January 1973, p. 50.

1. Prices are too high in comparison to those charged by rivals, relative to the benefits of the product. (Prices might be too high in a few regional markets and very appropriate elsewhere.)
2. Price is too low, again in certain markets and not in others.
3. The company is regarded as exploitative of customers and not to be trusted.
4. The price differentials among items in the product line are objectionable or unintelligible.
5. The price is destabilizing the market, which had finally become stabilized after great difficulty.
6. The firm is offering too many price choices, thereby confusing its customers and resellers.
7. The firm's price attracts undesirable kinds of customers, who have no loyalty to any seller.
8. The firm's pricing behavior makes customers unduly price-sensitive and unappreciative of quality differences.[13]

Establishing price objectives supportive of the marketing strategy and the overall goals of the firm is one of the most important price decisions. Without explicit price objectives that can be evaluated, the firm has no way of knowing the success of its other price decisions.

DETERMINANTS OF PRICE

We assume that you are familiar with classical economic determinants of price, including supply, demand, cost, and competition. There are also other determinants that affect price decisions—legal or regulatory forces, internal policy constraints, product life-cycle stages, and consumer behavior. Determinants of price depend on the situation; no generalization can be made as to what the most important will be in a specific situation.

> Fleischmann's gin had lost sales in the late 1970s because fewer gin drinkers were patronizing bars and lounges where much of Fleischmann's was sold. Evidently more gin drinkers were drinking at home—and Fleischmann's gin was not a popular take-home liquor.
>
> Over a period of two years Fleischmann's raised the price of a fifth of its gin about a dollar to $5.50 which was more in line with popular take-home gins. The result is that sales, and more importantly revenues, were much higher soon after the price change. No other part of the marketing mix was changed, except for a small modification to the bottle shortly *after* sales began to rise. One analyst summed up the situation saying, "Everybody thinks people go about pricing scientifically. But very often, the process in incredibly arbitrary."[14]

---

[13]Ibid., p. 50

[14]Jeffery H. Birnbaum, "Pricing of Products Is Still an Art, Often Having Little Link to Costs," *Wall Street Journal,* November 25, 1981, p. 25.

It is important to realize that prices are not always pulled out of the air as described above. Very often the calculation of a price requires only the application of a straightforward formula (Material + Labor Costs + Overhead + Other Expenses + Allowance for Profit ÷ Number of Units Produced = Price). In industries where competition is keen or products are standardized or both, a price may have to be precisely determined—for example, in selling cans to the beverage industry.

Let us now review several fundamental economic and competitive price determinants, variables that tend to be major considerations in price decisions.

Economic Determinants

Marginal analysis, from the field of economics, provides a theoretical framework or departure for understanding the relationship among costs, revenue, supply, and demand. The following concepts (you should be familiar with all of them) are used to determine the ideal price for maximum profits:

Marginal revenue (MR) is the change in total revenue (TR) that occurs after selling an additional unit of a product.

Average revenue (AR) (equal to demand) is determined by dividing total revenue by quantity (Q).

Average cost (AC), a factor determining the amount supplied, is determined by dividing total costs (TC) by quantity (Q).

Marginal cost (MC) is the cost associated with the production of one more unit of the product.

If cost and revenue concepts are combined and analyzed, pricing for optimum profits can in theory be determined. As we illustrate in Figure 13-2, optimum profit is obtained by pricing at the point where marginal costs are equal to marginal revenue. This analysis illustrates the fact that increasing costs due to inefficiencies of production interact with the slope of the demand schedule. If one more unit of output is produced beyond the point where MC = MR, the increase in costs is greater than the increase in revenue.

If we could hold all external environmental and internal organizational variables constant, this model could be used to make most price decisions, and price setting would be precise and controllable. In practice, the variables in this analysis are dynamic, so the model is difficult to use for new products before costs and revenues can be established. Also, the activities of competitors can quickly undermine revenue expectations. Marketers agree that the variables in this model are determinants of price; the problem is in measuring and evaluating them in a dynamic environment. But producing and pricing at MC = MR is an ideal model to work toward, and therefore it is a consideration—but only one—in determining the final price.

FIGURE 13-2 Using marginal analysis to price for optimum profits

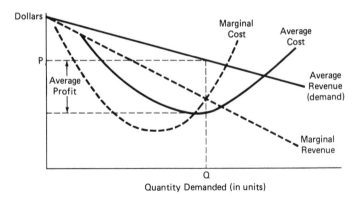

Competitive Determinants

Competitor's prices must be gathered as a regular research function in competitive industries or as a research input in price decisions. It is impossible to ignore the impact of price competition, especially for products where product differentiation may be difficult. Consider the intense price competition between General Foods and Procter & Gamble in the East Coast coffee market. Folger's (P&G) cut prices in New York, causing smaller competitors to lose a large portion of their market share, and many of these lesser firms were forced to liquidate. Maxwell House (General Foods) was being sold at up to 70 cents a pound less in the Pittsburgh market than in nearby Wheeling, West Virginia. The price war became so intense that the FTC even conducted a preliminary investigation to determine if predatory action had occurred. Another example, from the retail book industry, should be helpful:

> Discount bookstores have begun to flourish across the country. Barnes & Noble and Crown books were the first major low-priced bookstores and had grabbed 5% of the $5 billion book business by 1981.
>
> The market for discount books looked so good that B. Dalton Booksellers opened the first of what it hopes will become by far the largest chain of discount book houses in the country. B. Dalton plans to open at least 150 Pickwick Books stores which will sell books at up to 35% off list price; the Crown chain was already pushing best sellers at 45% off list price.
>
> Because chain store operations like B. Dalton and Pickwick can maintain a pretax margin of 8% of sales compared to an average 3.5% margin for independent book stores, the independents are likely to be squeezed out of the discount market. They simply can't price their books competitively and earn a sufficient return to cover their higher costs.[15]

---

[15]"Booksellers Try Discounting," *Business Week*, October 26, 1981, pp. 115–20.

Thus we see that price decisions in such a dynamic and competitive product and price environment would be meaningless without the consideration of price tactics used by competitors.

Internal Policy Determinants

Price policies are guidelines that direct the firm toward its objectives. Price policies facilitate price setting by identifying and limiting the acceptable alternatives, they provide general directions for price objectives, they serve as a bridge in moving from objectives to the final price decision, and they answer questions about the role of price as a strategic implement. Price policies do not provide procedures or tactics for day-to-day price implementing. Rather, they offer parameters for attaining objectives. As we stated earlier, policies enter the series of strategic decisions as a contingent constraint on the range of acceptable alternatives.

The price policies adopted are an important part of marketing-strategy development. They form the important link between the development of price objectives and price-setting activities in implementing the marketing strategy. The actual price set may remain flexible, so that salespeople can have some direct control in implementation of the marketing strategy. The price variable, as we have mentioned, is of strategic importance because of this flexibility. But all price decisions must be evaluated on the basis of price objectives and policies.

A firm may have one or several price policies. A few of those more widely used follow.

Symbolic. Prices are sometimes used to provide a product image of prestige or quality. A well-known Scotch whiskey was first introduced years ago as a low-priced brand. When the product failed, the producer changed the package, came up with a new, quality-image brand name, increased advertising, and doubled the price. Today it is regarded as a high-status, prestige Scotch whiskey.

Apparently, consumers often associate quality and status with a higher price. It is possible to price some products so low that consumers feel that they are of low quality. Therefore a price policy can be to price the product at a high level to give symbolic meaning (prestige) to the product. In some cases, the policy may be to price the product at higher base price than competing products.

Price Lining. This is another psychologically oriented policy. A limited number of prices are used for different product lines. For example, Dannon (Beatrice Foods Co.) sells all its yogurt flavors at the same price, even though there may be higher and varying costs associated with fruit-flavored yogurt than with plain yogurt. Price lining simplifies consumer decision making, and it may lower marketing costs. It is believed that by elimination of some price comparison (and confusion), consumers are more willing to buy.

Price-lining policies assume that the demand is inelastic for various product lines. Consumers are not expected to respond to slight changes in price. For example, a store may carry various lines of men's suits—in one area, $200 suits; in another, $100 suits; in still another, $70 suits. It is assumed that holding price constant for a category of similar products enables the consumer to concentrate on style or some other product variations.

Discount. Discounts are often an important part of price policies. Differences in size of purchase, type of customer, geographical area, and transportation considerations may result in legitimate discounts to reflect economies of scale, competitive situations, or the costs of serving different segments. The Robinson-Patman Act (discussed in Chapter 8) prohibits price discrimination that lessens competition. But discounts are legal if they can be justified by costs or the necessity to meet competition, or if the discounts are offered on a nondiscriminatory basis. Discounting policy is often a collateral policy to help achieve a price objective such as target on investment. The current base price is often only the bargaining point in some industries. When a discount policy is adopted, it provides a standing answer to salespeople who need to know how price will be used in the marketing strategy to attract certain types of buyers. Oversupply or economic conditions will often make price discounts a way of life. With the California wine industry in overproduction and a flat demand, jug prices have dropped 40 to 50 percent in recent years.[16]

Product Life-Cycle Price Determinants

Price decisions vary as the product is developed and goes through stages in the life cycle. Table 13-2 provides a few examples of price decisions that may be affected by the product life cycle. Price decisions related to strategy are important during product development. The selection of price objectives and a decision on the role of price in the marketing strategy will influence all other price decisions.

Establishing an introductory base price for a new product is a fundamental decision. In the chemical industry, for example, DuPont sets high prices on its new products in an attempt to generate immediate profits or recover development costs or both, whereas Dow Chemical sets base prices low and attempts to gain market share. The pricing policy used by DuPont is called *skimming*. The low-base-price policy used by Dow Chemical is called *penetration pricing*. Note that skimming focuses more on investment considerations of profit and costs (target-return-on-investment price objectives), and penetration focuses more on market-share price objectives.

Advantages of skimming include (1) price flexibility (it is easier to lower a

---

[16]Gilbert Sewall, "Trouble for California Wine Makers, *Fortune,* April 18, 1983, pp. 55–56.

TABLE 13-2 Product life-cycle determinants and price decisions

Product life-cycle stages	Price decisions
New-product development	Establish price objectives: analyze determinants of price—i.e., costs, competition, supply, demand, legal and other environmental variables; determine price and value perception relationships.
Introduction	Establish skimming or penetration introductory price, or skimming price for premium product variations and penetration price for low-end product variations; trade and consumer discounts to encourage purchase.
Growth	Consider price reductions to establish market position if production costs decrease; customary trade discounts; attention to broadening the market by using price to combat competition, strengthen dealer relations, and improve the price/value perception.
Maturity	Price defensively to protect position against competition; search for incremental pricing opportunities through premium-priced product variations; increase options, service, and quality to any market willing to accept higher prices; introduce lower-priced "fighting-brand" product variations; increase volume through private-label marketing channels with lower prices.
Decline	Price to maintain profits without regard to effects on market share; adjust price to changes in costs; special price reductions to close out or withdraw from the market; increase prices to loyal market to maintain profits or cover costs.

Source: Some of these ideas have been adapted from David J. Luck and Arthur E. Prell, *Market Strategy* (Englewood Cliffs, N.J.: Prentice-Hall, 1968), pp. 183–88; and Chester R. Wasson, *Dynamic Competitive Strategy and Product Life Cycles* (St. Charles, Ill.: Challenge Books, 1974).

price than to raise it), and (2) quick recovery of developmental costs (especially desirable if a short life cycle is expected). On the other hand, a penetration price may (1) discourage competitors, and (2) build a market share that provides a long-run profit base. Of course, in practice, firms often develop new-product price policies that are in between the polar extremes of skimming and penetration.

During product introduction, the use of price incentives to gain trial by early adopters and of price discounts to minimize risk is helpful in gaining widespread acceptance. Since buyers associate price with product value, in the introduction phase it is important that price matches the value perception of buyers.

During the growth stage, it is easier to lower prices to establish market position than to raise prices, although the price can be raised if costs increase or if the product's value needs to be increased symbolically. Typically in the growth stage, price discounts become more stable and new price lines (low-priced models and high-priced models) may be established to satisfy different market segments.

There is usually more price variation in the maturity stage of the product life cycle than in any other stage. The firm must be ready to make defensive price decisions to protect its market share. Price decisions to increase sales include new-product variations (lower-end and upper-end values), private brands, and the selection of an expanded number of market segments. Prices that penetrate new markets and maintain a table competitive environment are viewed as desirable.

Price decisions in the decline stage of the product life cycle should be profit-oriented. It should be recognized that the product is phasing or dropping out of the market, and therefore market share and product images are not as important (although some core markets may be willing to pay higher prices to obtain the product). The firm should plan to use price reductions to close out or saturate the market to provide a last-minute spurt of profits.

Portfolio Analysis and Price Decisions

Another framework within which we can examine pricing decisions is the Boston Consulting Group (BCG) model, commonly called product portfolio analysis. The BCG model assumes that cash flow and profitability will be closely related to sales volume. Products are classified according to their relative share of the market, and by the growth rate prevalent in the industry.

"Stars" hold a large share of a fast-growing market. "Cash Cows" are also market leaders, but they are found in low-growth markets. "Dogs" own only a small share of the market and experience little or no growth. "Problem Children" show great potential in that they are in a fast-growing industry but currently hold only a small share of the market.

Problem Children probably provide the greatest chance for price manipulation. Depending on the philosophy of the firm, it may want to set a high initial skimming price and quickly regain its investment (this firm would hold a rather pessimistic view of the product's future potential). An aggressive, optimistic firm would no doubt set a lower penetration price in an attempt to increase its market share and turn the Dog into a Star.

Once the product has reached the Star Stage, pricing policies may again be evaluated. The firm may set a high price if it feels it has a loyal consumer base or if it wants to recover research and development expenditures. Should competition be heavy, as in the small-computer industry, a low price may be necessary in order to retain market share—and of course if market share declines, the company may no longer have a Star.

Experience Curve Pricing

In experience curve pricing, a company fixes a low price that high-cost competitors cannot match and thus expands its market share. This is possible when a firm gains cumulative production experience and is able to reduce its manufacturing costs at a predictable rate through improved methods, materials, skills, and machinery. Texas Instruments used this strategy in the marketing of both its computers and its calculators. The experience curve depicts the inverse relationship between production costs per unit and cumulative production quantity. To take advantage of the experience curve, a company must gain a dominant market share early in the product's life cycle. An early market-share lead, with the greater cumulative production experience that it implies, will place a company farther down the experience curve than its competitors. To avoid antitrust problems, companies must objectively examine the competitive structure of the market before and after implementing experience curve strategy. The strategy should not be anticompetitive, and the company must have specific and accurate data that will be unshakable in a court of law. With suitable precaution and sound legal counsel, this method of pricing is perfectly acceptable where it can be successful as a pricing policy.[17]

PRICE IN THE STRATEGIC-PLANNING PROCESS

Three elements of strategic planning (current assessment, future assessment, and strategy formulation) should result in a delineation of the role of price in the marketing strategy. Price is a variable in the strategy in that it is an instrument or force used to reach objectives. The entire strategic-planning process is concerned with some aspect of price. Price is important in (1) strategy, (2) the marketing mix, (3) plans, (4) the offering, and (5) understanding of the perception and behavior of buyers (marketplace feedback). Current performance and market feedback (buyer reaction to price) provide inputs that are used to bridge the current-planning gap. Price is probably influenced more by environmental changes than is any other controllable variable.

Diagnosis of competitors' prices, government regulation, inflation/deflation, demand, supply, and general economic conditions is very important in the current assessment.

The prognosis (sales forecast, assuming different prices) yield the future-planning gap that would be experienced if the status quo (role of price in current strategy) remained the same during the future period. If there is no difference between performance, current price objectives, and the prognosis (no negative gap), then no strategic adjustments may be needed. If a gap is encountered, a strategy is needed that would permit the closing of the gap. In the strategy search, the firm may look for a differential advantage as it relates to price. The advantage may be that lower production costs permit the firm to engage in aggressive price competition. Another option could be that price is de-emphasized and other controllable variables are emphasized. Most life insurance companies stress product and promotion in their strategy, with price

---

[17]Alan R. Beckenstein and H. Landis Gabel, "Experience Curve Pricing Strategy: The Next Target of Antitrust?" *Business Horizons*, September–October 1982, p. 71–77.

(in terms of cost) not always a major consideration. The firm should develop a repertoire of price options to aid in the overall strategy search.

After strategy selection, the efficiency, visibility, and flexibility of price in the marketing mix and plans are important in strategic planning. The price is efficient if it produces desired effects (reaches objectives) without negative side effects on other marketing-mix variables. Price is visible when it is seen as a major support or reason for purchasing. In some situations, the marketing planner may not want price to be a visible part of the marketing mix; then, price will play a minor role in marketing strategy. Price is flexible when it can be changed or adapted to different situations. If the demand for the product is relatively elastic, price flexibility may be an important part of the marketing mix. Since price decisions interface with all functional strategies in the organization, they are a consideration in all strategic-planning processes.

SETTING AND EVALUATING THE PRICE IN PRACTICE

Opportunities for using price as a controllable variable can best be assessed by examining how the "value exchange" fits with the overall marketing strategy. For example, home carpeting and built-in household-appliance sales boomed after builders decided to make these items part of the total offering and finance them on a long-term basis. Some firms have increased sales and profits by pricing their products as a direct expense rather than a capital investment. Renting or leasing equipment to industrial buyers may allow a tax advantage that lowers the overall cost to the product user. Thus we see that buyers are concerned with the total offering and not just the price variable.

Firms should be systematic in setting prices. In practice, price decisions do not always follow a logical sequence as described in this text. As we have said, price setting is more of an art than a science. Theories and projections of supply, demand, competition, and other environmental relationships serve as a rough guide directing the thrust of price setting. But for most products, the marketer must decide what price to charge while taking into account the effect of many dynamic uncontrollable variables. Also, the marketer must keep in mind organizational goals (especially investment and profit considerations), marketing objectives, and the overall marketing strategy.

Once the price is established, the job of the marketing planner is not over. As with other strategic implements, the firm must continually monitor price performance: What impact does the price have on customers, competitors, and relevant publics such as regulators? Most firms conduct intelligence activities to systematically collect data on prices. For example, the grocery industry continually monitors the prices charged by other stores. A store manager may simply send an employee to a competitor's store with instructions to write down the prices of twenty commonly purchased consumer and grocery items. When the employee returns with the information, the manager can then determine if prices are in line with those of the competition.

Figure 13-1 illustrated the role of control and revision (feedback dimension) in making price decisions. With marketing intelligence about price performance, the marketers is in a much better position to improve these decisions.

SUMMARY

Price has unique strategic value because of its flexibility. Its importance to buyers makes price a controllable variable that can strongly affect the sales level. The impact of sales caused by a price adjustment can help to synchronize strategies and plans.

Because price is a very complex variable, it is impossible to identify every determinant of it. Also, product, promotion, and distribution decisions are major considerations in determining the role of price in the marketing strategy and the marketing mix.

In this chapter, we examined strategic price decisions. We focused on the establishment of price objectives; price in the planning process; determinants of price (including internal price policies, product life-cycle determinants, portfolio price decisions, and experience curve pricing; and the setting and evaluation of price in practice. If decisions are made systematically, price should be a useful force in the marketing strategy. But the price set in a specific exchange transaction is based on the judgment and experience of the marketer as well as the systematic price decisions discussed. Also, the efficiency, visibility, and flexibility of price in the marketing mix determine the detailed and systematic formulation of price in the marketing plan.

We turn now to promotion. Distribution will be discussed in Chapter 15.

REVIEW QUESTIONS

1. *What is the relationship between price and value?*
2. *Can price really be adjusted quickly and frequently to match supply or demand fluctuation? What are the limitations of price flexibility?*
3. *Compare the importance of price in creating symbolic value with the importance of promotion in creating symbolic value.*
4. *When are market-share price objectives appropriate?*
5. *Why are policies important in moving from price objectives to the final price decision?*
6. *Getting and evaluating price in practice can be difficult. How should the final price be determined by a decision maker?*
7. *How should the role of price in the marketing strategy be established?*
8. *Does the importance of price vary for different product categories?*
9. *When is barter trade a good price strategy?*

Eastern Airline's Unlimited Mileage Fare

In the summer of 1981, Morton Ehrlich, senior vice president of planning, Eastern Airlines (EAL), was sitting in his office, trying to decide what to do about the Unlimited Mileage Fare (ULM): whether to leave it alone, change it, or cancel it altogether. The ULM fare, initiated in 1977, had originally been designed to stimulate off-season traffic and demand for EAL's long-haul flights from Miami and Atlanta to the West Coast. Eastern believed the ULM fare, which allowed passengers to travel to many cities on one ticket at a reduced rate, would be attractive to, for example, the recently retired couple who was either looking for a vacation spot or for a second home. Also, for West Coasters in general, Eastern's ULM fare offered a vacation in the Caribbean as an inexpensive alternative to going to Hawaii. Eastern also believed the fare would be attractive to young travelers interested in seeing different parts of the country.

Recently, though, Eastern had entered the "transcon" market (New York to Los Angeles and San Francisco) which had long been dominated by United, American, and TWA. The ULM fare was seen as a potential means of getting passengers away from the other three and onto Eastern's transcon flights which had been flying at less than full capacity and were less full than its competitors.

COMPANY BACKGROUND

EAL is a certified air carrier with domestic routes that run predominantly north-south, but since deregulation, the company had added several new flights between the East and West Coasts. EAL also provided international service to the Caribbean, Bahamas, Bermuda, Mexico, and Canada.

In 1980, for the second straight year, EAL had carried more passengers than any other airline in the free world. This success was at least partially a result of an aggressive posture adopted by the company at a time when many other trunk airlines had been pulling back. EAL went into new markets and, in particular, entered the nonstop transcontinental market between New York City and California and added new service between the southeast and the West Coast.

The airline also was able to maintain itself in its important north-south markets in the face of heavy competition. It mounted effective promotional campaigns and built on its reputation as an airline that provided frequent and conveniently timed service in these markets.

EAL was one of only two airlines to show an operating profit in 1980, a year considered by many to have been the worst year up to that time for the industry's finances. Even so, EAL suffered a net after-tax loss of $17.4 million as compared to a net income of $57.6 million the year before (see Exhibit 1). The airline industry as a whole suffered from a huge

---

This case was prepared by Marilyn Edling, Research Assistant, under the supervision of Professor John Meyer, as the basis for class discussion rather than to illustrate either effective or ineffective handling of an administative situation. Copyright © 1982 by the President and Fellows of Harvard College.

increase in fuel prices and from a slowdown in the economy. Eastern's fuel costs increased 51% in 1980 and accounted for 29¢ of every expense dollar; in 1973, fuel only accounted for 10¢ of every dollar spent. The slowdown in the country's economy was reflected in passenger air travel, with EAL's passengers dropping to 39.1 million, a 3.1 million decrease from 1979. Revenue passenger miles (RPM) for EAL decreased 2.4% to 28.2 million and passenger load factor decreased to just over 61%. The rest of the industry suffered a much larger decrease in traffic, approximately 5.4%. This rapid downturn followed a very strong three-year period for EAL and for the industry.

FINDINGS ON THE ULM FARE

Analysis indicated that the ULM fare had been successful in hitting its target population of personal travelers and vacationers. Of the people who used the fare in 1980, 73% were personal travelers, while 27% were business travellers. Although the fare was originally designed as a West Coast fare, it wasn't until after 1978, with the introduction of more West to East Coast flights by EAL, that a significant number of passengers using the ULM fare originated in the west (see Exhibit 2).

The ULM fare was priced on an incremental rather than full-cost basis. According to a survey conducted by Eastern in the third quarter of 1978, the pretax contribution was $2.6 million (see Exhibit 3) calculated by breaking down the passengers into three groups:

1) *Fully generated*—Those who would not have traveled to any of the cities on their itineraries if the ULM fare had not been available.
2) *Partially generated*—Those who would have traveled to some but not all the cities.
3) *Diverted*—Those who would have traveled on Eastern at full fare if the ULM excursion had not been available.

In an update of the analysis, the same breakdown was assumed between the three passenger groups and these percentages applied to third quarter 1980 usage. This yielded just under $5 million as ULM's pretax contribution (see Exhibit 4).

To avoid inbalancing load factors, EAL instituted a number of procedures to control ULM demand on certain heavily used flights and at certain times of the year. These controls ranged anywhere from limiting the number of seats available to ULM passengers on certain international flights to excluding ULM travel altogether on certain flights and certain days (blackouts). In addition, EAL added peak and off-peak pricing to keep usage down during peak demand periods and to increase it during off-peak periods; these controls were constantly changing, depending on Eastern's anticipated load factors and other such considerations (see Exhibit 5 for tariff history).

POLICY ALTERNATIVES

Eight possible changes or recommendations emerged from EAL's deliberations on the ULM fare in the spring of 1981, all of which were intended to refine the initial ULM fare and increase its use.

1. *Separate Class.* The first recommendation was to designate the ULM as a separate class. This would allow easy future evaluation of the fare's effectiveness. As it was, the ULM fare was treated as a coach class on domestic flights and as a discount fare on international flights.

This lumping of ULM passengers together with other fare classes led to problems in booking passengers correctly. Because the ULM fare could only be used under certain conditions, as shown in Exhibit 5, it was important that booking agents know how many ULM passengers reserved seats on a particular flight. Without easy access to this information, coupled with the fact that ULM travelers had to book seats 14 days in advance, many agents unwittingly circumvented ULM capacity controls on certain flights. For example, sampling of the Barbados-Miami route found a ULM usage of 40% individual passengers when no individual ULM fare was available.

If EAL introduced a separate class, it would alleviate these problems and it would also be a fairly straightforward task to evaluate the contribution of the fare to the system's revenues. As it was, EAL used an historical percentage estimated from a random sample of itineraries to do these evaluations rather than actual flight data.

2. *Capacity Controls.* Most airlines aimed for an average load factor of 55% to 60% (so as to be able to accommodate business travelers without having to deny too many last minute requests for space, etc.). After running the correlation between the number of ULM passengers and average load factors between city pairs, continuing capacity controls were indicated to prevent ULM passengers from squeezing out full-fare passengers on popular flights (see Exhibit 7). As an alternative to holiday and other such blackouts, seat limits on individual high-density flights were considered better. Under such a procedure, the ULM share could fluctuate with the number of full-fare bookings up until departure time. On those flights that generally had a high load factor, a 100% capacity control could be imposed, essentially blacking out that flight to ULM passengers.

Additionally, this system could be used to divert ULM passengers to low-density routes as the fare allowed a passenger to choose different routes to reach his destination. For example, if a passenger ultimately wanted to reach San Juan, Puerto Rico, and he was boarding in Los Angeles, he could fly either to Atlanta and then Miami and then to San Juan, or if that transcontinental flight was full or blacked out, he could first fly to New York City and then take another flight to Miami and then on to Puerto Rico. In any case, the passenger need not be greatly inconvenienced as Eastern had an extensive north-south network as well as many route alternatives west to east.

3. *Price.* The adult fare had originally been set at $299. Approximately one year later, in November 1978, it was raised to $369. As a consequence, ULM RPMs then dropped off sharply at a time when Eastern's total systemwide RPMs were increasing (see Exhibit 9). The next year the fare was dropped back to its former level only to start climbing again at the end of 1979 (see Exhibit 8). By December 1980, the fare had climbed to $479. These price changes were intended to help control the seasonal demand for ULM tickets, as well as compensate for even higher fuel and operating costs. Presumably, if the fare were hiked enough, demand would fall off and, if lowered, ULM demand would increase (cf. Exhibits 8 and 9).

Some at EAL considered the 1981 price to be too high and not properly linked to its competition. For example, instead of viewing the fare as mainly providing an alternative to the West Coast-Hawaii vacation, ULM could be seen as essentially a transcontinental fare and hence should be linked to competitors' transcontinental fares. In such a view, the ULM price floor should be set during the off-peak season just above the competitors' transcontinental fares and, as a ceiling, roughly equal to the lowest fare from the West Coast to Miami that included two additional stops.

This pricing scheme, it was hoped, would increase EAL's transcon load factors, and with the judicious use of capacity controls, would put the short-hauls from the ULMs on EAL's less popular routes. It was felt that this scheme would work because, as pointed out above, the fare had appeared to be price sensitive in the past. The estimated price elasticity of demand for ULM had been estimated at -1.4% relative to the transcontinental fare.[1]

Complementing the recommendation of tying the fare more closely to transcontinental fares, it was also suggested that (1) individual travel on ULM be continued; (2) the surcharge on all Caribbean travel be continued; and (3) peak and off-peak pricing be continued.

4. *Target Market.* EAL was, to a considerable extent, a vacation airline, with over 60% of its passengers using the airline for personal travel and only 40% for business. For most trunk airlines, these percentages were just reversed. The ULM fare had worked well in attracting West Coast vacationers, its original target, but it had not been as successful in attracting business travelers. In 1978, 24% of the passengers traveling on ULM tickets were on businesses; in 1980, it was still only 27%.

The ULM ticket offered a unique opportunity for the business traveler to add on an inexpensive vacation. An advertising campaign could be launched explaining the fare and the vacation possibilities for the business traveler and spouse as well as children. To be effective, it was felt that Eastern would have to take ads out for the ULM in the business journals—e.g., *Business Week, Fortune, The Wall Street Journal*—media that Eastern had not traditionally used for advertising the ULM fare.

5. *Advertising Campaign.* Restructuring the whole advertising strategy for ULM was indicated. In addition to including the business media, the advertising should be concentrated during those seasons that Eastern wanted ULM travelers. A media blitz just prior to the off-peak seasons in cities where Eastern was interested in building up demand would probably be most effective.

6. *Reservation Days.* ULM ticket holders were required to make reservations 14 days in advance. Technically, this restriction allowed Eastern to control the number of ULM passengers on any one flight. But as was discovered (see p. 403), this had not always worked and bookings sometimes exceeded capacity controls. This discovery, as well as the recommendation to go after the business traveler who usually was not in a position to make travel plans so far in advance, suggested the reservation requirement might be discontinued.

7. *Blackout Days.* If flexible capacity controls were instituted, blanket blackouts to control ULM demand should no longer be needed.

8. *Number of Segments.* The ULM fare allowed 21 stops per ticket. There seemed to be no need to change this as survey data indicated that 95% of ULM passengers traveled less than 15 segments and 60% stopped between 5 and 10 times. At the same time, it was felt that ULM passengers should still be required to make at least two stops en route with the additional requirement of traveling at least 7 days but no more than 21 days. This provision would prevent the pure business traveler from using the discount fare but, at the same time, would leave the ULM fare attractive to the business/vacation traveler.

RECENT DEVELOPMENTS

During the summer of 1981, EAL instituted an Anywhere Fare aimed mainly at long-distance and transcontinental markets. For $179, a peson could travel between the East and

---

[1]The elasticity of demand measures the percent change in quantity demanded as a result of a 1% change in price.

West Coasts. The only restrictions were that reservations had to be made 14 days in advance and there had to be one Saturday night stopover.

Ehrlich still had to grapple with what to do about the ULM fare in the fall. The analyses had turned up a lot of information and he had to decide which, if any, of the recommendations to adopt.

EXHIBIT 1 Eastern Airline's unlimited mileage fare

	Year ended December 31		
All amounts in thousands	1980	1979	1978
Operating Revenues:			
Passenger	$3,151,798	$2,628,721	$2,156,182
Cargo	163,472	137,791	121,714
Incidental and other revenues	137,272	115,014	101,668
Total Operating Revenues	3,152,542	2,881,526	2,379,561
Operating Expenses:			
Flying operations:			
Aircraft fuel	1,019,546	672,689	425,191
Other	381,357	321,558	297,517
Maintenance	396,174	344,625	304,202
Passenger service	314,639	280,997	232,795
Aircraft and traffic servicing	550,685	481,320	409,511
Marketing and administrative	520,470	438,043	375,922
Depreciation and amortization	200,572	174,769	166,331
Cost of incidental revenues	67,242	56,158	71,313
Total Operating Expenses	3,450,685	2,770,159	2,282,782
Operating Profit	1,857	111,067	96,782
Non-Operating Income and (Expense):			
Interest income	11,118	28,877	13,113
Interest expense (exclusive of $10,276, $6,303			
and $2,274 capitalized)	(109,836)	(84,335)	(74,980)
Profit on sale of equipment	17,886	5,723	25,084
Gain on extinguishment of debt	—	—	4,368
Other, net	2,708	(922)	2,890
Total	(48,124)	(50,657)	(29,525)
Income (Loss) Before Income Taxes			
and Extraordinary Item	(46,267)	60,410	67,257
(Reduction in) provision for income taxes	(4,255)	2,779	—
Income (Loss) Before Extraordinary Item	(42,012)	57,631	67,257
Extraordinary item—net of a provision			
in lieu of income taxes of $2,498	21,654	—	—
Net Income (Loss)	(17,358)	57,631	67,257

continued

EXHIBIT 1 *(continued)*

All amounts in thousands	Year ended December 31		
	1980	*1979*	*1978*
Earnings (Deficit) Retained for Use in the Business:			
Balance at beginning of year	78,273	27,123	34,621
Loss on distribution of Treasury Stock to employees	(529)	—	—
Amortization of excess redemption value of Preferred Stock over carrying value	(96)	(56)	(27)
Cash dividends—Preferred Stock	(4,035)	(6,725)	(5,186)
Balance at end of year	$ 56,255	$ 78,273	$ 27,123
Earnings Per Common Share: (Note K)			
Income (Loss) before extraordinary item	$ (1.96)	$ 2.10	$ 2.91
Extraordinary item (Note B)	.99	—	—
Net Income (Loss)	$ (0.97)	$ 2.10	$ 2.91
Fully Diluted Earnings Per Common Share: (Note K)			
Income (Loss) before extraordinary item		$ 1.61	$ 2.41
Extraordinary item (Note B)		—	—
Net Income (Loss)		$ 1.61	$ 2.41

EXHIBIT 2 Eastern Airline's unlimited mileage fare

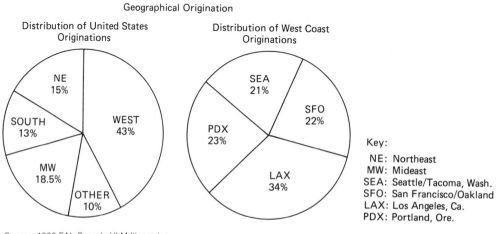

Geographical Origination

Distribution of United States Originations

Distribution of West Coast Originations

NE 15%
SOUTH 13%
WEST 43%
MW 18.5%
OTHER 10%

SEA 21%
SFO 22%
PDX 23%
LAX 34%

Key:
NE: Northeast
MW: Mideast
SEA: Seattle/Tacoma, Wash.
SFO: San Francisco/Oakland
LAX: Los Angeles, Ca.
PDX: Portland, Ore.

Source: 1980 EAL Sample ULM Itineraries.

EXHIBIT 3   Eastern Airline's unlimited mileage fare

Profit impact analysis
Quarter ended September 30, 1978

Traffic (Originating Passengers)	
Full Generation	29,761
Partial Generation	8,430
Diversion	18,388
Total Usage	56,579
Profit Impact Analysis	
Revenue Generation	
—Fully Generated	$ 8,898,539 *
—Partially Generated	676,255 **
Revenue Dilution	(2,375,362)***
NET REVENUE INCREASE	$ 7,199,432
Less: Incremented Costs	
—Fully Generated Passengers	(3,138,506)#
—Partially Generated Passengers	(497,450)##
—Diverted Passengers	(919,497)###
PRETAX CONTRIBUTION	$ 2,643,979

Key:

   * = 29,761 Fully generated passengers × $299 (the ULM fare in 1978).

  ** = 8,430 Partially generated passengers × $80.22 (the additional contribution from ULM).

 *** = 18,388 Diverted Passengers × $129.18 (the loss from diverting full fare passengers to ULM).

   # = Based on $92.60 incremental cost (average 10 segments at $9.26 per segment) plus commission costs at 4.3% of generated revenues.

  ## = Based on $55.56 incremental cost per passenger, reflecting 6 additional segments plus commission cost increase calculated on 4.3% of generated revenues.

 ### = Based on $55.56 incremental cost per passenger, reflecting 6 additional segments less commission cost decrease calculated on 4.3% of diluted revenues.

EXHIBIT 4   Eastern Airline's unlimited mileage fare

Profit impact analysis
Quarter ended September 30, 1980

Traffic (Originating Passengers)	
Full Generation	30,640 *
Partial Generation	8,679 *
Diversion	18,932 *
Total Usage	58,251
Profit Impact Analysis	
Revenue Generation	
—Fully Generated	$ 13,268,958 **
—Partially Generated	1,462,932 ***
Revenue Dilution	(3,792,080) #
NET REVENUE INCREASE	$ 10,939,810
Less: Incremented Costs	
—Fully Generated Passengers	(4,011,012) # #
—Partially Generated Passengers	(710,508) # # #
—Diverted Passengers	(1,235,625) †
PRETAX PROFIT CONTRIBUTION	$ 4,982,665

Key:

    * = Calculated using the 1978 percentage breakdown between the three groups.

   ** = Estimate: 30,640 × $433.06 (the weighted average ULM fare for quarter).

  *** = Estimate: 8,679 × $168.56 (from EA's 1980 survey of ULM).

    # = Estimate: 18,932 × $200.30 (from EA's 1980 survey of ULM).

  # # = Estimate: Based on $111.42 incremental cost (avg. 9 segments at $12.38/segment) plus commission costs at 4.5% of generated result.

= Estimate: Based on $74.28 incremental cost per passenger, reflecting 6 additional segments plus commission cost increase calculated on 4.5% of generated revenues.

    † = Estimate: Based on $74.28 incremental cost per passenger, reflecting 6 additional segments less commission cost decrease calculated on 4.5% of generated revenues.

EXHIBIT 5   Eastern Airline's unlimited mileage fare

ULM Fare History

9/77— Adult	$299.00
Child (12 or under)	$199.00

Fare Restrictions

- Applicable throughout Eastern's system except to/from Canada for group of 2 or more passengers, who must travel together for the entire itinerary.

- The entire itinerary must be determined and tickets issued at least 14 days prior to the date of departure on the first segment of travel. Itinerary cannot be changed after commencement of travel. Travel is restricted to Eastern's on-line service.

- Minimum stay: 7 days; maximum stay: 21 days.

- A stopover at the same intermediate point more than once during the period of travel is prohibited. However, travel via the same intermediate point for connections is permitted.

- A stopover at the passenger's point of origin at any time during the period of travel is prohibited. A minimum of 2 stopovers in addition to the outward destination is required.

- Applicable September 11, 1977 through September 10, 1978 except for blackouts as follows:

  November 22, 23, 27, 28, 1977
  December 21–26, 1977
  December 31, 1977–January 3, 1978
  February 15–19, 24–27, 1978
  March 17–18, 23–24, 1978
  April 1–2, 1978

6/15/78—

- Extended System Excursion Fares from 9/10/78 to 12/14/79

- Added Peak/Off-Peak fares

  Peak—$369—to apply from
  12/15/78 to 4/26/79 and
  7/01/79 to 8/31/79

  Off-Peak—$299—to apply from
  9/11/78 to 12/14/78
  4/27/79 to 6/30/79 and
  9/01/79 to 12/14/79

10/78—

- Added 1978–79 holiday blackouts.

- Added a discretionary capacity control provision.

- Established all-year fare levels in lieu of off-peak/peak fare levels, *for travel commencing 11/1/78:*
  —Adults—$369; Accompanied Child (2–11)—$199.

12/78—

- Added 7-day advance reservation/ticketing requirement for transportation originating at SLC/SFO* between 12/13/78 and 1/15/79. (Requirement remained 14 days for other cities.)

12/78—

- Added 7-day advanced reservation/ticketing requirement for transportation originating at AUS* between 12/24/78 and 1/22/79. (Requirement remained 14 days for other cities.)

3/79—

- Cancelled April–September, 1979 holiday blackout dates.

continued

EXHIBIT 5   *(continued)*

5/79—

- Cancelled all remaining holiday blackout dates.
  (November 1979.)

6/79—

- Reduced advance reservations/ticketing requirement from 14 to 7 days.
- Added fares for individual passengers.
  —Adult—$469; Accompanied Child (2–11)—$199

9/79—

- Extended expiration date from 12/14/79 to 12/14/80.
- Reduced minimum number of stopovers from 3 to 2.
- Added 1979–80 holiday blackouts for travel to/from DAB/FLL/FMY
  GNV/JAX/MLB/MIA/ORL/SRQ/TPA/PBI*
- Added reduced fares for period 9/1 to 12/14/79:

	Group of 2 or more	Individual
—Adult	$299 per Psgr.	$399
—Accompanied Child (2–11)**	199 per Psgr.	199

- Fares for the period 12/15/79 and after:

	Group of 2 or more	Individual
—Adult	$369 per Psgr.	$469
—Accompanied Child (2–11)	199 per Psgr.	199

4/80   *For Travel 4/1/80 or After*

	Group of 2 or more	Individual
—Adult	$425	$525
—Accompanied Child (2–11)	225	225

6/80   *For Travel 6/17/80 to 12/14/80*

	Group of 2 or more	Individual
—Adult	$425	$525
—Accompanied Child (2–11)	225	225

6/80   *For Travel 12/15/80 to 5/31/81*

	Group of 2 or more	Individual
—Adult	$479	$579
—Accompanied Child (2–11)	249	249

8/80   *For Travel 8/6 to 9/1/80*

	Group of 2 or more	Individual
—Adult	$425	$525
—Accompanied Child (2–11)	225	225

For Travel 9/2 to 12/14/80

	Group of 2 or more	Individual
—Adult	$459	$659
—Accompanied Child (2–11)	259	259

For Travel 12/15/80 to 5/31/81

	Group of 2 or more	Individual
—Adult	$525	$725
—Accompanied Child (2–11)	325	325

11/80   *For Travel 11/15 to 12/14/80*

	Group of 2 or more	Individual
—Adult	$459	$659
—Accompanied Child (2–11)	259	259

continued

EXHIBIT 5 *(continued)*

For Travel 12/15/80 to 5/31/81

	Group of 2 or more	Individual
—Adult	$540	$740
—Accompanied Child (2–11)	340	340

12/80—

- Individual Travel Fare Cancelled
- Increased advance reservations/ticketing requirement from 7 to 14 days.

1/81—

- Extended System Excursion fares from 5/31/81 to 12/14/81.
- Added peak fares for traveling during the period of 6/1 to 9/14/81.

For Travel 1/18 to 5/31/81 and 9/15 to 12/14/81—

—Adult	$540.00
—Accompanied Child (2–11)	340.00

For Travel 6/1 to 9/81

—Adult	$625.00
—Accompanied Child (2–11)	425.00

Spring 81—

- Individual travel fare reinstated.

*See Exhibit 6 for key to city acronyms.
**No change in child's level.
Note: All fares exclude tax.

EXHIBIT 6 Eastern Airline's unlimited mileage fare

Key to city acronyms

ATL	=	Atlanta, GA
AUS	=	Austin, TX
CHI	=	Chicago, IL
DAB	=	Daytona Beach, FL
DFW	=	Dallas/Ft. Worth, TX
FLL	=	Ft. Lauderdale, FL
FMY	=	Fort Myers, FL
GNV	=	Gainesville, FL
JAX	=	Jacksonville, FL
LAX	=	Los Angeles, CA
MCO	=	Orlando, FL
MIA	=	Miami, FL
MLB	=	Melbourne, FL
NYC	=	New York City, NY
PBI	=	West Palm Beach, FL
SFO	=	San Francisco/Oakland, CA
SJU	=	San Juan, PR
SLC	=	Salt Lake City, UH
SRQ	=	Sarasota/Bradenton, FL
STL	=	St. Louis, MO
TPA	=	Tampa, FL

EXHIBIT 7   Eastern Airline's unlimited mileage fare

Correlation coefficients between ULM passengers and load factors by city pair (by month—ending Feb. 1981)

City pair	Coefficient	No. of monthly observations	Estimated average load factor
ATL-ABQ	.31	16	70
ATL-CHI	.17	16	55
ATL-DFW	.39*	16	63
ATL-FMY	.08	15	67
ATL-STL	−.22	16	66
MIA-LAX	−.07	8	49
MIA-SFO	.53*	8	48
NYC-LAX	.23	8	42
NYC-SFO	.47	8	40
ATL-LAX	.55*	16	49
ATL-NYC	.39*	16	62
ATL-MCO	.48*	16	57
ATL-RDU	−.18	16	56
ATL-SFO	.79*	8	53

* = Significant at .05 probability level.

EXHIBIT 8   Eastern Airline's unlimited mileage fare

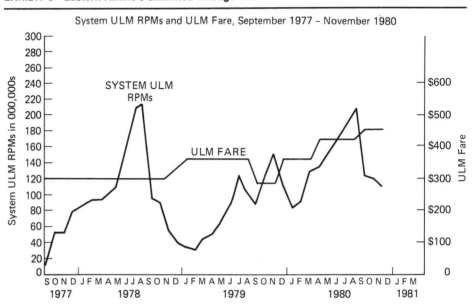

System ULM RPMs and ULM Fare, September 1977 – November 1980

EXHIBIT 9
Eastern Airline's unlimited mileage fare

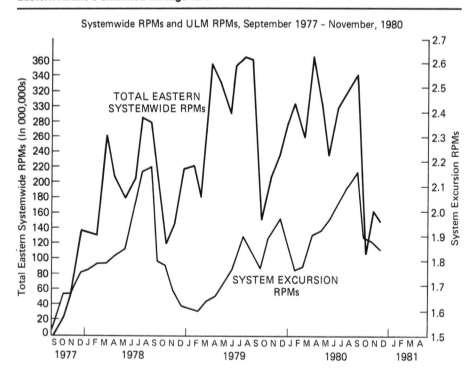

Systemwide RPMs and ULM RPMs, September 1977 – November, 1980

DISCUSSION

Place yourself in the position of Morton Ehrlich, in studying the data and recommendations and in then making the strategic planning decisions about the Unlimited Mileage Fare.

1. What is your general conclusion about the desirability of continuing to offer ULM fares during the fall of 1981 and in 1982?
2. What would you recommend in prices—and in reference to the target markets that EAL would be appealling to?
3. What other policy decisions would you make with regard to the other alternatives, on which there have been recommendations?
   For each answer, state the basis on which you reached it.

14

Promotion

Promotion decisions are often made simultaneously with other marketing-mix decisions—those dealing with product, price, and distribution—not subsequent to them. They should therefore be coordinated with these other decisions to create a marketing mix.

This chapter begins by reviewing promotion concepts and examining the significance of promotion in marketing strategy and plans. We will then look at an approach to making strategic promotion decisions. Some steps in developing a promotion strategy that we will examine include finding target markets and audiences, determining objectives and tasks, budgeting for promotion, and selecting the promotional mix. Evaluating promotional effectiveness and controlling the promotion elements are the final topics covered in the chapter.

Promotion is examined here from a strategic viewpoint; we do not cover the implementation techniques that must be used to conduct promotion activities, such as how to write advertising copy. Also, we do not cover most fundamentals and principles of promotion; these can be found in a basic promotion text.[1] Our concern is how to use promotion effectively as a strategic variable in the marketing strategy, the marketing mix, and the marketing plan. The fol-

---

[1]Richard E. Stanley, *Promotion*, 2nd ed. (Englewood Cliffs, N.J.: Prentice-Hall, 1982).

lowing example illustrates the importance of promotion in developing a marketing strategy:

> Although 7-UP has captured 60 percent of the clear-colored soft-drink market, it is unhappy with its meager 6 percent share of the total soft-drink industry. The company has developed a promotion strategy that may strengthen its position in the cola-dominated marketplace.
>
> The company has positioned 7-UP as a "pure" soft-drink alternative to colas, which account for two-thirds of the total market, and had advertised that 7-UP has no caffeine, artificial colors, or artificial flavors. While several competitors considered filing suit against the company because its advertising implies that any absence of artifical additives is positive, 7-UP maintains that it is only advertising product attributes; it is not saying that these ingredients found in many competitors' drinks are harmful. But, if the public views these ingredients as harmful, it could hurt sales of all colored soft drinks—and 7-UP could greatly increase its market share.[2] This example indicates the potential of an effective advertising campaign.

CONCEPTS AND SIGNIFICANCE

The term *promotion* embraces influence processes exerted by the sellers of products on those they seek to be buyers. Personal selling, advertising, sales promotion, and publicity—the four elements of promotion—can be summarized as follows:

> *Advertising* is any paid form of nonpersonal presentation or message (mass communication). Advertising messages are transmitted through the mass media—radio, television, magazines, and newspapers—and are intended to inform or persuade existing or potential buyers and relevant publics. Advertising always has an identified sponsor. Advertising decisions are concerned with determining objectives, issues, and message development, media (channel) selection, and the evaluation of advertising effectiveness. In addition, by communicating symbolic significance, advertising can add value to products.
>
> *Personal selling* involves interpersonal communication to inform and persuade. The salesperson communicates directly with a client or prospect and obtains direct feedback. Personal selling is a powerful promotional tool in informing and persuading because of the ability of the salesperson to talk back, explain, question, or refute objections. This type of personal interaction is not possible in advertising. Personal selling should not use coercion to obtain its goal; the potential buyer listens to the biased appeal of the salesperson and then accepts, rejects, or delays action on the appeal before a decision is made.

---

[2]Richard Morgan, "Critics Charge Seven-Up with 'Scare Tactics,'" *Adweek*, May 30, 1983, p. 16.

Sales promotion is a term often used to describe any promotional activity that cannot be classifed as advertising, personal selling, or publicity. Generally, it involves a direct inducement, possibly offering an incentive (or added value) to the offering. Sales promotions directed toward consumers include demonstrations, contests, cents-off coupons, free samples, and special packaging. Other sales-promotion activities are designed to encourage resellers and salespeople to sell the product, perhaps through sales contests, free merchandise, displays, and awards. Sales promotion differs from advertising and personal selling in that it is nonrecurrent and that the focus is usually to increase sales in the short run. Sales-promotion techniques such as free samples and point-of-sale displays gain attention and involve, persuade, and reinforce the buyer. Sales promoting is often used along with advertising and/or personal selling.

Publicity is nonpersonal communication about a product or organization that is not paid for by the sponsor. Publicity differs from advertising in that there is no sponsor identified. The message reaches the public because it is newsworthy and not from the direct purchase of media time or space, although the seller has to pay personnel to manage press releases and plan other external communication. Also, advertising messages can be controlled and focused to a target market, whereas there is less control over the news media that carry publicity.

Before examining how these elements illustrated in Figure 14-1 can be used and coordinated to achieve promotion objectives, let us examine the significance of promotion as a controllable variable in influencing purchase decisions.

FIGURE 14-1. Promotion mix

Promotion as a Key Strategic Variable

The marketer uses promotion to stimulate the buyer and obtain a desired response. Therefore, inducing awareness, trial, acceptance, and preference are typical goals of promotion. Promotion is persuasive and is usually designed to change attitudes and behavior in a desired direction, although it is not really possible to control behavior or the extent of attitude change.

The marketer must guide promotional messages so that they are consistent with the buyer's existing cognitive structure. As the buyer becomes psychologically involved with a product (gains knowledge and begins to develop attitudes), he or she maintains control over where to look for information, what messages are perceived, and how the information is interpreted.[3] Therefore, promotion should be planned to reduce conflict with the buyer's existing knowledge and to communicate benefits (or attitudes) that are acceptable.

Promotion is also an important variable in developing product symbolism, as the following example shows:

> Different products generally require differing promotional appeals. When marketing beer, for instance, "user imagery" or symbolism becomes very important, whereas a soap marketer would probably use logical rather than emotional appeals.
>
> Stroh Brewery Company has used symbolism extensively to market its premium beer—Signature. The Signature bottle has a simple, classic appearance to promote a "high-class" image. The graphics on six-pack cartons convey the same image. Even the truck drivers who deliver Signature beer to local stores wear uniforms that have been carefully designed to further promote Signature's image as a top-line product.[4]

Symbolism is especially important in increasing the value of products that consumers use in self-expression. Clothes, like beer, are good examples of such products. Clothes have social significance, and therefore their symbolic attributes are important. Among style setters, for example, signature clothes characterized by the Izod alligator and the Ralph Lauren polo player have value. Consider how promotion can increase the value of a product to consumers by developing a desirable image:

> The Cadillac Cimarron and the Chevrolet Cavalier are both members of General Motors' J-car product line. For all practical purposes, the cars are mechanically the same except for differing body styles. The cars appeal to different markets, however, and the supposed differences may be more symbolic than functional. A Cavalier could be given all the options usually available on the Cimarron, but it is doubtful whether it would be able to appeal to the same market because the car-buying public views Chevrolets and Cadillacs differently. The Cavalier is aimed

---

[3]Everett M. Rogers and F. Floyd Shoemaker, *Communication of Innovations: A Cross Cultural Approach,* rev. ed. (New York: Free Press, 1971), p. 109.

[4]"Marketing Emphasis Is on Consistent Imagery When Selling Beer: Stroh Exec," *Marketing News,* March 4, 1983, p. 10.

at an economy-minded market, whereas the higher-priced Cimarron is carving a niche in the luxury-car market. While on the inside these two cars are very similar, on the outside the symbols related to appeals are very different.

Promotion (and price) help create the Cadillac image. For many products the symbolic appeal is enhanced through promotion.

The marketer must discover circumstances favorable to the use of promotion elements in the marketing strategy. Since promotion is a key consideration in strategic planning, it should be viewed as an implement for making use of market opportunities. The promotion element used is structured by the environment, especially the nature of buyer demand. Promotion has a catalyic function in the marketing strategy, and since demand is one of the most uncontrollable forces to deal with, promotion is used to shift demand and expedite the buyer decision process. Therefore, opportunities for developing an effective promotion plan start with an analysis of markets and understanding of forces underlying demand, as well as the firm's goals and market position.

> While sales have been increasing steadily for several years in the U.S. wine market, the sales growth of domestic brands has gone flat. In fact, shipments of California wines were down 13 percent in early 1983. Through the 1970s and early 1980s wine producers had fought to secure their niche in a growing market, but now wine makers must wrestle market share away from others if they hope to continue their own sales growth.[5]

Industry leader Gallo Winery has thus far done the best job of capturing additional market share through increased marketing efforts—specifically sales promotion. Gallo has made up for the lower prices by increasing the volume of its product sold. Because of its strong hold on the U.S. market (Gallo has a 27 percent market share, three times the size of its nearest competitor), and because it operates with the greatest economies of scale in the industry, it correctly believed that its increased spending on sales promotion and advertising was justified and would provide greater returns. Advertising kept the Gallo name on consumers' minds and projected a quality image to the public despite price cutting. Discounts provided to dealers help to generate greater volume in a slow market, as well as ensuring their distribution channels will be maintained. Thus we see that promotion can be a key variable in strategic planning, but it must be planned and synchronized with other elements of the marketing mix.

The promotion plan should be designed to induce buying action or to support the buyer decision process (Figure 14-2). The function of promotion in the marketing strategy is to catalyze transactions. If effective, it results in transactions that would not otherwise have occurred, because promotion moves the buyer to a decision by facilitating the flow of information that can persuade the buyer to purchase. Then, after identifying the product attributes

---

[5]"The Wine Wars Get Hotter," *Business Week*, April 11, 1983, pp. 61–65; and Gilbert J. Sewall, "Trouble for California Wine Makers," *Fortune*, April 18, 1983, pp. 54–59.

FIGURE 14-2. Stages of the buyer decision process

Source: Patterned after John Dewey, *How We Think* (New York: Heath, 1910); and Orville Brim et al., *Personality and Decision Processes* (Stanford, Calif.: Stanford University Press, 1962).

and benefits desired by the target market, promotion makes the offering visible to buyers.

Holding all the marketing-mix variables constant (price, product, and distribution), promotion can direct the marketing strategy to the desired target market. For example:

> When Union Carbide launched Glad 3-Ply Trash Bags, the firm had to overcome a major problem—how to convince buyers that the new three-ply bag was better than competing brands and yet cost no more than the Glad two-ply bags, which had been introduced earlier. To solve this problem, Union Carbide employed a massive promotional program. Consider some of the promotional efforts used by Union Carbide.
>
>> The company launched an advertising campaign that consisted of intensive television, radio, and print advertisements. Tom Bosely was the television spokesperson.
>>
>> Several sales promotion activities, such as coupons and sweepstakes, encouraged consumers to try the new bags.
>>
>> Fifty-five key sales representatives were introduced to the product at a national sales meeting. A specially prepared, extravaganza videotape presented the product in sales-training sessions.
>>
>> Sales personnel participated in a sales incentive program. Everyone who made his or her sales quota could win a trip for two to Cancun, Mexico. All sales managers and representatives did win their trip.
>>
>> Publicity activities included press conferences, presentations at the Association of Extension Home Economists Convention, and sponsorship of a project to encourage home gardening. The company donated bags to help clean up Times Square.

This example demonstrates how a company was able to solve a problem by developing and implementing an effective promotional program.

The target market is very often defined on a multisegment basis. Therefore, different promotion messages using different media may be aimed at specific market segments. Also, various market segments can be in different stages of the buyer decison-making process. Therefore, different elements of the promotion mix may be used. For example, advertising and publicity (mass communication) can be especially important at the knowledge stage of buyer decisions for widely distributed products purchased on a mass-consumption basis. Personal selling and sales promotion can be important at the persuasion and decision stage for many goods.

Role of Promotion in the Buyer Decision Process

The stages of the buyer decision process are need recognition, search, evaluation of alternatives, decision to purchase, and product usage. Each stage shown in Figure 14-2 indicates a range of promotional opportunities available.

The firm's promotional objective during the need recognition stage should be to get customers to realize that they have a specific need or want. Many new, and even existing, products are advertised on the basis that they solve a need that no other product addresses. A common personal-selling technique is for the salesperson to first get the customer to admit a need, and only then to attempt to "make the sale" by solving the need. Advertising can be used to illustrate a need for new consumer products like men's cosmetics or a cat food for kittens.

Buyers should learn more about the product in search stage—the information-gathering stage. Advertisements for new products often contain a great deal of information about the product, such as advertisements for small computers or turbo diesel engines for compact cars.

In the evaluation-of-alternatives stage, promotion can be used to help consumers make a choice between competitive products. Comparative advertising, such as the Pepsi Challenge, may be effective in this stage.

FIGURE 14-3. Buyer decision process models
Source: (A) E. K. Strong, *The Psychology of Selling* (New York: McGraw-Hill, 1925); (B) Everett M. Rogers, *Diffusion of Innovations* (New York: Free Press, 1962), pp. 79–86. General framework suggested by Philip Kotler, *Marketing Management*, 5th ed. (Englewood Cliffs, N.J.: Prentice-Hall, 1984), p. 612.

Stages	Decision Process	AIDA (A)	Product Adoption (B)
Cognitive	Need Recognition ↓	Attention ↓	Awareness ↓
Affective	Search ↓ Evaluation of Alternatives ↓	Interest ↓ Desire ↓	Interest ↓ Evaluation ↓
Behavioral	Decision to Purchase ↓ Usage	Action	Trial ↓ Adoption

Personal selling is usually the most effective promotional tool available to the marketer in the decision-to-purchase stage, because salespeople can deal directly with a prospective buyer and answer his or her questions. Obviously, other forms of promotion do not have this flexibility.

Once consumers have decided to use a product, it is important that promotion still be used to continue communicating with the buyer and to reinforce his or her buying decision. Salespeople should follow up their sales to ensure that the customer is satisfied. Reminder advertising is used to keep the product on consumers' minds. It is important to remember that a company must generate repeat sales to survive in the long run.

Promotion plays a key role across each of the stages in the buyer's decision-making process. Promotion's role will of course be determined by many factors, especially the target market. The target market's behavior will determine many aspects of the promotional message.

The above "model" of the decision process is shown graphically in Figure 14-3, along with two other similar models. The AIDA model shows how the buyer progresses through the stages of attention, interest, and desire and finally reaches the action stage and makes the actual purchase. Promotion efforts under this scheme first attempt to gain the buyer's attention, or to let the buyer know that the product is on the market and that he or she should be aware that it exists. Advertisements stressing product benefits then follow to first stimulate interest and then later create desire for the product. Finally, the buyer is asked to take action, such as in a personal-selling situation.

The third model, the product-adoption model, consists of the following stages:

1. *Awareness.* The buyer becomes aware of the product.
2. *Interest.* The buyer seeks information and is receptive to learning about the product.
3. *Evaluation.* The buyer considers the product benefits and determines if it should be tried.
4. *Trial.* The buyer examines, tests, or tries the product to determine usefulness or utility.
5. *Adoption.* The buyer purchases the product and can be expected to use the product to solve problems.[6]

This conceptualization of the adoption process has been highly favored by marketing researchers in the past. But recent critics of this model point out that it is too simple. Among its numerous deficiencies are these:

1. It implies that the process always ends in adoption decisions, whereas in reality, rejection may also be a likely outcome. Therefore a term more general than "adoption process" is needed that allows for either adoption or rejection.

---

[6]Everett M. Rogers, *Diffusion of Innovations* (New York: Free Press, 1962).

2. The five stages do not always occur in the specified order, and some of them may be skipped, especially the trial stage. Evaluation actually occurs throughout the process rather than just at one of the five stages.
3. The process seldom ends with adoption, as further information seeking may occur to confirm or reinforce the decision, or the individual may later switch from adoption to rejection (a discontinuance).[7]

Figure 14-3 also lists the cognitive, affective, and behavioral stages. The marketer may use promotion to gain a response in one of these three stages from the target market. The purpose of promotional activities during the cognitive stage is to put something in the consumer's mind, or specifically to make the consumer more familiar with the product. You can see how each of the three models parallels the cognitive stage. In the affective stage, it is hoped that promotion will have an effect on the consumer's attitude toward the product. And it is hoped that the effect will be to generate interest in the product and bring the consumer closer to purchasing the product. Finally, in the behavioral stage, promotion attempts to get the prospect to undertake some purchase action.

PROMOTION DECISION SEQUENCE

The promotion decision must be developed after organizational goals and marketing objectives have been established. Our strategic viewpoint focuses on planning and evaluating promotion's effects on buyers. The steps we view as most important in promotion decisions from a strategic perspective are (1) finding target markets and audiences, (2) determining objectives and tasks, (3) preparing a promotion budget, (4) selecting a promotional mix, and (5) evaluating and controlling the effectiveness of promotion. Figure 14-4 illustrates this promotion decision sequence.

It is important to determine the role that promotion will play in the firm's marketing strategy. Generally, promotional tools such as advertising and personal selling are central to a marketer's strategy. It is also important to understand promotion's role relative to the other marketing mix components and to keep all of these components working together to best market the firm's product.

Target Markets and Audiences

After the target market has been found, target audiences should be selected to receive messages. In the case of consumer products, decisions must

---

[7]Rogers and Shoemaker, *Communication of Innovations,* p. 101.

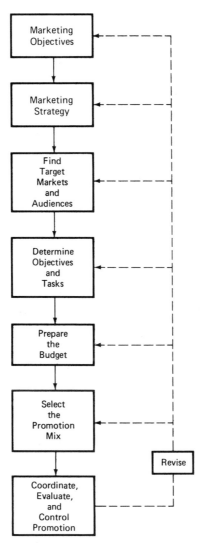

FIGURE 14-4. Strategic promotion decision sequence

be made as to whether both middlemen and consumers are to receive messages, and also:

1. What is the role of interpersonal communication vs. mass media communciation?
2. What type of promotion campaign will be most effective?

Specific questions to be answered for industrial markets include:

1. What is the role of product users, influencers, and purchasers in the buying process?
2. What purchasing groups of individuals make purchase decisions?

A fundamental strategic decision will be whether to pull the product through the channel by concentrating on final purchasers or whether to push it through by gaining the cooperation of middlemen. A decision to push or to pull the product will determine where to aim messages or where to send salespeople.

Figure 14-5 indicates how promotion efforts move through marketing-channel members when a push or a pull decision is made. Personal selling and sales promotion are used most often in a pushing decision. When the pulling approach is used, communication from the producer encourages the buyer to make special efforts to obtain the product from middlemen. Mass communication (advertising and publicity) is used most often in pulling decisions. Of course, a firm can use a combination of pushing and pulling approaches, but usually there is more emphasis on one of them. Consider how marketing giant Procter & Gamble uses both pulling and pushing approaches to promotion:

> For many years now Procter & Gamble has led all U.S. firms in terms of number of dollars spent on advertising. Obviously Procter & Gamble relies heavily on a pull strategy to sell its wide line of consumer goods—or does it? It also has one of the most aggressive sales forces in the industry, typically hiring only top students to fill vacant sales positions each year. Procter & Gamble relies on this sales force to ensure adequate distribution of its products and to gain shelf space for new goods.

Promotion Objectives and Tasks

After the target market and audiences are identified, the marketer should determine promotion objectives and tasks. The objectives should state what is to be accomplished and what buyer responses are desired. The promotion tasks should be oriented toward these objectives, as activities designed to expedite the buyer decision process. In other words, promotion objectives state the desired end result, whereas promotion tasks indicate what needs to

FIGURE 14-5. PUSH vs. PULL decision

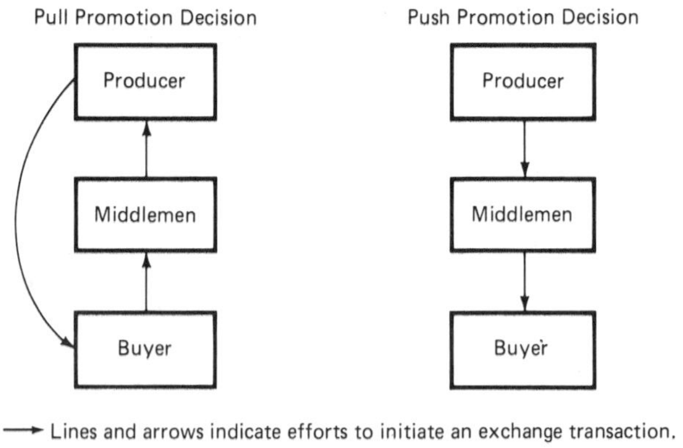

Lines and arrows indicate efforts to initiate an exchange transaction.

be done to achieve it and, by selection of the promotional mix, what instruments are to be used.

> After years as the leading "middle-market" priced motel chain, Holiday Inn is entering a new market. The firm has budgeted $200 million through 1985 to build the first eight Crowne Plaza hotels which will offer luxurious rooms, fine dining, and such extras as hand-held hair dryers, remote control TV's and videodisk players in some rooms. The target market for Crowne Plaza is defined as the "upscale business traveler." The promotion objective is to persuade the businessman to stay at a Crowne Plaza hotel rather than a Marriott, Hilton, Sheraton, or Hyatt hotel. Promotion tasks are to upgrade the Holiday Inn image (49 Inns judged to be of poor quality were dropped by the chain in a recent year); offer business and other upscale travelers a luxurious, but affordable hotel value; and to avoid competition between Crowne Plaza and Holiday Inn.[8]

In stating promotion tasks, the marketer determines what message should be aimed at the target market to gain product acceptance. The tasks to be performed specify the basic substance of the communication message in general terms. The details of execution are often handled by promotion specialists.[9]

Whereas the promotion objectives define the role of communcation in supporting the overall marketing objective, the promotion tasks translate the objectives into issues.

The Promotion Budget

It is difficult to determine exactly how much should be budgeted for promotion, although most firms have an upper limit on expenditures based on resources and projected sales. "At best, available methods of budgeting are only rough approximations of an ideal expenditure level."[10] We approach the topic by providing some accepted methods for determining the budget. In practice, trial and error is used by necessity.

Obviously, the budget should be adequate to achieve the promotion objectives and tasks discussed in the preceding section. Still, many firms use arbitrary budgeting methods without the measurement of promotion effectiveness. The following are some of the widely used methods.[11]

Percentage of Sales. The establishment of a promotion budget based on expected or past sales appears on the surface to have no logical justification, but there are several reasons why it is popular: A formula is provided that per-

---

[8]"Holiday Inn Opens Doors for the Upscale Traveler," *Business Week*, April 25, 1983, pp. 101–54.

[9]James Engle, Martin Warshaw, and Thomas Kinnear, *Promotional Strategy*, 5th ed. (Homewood, Ill.: Richard D. Irwin, 1983).

[10]Ibid., p. 192.

[11]These methods have been adapted from Joel Dean, *Managerial Economics* (Englewood Cliffs, N.J.: Prentice-Hall, 1951), pp. 364–75.

mits the budget to fluctuate with the ability to pay (revenue); and the formula, if widely used in an industry, tends to develop competitive stabilization of promotion expenditures. For example, most airlines spend less than 1.5 percent of their sales on advertising, and major oil companies spend less than 0.5 percent of their sales on it.[12]

On the other hand, this budgeting method appears to be illogical because promotion expenditures should be the cause of sales, not the effect. Also, if sales are increasing owing only to external environmental forces, a firm using the percentage-of-sales budgeting method may increase promotion expenditures unnecessarily. However, many firms use this method because they find that it gives them control over promotion expenditures and that—although this may be an illusion—sales, promotion budgets, and market opportunity become intertwined.

Maximum Promotional Budget. This method, too, appears on the surface to be irrational; but it does assume that promotion expenditures may cause an increase in sales. And since the effects of promotion, especially advertising, may be long-lasting (similar to capital investment), corporate income taxes favor maximum expenditures on promotion to increase the long-run profit base.

There are several marketing objectives that suggest maximum expenditures on promotion. A marketing objective of increasing market share may require the firm to outspend competitors. A marketing objective of maximum sales growth suggests maximum promotion expenditures.

The limit of funds available for the promotion budget is determined by the financial resources of the firm and its ability to borrow outside funds. Most firms have a real limit on what they can spend, and in most cases, the limit is based on resources available within the organization.

Return on Investment. Setting a budget based on the return on investment appears to be a very logical approach to promotion budgeting. The main problem is the difficulty of measuring the rate of return on promotional expenditures. Promotion may increase sales today and generate goodwill or product knowledge that will increase sales tomorrow. Therefore, even if the effects of promotion could be measured, it might be impossible to know for many years its total impact. For example, Reynolds Industries has spent millions of dollars promoting Camel cigarettes over the past 40 years, and today this item still ranks in the top sales of all cigarette brands and brand variations. The brand image and consumer knowledge about the product, developed over the years, would continue to make this a profitable product for some time even if Reynolds terminated all promotion activities.

Objective-and-Task Method. This method logically follows our second step in developing a promotional strategy—determine promotion objectives

---

[12]"100 Leaders' Advertising as Percent of Sales," *Advertising Age*, August 29, 1977, p. 30.

and tasks. After objectives are defined, tasks are identified, and then a budget is developed that is sufficient to accomplish the tasks.

This method is straightforward and could be used to develop any promotion budget. The difficulty lies in determining the value to be derived from attaining objectives. In other words, the technique places the emphasis on determining what objectives are worth attaining and although cost can be measured, only rarely can the real value of obtaining the objective be measured.

The technique is useful and integrates well with our other steps in making promotion decisions. For example, a recent candidate for president developed a campaign objective of clarifying his image as warm and dynamic, with great integrity. Toward this objective, $10 million was budgeted for advertising and two months' aggressive campaigning (personal selling) was conducted. Advertising attempted to show the candidate as strong and forceful on major issues. Personal selling focused on making him appear to be in control, based on his accomplishments. Also, the objections raised by the opposing candidate were countered. Although this candidate narrowly missed being reelected, many of his promotion objectives were reached.

Competitive-Parity Approach. This method bases promotion expenditures on the expenditures of other firms in the industry. For instance, two major airline competitors spend approximately the same amount on advertising. In one recent year, Airline A spent $24.6 million and Airline B spent $23.9 million. It may be necessary to spend as much as your competition to offset any advantage gained through promotion. This approach comes closer to collusion in setting the limits of competition than to actual determination of the benefits from promotional expenditures.

Sales Responsiveness Considerations in Budgeting. Promotion responsiveness is the relation of changes in sales to changes in promotion expenditures with other variables constant. A distinction should be made between (1) industry responsiveness and (2) market-share responsiveness.

Retailers and wholesalers often stock up on discounted merchandise near the end of a sales promotion campaign and may not buy at list price again for weeks. Consider two pet food sales promotions. The first allowed a 26 percent discount to retailers and encouraged large orders, while the second allowed a 21 percent margin and policed purchase quantities more carefully. The first promotion resulted in huge sales during the promotion, but the company lost $100,000 because it took two months for retailers to sell off the excess inventory and begin buying again at regular prices. In the second situation retailers began purchasing again only two weeks later, and the firm broke even while still selling an additional 100,000 cases.[13]

There may be untapped potential in the market. Some years ago Tylenol increased its advertising budget substantially in response to increased advertising undertaken by a competitor. As a result, Tylenol captured an additional 4

---

[13]"The No-Win Game of Price Promotion," *Fortune,* July 11, 1983, pp. 92–102.

percent of the market and the competitor gained two market-share points. In other words, the market was responsive to promotional expenditures for the industry (nonaspirin pain relievers), and the products' (Tylenol and Datril) sales were responsive to increased promotional expenditures.

Developing an accurate formula of promotional responsiveness in competitive industries is very difficult because

1. The amount and quality of competitors' present and past promotion influence responsiveness of sales to the firm's own promotion. Selling costs are likely to vary in accordance with the activities of rivals.
2. Competitors may react defensively to a firm's promotion plan by adjusting their own promotion plans.
3. External environmental variables can quickly change buyers' demand patterns.[14]

During product introduction and growth, there is greater promotion responsiveness for industry sales. Later, as the product moves to maturity, industry sales will be less responsive to promotion, but a brand may gain in market share for the industry and therefore be responsive to promotion.

There can still be promotion responsiveness for a firm's products even when industry sales are declining, although promotion expenditure to gain a larger share of a declining industry is a questionable strategy in most cases.

Since there are so many uncontrollable variables that influence the sales responsiveness of promotion, there is a need to combine marketing intelligence and intuition to project how promotion may influence sales. Even though we know a relationship does exist and models help explain it, responsiveness is discovered more often by trial and error than through a formula or model.

The Promotion Mix

After the determination of the amount to budget for promotion, an allocation of funds to advertising, personal selling, sales promotion, and publicity is in order. The promotion mix rests on the notion that promotion elements are interchangeable, within limits, but that some promotion elements are best to attain certain objectives. Some tasks can be accomplished with advertising or personal selling or sales promotion or publicity. Therefore, an attempt should be made to select the optimum combination of methods—the combination that is most efficient and effective in obtaining results from the appropriated budget.

Advertising can be a very cost-efficient promotional tool because it can reach a specific target market at a low cost per person. Each time a car drives

---

[14]Joel Dean. *Managerial Economics* (Englewood Cliffs, N.J.: Prentice-Hall, 1951), p. 354. Reprinted by permission of Prentice-Hall, Inc., Englewood Cliffs, N.J.

by a billboard or someone flips through a magazine the message will be repeated, thus reinforcing the firm's message and lowering the cost still further. Advertising allows a firm to project a specific image to the public, such as the quality image of Cadillac, Chivas Regal, and E. F. Hutton.

Despite the low cost per person reached, the absolute cost of advertising may be too high for some firms. The persuasive impact of advertising on consumers is lower than, say, personal selling, and it does not allow for feedback from unconvinced or confused potential customers. Advertising is, however, an integral part of the promotion mix of many firms. For example, advertising expenditures of the nation's top one hundred advertisers have consistently risen over the past two decades, with total expenditures for the group reaching almost $15 billion in 1981. Procter & Gamble has been the nation's leading advertiser every year since 1964, and it believes that its huge advertising expenditures have been responsible for making it such a successful company today. Procter & Gamble spent $671.8 million on advertising in 1981, about 23 percent more than the next-largest advertiser, Sears, Roebuck, & Company.[15] Clearly, these marketing giants have no qualms about investing heavily in this form of promotion.

Personal selling is typically aimed at one or a few individuals, whereas advertising is aimed at an entire market and therefore the cost per contact is high. Because personal selling allows the prospect to provide feedback, it has a greater impact on customers than does advertising. The salesperson gives this method of promotion greater flexibility because he or she has the ability to change the message being communicated after gauging the prospect's frame of mind.

While there are no costs for broadcasting publicity, as there are with advertising, there are other costs to consider. Usually a firm that uses publicity extensively either must have employees in the firm who prepare news releases or must hire a public relations or advertising agency to perform these duties.

Publicity usually cannot support a firm's entire promotional burden, but it is often a key ingredient in an effective advertising campaign. Publicity must be planned so that it is compatible with, and supportive of, other elements in the promotion mix.

Sales promotion encompasses all other forms of promotion that do not fit into the categories of advertising, personal selling, or publicity. Marketers often use sales promotion to improve the effectiveness of other promotion-mix ingredients. For example, major soft-drink makers have recently used contests in which consumers can win money and prizes simply by purchasing the drink and checking the bottle cap or can tab for a possible prize. This sales promotion scheme has been used in accordance with the firms' regular advertising program. Occasionally, a firm may use sales promotion as its primary promotion method. For instance, a local sausage producer who cannot afford an advertising campaign may offer free samples to customers in retail stores as its major means of promoting the firm's product. This is unusual, however.

---

[15]"100 Leaders Spend 14% More in 1981," *Advertising Age*, September 9, 1982, p. 1.

The various elements of the promotion mix must be synchronized to attain marketing objectives. Decisions and overall planning for the promotion mix should be under the direction of the manager or managers in charge of strategic planning. The promotion mix is only one variable in the marketing strategy, and the objectives set for the various promotion elements should support and reinforce overall marketing objectives.

On the other hand, promotion managers (sales manager, advertising manager, sales promotion manager, and publicity manager) should have clearly delegated duties, and the necessity for securing top-management approval should relate to coordination and integration of promotion in the marketing mix and strategic matters relating to budgeting. For example, strategies should view promotion elements as somewhat interchangeable, and some decisions should be made or altered by promotion managers to accomplish tasks and achieve results. If one advertising medium seems to yield poor returns, part of the budget for it may be shifted to another medium to improve results. This type of decision may be made by a promotion manager.

Evaluate and Control Promotion

At the heart of budgeting and selecting a promotion mix is assessing promotion effectiveness. On one point, most experts agree: Marketers should try to ascertain the optimum promotion exposure level for a generic product, for the firm's brand, and for the target audience. At least some attempt should be made to recognize when promotion is inadequate and when it is excessive, wasteful, or perhaps irritating.[16]

Promotion complements the other marketing-mix variables, and it varies in intensity from one product class to another. After reviewing the literature on the effectiveness of industrial promotion, Lilien et al. indicate that the following questions should be asked:

1. *Economies of scale.* Is there some relevant range in which additional investments of promotion yield increasing returns?
2. *Threshold effects.* Is there some minimum level of exposure that must be exceeded for promotion to have a discernible effect?
3. *Interaction effects.* Does the promotion mix interact to produce effects that are greater than the sum of its separate effects? For example, do advertising and personal selling interact to be more effective when used together than the same resource using only advertising or personal selling?[17]

---

[16]Herbert E. Krugman, "What Makes Advertising Effective," *Harvard Business Review,* March–April 1975, p. 99.

[17]Adapted from Gary L. Lilien, Avis J. Silk, Jean-Marie Chaffray, and Muralidhar Rao, "Industrial Advertising Effects and Budgeting Practices," *Journal of Marketing,* published by the American Marketing Association, January 1976, p. 17.

The measurement of advertising, personal-selling, publicity, and sales-promotion effectiveness requires marketing intelligence activities, which may include marketing research as well as the systematic collection of performance results on a regular basis. The basic approach to evaluating any promotion element should be to (1) determine clear objectives for the promotion, (2) compare promotion performance results with expected performance stated in the objectives, and (3) evaluate and improve overall effectiveness of utilizing promotion research and managerial judgment.[18]

A general philosophy for budgeting and controlling promotion expenditures can be found in the economist's principle of marginal analysis: Does the expenditure of one additional promotion dollar make a contribution to profit in the long run?[19] Although this question cannot always be answered, it should be a guiding principle. It is easier in the short run to measure whether objectives such as product awareness and level of product knowledge have been achieved.

SUMMARY

The third marketing variable we are discussing is promotion. Promotion decisions are sometimes made simultaneously with product decisions—especially when product benefits may be created through symbolization. We explained the buyer decision process and related several decision models to promotion and strategic planning. Next, we presented a promotion decision sequence:

1. Define marketing objectives.
2. Plan marketing strategy.
3. Find target markets and audiences.
4. Determine objectives and tasks.
5. Prepare the budget.
6. Select the promotion mix.
7. Evaluate and control promotion effectiveness.

Since the development of organizational goals and marketing objectives was discussed earlier, we covered steps 3 to 7 in Chapter 14, limiting our discussion to some considerations in strategic planning rather than expanding it to implementation activities such as training the sales force or writing advertising copy.

---

[18]David W. Cravens, Gerald E. Hills, and Robert B. Woodruff, *Marketing Decision Making: Concepts and Strategy* (Homewood, Ill.: Richard D. Irwin, 1976), p. 647.
[19]Jean-Jacques Lambin, "What is the Real Impact of Advertising?" *Harvard Business Review*, May–June 1975, p. 145.

1. *In managing the promotional efforts, what typical objectives does a firm's management desire? How are the promotional objectives related to marketing objectives?*

2. *What is the relationship between the promotion mix and the promotional objectives?*

3. *"Promotion can be the key strategic variable." Evaluate this statement from the viewpoint of the strategic planner.*

4. *Why is promotion so closely linked to the buyer decision process?*

5. *Why is the method used to determine the promotional budget so important to the strategic-planning process?*

6. *"The marketer must guide promotional messages so that they will be consistent with the buyer's existing cognitive structure." Evaluate and discuss.*

7. *"Product symbolization is created at least in part by the promotional efforts of the firm." Relate the concept of product symbolization to our concept of the offering described in Chapter 1.*

8. *Why is it necessary to know the effect of interpersonal communcation versus mass media communication in planning a promotional campaign?*

9. *How should the promotion decision sequence presented in this chapter be linked to the strategic planning process?*

Computer Boutique

INTRODUCTION

George Johnson first became interested in home computers in his role as a math teacher at a Centerville high school. After reading a number of reports in business magazines, George became convinced that the market for home/personal computers was worth looking into. Even the least optimistic predictions seemed to indicate a very good potential for growth. Discussions with other faculty members, as well as local businessmen, convinced George further that sufficient demand potential existed in his local market area, which was situated in a medium-sized town in the western part of Kentucky, to support a dealership for one of the major home computer brands. He also felt that his own past experience in teaching business courses would prepare him, to some degree, to be a part time salesperson.

His wife, Brenda, was also enthusiastic about the proposed business venture. After some evaluation of the various brands available, George became convinced that the Apple computer offered the best value and best growth prospects for the near future. The two of them decided to open a dealership to sell Apple computer products.

Brenda had been employed with large accounting firms in Chicago and New York and, more recently, with a local company as a systems analyst. She was quite familiar with the design and installation of computers in the business environment. Brenda was anxious to strike out on her own and felt that by leaving her present job with the firm and entering into a partnership with her husband she could gain some freedom to do the type of work she really enjoyed. She also felt that the long-term profit prospects were much better in this industry for the independent dealer than for the career programmer/analyst. Thus in the summer of 1981, George and Brenda entered into a partnership to distribute the Apple computer in their market area which covered about 100 square miles of western Kentucky. They named their new business "The Computer Boutique."

Under the terms of the new agreement, Brenda was to manage the organization, and act as a primary sales and technical resource person. George was to serve as a consultant to the firm, concentrating on educational and individual small business clients. Additional salespeople would be hired as business grew. They would be paid by a combination of salary and commission.

PRESENT SITUATION

The Apple Computer Company was founded in 1976 by two college dropouts named Steve Jobs and Steve Wozniak. The two had done time as design engineers in California's Silicon Valley where they became intimately familiar with the technology required to build a

---

This case was prepared by Professors Phillip Niffenegger and Fred Miller of Murray State University. It is used with their permission.

microcomputer. After building a number of models for their friends, they decided to enter the commercial market. By mid 1977, they had introduced the Apple II computer, which sold for as little as $1,500 and was aimed at the home hobbyist market. The Apple II was extremely successful, and by 1979 the incorporated firm had attained a total sales of $60 million, up from total revenues of under $2 million its first year of operation. Success continued for the company with the introduction of the Apple III computer in May of 1980, leading to total 1980 sales of $165 million—up 175 percent.

During this high-growth period, Apple also had undergone several changes in their distribution structure. In early 1980, Apple terminated independent distributors and established company-owned regional support centers for its dealers. This was aimed at providing better support to Apple's 850 domestic dealers.

The Johnsons had applied to Apple and had been accepted as a dealer for Centerville, which had a population of about 50,000. It was located in a rural area of the state, and the Johnsons believed that in addition to local businessmen, professionals, and home hobbyists, the large-scale farm operators would also provide potential customers. Furthermore, George commuted to his high school teaching job in an adjacent town, about 50 miles from Centerville, in which was located a university. The town also had a population of about 20,000 people. Under the terms of his dealership agreement, the Boutique was allowed to make sales in the nearby university town. According to their calculations, the total population of his potential market area numbered close to 100,000 people, which he felt should be adequate to support his projected sales target.

The plan was that George would sell part-time in the university town as well as in Centerville to assist Brenda, who would manage the firm and be its primary salesperson. Through his ties with the university, George hoped that he could also develop a pool of potential people who could write custom programs (software) for users who needed specialized applications.

George and Brenda made arrangements with a local distributor of business machines to lease 500 square feet of floor space on the first floor of the office equipment firm. They believed this provided an ideal location both because potential business users for other business machines would pass by his display area, and because it was within a few minutes drive of most of the major businesses located in Centerville.

The Johnsons planned a sales program based around in-store equipment demonstrations as well as sales calls in the field, with and without computer equipment. They planned to use local advertising which aimed at small business users and identified the Boutique with Apple's national advertising campaigns. As manager, Brenda prepared a pro forma income statement (Exhibit 1) to guide the first year's operations and expenditures.

Brenda was quite optimistic that the long-term growth opportunities in the personal computer market were excellent. She based this assumption on a number of projections done by private industry analysts. Informed projections of yearly sales growth in the total industry through 1985 ranged from 32 percent to nearly 50 percent; and in just six years total industry revenues had grown from nothing to over 1.5 billion dollars. Personal computers were expected to approach the 5 billion dollar level by 1985. (See Exhibit 2.)

The Johnsons felt that the area they served was relatively unsophisticated in its knowledge and use of microcomputer products, and that therefore a well established and recognizable brand was particularly important to their success. They felt that given the nature of the competitive environment in this industry and idiosyncrasies of the local environment, one of three potential growth patterns was possible. First they could remain primarily an Apple Computer dealer and expand by incorporating new lines of peripheral products for that system. Secondly, Computer Boutique could become a dealer for other computer systems, offering a breadth of choice, in place of depth of offering in the single product line for its customers. The potential introduction of new equipment by large computer companies such as Xerox and IBM, as well as the entry of Japanese firms into the market, might necessitate such a move. Third, the division could expand into other cities within the region, perhaps using a franchise arrangement to secure local capital.

PRODUCT DATA

The Apple product line consisted primarily of two models: The Apple II computer, which ranged in price from about $1,500 to about $3,500, depending on the size of the memory and the associated accessory equipment desired by the customer. Additional equipment included the choice of black and white or color T.V. monitor, disk drives to store additional programs and data files, and a range of output printers which could produce everything from letter-quality documents to a fairly simple printed record of the data output. The Apple III computer was priced from about $4,500 to over $6,000, depending on the options selected by the customer. Its major advantage was its larger memory and ability to handle more complicated types of data analysis.

But no matter how good the computer product (hardware) it would be of little value without the right program of instruction to make it suitable for a particular application (software). One benefit of the Apple system was that because it was the first widely marketed personal computer, a great variety of software had been developed by interested individuals and was now marketed through a series of software houses. The price of an individual program, which might range from a video game through a complicated sales forecasting program, could range from $15 to $2,000. Generally, the software was written for specific user groups such as home hobbyists or small businesses; a representative listing of the types of software available is provided in Exhibit 3.

The Johnsons believed that an important part of the product was the personal service necessary to acquaint the potential user with the operation of the machine, as well as guide him to standard programs which were adaptable to his particular needs. It had been their impression that the major gap or lack in the industry was for a customer-centered organizational philosophy that was aimed at identifying and meeting customer needs. They felt that this type of philosophy would be even more important as the market served by the microcomputer industry changed from that of the hobbyist to the small business and professional environment. They believed this to be especially true in their sales region which had not been served by a microcomputer dealer previously. It was relatively remote, and microcomputers had not to date made a significant impact in the area. For this reason, local small businesses and professionals were rather wary of the microcomputer products. Potential buyers did recognize their need for information processing capability, but were reluctant to purchase the equipment that could supply that need without a good deal of local help, service, and support.

To respond to this opportunity, the Johnsons provided low cost training to their clients through a series of workshops which were held during evening hours at the Centerville Office Machine Store. The Johnsons thought that one competitive advantage that they could offer versus other suppliers of personal computers was their ability to sit down with customers and show them via a one to two hour demonstration how a particular Apple equipment combination could be adapted and programmed to suit the specific needs of the customers. Stores like Radio Shack often could not provide such a personalized presentation. They believed that the provision of such a service could furnish them with a strong competitive advantage over other sellers in the area. As one industry source had put it, "There has been a missing link from day one: Nobody has started with the customer to find out what he wants in a small computer. Instead of homing in on market segments and smoothing the interface between man and machine, they build stuff for technical people to play with. They think they are appealing to the laymen, but they are really not."

MARKET ANALYSIS

Since the original introduction of the personal computer in 1976, the market had changed radically. The hobbyist market slowed down beginning around 1978. George felt that the biggest potential for sales was in the small business market, and professionals such as doctors and lawyers. He based this belief on national trade surveys which identified the following five basic types of customers:

1. The hobbyist
2. Small business
3. Professional users
4. The agricultural community
5. The educational community

In the initial phase of growth in the microcomputer industry the home user or hobbyist provided the majority of demand for the product. Generally, they are innovators with great interest in the technical details of equipment and computer programming, but with relatively little interest in prepackaged software. Current estimates are that 6.9 percent of microcomputer sales goes to the hobbyist or home market. The hobbyists typically make a modest initial acquistion in terms of equipment. Their needs for mass storage devices are not as great and they tend to use cassette as a storage device rather than disk. Also, the hobbyists are very price conscious and low cost is often the dominant benefit sought. For this reason, they may be lost by the retail computer dealer to mail-order houses who offer substantial discounts which the retailer is not able to meet.

Moreover, the hobbyists are generally not impressed with the offsetting advantages which the retailer can offer, such as fast local service, since time is not a big problem when equipment problems arise. The home user is more willing to consult manuals and to spend time working to solve his or her own problems than either the business or professional user.

The second market identified by the Boutique is that of small business. This group contains a number of small, local businessmen in the area who have information and managerial information needs which are not adequately handled by their present manual systems and who may benefit from computerization of their business. The average system purchased by this group ranges in the neighborhood of $8,000 to $10,000. The benefits which they seek are: (1) accuracy of information ; (2) ease of obtaining accounting information; (3) automation of manual bookkeeping services so as to free up managerial time; (4) the availability and accuracy of managerial reports on a timely basis to be used for diagnostic purposes in the management of their businesses.

This group is very concerned with local service for any computer system which they buy and with help in setting up and maintaining computerized accounting systems. Thus the retail outlet has an advantage over mail-order firms since they are able to provide the local service and support desired. Although a wide range of prepackaged software is available for this market, many small business users are unwilling or unable to mold their operations to what is available. Thus, this customer type can also be a significant source of sales for program development, seminars in accounting software, and courses in computer usage.

Included in the professional category are accountants, lawyers, doctors, dentists, veterinarians, engineers, and surveyors. At one level, the needs of this group are identical with those of the small business, since both groups need standard accounting applications to maintain their accounting records. However, the groups differ in that the professional community tend to be businessmen by chance and not by choice. They are concerned with maintaining books for government and tax record requirements. However, their primary interest is in the ability of the computer to help them perform their specialized professional tasks. For this reason, this group is very demanding in terms of the software packages that the retailer is required to locate.

It is not unusual for the computer retailer to be approached by a member of one of these professions who is seeking a computer system that will handle a software package that they have located elsewhere. This represents a sale for which the dealer has had to extend very little effort. Also, once the initial purchase has been made, the professional may be approached for other software applications which can result in future sales. The professional accounts for about 17 percent of the personal computer market with an average system price of just under $7,800.

Current estimates are that some 5 percent of the farm community is using microcomputers in the analysis of their business and farming needs. Estimates project that within the next 10 years that figure could rise to as high as 85 percent. Since the region in which the Computer Boutique is located is largely rural, it seems to represent good potential for development. In general, farmers are looking for specialized accounting applications like single entry accounting systems designed for use on the farm. In addition, they need budgeting and forecasting tools, as well as programs which allow them to assess the different variables that play a role as they make their day-to-day farm operating decisions. In the absence of [a] computer system these calculations can be very time consuming, and take the farmer away from the demands of his real job, farming operations.

Sales to farmers tend to be cyclical, running with the seasonal harvests. Farmers are not averse to making large capital investments if the benefits of those investments can be shown to be cost effective. The farmer is accustomed to investing large sums of money in implements for farm usage, based upon extensive pay out planning. Farmers generally have well-established lines of credit and therefore are able to acquire financing on their own much more easily than other types of business firms.

The educational market is composed primarily of elementary and high school teachers who anticipate using the computer in the school room, either to teach computer literacy or to use as an educational aid in other subject areas. Due to recent cutbacks in federal and state budgets, this market presently does not have a great deal of investment capital available to it. Furthermore, prices which can be charged for this market are governed by state contract.

Although the Computer Boutique was not successful in its bid for the state contract, it does have the option of matching contract prices to achieve educational sales. However, the prices are low and leave it very little operating margin.

Computer Boutique would like to meet state contract prices and pursue the educator market for two reasons. First, as the economy improves, making more money available to the educational community, and as the benefits of the computer in the classroom become more apparent, the number of acquisitions should increase. An increase in volume could offset the low prices, adding to profits. Second, as young people become acquainted with the capabilities of microcomputers in the classroom, they will develop into potential markets for home use. And the system which they utilize in the classroom will tend to be the one they purchase for home use.

Since price is already established, service is important to the educator market, in two aspects: (1) helping the teacher to master the equipment and stay ahead of the students; and (2) helping educators to locate and keep up to date on the latest software.

In terms of competition at the national level, Brenda found some marketing research data from a trade magazine which showed that currently Apple had the largest share of the market with about 23 percent of the total estimated 1981 dollar sales. They were followed by Tandy (Radio Shack) with 16 percent, and Commodore with 10 percent. (See Exhibit 2). When they had decided to establish an Apple dealership, the Johnsons foresaw no strong competition in this market area, since the only local outlets for personal computers were Radio Shack stores in Centerville and in the university town. Based on his philosophy of the importance of personalized service, [Johnson] felt they did not constitute serious competition in this particular product category.

However, three months after Computer Boutique set up shop, IBM Corporation, the nation's largest seller of large-size computers, announced their entry into the personal computer market. Although there was no local dealer for the IBM product line, IBM was planning to sell through a series of franchised computer stores (Computerland), as well as through a chain of specialized Sears, Roebuck business product stores which were planned for large-city areas. In addition, IBM's regular sales force will sell the new personal computer line. IBM's line was roughly comparable to the Apple. The lowest-priced system cost $1,565 but offered no visual display screen. The most elaborate, offering a capacity to display data in graphic form in 16 colors and a memory system that could store more than 250 typewritten pages of information, would cost more than $6,000.

Industry observers felt that the major strength IBM brought to the market was their strong reputation for reliability and service, even though their new microcomputer line did not offer any real technical breakthroughs. IBM planned to offer its own software, as well as software packages similar to those available for the Apple. Some industry analysts felt that the entry of IBM into the personal computer market would be good for all of the large producers, since they would validate the importance of this particlar market segment. Certain analysts also predicted that the large infusion of advertising and merchandising dollars by IBM would stimulate the growth of the entire market, much as the entry of Kodak into the instant-picture market helped to increase the sales of Polaroid.

PROMOTION

Brenda felt that the area of promotion presented both challenges and opportunities to the Boutique. She was uncertain as to how the promotional budget should be allocated to advertising and personal selling. Further she was unsure as to the maximum media allocation for advertising dollars.

The area of personal selling demanded much thought and necessitated many important decisions. How many sales people should the Boutique hire? How should they be compensated? Should they concentrate on inside or outside sales? Should they be assigned sales territories, vertical markets, or no markets at all? What sources should they use to find leads for the Boutique? What types of approaches should be used for each of the markets which the Boutique desires to reach? Brenda felt that proper decisions on these questions would be crucial in determining the success of the new business.

FINANCES

Based on her projected 12-month budget, Brenda felt that the Boutique could provide an acceptable end-of-year profit if it sold between four and six Apple Systems per month. This would work to a total monthly sales volume of about $29,000. Monthly sales for the first three months of operation averaged $22,000. However, the Apple organization felt that each distributor should be capable of selling between eight and ten Apple Systems per month. There was some danger that if the Computer Boutique did not realize this latter sales level, Apple would not renew the franchise, but give it to a more successful dealer who was now operating in an adjacent city about 60 miles to the north.

PRICING

The policy of Apply Computer Incorporated is to formally discourage discounting from its basic margins of 30–35 percent. In theory the Boutique adheres to this practice of no discounting. However, there are significant exceptions. The first is the educational market in which the price level is set by the state contract. Another source of downward pressure on price comes from the home user market. The hobbyists tend to search the numerous publications of the microcomputer industry to locate a mail-order firm advertising exceptionally low prices for Apple equipment, then bring these prices to the attention of a local Apple dealer, and demand equivalent discounts. One of the most perplexing problems which

Computer Boutique faces is how to respond to this type of downward price pressure from the hobbyist.

Bidding pressure on prices can also develop from the retail Apple dealers in adjacent regions. Thus far, the policy of Computer Boutique has been to maintain the price level suggested by Apple, in order to provide the margin necessary to support services such as consultation and repairs, as well as to maintain the quality image of Apple products, so painstakingly built by the manufacturer. Discounts have been considered, however, when the Johnsons felt they were justified by volume, the prospect of future business, or in competitive bidding situations.

EXHIBIT 1   Pro forma income statement
First year's operation

		Dollars	*% Sales*
Sales: 70 systems @ $5000		350000.00	0.98
Consultation & instruction fees		6000.00	0.02
Total revenues		356000.00	1.00
Cost of sales		234500.00	0.66
Gross margin		121500.00	0.34
Administrative salaries	18000.00		0.05
Allowance for advertising	48500.00		0.14
and sales force compensation			0.00
Instructor's fees	3000.00		0.01
Rental of office space	6000.00		0.02
Miscellaneous	5000.00		0.01
Total expenses	80500.00	80500.00	0.23
Income before taxes		41000.00	0.12
Provision for income taxes		9020.00	
Net income		31980.00	0.09

**EXHIBIT 2 Total market size and division
of the market**

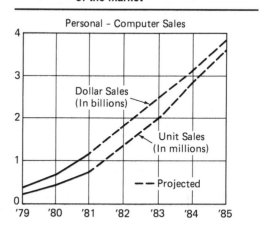

Personal – Computer Sales

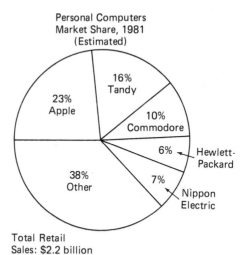

Personal Computers
Market Share, 1981
(Estimated)

23% Apple

16% Tandy

10% Commodore

6% Hewlett-Packard

7% Nippon Electric

38% Other

Total Retail
Sales: $2.2 billion

EXHIBIT 3   Types of software programs available for Apple

PHYSICIANS
Medical Secretary
Medical Billing
Medical Ed. Programs
Data Base
Word Processing

LAWYER
Word Processing
Professional Time Management
Client Billing System
Budgeting
Desk Top Planner
Speechlink 2000
Supertalker
Case History

BANKER
Interest and Loans
Desk Top Plan
Loan Analysis
Stock Evaluator

SMALL BUSINESS OWNER
General Ledger
Accounts Payable
Accounts Receivable
Payroll
Inventory
Word Processing
Aardvark Tax Programs

DENTIST
Patient File
Dental Management System
Mailing List
Case History

SALES MANAGER
Desk Top Plan
Mail List Manager
Order/Entry Invoicing
Information Master

CONTRACTOR
General Ledger
Accounts Payable
Accounts Receivable
Job Costing
Payroll
Project Management

ACCOUNTANT/BOOKKEEPER
General Ledger
Cost Accounting
Mail List
Master Tax
Payroll

SECRETARY
Word Processing
Mail Lists
Appointment Calendar

MANUFACTURING
Warehouse/Distributor Pkg.
A/P, A/R, Job Costing
Machine Part Quoting
Order Entry

DRUG STORE
General Accounting System
Patient File History

RESTAURANT
Payroll
Inventory

REAL ESTATE
Listings
Financial Pkg.
Income Property Analysis
Lease Management
Data Base

RETAILER
Accounting
Cash Register
Inventory

PLANT MANAGER
Records Employee
Budgeting by Department
Cash Flow Analysis

AGRICULTURAL
Crop and Herd Planning
Farm Accounting Systems
Depreciation Records
Linear Programming

DISCUSSION

1. Upon what market segments should the Computer Boutique concentrate its marketing efforts? Why?
2. Should the promotional budget be concentrated on advertising, on personal selling, or on a combination of the two?
3. If a combination of advertising and personal selling, what proportions of the $48,500 allowed in Brenda's pro forma income statement should be allocated to each of these functions? In reaching this decision, you may consider the roles payed by each and estimate the sale personnel that would be needed.
4. Would you recommend that the sales-force personnel be specialized, each on certain market segments (or all sell to all segments)? Should a separate advertising campaign be run for certain segments? Why?

CASE 14-2

Ralston Purina Company

In 1975, the Ralston Purina Company had grown to one of the largest food manufacturers in the world. Its sales volume was exceeding $3 billion, and its sales and profits were continuing to climb impressively. Its major fields of operations were divided into agribusiness, consumer products, and restaurants. Although the first group was obtaining a greater share of sales volume, the consumer products lines were earning nearly half of Ralston Purina's profits. These included cereals, tuna, mushrooms and—especially—pet foods, in which it was the world's leader. The largest category among pet foods was those for dogs.

The company's greatest surge forward in dog food occurred in 1956, when it successfully tested a novel extruded dry food. Placed on the market under the name of Purina Dog Chow dog food, within a few years it became the leading brand of dry dog food, a position held to this day. Total dry dog food sales of all brands experienced steady increases in market share of all dog foods to the level of 42 percent share of market in 1962. At that time, General Food successfully innovated moist dog food (Gainesburgers), which temporarily checked growth in the dry product segment. Soon the dry share began further market share growth, at a dramatic rate after 1973 and reached 49 percent of total dog food sales in 1975.

BACKGROUND OF PUPPY CHOW

Ralston Purina's research laboratories had discovered that puppies have special nutritional needs that are not met with foods formulated for mature dogs. Developmental work found that a special dry product for puppies was feasible. Market analysis reported that

---

Courtesy of Ralston Purina Company. "Chow" is a registered trademark of Ralston Purina Company.

approximately 20 percent of pet dogs are under one year old and should be considered to be puppies. Surveys were launched to identify and understand the uses and purchasers of foods for puppies.

Some key findings of this survey included these:

Most puppies are purchased by young households, those with adults under 35 years of age. The purchase of the puppy's food is a task of the young housewife, who finds herself in need of information on how to care for a puppy. She may turn to a veterinarian for advice, but it was found that even these "pet influentials" often know little about the special nutritional needs of puppies.

The housewife tends to think about the puppy as she does about her own children. She would realize that the puppy has nutritional needs different from grown dogs—or if not aware of this, she could be easily convinced of it.

It was decided to proceed with the new product for puppies, which would resemble the firm's leading dry dog food, Purina Dog Chow, but would have a differentiating name: Puppy Chow puppy food. A decision was necessary also regarding how to "position" the product in the buying public's minds. After much study of market data and creative thinking, the following strategy was selected, which we will call the #1 strategy, since it was the first one adopted.

Strategy #1: Special-needs strategy. This would stress the infancy of the puppy, which would require special feeding. It would be most effective on television, which would dramatize the similarity between a playful little puppy and a baby.

This advertising strategy was adopted and rendered into several very attractive TV commercials. These spearheaded the market launching of Puppy Chow in 1964.

Puppy Chow contained extra nutritional ingredients not found in Dog Chow, so it was given a premium price of 15 percent over Dog Chow. A milk coating was put on the product to enhance its puppy orientation. The packaging was 5- and 10-pound bags. In its first full year of sales, it obtained 0.3 percent of total dog food sales, a small share but in line with Ralston Purina's expectations. A second variety was added, around 1970, which had a beef flavor, and with the addition of water, made gravy.

Puppy Chow puppy food was growing in sales in 1972, but a market study revealed that it had failed to penetrate well one segment of its market.

The first market segment for Puppy Chow was identified as being puppies of under six months' age. In that bracket, approximately two out of three owners had tried Puppy Chow puppy food or a comparable competitive specialty for puppies, although only half of these continued to serve it for long. However, Puppy Chow was being highly successful in that it was winning over 85 percent market share of those who did use a special puppy food.

In nutritional terms, a dog remains a puppy until it nears a year's age, according to Ralston Purina laboratories. In the six-month-to-a-year segment, the picture was different from that for the younger pups. Most of the owners were then shifting to feeding adult dog foods, with only about 15 percent staying with the special puppy foods. Consumer evidence indicated that the housewife then felt that the puppy had grown into an adult and could be fed the regular (and cheaper) adult dog food.

In response to this low market segment presentation, a different advertising direction was adopted for Puppy Chow.

Strategy #2. This one showed the little puppy grown into a definitely larger dog, but stressed that it is really still a puppy until it reaches a full year old. This theme was utilized in new commercials for Puppy Chow. It was given the name, in the company, of the extended-use strategy.

At that point Puppy Chow puppy food held a market share of about 2 percent of the total dollar dog-food market, or nearly 5 percent of dry dog food. This was a strong and profitable market position. The shift of advertising to the extended-use theme, again employing mainly the TV medium, brought a definite market-share increase and approximately doubled the 6- to 12-months-segment of the market using puppy food. Considering that a dog 10 to 12 months old eats about three times as much as a 3-month-old puppy, the sales potentials in that segment are impressive. A 25-pound-bag size of Puppy Chow had been brought out that should appeal to this segment, as its price came to about 25 percent less per pound than the 5-pound size.

In early 1975, as the product manager for Puppy Chow approached that brand's plans for the next year, another external factor seemed to be of importance—the rise of competition in the product category:

> Another brand of puppy food had been introduced by another strong company around the time that Puppy Chow food first appeared. It was Carnation's "Friskies Puppy Food." That brand had never been given effective enough promotion to develop into a real threat to Puppy Chow puppy food, which still held most of the market, but it was still something of a threat in view of its manufacturer's capabilities generally.

> Recently two other brands had appeared, both by regional marketers. One was by Blue Mountain in the Northwest, and the other was "Puppy Love" by Jim Dandy in the Southeast. The latter brand sold so well that in its first month, it pushed into second place in the Southeast.

Although these new brands might not spread far from their regions, because their companies had not marketed outside them, such a potentiality was real. And there was a significant possibility that some other strong dog-food company (say, General Foods or Quaker Oats) might decide to enter the profitable puppy category. The product manager therefore felt that serious consideration should be given to a third strategy:

> Strategy #3: this would be a brand-oriented advertising emphasis. Whereas the earlier two strategies had been primarily educational, to convince dog owners of the need for a special puppy food (with the brand name secondary), the new theme would be a selective appeal. That is, it would stress first that Puppy Chow is the ideal brand to buy, only secondarily explaining the general need for a special puppy food.

These, then, were the advertising strategy alternatives that the product manager considered in contemplation of the 1975–76 marketing plan. The choice would hinge, assuming that an effective TV commercial could be created to communicate each of these three options, on the still-unrealized potential sales in the two market segments (pups up to six months; and those over six months) and on competitive expectations. The options were (1) to continue with the extended-use strategy; (2) to revert to the special-needs strategy; and (3) to develop the brand-oriented one.

DISCUSSION

1. What promotional problems did Ralston Purina face in the introduction of Puppy Chow in 1964?
2. What promotional problems did Ralston Purina face with Puppy Chow at the time of the case (1976)?
3. Which of the three strategies being considered in 1976 would you prefer? Why?
4. Suggest uses of sales promotion, personal selling, or nonselling marketing functions that would be consistent with and enhance the advertising strategy you picked in question 3.

15

Distribution

Distribution is a major consideration in strategic planning, despite its being last in our sequence of controllable variables. Distribution decisions may be made prior to or simultaneously with other controllable variables used in strategy formulation. Although distribution decisions tend to be relatively inflexible, a change in distribution or a new marketing channel could result in a distribution-oriented strategy. When International Business Machines made its entry into the personal computer market, the company—in a radical departure from previous marketing practices—established a new method of distribution. Rather than using its own sales force, IBM sold its new machines through such retailers as Sears, Roebuck and Computerland. IBM needed to develop a new marketing channel in order to compete with Apple Computer, Tandy Corporation's Radio Shack, and other marketers of personal computers. Sears, which is one of the marketing outlets for IBM's personal computers, is establishing a nationwide chain of business machine stores that will operate independently of the Sears department stores. Obtaining IBM's line of personal computers gave a strong boost to Sears' new method of distribution.[1]

In reading this chapter, you should remember that this text is about marketing strategy. We will cover some strategic dimensions of distribution impor-

---

[1]Some facts adapted from "IBM's New Line Likely to Shake Up Market for Personal Computers," *Wall Street Journal*, August 13, 1981, p. 21.

tant in planning and omit some major concepts relating to marketing channels and physical distribution with which the strategist should be familiar.

We provide, first, an overview of the significance of distribution and important decisions in strategic planning. Next, we identify distribution options in strategy formulation and distribution performance opportunities. Finally, we cover the evaluation of distribution in the strategic-planning process.

CONCEPTS AND SIGNIFICANCE

Our discussion of distribution will include decisions regarding the following areas:

1. *Marketing channels* (or channels of distribution, or trade channels) consist of intrafirm units and extrafirm middlemen that direct the flow of products from producer to buyer. Marketing-channel intermediaries include merchants and agents. Merchants buy, take title to, and resell products. Agents negotiate purchases or sales for a commission but do not take title to products.
2. *Physical distribution* deals with creating time and place utility—i.e., getting products where they are wanted at the right time. Physical-distribution decisions (logistics) concern transportation, storage, material handling, inventory control, distribution-related communications, and data processing.

In Chapter 13 we mentioned that price was one of the more flexible variables in the marketing strategy. Distribution, in contrast, is usually the least flexible. Distribution decisions often involve long-term commitments to internal resources and to external intermediaries that make the firm's products available. There may be, at various distribution stages, individual decision makers that act independently. Therefore, customary procedures and institutionalized channel arrangements may be established that a producer may be forced to use owing to competitive structure, or possibly because the channel system is based on market considerations. Channels are partially (but seldom wholly) *un*controllable variables, from either the producer's or the middleman's viewpoint, and they are slow to change. Further, it takes investments and planning to establish a smoothly working channel.

> Warehouse grocery stores captured a larger than expected chunk of the grocery business during the recession of the late 1970s and early 1980s as consumers became more price-conscious. These no-frills warehouse stores often put products on the display floor without removing them from their shipping cartons and usually asked customers to box and carry out their own purchases. However, they offered prices that averaged 15 percent less than those of the traditional supermarkets.
>
> Many large grocery chains have been concerned about the sudden increase in competition—and many put the blame on large manufacturers like Procter &

Gamble and Colgate-Palmolive, which sell to both types of stores. While the supermarkets naturally want products from these giant distributors on their shelves year round and thus purchase the bulk of these goods at regular prices, the warehouse seldom buys at all unless the manufacturer is running a special promotion. P&G has attempted to combat this problem by adjusting its selling policies. The marketing giant will sell its consumer products at discounts during special promotions only if the store "regularly stocked the promoted brand size for 90 days prior to the promotion" or if it placed an order for the item at the regular price, intending everyday selling of the item in the future.[2]

To develop a common understanding of marketing channels, we will briefly outline typical channel arrangements, physical-distribution considerations, and structure. Our chief concern in this chapter is distribution planning as an integrated part of the total marketing strategy. Therefore, strategy, marketing mix, and plans are our focus. Although some textbook descriptions of marketing channels examine mainly extrafirm merchant and/or agent middlemen, we consider intrafirm units just as important in overall planning.

TRADITIONAL MARKETING CHANNELS

The marketing channel structure defines the arrangement and linkage of its members. Figure 15-1 shows typical marketing channels for consumer products. It is important to realize that consumers may want, and organizations can design, almost any number of different distribution paths.

Each successive channel in Figure 15-1 is more complex than the preceding one. Channel A illustrates the direct movement of a product from the producer to the consumers. Mail-order catalogs, telephone sales, or the producers themselves could sell directly to consumers. You can see this type of channel in action as local farmers sell small quantities of their fruits and vegetables from trucks parked on the side of a busy road. Channel B might be characterized by a large retailer such as Sears that purchases many products directly from the manufacturer and in turn sells these goods to consumers. Also, some producers such as Goodyear own their retail stores, but the retail function is still performed.

Perhaps the most traditional channel is outlined in channel C, with the product flowing from the producer to the wholesalers who supply the retailers, who in turn sell to the public. Many products are distributed in this manner. For instance, Foremost-McKesson Company acts as the wholesaler in the distribution of chlorine for swimming pools. Foremost-McKesson accepts shipments from chlorine producers and then stores these shipments in its network of McKesson chemical warehouses across the country. These warehouses distribute chlorine to local chemical resellers and retailers, who then sell to the consumer market. Channel D shows a similar channel, which in addition uses

---

[2]Margaret Yao, "Supplier Policy on Price Roils Food Retailers," *Wall Street Journal*, September 25, 1980, p. 15.

FIGURE 15-1. Consumer goods marketing channels

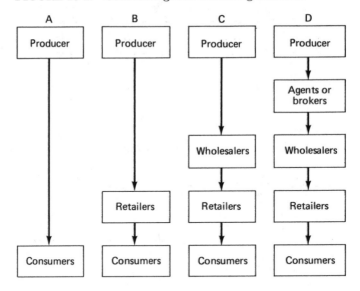

agents or brokers who further negotiations by bringing buyers (wholesalers) and sellers (producers) together.

Figure 15-2 shows the typical channels used for industrial products. Products sold to large industrial buyers are often sold directly to those buyers, as in channel E. As the number of customers increases, the direct distribution approach becomes less effective and industrial distributors—merchants who take title to products—may be brought into the channel.

FIGURE 15-2. Typical industrial product-marketing channels

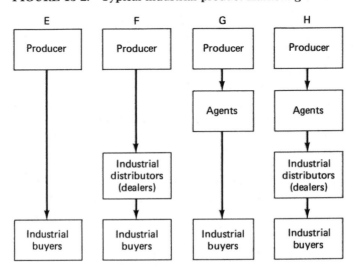

FIGURE 15-3. Mitsubishi's distribution networks

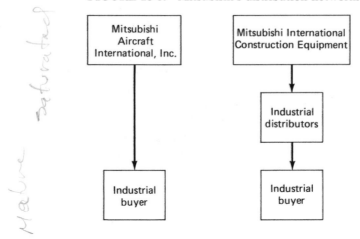

Mitsubishi Aircraft International sells corporate jet aircrafts directly to corporate buyers. However, when Mitsubishi began marketing industrial and construction products, industrial distributors were brought in to help reach the larger number of customers existing in this market (see Figure 15-3).

Agents may be used in the channel, as in channel G, when standardized products are being sold and information gathering and selling functions are important. When a more complex situation arises, a more complex channel, like channel H, may be needed. For example, channel H could be used for import agents who sell to distributors serving small manufacturers.

Decision Factors and Methods

Distribution decisions, like all other marketing-strategy decisions, are structured by organizational goals and marketing objectives. And assessment of the market opportunities that structure distribution alternatives is necessary before other systematic steps can be taken to formulate an approach to distribution. Failure to assess market opportunities before launching a new product led to declining profits for the Singer Company. Singer attempted to distribute TV and audio products through its sewing-machine stores. Later it discovered that people who patronize sewing-machine stores are not decision makers for TV and audio products.[3] Marketers must go beyond market and sales potentials to determine where, when, and how to make products available.

After market opportunities are understood, it is necessary to identify and design marketing channels and physical-distribution systems to make products available. Note that we did not say, "to *select* marketing channels," because most marketers do not have access to or control over all or even a great num-

---

[3]"Why the Profits Vanished at Singer," *Business Week*, June 30, 1975, p. 106.

ber of channel alternatives. This step relates to decisions about the intrafirm units and external intermediaries that may be used to distribute the firm's products. Also, one must understand the marketing-channel leadership role to know what channel member will exert most control decisions.

Developing efficient and customer-oriented physical distribution is an important and costly distribution activity. Physical distribution is a consideration in analyzing market opportunities and identifying and designing marketing channels. Physical-distribution decisions are often made simultaneously with these decisions, because logistical considerations may represent major opportunities or constraints. The physical-distribution requirements of the product can determine what marketing channel is utilized, or structure the selection of a market to serve.

Intrafirm and Extrafirm Options
in Channel Management

Distribution-related strengths and weaknesses will determine the role of intrafirm units in the marketing channel. Figure 15-4 illustrates vertical integration (vertical marketing system) from the viewpoint of the producer, wholesaler, and retailer. To develop control over the marketing channel, the firm must operate from a position of strength and maintain a leadership position.

A firm that has strong finances and consumer acceptance of many products is best able to develop its own distribution system. For these reasons, Procter & Gamble and General Foods are in an excellent position to direct and control the flow of their products to retail food stores. Both companies have large sales forces, with sales branches and sales offices to manage channel activities. But the small firm may also recognize opportunities to take over channel activities to improve distribution.

> In the early 1970s Worth Sports Company was a small firm producing and selling poor-quality baseballs, primarily to carnivals. Worth believed this market was deteriorating and was looking for new markets with growth potential. In 1969 a Pittsburgh inventor had developed the first aluminum bat, but it had not yet reached the market. Worth took the idea, improved the bat's design, developed an entire range of bats varying by size and weight (the original bat came in only one small "kids size"), and sent an enlarged sales force out on the road. The aggressive sales force was able to get Worth equipment into major sporting goods stores and retail outlets for the first time. The result is that Worth instantly claimed 50 percent of the aluminum bat market, stealing the market from the better-known Hillerich & Bradsby Company (maker of the Louisville Slugger).[4]

The nature of the product or the established marketing-channel structure may affect the firm's degree of involvement in the channel. For example, lack of marketing channels may be a major obstacle shaping the decision. In

---

[4]Curtis Hartman, "Changing How the Game Is Played," *Inc.*, March 1983, pp. 94–102.

FIGURE 15-4. Comparison of conventional
marketing channels and a vertical
marketing system

Source: From *Strategic Marketing* by David
T. Kollat, Roger D. Blackwell, and James F.
Robeson, copyright © 1972 by Holt, Rinehart
& Winston, CBS College Publishing.

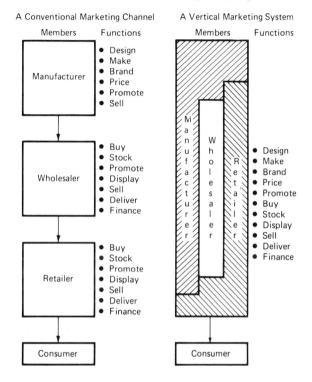

the United States, tobacco wholesalers develop an assortment of competing cigarette brands and distribute this assortment to retail stores and vending machines. R. J. Reynolds, therefore, can launch a cigarette with the assurance that existing middlemen are available to affix state tobacco-tax stamps, stock retailers' shelves, and assist with transportation and storage.

In the above example we saw how Worth was able to open up new channel members (retail stores). Previously, Worth salesmen had been able to sell to few retail outlets. It took a tremendous innovation for Worth to change its distribution channel. Thus, the middlemen available and tradition structure the design of the marketing channel.

We assume that you are familiar with the various types of merchant wholesalers, agents, and brokers that can facilitate distribution.[5] Our concern here is with strategic decisions, the identification and designing of a market

_____

[5]These middlemen are described in William M. Pride and O. C. Ferrell, *Marketing: Basic Concepts and Decisions* (Boston: Houghton Mifflin, 1983), pp. 208–14.

channel that can efficiently and effectively contribute to the marketing performance.

As we have mentioned, intrafirm units can develop, coordinate, and implement the distribution function. Vertical marketing systems, in contrast to conventional marketing channels, consist of horizontally coordinated and vertically integrated distribution systems.[6] Note, in Figure 15-4, that manufacturers, wholesalers, or retailers can administer the distribution activities (design, make, brand, price, promote, buy, stock, display, sell, deliver, finance) as the product moves to the consumer.

When a manufacturer takes command and directs most channel activities, wholesaling and retailing activities are still performed. For example, if the wholesaler as an establishment is deleted, then sales offices and/or sales branches may be developed by the manufacturer. The U.S. Census of Business includes manufacturer's sales offices and sales branches within its definition of wholesale establishments. Also, vertical marketing systems usually treat retailing as a separate entity. The retailer may be treated as if it were an extrafirm organization even when it is company-owned. Examples of manufacturer-directed vertical marketing systems include Goodyear, Firestone, and B. F. Goodrich. These firms produce automobile tires, make distribution decisions (maintain sales offices and sales branches), and even have some company-owned retail stores.

A wholesaler-directed vertical marketing system makes most distribution decisions, as illustrated in Figure 15-4. Super Valu, for instance, is the largest food wholesaler. In its contractual vertical marketing system, independent retailers join with the wholesaler to achieve operating economies and improve distribution performance. The Super Valu wholesale channel leader controls many aspects of the marketing strategy (including private-brand labels) and directs the distribution effort at the retail level.

Some larger retailers now control their distribution systems and part of their manufacturing facilities such as suppliers of Sears private-label products. Another corporate system, Holiday Inns, has developed a self-supply network that includes a carpet mill, a furniture manufacturer, and numerous distribution facilities (warehousing storage, sales branches).[7]

Multiple Marketing Channels
as a Strategic Alternative

Some firms use both traditional marketing channels and vertically integrated marketing channels (including vertical marketing systems), as well as other arrangements that can be developed to distribute products. The marketing channels used by a manufacturer of automobile and truck tires is illustrat-

---

[6]Based on material developed by Alton F. Doody, William R. Davidson, and Bert C. McCammon, in David T. Kollat, Roger D. Blackwell, and James F. Robeson, *Strategic Marketing* (New York: Holt, Rinehart & Winston, 1972), pp. 287–92.
[7]Ibid., p. 289.

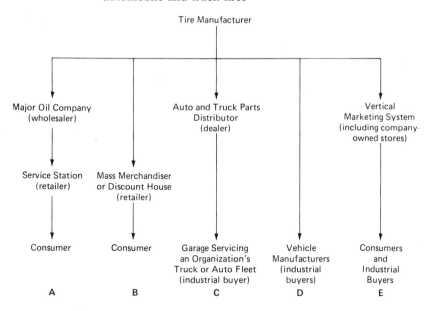

FIGURE 15-5. Multiple marketing channels of a manufacturer of automobile and truck tires

ed in Figure 15-5. Note variations in intrafirm control and distribution decision making in the various marketing channels. Although the same good (automobile tires) may move through each of the five channels illustrated, the intrafirm control and involvement would be different. For example, in channel A, the major oil company would direct the tire to its service stations and consumers. It would stock, promote, display, sell, deliver, and finance the product. Vehicle manufacturers in channel D would be using the tire as an industrial part in the assembly of new vehicles. They would want large quantities, with display, promotion, and selling of tires not a consideration. Channel E would be totally controlled by intrafirm units, and contact with the public would be through company-owned retail stores. Many Goodyear retail stores service both industrial buyers (fleet operations) and consumers seeking tires for their automobiles.

Multiple channels offer great opportunity for the manufacturer, because different markets can be served by adjusting all forces (including distribution) in the marketing strategy to satisfy their wants. Also, a specific marketing channel may be used to appeal to one market segment (say, discount-house purchasers, channel B) without affecting the sales of other channels (for instance, vehicle manufacturers, channel D). If sales of the manufacturer's brand are hurt by discount-house sales, a change in product, using a private-brand name rather than the manufacturer's brand, could eliminate this problem.

These examples should illustrate that channel decisions can be very complex, and that they are highly interrelated with decisions about other controllable variables.

Understanding Channel Role Relationships

Channel members interact in carrying out the marketing tasks, and they develop perceptions about their own roles and the roles of other channel members. As a channel member plays a more successful role in directing the channel, other channel members come to regard this behavior as customary. Therefore, they prescribe behavior for channel members in accordance with this conception and overtly enforce their prescriptions by means of sanctioning behavior.[8]

One of the most important considerations in designing a channel is who the channel leader will be. Some channels may operate on the basis of consensus, with all efforts coordinated for mutual benefit. Most channels, however, can identify a leader who is looked to for establishing channel policies and coordinating distribution efforts. It is not necessary to exercise power and be the channel leader in order to be successful. It *is* necessary, however, to determine who the appropriate leader is and why that leader can best serve the interests of all channel members and target markets. Cooperation is required for the channel to operate as an effective and responsive system. Each role (including the leadership role) in the channel represents an expected mode of conduct and defines the contribution of that unit to the system.[9] Adel I. El-Ansary summarizes one approach to decreasing channel conflict and increasing channel cooperation:

> Two conditions are necessary to minimize and contain conflict and increase cooperation among channel members. First, the role of each channel member has to be specified. In reality, role specification is a specification of performance expectation from each channel member for the functions he performs. Role specification enhances the ability of channel members to predict one another's behaviors. Therefore, role specification, clarification, and agreement enhance the potential of cooperation in channel relations. Role ambiguity and disagreement enhance the potential of conflict among channel members. Second, certain measures of channel coordination have to be undertaken. Coordination in an interorganizational setting requires leadership and the exercise of control. Control is a two-edge sword. If exercised benevolently, it enhances channel member cooperation. Otherwise, it may fuel conflict among the channel members.[10]

Power bases for developing channel leadership include authority, coercion, rewards, referents (reference groups), and expertise. Channel power relates to the ability of one channel member to facilitate or hinder the goal attainment of another channel member. Figure 15-6 illustrates the components

---

[8]Lynn E. Gill and Louis W. Stern, "Roles and Role Theory in Distribution Channel Systems," in *Distribution Channels: Behavioral Dimensions,* ed. Louis W. Stern (Boston: Houghton Mifflin, 1969), p. 36.

[9]Louis W. Stern and Ronald H. Gorman, "Conflict in Distribution Channels: An Exploration," in Stern, *Distribution Channels,* p. 157.

[10]Adel I. El-Ansary, "Perspectives on Channel System Performance," in *Contemporary Issues in Marketing Concepts,* ed. Robert F. Lusch and Paul H. Zinszer (Norman, Okla.: University of Oklahoma Press, 1979), p. 50.

FIGURE 15-6. Channel leadership components

Source: Adapted with permission from *Marketing Channels and Strategies*, 2nd Ed. by Ronald D. Michman and Stanley D. Sibley, Grid Publishing, Inc., Columbus, Ohio, 1980.

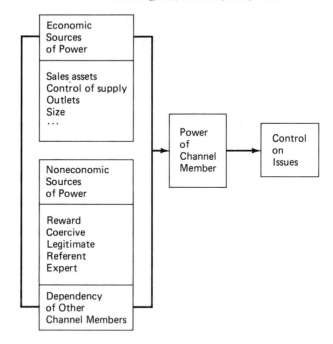

of channel leadership. Note that a firm could use one or several bases of power to exert channel leadership.

> Several conditions are necessary for the emergence of channel leadership. A channel member has to command a comfortable margin of power over other channel members with regard to issues of channel relations, e.g., price, discount structure, and promotional expenditures. Next, this channel member has to have the desire to influence the behavior of other channel members and actually use this power. Finally, other channel members have to tolerate the use of power to achieve control. Channel members' tolerance of control depends to a large extent on their satisfaction with their own power position and the payoff or rewards they reap as a result of improved channel performance. In other words, control will be tolerated only if benefits of such control are understood, realized, and shared equitably by the channel members involved.[11]

Through the years manufacturers have typically been the leaders of their own distribution channels, but in the grocery industry the retailers are now taking the upper hand. Manufacturers once had control because they used large ad-

---

[11]Ibid.

vertising and sales promotion budgets to "pull" customers into stores. But recently the retailers have begun to win minor battles with the distributors, and they no longer blindly carry only the products the manufacturers tell them to carry. If a product does not turn a reasonable profit, it may be off the shelves long before the manufacturer has given up on it.

Manufacturers, however, can undertake a promotion blitz of a product, and customer demand will force retailers to carry the product. Thus there now seems to be a balance of power in the distribution chain, but it will definitely cost more. Manufacturers will have to spend more to get retailers to cooperate.

STRATEGIC DISTRIBUTION DECISIONS

It is necessary to systematically plan and evaluate distribution as a controllable variable. Distribution decisions are a part of all phases of the strategic-planning process (Figure 15-7). We have discussed the need for market and environmental analysis (current assessment) and the need to develop distribution as an implement to overcome the future-planning gap (future assessment).

FIGURE 15-7. The channel design process
Source: William Lazer and James Culley, *Marketing Management* (Boston: Houghton Mifflin Company, 1983), p. 619.

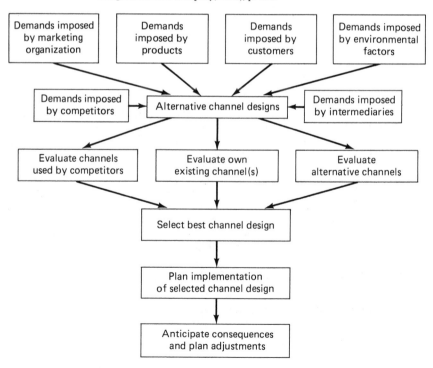

Now we focus more on distribution options and decisions in the strategy-formulation stage of the strategic-planning process.

Developing Options by Identifying Performance Opportunity

Figure 15-7 illustrates the channel design process. The requirements of the channel depend on demands imposed by the company and its products, customers, environment, competitors, and intermediaries. Through an evaluation of these demands, the organization will be able to identify alternative channel designs available to it.

To develop the best channel possible, the firm should look at its existing channel structure and compare this channel with competitors' channels currently being used, and with the alternative channel structures just identified. This analysis will enable the organization to determine which channel is the best for it to use, given its objectives concerning the cost of operating the channel, the degree of control sought, the possibility of a competitive advantage being created with the new channel, and the degree of integration desired.

Of course at this stage the firm may determine that its channel is the optimum channel and will thus not need to proceed further. However, once a new or revised channel has been discovered, the firm should make sure that it is properly implemented. Planning the implementation involves setting standards for channel members and then selecting members who can work together and thus avoid problems in the future. But even the best-laid plans sometimes go astray, and therefore the firm must continually monitor its channels of distribution and "fine-tune" any problems that develop.

Physical Distribution in Strategic Planning

Physical-distribution decisions include considerations in identifying both market opportunities and channel alternatives. This is because alternatives for the physical distribution of goods structure what markets should be served and what marketing channels will be most efficient. It is possible that an innovation in physical distribution can be the most important element of the marketing strategy. We restrict our discussion here to the major decisions involved in blending physical distribution into the overall marketing strategy. It is assumed that you have some background in the basic concepts, methods, and activities involved in physical distribution.

We view physical distribution as a channel flow that must be coordinated to provide the service level desired by target markets and to do it at acceptable costs. The principal elements of the physical distribution system are

1. Inventories—carried as buffers between operations to permit economical and effective system operation

2. Transportation—the key characteristics of the transportation system being its cost, speed, and reliability of performance
3. Warehousing and materials handling—of particular importance, the capital invested in facilities and the cost of moving material into and out of stock point
4. Communications and data processing—affecting the order-processing capability of the system, integration of system elements, the cost balance of the system, and the capability of controlling the system.[12]

Marketing strategists must accept a substantial responsibility in designing the physical-distribution system. The financial control system within the firm may emphasize the reduction of costs and efficiency within the distribution system, but marketers must keep an eye on the services the customers want. For example, the increased costs of air transportation may be justified for a heavy replacement part if speed of delivery is the key consideration of the market. In other words, control over physical distribution can produce a value (reliability, speed, availability) that can be a part of the total offering. Also, costs or difficulties of physical distribution impose constraints on freedom of marketing action.[13] For example, in Bolivia it would be impossible for cattlemen to get beef to the marketplace without the services of expert pilots who fly World War II-type planes. Consider a typical transportation method used to move beef from a remote area to La Paz:

> The department, or province, of Beni has no roads. To get beef to market in La Paz, cattlemen butcher steers at one of the areas's 50 airstrips, and the carcasses are loaded onto waiting planes. Because of the tropical climate, butchered beef would spoil quickly if planes couldn't get in to pick it up. The most popular pilots among cattlemen are the ones who will defy practically any weather to get through.[14]

This example also illustrates the importance of adapting the physical-distribution system to the environment. With the refrigerated rail and truck systems in the United States, air transportation of beef would be highly inefficient. But as the environment or markets change, the marketer must be alert to adjust the physical-distribution system to fit the situation.

One major decision to be made in determining an optimal distribution channel relates to the trade-off between transportation cost and storage cost shown in Figure 15-8. As the number of units shipped through the channel increases, shipments will bring about associated higher storage costs as the volume of inventory increases. The key is to find the lowest *total cost* that still allows the firm to meet its distribution objectives. In highly competitive industries where products are homogeneous, the least-cost, most-efficient method

---

[12]John F. Magee, *Physical Distribution Systems* (New York: McGraw-Hill, 1967). pp. 46–47.
[13]Ibid., p. 31.
[14]Everett Martin, "Getting Bolivian Beef to Market Can Make You a (Gasp) Wreck," *Wall Street Journal*, April 2, 1976, p. 1.

FIGURE 15-8. Trade-off between transportation cost and storage cost

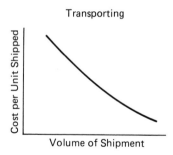

Transporting

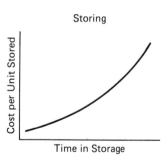

Storing

may provide a competitive advantage. Consider the lower beef-distribution costs developed by Iowa Beef Processors, Inc. (IBP):

> IBP developed a process of shipping beef cut into primals or subprimals, sealed in vacuum bags, and placed in shipping cartons. This process has become known as "Boxed Beef" and offers supermarkets economic advantages over traditional carcass beef that can amount to $30 to $40 per head. The savings are realized in many areas of the distribution system, including (1) reduced freight costs because excess fat and bone are removed prior to shipment; (2) increased handling efficiency at the warehouse; (3) fewer deliveries; and (4) minimum product shrink and increased product life due to vacuum packaging.[15]

EVALUATING DISTRIBUTION PERFORMANCE

Although a firm usually has strong commitments of its channel structure, evaluation and control of distribution performance are necessary to cope with the varying environments. If distribution is to be an effective force in the marketing strategy, the marketer must go beyond identifying market opportunities, and make distribution effective by evaluating and modifying the distribution system to improve channel performance. Stern and El-Ansary point out that "if it is found that one channel member cannot perform an activity as efficiently or effectively as another, then it is detrimental to the output of the channel not to reallocate the activity."[16] This reallocation process is a primary task in controlling channel performance.

To evaluate any system, there must be clearly defined objectives. Distribution objectives must, of course, support organizational goals and marketing objectives, and they cannot be totally isolated from the objectives of other controllable variables. Some of the areas that must be considered in order to

[15]Adapted from J. Fred Haingler, "IBP: News of Boxed Beef Distribution," *Handling and Shipping,* Fall 1976, p. 62.
[16]Louis W. Stern and Adel I. El-Ansary, *Marketing Channels,* Second Edition (Englewood Cliffs, N.J.: Prentice-Hall, Inc., 1982), p. 31

achieve successful distribution performance for the development of objectives are these:

1. Percentage of the market covered by various marketing channels
2. Expense and service levels to be attained through physical-distribution systems
3. Intensity of product exposure designed in the distribution system—i.e., intensive, selective, exclusive
4. Product-mix and product-line requirements in the inventory of the firm and of middlemen
5. Price and promotional considerations as they relate to different members of the marketing channel
6. Role relationships that influence cooperation, conflict, and leadership in the marketing channel.
7. Return on investment associated with different marketing channels

Actual measurement of the distribution system can be developed through the marketing information system. Also, in special problem situations, marketing research may be used to investigate problems or opportunities that relate to distribution performance. For example, at what sales level will it be more profitable to develop a sales force and company sales branches than to continue using merchant wholesalers? A decision this important should be based on marketing intelligence.

The control of distribution performance goes beyond the decision to modify or improve an activity or behavior. The control dimensions must consider overall distribution performance, by considering the impact on other controllable variables in the marketing strategy and the goals and objectives of the organization.

SUMMARY

Distribution as a controllable variable involves strategic decisions about marketing channels and physical distribution. These two areas of decisions are interrelated and structured by market opportunities. All distribution decisions should be based on the wants and behavior of the end user or consumer.

Distribution is one of the more inflexible strategic variables, owing to customary procedures and structure. Furthermore, the investments required and the coordination of independent middlemen make channels slow to change.

In this chapter, we presented a logical and systematic approach to making strategic distribution decisions, without including the various activities and procedures necessary to implement strategic decisions. As with other strategic implements, distribution decisions must be based on organizational goals and marketing objectives. Market-opportunity assessments are necessary to determine distribution alternatives. Next, distribution deficiencies in the current strategy are discovered, and strategic distribution options must be developed.

Finally, distribution performance should be analyzed, evaluated, and controlled, and revisions made if objectives are not achieved.

One final point: With the background of our discussion in Chapter 15, there must be constant vigilance that distribution activities, especially control placed on channel members, do not result in legal conflict. Courts and regulatory agencies are alert to distribution decisions that will injure competition or result in unfair trade relationships. And other aspects of the environment, such as technology, competition, and social trends, can also affect the structure of distribution.

REVIEW QUESTIONS

1. Compare the advantages and disadvantages of the vertical marketing system as a strategic approach to distribution. Products and industries where the vertical marketing system works best should be discussed.

2. "Distribution is inexpensive if you have a large share of the market, but with a small share it is expensive." Comment on this statement. What are the strategic implications?

3. How should decisions about marketing channels and physical distribution be integrated in the strategic-planning process?

4. Why is distribution sometimes an inflexible variable in strategic planning?

5. Compare the strategic importance of distribution with the strategic importance of product, price, and promotion.

6. Suggest some strategic variations in distribution as the product moves through the product life cycle.

7. What are some of the behavioral dimensions of distribution decisions? What role do power and leadership play in channel control?

8. What are the steps in the channel design process?

9. How should a firm evaluate its distribution performance?

Levi's for Feet

Practically everybody in the United States is familiar with Levi's,[1] and many know how Levi Strauss drove his wagonload of blue denim to California during the 1850 gold rush. It was miners' demands for blue jeans that made Strauss very successful and his first name a household word. In modern times, of course, the demand for the riveted blue denim jeans has been general among Americans, bringing to the firm, Levi Strauss & Company of San Francisco, a sales volume now rising over $1 billion annually.

The attractive power of the Levi's name has been measured by the firm's surveys, which have found that 99 percent of Americans aged 14 through 24 are familiar with it, a level unequaled by any other brand. Taking advantage of its name and image, the company had been expanding to other garments for young males and starting to cater to girls and adults. As the Levi Strauss firm investigated other potential lines, shoes entered consideration—and also the name of another venerable firm, the Brown Shoe Company. This firm had been founded in St. Louis 1878 and, like Levi Strauss, was still headquartered in its original city. Now, in 1976, it was the lead manufacturing company of the Brown Group, and the parent company also owned shoe chains and other businesses. What transpired between these two companies is told in this quotation:

> The decision to enter the shoe business was no sudden move for Levi Strauss. Gerald O'Shea, Levi's vice-president of marketing, says the company heard from 20 manufacturers who wanted to market shoes under the Levi brand. "We have long considered the idea of expanding Levi's franchise, but we didn't want to go into the shoe business as such," Shea notes. Of all the suitors, he says, Brown was the most natural partner. "The two companies have the same kind of people, ethics, and quality standards."[2]

Brown Shoe was also a logical partner in that it is the largest branded shoe manufacturer in the nation. A licensing agreement was arranged between the companies under which Brown would design, make, and market the shoes, with Levi Strauss receiving royalties and acting in an advisory capacity.

Market and product strategies were determined jointly by the two companies. The target was males between 18 and 24 years old. At that time, approximately 80 percent of Levi's jeans sales were to males, and 60 percent of their buyers were between 18 and 24.

The project had moved far toward commercialization by the spring of 1975. A line of shoes had been designed and submitted to focus groups of young males. Their responses turned out to be most enthusiastic, and the companies felt assured that the styles were right. The marketability would not be demonstrated, however, unless an actual market test was conducted. This was planned for the summer of 1975 in Sacramento and St. Louis, two cities where the respective companies could observe results most effectively from their headquarters.

In preparation for the market test, product and pricing decisions had been made by

---

This case is published with express permission of the Brown Shoe Company, Division of Brown Group, Inc., and of Levi Strauss & Company.

[1]Levi's is a registered trade name of Levi Strauss & Co.

[2]*Business Week,* November 10, 1975, p. 124–27.

Brown Shoe Company, but key aspects of merchandising and distribution strategies still had to be decided. Following are the product, pricing, and distribution situations at that time.

PRODUCT

The designers of "Levi's for Feet" sought a natural, casual life-style that would have universal appeal to youth. Besides being casual, the shoes were to convey the same atmosphere as Levi's blue jeans, and they would be tied to the Levi's image by attaching the famous orange Levi's label and a permanent, visible Levi's tag. There were such brand-visibility tags on some of the new "competition" or athletic shoes, notably the German import of Adidas, but for American shoes in normal wear, it was a rash innovation.

There would be twelve styles in the new line, including sandals, modified hiking boots, athletic shoes, and general casual styles. All would have leather uppers except a blue denim sneaker and a nylon athletic shoe. The styling would have some originality, but the main differentiation would lie in the Levi's name.

Another difference would be in the sizes offered. There would be twelve lengths, which would accommodate nearly all feet in that respect, but rather than having a number of widths, the Levi's footwear would come in only width D, the most typical.

Product policy regarding new styles would also be unusual. The initial twelve models were intended to be stable and kept in the line indefinitely. When some weakened, and as fashions changed, new styles would be fed in gradually. This would avoid serious obsolescence of stock held at retail, while the total assortment would be held near the initial dozen styles.

PRICE

The suggested retail prices were to range from $13 to $32 a pair. The lowest-price item would be sneakers, and most leather-uppered shoes would be suggested to retail between $25 and $30. Although this was not an inexpensive price range, it would be characteristic of good-quality shoes and in line with popular items for young men. A suggested retail markup was provided at a normal percentage for the good-shoe trade. With the line's attractiveness, it was believed that no unusual trade discounts would be needed to induce retailers to take on the line at its introduction.

DISTRIBUTION

Distribution plans were still under formulation, and the current retail shoe scene had to be given deep study. Quality shoes at this time were distributed largely through three types of outlets:

1. Department-store shoe departments, where there were three distinct departments for men's, women's, and children's shoes
2. Specialty shoe stores, usually catering only to women or to men, tending to feature exclusive, prestige brands
3. Family shoe stores

The third group contained the largest-volume outlets and was organized largely in chains, some of which were Brown Group subsidiaries. Second in volume was department stores.

Some relevant characteristics of conventional shoe retailers were these:

1. The shoes out on display were only a fraction of those carried, as there was limited space on the selling floor. Most of the shoes were kept in the back room. And as only one shoe of a pair would be put on display, self-service was impossible.

2. Clerk service involved a long routine in waiting on each customer: (a) hearing the customer's request; (b) measuring the customer's size; (c) interpreting what the customer really wanted in connection with what was in stock; (d) selecting two or three pairs from stock and bringing them out to the customer; (e) putting each shoe on the customer's foot and advising about its fit; (f) pointing out good features and encouraging purchase; (g) returning to the stockroom for more items, if the first selection was not acceptable or was ill-fitting; (h) if a sale was made, writing the sales check, boxing and tying the shoes, and completing the transaction; and (i) returning the unsold shoes to the back-room stock.

3. Shoe clerks were expected to have expertise in fitting, and many were very proud of their skill.

4. A single line of shoes might encompass as many as sixteen lengths and five widths (or more, if it included such unusual sizes as AA or EE). Most of these sizes might be carried for each style and color in the line. A full line like Brown's "Roblee" could entail 1,200 square feet of floor space.

5. Turnover of shoes tended to be slow, averaging under 1.9 times a year. Some unusual sizes or unpopular items in a line would have far poorer turnover. Where there was low turnover and many stock-keeping units to be managed, reorder practices by retailers tended to be loose. Out-of-stocks were far too common.

6. Shoe manufacturer's sales representatives often made extravagant promises of fast service on reorders. Most manufacturers actually gave slow turnaround on reorders and were unreliable in this regard. Low credibility of order service was a factor that discouraged retailers' refilling stocks, especially on seasonal models.

The description above concerns conventional shoe channels at that time. Those channels, however, were seldom patronized by American males of the 18–24 age bracket. These young people were thronging to different types of clothing outlets, either (1) the youth or jeans departments in department stores, or (2) specialized jeans shops that were multiplying in suburban shopping centers. These two types were Levi's main channels.

Jeans shops or departments differed radically from conventional shoe outlets in both atmosphere and merchandising methods. Their ambience was casual, matching their patron's moods. Clerks also were casual, and their expertise was in fitting jeans snugly. Merchandise was displayed on racks or tables, wall-to-wall, for self-service. Merchandise turnover was fairly rapid, and back-room stocks were limited by space, so most of the merchandise was out on the floor. Managers had been accustomed to dependable order service from Levi Strauss and other suppliers.

THE PROBLEM

The manager of the Levi's for Feet Division at Brown Shoe Company recognized that a number of decisions had to be made before the testmarketing plan was ready. Product, price, and promotional decisions were either complete or largely resolved. In distribution, however, the fundamental strategies had not yet been found. It was vital that the right type of outlets be determined, whether among conventional outlets or in jeans departments or jeans specialty shops. The best outlets would not be willing to take on Levi's for Feet unless a retail program was offered that would be profitable and manageable for them, in terms of their operating characteristics and needs.

DISCUSSION

1. Which types of outlets should be selected for the distribution of Levi's for Feet? Why?
2. Identify the obstacles or difficulties that Brown Shoe Company would face with the selected type(s) of retailers in inducing them to (a) take on the Levi's line, and (b) efficiently stock, display, sell, and manage the line.
3. Describe a strategy for Levi's for Feet that would be likely to obtain and maintain an efficient distribution system at the retail level.

16

The Marketing Plan

After the strategic program has been determined, the marketing plan is prepared. Because most of this book has been devoted to strategic decision making, the reader may infer that the stage of preparing the plan is less important than strategy formation. Managers of a strategic unit would probably disagree. A great deal of effort and personal commitment are required to implement a marketing plan.

The term *plan* must first be defined, since it has various meanings. Next we will discuss the purposes served by the plan. Organizational aspects constitute the third topic. Four components of the actual marketing plan will then be described: structure, quantitative analysis, writing, and presentation. Skill in creating a written plan is much more valuable to managerial careers than a college student is likely to appreciate: Business firms find that very few people can write and present plans effectively.

NATURE OF THE MARKETING PLAN

Two definitions of the word *plan* are found in current dictionaries:

"An orderly arrangement of parts of an overall design or objective."
"A detailed formulation of a program of action."[1]

---

[1]David S. Hopkins, *The Marketing Plan* (New York: The Conference Board, 1981), p. 1.

Those quotations came from a monograph that reported on a survey of marketing executives in 267 manufacturing and service corporations. The monograph also contains the following comment:

> ... *the marketing plan* is seen by many executives in the survey as the very symbol and essence of purposeful marketing management. They regard a formally prepared, written marketing plan as the means of linking the marketing function with the principle of management by objectives. ... Unless all the key elements of a plan are written down, they say, there will always be loopholes for ambiguity or misunderstanding of strategies and objectives, or of assigned responsibilities for taking action.[2]

The plan, then, is formally prepared and written and is a detailed formulation of the action program necessary to carry out the strategic program. This word is a noun and is not the verb "to plan"—or planning—as the latter embraces the entire planning process from objectives to the point of implementation. This can be clarified by a diagram that indicates what precedes and what follows the marketing plan:

STRATEGIC PLANNING

Objectives
Definition of Business Area
Strategic Program
Resource Requirements

THE MARKETING PLAN
and its approval

IMPLEMENTATION

The core strategy and the key elements of the marketing program should have been put in writing, in specific terms, during the strategic-planning process (in the first box of our diagram). The strategist does not clutter the presentation of those ideas, however, with specific details. Instead the strategy is described in rather broad strokes. Such a general statement is not suitable for directing the strategy's implementation, nor is it intended to. The marketing plan is the action document.

One definition of an annual marketing plan is the following used by the Best Foods Division of CPC International, Inc.:

> *DEFINITION:* The Annual Marketing Plan states the facts, establishes the objectives, defines the strategy, and details all the marketing efforts for each product. The plan should state where the product is now, where it expects to be at the end

---

[2]Ibid., pp. 1–2.

of the plan year in terms of specific objectives, and how it expects to meet those objectives.[3]

Strategic plans for long-range periods should include a marketing plan for that period as well as shorter-range annual or periodic plans. There would also be a plan for an SBU and a plan for each PMU in very large firms. The following quotation, from a forest products company, presents an interesting description of how the plan has been evolving in one firm:

> Formalized market planning began in 1968. At that time, the focus of the plans was upon the prior identification of end-use markets and the company's position in those total markets. There was only slight recognition of market segmentation and product position. [More recently] the significant change has been in financial orientation, targets and measurements. The marketing plan is now presented as part of a business and profit plan. That plan includes detailed financial data, production, personnel audit, research and development and so forth.[4]

We have indicated that there may be more than one plan (e.g., one for short-term and one for long-term periods; one for finance and one for marketing; one for each PMU and one for each SBU). We speak of *the* marketing plan, however, because there is just *one* plan that *governs* the operations for each planning period (for the particular planning unit).

PURPOSES AND SIGNIFICANCE

The purposes of a marketing plan must be understood to appreciate its significance. The principal functions of a marketing plan are these:

1. It *explains the situation*, both present and future, of the planning unit or PMU. This would include the market environment and the PMU's position in it; it would also state the unit's current planning gap and project its future planning gap. The proposed plan could be understood only with this background.
2. It *specifies the results* that are expected, so that the organization can anticipate what its situation will be at the end of the planning period.
3. It *identifies the resources* that will be *needed* to carry out the planned actions, so that a judgment can be made about the wisdom of such expenditures for such a purpose.
4. It *describes the actions* that are to take place, so that the responsibilities can be assigned for implementing the campaign.
5. It *permits monitoring* the ensuing actions and results, so that controls may be exerted.

The marketing plan should cover those five areas in detail.

---

[3]Ibid., p. 45.
[4]Ibid., p. 6.

The five main purposes set forth above are very important ones to various persons in the firm. The line managers who are to carry out the plans are most interested in the fourth purpose. The strategic planner and that manager's superiors have a special interest in the fifth purpose, as they want to ensure that tactical changes can be made if needed, during implementation, and they must be able to evaluate why the strategy does or does not succeed. The high-level executives who have the authority to approve or reject the proposed strategic plan would have particular interest in the second and third purposes.

The most pressing concern for the strategic planner may lie in the third purpose. The marketing plan is the means of communicating the strategy to those making the critical decisions on resource allocation. That is the do-or-die event in the strategy process, the one about which the strategist is most anxious. A related more personal goal for the strategist may involve his or her exposure to higher management. Evaluation of the planner's ability and performance may be based on that plan.

ORGANIZATIONAL ASPECTS

The person who *prepares* the marketing plan should be the same one who devised the strategic program. This person is the one who is most knowledgeable about the strategy and its purposes. In large firms with PMUs, this person would be the product manager (or brand or market manager). Many firms, however, place this responsibility in the hands of a higher marketing executive. The Conference Board survey, quoted above, found that among manufacturing firms nearly twice as many gave this responsibility to a marketing vice-president or director than to someone on the PMU level. Those data do not necessarily refute the logic of having the PMU manager prepare the plan. Many of the firms responding may not have the PMU type of organization, whereas in many that do, the marketing director may feel responsible for the product manager's work. A product manager should want and expect a higher marketing executive to participate in ideas for the plan.

Approval of marketing plans must be lodged in higher-level executives who have been given final authority. In the Conference Board survey, around three-fourths of the service firms and half of the manufacturing firms assigned marketing plan approval to the CEO or executive vice-president. In some firms with SBUs, the plan goes up only to the head executive of that unit for approval. Many companies also have committees of executives who evaluate and screen marketing plans before they are submitted to the approving executive. Therefore, when a PMU manager writes a marketing plan, it must be clear and persuasive in order to win approval by the series of decision makers through which it is routed.

There is often a planning specialist or a staff of such specialists in today's corporation, usually attached to the CEO's office. This function is normally of such importance that the head of planning is a vice-president. These individuals may do most of the work underlying the corporate plan, but that final plan is the creation of any strong CEO. Regarding the planning activity and writing of plans at lower levels, on which we are concentrating, these central planners should not wish to participate or interfere. They are vital to the lower-level planners, though, as source people whenever data or advice is needed and as stimulators of planning interest around the firm.

Both long-term and short-term plans should be prepared, typically by the same planner. Figure 5-3 shows the relative timing of the parallel long-range (program) and annual (period) plans in the IBM organization. A firm may need more plans—perhaps four types, as in the "four-loop" system of Texas Instruments, Inc., which is charted in Figure 16-1. These four types include (1) long-range (ten-year) plans; (2) intermediate plans that concentrate on the next year but also project three more years ahead; (3) the "rolling plan" with quarterly updates of the coming twelve months; and (4) four-month forecasts of business. The intermediate plans are useful for deciding on new products, personnel needs, and capital needs. The rolling plan is intended for quick response to changing business conditions. Obviously TI places strong emphasis on planning work.

Smooth functioning of an organization requires that all important tasks be stated and scheduled in written form. Such a schedule is essential for the person assigned the formulation and preparation of the marketing plan. A planning calendar used in the drug firm of Merck, Sharp & Dohme is shown in Figure 16-2. You may imagine Chester Trimble, the product manager for cer-

FIGURE 16-1.   Texas Instruments, Inc.'s, "four-loop" planning system

Source: "Texas Instruments Management Philosophies and Growth Experience," an address by L. M. Rice, Jr. to Institute Panamericano de Alta Direction de Empresa in Mexico City, May, 1980. (Dallas: Texas Instruments, Inc., 1980), p. 13. Used with permission.

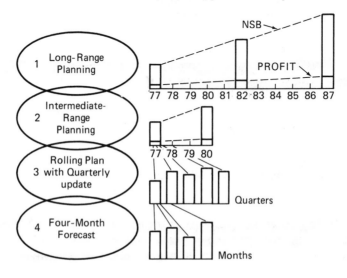

FIGURE 16-2. Marketing planning cycle of Merck, Sharp & Dohme division of Merck & Company, Inc.

Source: David S. Hopkins, *The Short-Term Marketing Plan* (New York: The Conference Board, 1981), p. 72.

First Quarter	– Product Managers' Quarterly Reports (previous quarter's results).
Second Quarter	– Sales Forecasts—Current year estimated actuals and forward planning for next two years.
	– Product Managers' Quarterly Reports (previous quarter's results).
	– Annual Marketing Strategy Review Meeting.
	– Prepare Marketing Strategy Profiles for next year.
	– Cost Promotion Program for next year.
	– New Project proposals sent to Research.
	– Prepare guest physician program for next year.
Third Quarter	– Sales Forecasts—Current year estimated actuals and forward planning for next two years.
	– Finalize next year's Promotion Programs.
	– Product Managers' Quarterly Reports (previous quarter's results).
	– Marketing management formal review of next year's Promotion Program.
	– Review next year's profit plan with divisional management.
Fourth Quarter	– Sales Forecasts—Current year estimated actuals and forward planning for next two years.
	– Product Managers' Quarterly Reports (previous quarter's results).
	– Review next year's profit plan with corporate management.
	– Complete Marketing Strategy monograph for next year.
	– Prepare next year's strategic plan (5-year long-range plan).

tain brands in another drug firm, whose strategy was discussed early in Chapter 1, working with such a schedule.

In this schedule, one or more decisions or forecasts are due in every month except the ninth one. At this point, though, the product manager is much involved in creating the "marketing strategy plan" due in the eleventh month. The schedule shows that the marketing strategy is first drafted during the second month and its elements are resolved during the ensuing nine months. Every item in Figure 16-2 would require some sort of written report from the product manager. The analytical and writing work in marketing planning is a year-round job.

STRUCTURE OF THE PLAN

Anyone writing a paper of some complexity should structure the subject matter before starting to write. In most corporations the general structure of the marketing plan has already been outlined for the planner. A standard format for marketing plans is issued, with instructions on what to cover. The various managerial people who will evaluate a number of plans usually require a uniform format to aid examination and comparison.

A good deal of variation is found among the formats used in different corporations. Two formats are shown in Figures 16-3 and 16-4. These firms' industries (chemicals and banking services) are different, but unique executive tastes in a corporation would also account for some of the variation in format. There are, however, some common subjects, such as opportunities, objectives, and marketing strategies, covered by most if not all marketing plans. The Du-Pont plan (Figure 16-3) seems to emphasize objectives and strategies more

FIGURE 16-3 **Table of contents for a marketing plan of a division of E. I. DuPont de Nemours & Co., Inc.**
Source: *The Marketing Plan*, The Conference Board, Conference Board Report No. 801 (1981), p. 62.

ANNUAL U.S. MARKETING PLAN

SITUATION ANALYSIS

- Sales History
- Market Profile
- Sales versus Objective
- Factors Affecting Sales
- Profitability
- Factors Affecting Profitability

MARKET ENVIRONMENT

- Growth Rate
- Trends, Changes in Customer Attitude
- Recent or Anticipated Competitor Actions
- Government Activity

PROBLEMS AND OPPORTUNITIES

- Problem Areas
- Opportunities

MARKETING AND PROFITABILITY OBJECTIVES

- Sales
- Market Profile
- Gross Margin

MARKETING STRATEGY

MARKETING

- Marketing Programs

PRODUCT ASSUMPTIONS

FIGURE 16-4. Marketing plan outline of the Fidelity Bank, Philadelphia

Source: *The Marketing Plan*, The Conference Board, pp. 63–64.

MARKETING PLAN OUTLINE

For each major bank service:

I. MANAGEMENT SUMMARY

What is our marketing plan for this service in brief?

This is a one-page summary of the basic factors involving the marketing of the service next year along with the results expected from implementing the plan. It is intended as a brief guide for management.

II. ECONOMIC PROJECTIONS

What factors in the overall economy will affect the marketing of this service next year, and how?

This section will comprise a summary of the specific economic factors that will affect the marketing of this service during the coming year. These might include employment, personal income, business expectations, inflationary (or deflationary) pressures, etc.

III. THE MARKET—qualitative

Who or what kinds of organization could conceivably be considered prospects for this service?

This section will define the qualitative nature of our market. It will include demographic information, industrial profiles, business profiles, etc., for all people or organizations that could be customers for this service.

IV. THE MARKET—quantitative

What is the potential market for this service?

This section will apply specific quantitative measures to this bank service. Here we want to include numbers of potential customers, dollar volume of business, our current share of the market—any specific measures that will outline our total target for the service and where we stand competitively now.

V. TREND ANALYSIS

Based on the history of this service, where do we appear to be headed?

This section is a review of the past history of this service. Ideally, we should include quarterly figures for the last five years showing dollar volume, accounts opened, accounts closed, share of market, and all other applicable historical data.

VI. COMPETITION

Who are our competitors for this service, and how do we stand competitively?

This section should define our current competition, both bank and non-bank. It should be a thoughtful analysis outlining who our competitors are, how successful they are, why they have (or have not) been successful, and what actions they might be expected to take regarding this service during the coming year.

VII. PROBLEMS AND OPPORTUNITIES

Internally and externally, are there problems inhibiting the marketing of this service, or are there opportunities we have not taken advantage of?

This section will comprise a frank commentary on both inhibiting problems and unrealized opportunities. It should include a discussion of the internal and external problems we can control, for example, by changes in policies or operational procedures. It should also point up areas of opportunity regarding this service that we are not now exploiting.

VIII. OBJECTIVES AND GOALS

Where do we want to go with this service?

This section will outline the immediate short and long range objectives for this service. Short range goals should be specific, and will apply to next year. Long range goals will necessarily be less specific and should project for the next five years. Objectives should be stated in two forms:

(1) qualitative—reasoning behind the offering of this service and what modifications or other changes do we expect to make.

(2) quantitative—number of accounts, dollar volume, share of market, profit goals.

IX. ACTION PROGRAMS

Given past history, the economy, the market, competition, etc., what must we do to reach the goals we have set for this service?

This section will be a description of the specific actions we plan to take during the coming year to assure reaching the objectives we have set for the service in VIII. These would include advertising and promotion, direct mail, and brochure development. It would also include programs to be designed and implemented by line officers. The discussion should cover what is to be done, schedules for completion, methods of evaluation, and officers in charge of executing the program and measuring results.

(five sections) than the Fidelity Bank plan (Figure 16-4) does (two sections), but we do not know the length and amount of detail included in these very important subjects. In the bank's outline, we have included instructions pertinent to each topic to give some idea of what would be wanted.

Business reports must be concise and right to the point. Language must be clear and fairly simple. Data to support the assertions and programs in the marketing plan are required but should be given sparingly and often communicated with graphs. The number of subjects listed in Figures 16-3 and 16-4 seem to require fairly hefty documents (for instance, eighteen subjects are listed in the DuPont format). The planners, however, should condense the reports that will be read at higher levels—even though they should have complete plans for their own files and later reference. The Fidelity Bank specifies a one-page length for the management summary (possibly the only page read thoroughly by some executives), but each of the other sections should probably be held down to a few pages.

A very condensed statement of the plan and its main supporting data may be required for top-level review and approval. There are corporations with hundreds of PMUs, and their CEOs simply cannot afford the time to scan more than one or two pages on each of them. Anyone who has experienced difficulty in confining a topic to a few pages would find such conciseness a challenge. Let us recognize, though, that the CEO of a large corporation is concerned primarily with the plans of each SBU, which are expressed in some detail. This CEO would closely examine only PMUs with critical problems or outstanding performance.

Now that you have observed the content of marketing plans and understand their diversity, we will discuss and develop a single format. We will begin with the economic and financial analysis and projections that provide the foundation for the plan. A case presented earlier will serve as an example. We will then explain what the marketing planner might write in each section of the report.

ANALYSIS AND PROJECTIONS

The marketing plan document would contain not only qualitative statements about the situation, proposed program, and its rationale but also quantitative data relevant to the proposal. The planner would have been making numerous analyses as the strategic planning proceeded. In order to assess and choose the best strategy, projections of the effects of various alternatives would have been required. For such projections, however, general numbers would suffice. After a planner has chosen a strategy and described its program in specific detail (usually with help from functional departments and reactions from his or her superior), detailed figures for that program are developed. This is a formidable job and must be based to a degree on assumptions and estimates, since future markets hold many unknowns.

One of the toughest quantitative tasks underlying the marketing plan is computing the effects of the marketing actions contemplated—evaluating market response. How much sales response should be anticipated for a variable in a proposed marketing mix? (That is, what incremental change would it produce?) Consider estimating the effects of some dollar expenditure on a particular type of activity—say, advertising. For that a ratio or "response coefficient" is used.

Let us say that advertising is expected to have a response coefficient of 0.2, meaning that the sales variation resulting from an advertising expenditure would be 20 percent of that ratio. If advertising expense went up by 50 percent, then a 10 percent growth in sales would result ($.50 \times .2 = .10$). Take a firm that has been spending $100,000 on advertising and selling $3 million of the advertised product. If a 0.2 coefficient applies, then when advertising is increased by $50,000 (or 50 percent), sales would increase by $300,000 (or 10 percent).

We would expect different coefficients with regard to other marketing variables in the mix. Price would have a negative coefficient, since volume should move in the direction opposite to the price change.

The firm, let us hope, has empirical evidence from its own past advertising and traceable sales results (or observed effects for similar other firms) to set a reasonably accurate response coefficient. To reflect on this problem, observe our graph in Figure 16–5, which portrays the example above. The solid line represents the $300,000 rise in sales volume that is estimated as the result of a $50,000 rise in advertising expense. The decision maker may feel confident about that relationship, but consider his or her carrying that logic to extremes.

FIGURE 16-5. Sales response to advertising expenditures. The sales growth imputed to a 50 percent increase from $100,000 to $150,000 is shown by curve S_1. A theoretical curve of response over a full range of advertising expenditure is shown by curve S_2. (Data hypothetical.)

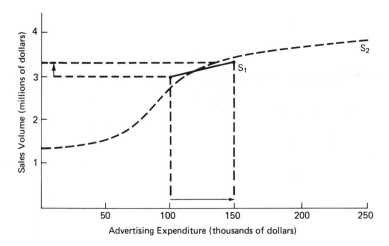

If advertising outlay were raised by 1,000 percent, would sales triple (up 200 percent)? Given the limitations of the potential market size and of probable competitive reaction in the face of such aggression, such a sales increase seems improbable—and so the response coefficient for such a huge increase would presumably be significantly less. Or, if advertising expense were wholly curtailed, would sales drop by only 20 percent? The point, then, is that this linear relationship between advertising and sales, which is the solid line S_1 in Figure 16-5, is valid at best only over a limited variation in the advertising-expense factor.

The curve S_2 in Figure 16-5 is a more likely approximation of the relationship between advertising expenditure and sales volume. The same general theory and an S curve tend to be applicable also to any other marketing activity in which a very small expenditure produces no results up to a threshold level, while very high level expenditures produce rapidly decreasing returns. (Response to price change is along a different curve; but at the extremes, the same theory operates.) The planner should if possible be armed with empirical evidence of how advertising (or any other marketing effort) does tend to behave for the type of market and product involved.[5]

But projecting the effects on sales of a single variable, which we have been doing above, would be quite artificial and misleading. In actuality, a

---

[5]A compilation of the various elasticities of demand relative to advertising, which were reported in published studies between 1969 and 1975, is provided in Randall L. Schultz and Robert P. Leone, *A Study of Marketing Generalizations,* Paper No. 563 (West Lafayette, Ind.: Krannert Graduate School of Management, Purdue University, 1976), p. 10.

number of marketing variables act conjointly, with interaction, and if the strategy is well devised, they produce a synergy. That is, the market response to changes in expenditure on variables A and B acting together tends to be greater than the sum of the responses to each variable acting alone.

Let us say that the response coefficient to price changes for Product J, within some range from the current price, is -3.0. That is, for a reduction in price of 1 percent, an increase in sales volume of 3 percent would occur. Advertising's coefficient, as in our earlier example, let us say is 0.2; so if advertising expenditure were increased by 10 percent, we would anticipate a 2 percent rise in sales volume. The total of these two projected changes, as actions performed independently of each other, would be 5 percent sales growth.

Now suppose we devoted the additional advertising space or time to promoting the price decrease. Since many more buyers would now be aware of the price drop, it would probably attract many more and produce substantially greater effect than the -3.0 rate of change. If it resulted in an 8 percent sales increase, these variables would be said to be synergistic, with the extra increment of 3 percent yielded.

The task of projecting the joint sales effects of a number of simultaneous changes in the marketing mix effort is, of course, complex. It demands much greater insight or empirical data than in their being projected singly. The equation for doing so was well described by Kotler some years ago, in an article that remains the classic explanation.[6] We will employ his equation and adapt his example below:

To estimate sales, relative to the effects of three marketing variables, the general functional equation is:

$$Q = f(P, A, S)$$

where

Q = estimated sales
P = price
A = advertising (expressed in dollars)
S = selling (expressed in dollars)

To take into calculation the unit sales volume and the individual sales-response coefficients for each of the marketing variables, one would use a multiple exponential form of equation to reflect each demand function:

$$Q = kP^a A^b S^c$$

where

k = a scale factor to translate the dollar values of the three variables into units
a = the price-response coefficient
b = the advertising-response coefficient
c = the selling-response coefficient

Let us again assume that the price and advertising coefficients are respectively -3.0 and 0.2 and that the selling coefficient is 0.1. Also let us say that 10,000 is

---

[6]Philip Kotler, "Marketing Mix Decisions for New Products," *Journal of Marketing Research*, February 1964, pp. 43–49.

the proper scale value in this instance for k. Inserting these values into the formula gives us the following:

$$Q = 10,000 \, P^{-3} A^{1/5} S^{1/10}$$

Let us note that a vital step in this calculation is setting the value of k, which represents the size of the market prior to introducing the several changes in the marketing factors.

The portion of Kotler's solution that we have used refers only to estimating sales volume. This is one stage in calculating the estimated profit for a given marketing-expenditure mix, and we will refer to it again later in connection with the integrating decision.

It may be noted that Kotler's model above is multiplicative and uses fixed exponents. Such an exponent may accurately predict the response or demand elasticity of a variable in the marketing mix, for one or more segments in the market. However, it becomes grossly inaccurate for other segments. These dynamics make the response exponents very tricky, and there is also great difficulty in estimating the interaction between variables.

An issue we have not yet addressed is the relative quality or potency of various alternatives of each marketing functional tool. That is, substantial difference (apart from their scale or dollar costs) often exists between the effectiveness of alternative advertising appeals and their renditions of different advertising media, of various sales-promotion methods, of alternative new packages, and of other variables. (Note that we used only three variables in our equation, but there may be significant change in others to be taken into reckoning.) If the planner can obtain any reliable indications of relative effectiveness among alternatives, these should be used.

> The Q Company's marketing planner for Project J is projecting the likely effect on sales volume of a proposed marketing program. It includes a 5 percent increase, in real dollars, in advertising expenditure, which also means that about 5 percent more potential buyers will be reached by the message. The proposed advertisements themselves have been given some thorough pretesting on typical consumers by the advertising agency. The consumers have rated these new advertisements with a measurement of buying interest that has become the agency's standard index of probable effectiveness. According to this tested measurement, the new advertisements score 15 percent better results than the old ones. The planner may therefore increase his or her projections of sales response to the advertising for this quality index—to whatever extent the planner has found or estimates that such superior quality would stimulate greater sales during the period concerned.

But marketing management, you might well protest, rarely has accurate data on each variable's effects on sales volume. And even when it does, those data tend to be limited to a handful of observations or a narrow range of intensity—or to relate to other products or market situations than the particular one being faced. Granting this, it is desirable to employ a market-response formula, even if all the ratios used are intuitive and the basic market size is questionable. Any decision maker who determines the amount of marketing expenditures or effort for any product, function, or firm can do so rationally only with implicit assumptions of such relationships. The use of a model and actual calculation forces the decision maker to explicate his or her calculations and thus realize how the decision is being reached and with what assumed values. This discipline raises the right questions and should stimulate the search for sounder and more real bases or data. It also provides a good learning process in this aspect of strategic thinking.

These estimates of the sales response to the variables in the proposed marketing mix are to be used in *predicting the outcome of the proposed plan.* Projections of the various elements in the plan should be brought together in a quantified fashion to create a pro forma income statement for the unit (e.g., a PMU) for which plans are being made. The planner needs a system or formula with which to arrive at the needed predictions. A model to be followed in the nine-stage flow chart is shown in Figure 16-6. After some comment, we will demonstrate the model's use with calculations in a hypothetical example.

The diagram in Figure 16-6 is similar to that in Figure 5-8, which displays steps in a PMU's strategic-planning process. These two diagrams show the same process, but their similarity may not be obvious. In Figure 5-8 the steps are arranged horizontally, but the vertical dimension shown in Figure 16-6 is the normal one for calculations. Omitted from Figure 16-6 are the preceding steps of situation analysis and definition of market targets. Those steps would have complicated Figure 16-6 unduly, but recall that the PMU manager, Chester Trimble, discovered an opportunity through his situation analysis and made a key decision in targeting pediatricians and young children.

There are three interlocking series in Figure 16-6. Through determining the impact of the new strategy (3), one calculates a changed market-share (2) projection for the brand. That market share is multiplied by the total market (1) to estimate the sales volume, which in turn is the key to developing a projected profit and loss statement for the brand. The steps may be grasped more easily when seen in numbers—Table 16-1 displays the figures used by Trimble and will form the basis of our discussion.

Industry sales of the type of product being planned, step 1, may be arrived at through various sources. In the specific case of Brand C (Trimble's responsibility), the U.S. Department of Commerce publishes dollar sales of penicillin—at manufacturers' prices—in its *Survey of Current Business.* A planner must first determine what product category is relevant (in this case penicillin for oral administration), which may be a hard question to answer. A broader definition than desired may be necessary because data are not available for the specific type of product or industry. Projecting the existing figure to future industry volume may be done by using a number of causal factors' trends or forecasts, but undoubtedly some judgment will enter as well.

Trimble had data measuring actual current penicillin sales for figuring current market share, and that for the forthcoming year was based on the rate at which Brand C's share had been eroding over the past three years (2). More difficult would be the estimates in step 3 of Table 16-1, the effect of the new strategy on consumer response to Brand C. The marketing program may con-

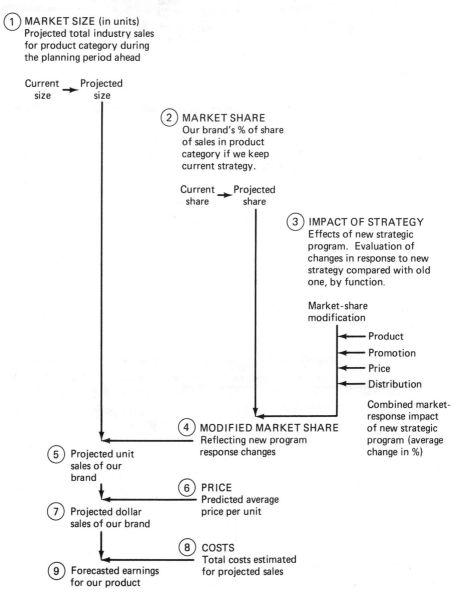

FIGURE 16-6. Systematic model for predicting effects of a proposed strategic program

(1) MARKET SIZE (in units)
Projected total industry sales for product category during the planning period ahead

Current → Projected
size   size

(2) MARKET SHARE
Our brand's % of share of sales in product category if we keep current strategy.

Current → Projected
share   share

(3) IMPACT OF STRATEGY
Effects of new strategic program. Evaluation of changes in response to new strategy compared with old one, by function.

Market-share modification

← Product
← Promotion
← Price
← Distribution

Combined market-response impact of new strategic program (average change in %)

(4) MODIFIED MARKET SHARE
Reflecting new program response changes

(5) Projected unit sales of our brand

(6) PRICE
Predicted average price per unit

(7) Projected dollar sales of our brand

(8) COSTS
Total costs estimated for projected sales

(9) Forecasted earnings for our product

sist of several new actions and in more than one of the marketing variables, so the effects in each function must be predicted and interactions between them reflected. How Trimble came out with these particular ratios will be discussed in the next section where the plan's content is examined. You may have noticed that what Trimble has calculated in stage 3 differs from what we earlier said about response coefficients. There our subject was the basic determina-

TABLE 16-1 New marketing strategy's projections for 1985, for Brand C

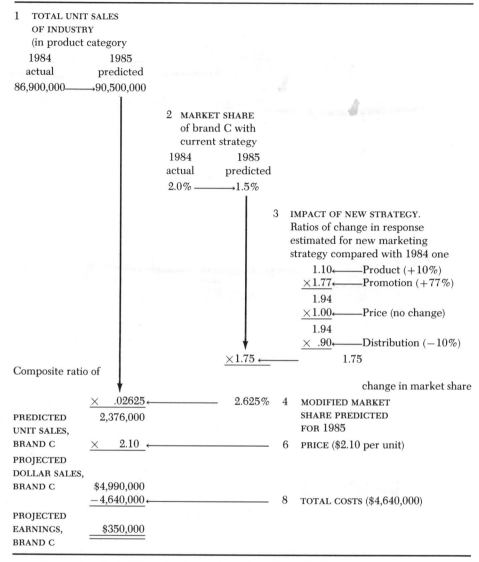

1 TOTAL UNIT SALES
OF INDUSTRY
(in product category

1984	1985
actual	predicted

86,900,000——→90,500,000

2 MARKET SHARE
of brand C with
current strategy

1984	1985
actual	predicted

2.0% ———→1.5%

3 IMPACT OF NEW STRATEGY.
Ratios of change in response
estimated for new marketing
strategy compared with 1984 one

1.10←——Product (+10%)
×1.77←——Promotion (+77%)
1.94
×1.00←——Price (no change)
1.94
× .90←——Distribution (−10%)
×1.75 ←———   1.75

Composite ratio of

× .02625←————— 2.625% 4 MODIFIED MARKET
change in market share

5 PREDICTED   2,376,000   SHARE PREDICTED
UNIT SALES,   FOR 1985
BRAND C   × 2.10 ←—————— 6 PRICE ($2.10 per unit)

7 PROJECTED
DOLLAR SALES,
BRAND C $4,990,000
               −4,640,000←—————— 8 TOTAL COSTS ($4,640,000)

9 PROJECTED
EARNINGS, $350,000
BRAND C

Data are hypothetical. The calculations and model are discussed in the text.

tion of the coefficients, whereas Trimble is estimating the incremental effects of (the changes in) each function's different character from that in the old strategy. For the calculation of incremental effects, we would enter the symbol for change in the equation shown on page 477 like this:

$$\Delta Q = k\Delta P^a \Delta A^b \Delta S^c$$

Determining or estimating the sales response coefficients themselves is much more difficult than estimating the coefficients of changes in programs. If there is solid evidence of the effects, these are more likely to be known for a whole corporation or SBU than for any single PMU. The work of determining such coefficients is now at the frontier of marketing knowledge, but they are of great importance in strategic decisions.

The strategist is on somewhat safer ground in predicting prices, but bear in mind that a relatively small percentage price error would mean a large error in estimated earnings. Costs are likely to involve the least chance of serious error, but their determination requires obtaining substantial data and cooperation from accountants and others. The amounts of the marketing costs would have been decided while the strategic program was being formulated. Now that Trimble has completed all of these calculations, we turn to the matter of presenting them.

CONTENT OF THE PLAN

The strategic program and other portions of the marketing plan *must* be stated clearly and persuasively, yet with such honesty that the proposal is given credence by the executives who will evaluate and judge it. Skill in organizing ideas and data and in written expression pays off in this task. The manager who created and is proposing the strategy is normally the one who writes the proposal, using both words and numbers—and sometimes graphics. The format, style, and number of pages have probably already been prescribed. Usually a straightforward and rather sober style is wanted, and fancy charts or language would detract seriously, even if permitted.

Actual marketing plans are always the proprietary information of a firm, and since they are kept confidential, we do not exhibit one. Nor is this the place for instruction on good business report writing, on which many books are available.[7] An exercise for writing a marketing plan is provided in Case 16-1, which has the background and data for such a plan.

Brevity in a marketing plan document is imperative. Executives who are to evaluate the plan must be able to read it in a reasonable length of time and grasp the points that the planner wants to emphasize. The Conference Board report on marketing plans stresses keeping the plan short with these passages:

> ... marketing planners in a number of companies have been warned that plans will be judged by the quality of thinking that has gone into their preparation, not by the quantity of material presented. The plan is intended to focus on the main issues and proposals, so as to ensure that it [will] be carefully read, noted and acted upon.
>
> Certain guidelines for planners ... specify the number of pages—or even half-pages—to be devoted to each topic. A case in point is a grocery products firm

---

[7]See, for example, Raymond V. Lesikar, *Report Writing for Business,* 5th ed. (Homewood, Ill.: Richard D. Irwin, 1977); and L. Brown, *Effective Business Writing,* 3rd ed. (Englewood Cliffs, N.J.: Prentice-Hall, 1973).

where it is a rule that no brand marketing plan may be longer than five pages, plus key supporting material. Says the marketing director: "The product manager is forced to focus in tightly on those areas that are critical to attaining volume and profit objectives."[8]

Although we are not going to present a plan here, we do want to indicate something of the brevity that is desirable. For this purpose, we will show how Trimble might have begun a report that followed the table of contents given in Figure 16-3. The first item with regard to Brand C might begin in this way:

1985 marketing plan—Brand C
Situation analysis

Sales History:
Brand C's dollar sales declined sharply during the past two years. Its unit sales and share of market have dropped for five years at a worsening rate.

	1980	*1981*	*1982*	*1983*	*1984*
Sales in $	$4,700,000	$4,703,000	$4,805,000	$4,410,000	$3,630,000
Sales in units	3,208,000	3,102,000	2,719,000	2,260,000	1,740,000
Change from previous year	−1%	−3%	−8%	−17%	−19%
Share of market	4.2%	3.9%	3.3%	2.6%	2.0%

Sales versus Objectives:
Brand C kept close to its objectives until falling seriously below in 1983 and 1984.

	1980	*1981*	*1982*	*1983*	*1984*
Unit sales:					
Objective	3,100,000	3,200,000	2,800,000	2,500,000	2,100,000
Actual	3,208,000	3,102,000	2,719,000	2,260,000	1,740,000
% of Objective	103%	97%	97%	91%	82%

Note: objectives have been lowered since 1982 because of company's shifting of promotional funds to Brand E penicillin.

Trimble would go on to finish the "Situation Analysis" topics (of Figure 16-3) using mainly figures rather than words, because they tell the story so succinctly and can quickly be grasped by the executives. Highlights or comments must of course be in words. Later sections of the report may also have to be presented in words—where the message cannot be expressed in numbers (e.g., the section on "Government Activity" or description of the marketing strategy).

For the remainder of the proposal of Brand C's strategy, Trimble would hope to display an impressive knowledge and insight into the situation and creativity. This planning document may be the best opportunity to gain per-

---

[8]Hopkins, *Marketing Plan*, p. 12.

sonal visibility with higher executives, as well as being the critical step in winning support for his program.

The objectives may be quite troublesome for the product manager (or whoever bears responsibility for seeing that the plan succeeds). If instead the product manager is supposed to initiate the objectives (for approval at a higher level), he or she may be in a quandary about what level to set. If the objective is set lower than anticipated results, it may easily be attained. Will higher management, however, put many resources behind a product that is expected to do rather poorly—especially when compared with other products whose planners have submitted optimistic objectives? On the other hand, overpromising may win large resources, but the manager risks being discredited when the high goals are not realized. Trimble's sales goal of more than 2.3 million units, as given in Table 16-1, presented a stiff challenge indeed—this meant raising an ailing brand's sales by 25 percent.

In the "Marketing Strategy" section (still following the Figure 16-3 format), Trimble would briefly describe the features of his plan and support them with a rationale (why this strategy would bring success in 1985). Features for Brand C might include the following:

- Market focus on young children and particularly strep throats.
- Program directed at pediatricians primarily—and secondarily at family physicians, who would prescribe Brand C.
- A product improvement with a small-size tablet for children.
- Advertising dollars concentrated on media specialized for target physicians.
- Sales promotion device that meets these doctors' expressed need for ensuring that proper dosage is taken.

Trimble should write strong and honest arguments for that strategy, showing how it (1) would achieve product differentiation important to the market; (2) would strike while the strategic window was open, ahead of competition, since the doctors strongly feel this need; and (3) would attract a market segment large enough to justify the cost and to fulfill the sales objective.

The heart of the proposal would be the projected profit and loss statement for the PMU. In Figure 16-3 there is no indication of where that would be placed, but it seems logical to include it in the "Marketing Strategy" description. Since corporations usually require a first-page summary of the plan, and since these projections would be of the greatest interest to the executives, the numbers for the key projections should also be given there.

Underlying those projections are the planner's estimates of the sales response to the marketing plan—to the main features of the marketing mix as well as their joint effects. The ratios of change in response (against the existing strategy) are given in Table 16-1. Those should have been arrived at following extensive analysis and perhaps some marketing research work. Then the planner has to draw some conclusions. In Trimble's case, the reasoning could have run like this:

> The heart of the strategy is in sales promotion, the cardboard blocks that our sales force is going to give to physicians and, through the physicians, to mothers to keep track of their children's dosage. For the certain types of physicians on whom we will concentrate (the market segments), we have good figures on the volume of penicillin prescribed. Our market survey indicates that at least 20 to 25 percent of them would switch to prescribing Brand C. That alone would increase our market share by 40 percent.
>
> This improvement would be compounded because our product would gain visibility with physicians through a new focus of our advertising media, gaining more effects per dollar. Past advertising research by our SBU suggests that this would increase our share by another 20 percent. And with the 5 percent increase in my 1985 advertising budget, this all nets out to an overall projection that the promotion response will bring a 77 percent increment in the brand's sales.
>
> Then there is also the smaller size that we will put out for children, a product improvement. While that will substantially add to Brand C's attractiveness, our past experience is that competitors rapidly copy such a simple change. Still, at least an additional 10 percent response to the product should be gained in sales. In distribution I have to face a negative factor, as a number of retailers were dropping Brand C this past year, and its sales momentum cannot occur fast enough with the new program, in 1985, to turn this distribution trend around. I estimate that the distribution function will have a negative impact on sales, about 10 percent for the year. And about price? As one of the lesser brands, we simply tag along with competition in Brand C's pricing, meeting others' prices. And so the price factor would have no effect.

Following the marketing strategy's statement and supporting reasoning would come a more-detailed section on the marketing plan. It would explicitly say what was going to be done to implement the strategy, by what departments, and with what expenditures. This would include such details as advertising media, time or space, and schedules; sales-force calls and materials; quantities and costs of sales promotion material or campaigns; prices and discounts; product improvement costs; and other marketing activities.

PRESENTATION AND APPROVAL

Except in organizations so small that one person combines the functions of both creating a plan and approving it, the authority to approve the marketing plan is vested in executives higher than the planner's level. The plan in final form is therefore submitted to that person, group, or committee. The writing of the plan is not the critical thing: rather it is that the people who hold the power of approval will understand and favor the plan.

Where there are only the planner and one person at the higher level of approval, these two would discuss the plan and have ample communication —and the formal statement of the plan would be of minor importance. In large firms that is not the case, but the planner (e.g., a product manager of a

PMU) should be able to make a personal presentation at the next level up and probably to the CME or a marketing committee of executives. These presentations are very important and carefully prepared. Besides going through the written proposal page by page, a PMU manager would want to have some visual aids to show the higher executives, to facilitate interest in and understanding of the plan. The PMU manager would rarely be enabled to make presentations (in large corporations) to top executives when they are considering final approval of all proposed plans. If the SBU executives are strongly sold on a plan, though, they should serve as strong advocates at the top level. The written statement of the plan (normally boiled down to a few pages for the CEO) must be able to carry the message clearly at higher levels.

The approval process becomes very complicated in multiproduct corporations. One problem relates to the blending of a number of submitted plans. If the firm is divided into SBUs, their head executives will receive proposals from each of the PMUs in their unit that have to be combined. They will also receive plans from each function. Similarly at the corporate level, plans for the various SBUs would be submitted. All of these must be combined, and the whole must be consistent with the total plan of the corporation and the particular SBU.

The corporate or an SBU plan may be viewed as (1) an *aggregate* of the individual function and SBU (or in an SBU, its PMUs) plans that correctly reflects their anticipations and summarizes their total income and outgo projections, or (2) the *master plan* to which all the more-detailed plans must conform. Both views should be accommodated to some degree, and agreement would be reached through negotiations between planning levels. Besides this articulation between levels, there is the dimension of time, interrelating long-term and short-term plans. At the top level is the longest perspective and knowledge of long-term conditions and objectives, and so it is there that the melding of the submitted annual plans with long-term plans tends to take place.

At the approval stage, two salient questions would be: (1) Does the proposed plan meet or exceed the objectives? and (2) Are there any alternative uses of resources that would meet the corporate (or SBU) objectives better than the marketing plan that has been submitted? The executives at the approval stage have to make efficient decisions—as the time is short before the plans have to go into action—on a complex set of alternatives. Thus they need a broadly useful decision model that accurately reflects the right objectives. An attractive model has recently been proposed by Sheth and Frazier, which they call a "margin-return model."[9] They describe their model's purpose in this way:

This paper develops a model for strategic market planning using the corporate goals of margin and return on investment as its foundation. Based on whether or

[9]Jagdish N. Sheth and Gary L. Frazier, "A Margin-Return Model for Strategic Planning," *Journal of Marketing*, Spring 1983, pp. 100–109.

not an organization's net profit margin and return both reach targeted levels, the model shows how different strategic objectives should be sought and how different strategies should be utilized to achieve the organization's ultimate margin and return goals.

Sheth and Frazier explain why net profit margin and return on investment are the most common goals of corporations. They have also created a model for classifying a firm's various planning units and specifying the type of strategy appropriate for each of them. This involves a four-cell matrix shown in Table 16-2. On the horizontal dimension, the planning is divided between those with satisfactory or with unsatisfactory targeted returns on investment. (Of course the criterion for being "satisfactory" must be defined in each firm.) Likewise, each unit is placed in a quadrant for its degree of satisfying profit margin targets. We have shown only the two general types of strategy that Sheth and Frazier would assign in each quadrant and in their language. We will not protract this discussion with further delving into their strategy categories but suggest to the reader that this may prove to be a useful model for deciding approval of strategies and resource allocations.

The results possible in this approval process are either (1) the marketing plan is turned down and returned for replanning and resubmission when it meets the requirements stipulated by the higher executive(s) or (2) it is approved. In the latter case, budgetary authority is thereby given to allocate the specified funds, and the functional departments are authorized to take the actions that implement the strategy.

SUMMARY

Chapter 16 has carried us beyond the determination of strategy, into its translation into a specific marketing plan. We naturally began with a description of the plan's nature and functions. Five purposes of the plan were stated: (1) ex-

TABLE 16-2   The margin-return model

	Targeted return	
	Satisfactory	*Unsatisfactory*
Satisfactory	Quadrant One 1. *Market Entrenchment* 2. *Market Expansion*	Quadrant Two 1. *Volume Improvement* 2. *Capital Restructuring*
Targeted Margin Unsatisfactory	Quadrant Three 1. *Margin Improvement* 2. *Product Improvement*	Quadrant Four 1. *Corporate Retrenchment* 2. *Corporate Restructuring*

Source: Condensed from Jadish N. Sheth and Gary L. Frazier, "A Margin-Return Model for Strategic Market Planning," *Journal of Marketing*, Spring 1983, p. 102.

This is the model for decisions on approving strategic plans that is discussed in the text.

plaining the situation; (2) specifying the results that are expected; (3) identifying the resources that will be needed; (4) describing the actions that are to take place; and (5) permitting the monitoring of the plan's implementation.

Organizational aspects dealt with (1) who should propose the marketing plan and (2) who should approve it. There are complications in having both short-term and long-term plans to be proposed and coordinated, as well as those from a number of PMU and functional units. A more-sophisticated "four-loop" system of Texas Instruments was also shown.

We described how the plan may be structured and showed two examples to indicate the variations in plans' formats between firms. We then discussed the critical task of projecting the response to proposed marketing actions. This basic judgment underlies the projection of any strategy. We presented a model for predicting a strategic program's results and then diagrammed some calculations with the model.

Some principles of writing plans were than used in a concrete example—the story of how our hypothetical product manager might develop the rationale for the plan to be proposed for Brand C.

We then discussed the presentation of the plan and, finally, the important matter of evaluating and approving the plan.

REVIEW QUESTIONS

1. *Distinguish between* strategy *and* plan *in the sense used in this chapter.*

2. *What would be the practical accomplishments and benefits to a firm in creating marketing plans that are adequate and realistic?*

3. *Does it suffice for a firm to prepare only a marketing plan and no others? If that were the case, what sort of difficulties might happen?*

4. *Take the viewpoint of the person who is preparing a marketing plan and will be responsible for its realization, such as a product or brand manager. To this person, what would be the plan's most important element or quality with respect to (a) obtaining its higher-up approval; and (b) when the plan is put into effect, determining what happened and why?*

5. *In a large modern organization where are the following responsibilities usually assigned: (a) approving of marketing plans, and (b) creating those plans? What is the logic of this?*

6. *Look at the "four-loop" planning system used by Texas Instruments. How does it differ from the conventional planning of a year and five years ahead? What advantages or problems do you see in TI's method?*

7. *Examine the two tables of contents of marketing plans, Figures 16-3 and 16-4. On the basis of those outlines, which may more effectively convey a marketing strategy and its rationale to top management? If you see any significant difference between the outlines, is that attributable to the nature of the particular industries (chemical manufacturing and banking)?*

8. *What is a* response coefficient? *Would you consider its determination to be one of the critical tasks or not? One of the more difficult? Explain your views.*

9. *Describe what is involved in determining a marketing mix for a particular PMU. How would you approach that job?*

10. *Describe the steps through which one should proceed in estimating the probable effects of a possible strategic program. Which items have to be projected in following our systematic model? How much effort is that task worth?*

11. *A new marketing planner has to write his first strategic marketing plan. What are some of the helpful suggestions you would offer?*

12. *Consider the work of an executive who must evaluate and then either approve or disapprove marketing program proposals from some thirty PMUs during one week of November, annually. To do that efficiently, what key questions or criteria should this executive raise when evaluating and comparing the proposals?*

Charmers, Inc. (A)

Marketing strategy and its written plans were formulated by product managers in the firm of Charmers, Inc. There were six product managers in 1983, and they reported to the chief marketing executive (CME), Paul VanArp. The deadline for submitting annual plans was November 15, at which time each PMU's manager would appear before the Marketing Committee to discuss the strategic proposals that had already been circulated to its members.

One of the product managers was Irene Moroni. Her domain was hair-care products, which consisted of three brands of shampoos and two brands of rinses. The analytical and logical processes that she went through in deciding each year's plans were naturally complex, but we will attempt to describe them—and then ask the reader to evaluate them. Only the plans for the coming year will be discussed, although the product managers had to determine longer-range ones too. Our discussion will consider only one of her bands.

THE COMPANY

In 1983 Charmers, Inc., had existed for over sixty years. Originally a maker of only cold cream, it eventually added a line of complexion products and some cosmetics. Until 1972 the company's volume and profit growth had surpassed those of the total cosmetics industry, of which it was a relatively small member. Its product policy was conservative: Make and sell a limited number of brands and items in cosmetics and skin creams, concentrating selling efforts in major metropolitan areas. Charmers' careful nursing of its advertising dollars was partially offset by relatively heavy sales promotion outlays. It emphasized trade promotions to induce merchants to stock its products and use its point-of-sale displays and demonstrators.

After 1972 came a different era for the company. A faster pace of competitive new brands and products forced Charmers to increase its new products and features—with correspondingly heavier marketing costs. In 1983 it had three main product segments, and its dollar sales were divided among them as follows:

Cosmetics	44%
Skin-care products	35
Hair-care products	15
Other toiletries	6
	100%

Since Charmers could not begin to match the marketing power of such big rivals as Procter & Gamble and Revlon, it had to carefully dole out its expenditures, as already mentioned. This strategy was not quite succeeding in keeping its business competitive with the overall cosmetics industry. In terms of "real" shipments (sales dollars adjusted for infla-

Names and data in this case are fictitious.

tion), year-to-year changes compared with those of the industry are shown in the following table:

	Percentage changes in real shipments	
Years	Cosmetics industry	Charmers, Inc.
1973–77 (average)	+4.7%	+4.2%
1978	+4.7	+3.7
1979	−4.4	−4.9
1980	0.0	−0.3
1981	+0.6	+0.1
1982	+1.7	+0.5
1983 (projected)	+3.5	+2.0

Due to generally rising prices, Charmers' financial statements presented a greater apparent growth. Moroni was interested in the more recent trends, as shown below:

Charmers, Inc.
Operating results, 1981–83
(in millions of dollars)

Years	Sales	Net income	Advertising
1981	$283	$20	$24
1982	301	23	26
1983	323	28	30

The level of sales volume might indicate that Charmers was a large firm. For the cosmetics industry it was not, as it held barely a 3 percent market share overall.

PRODUCT LINE

Sales of the hair-care products PMU were mainly in shampoos, which constituted $40 million of the $47 million sales that the line would sell in 1983. Shampoo was added by Charmers in 1960, but its three brand entries had indifferent results until 1978. Then it introduced a brand named "Crowning Glory," which featured demonstrably superior hair-cleaning ability. Its first-year sales were an encouraging $11 million but soon leveled off. In mid-1980 a new version was introduced combining both shampoo and conditioner, and the word "Combo" was added to the name. In 1983, Crowning Glory–Combo was going to sell over $33 million volume.

Moroni detected, however, that the popularity of Combo was starting to wane under competitive attacks. She still had two other brands that had been around longer. One was beginning to lose money seriously and ought to be dropped. The other had a nice niche among female senior citizens but little potential elsewhere. For the short range, the company would have to defend its shampoo market position with Crowning Glory. But how?

MARKET POSITION

Several brands held much larger shares of the total shampoo market. Moroni identified the following as the major competitors and placed their sales volume in the following order:

Head & Shoulders (Procter & Gamble)
Flex (Revlon)
Silkience (Gillette)
Pert (Procter & Gamble)
Johnson's Baby Shampoo (Johnson & Johnson)
Agree (S. C. Johnson)
Suave (Helene Curtis)

Brands that catered mainly to dandruff control are not listed, since they were not directly competitive. There were dozens of other brands that did compete, some of them strong in a few markets. Even to hold a number-ten position in this throng took diligent effort.

The initial image sought by Crowning Glory was simple and straightforward. It could be expressed as "It gets your hair cleaner, and we have laboratory proof." Indeed Charmers could feature independent laboratory findings that supported this. Its physical qualities were most like J&J Baby Shampoo (for which Johnson & Johnson was then waging a market extension strategy that led mothers to use the baby's gentle shampoo for themselves). Studies of how consumers perceived Crowning Glory, though, found them identifying it with Pert and Agree.

When conditioners were added a few years later (the Combo version) a new image —convenience—was promoted: "A single product now both cleans and conditions your hair." This was beamed at busy young women, whose attraction almost doubled market share. A secondary benefit of economy might have been stressed (but was not): "You only have to buy one product."

While sales and profits grew, Combo was still number ten in sales rank in 1983. In its target segment of youngish working women, though, it was number five. Consumers now perceived it as being similar to Pert, Flex, and Suave. Moroni might try to position its marketing strategy against any one of these:

1. Pert had a large volume to attempt to penetrate, nearly three times Crowning Glory's, and it was fairly similar. It would take a lot of nerve to go up against P&G, however.

2. Flex was battling for top position in the market and was the fastest-growing brand in dollars. However, it had enriching ingredients that actually made it unlike Crowning Glory, and Revlon was expected to launch huge new marketing efforts in 1984 to regain its total growth momentum.

3. Suave was the most similar brand in formulation, and its producer (Helene Curtis) had corporate marketing strategies very much like those of Charmers. Still, its sales volume only slightly exceeded that of Crowning Glory, so it was not such a fine target.

Moroni felt that the best choice among rival brands was to position against Suave with sales promotion efforts. Some really innovative feature that could draw sales away from various brands, however, ought to be the focus of advertising. Fortunately, the firm's laboratories had some new feature options for her.

PERFORMANCE AND OBJECTIVES

The financial performance of each brand was very important background in determining strategy, since it would be necessary to find a means of bettering it—if at all possible. The "bottom line" that product managers most tried to excel was a brand's "contribution margin." This was composed of cost of goods sold (manufacturing and shipping costs) and direct promotion costs (advertising and sales promotion). The performance figures for Crowning Glory during 1981–83 were (in thousands of dollars):

	1981	1982	1983
Sales	$23,605	$29,781	$33,216
Cost of goods sold	12,747	15,784	16,940
Gross margin	10,858	13,997	16,276
Advertising	4,013	5,062	4,982
Sales promotion	3,777	3,872	3,986
Direct promotion	7,790	8,934	8,968
Contribution margin	$ 3,068	$ 5,063	$ 7,308
Contribution % of sales	13.0%	17.0%	22.2%

When net profit is calculated from the contribution margins given above, Crowning Glory's had grown from about 4.8 percent of sales in 1981 to 8.0 percent in 1983. That was a nice improvement but only came up to the company's overall profit rate.

The task of the product managers was not to equal the past records but to meet the objectives set for the period ahead. The president of Charmers, Inc., had established a 15 percent growth in dollar sales as the target that the PMUs were supposed to meet. In the interest of restoring the firm's profit level, he also decreed that marketing expense should not rise by over 8 percent.

Outside forecasts on the market for shampoos in 1984, in dollars, indicated an 11 percent gain in 1984. Also it was forecasted that the employment of women would grow very slowly. This implied only about a 9.5 percent growth in shampoo purchases of Crowning Glory's principal market segment. In short, to meet the objectives of an 18 percent growth in contribution margin (or profits), Moroni would have to figure a way to earn an $8.7 million margin in a sluggishly growing market.

ANALYSIS AND STRATEGIES

Keeping the status quo—that is, continuing the same strategy for Crowning Glory—just would not work. To meet the earnings objective, this would require cutting back promotional costs. In the face of immense competition and the contingencies of some new attacks by mighty firms like J&J, P&G, or Revlon, that would be the way to lose market share and court disaster. Instead something different must be found that would increase sales without a corresponding increase in costs. Moroni felt that a bright new strategy might tease out more dollars than the president had indicated, so she especially looked for one.

Eventually—and after many ideas had been rejected—three optional strategies remained. She gave each a name, as follows:

Strategy 1—"Combo Hype." This would continue to hammer the appeals of wonderful cleaning power and of convenience, which consumer surveys found were still potent. However, a new way of presenting it had been created by the ad agency and had tested very well. This would be a compromise in its results: a modest rise in promotional costs would bring a modest sales growth.

Strategy 2—"Extended Usage." This was a twist on what J&J had done with its baby shampoo in adding the babies' mothers to its buyers. Crowning Glory would move the other way, convincing young mothers (having many of them among its present loyal buyers) that this was the pure shampoo they should also use for the baby. Again, a new advertising approach was ready to sell it. The main element in this campaign, however, would be sales promotion. Heavy couponing of young parents would add the impact of money saving when they also tried this brand for the baby.

Strategy 3—"Neat 'n Easy." This strategy would be based on a packaging innovation. Moroni had noticed that the supplier of closures for Charmer's bottles also made dispenser caps that are used on liquor bottles, to pour exact quantities. She had asked the supplier about a simplified one for pouring shampoo, and the supplier had designed and tested one. Now Charmers had taken an option for exclusive use on toiletries, and the dispenser top had been consumer tested. Both home testing and a sales wave experiment had shown a strong liking and purchase preference for this feature.

This third strategy would add new and unique appeals. One was again a form of convenience: no need to take the cap off in the shower and fumble around. It added to the economy appeal: no waste. And it brought a sort of science to shampooing, as the laboratory had found the optimal quantity that the cap would pour for normal hair (and twice pouring for oily hair).

Moroni went into much more detail than has been given above. All the important analyses and research reports went into her files, as also did her rationale for each strategic option. The next important step was to forecast the financial results of each of the final strategies. The figures that she arrived at are given below (again in thousands of dollars):

	Strategy 1 "Combo Hype"	Strategy 2 "Extended Usage"	Strategy 3 "Neat 'n Easy"
Sales	$36,370	$38,530	$41,500
Cost of goods sold	18,450	19,330	22,400
Gross margin	17,720	19,200	19,100
Advertising	5,320	5,500	6,500
Sales promotion	4,400	5,800	4,000
Total direct promotion	9,720	11,300	10,500
Contribution margin	$ 8,000	$ 7,900	$ 8,600
Contribution % of sales	22.0%	20.5%	20.7%
Share-of-market estimate	3.0%	3.2%	3.5%

Moroni strongly preferred strategy 3. It would yield a good 18 percent growth in earnings (contribution). Of much significance to her, it would also strengthen market share—which would aid future earnings. She recognized that the 17 percent rise in promotion costs ran counter to the president's directive to hold that to 8 percent. Actually she wished that much more could be put into advertising because such a salable feature was being added (she anticipated). However, she had found a way to steer around the objection to her requested $1.5 million ad increase. She was recommending dropping the weakest shampoo brand and also cutting back advertising of her second shampoo brand. Together this could switch $1.1 million to Crowning Glory. And this would mean that her net increase in total shampoo advertising would meet the 8 percent constraint.

Moroni's role was to analyze, conceive, and propose strategic plans, not to approve them. They would have to be submitted to the Marketing Committee. Although VanArp had given her some guidance and encouragement, her proposals might undergo quite a battering by that committee. She would make a personal appearance in their behalf, but before that the plan must be written, using the prescribed format. When she and the committee reached an agreement or compromise, that written plan would be evaluated at the top level and (maybe) approved there.

DISCUSSION

1. If you had Moroni's job, what specific reasons and calculations would you submit to support your proposal?

2. If instead you were a marketing executive with this company and were to evaluate the plans that the six product managers presented: (a) What specific criteria would you use to judge and to compare these various plans? (b) With respect to Moroni's plan for Crowning Glory, what would you identify as the serious problems faced and the assumptions that were made? (c) Which of your main doubts would she have to dispel?

3. Write a statement about Moroni's strategic program. Confine that statement to two pages, if typewritten. The Charmers, Inc., management has established the following outline of topics, so follow the sequence below (inserting a heading before each main section):

    I. Situation Analysis
       Sales, market, and earnings history. Major factors affecting the brand's past sales and popularity; major competition.

    II. Problems and Opportunities
       Major obstacles to overcome; major sales potentialities

    III. Market and Product Objectives
       Projected profit and loss statement
       Reasons for selection of these objectives (and for deviations from corporate goals)

    IV. Marketing Strategy
       Description of strategy
       New features and methods
       Effects on market and competitive positions
       Explanation of how program would reach its objectives

CASE 16-2

Charmers, Inc. (B)

Lee Soong, the Director of Information Services in Chamers, Inc., lunched with Paul Van-Arp one wintry day. Soong was in charge of all information systems, computers, and tele-communications. Charmers, Inc., was a moderately large member of the cosmetics industry (further details on the company are given in Case 16-1).

As his department's success depended on being well informed of the needs of clients around the company, Soong tried to meet with each important executive monthly. VanArp, as the chief marketing executive, was in that category. A subject stressed by Van-Arp during lunch was his relief at having completed the annual planning cycle, which he called the "yearly headache." Chatting after lunch he expanded on that problem, saying this about the plans that the product managers submitted:

Names and data in this case are fictitious. Adapted from the "Concorn Kitchens" case that was published in H. W. Boyd, Jr. and R. T. Davis, *Marketing Management Casebook,* (Homewood, Ill.: Richard D. Irwin, 1976). Reprinted with the permission of the publishers, Stanford University Graduate School of Business. © 1973 by the Board of Trustees of the Leland Stanford Junior University.

"The heart of each PMU manager's plans for each brand is a projected profit and loss statement. We must rely heavily on those projections in judging a strategy's effectiveness and what it justifies in allocating funds. These plans are intended to be a product manager's commitment to reach its projected sales and profit figures. These supposedly are based on the marketing program submitted with them. But I have my doubts; for instance:

1. Are those figures a sincere commitment or are they playing games to maximize their budgets?
2. Is there actually any relationship between those plans and past performance? What meaning should I give to those projected figures?
3. How do the sales figures relate to specific marketing inputs? If there were different expense allocations, how would they affect sales? How much thought has been given to such alternatives?
4. Should I look at those projections as a firm forecast or just a hopeful wish?

VanArp cited a recent case in which a product manager had made such glowing projections that a brand was given remarkably high funding. Because of this, actual results had been so much lower and better-performing products so underfunded that the company had missed some large profit opportunities.

Soong said he believed that a computer planning model could be designed that would largely solve those problems and also expedite the planning work. VanArp was deeply interested, so Soong promised to have a model ready soon. He and his staff were excited about this chance to serve marketing, and within two weeks he described his model in the following:

MEMORANDUM

To: Paul VanArp
From: Lee Soong
Subject: Proposed computer planning model: COSMETRIC

As promised, we have designed a computerized planning model with which your product managers can quickly compute and display forecasted results for each brand. Also they can easily experiment with optional plans, testing alternatives until they reach an optimal mix of marketing expenditures. I am naming the model "COSMETRIC."

There would be three stages in the process:

Stage 1 *Historical file.* A printout of eleven components of past performance of that brand.

Stage 2 *Planning base.* This projects and displays projections for that brand over whatever future horizon you are using (and my example is for 5 years). There are two phases of this: (a) a planning base of the key components, those that produce the performance results; and (b) the planning base profit and loss statement, which contains those projected results.

Stage 3 *Experimentation with options.* This will enable the planner to substitute any change into the planning base and to see whether it would improve the results.

Stage 1 would mainly use data about 5 years' performance, from our information system. If your people will also give me their figures on market size and our share for each brand, we will store these also for stage 1. Incidentally, for brands that we have had for less than 5 years, we will of course have a briefer historical base.

Stage 2 is extrapolated by the computer from the planning base, as straight-line projections. Being mechanical in nature, these projections will not always be appropriate. These initial projections are meant to indicate what results would be if the strategies used in the base period are continued.

In stage 3 various changes may be made, as the planner wishes. Unless very complex, they could be done on a desk calculator. For the advantage of speed and accuracy, permitting repeated iterations to test varied inputs, the computer program is recommended for stage 3. Changes may be of two types: (a) when you or your planners feel that the planning base projections erred in estimating the future market environment, and (b) when the planner wants to test alternative marketing fund allocations.

The person experimenting with optional marketing plans must have some specific estimate of the way that sales would respond to each of the marketing variables. That is a "response coefficient" that expresses, numerically, the ratio of change in sales volume for a given change in the marketing variable. That coefficient is determined by the following ratio:

$$\frac{\text{\% change in \$ sales}}{\text{\% change in \$ input of the variable}}$$

For instance, we might use the following figures for advertising:

$$\frac{\text{10\% increase in \$ sales}}{\text{100\% increase in \$ advertising}} = +.1 \text{ response coefficient}$$

Thus if you wanted to find the effect of raising advertising from $200,000 to $300,000 (a 50% increase), sales would have a resulting increase of (.1 x 50%), or 5%. And so, if sales project to $4,000,000 when advertising spending is $200,000, such a 50% increase in ad dollars would boost sales by 5% to $4,200,000. Thus $100,000 additional advertising would yield $200,000 sales gain. Of course the model would need to deduct all other expenses too, so this would be an unprofitable idea. I feel sure that we will find response coefficients to be higher than that, as with the following sales effects occurring with 0.2 and 0.4 advertising-response coefficients.

Change in advertising (percent change from planning base)	Percent change in sales for an advertising-response coefficient of:	
	.2	.4
+20%	+4%	+8%
+10%	+2%	+4%
Same Adv. as in Planning Base	Same Sales as PB	Same Sales as PB
−10%	−2%	−4%
−20%	−4%	−8%

The same thing would apply to price changes except that the effects would be inverse, since raising prices lowers sales. Therefore, price-response coefficients would be negative, as shown below:

Change in price (as % of price planning base)	Percent change in sales for a price-response coefficient of:	
	−1	−2
+10%	−10%	−20%
No change	No change	No change
−10%	+10%	+20%

I am going to illustrate how this works, in the three stages, with an example of an imaginary product that will be referred to as Brand A. I believe that the nature of the variables and the tables will be clear. I should say that we are using our factory prices, not retail. Also we carry this so-called profit and loss statement only down to the contribution margin, since that is the goal that your people plan against at the brand level. The stubs indicate whether the measurement is units (cases of 24s) or dollars and the deletion of thousands (000s). Also I am simulating a bit of dialogue with the computer as the planner sits as the keyboard.

Which brand do you want to consider?
$ Brand A

Historical file Brand A

	1979	*1980*	*1981*	*1982*	*1983*
1. Market—total cases (000s)	2,000	2,250	2,400	2,650	2,800
2. Share	.30	.29	.28	.27	.26
3. Price per case $	24.00	24.50	25.00	25.50	26.00
4. Cost of goods sold per case $	15.00	15.40	15.75	16.15	16.50
5. Gross margin per case $	9.00	9.10	9.25	9.35	9.50
6. Sales volume—cases (000s)	600	652.5	683.2	715.5	728.
7. Sales—$ (000s)	14,400	15,986	17,080	18,245	18,928
8. Gross margin—$ (000s)	5,400	5,938	6,320	6,690	6,916
9. Advertising—$ (000s)	2,000	2,500	3,000	3,500	4,000
10. Sales promotion—$ (000s)	1,000	950	900	850	800
11. Contribution margin—$ (000s)	2,400	2,488	2,420	2,339	2,116

Planning base Brand A

	1984	*1985*	*1986*	*1987*	*1988*
1. Market—total cases (000s)	3,000	3,200	3,400	3,600	3,800
2. Share	.25	.24	.23	.22	.21
3. Price per case $	26.50	27.00	27.50	28.00	28.50
4. Cost of goods sold per case $	16.875	17.25	17.625	18.00	18.375
9. Advertising—$ (000s)	4,500	5,000	5,500	6,000	6,500
10. Sales promotion—$ (000s)	750	700	650	600	550

Planning base P&L Brand A

	1984	*1985*	*1986*	*1987*	*1988*
6. Sales volume—cases (000s)	750	768	782	792	798
7. Sales—$ (000s)	19,875	20,736	21,565	22,176	22,743
8. Gross margin—$ (000s)	7,219	7,488	7,722	7,920	8,120
9. Advertising—$ (000s)	4,500	5,000	5,500	6,000	6,500
10. Sales promotion—$ (000s)	750	700	650	600	550
11. Contribution margin—$ (000s)	1,969	1,788	1,572	1,320	1,070

After examining the base file, historical and projected, the planner in my example would input the response coefficient for any variable that is to be tested. In my case only price is to be experimented with. A slightly elastic coefficient has been determined for the effects of price, in our case, of −1.2. Next, the planner inputs the new values for price that are to be considered, which first will be a lower price at a constant level over the five years. Next, a higher price level is tested, with progressively higher levels over those years, which proves to be more profitable. After that, other prices could be tested to find the optimal projection of earnings (contribution margin). In similar fashion, sales promotion or advertising could be tested at various expenditure levels.

Do you wish to override any projections? "yes"
Which line? 3
Input new values for line 24, 24, 24, 24, 24
Any others? "no"
Specify response coefficient to be used for each of 5 years
Price −1.2, −1.2, −1.2, −1.2, −1.2

Revised P&L Brand A

	1984	1985	1986	1987	1988
6. Sales volume—cases (000s)	819	839	854	865	872
7. Sales—$ (000s)	19,063	20,135	20,502	20,764	20,922
8. Gross margin—$ (000s)	5,837	5,663	5,436	5,190	4,904
9. Advertising—$ (000s)	4,500	5,000	5,500	6,000	6,500
10. Sales promotion—$ (000s)	750	700	650	600	550
11. Contribution margin—$ (000s)	588	(37)	(714)	(1,410)	(2,147)

Any others? "yes"
Which line? 3
Input new values for line 27, 28, 29, 30, 31
Specify response coefficient to be used for each of 5 years
Price −1.2, −1.2, −1.2, −1.2, −1.2

Revised P&L Brand A

	1984	1985	1986	1987	1988
6. Sales volume—cases (000s)	733	735	731	724	714
7. Sales—$ (000s)	20,155	20,549	21,194	21,724	22,136
8. Gross margin—$ (000s)	7,206	7,889	8,313	8,689	9,051
9. Advertising—$ (000s)	4,500	5,000	5,500	6,000	·6,500
10. Sales promotion—$ (000s)	750	700	650	600	550
11. Contribution margin—$ (000s)	1,956	2,189	2,163	2,089	2,051

Any others? "no"

If this model appeals to you, it might be tried with data of some of our actual brands. Let me know how we can assist you in that.

After he had absorbed Soong's ideas, VanArp was aware that he should also become informed about the availability of response coefficients. He asked the marketing research department about this and soon received the following reply.

MEMORANDUM

To: Paul VanArp, Vice President—Marketing
From: Linda Halasnik, Marketing Research
Subject: Sales response coefficients

This will answer your request for information on estimated levels of sales response to marketing variables (in dollars) that are critical ones in your strategic planning.

Regarding advertising, we can base a coefficient on three market tests of new products in which two levels of advertising expenditure were tested. These were for varied *new* products during 1981–83. In each test the relative levels of advertising outlays were similar, and the sales results were consistent, so we feel some confidence about this variable for new products. Established products might have different response rates, so we and the ad agency have studied a number of cases after the fact (not experimentally), concluding that the response coefficient is moderately lower than with new products. On this basis, we estimate that the figure given below is within 10 percent of actual response for established products.

We have more doubt about sales promotion, on which nothing has been done experimentally. We have tried to track results for the sales department on ten cases, with no control for other variables. We find that this is the most volatile variable and is least constant between product categories. I judge about ± 25 percent error should be allowed in the coefficient given below.

Price has been the most studied variable, for we have tracked 25 price changes by us and by competitors in the past few years. These observations have not been designed as experiments, and we have found substantial variations in response between product categories. I would assume a 10–15 percent error margin in that coefficient, at this time.

I have given you all those caveats so that our figures will be used with due care. The response coefficients are:

Advertising	0.3
Sales promotion	0.2
Price	-1.7

Historical file Crowning Glory

	1979	1980	1981	1982	1983
1. Market—total cases (000s)	20,914	21,820	22,872	23,759	25,630
2. Share	.014	.023	.024	.029	.030
3. Price per case $	36.00	39.26	41.25	43.20	43.20
4. Cost of goods sold per case $	20.07	21.57	22.27	22.92	22.04
5. Gross margin per case $	15.93	17.69	18.98	20.20	21.16
6. Sales volume—cases (000s)	356	502	572	689	769
7. Sales—$ (000s)	12,800	19,310	23,605	29,781	33,216
8. Gross margin—$ (000s)	5,670	8,881	10,858	13,957	16,274
9. Advertising—$ (000s)	2,040	3,500	4,013	5,062	4,982
10. Sales promotion—$ (000s)	2,100	3,100	3,777	3,832	3,984
11. Contribution margin—$ (000s)	1,530	2,281	3,068	5,063	7,308

Planning base Crowning Glory

	1984	1985	1986	1987	1988
1. Market—total cases (000s)	26,809	27,988	29,167	30,346	31,525
2. Share	.034	.038	.042	.046	.050
3. Price per case $	45.00	46.80	48.60	50.40	52.20
4. Cost of goods sold per case $	22.53	23.02	23.51	24.01	24.50
9. Advertising—$ (000s)	5,717	6,452	7,187	7,922	8,657
10. Sales promotion—$ (000s)	4,455	4,926	5,397	5,868	6,339

Planning base P&L Crowning Glory

	1984	1985	1986	1987	1988
6. Sales volume—cases (000s)	872	975	1,078	1,181	1,284
7. Sales—$ (000s)	39,240	45,630	52,391	59,522	67,025
8. Gross margin—$ (000s)	18,926	21,578	24,230	26,882	29,534
9. Advertising—$ (000s)	5,717	6,452	7,187	7,922	8,657
10. Sales promotion—$ (000s)	4,455	4,926	5,397	5,868	6,339
11. Contribution margin—$ (000s)	8,754	10,200	11,746	13,112	14,538

If you decide to use the computerized planning model, there should be more intensive study to arrive at accurate response coefficients. We would be glad to tell you about the possibilities.

VanArp decided that he wanted each of the six product managers to try using COSMETRIC to enable them to participate in deciding whether to use it in the future. He chose Crowning Glory as an actual brand with which to illustrate the model. He asked Moroni to supply the 5-year historical data and then had Soong run the planning base data with her figures, as if they were doing the 1983 planning work again with the model.

As he told Soong, he would expect that a product manager might modify the straight-line projections of the computer's, but that manager would have to write a logical justification. After completing the base plan, each product manager would be asked to set 1984–88 goals with respect to the following: (1) the brand's case sales, (2) its dollar sales, and (3) its contribution margin. Next the product manager would have to determine how to attain such goals. Prices would already have been set (to figure dollar sales). Advertising and sales promotion expenditures, as well as prices, would have to be set for improving—and eventually optimizing—the marketing mix. These changed plans would also need to be supported by explanations.

VanArp said that if the goals set up in such a plan were found to be unattainable, the product manager would explain why and then set new goals. If the new ones were projected to be attainable, the product manager would be asked to try a still higher goal. "In this way," he remarked, "we hope to come close to an optimization scheme through interactions that match inputs with outputs. While I am interested in the numbers that come out of this planning exercise, my greater interest is in how a product manager reached them. This will put that planner's thinking on display, starting with the size of the planning gap—which is the difference between one's goals and the planning base."

Early in February, VanArp held a product manager meeting where the managers were asked to repeat their 1984–88 planning, but now using the COSMETRIC model. He gave them copies of Soong's description as well as the planning base for Crowning Glory. He told them to go through these six steps:

1. Gather the planning base data on one of your brands, and have the Information Services people run the projections for 1984–88.
2. If you find that the projected data fail to show the historical trends accurately, make necessary changes. Explain them.
3. Set your goals for this brand annually, 1984–88, for each of the following: sales in cases; market share; and contribution margin.
4. Determine how much gap there is between your planning base P&L (step 2) and your goals (step 3).
5. Find new expenditure strategies that would achieve these goals.
6. Alter your goals upward or downward, if necessary, in order to gain optimal benefits from expenditures (with justifications).

DISCUSSION

1. Looking at the COSMETRIC model and its outputs from VanArp's viewpoint: (a) Which of his expectations does it seem to fulfull? (b) Which would it not offer? (c) How should he evaluate it as a desirable planning tool?
2. Looking at COSMETRIC from a product manager's viewpoint, particularly Moroni's: (a) In what ways would it benefit her? (b) In what ways would it make her planning work less efficient or possibly misguide her? (c) Do you believe that she should be in favor of adopting COSMETRIC or not? Why?
3. As you see it, what is needed in efficient, thorough, and creative planning that this model lacks? Have you any ideas for overcoming such deficiencies?

$$17$$

Implementation and Control

> *"The best laid schemes o' mice and men*
> *Gang aft a-gley."*[1]

Thus did the Scottish bard express, some two hundred years ago, the truth about what happens to plans. About mice we do not know, but the plans of businesses usually have somewhat different results than had been anticipated. In today's vocabulary, we might speak of the operation of the first "Murphy's Law" (to the effect that if anything can possibly go wrong, it will). This final chapter discusses the two phases of management that deal with plans' outcomes: *implementation* and *control*.

IMPLEMENTATION

Implementation, or execution, is where the payoff of strategy lies. "Getting the job done" is a terse way of describing the implementation phase of management. Formulating an appropriate strategic program alone is not enough, as the following examples show:

The marketing manager in a company that manufactured consumer paper products discovered that in the southeastern region, its brands had excellent distribu-

---

[1]Robert Burns, "To a Mouse" (1785), stanza 7.

tion in cities like Atlanta and Tampa but very inferior coverage in small towns. To remedy this, a strategy was devised: a point-of-sale and advertising support program for the retailers, including cooperative payments. The southeastern sales force was instructed to push this program with their small-town and rural outlets as a means of increasing sales in those outlying areas. When checking into this later, the manager found no growth in those outlying areas. Then an inquiry revealed that the representatives instead had lavished the program on their city outlets. Why? These salespeople were paid substantially by commissions on sales, and they perceived much better sales response (and thus commissions for themselves) by giving the program to their good city accounts.

A large ethical drug manufacturer had a wide line of brands that its sales force sold through the medical profession, hospitals, and drugstores. The salespeople made a complete round of their customers each three months, so sales campaigns were set up on a quarterly basis. For each three months, one brand was chosen as the featured one in a quarterly advertising campaign, which was to be coordinated with personal selling. During those months, the designated brand was to be brought up in every sales interview. Another brand would be featured during the following quarter. A time-and-duty study with sales representatives, which had another purpose, happened to find that during July (first month of the *third* quarter) about 45 percent still were pushing the featured brand from the *second* quarter. The strategic synergy of selling and advertising there was lost.

The possibilities of strategic plans miscarrying are always threatening. Our product manager, Trimble, depended on salespeople to carry his promotion to the physicians and faced risks that other functions might fail to carry out their assignments. This book has stayed within the scope of its title, *Marketing Strategy*, but would be remiss to ignore the interlocking work of implementation.

The relationship between strategy and implementation does not work in just one direction. Bonoma speaks of this and then offers the following example:

> Marketing strategy and marketing implementation form a circle or cycle, each affecting the other. While it is well known that strategy affects acts, an equally important generalization is that execution affects marketing strategy, especially over time.
>
> Despite this fuzzy boundary, it is not difficult to diagnose marketing implementation problems, or to distinguish them from strategy shortfalls. When a 50-person computer terminal sales force sells only 39 of the company's new line of "smart" microcomputers during a sales blitz in which 500+ units were forecast to be sold, is the problem with sales force management or with the strategy move to smart machines?
>
> In this example, assigning the symptoms to strategy causes does not fit well with the available evidence. . . . Assignment of the poor sales performance to marketing implementation better fits the problems. The average company sales representative earns over $50,000 annually. Consequently, there is little sales force hunger to struggle with an unfamiliar new product. Worse, sales incentive compensation on the new machines was set lower than on the old ones, a puzzling implementation move. Also, the old terminals have a selling cycle one-half as long as the new ones, and require no software knowledge or support. Here is a case where poor execution stifled good strategy.
>
> The computer example asserts an important diagnostic rule about strategy and implementation problems. When strategy is good, poor implementation can dis-

guise that fact. . . . When both strategy and implementation are on target, all that can be done to assure success has been done. When strategy is inappropriate and implementation poor, failure is the probable result. However, such failures will be intractable, because management may not see the strategic inadequacy through the mask of implementation shortcomings.[2]

Implementation work lies beyond the scope of the planner's own responsibility or authority. Nevertheless, it importantly affects what the marketing planner does. One way in which the planner can promote good implementation is to make the plan's intentions and methods clear and to follow through by making sure that the people who will direct implementation receive and understand the plans. A product manager, for instance, should maintain contact and interaction with various functional managers who would be involved in executing the plans. Arrangements are often made for a product manager to speak at sales-force conventions and occasionally to travel with some sales personnel. Another means of enhancing implementation is to know the limitations of the firm's personnel and facilities before setting plans, so that those adopted will prove feasible. Compliance with a marketing plan can also be achieved by inviting functional managers to participate by offering advice on the plan, so that they will have favorable attitudes when the time of execution arrives.

A prominent study of successful corporations has highlighted the importance of execution. Peters and Waterman have observed that

> the crucial problems in strategy were most often those of execution and continuous adaptation: getting it done, staying flexible. And that, to a very large extent, meant going far beyond strategy to issues of organizing—structure, people, and the like.[3]

The marketing strategist should have accurately assessed the organization's implementation abilities in order to judge whether in that organization a certain difficult strategy can be carried out. It is equally vital, after implementation, to determine whether performance shortcomings should be attributed to poor execution or poor strategy. Again consider what Bonoma says:

> Two points stand out to help managers diagnose marketing implementation problems for this analysis. First, poor execution masks both strategic appropriateness and inappropriateness. Therefore, when unsure of the causes of poor marketing performances, look first to marketing *practices* before making strategic adjustments. Second, a careful examination of the *how* questions, the implementation ones, often can identify an execution culprit responsible for apparent strategic problems.[4]

---

[2]Thomas V. Bonoma, Textual Note 6: *Managing Marketing*, 9-584-007. (Boston: Harvard Business School), pp. 2 and 3. Copyright © 1983 by the President and Fellows of Harvard College. Quoted by permission of Harvard Business School.

[3]Thomas Peters and Robert Waterman, Jr., *In Search of Excellence: Lessons from America's Best-Run Companies* (New York: Harper & Row, 1982), p. 13.

[4]Bonoma, *Managing Marketing*, p. 4.

The skill of monitoring is a part of control, our next and final section. Let us have a last word about good implementation and its linkage with strategy by again quoting Bonoma:

> When all is said and done, quality in marketing practice is not a guarantee of good marketplace results—there's just too much luck, competitive jockeying, and downright customer perverseness to hope for that sort of predictive accuracy. Rather, good marketing practice means high quality of management's coping behavior when faced with the inevitable execution crises threatening to blur its strategies for managing customers and middlemen. Individually, such day-to-day threats are not much to fear. Taken collectively, they are strategy-killers.[5]

CONTROL

This, our final section, is concerned with control, a process that is conducted during the implementation of the strategic plan. Control—a continuous part of the strategic-planning process—is needed to implement plans and revise strategy. We will describe what control means and includes and will relate it to the strategic-planning cycle. Next we will discuss the establishment of control, including control variables and standards. Then we will present an example of performance analysis using such standards. Finally, we will discuss diagnosis, adaptation, and contingency planning—which will lead us full cycle to control's contributions to the initial steps of the strategic management process.

Control Concepts and Purposes

Control includes the actions taken to keep the firm directed toward objectives and to bring performance and desired results closer together. Two types of activities are necessary for control: First, actions must be monitored to determine outcomes. Second, if necessary, steps must be taken to match performance with desired results, or else objectives must be adjusted to reflect attainable performance levels. Control can be both tactical (taking actions toward keeping the current periodic plan on course) and strategic (reshaping the programs to be implemented during future periods).

> The value of maintaining control over marketing strategy's implementation is exemplified in the toy industry. Its consumer demand often changes rapidly, competitive products stream into the market, and average product life is short. The toy industry may never have been more hectic than between 1981 and 1983 when video games had their bonanza.
>
> According to *Fortune* magazine, video toys rose to 30 percent of the toy industry's $6.7 billion wholesale volume in 1982. Yet in 1983 that segment of the toy industry became a disaster area. "Atari, which vaulted to the top of the toy industry and reached sales of $2 billion in 1982 lost an estimated $500 million [in 1983]. . . . After losses of more than $200 million in its electronic division, Mattel

---

[5]Ibid., p. 15.

discontinued production of its Aquarius computer, but denies rampant rumors that it will write off its entire electronics division after New Year's."[6]

Fortune contrasted companies like Kenner and Hasbro, members of the toy industry that had not plunged into video games and had prospered through that period. One reason cited was their recognition of market segments: "Their common, correct perception was that the toy industry isn't a monolith but a series of market segments. On these diverse playing fields, different moves are needed."[7]

Their other important strength was in controls, which was notable particularly in Kenner toys. As *Fortune* said, "Kenner Products, part of the General Mills Toy Group, has played a much more dangerous game with exceptional skill. It is the master of the high-rolling, hype-dependent side of the business: acquiring and exploiting licenses to the latest fad, usually characters from movies or TV shows. The failure rate is high and expensive. Yet Kenner has struck pay dirt not once but three times with a trio of the hottest licenses in history. . . . As Mendelsohn (president of the Kenner division) tells it, the trick is not so much getting new licenses fast as cutting your losers fast and exploiting the winners."[8]

Clearly, Kenner's success was mainly due to controls. It is a subject very worthy of our study.

Let us consider the managerial responsibility of controlling the activities that bring the plan to fruition. Normally, this monitoring of implementation is placed in the hands of the person who was responsible for the creation of the plan. Therefore, the role of "controller" is often associated with that of planner.

The purpose of control is to direct activities so that the plan will be achieved to the extent feasible. An adequate control system would be able to do these four things:

1. Detect when and where there are deviations from the planned results.
2. Measure the extent of deviation or falldown so that priority can be given to the worst shortcomings.
3. Permit the cause of deviation to be recognized.
4. Cope with the situation and, if possible, bring activities back in line with the plan.

In order to achieve those aims, the following items must be provided to—or within the ability of—our planner/controller:

1. *Yardsticks,* or comparative standards. These show what *should* happen when the plan is being met. A well-structured and explicit plan includes use of those yardsticks at frequent enough intervals that timely action may be taken.
2. A *feedback* or performance information system that reports often enough the results attained. It should be in the same units as and synchronized with the yardsticks for immediately reading the results.

---

[6]Steven Flax, "The Christmas Zing in Zapless Toys," *Fortune*, December 26, 1983, p. 104.
[7]*Fortune*, December 26, 1983, p. 99.
[8]Ibid., pp. 100 and 104.

3. *Diagnostic* ability and system, to analyze what has happened and to unearth the causal factor or factors. This depends not only on the personal insights and constructive problem-solving ability of the manager but also on the availability of the information on what is happening.
4. *Contingency plans* and methods and the ability to make tactical changes that tend to correct the diagnosed difficulties.

The manager of the annual plan finds that most of the year is spent in controlling the plan's execution. Return to the annual-planning calendar of Merck, Sharpe & Dohme in Chapter 16 (Figure 16-2), and you will notice the interim timing of progress reports. An alert manager receives feedback, analyzes it, and acts much more frequently than that schedule indicates.

The manager's response to some detected and analyzed deviation from plan may be any of these:

1. Take corrective action that removes the cause of the deviation.
2. Adapt to deviations that are beyond the firm's control, changing plans tactically to make the best of a changed situation.
3. Allow both the plan and the condition to continue, but profit by the experience in devising the right strategy and projecting plans for the next planning period (or year).

Naturally, the first type of action is preferred, but often it is some *un*controllable variable that is responsible. Adaptation is the next most desirable, provided that the organization has sufficient ability to adapt. Although the third alternative may seem the worst, often the deviation is too minor to make either of the other actions worthwhile. Also, it is wise to recognize when the firm faces some inexorable obstacle to its plans and not waste effort and resources in trying to combat what is beyond its influence.

A Monitoring System

The manager responsible for a strategic-marketing plan should maintain a vigilant watch over its execution. It is important to know both (1) the extent to which the desired actions were in fact implemented and (2) how effective they were. The first of these aims is the more feasible, particularly with respect to those actions taken by personnel within the firm or by some outside agency that reports accurately to the client firm. Effectiveness is much harder to determine. In the external environment many forces may be actively affecting the program, but it can be highly profitable to isolate the program's outcomes and, even better, one major element in the program. The manager's superiors in the firm may also be acutely interested in the program's results—as well as in judging that manager's ability to plan realistically and to choose winning strategy.

A monitoring system has two main parts: an information system to keep the management informed and a set of standards for implying what the information means. These are the *statistical* aspects of control that we will discuss here.[9]

Performance Information System

A strategic manager depends heavily on obtaining information. A firm's marketing information system (MIS), if one exists, should be the prime source. However, it is difficult to distinguish between an MIS and other information systems that operate in well-developed corporations. It would also be difficult to describe all the kinds of data that a manager might find to be worth the cost of acquiring and the time of interpreting. We simply state that a regular and systematic flow of information is essential to control, and we will call this flow a "performance information system." This system is connected with the total cycle of strategic planning in Figure 17-1.

In Figure 17-1 we note that what is learned during the monitoring of performance—and later when taking the action itself—creates information that should be fed back into the system. Also outputs from the information system benefit control in both the monitoring and the action-taking stages and, in addition, feed into the determination of future strategy.

Figure 17-1 is quite simplified and could be made complex if all flows were included. Information does not come solely from buyers (which would probably be in the form of surveys or consumer panel reports). It also comes from the monitoring of products' flow through the distribution channels and in various data obtained on distributors, on competitive actions, on relevant environmental changes, and on internal activities of the firm itself. Some data are reported regularly through the accounting and marketing organizations. Other data are gathered as needed—this includes specific marketing research aimed at solving unique problems facing a product, at uncovering certain market characteristics, or at defining market position.

Standards and Control Criteria

It is impractical to attempt to monitor all the actions taken to implement the marketing plan; and it is impossible to measure all relevant environmental changes. Therefore selectivity must be exercised in choosing the marketing and environmental variables that are to be measured for periodic scrutiny. Also, to establish control, one must set standards and criteria based on marketing objectives.

The marketing plan is a detailed and systematic formulation of actions to take place, including the resources to be used. The effectiveness and efficiency of performance are evaluated based on established standards. A standard is a

---

[9]A specific illustration of a monitoring system is given in our Case 17-1 at the end of this chapter. Rather than duplicate such material during this discussion, we refer you to that case.

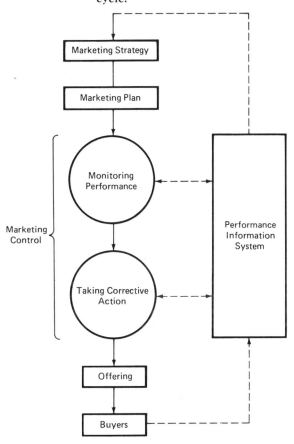

FIGURE 17-1. Marketing control and the performance information system. The broken lines represent decision inputs into the strategy cycle.

criterion, or acknowledged measure of comparison. The chosen standards should reflect the uniqueness of the organization and its resources, as well as the more critical achievements needed to realize the strategic plan. Frequent comparison of the selected variables' levels of achievement with the marketing plan may keep the organization on course to reach its objectives. Attainment of objectives also depends on the ability to take corrective actions when significant variation is discovered.

The selection of standards and criteria levels should flow from the marketing plan. It is important that the standards support the strategic decisions and the entire strategic-planning process. Suppose, for example, that all salespeople are issued a standard of making twenty calls per week. A salesperson

FIGURE 17-2. Selecting variables to establish standards and to control performance

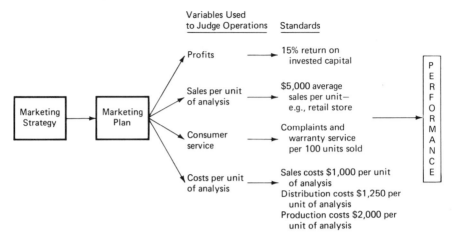

could meet this standard by arranging travel plans that would simply involve making twenty contacts with the most convenient customers rather than focusing on those who are the main targets of the current strategy. In addition, such a standard obviously would not optimize the sales calls, because it makes no allowance for varying travel times and could lead to brief calls that are ineffective in the larger territories.

Figure 17-2 contains a bare outline of steps in a systematic approach to selecting variables for control. This merely shows examples of the types of variables that may be selected. The specific marketing plan and type of organization should structure that selection. The standards indicated in Figure 17-2 are merely some averages, but in practice various standards may be set for categories of units or put on sliding scales (e.g., $20,000 sales for the largest category of supermarket; $4,000 for the average convenience store; distribution costs $117 per 1,000 pounds in zone 9).

Taking Corrective Action

Once a manager has the data and adequate comparisons of performance against standards, steps should be taken to determine whether any corrective action is needed and would be warranted, considering the cost and interval before such action could take effect. The first step in this will be called "performance analysis"—in which the data are broken down to facilitate their interpretation. This would be followed by diagnosis and determination of any action. Our friend Chester Trimble and his penicillin Brand C will again serve as the example.

Performance Analysis: A framework developed by Hulbert and Toy for marketing control integrates the concepts of marketing strategy and plans

TABLE 17-1 Brand C: Variance between planned and actual performance, first quarter of 1985

Item	Objective	Actual	Variance
Sales			
Units sold	580,000	576,000	(4,000)
Price per unit ($)	2.10	2.18	+.08
Dollar sales ($)	1,218,000	1,255,700	+37,700
Total market (units)	29,000,000	32,000,000	+3,000,000
Share of market (%)	2.0	1.8	(0.2)
Costs			
Variable cost per unit ($)	1.65	1.75	+.10
Contribution margin			
Per unit ($)	.45	.43	(.02)
Total contribution ($)	261,000	247,700	(13,300)

Source: Format based on James M. Hulbert and Norman E. Toy, "A Strategic Framework for Marketing Control," *Journal of Marketing*, April 1977, p. 13.

    Data are hypothetical.

with the concepts of managerial accounting.[10] The focus of their approach is to evaluate marketing performance versus the marketing plan. However, the marketing plan may provide inappropriate criteria, or unanticipated events may have occurred during the planning process. Therefore, this framework takes these kinds of planning variances into acccount.

    The first step in strategic control is to evaluate performance according to standards derived from the marketing plan. Table 17-1 shows the result of operations for Brand C during the preceding time period. The analysis of differences between actual and planned performance has limited potential for diagnosing the causes of problems. Rather, its major benefit is in the identification of areas where problems exist.

    Sources of variance for Brand C may be differences between (1) actual and planned total market size, (2) actual and planned market share, or (3) price/cost per unit. A variance decomposition of these three variables aids in understanding causes of variance and should relate to strategy variables in marketing planning. The procedures used for decomposition are consistent with recommended accounting practice.

    The following symbols are used in the analysis:

$$S = \text{share of total market}$$
$$M = \text{total market in units}$$
$$Q = \text{quantity sold in units}$$
$$C = \text{contribution margin per unit}$$

---

[10]This section has been adapted from James M. Hulbert and Norman E. Toy, "A Strategic Framework for Marketing Control," *Journal of Marketing*, published by the American Marketing Association, April 1977, pp. 12–20.

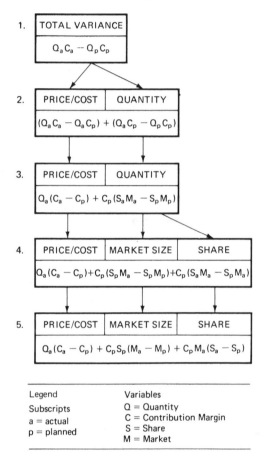

FIGURE 17-3. Decomposition of variances in comparison with marketing plan. This analysis is based on standards developed in the marketing plan.

Source: Hulbert and Toy, "A Strategic Framework for Marketing Control," p. 19.

The subscript *a* denotes *actual* values, and *p* denotes *planned* values.

The process of calculating the variances in Hulbert and Toy's method is charted in Figure 17-3. Note that steps 3 and 5 are optional equations that may be simpler to calculate. We next illustrate the application of Figure 17-3 in the case of Brand C that we have been following, using data from Table 17-1. These calculations are displayed in Table 17-2 through step 4, which suffices for our discussion.

TABLE 17-2 Calculation of variance decomposition compared with marketing plan
for Brand C

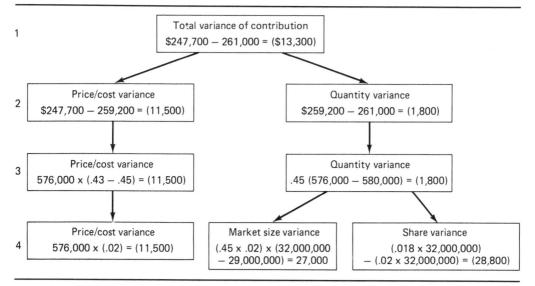

Data are hypothetical. These calculations follow the model shown in Figure 17-3.

Following the process in Figure 17-3, the price/cost variance is given by

$$(C_a - C_p) \times Q_a = (.043 - .045) \times 576,000$$
$$= -\$11,500$$

and the quantity variance is given by

$$(Q_a - Q_p) \times C_p = (576,000 - 580,000) \times .45$$
$$= -\$1,800$$

The sum of these contribution variances yields the overall unfavorable contribution variance of $-\$13,300$.

The second stage of the analysis is the further decomposition of the quantity variance in contribution into the components due to penetration (share) and total market size.

The variance in contribution due to share is given by

$$(S_a - S_p) \times M_a \times C_p = (.018 - .02) \times 32,000,000 \times .45$$
$$= -28,800$$

and the market-size variance is given by

$$(M_a - M_p) \times S_p \times C_p = (32,000,000 - 29,000,000) \times .02 \times .45$$
$$= +\$27,000$$

The sum of the market-size and share variances yields the overall unfavorable volume variance in contribution of $1,800.

The variances can be summarized as follows:

Planned profit contribution		$261,000
Volume variance		
Share variance	$ (28,800)	
Market-size variance	27,000	
		(1,800)
Price/cost variance		(11,500)
Actual profit contribution		$247,700

Variances may occur owing to problems in forecasting market potentials or environmental changes. This would be a mistake in the future-assessment stage of our strategic-planning process. But whatever the variances are, there should be attempts to *assign responsibility,* whether it is for poor planning or poor execution of the plan.

At this point a planning gap is identified for Brand C, but more analysis is needed to understand the variance. So far, the analysis has used the existing marketing plan to review performance. From this point an additional decomposition of variance could be made after determining a revised plan, a further stage in the Hulbert and Toy method that we have been describing—but which will not be included here. By such analysis, the extent to which planning was responsible for the variance could be isolated from that which was due to performance of the plan.

The product manager for Brand C is likely to be more interested in something else: in determining *why* the performance deviated from the plan's objectives. The product's contribution to profits (which is a margin earned before certain indirect charges and income taxes) fell just 5 percent short of the objective. Upon closer examination, however, we find the results to be even more unfavorable. That the actual market turned out to be 10 percent greater than forecasted was a break for which the manager could take no credit. Without that greater market, the contribution would have been about 17 percent worse than planned. As Table 17-2 tells us, the widest deviation in earnings was due to falling short in market share, and less than one-fourth of the shortfall was attributable to price/cost variance.

As manager, Trimble would dissect the data in Table 17-2 as much as possible. He might observe further that costs overran the objectives to a substantial degree, and had prices not risen, the cost variance would have exceeded $50,000. Did prices rise because the industry was affected by rising costs of materials or other items? If costs did not rise due to such causes, did the fault lie in anything that would be controllable? What? Are prices—or costs—likely to stay up or even continue to rise?

Other aspects of the variance should be studied also. For instance, was the high level of industry sales relative to Trimble's objectives his error in forecasting or not? If it was, he may learn how he went wrong. If it was not, what causes were behind rising demand—and will they last? The market-share deviation also poses problems. While a mere 0.2 percent of market deviation may seem small, it was one-tenth short of the planned share. Was it the fault of the strategy? Or was it due to competitors staging a more vigorous marketing effort than expected? Or spending too little? Or what? On the other hand, considering that 1.8 percent represented a gain over the predicted current planning gap of 1.5 percent, is it a bit too early to judge how much the strategy will stimulate sales? This deviation also raises a question of timing: Should Brand C's strategy be changed now in the second quarter of the year? Or should change await the plans for next year? This raises the matter of whether Trimble has any options right now and, if so, how long it would take to implement any change.

We have mentioned only a few of the many ideas or hypotheses that can be gleaned from the analysis of feedback data and comparisons with standards. Their richness depends on the planner's depth of experience and grasp of the current environment. The data owe their existence to someone's forethought, someone who anticipated the problems and questions that would arise. In our era of telecommunications and computers, enormous amounts of data are available from data banks and information systems. These are easily processed into miles of computer printouts—but that is not what the strategic planner needs and can in fact become a paper blizzard. The planner merely needs well-selected data and appropriate calculations to make possible efficient analysis and find the strategic angles.

Diagnosis. Beyond the analyzed data comes *diagnosis*, which explains the situation and its causes. The significance of any unearthed problems should be assessed, and judgment should be made about whether or not specific factors in the situation are controllable by the firm. If controllable, a decision is needed on what action would be effective and whether it is warranted (given time, cost, and risk assessment). If uncontrollable, the decision is how to adjust and make the best of the situation.

Contingency planning can be invaluable in the control process. This involves careful advance vision of what important deviations from the planned environment may materialize. Doing this by creating alternative scenarios of the future (multiple scenario analysis) was discussed in Chapter 2. The second essential part of contingency planning is to have predetermined courses of action to be implemented if a particular contingency requires some time to design and conduct (and so its needs should be anticipated). Both types of research are needed for control: tracking to indicate where there are problems or new opportunities, and diagnostics to find what to do about it.

A competent marketing planner has gained insights that help him or her detect new developments and evaluate their significance. This planner has also had experience or can use the experience of others to form principles for choosing actions. The competent planner does not depend on the firm's internally generated data on sales or other data from the accounting system. For the strategist such data are largely history—and a superficial view of marketing history at that. Strategists need external sensors that may identify a groundswell long before its results become evident to less-alert watchers. They do not learn and interpret important developments by chance, but rather by being prepared and knowing what to look for.

A textbook cannot arm its readers with such investigative ability, but it can emphasize the value of such skills if marketing is one's career. The strategist particularly looks for indicators of important turning points in market behavior and needs, in new technology that is relevant to his or her strategic unit, and in the life stages of product categories and brands.

As a product is approaching readiness for market launching, for example, the strategist seeks the optimal situation for the product launch and is very interested in reported prices or unusually vigorous promotions of the firms already in the target market. After launching, sensitive data may include the extent of distribution, brand awareness and acceptance, and extent of repeat buying. When strong growth has happily begun, monitoring would shift to watching competitors' strategies and market shares. Market testing of new ideas for keeping one's product differentials ahead of competitors may be timely. Data that define markets would now have to be refined to search for any distinct and worthwhile segments of buyers, as well as how to win them. These data would anticipate the slackening growth that all the rivals are enjoying and a more savage struggle ahead when the fittest will survive in saturated markets. As that period is approached, the strategist will want to not only identify users' product dissatisfactions and unfilled needs but also stimulate R&D to come up with product improvements and proliferations that can strengthen the brand's market position. Turning points, then, need to be anticipated and correctly identified when they do occur so that marketing action will be timely. We have merely sketched a few ways in which developments are to be watched for and interpreted, to emphasize that control should be a very active and imaginative stage of strategic management.

Control has an important benefit in aiding decisions about when new products should be brought out, or other methods such as acquisition should be used, to preserve the firm's marketing position and keep it dynamic. This input to the planning of future short- and long-range periods brings us full cycle to the beginning of a strategic plan. There is a second link between control and future marketing planning too: The control process should have increased the knowledge and the planning skills of the strategists. Competent control will build more competent strategists.

SUMMARY

In this two-part chapter, the first part discussed the *implementation* of strategy. Good strategies can be frustrated when their implementation fails. We said that implementation is as vital as strategy, whose crucial problems most often lie in execution. This is a vast subject on which there was room only for comment.

Control formed most of the content of this chapter and was defined as the actions taken to keep the firm directed toward objectives and to bring performance and desired results closer together. Four purposes of an adequate control system were stated (detecting deviation, measuring the extent of deviation, recognizing the cause, and coping with the situation). To achieve those purposes, four things must be provided in the control system: standards, feedback, diagnostic ability, and contingency plans.

A system for monitoring implementation was diagramed and briefly described. Then the matter of steps for establishing standards was considered. A process for decomposing variances in order to guide corrective action was described. This was then applied to our prior example of Brand C. We discussed some angles and some questions that would particularly intrigue the brand's manager. Contingency planning's nature and vital role was the fourth part of the system discussed. Finally, we covered diagnostic information and analysis and some of the specific developments that may confront a product's manager (or general marketing management).

The book ends here, but strategic planning would continue in its long- and short-range cycles. Control, it was pointed out, feeds into planning for future periods.

REVIEW QUESTIONS

1. *In the following pairs of activities, state which—if either—is more essential to a firm's operations: (a) control or implementation? (b) implementation or strategy? (Another way of viewing this question would be: In which activity would you want to allocate the best and top-paid talent if you were the CEO?)*

2. *Product managers like Chester Trimble have serious need for the field sales representatives to implement their strategic plans, in contacts with buyers. What might Chester do to gain such cooperation?*

3. *Looking at the topic of question 2 from the opposite viewpoint, what difficulties might the sales manager face because the organization has put products under a number of product managers? What might a CME (like VanArp in Case 16-1) do to avert or minimize such difficulties?*

4. *What principal things should a control system accomplish in order to enable effective management?*

5. *What must a planner possess in order to exercise ample marketing controls?*

6. *Due to a tragic accident, in 1980 the Ford Motor Company faced a crisis with its Pinto line, which had been one of the most popular subcompact cars. When a passenger was killed in a fire alleged to have been caused by*

bad location of the fuel tank, the notoriety that resulted gravely affected Pinto sales. (a) Would you say that this problem arose from a controllable or an uncontrollable force? (b) If the company had an almost perfect control system, what could it have contributed to Ford's coping well with that crisis (after the accident had happened)? It may be helpful first to identify some of the options that might have been followed and then consider how a control system might spotlight or reveal them.

7. *Study Figure 17-2. (a) How might the system charted there benefit performance? (b) What is missing or what are the serious limitations in that system, as there presented?*

8. *What is meant by* decomposition of variances? *How does that aid a manager? What kinds of data or knowledge does it require?*

9. *When noting a significant deviation (or gap) or actual results versus plans, what specific questions should a manager ask before taking any action?*

10. *Define* contingency planning. *Your book describes it as "invaluable." Does that mean that strategic planning cannot exist without it? Explain.*

11. *It is said that an excellent marketing strategist has great abilities in (a)* tracking *and (b)* diagnosis. *What do those terms mean, in plain words? What does that person require in order to track and to diagnose?*

Charmers, Inc. (C)

Charmers, Inc., was a manufacturer of cosmetics and toiletries that were sold nationally in the United States, to consumers through retail outlets. The firm, its market position, and its strategic planning were described in Case 16-1. That case focused on the planning tasks of a product manager, Irene Moroni, and a brand of shampoo for which she was responsible, called Crowning Glory. This case will also deal with that brand with regard to its performance when the 1984 strategy was implemented.

The product managers closely monitored the actual results attained by their brands and took such steps to counter deficient performance as were practicable. They naturally sought to fulfill or even surpass their annual objectives. Sometimes they were dealing with quickly controllable variables that could bring results back into line with objectives. When that was not possible, an accurate diagnosis might lead to more accurate expectations and more effective strategies in the future.

A product manager usually had quick weekly feedback on sales data from the factory level, but the management information system (MIS) provided feedback monthly or bimonthly on most internal factors. It also provided reports of data purchased from market data services. The MIS was supplemented with custom surveys that obtained more special insights into situations at the consumer or distributor levels.

Informally, the product managers often discussed developments with marketing executives. Formally, there were quarterly sessions at which all the product managers and executives met, often for a full day, to receive each brand's report and to discuss optional actions. These quarterly reviews were major events for a product manager and were preceded by weeks of analyzing and conceiving changes in programs. That was what Moroni had been doing, for instance, as she prepared for the quarterly review on July 9, 1984. She had succeeded in gaining approval for her strategy 3 in Case 16-1, and we will read some of the data on its results for the first six months of 1984.

PERFORMANCE FEEDBACK

The marketing management at Charmers, Inc., had designed a condensed form on which the MIS reported the key items of feedback to each product manager. This was the main document on which each manager concentrated. It was issued for each month, with cumulative reports also for each quarter. It included the three kinds of performance of greatest interest: sales revenues, costs, and contribution margin earned by the brand. The standard format had four columns: (1) comparison with the past performance, (2) planned current performance, (3) actual performance, and (4) variance from plan.

The first exhibit will be that of this key performance report on Crowning Glory for the first six months. This is one of several such pages that Moroni received in this format, as there were also monthly and quarterly reports (comparing the identical period of the previous year). The one shown below is illustrative and appropriate to this case.

Names and data in this case are fictitious.

Crowning Glory performance analysis
January–June 1984

| Item | 1983—Year | 1984—First six months | | |
	Actual	Planned	Actual	Variance
Revenues:				
Sales (case units)	769,000	469,000	438,000	(31,000)
Price per case $	43.20	43.10	43.14	.04
Revenues $	33,216,000	20,200,000	18,895,000	(1,305,000)
Total market (cases)	25,630,000	13,747,000	13,900,000	153,000
Share of market	3.0%	3.4%	3.15%	(.25%)
Costs:				
Variable cost per case $	22.04	22.20	22.44	.24
Contribution:				
Per case $	9.50	9.60	8.29	(1.21)
Total $	7,308,000	4,502,000	3,629,000	(873,000)

The data shown above were only some key variables and provided the first stage of perfor-mance analysis. Many other variables could be dissected and reported by the firm's MIS.

SALES ANALYSIS

Sales statistics were continually monitored by the product managers as well as various marketing executives. The MIS provided those for actual shipments from the Charmers factory on a weekly basis. Data were given on sales in both dollars and in units (usually cases). Moroni was more concerned about unit sales, since they avoided distortions of changing prices. To avoid detail, we will exhibit the data fed back to her, of case sales, on a monthly basis, giving the actual results for the first six months of both 1983 and 1984, as well as plans for the present year.

Factory sales of Crowning Glory
First six months of 1983 and 1984
(in thousands of cases)

	1983 actual	1984 planned	1984 actual
January	66	76	70
February	62	73	63
March	68	80	63
April	68	81	77
May	71	84	81
June	62	75	78
Total	397	469	432

The sales statistics from the MIS could be provided for any of the sales-force dis-tricts, as well as for the four sales regions into which the salespeople were organized. The case sales for the first two quarters and for the combined first half are given below, com-pared with Moroni's sales objectives for the 1984 first half.

Factory sales of Crowning Glory by selling regions
First half of 1983 and 1984
(in thousands of cases)

	First quarter		Second quarter		Total first half			
	Actual		Actual		1983	1984	1984	
Sales Region	1983	1984	1983	1984	actual	planned	actual	Variance
East	42	43	43	60	85	101	103	+2
Central	47	48	48	55	95	112	103	−9
South	67	63	69	67	138	161	130	−31
West	40	42	41	54	81	95	96	+1
Total	196	196	201	236	399	469	432	−37

The factory sales data were also tabulated by size of cities or counties, by key distributor accounts, and by order size. A marketing manager also could make special requests for analyses.

RETAIL AUDIT DATA

Charmers, Inc., was a subscriber to a national audit service that measured the movement of merchandise at the retail store level. These data were much more sensitive to the

Retail sales of Shampoo and Crowning Glory
January–April 1984
(based on retail store audits)

	Percentage of total U.S. sales	
Territory	All shampoo brands	Crowning Glory
East		
New England	5.6%	5.7%
Metropolitan New York	3.5	2.5
MidAtlantic	12.1	15.5
Subtotal	21.2	23.7
Central		
East Central	14.4	15.6
Metropolitan Chicago	2.9	1.6
West Central	6.9	7.0
Subtotal	24.2	24.3
South		
Southeast	22.8	20.4
Southwest	11.3	9.8
Subtotal	34.1	30.2
West		
Metropolitan Los Angeles	3.6	5.6
Pacific and Mountain	16.9	16.2
Subtotal	20.5	21.8
Total U.S.	100.0%	100.0%

changes in consumer purchase levels than the factory data. However, they were reported on only bimonthly periods. The reports for the first two such periods had been analyzed when Moroni was evaluating Crowning Glory's position at the beginning of July 1983. As the May–June period results had not arrived, only the first four months could be used as she prepared for the review meeting.

The audit service gave the retail sales movement for all major brands of shampoos and for private labels, but we are showing only those on Crowning Glory. The audit data were divided into territories that corresponded with boundaries of Charmers' sales organization, within each of the four regions. The following table lists the first four-month results for these areas with regard to the distribution of sales volume for the total of all shampoo brands in comparison with that of Crowning Glory.

Another series of data from the retail audit reports was the share of market (i.e., percentage of total shampoo sales) that Crowning Glory was obtaining. Also reported was the number of and percentage of audited retail stores that were stocking Crowning Glory during the audit period. The combined data for the first four months of 1984 and of Moroni's market-share objectives are as follows:

Retail market share and distribution of Crowning Glory
January–April 1984

Territories	Market share % of total sales		% of outlets stocking Crowning Glory
	Planned	Actual	
East			
New England	2.6	3.1	75%
Metropolitan New York	3.1	2.6	68
MidAtlantic	3.6	3.9	84
Average	3.2	3.5	77
Central			
East Central	3.6	3.5	88
Metropolitan Chicago	2.4	1.4	59
West Central	2.9	2.9	80
Average	3.1	3.0	81
South			
Southeast	3.3	2.7	60
Southwest	2.6	2.0	62
Average	3.0	2.3	61
West			
Metropolitan Los Angeles	5.0	4.7	90
Pacific and Mountain	3.2	3.1	82
Average	3.7	3.4	84
Total U.S. average	3.3	3.0	73%

Note: Metropolitan area figures are excluded from adjoining territories.

The above types of data were furnished for all major brands and for each reporting period. Also the size of city or county and types of stores (chain or independent and sales volume bracket) were reported. Charmers had been obtaining such data on Crowning Glory for over five years.

OTHER DATA

One other syndicated data service was retained to report market data. This was a firm that maintained consumer panels, people who recorded their purchases and related data on a frequent basis. This data service furnished monthly data. We will show the cumulated data from January through May, which Moroni had in hand when making her diagnosis of Crowning Glory's position, on women's shampoo purchases. Alongside those figures we are indicating the relative importance of age segments with data on the proportions of U.S. females, aged 18 and over, by age bracket.

Females who purchased Crowning Glory
January through May, 1983 and 1984
(percentage of panel members reporting)

Age bracket	Percentage of U.S. females in age bracket in 1983	Percent in bracket who purchased Crowning Glory	
		1983	1984
18–24	17.1%	4.7%	3.5%
25–34	22.3	5.4	4.6
35–44	15.8	4.9	4.1
45–54	13.5	3.6	3.0
55–64	13.4	3.3	2.9
65 and over	17.8	3.6	4.5
Total	100.0% average	4.4%	3.9%

For the panel data, too, there were a number of breakdowns and variables beyond those shown above. These included purchases of other brands, region, size of community, and type of store where purchased.

Beyond the kinds of data illustrated, there were those from an annual survey conducted by Marketing Research on consumer brand attitudes and images, for the main products sold by Charmers. The brand's advertising agency routinely had survey data on brand awareness, advertising viewing or readership, and advertising audiences. Moroni's files already contained data from such studies made at some point during the first half of 1984 and comparable reports from the past few years. The Marketing Research department was ready to design and conduct various other studies upon request. Also the various data services could perform custom analyses of their data beyond those already subscribed for. These additional services involved substantial charges against a brand and therefore were ordered only after careful consideration. Normally it would also involve a one-month to three-month wait to receive customized data.

Moroni approached her study of the various feedback data with the objectives and anticipations in the 1984 Crowning Glory strategic plan in mind. Her plans and underlying analysis have been described in Case 16-1. She also had a wealth of information on events that had already taken place during 1984. This case presentation is not extended to describe what had been happening in the outside environment during that period. Within the firm, the intended actions for Crowning Glory had mainly been implemented. One difficulty had arisen with regard to the new dispenser cap. The factory had initially encountered serious quality problems with the assembly-line installation of that cap. A minor number of faulty packages had mistakenly been released for distribution in January. The delay in production while those problems were being solved lost about 4 percent of orders placed for January. Also the new cap cost about five cents more than expected. One other negative factor was that the sales-training and presentation material for the 1984 Crowning Glory campaign did not reach some sales districts until late in January (instead of reaching them before Christmas). On the whole, however, the marketing plan had normal implementation.

DISCUSSION

1. Perform a variance-decomposition comparison with the marketing plan for Crowning Glory. This analysis would utilize the formula that was charted in Figure 17-3. The data are given in the first table of this case, entitled "Crowning Glory Performance Analysis." After you have completed your calculations, study them. What does your analysis suggest regarding the aspects or problems that need closer study?

2. Reconsider the objectives, anticipations, and logic underlying the strategic program that Moroni had recommended in Case 16-1. What significant developments or experiences occurred during the first half of the planned year, 1984? Where have the favorable or adverse results taken place? What are your hypotheses regarding the causes of those results?

3. On the basis of the incomplete evidence that has been shown to you, what seem to be the relevant actions that Moroni might take tactically during the balance of the current year (1984)? What does your analysis suggest with regard to changing strategy for the future, especially for 1985 marketing?

4. The data given in this case have been somewhat inadequate to enable you to answer the above questions with much assurance. Make a list of other data that you would like to have in order to make a sufficient analysis to identify clearly the problems of Crowning Glory. What would you also like to find out to aid the product manager in determining more effective marketing strategy? (Some of the desirable data may have been mentioned in the case, but your imagination may conceive of other valuable data.)

ADDITIONAL CASES

CASE A

Bloomington Bank and Trust Company

Bloomington Bank and Trust (BBT hereafter) is a state-chartered commercial bank located in an affluent eastern state. The bank's assets currently stand at approximately $35 million, a figure which ranks the bank as medium-sized in comparison to the other commercial banking institutions of the state. At the close of 1975 BBT found itself in better shape than ever, at least in pure numbers. Demand deposits had increased 14.6% during 1975 (55% since 1970); likewise, time deposits had grown 10% in the past year and 75.4% in the recent five-year period. Also, total assets had risen 62.3% and total capital had grown 43.5% since 1970.

The bank's market had also grown geographically in recent years, as branches had opened in three area towns, and plans were being formulated for the creation of two more. Formerly bank management had been hesitant about expanding into new towns, fearing that the bank would lose its close identification with Bloomington residents. However, at the same time, larger commercial banks were not hesitating to install branches of their own in Bloomington, and as a result, BBT had gradually been losing market share. BBT's first branch opening was experimental in nature but its resulting success encouraged bank officers to plan for more in the future.

Now that BBT had established itself as a highly successful bank not only in its base town but in the state's most competitive banking region as well, its president, Jim McGowan, felt it an opportune time to retire. He announced his plans in June of 1975, and a search for his successor, who would take office at the start of 1976, was immediately initiated.

On January 2, 1976, McGowan's successor, Brian McQuade, began his stewardship as president of BBT. McQuade had been a vice-president of the state's largest commercial bank before accepting his new post and possessed an exceptional financial background, developed from previous executive positions at banking institutions throughout the East. The bank's Board of Directors was extremely satisfied with its selection, and McQuade felt confident that he would continue where Jim McGowan left off.

The new president's first task involved an investigation of BBT's past and present strategies. He studied all memos left to him by the bank's former president and analyzed the programs employed by the institution, but still, after weeks of painstaking research, McQuade felt his efforts were wasted. Upon accepting his executive role, McQuade had pledged to the Board of Directors that he would continue to lead BBT toward highly successful operation, that he would continue to strive for goals toward which the bank had progressed under the leadership of Jim McGowan. Unfortunately McQuade could not determine what these goals were. Nowhere had the former president explicitly stated any formal goals or objectives by or towards which the bank would operate. In fact, the only material that McQuade could proceed on was a list, compiled by himself, of various strategies BBT had undertaken in the last 15 years. This list, however, was an inadequate basis from which to plan future programs.

Next, McQuade conferred with four of the bank's top executives in hope that they might clarify the problem. He found that all were top-flight and knowledgeable concerning strategies they were responsible for, and information gathered from these meetings was helpful to McQuade in determining the commercial and consumer markets toward which BBT concentrated activity. Nevertheless, McQuade still could not uncover a list of specific goals or objectives around which past strategies were planned or toward which future strategies might be geared.

Finally, the new president decided to meet with Jim McGowan himself. The meeting lasted approximately three hours, and McQuade left the McGowan home with a clearer picture of the past administration's planning process; however, planning for the future was as vague a concept as ever. In his conference with BBT's former chief executive, McQuade confirmed what he had suspected; that is, all programs had been initiated *instinctively* by McGowan. Whenever McGowan had felt that a new program was "right" for the bank, he had ordered it implemented. Perhaps McGowan had acted toward some type of long-term goals subconsciously, but they were not formal or written objectives. Moreover, McGowan himself could not articulate these subconscious goals for McQuade.

Now McQuade knew that the greater part of his first year as BBT's president would have to be spent formulating goals and objectives by which the bank would operate. He felt that BBT, especially now that it was expanding significantly each year, could no longer be operated according to an executive's intuition. What the bank needed now was a written operating plan. If such a plan could be drawn up, he felt, new strategies could be implemented as part of the plan. Also, any proposed strategy would be considered by management only if that strategy was consistent with the goals set forth in the plan. Conceptually, the idea seemed perfect, but McQuade knew that it could fail in actual practice. In fact, McQuade's former bank had attempted to utilize an operating plan. In theory that plan was still in existence; in practicality it was all but useless. Still, McQuade felt that the situation was different in Bloomington. BBT was but $\frac{1}{60}$ the size of the other bank (by assets), and interests here were not as diverse and uncontrollable as those in the larger bank. McQuade knew that an operating plan could work at BBT if it were wisely and efficiently conceived.

McQuade also knew that he wouldn't be able to draw up the plan himself. Consequently, he informed his four top aides of his plans and asked them to think about the bank's operations: where they presently stood and where they should head in the future. McQuade also realized his limitations as a professional planner; therefore, he called an outside consultant, Dr. Richard Baker, whom he knew to be an expert in business planning.

On May 4, 1976 McQuade and Baker met in McQuade's office. The bank president explained the situation to Baker stressing the need for an operating plan that would be specific enough to establish direction towards predetermined goals yet flexible enough to encompass innovative strategies. Baker responded favorably to the idea and felt confident that a written operating plan was a viable system for management of BBT. He immediately suggested that a schedule be drawn up for the completion of the various stages involved in creating the plan and that every effort be made to follow the timetable. The two men spent the remainder of the evening developing the schedule (Exhibit A). As the meeting ended, Baker suggested to McQuade that work begin on accomplishing Task #1 as soon as possible.

The suggestion was actually unnecessary as Brian McQuade had already planned to confer with his department heads the very next morning. McQuade was now firmly committed to the planning idea, and made this known to his officers when he arrived at the bank on May 5. A meeting was arranged for May 18 at which Baker and McQuade would meet with McQuade's four top aides: Jim Carlson (Commercial and Mortgage Lending, Marketing), Bob Delaney (Operations, Personnel), John Erickson (Trust, Portfolio Investments),

EXHIBIT A Bloomington Bank and Trust Company—Planning Milestones

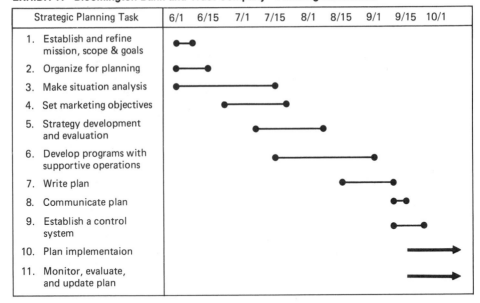

Strategic Planning Task	6/1	6/15	7/1	7/15	8/1	8/15	9/1	9/15	10/1
1. Establish and refine mission, scope & goals									
2. Organize for planning									
3. Make situation analysis									
4. Set marketing objectives									
5. Strategy development and evaluation									
6. Develop programs with supportive operations									
7. Write plan									
8. Communicate plan									
9. Establish a control system									
10. Plan implementaion									
11. Monitor, evaluate, and update plan									

and Ted Fredericks (Consumer Lending, Credit and Debit Cards). That meeting opened as McQuade introduced Baker to the executives and explained the nature of the meeting:

McQuade: Gentlemen, today we're to lay the groundwork for an operating plan which I hope will serve as a management guide for all of us. By November, it is hoped that a strategic operating plan for the year 1977 will have been developed. But the development of a short-term plan necessitates reference to longer-term strategic goals. Therefore, today, through a brainstorming session of sorts, we will attempt to devise BBT's mission and its goals. Later, we'll attempt to build strategies that can be used to attain those goals. Before we begin, are there any questions that you would care to ask either Dr. Baker or myself?

Delaney: I'm a little confused. Many concepts that are considered to be goals are but means towards achieving more generally defined goals. Are we distinguishing between the two?

Baker: That's very true, Bob, but today we're just trying to assemble a list of any objectives for the operation of BBT. After we've compiled the list we might separate the goals into separate groups; for instance, *ends* goals and *means* goals. But again, the separation can be done some other time. Today we want to get all of the objectives down on paper.

McQuade: OK; I guess we're all set now. Let fly with any concepts which you feel best describe what we're trying to achieve here at BBT. I'll be taking the minutes of the meeting.

Erickson: Well, for starters, I feel that one of our main objectives is to provide a full range of banking services to the markets in which we're located.

McQuade: Good! In fact, that may even be our mission here.

Carlson: Another goal might be to increase profits substantially.

Baker: Can we make it more specific than that? To be effective, the goal should contain a fairly exact range to strive towards.

Carlson: I see. Well, how does 8–10% sound? Increasing profits after taxes 8–10% compounded annually.

McQuade: Much better. Some more ideas . . .?

The meeting continued for three hours as goals of the institution were established and a division of responsibility in the planning process was discussed. As the men became more involved, possible strategies to be used in 1977 were discussed, but it soon became apparent that an exhaustive inventory of possible strategies could not be accomplished in just one evening. Therefore, McQuade cut short the session and suggested that all concerned deliberate for a few weeks upon further proposals. On June 1 he issued the following memo, a recapitulation of the thoughts that were expressed on May 18.

MEMO

TO: James Carlson   June 1,1976
    Robert Delaney
    John Erickson
    Ted Fredericks
FROM Brian J. McQuade
SUBJECT: PLANNING

Here is a first stab at outlining the goals, objectives, and strategies we have been discussing. During the next several months, we will be working to develop a marketing plan for late 1976 and 1977, a 1977 budget and the foundation for a longer term strategic plan. Your suggestions and comments are essential.

1. *BBT Goals*
    A. Provide full range of banking services to market in which located
    B. Increase profits after taxes 8–10% compounded annually
    C. Build and retain capital to maintain capital to deposit ratio of 1:12–15
    D. Increase stock value steadily over time
    E. Provide a "stimulating" and financially rewarding work atmosphere for employees
    F. Maintain and build an image of BBT as a quality, imaginative, service oriented and "professional" institution
    G. Maintain size and profitability advantage over other banks in town
    H. Build toward a profit goal of 1% + of assets (reduced by check deposit float)
    I. Specifically develop the capacity of BBT to meet the operational, investment and lending needs of commercial and professional customers and prospects in our marketing area
    J. Increase demand deposits 8–12% ± annually
    K. Increase time deposits 10–15% ± annually
    L. Build from the present 50% + loan to deposit of ratio to one of 67–70% by 1980
2. *Planning*
    A. The overall bank planning shall be directly the responsibility of the president
    B. Primary assistance will come from four department heads:

    James Carlson   —Branch Administration
                                         Commercial and mortgage lending
                                         Marketing
    Bob Delaney   —Operations
                                           Personnel
    John Erickson   —Trust
                                          Portfolio Investments
    Ted Fredericks   —Consumer Lending
                                          Credit and Debit Cards

    C. All officers and key supervisory personnel will be encouraged to participate in the planning function through submission and reaction to ideas and periodic meetings.
3. *Strategies*
    A. Intensify BBT—commercial/professional exposure
        a. direct call program
        b. direct mail program
        c. educational forums/seminars
    B. Activate statement saving d/d–d/w

C. Issue debit card to DDA and savings customers
D. Telephone transfers including non-BBT/DDA a/cs
E. Alter NOW charges—perhaps full analysis basis (?)
F. Offer personal reconciliations via serialized checks onto statement
G. Make master charge picture card optional
H. Install a personal/commercial revolving credit service
I. Install equipment for competitive check clearing service
J. Institute "Working Trust" service
K. Extend drive-in hours for commercial activity
L. Institute account receivable financing service
M. Branch into more commercially developed areas such as East Harrington, Jackson, Westfield, etc.
N. Open Cookston Branch on Sunday
O. Eliminate 78 method on installment loans—go to simple interest
P. Intensify bill paying services
Q. Offer account reconciliation services
R. Provide lock box service
S. Intensify and formalize government securities facilities including perhaps repurchase agreement handling

   We have a Planning Meeting scheduled for 2 P.M. on Thursday, June 3. Please be prepared to comment on the items in this memo and to add your own suggestions. Particularly as relates to your area of responsibility, let's get all ideas "out on the table" regardless of what you feel might be their final disposition after more thorough study.
   (Signed)
   Brian J. McQuade

   On June 3 all six men met again in order to complete the file of possible projects to be implemented in 1977. Once again, the president of BBT displayed his commitment to the operating plan by recording the minutes of the meeting.

McQuade: Gentlemen, today we're going to go through another brainstorming session. Our meeting of May 18 was highly successful; still, it was only a beginning. Today I want to hear your ideas concerning possible programs that might contribute to our objectives. We won't be discussing the viability of the various programs today; therefore, I want to hear of any ideas that come to mind. Assessment of their significance or workability can wait until later. To keep some semblance of order, Dr. Baker has suggested that we divide our ideas among four categories: loan service oriented programs, deposit/operations service oriented programs, public relations oriented programs, and other or multiple service oriented programs. I think that we can start with those projects that are loan-oriented. Of course, Jim and Ted, since these are your areas of responsibility, we may be looking to you for many suggestions. However, we're looking for recommendations from the entire group; therefore, I hope, Bob and John, that you won't hesitate to contribute whenever an idea comes to mind. OK, I guess we're ready now. Please feel free to start.
Delaney: How about if we develop contractor and dealer business in the home improvement and construction areas.
McQuade: Got it. Anbody else?
Fredericks: I think that our commercial customers would benefit if we provided financial analysis programs for them. We might be able to do this through time sharing facilities.
McQuade: Definitely something to investigate. Some more ideas . . .?

   The session went on for five hours, and when the six men broke up that night, they had compiled no fewer than 113 possible programs. The president took the list home with him that night and reviewed it with mixed emotions. He was extremely pleased with the production of the meeting. Nevertheless, he now faced a fresh problem; that is, deciding upon the priority of the various programs. Certainly, it was impossible to implement each of the suggestions, but choosing the more viable alternatives was not an easy task. The next morning he called Dr. Baker and informed him of his dilemma. The consultant didn't appear surprised by the suggestion that some type of collaborative rating system be used. He recommended that the president and his department heads rank each of the programs on a scale in terms of meeting the goals of the institution. McQuade accepted the advice and drafted the following memo. The complete list of programs was attached and appears as Exhibit B.

MEMO

TO: Department Heads   Date: June 15, 1976
FROM: Brian J. McQuade
SUBJECT: Planning

Based on our 6/3 meeting and my 6/1 memo, we broadly defined BBT goals as meeting specifics to do with:

1. Increased profits
2. Improved employee effectiveness
3. Meeting of growth objectives
4. Meeting of market share objectives
5. Meeting of service objectives

We came up with one hundred thirteen possible ideas that might contribute to these objectives. Please review the attached list and rate each idea on a scale of 1 (low) to 10 (high) in terms of meeting the broad goals outlined above. Obviously, your rating will be based on less than full understanding of each idea but give it a try.

I would appreciate your giving your copy to Jean by 9 A.M. Wednesday. You should be able to complete this in thirty to sixty minutes.

(Signed)
Brian J. McQuade

On June 17, McQuade sent the final compilation of the ratings to his department heads and to Dr. Baker. On that same day a meeting between the six men was scheduled for the purpose of making preliminary decisions concerning projects to be undertaken. The memo is followed by Exhibit B, the rating results of the various proposals.

MEMO

TO: Department Heads   June 17, 1976
FROM: Brian J. McQuade
SUBJECT: Planning

Attached is a resume of the responses to my memo of June 15 on ranking the ideas generated on June 3. The highest rated twenty-five items have been so annotated to the right of the total weight column. Also attached is a sheet showing the distribution of responses for the entire one hundred thirteen ideas submitted.

We will be discussing this further at our session this afternoon. The results of this survey should be viewed simply as advisory and one of a number of inputs that will go into a specific action plan.

(Signed)
Brian J. McQuade

EXHIBIT B Loan service oriented

A. Program	Points received	Rank
1. Make Master Charge Picture Card optional	38	24
2. Install a personal/commercial revolving credit service	40	12
3. Institute an accounts receivable financing service	24	
4. Eliminate 78 method on installment loans—go to simple interest computations	23	
5. Develop contractors/dealer business in home improvement and construction areas	38	25
6. Provide financial analysis programs for commercial customers—perhaps via time sharing facilities	30	
7. Install a lease financing program	21	
8. Utilize Master Charge for under $500 loans	36	
9. Computerize commercial loan function	37	
10. Institute short term line of credit facility for both individuals and businesses	38	
11. Intensify sales effort for large dollar direct installment loans	44	1
12. Develop a second mortgage loan program	41	11
13. Develop a formalized house-to-house loan program	35	
14. Develop a MGIC and other low down payment mortgage program	26	
15. Expand dealer financing on selective basis	32	
16. Develop a mortgage product with ascending amount payments	26	
17. Formalize a skip payment installment loan program	33	
18. Install a variable rate mortgage program	33	
19. Extend new car installment loans to forty-eight months	36	
20. Institute a balloon payment installment loan program	22	
21. Give rate breaks on Master Charge finance charges to employees and preferred customers	27	
22. Provide coupon books for mortgage payments	33	
23. Activate automatic installment loan and mortgage payments	29	
24. Institute a private label credit card program using Master Charge facilities	32	
25. Add BankAmericard to present Master Charge program	28	
26. Install American Express Gold Card program	27	

B. Deposit/operations service oriented		
27. Activate statement savings d/d/—d/w	40	13
28. Issue debit card to DDA and savings customers	42	6
29. Install telephone transfer service including facilities for non-BBT, DDA customers	38	
30. Alter NOW charges—perhaps to full analysis basis	31	
31. Offer personal reconciliations via serialized checks on the statement	32	
32. Install equipment for competitive check clearing service	40	14
33. Extend drive-in hours for commercial activity	38	
34. Intensify bill paying services	33	
35. Offer account reconciliation services for commercial DDA customers	32	
36. Provide a lock box service	29	
37. Institute a "goal" savings account program	28	
38. Make available for sale, packages of foreign currency	20	

B. Deposit/operations service oriented (continued)	Points received	Rank
39. Institute a courier deposit pick-up service for commercial businesses	40	15
40. Intensify bank by mail program	26	
41. Institute an emergency 24-hour, wide area money transfer facility using outside sources	24	
42. Institute an automatic savings program for BBT customers with and without our checking accounts	32	
43. Institute GIRO bill payments product	27	
44. Expand automated tellers to other offices	19	
45. Install complete in-house computer facilities	32	
46. Install lobby depositories and/or automated tellers	27	
47. Install mini-max checking account	30	
48. Provide facsimile transmission among our offices	21	
49. Institute a pre-paid interest program using dollars or premiums	27	
50. Expand branch courier service	28	
51. Install out-going WATS	20	
52. Institute service charges for checking accounts	30	

C. Other or multiple service oriented

	Points received	Rank
53. Intensify commercial/professional direct call program	44	2
54. Intensify commercial/professional direct mail program	40	16
55. Institute "Working Trust" service	26	
56. Branch into more commercially developed areas such as East Harrington, Jackson, Westfield, etc.	42	7
57. Open Cookston Branch on Sunday	22	
58. Intensify/formalize government securities service	30	
59. Provide a commercial service information kit	38	
60. Provide a more formalized municipal finance assistance program	32	
61. Create and staff a new marketing department	28	
62. Expand East Harrington Branch with safe deposit facilities, etc.	31	
63. Provide more service "breaks" for senior citizens	23	
64. Simplify paperwork on a bank-wide basis	26	
65. Develop a more formalized advertising program	44	3
66. Create a consumer advisory service	30	
67. Create and staff a new business development sales force	43	4
68. Expand through acquisition of other banks	32	
69. Develop a physical facilities plan	36	
70. Institute a 24-hour telephone transfer service	31	
71. Improve customer forms bank-wide	36	
72. Provide MICR encoded coupons for all customer transactions possible	31	
73. Increase use of premiums	27	
74. Install free incoming WATS line	22	
75. Install close circuit TV facilities between offices	16	
76. Purchase Texas Instruments high-powered calculator	40	17
77. Expand Cookston parking facilities through property acquisition	31	

D. Public relations oriented

	Points received	Rank
78. Intensify commercial/professional educational forums/seminars	40	18
79. Play music on telephone holds	21	

D. Public relations oriented (continued)	Points received	Rank
80. Acquire Jai Alai passes for and with customers	20	
81. Provide service starter kits for individuals	37	
82. Intensify local school education program	28	
83. Institute merchants relationship program	35	
84. Institute new apartment dwellers call program	29	
85. Institute a home consulting program	27	
86. Institute a business consulting program	37	
87. Institute a consumer information program	34	
88. Run a photo contest for a BBT calendar	42	8
89. Make available a BBT "24-hour" tee-shirt	25	
90. Install coffee bars in branches for customers	18	
91. Renovate main office stairway	25	
92. Redecorate East Harrington Branch	32	
93. Construct a children's waiting facility at main office	32	
94. Procure benches and/or fountains, bird baths, etc. for main office outside	21	
95. Improve outside lighting for main office	30	
96. Provide customer service area in Operations Department	32	
97. Utilize more "exhibits' in main office	34	
98. Acquire season tickets for pro hockey games for and with customers	40	19
99. Acquire Pro Am slot at Greater Columbia Open	26	
E. Employee effectiveness oriented		
100. Provide customer contact employees with uniforms	20	
101. Enlarge employee lunchroom	40	20
102. Constitute an employees' club for discounts, joint activities, etc.	36	
103. Improve employee job descriptions, salary ranges, etc.	43	5
104. Eliminate cash pay day for employees	36	
105. Provide payroll deduction facilities for employees	39	22
106. Institute an employees' sales incentive program	42	9
107. Activate a formalized employee training and education program	40	21
108. Conduct thorough staffing evaluation survey throughout the bank	42	10
109. Institute a profit center accounting system	35	
110. Institute an officer bonus/incentive program	39	23
111. Eliminate employee Christmas bonus with base pay increases	34	
112. Conduct off premises and non-work day educational program for employees	30	
113. Conduct off premises and non-work day educational program for Board of Directors	35	

On June 28 another meeting was held at which 62 of the 113 proposals were designated as workable for the year 1977. Each of the officers was assigned responsibilities for the implementation of programs covered by his department. The projects to be effected and those responsible for the systematic planning of their implementation were presented to all officers. Items were designated as the sole responsibility of one officer, the joint responsibility of two or more officers, or delegated to other employees. Also several programs needed review by Bob Delaney prior to receiving a go-ahead. All officers were expected to have completed all planning reports by August 9 when another meeting was scheduled.

On August 9, BBT's officers met in order to submit final planning reports concerning strategies from their respective departments. Each of these department heads had spent a considerable amount of time constructing schedules and plans for the projects' implementations, and their resultant work was top-rate.

For the next month, McQuade reviewed the minutes of the meetings of the past four months and gradually completed a preliminary draft of a 1977 Operating Plan. To do so, he, along with Dr. Baker, first re-examined the list of goals which had been prepared at their May 18 meeting. A further subdivision was made as approximately one-half of the objectives were categorized as general goals while the remainder, "means goals," were included as a plan to meet the more general goals. The two men also reviewed the reports that had been submitted by the department heads and incorporated ideas under appropriate headings. The preliminary plan was submitted to each of the department heads on September 6 to make certain that their findings had not been distorted in any manner, and finally, after minor revisions, the plan was submitted to BBT's Board of Directors for final approval on September 22.

MEMORANDUM

TO: Board of Directors and Officers   September 22, 1976
FROM: Brian J. McQuade
SUBJECT: 1977 Operating Plan

This plan has been developed over the last several months through input, discussion, and suggestions from customers, employees and directors. To plan for one year necessitates reference to longer term strategic goals. We have just begun to formalize a strategic plan and have done enough to construct the shorter term operating plan. This plan is intended as a guide, a summary, and a reference point. It should be studied in detail by all officers.

Mission of BBT: To provide to our market a full range of conveniently delivered banking services of high quality at competitive prices. At the same time, developing a record of growth and profitability which will be financially rewarding to our stockholders.

A. *Goals*
   1. Increase profits after taxes 10–15% compounded annually.
   2. Build towards a profit goal of 1% return on assets (less check-float-created due from balances).
   3. Build towards realizing a return on invested capital of 10–12%.
   4. Build and retain capital to maintain capital to deposit rates of 1:12–15.
   5. Increase stock value steadily.
   6. Maintain and build BBT as an imaginative, service oriented and professionally operated institution.
   7. Provide a stimulating and financially rewarding work environment for employees.
B. *General Plan to Meet Goals*
   1. Increase demand deposits 8–12% annually.
   2. Increase savings and time deposits 10–15% annually.
   3. Build from the present 50%+ loan to deposit ratio, to one of 65–70% by 1980.
   4. Adopt a posture of more aggressive sales through a combination of more rapid product enhancement and development, improved and intensified advertising, improved development and communications, intensified calling on the business community, and a progressive branching program.
   5. Specifically develop the capacity of BBT to meet the operational, investment and lending needs of professional and commercial customers in our marketing area.
   6. Increase market penetration in towns having branches with particular emphasis on Bloomington. Intensify efforts to penetrate more fully towns contiguous to those in which branches are located.
   7. Intensify efforts to improve the profitability of that part of the investment portfolio which prudently need not be considered primary reserves.
C. *Prime 1977 Programs*
   Some of the '77 programs may be implemented during the remainder of 1976 but are included here to solidify this initial written operating plan. Quantitative details will be developed during a budgeting process to be conducted in the fourth quarter.

1. *Organizational Structure*
   a. President—will be responsible for overall results and management including planning. His role will include a major public relations effort, sales initiatives, with selected prominent prospective customers, and contact with current major customers. He will be assisted by three department heads, each reporting directly to him.
   b. Department Heads
      1. James Carlson
         (a) banking services including commercial lending
         (b) branch administration
         (c) marketing
      2. Bob Delaney
         (a) operations
         (b) financial reporting
         (c) personnel administration
      3. John Erickson
         (a) trust marketing and operations
         (b) investment services
         (c) investment portfolio management
2. *Intensify Lending Activities*
   a. Install a personal/commercial revolving credit service (in addition to Master Charge).
   b. Institute a short term line of credit facility for both individuals and businesses.
   c. Intensify installment lending activity
      1. Formalize a deferred/tailored installment loan program.
      2. Develop contractor/dealer business in home improvement areas.
      3. Intensify efforts to develop a more competitive pricing posture consistent with BBT goals.
      4. Develop a second mortgage loan program.
   d. Implement a formalized house-to-house loan program.
   e. Computerize the commercial loan function.
   f. Make Master Charge Picture Card optional.
3. *Intensify Overall Marketing Effort on a Wide Basis*
   a. Hire an advertising agency.
   b. Institute a formal officer call program.
   c. Initiate a program of business/professional seminars/forums.
   d. Intensify social program for selected major customers and prospects.
   e. Add to staff a business development officer to concentrate on non-customers in Bloomington and selected parts of E. Harrington in 1977.
4. *Improve and Intensify Non-lending Product Lines and Sales Effort*
   a. Institute d/d–d/w statement savings.
   b. Institute serialized check service.
   c. Issue a debit (noncredit) card for automated teller activation.
   d. Institute a telephone transfer service.
   e. Investigate and implement if feasible a deposit pick-up service for businesses.
   f. Investigate and implement if feasible a mini-max checking account service.
   g. Revise NOW account service charges to present more competitive product.
   h. Implement a formalized government security service.
   i. Investigate and implement if feasible "The Working Trust" service.
   j. Develop operational service "starter kits" for individuals and businesses.
   k. Review service pricing schedules and revise to increase revenues where possible.
   l. Build customer service conference area outside Bookkeeping Department.
5. Open Westfield Branch in early 1977.
6. Open Four Corners and/or Buckingham Branches in late 1977, early 1978.
7. *Improve Internal Operations*
   a. Accounting
      1. Install remote entry data processing equipment
      2. Place all loan accounting functions in one centralized "back-office" operation.
   b. Financial Reporting
      1. Automatic investment portfolio accounting.
      2. Eliminate cash basis accounting and install a full accrual system (while retaining cash basis tax reporting while advisable).
      3. Progress towards a profit center accounting system.

c. Formalize a facilities plan and ongoing facilities plan procedure for action to be taken in 1978 and beyond.
   d. Develop formalized job descriptions (and possibly salary ranges).
   e. Develop a more formalized officer evaluation program.
   f. Evaluate and implement better performance oriented compensation programs for officers.
   g. Intensify communications between Board of Directors and Cookston Advisory Board and bank management.
   8. Investigate and where possible implement changes in Trust services and charges consistent with overall BBT goals.
   9. Complete Main Office banking floor renovations.

D. *Five Year Financial Scenario*

Tables I–V [follow and] describe a possible course that could develop based on tentative longer range goals and the continuation of the overall philosophy of business being developed in this plan. From our current vantage point, the 1976 and 1977 net income projections may be difficult to achieve. Hopefully near term deficiencies may be overcome during the period 1978–1981.

E. *Conclusion*

The planning process is a continuing one involving all personnel in management positions. I believe that the meetings, memos, studies, discussions, and surveys that have gone into this initial plan have already proven beneficial to the individuals involved and the bank. Bloomington Bank is a solid and respected institution—it has performed well in its marketplace and for its stockholders. We have the opportunity to create an even more interesting and exciting institution—one that can serve its present and an expanded marketplace better than it has. We have the opportunity to create a more dynamic work environment for all employees and to obtain better financial results for stockholders and employees. The task is not an easy one. The business of banking shares with other businesses the pressures of regulation, increasing costs, and the resultant squeeze on profits and increasing competition.

I suggest that we view our challenge as opportunities to grow personally and as an institution. Better management in its broadest sense, and including all levels, is the greatest need in banking today—I believe we can learn together to manage better.

1977 will be an exciting and interesting year for Bloomington Bank. Much of what we have planned is basic and simply positions us better vis-a-vis our competition. In the planning process we have deferred for 1977 some of the more creative steps that we may have wished to take. Experience confirms the wisdom of learning to walk before running. We have chosen to walk more quickly—we may or may not ultimately decide to run.

I seek both your support and cooperation and in turn offer you mine.

(Signed)
Brian J. McQuade
Approved by Board of Directors on
September 22, 1976

Budgets for each of the programs were prepared, and the plan began operation in November, 1976, two months ahead of schedule.

After six months of painstaking work by all involved, Bloomington Bank and Trust was operating according to a formal written plan for the first time in its history, and its president, Brian J. McQuade, felt confident his bank was headed toward even greater success.

TABLE I   Total deposits

	HISTORICAL	
	Total deposits	% increase
1970	17,805,000	
1971	19,923,000	11.9
1972	22,082,000	10.8
1973	23,304,000	5.5
1974	26,646,000	14.3
1975	27,818,000	4.4

(5 Year: 56.2%)

	PROJECTION	
	Low growth projection	High growth projection
1976	30,960,000	31,890,000
1977	33,846,000	36,358,500
1978	37,003,800	41,459,475
1979	40,459,236	47,283,260
1980	44,240,602	53,933,196
1981	48,378,958	61,527,516

TABLE II   Total loans

	HISTORICAL	
	Total loans	Deposit to loan ratios 1:–
1970	8,708,000	.489
1971	10,073,000	.506
1972	11,927,000	.540
1973	13,271,000	.569
1974	14,372,000	.529
1975	15,118,000	.507

(5 Year: 73.6%)

	PROJECTION	
	Low growth projection	High growth projection	Projected low to dep. ratio
1976	16,718,400	17,220,600	.54
1977	19,292,220	20,724,345	.57
1978	22,202,280	24,875,685	.60
1979	25,489,318	29,788,453	.63
1980	29,198,797	35,595,909	.66
1981	33,865,270	43,069,261	.70

TABLE III   Net income

	HISTORICAL	
	Net income	% increase
1970	160,000	
1971	174,500	9.1
1972	135,100	(22.6)
1973	216,200	60.0
1974	245,000	13.3
1975	230,000	(6.1)

	PROJECTION	
	10% growth projection	15% growth projection
1976	236,500	247,250
1977	260,150	284,337
1978	286,165	326,988
1979	314,781	376,036
1980	346,259	432,411
1981	380,885	497,308

TABLE IV   Capital

	HISTORICAL	
	Capital	% increase
1970	1,761,000	
1971	1,874,000	6.4
1972	1,951,000	4.1
1973	2,163,000	10.9
1974	2,381,000	10.1
1975	2,527,000	6.1
(5 Year: 43.5%)		

	PROJECTION	
	Low	High
1976	2,641,900	2,662,250
1977	2,797,990	2,847,687
1978	2,969,689	3,060,940
1979	3,170,004	3,286,562
1980	3,377,760	3,546,027
1981	3,606,291	3,844,412

TABLE V   Ratio—deposits to capital

	HISTORICAL		
	Total capital	*Deposits*	*1:-*
1970	1761.1	17805.2	10.1
1971	1874.1	19923.1	10.6
1972	1951.5	22082.5	11.3
1973	2163.1	23304.1	10.8
1974	2382.6	26646.6	11.2
1975	2527.6	29818.1	11.8

	PROJECTION	
	Low	*High*
1976	11.7	12.0
1977	12.1	12.8
1978	12.5	13.5
1979	12.8	14.4
1980	13.1	15.2
1981	13.4	16.0

DISCUSSION

1. What principal steps has McQuade taken to improve the planning of the Bloomington Bank and Trust Company? Specify the benefits that BBT seems likely to gain from this formal planning system.

2. Compare what McQuade and his associates have done with the strategic-planning system that has been set forth in Chapter 1. What are the evident differences? What, if anything, has the BBT plan omitted? How, if at all, would such omissions be likely to affect the BBT?

3. Stipulate the ways in which McQuade should have modified the planning system when preparing strategic plans for the following year, 1978. Justify your recommendations.

Baltimore-Washington International Airport

Standing on the wind-blown observation deck of Baltimore-Washington International Airport (BWI), Mr. Karl Sattler was lost in thought. Oblivious to the thunder of a departing Boeing B–707, he was considering his current task as Director of Planning and Development for the Aviation Administration of the State of Maryland. He had been asked to recommend whether the airport, despite its new name, was to be defined as a local facility, serving Baltimore primarily, or as a regional facility serving the metropolitan areas of both Washington, D.C. and Baltimore. It was clear to Mr. Sattler that BWI would need to modernize its facilities in either case. But even though, historically, BWI had served more than the Baltimore area alone, the magnitude of the task of turning the airport into a major regional air center was far greater than that of modernizing it for local use.

Mr. Sattler was aware that, aside from the higher construction and marketing costs required to turn the airport into a regional facility, a differentiated image would have to be developed for BWI to compete for regional air traffic with Washington National and Dulles airports. He also believed that airlines already established at those two airports would have to be convinced either to switch or to open up new offices at BWI. However, if the airport were to be defined as a regional facility, the airport's management would have an easier time attracting airlines which were primarily interested in serving the Washington, D.C. area. Similarly, air passengers resident in or destined to Washington, D.C., as well as air cargo shippers and consignees, would be more likely to use a regional airport rather than a local facility. Identifying BWI as a Baltimore-only airport meant planning a smaller facility, more directly related to the needs of Baltimore and the State of Maryland, rather than the dominant needs of the larger Washington, D.C. market. Not only would capital expenditure and operating fund requirements be substantially less, but, as a local airport, BWI could use its unique identity to promote new air services which would not come into direct competition with those of the Washington airports.

Because of the airport's historical role as a link between the cities of Baltimore and Washington, D.C., and of the airport's need to update its facilities in any case, the development of a regional air center seemed the preferable alternative. But Mr. Sattler believed that he could recommend it only if he felt that the regional facility could be operated profitably. And he did not think this was possible unless he could demonstrate that a modernized BWI would indeed be an attractive alternative to a sizable segment of the regional air traffic market. Both he and his staff agreed that the key to his recommendation would be his analysis of the characteristics of present and potential air passengers in the Washington/Baltimore area.

THE COMMERCIAL AVIATION INDUSTRY

Commercial air travel had grown rapidly since its beginning in 1919. The increase was particularly marked in the United States. Between 1956 and 1966, for instance, the number of revenue passenger miles[1] flown by U.S. domestic truck airlines[2] grew from 21.6 billion to 56.8 billion. The increase in international traffic was similarly dramatic: between 1963 and 1973, the number of passengers handled on scheduled services on the North Atlantic routes alone jumped from 2.422 million to 10.029 million.

This increase in air passengers and passenger-miles flown was related to the appearance of new aircraft. In the late fifties, piston-engined propellor aircraft were exchanged for jet transports, such as the four-engined Boeing B–707 and the Douglas DC–8 or smaller two-engined and three-engined jets. In 1970, the second generation of jet transports came into service. Over twice as large as the B–707, Boeing's B–747 could take off with nearly 400 passengers and their baggage, mail, and cargo from runways slightly shorter than those required by its four-engined predecessors. But the heavier weights and higher take-off landing speeds of these aircraft required longer and stronger runways than were often built previously, and their greater seating capacities required larger passenger terminals.

Air travellers, however, still represented a relatively small percentage of the number of people travelling by the various modes of transportation. According to the 1967 U.S. Census of Transportation, 86 percent of all trips taken by individuals in the U.S. each year were by car. The Census also revealed that air travel seemed to draw people with different socio-economic characteristics from those using the other major transportation modes—automobile, bus, and train. A significant majority of trips taken by these other modes of transport were for other than business-related reasons, while most trips on commercial airlines were business-related. Over two-thirds of all trips by automobile distanced less than 200 miles. Trips of these distances accounted for 61 percent of the total bus trips and 42.4 percent of train trips, but only 7.8 percent of commercial airline trips. Airline passengers, moreover, generally had higher incomes than travellers using the other transport modes. Travel by members of families with incomes over $15,000 accounted for 9.5 percent of auto trips, 6.7 percent of bus trips, 9.8 percent of train trips, but 28.2 percent of airline trips. Professionally or managerially employed household heads constituted the largest single group of commercial airline users, while blue collar workers accounted for the largest single group using the other transport modes.

THE REGION'S AIRPORTS

BWI

On June 24, 1950, some three years after construction began at a site in Anne Arundel County ten miles south of Baltimore, Friendship International Airport (only recently renamed Baltimore-Washington International) was formally dedicated by President Harry S. Truman. The original facility, including terminal buildings, access roads, car parks, and runways, cost approximately $18.2 million. Scheduled services began one month later with the arrival of an Eastern Airlines DC-3 on a flight from Atlanta to Newark. From then until about 1962, Friendship International acted as both the main airport for Baltimore and the State of Maryland and the international facility for the Baltimore/Washington, D.C. region.

---

[1]A revenue passenger-mile is the carriage of one revenue-paying passenger one mile.
[2]A domestic truck airline is a U.S. airline which operates a transcontinental service or an extensive service in at least one-half of the country.

The airport's design was innovative. Ten aircraft could be handled simultaneously. The passenger terminal separated the flows of inbound and outbound passengers to upper and lower levels. All of the runways were constructed to handle aircraft with operating weights up to 450,000 pounds, which was exceptional since the Douglas DC–4 aircraft, then one of the largest air transports in operation, had a maximum operating weight of only 73,000 pounds. Only with the appearance of the Boeing B–747 wide-bodied aircraft in 1970, with operating weights of 775,000 pounds and more, was the runway system's capacity finally exceeded. Furthermore, the runways were longer than was necessary at the time, each of them measuring at least 1,000 feet over what was necessary for any aircraft at the time. The main east-west runway, measuring 9,450 feet, was more than adequate for the largest transports until the early nineteen-seventies.

In 1972, the State Aviation Administration of Maryland, one of seven groups under the newly formed Maryland Department of Transportation, purchased Friendship International Airport from its original owners (Baltimore City) on behalf of the State. The name Friendship International was changed to Baltimore-Washington International following the purchase. However, while the name of the airport had been changed, the planners in the SAA were not sure of the extent of its potential market area. They expressed concern that the existing facility, while one of the most advanced when it was opened, was now woefully inadequate for the nineteen-seventies and beyond.

During the first full year of operation, a total of 211,236 passengers arrived and departed through the airport. Between 1950 and 1962, the number of passengers handled at Friendship International increased at an average annual rate of 19 percent to 1,436,361. (See Exhibit 1 for passenger statistics at BWI.) Through 1960, the number of enplaning passengers exceeded the number of those deplaning, but from 1960 on, the reverse was more often the case. The number of charter passengers grew from nearly 13,000 in 1968 to over 53,000 in 1973. However, for the 11 years following 1962, the average annual increase in total air passengers had fallen to 6.6 percent, the total approaching three million in 1973. Even more disturbing, the kind of traffic handled at Friendship changed after 1962, largely as a result of the opening of Dulles Airport. Although Friendship's share of passengers flying less than 600 miles increased, there was a dramatic decline in the share of those flying distances greater than 1,000 miles. (See Exhibit 2 for statistics on Friendship's share of traffic.)

But despite declining passenger volumes, the operation of Friendship International Airport continued to be profitable. During the period from September 1, 1970 through June 30, 1971, the airport generated nearly $3.8 million in various revenues, which resulted in a net income of $86,185. Operating expenses totalled over $3.5 million.

Washington National Airport

In 1941, the first airport constructed, owned, and operated by the Federal Government was opened. Washington National was built on land reclaimed from the Potomac River. Its four runways ranged in length from 4,100 to 6,855 feet. One of them closed by the late 1960s, but the lengths of the remaining three were not increased to compensate for the loss. During 1942, the first full year of operation, a total of 459,396 passengers were handled at the airport. In 1946, that figure reached above one million, which necessitated the expansion of the terminal. By 1958, three separate expansions increased the size of the original terminal by almost 37 percent.

In November, 1959, all jet operations by airlines were banned from the airport. However, with the rapid retirement of propeller-powered aircraft, the ban was lifted for two-engined and three-engined jets. While the larger aircraft, such as the Boeing B–707, were not allowed to land or take off at the airport, the smaller Boeing B–727 and the McDonnell—Douglas DC–9 could. Traffic growth, by 1966, reached levels that required restricting the number of take-offs or landings during each hour to a range of 650 miles, although some exceptions—four routes to Florida, and one each to Memphis, St. Louis, and Minneapolis/St. Paul—were permitted. In 1970, jet air carrier operations were further restricted to the hours between 7 A.M. and 10 P.M. But despite these restrictions, the number of passengers using Washington National continued to increase. (See Exhibit 3 for traffic volumes at the region's three airports.)

Dulles International Airport

Dulles International Airport was opened on November 17, 1962 on a 10,000 acre site in Loudon County, Virginia. Two parallel north-south runways, each 11,500 feet long, crossed a third (east-west) runway of 10,000 feet. Several taxiways, designed for use by smaller aircraft, were also constructed. All the facilities, including the terminal, were designed so that they could be expanded as required by traffic growth. Building and outfitting Dulles cost a total of $108.3 million, including $15.9 million for the passenger terminal, $19.3 million for an access highway from the Capital Beltway, and $20.7 million for the runway system. In the one and one-half months of operation in 1962, 52,000 passengers used the airport. In 1973, that figure reached 2,645,000.

In contrast to the usual airport facilities, airliners were parked away from the passenger terminal, which eliminated both congestion around the terminal and the need for special vehicles to maneuver the aircraft into tight spaces. Passengers were transferred from the terminal to the aircraft by means of special "mobile lounges." These were designed to work with both the first generation of jet transports (such as the Boeing B–707) and the wide-bodied jets which were then still on the drawing board.

The Washington-Baltimore Region

In approaching the decision before him, Mr. Sattler looked first at data provided by the 1970 Census on the Baltimore/Washington region, since the majority of people using the three airports lived within the area. A total of 4,672,213 people resided in the two standard metropolitan statistical areas (SMSAs) of Washington, D.C. and Baltimore. (See Exhibit 4 for a map of the two areas and Exhibit 5 for selected Census information.) The Washington, D.C. SMSA, which includes counties and cities in Virginia and Maryland as well as the District itself, accounted for 56 percent of the total, or 2,601,545 people. The largest population concentrations, as might be expected, were found in the two cities proper, Washington with 756,492 and Baltimore with 905,757 people. Counties and cities in Virginia accounted for 661,680 persons, and the larger part of the remaining population resided in the Maryland counties of Prince Georges and Montgomery.

The concentrations of residents attaining certain levels of income and education, and working at specific types of jobs, varied widely from city to city and county to county in the two areas. The highest concentrations of residents with some college education were in Washington, D.C., Fairfax, and Montgomery Counties. Almost 50 percent of the population in Montgomery had gone to college, whereas, by contrast, in Alexandria, Virginia, only 9.3 percent of the residents had gone beyond the high school level. Blue collar workers comprised the largest single occupational group of residents in the region, although white collar workers accounted for 47 percent of the total working population. Only in Montgomery County, the County and City of Fairfax, and in Falls Church did the number of white collar workers exceed all other groups. Fifty-five percent of the recorded family incomes fell within the range of $5,000 to $14,999 per year. Only 9 percent of the total had incomes in excess of $25,000, and those were spread unevenly across the statistical areas.

After looking through the census reports, Mr. Sattler also reviewed a number of population projections for the State of Maryland through 1990. (See Exhibit 6.) With the exception of the City of Baltimore, all of the areas in Maryland were expected to increase the numbers of their residents. According to the estimates, the total population of the Maryland cities and counties within the two SMSAs was expected to increase by 26.2 percent during the twenty year period to over four million people. Howard County's population was expected to register the single most dramatic increase of over 200 percent.

Population estimates for the Baltimore SMSA predicted an increase in working population from 885.8 thousand in 1970 to 1,191,900 by 1990. Manufacturing employment was expected to decline from 197,000 to 167,300 in the twenty years; but civilian government (federal, state, and local), wholesale and retail trade, financial, insurance, real estate, and service-related employment were all expected to increase. The number of civilian government workers was expected to jump from 17.1 percent of total employees in 1970 to 23.1 percent in 1990. Employees in wholesale and retail trade activities were expected to account for the largest single percentage of workers.

PASSENGER SURVEY

An extensive survey of air passengers, conducted on behalf of BWI and the Maryland Department of Transportation, also came under Mr. Sattler's scrutiny. Flights from the three area airports were surveyed during the periods of November 7–14, 1973; November 28–December 13, 1973; and January 9–23, 1974. A total of eleven airlines participated. The initial sample of flights was drawn from the top one hundred markets of the Washington and Baltimore airports, which was then reduced to the top thirty. One market was added from the remaining seventy and a second from the commuter flight market within Maryland. Flights of non-participating airlines were dropped from the sample, and the master list was then divided according to times of departure: 6:01 A.M. to 10:00 A.M.; 10:01 A.M. to 4:00 P.M.; 4:01 P.M. to 3:00 P.M.; and 8:01 P.M. to 6:00 A.M. From a total of 11,995 flight departures per week, the researchers selected a target sample of 555 flights. Including the two additional markets, the target sample increased to 730 flights during the five week period. Fifty-nine percent of the questionnaires were completed, yielding a total of 16,829 surveys.

Among other things, the survey collected information on the age, income, travel purpose, point of origin, and airport preference of each respondent. The data was separated by departure airport to allow the researchers to compare passenger profiles. At all three airports, those passengers with incomes below $10,000 per year accounted for a small percentage of all those passengers surveyed. Those passengers with incomes of $25,000 and more accounted for only 50 percent of all respondents at both National and Dulles airports, but only 41.8 percent of these at BWI. Passengers at Dulles were most often on government-related business, while at both BWI and National airports, over one-third of the trips were related to other business activities. Regardless of the purpose of the trip, most passengers left for one of the three airports from their residences. Dulles was preferred over BWI as a long-haul airport, but BWI was preferred slightly more than Dulles overall. Over one-half of all respondents, however, preferred to use Washington National over either of the others.

Seven factors in selecting one of the airports were graded according to the passenger's perceived importance. (See Exhibit 7 for a breakdown by airport.) Overall, the convenience of the airport's location was the most important selection factor mentioned by all respondents. The availability of direct flights and convenient flight times were the second and third most important factors, respectively. Cost and time required to travel by public transportation, better access roads and parking, better ticketing and baggage facilities, and seat availability were not considered very important. Passengers using BWI and National most often cited its convenient location as the most important factor in their choice. Passengers at Dulles, in contrast, were often attracted because it was the only one of the three airports with direct flights to their destinations.

The air passenger survey also collected data on the geographic origins of the air travellers at each of the three airports. National Airport, it appeared, was the only facility which served the entire Washington, D.C./Baltimore region. Passengers from as far north as Howard and Carroll Counties in Maryland boarded flights at National. BWI's service area was slightly smaller, excluding half of Fairfax County and almost all of Loudon. Dulles' service area was even more restricted, drawing no passengers from the City of Baltimore, Anne Arundel, Harford, and Baltimore Counties. Moreover, BWI and Washington National each drew more than 75% of certain counties' total air travellers, whereas Dulles drew only between 50 and 74 percent from Loudon, the county in which it was situated.

Primary and secondary service areas were determined for each of the three airports from these figures and from the application of observed driving times. BWI's primary service area included all of Maryland and Washington, D.C., an area comprising 80 percent of the region's population. The northern boundary of the primary service area of Dulles was the northern boundary of Montgomery and Prince Georges Counties, an area comprising 59 percent of the region's population. Only the City of Baltimore, Baltimore, Carroll, and Harford Counties, together holding 33 percent of the region's population, were excluded from Washington National's primary service area.

Some of the driving times used to help determine the service areas of the airports came from a study done shortly after Dulles opened. Mr. Sattler also looked at this original study, which included the length of time required to travel from selected points in the region to both BWI and Dulles and then to board the aircraft. (See Exhibit 8 for time and comparisons.) Aside from points in Washington, D.C. and Baltimore proper, all of the departure points were located within five miles of the northern boundary of the Capital District. Twenty minutes was added to the driving times to both airports for passenger check-in. An additional fifteen minutes was added to these times at Dulles to cover the use of their mobile lounges in boarding the aircraft there. From every point, getting on a flight at BWI required less time than that required at Dulles, the differences in travel times varying between 15 minutes and 2 hours and 10 minutes. Mr. Sattler was particularly surprised to find that it was quicker to get on a flight at BWI even from downtown Washington, a fact that contrasted sharply with the general perception that BWI was located too far away for use by people residing in the District.

THE ALTERNATIVES

If Mr. Sattler made the decision to develop BWI as a regional facility, significant work would be required on the passenger terminal, ramp areas, taxiways, and runways to bring the airport's capacity up to the proposed 11 million passengers per year. The enlarged facilities under the regional proposal would permit the airport to handle both medium and long-haul flights as well as local services—to function, in other words, as more than a simple, short-haul origin-destination airport. And since the longer flights usually entailed larger aircraft, such as the B-747 and DC-10, the facilities would have to be expanded accordingly. The most recent estimate totalled $100 million, $70 million for a completely rebuilt and expanded terminal, and $30 million for the work on the ramps, taxiways, and runways. However, if the airport were to remain a local facility, the ramps, taxiways, and runways were adequate to handle the smaller airliners with only additional $5 to $6 million in repair work and new construction. Similarly, because the existing passenger terminal was of adequate size to handle even the long range predictions for local traffic, the total cost of refurbishment under this alternative would amount to $33.6 million.

In either case, BWI would have to sell performance bonds, a particular form of industrial revenue bonds, to finance the modernization. These bonds were the usual method of financing airport construction or development since the 1950's, when the financing for Chicago's O'Hare International Airport was worked out. "The airlines pledged that, if airport income fell short of the total needed to pay off the principal and interest on the bonds, they would make up the difference by paying a higher landing fee rate. Under this arrangement, landing fees—the amount billed to an airline each time one of its airplanes lands on a runway—are periodically raised or lowered to compensate for shortages or excesses in income in the preceding period."[3] These bonds are usually issued for 25 or 30 year terms, much longer than the customary terms offered on general obligation bonds. Interest rates, accordingly, ran higher—by the early seventies, from 6 to 10 percent.

Mr. Sattler had also collected some information about the public relations and promotion under each of the two alternatives. At present, the airport was spending approximately $50,000 per year for promotional advertisements in newspapers and magazines, both in Baltimore and in cities which had non-stop air links with Baltimore. He assumed that the amount could remain about the same if the airport was defined as a local facility. However, if BWI were to be developed as a regional airport, it would be necessary to increase media advertising. In addition to its present promotional efforts, a campaign would have to be developed to attract passengers from the Washington, D.C. area. One estimate of the cost of such a program forecasted an immediate doubling of promotional expenditures, followed by a subsequent increase to approximately $140,000 per year.

Personnel requirements would also change if the airport were developed as a regional facility. One proposal outlined the need for managers specializing in passenger service, air cargo, public relations, and press services. The current salary expenditures for the airport's management totalled $65,300, but with an expanded staff to manage the airport, this expenditure would increase to $122,220.

In addition to these various costs, Mr. Sattler had to consider how the airport would promote itself as either a regional or a local facility. He wondered how the airport would attract passengers and airlines from the Washington, D.C. airports. In most cases, because of a new resort or the emergence or expansion of an industry, the airlines would petition the right to serve a new city through the Civil Aeronautics Board. In other cases, however, the airport owners would approach the airlines in an attempt to entice them to begin service at their facility. If the airport "went regional," Mr. Sattler knew that an expanded staff would have to sell BWI actively to new airlines or to convince those airlines currently serving the airport to increase the number of destinations that they served on a non-stop basis.

Turning back to the many reports, data sheets, and documents in his office, Mr. Sattler was prepared to begin his review of the current and potential air passengers in the Washington, D.C./Baltimore region. He expected that his consumer analysis would provide the basis for a recommendation to define BWI as either a regional or local airport. Once the role of the airport was defined, he could then determine what marketing efforts would be needed to support the decision.

---

[3]"How They're Financing the Big City Airports," *Air Transport Report* (Washington, D.C.: Air Transport Association), March 1972.

EXHIBIT 1 Baltimore-Washington International Airport Passenger Statistics

Year	Deplaning	Enplaning	Charter	Total
1951	99,583	111,653		211,236
1952	—	—		234,597
1953	—	—		280,849
1954	—	—		305,542
1955	157,954	169,647		327,601
1956	166,841	177,014		343,855
1957	193,780	206,317		400,097
1958	189,569	198,713		388,282
1959	265,717	274,966		540,683
1960	370,301	376,389		746,690
1961	569,631	566,370		1,136,001
1962	719,631	716,730		1,436,361
1963	575,037	571,640		1,146,677
1964	741,534	717,768		1,459,302
1965	896,559	896,755		1,793,314
1966	998,864	1,002,901		2,001,765
1967	1,229,500	1,240,231	12,709	2,469,731
1968	1,437,772	1,443,103	29,283	2,910,158
1969	1,523,771	1,512,748	34,036	3,070,555
1970	1,495,993	1,490,412	33,236	3,019,581
1971	1,397,950	1,369,004	40,339	2,807,293
1972	1,430,652	1,403,020	60,720	2,894,392
1973	1,436,289	1,405,635	53,267	2,895,191

Source: State Aviation Administration, Maryland Department of Transportation.

EXHIBIT 2 **Baltimore-Washington International Airport**
Friendship's share of traffic

Market Distance/number of markets/ fastest and slowest growing	1962–1972 average annual growth	Friendship's share	
		1962	1972
0–200 miles (5)	5.6%*	10.2%†	12.5%‡
—Newport News	8.4		15.5
—Richmond	0.0		2.9
201–400 miles (15)	10.6	14.9	18.4
—Providence	18.3		15.3
—Greensboro	6.7		3.5
401–600 miles (10)	12.3	12.8	20.2
—Columbia, S.C.	18.6		13.9
—Dayton	7.1		6.5
601–800 miles (7)	10.4	29.4	20.7
—Memphis	13.8		11.2
—Milwaukee	9.2		14.3
801–1,000 miles (5)	12.4	37.7	27.9
—New Orleans	14.3		46.6
—Minneapolis/St. Paul	9.4		9.3
1,001–1,600 miles (3)	12.6	53.1	24.3
—Houston	14.5		36.2
—Denver	12.3		20.8
—Dallas/Ft. Worth	11.8		20.3
over 1,600 miles (5)	10.6	71.9	19.8
—Phoenix	16.7		15.1
—Seattle	8.2		32.8

Source: State Aviation Administration.

Notes:

*To be read as between 1962 and 1972 passenger traffic between the Washington/Baltimore region and those five markets located within 200 miles grew at an average annual rate of 5.6 percent.

†In 1962 10.2 percent of all passengers flying from the Washington/Baltimore region to all of the markets located within 200 miles departed from Friendship International Airport.

‡In 1972, 12.5 percent of all passengers flying from the Washington/Baltimore region to all of the markets located within 200 miles departed from Friendship International Airport.

EXHIBIT 3 **Baltimore-Washington International Airport**
Comparative airport statistics
Passenger traffic (in thousands)

Year	Washington National	Dulles International	Baltimore-Washington
1952	2,492		235
1953	2,720		281
1954	3,103		306
1955	3,635		328
1956	3,964		344
1957	4,463		400
1958	4,534		388
1959	5,006		541
1960	4,726		747
1961	4,646		1,136
1962	4,837	52	1,436
1963	5,464	667	1,147
1964	6,188	782	1,459
1965	6,773	838	1,793
1966	7,920	1,175	2,002
1967	9,383	1,565	2,470
1968	9,968	1,774	2,910
1969	10,248	2,176	3,071
1970	9,768	2,157	3,020
1971	10,377	2,245	2,807
1972	11,122	2,517	2,894
1973	11,716	2,645	2,895

Sources: Maryland Department of Transportation, State Aviation Administration—Baltimore-Washington Airport; Metropolitan Washington Airports—Washington National Airport, Dulles International Airport.

EXHIBIT 4   Baltimore-Washington International Airport

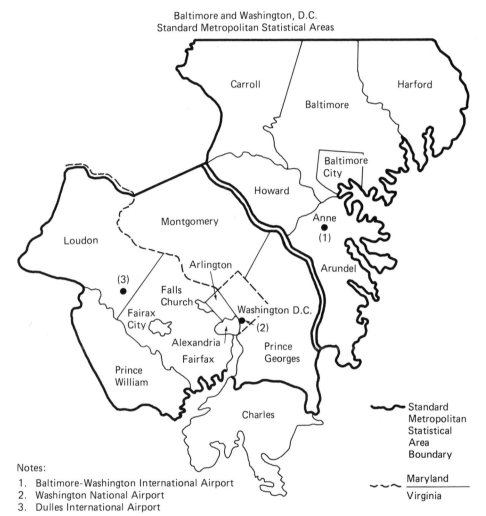

Baltimore and Washington, D.C.
Standard Metropolitan Statistical Areas

Carroll

Harford

Baltimore

Baltimore
City

Howard

Anne
(1)

Montgomery

Loudon

Arundel

Arlington

(3)

Falls
Church

Washington D.C.
(2)

Fairax
City

Alexandria

Prince
Georges

Fairfax

Prince
William

Charles

——— Standard
Metropolitan
Statistical
Area
Boundary

- - - Maryland
Virginia

Notes:
1. Baltimore-Washington International Airport
2. Washington National Airport
3. Dulles International Airport

EXHIBIT 5 Baltimore-Washington International Airport
Population demographics

Characteristics	Prince William	Loudon	Fairfax	Fairfax City	Falls Church	Alexandria	Arlington	Washington, D.C.
Total Population	111,102	37,150	455,021	21,970	10,772	15,572	10,093	756,492
Education*								
None	402	261	820	50	26	152	55	5,109
Elementary	8,393	5,313	21,693	1,095	676	2,996	1,678	96,274
High School	27,501	9,195	97,968	5,318	2,793	3,505	2,448	199,104
College	12,588	4,795	108,454	4,329	2,754	678	682	122,564
Total	48,884	19,564	228,935	10,792	6,249	7,331	4,863	423,051
Occupation†								
Prof./Mgr.	9,662	4,098	71,754	3,167	2,024	443	567	86,326
Clerical/Sls.	8,776	2,846	51,316	2,860	1,626	1,231	1,075	107,647
Blue Collar	14,721	6,595	38,991	2,315	1,058	3,936	2,033	127,977
Other	374	800	1,495	42	26	547	471	13,026
Total	33,533	14,339	163,556	8,384	4,734	6,157	4,146	334,976
Family Income‡								
$ 0.0–$ 4.9	2,811	1,486	7,108	326	216	73	216	33,475
$ 5.0–$ 9.9	7,813	2,714	18,283	1,100	653	282	508	66,146
$10.0–$14.9	8,894	2,738	28,580	1,426	780	241	457	37,005
$15.0–$24.9	5,576	1,825	43,399	1,989	916	205	368	27,924
$25.0 +	838	373	16,712	585	385	42	108	13,102
Total	25,932	9,136	114,082	5,426	2,950	843	1,657	177,652

continued

Source: U.S. Department of Commerce, Bureau of the Census, 1970.

Notes:
*Those people aged 25 years and over.
†Those people aged 16 years and over.
‡Family income in thousands of dollars.

EXHIBIT 5 (continued)

Characteristics	Prince Georges	Montgomery	Anne Arundel	Baltimore City	Howard	Carroll	Baltimore	Harford
Total Population	660,564	522,809	297,539	905,757	61,911	69,006	621,077	115,378
Education*								
None	1,789	1,807	1,487	8,746	165	637	3,140	429
Elementary	46,464	27,446	35,696	198,307	6,869	14,132	86,232	13,906
High School	174,612	111,330	79,113	223,523	15,087	18,996	177,799	29,552
College	96,978	142,112	34,393	65,835	10,351	5,058	76,991	13,031
Total	319,843	282,695	150,689	496,411	32,472	38,823	344,162	56,918
Occupation†								
Prof./Mgr.	86,197	101,252	29,987	63,887	8,750	4,939	71,446	11,257
Clerical/Sls.	92,819	66,756	29,690	92,744	5,944	5,462	81,613	9,315
Blue Collar	88,522	45,154	46,780	186,780	8,947	16,653	104,961	18,367
Other	1,867	2,332	1,316	9,289	372	289	1,331	426
Total	269,405	215,494	107,773	352,700	24,013	27,343	259,351	39,365
Family Income‡								
$ 0.0–$ 4.9	13,928	7,681	7,679	50,261	1,242	2,509	12,967	3,563
$ 5.0–$ 9.9	41,346	19,332	20,271	75,502	3,210	5,715	42,927	9,158
$10.0–$14.9	51,953	30,797	23,231	53,981	4,497	5,337	54,939	8,661
$15.0–$24.9	46,285	47,686	16,350	28,554	4,882	2,833	39,798	5,831
$25.0 +	9,888	26,435	3,904	7,535	5,851	576	11,744	1,193
Total	163,400	131,931	71,435	215,833	19,682	16,970	162,375	28,406

Source: U.S. Department of Commerce, Bureau of the Census, 1970.

Notes:

*Those people aged 25 years and over.
†Those people aged 16 years and over.
‡Family income in thousands of dollars.

**EXHIBIT 6 Baltimore-Washington International Airport
State of Maryland population projections**

County/City	1970 population*	1990 population†	1970–1990 percentage increase
Anne Arundel	299,899	500,353	66.8%
Baltimore	624,745	768,912	23.1
Carroll	69,411	107,749	55.
Harford	116,455	171,204	47.0
Howard	63,091	192,568	205.2
Montgomery	528,027	700,542	32.7
Prince Georges	671,516	866,053	29.0
Baltimore City	903,515	828,180	(8.3)
Total	3,276,659	4,135,561	26.2

Source: Maryland Department of State Planning.

Notes:

*Maryland Department of State Planning population estimates.

†Maryland Department of State Planning population estimate based on their 1970 estimate.

EXHIBIT 7 Baltimore-Washington International Airport
Airport choice factors

Factor	Not important	Important	Very important	Most important
Overall				
Convenient location	13.9%	15.6%	16.9%	53.6%
Cost and time of public transport	51.4	17.7	15.4	15.4
More convenient flight times	18.3	21.7	24.7	35.4
Better access roads and parking	52.3	21.9	14.2	11.6
Better ticketing/baggage facilities	58.1	23.3	10.6	8.0
Only airport with direct flight	31.0	14.6	14.9	39.5
Only flight with available seat	65.5	12.2	7.8	14.5
Washington National Airport				
Convenient location	12.0	16.9	18.8	52.7
Cost and time of public transport	45.6	19.3	17.8	17.2
More convenient flight times	15.4	20.8	25.9	37.9
Better access roads and parking	60.8	21.1	10.9	7.3
Better ticketing/baggage facilities	63.8	21.3	8.8	6.0
Only airport with direct flight	30.4	14.6	15.7	39.3
Only flight with available seat	64.0	12.5	8.2	15.3
Dulles International Airport				
Convenient location	32.4	20.9	15.6	31.0
Cost and time of public transport	66.5	16.6	10.5	6.4
More convenient flight times	18.8	21.7	24.0	35.6
Better access roads and parking	40.0	22.3	20.4	17.3
Better ticketing/baggage facilities	48.2	24.8	16.5	10.4
Only airport with direct flight	22.3	11.6	13.7	52.3
Only flight with available seat	71.0	11.0	6.5	11.4
Baltimore-Washington International Airport				
Convenient location	8.1	10.1	13.7	68.1
Cost and time of public transport	55.4	14.8	13.1	16.6
More convenient flight times	24.2	23.5	22.6	29.7
Better access roads and parking	42.8	23.4	17.0	16.8
Better ticketing/baggage facilities	52.3	26.5	10.6	10.6
Only airport with direct flight	38.2	16.7	13.9	31.1
Only flight with available seat	65.5	12.3	7.6	14.5

Source: Baltimore-Washington International Airport.

To be read: 13.9 percent of all the responses to the question about the importance of the airport's convenient location, stated that it was not important. Only 8.1 percent of those passengers using Baltimore-Washington responded in the same manner.

EXHIBIT 8 **Baltimore-Washington International Airport**
Comparative surface access time

	Destination		Time saved
	Friendship	Dulles	via Friendship
Origin	(minutes)		(minutes)
Mt. Rainier			
Heavy Traffic Periods	65*	110†	43
Other Periods	57	99	42
Cheverly			
Heavy Traffic Periods	40	121	81
Other Periods	40	94	54
Seat Pleasant			
Heavy Traffic Periods	52	121	69
Other Periods	48	103	55
Hyattsville			
Heavy Traffic Periods	57	120	63
Other Periods	53	105	52
Riverdale			
Heavy Traffic Periods	54	128	74
Other Periods	52	109	57
College Park			
Heavy Traffic Periods	57	130	73
Other Periods	50	111	61
Silver Spring			
Heavy Traffic Periods	75	111	36
Other Periods	70	100	30
Washington, D.C. (12th & K Streets)			
Heavy Traffic Periods	70	85	15
Other Periods	65	81	16
Baltimore			
Heavy Traffic Periods	30	160	130
Other Periods	20	140	120

Notes:
*Includes 20 minutes for terminal processing.
†Includes 20 minutes for terminal processing plus 15 minutes for the mobile lounge trip.

DISCUSSION

1. Prepare a market analysis of the territories that the Baltimore-Washington airport would probably serve as (1) a local airport and as (2) a regional airport. Besides determining current market population totals, determine your longer-range projections to 1990.
2. List the advantages of adopting each general strategy (that is, being a local airport and instead aiming to be a regional one).
3. State the reasons for your choice in question 2. Support them with whatever data you consider relevant.

CASE C

Public Service Company of New Mexico

In January, 1978, Dan Peck, Director of Load Management, was preparing for a long range planning meeting. The meeting was to be broad in scope and would consider Public Service Company of New Mexico's activities in the areas of load management, rate design, public relations, advertising and promotion, customer contact work, market research and forecasting. Responsibility for these activities was currently assigned to a number of organizational components. Generally these components worked well together in support of overall company objectives, assisted materially by good informal communication channels. There was concern, however, that as the company grew these informal communication channels would become less effective. It was felt, therefore, that consideration should be given to formalizing individual component objectives and to alternative forms of organization.

In 1975 load management had been defined as a key company activity. In preparing for the meeting Dan was well aware that decisions arrived at would have substantial impact on the load management function and, in turn, on the long range future of the company.

COMPANY BACKGROUND

PNM is the largest investor-owned utility in the state of New Mexico providing electric service to nearly one half of the state's residents. The company's primary service areas are the cities and towns along the Middle Rio Grande Valley and the communities of Las Vegas and Deming. The company also provides electric service to other areas of the state

This case was prepared by Professor H. Michael Hayes of the University of New Mexico Anderson School of Management as a basis for class discussion rather than to illustrate either effective or ineffective handling of an administrative situation.
Copyright © 1978 by H. Michael Hayes. Used by permission.

through sales to investor and publically owned utilities and federal agencies. Outside of its normal service area the company provides electricity to a number of uranium mines and mills near Grants, New Mexico. In addition, the company provides water service to residents of Santa Fe and Las Vegas.

PNM's history dates back to 1880 and includes over 25 companies in a series of mergers and acquisitions. In 1926 the New Mexico Power Co., controlled by the Federal Light and Traction Company, became the predominant predecessor to the company which evolved in its present form in 1949. In 1972 the Company was listed on the New York Stock Exchange (trading symbol PNM).

Load Characteristics

As part of the Sun Belt, New Mexico has experienced a population growth substantially above the national average. In the PNM service area population growth in the period 1974–76 was 2.2% and is projected to be 2.3%, twice the national average. Company operating statistics reflect this growth (See Appendix 1). From 1966–76 peak load grew at a rate of 7.2% compounded, hitting 633 Megawatts (MW) in the summer of 1976. In the same period the growth in the number of residential customers was 3.7% compounded. The number of company employees also increased; from 937 in 1972 to over 1500 in 1976.

As shown in Table 1, kilowatthour (KWH) sales and company revenues come primarily from residential and commercial customers. Despite a substantial growth in industrial revenues due to uranium mining and milling activities only 16.8% of KWH sales and 13.7% of company revenues came from industrial customers in 1976. Resale contracts are an important source of revenue and the company has successfully included time of day rates in a number of its resale contracts, assisting materially in improving the annual overall load factor to levels in excess of 70%.

TABLE 1 Selected 1976 operating statistics

Class of service	KWH sales (% of total)	10 year compound growth rate	Revenues (% of total)	Number of customers
Residential	25.5	8.1	34.1	156,116
Commercial	35.5	8.5	38.0	17,483
Industrial	16.8	3.8	13.7	489
Other	4.4	6.3	4.4	250
Resale	17.8	7.1	9.8	5

Organization

PNM is organized in eight functional areas, as shown in Appendix 2. Six electric operating divisions (Albuquerque, Belen, Bernalillo, Deming, Las Vegas, and Santa Fe) report to the Vice President for division operations. Albuquerque is the largest division (metropolitan area population approximately 350,000) and the company headquarters are located in Albuquerque.

Fuel Situation

Currently PNM is in a transition from gas to coal as its predominant source of fuel. Older plants in the Albuquerque, Santa Fe, and Las Vegas areas are gas or oil fired. In 1972 PNM acquired 13% ownership in two units at the Four Corners Generating Station (near Farmington, N.M.). In partnership with Tucson Gas and Electric the company has a 50% interest in the San Juan Generating Station, located in northwest New Mexico, and in Western Coal which controls approximately 60 million tons of coal suitable for strip mining adjacent to the San Juan site. The first San Juan unit rated 322 Megawatts (MW) went into service in November, 1973, with a second unit rated 330 MW following in December, 1976. Units 3 and 4 were scheduled for installation in 1979–1981. In 1972, over half the kilowatt hours generated came from gas fired plants and only 44% from coal. By 1976, 60% of the company's generation came from coal fired plants.

In addition to its heavy involvement in coal, PNM has a 10.2% interest in the Palo Verde Nuclear Generating Station near Phoenix, Arizona. Three 1270 MW units were currently scheduled for completion at Palo Verde in 1982, 1984, and 1986.

Rate of Return/Indexing

In common with all electric utilities, PNM faces continuing problems in attracting sufficient capital to finance additional plant expansion. To attract capital the company established as its basic financial objective a policy of paying dividends amounting to 8% of stockholders common equity. Achieving this objective in the face of increasing inflation required the company to seek frequent rate increases. Uncertainty as to the outcome of its requested rate increases reduced the attractiveness of the company's common stock and was considered to be jeopardizing the company's AA bond ratings.

Effective April 22, 1975 the New Mexico Public Service Commission (NMPSC) approved an indexing plan for PNM which eliminated the necessity for frequent and protracted rate increase hearings. Essentially, NMPSC agreed to a 14% return on common equity for PNM. It further agreed to a procedure in which a quarterly review is made of the rate of return. If the quarterly review indicates a rate of return above 14.5%, rates are reduced. If the review indicates that return is below 13.5%, they are increased.

As a result of indexing PNM believes that rate increases have come to half of what they otherwise would have been (rate increases for utilities across the country have averaged about 10% a year recently versus PNM's increases of 6%). The major reason for this, according to Jerry Geist, PNM's president, is that the earning stability brought about by indexing has enabled the company to markedly reduce its cost of capital. Since the advent of indexing the PE ratio of the company's common stock has increased by approximately 20%. It has maintained its AA ratings on bonds, believed to be worth 100 to 200 basis points.[1] As a result of indexing, the estimated interest savings in meeting 1980 capital requirements are estimated to range from 16–28 million dollars.

Indexing is not without controversy, however. Critics contend that incentive to keep costs down has been lost as a result of indexing. PNM's financial manager, Martin A. Clifton, answers this argument pointing out that the leeway between 13.5% and 14.5% can come to $1 million a year. "That's plenty of incentive to do better," he says. And speaking for the NMPSC, Robert L. Swarthout, executive director, says, "If you look at the performance of the company and the cost of debt since indexing, I believe the consumer has benefitted."

Solar Strategy

Despite the company's heavy involvement in coal and nuclear energy sources there is a strong belief that solar energy will be a major element of strategy in the future. In a recent article in *Business Week* PNM President Jerry Geist was quoted as saying, "Sun-

---

[1]100 basis points = 1% of bond's face value.

shine is a resource that we need to utilize. As things are, our customers are getting creamed with fuel price increases."

Abundant as sunshine is in New Mexico (in 1976 Albuquerque had 179 clear days, second only to Phoenix in major metropolitan areas), solar generation is currently more expensive than either fossil or nuclear. However, 1983 cost projections indicate[d] that existing gas/oil fired plants could be retrofitted to solar with resulting total generating costs of approximately 35 mills per KWH[2] versus 40–50 mills for oil fired plants. According to Geist there is as much as 10,000 MW of plant capacity in the southwest which could benefit from such retrofitting.

It is also felt that use of solar heat for home and/or water heating will play a significant part in holding down the future cost of electricity. According to David K. Summers, a PNM energy conservation engineer, time of day rates in conjunction with solar heat in residential applications may shift consumption to off peak hours; thus improving system load factor resulting in lower rates for all consumers.

Competition

The other major energy supplier in New Mexico is the Southern Union Company which provides natural gas service to 45 cities and towns in New Mexico including Albuquerque, Belen, Bernalillo, and Santa Fe. Despite some limitations, gas is generally available for new residential and commercial customers in the area. Gas prices at the retail level have increased substantially, however, reflecting an increase in the cost of purchased gas to Southern Union Co. from 25 cents per Mcf in 1972 to 93 cents in 1976.

In 1976 Southern Union Company implemented a number of organizational changes including:

1. A major change in New Mexico where all operations were combined in one division and designated the Gas Company of New Mexico.
2. Gas appliance merchandising was separated from utility operations and placed under a new division, the Gas Appliance Company.
3. The company entered the solar energy business by obtaining the rights to distribute products of a Denver, Colorado manufacturer of solar energy systems in Arizona, southern Nevada, and most of Texas and New Mexico. A new subsidiary, Enersol Company, was organized to handle this business.

To some extent these organizational changes reflected a change in the company's marketing philosophy. The shift from a consumption minded to a conservation minded public dictated a cessation of direct sales promotion. Instead, the company placed more and more emphasis on consumer information and education. As stated in the 1976 Annual Report:

> To protect the Company's markets from erosion, substantial marketing efforts are being aimed by the Gas Appliance Company at the replacement market by encouraging the use of modern, more efficient gas appliances which when used properly, actually bring about overall savings in energy consumption. In addition, the Company has actively maintained relations with traditional trade allies—manufacturers, distributors, dealers, and home builders. An objective of both these activities is to help reassure the general public that the Company will have gas available to continue serving high priority uses—principally residential and commercial loads—well into the future.

In the solar field, Southern Union Company was also actively involved with builders in testing combination natural gas/solar energy systems in homes and apartments; reflect-

---

[2]1 mill = $.001.

ing the company's belief that if solar energy develops as expected it would enable serving more customers for a longer period of time since solar energy can be used in the home as a supplement to natural gas energy.

MARKETING AT PNM

In 1972 marketing at PNM was restructured. A Marketing and Staff Services Department, reporting to a vice president of marketing, was established. Included in this new department were the previous activities of the Consumers Services and Home Economics Departments. In addition a Marketing Research Department was established. Objectives of the Marketing Research Department included the development of data to (1) develop a marketing program to improve systems load factor, (2) determine effect of various methods of pricing electricity, and (3) encourage a proper balance in the application of energy to end uses.

Throughout 1973 and 1974 efforts in the newly created departments were devoted to developing an appropriate data base and to developing selected marketing programs to increase off-peak use. During this period the first in-house company-wide residential customer attitude and awareness survey was completed.

Marketing Plan/1975

In October, 1975, a comprehensive proposal entitled "Planned Growth Through Marketing" was presented for top management consideration. The plan identified the importance of marketing and developed five broad business objectives as follows:

1. that energy sales should be expanded in a manner so as to minimize the capital-related and energy (fuel)-related components of PNM's retail rates;
2. that load management objectives proposed by the Federal Energy Administration for the electric utility industry should be vigorously pursued to the extent that these actions will be to the over-all benefit of our customers;
3. that our customers are to be provided with the information required for their wisest use of electricity and of substitute energy sources;
4. that the development and adoption of electrical products which provide a means of reducing pollution from present energy consuming applications and which provide the lowest cost alternatives to existing energy consuming applications are to be encouraged; and
5. that implementation of the elements of this plan must present a consistent impression which is in harmony with the broader goal of serving the welfare of our customers.

To achieve these business objectives the marketing plan identified 26 elements with defined activities, timetables and measures of accomplishment. Marketing goals and significant actions by plan element for 1977 are listed in Appendix 3.

In addition to making very specific recommendations regarding all 26 plan elements the marketing plan included a net benefit comparison for the years 1976 to 1985. This comparison contrasted estimates of potential earnings against program costs. "Most likely" estimates of net benefits were made for each year. On a levelized basis net benefit estimates amounted to $481,294 per year.

Organization Changes/1975

Throughout the utility industry 1974 and 1975 were the years of de-emphasis of marketing activities. Much of PNM's marketing plan was devoted to conservation activities and to load management, designed to shift energy demands to off peak hours. Rightly or wrongly, however, marketing had become associated with unlimited growth and this concept was not consistent with the mood for conservation that was sweeping the country as a result of the energy crisis. To reflect this national concern and because of certain internal considerations it was decided by PNM management that the marketing function as a clearly defined and separate entity should be discontinued.

Late in 1975 marketing activities were reorganized. Load research and market research were assigned to the Manager—Rates Department. Consumer services functions were moved into division operations. Responsibility for advertising and promotion was assigned to the vice president for public relations.

Further emphasis was placed on the load management program. Responsibility for the program was assigned to the Market Research section and in early 1976 the basic elements of the program were defined in the form of Interim Load Management Project (IMLP).

While much of the work of the former marketing department was being continued the organization changes were not without cost. There was serious concern in the minds of many about the future of marketing at PNM, particularly in the case of those involved in direct customer contact work. Dispersal of marketing activities created communication problems. In some instances employee morale was adversely affected.

A management and operations review by Theodore Barry and Associates recognized some of these problems and commented in part as follows:

> The load management program, while well defined in the market research department, appears to be somewhat fragmented. This fragmentation is a natural consequence of the multidiscipline approach, and is most effectively integrated through periodic review and policy definition by PNM's senior management. There is some confusion among the principal participants within the company regarding the direction of the program, its priority within the overall context of system-wide planning functions and its solidifications as the approved load management position of the company. This confusion can be attributed in great part to the relative newness of the program and its adoption in early 1976 on an interim basis.

In a summary of major recommendations included in the Barry Study, it was recommended that the load management program be formalized, with probable cost benefits of $1,800,000. Other benefits that might result from such formalization were seen to include clarification of corporate policies regarding marketing and load management.

Utility Conservation Action Now (UCAN)

On March 16, 1976 in response to a request by the Federal Energy Administration (FEA), PNM transmitted a draft version of its UCAN Action plan to the FEA regional office in Dallas. The action plan was identified as stemming from the October 1975 marketing plan. However, it was pointed out the marketing plan was still subject to final approval by PNM management, pending an upcoming review and approval hearing on advertising by the New Mexico Public Service Commission. Hence the action plan was submitted subject to the outcome of that review and approval process. (PNM's action plan received a letter of commendation from the FEA.)

The plan listed specific actions regarding load factor, system capacity factor, growth rates in KWH sales and KW demand. In addition it established objectives for oil consumption and electric generation, KWH output to be produced by coal and nuclear and increased end use efficiency of distributed electricity. Specific energy conservation and efficiency measures were identified in the following areas.

1. Structural Rate Reform
2. Load Management
3. Wisest Use of Energy-Promotion and Advertising

4. Consumer Education Program
5. Energy Consultation
6. Energy Efficiency Awards
7. Municipal Refuse Power Generation
8. Building Practices Revision Program
9. Electrical Transportation Program
10. Generation Byproduct Utilization
11. Predictive Models
12. Bulk Generation

Consistent with its UCAN Proposal, and anticipating federal requirements pertaining to mandatory hearings by state regulatory agencies, PNM and the other investor-owned utilities in New Mexico proposed (to the NMPSC) additional hearing topics for legislative consideration of utility rate reform as follows:

1. Time of Day Rates
2. Seasonal Rates
3. Cost of Service Pricing
4. Interruptable Rates and Management Techniques
5. Prohibition on Declining Block Rates Unless Cost Justified
6. Prohibitions or Restrictions on Master Metering
7. Procedures for Reviewing Automatic Adjustments
8. Procedures Prohibiting Discrimination in Rates and Other Practices Against Solar, Wind, and Other Small Systems
9. Procedures to Provide Adequate Information to Customers
10. Prohibitions on Charging Rate Payers for Certain Advertising
11. Procedures to Protect Against Abrupt Termination of Service
12. Lifeline Rates

It was the feeling of PNM, and the other investor-owned utilities, that covering these topics would provide the opportunity for a comprehensive and integrated approach toward energy conservation consistent with proposed federal law and that this would put New Mexico in a leadership position as regards responding to federal requirements.

Current Marketing Organization

Subsequent to the organizational changes of 1975, additional changes were made affecting marketing functions. The load management function was assigned to the corporate secretary and treasurer's office. Principal activities reporting to the Director of Load Management were Marketing Research and Residential and Commercial Development. This latter activity involved approximately 14 people and evolved from the customer service activity in division operations. Primary objectives of the new functions were to increase sales efficiently, and to assist in conservation practices both residential and commercial. Specific activities include such items as working with trade allies and developing standards for heating and cooling. In describing the new organization, Dan Peck said, "With just a few people in the organization and the significantly increasing trend toward total electric living, we no longer have the manpower to respond to customers on an individual basis. Hence we are trying to work through qualified builders and other trade allies in order to multiply our efforts."

Lanny Tonning was appointed Director of Public Relations, reporting to the vice president of public affairs. In this capacity, Tonning is responsible for all PNM advertising activities (including exhibits and displays), consumer education, the company's speaker's bureau and employee education plus special newsletters to opinion leaders and the company's annual report. According to Tonning:

> Every day we have to furnish an incredible amount of information to a wide variety of people outside the company. This information tends to fall in two major categories. First, there are matters of fact. Here I'm talking about such things as those aspects of the company's business which are a matter of public record, or such things as the efficiency of various kinds of generating equipment or the efficiency of various kinds of insulating systems for home heating. To the degree that we can, we try to refer these kinds of questions to experts within our company, recognizing at the same time that people who are experts in these matters cannot be expected to spend all their time answering outsiders' questions. On the other hand, we have a category which I call interpretive information. This tends to deal with matters of company policy and may involve such things as justification of our advertising progam or our rate structure. We spend a lot of time educating our employees to be good spokesmen for the company in these matters but the primary responsibility for such communication rests with my office and with top management.

Currently PNM has in place a load management committee chaired by Dan Peck. The committee is made up of representatives of financial planning, generation planning, transmission planning, load research, market research, rates, public information and division operations. According to Peck, "Load management activities take place on both sides of the meter. That is, we can control our plant load factors by the kinds of interchange contracts we negotiate with neighboring utilities or through energy storage systems such as pumped storage or through the use of peaking plants. On the customer's side of the meter we are looking at such things as time of day rates or load control as ways to improve system load as well as to effect energy conservation. The commitee's basic responsibility is to coordinate all load management activities."

The Residential Customer

The nature of residential demand for electricity with respect to price has been the subject of a number of investigations. Some studies have attempted to determine price elasticity from secondary data (i.e., from existing data on demand, consumption, price, income, etc.). Other studies have involved experiments to determine the impact of Time-of-Day (TOD) rates, peakload pricing, inverted rates, rates using Long Range Incremental Costing (LRIC), etc.

The difficulty in accurately determining elasticity of demand was described by the Committee on Interior and Insular Affairs (S. Res. 45, 92d. Congress) as follows:

> The effect of pricing policies on the level and growth of electric consumption is difficult to determine, since the measurement of price-responsiveness of demand (its elasticity) for either electricity in particular or energy generally is still in the embryonic stage. Elasticities are not necessarily the same in the different consuming sectors, nor yet in the long run versus the short run. Conceptually this presents no problem; on the level of measurement, however, it is a different story. Available data are not defined nor segregated in a manner which permits rigorous statistical treatment. Indeed, the data are not always what they purport to be, as, for example, data on commercial consumption may include small industrial consumption because of the way in which the reporting utility defines its customer classes.

Partly because of methodology and partly because of variability in the data across geographical boundaries, time periods, etc., results of elasticity studies have varied widely. In one group of recent studies calculated price elasticities ranged from −.23 to −2.09. (An elasticity coefficient of $-.23$ means that demand was found to decline .23 percent for a one percent increase in price.)

Few studies have been made regarding the impact of energy conservation information on demand for electricity. In one such study, however, Dr. Ray Battaglio of Texas Tech concluded that energy conservation messages *and* feedback on use had *no* effect on consumption.

Commenting on this subject Lanny Tonning said:

> Not everyone at PNM agrees with me but I seriously doubt that conservation messages will have any significant effect on our customers' use of electricity. The only way to really alter demand, as I see it, is through price or by some means of load control.

Current Marketing Activities

One of PNM's major activities evolving from the 1975 marketing plan is the SMART (Save Money and Resources Too) home program. The basic concept of the SMART home is a high level of insulation which reduces heating requirements by two thirds and costs no more to build than a conventional FHA unit. Since introduction of the concept the number of homes constructed to SMART standards has far exceeded PNM's expectations.

Currently PNM is involved in seven experimental solar projects at the residential level. Largest of these is a joint project with HUD (Department of Housing and Urban Development) and AMREP (a local builder) to install solar heating equipment with load management features in 25 new homes being constructed in the Albuquerque area.

Current Marketing Objectives

According to Dan Peck:

> I see our basic objective at PNM as one of meeting the growing energy needs of the state. That is, PNM should not be a constraint to achieving whatever destiny the state elects to pursue. From a marketing standpoint I see this as meaning that we focus on promoting the efficient use of electricity and reducing the state's dependence on gas and oil as sources of energy. From a load management standpoint I see this as requiring that we do everything we can to shape the load pattern in a manner acceptable to our customers so as to minimize revenue requirements. I think if we can do these two things we will carry out our obligation to the state of New Mexico and also to our stockholders.

APPENDIX 1   Comparative operating statistics

	1976	1975	1974	1973
ELECTRIC SERVICE				
SALES—KWH (Thousands)				
Residential	916,748	875,361	828,243	786,108
Commercial	1,277,025	1,177,953	1,128,576	1,110,147
Industrial	605,559	530,188	549,622	616,405
Other Sales	157,694	136,136	137,843	128,171
Total Sales to Ultimate Customers	2,957,026	2,719,638	2,644,284	2,640,831
Sales for Resale	638,207	578,037	250,901	122,656
Total Energy Sales	3,595,233	3,297,675	2,895,185	2,763,487
ELECTRIC REVENUES (Thousands)				
Residential	$ 32,423	$ 28,912	$ 23,314	$ 20,552
Commercial	36,198	30,851	25,403	22,283
Industrial	13,070	9,993	8,349	7,210
Other Revenues	4,168	3,361	3,004	2,613
Total Revenue from Ultimate Customers	$ 85,859	$ 73,117	$ 60,070	$ 52,658
Sales for Resale	9,340	8,241	2,782	1,074
Total Revenue from Energy Sales	$ 95,199	$ 81,358	$ 62,852	$ 53,732
Miscellaneous Electric Revenues	1,935	1,412	2,406	2,803
Total Electric Revenue	$ 97,134	$ 82,770	$ 65,258	$ 56,535
CUSTOMERS AT YEAR END				
Residential	156,116	151,111	147,516	143,201
Commercial	17,483	16,738 (2)	16,469	16,241
Industrial	489	515 (2)	298	295
Other Customers	250	246	231	229
Total Ultimate Customers	174,338	168,610	164,514	159,966
Sales for Resale	5	4	4	3
Total Customers	174,343	168,614	164,518	159,969
Reliable net capability—KW	858,000	727,000	727,000	617,000
Coincidental peak demand—KW	633,000	586,000	583,400	533,000
Average Fuel cost per million BTU	61.83¢	47.23¢	39.49¢	26.16¢
BTU per KWH of net generation	11,084	10,848	11,054	11.017
WATER SERVICE				
SALES—Gallons (Thousands)—				
Customer sales	2,959,209	2,859,783	3,013,508	2,855,673
Interdepartmental sales	4,014	9,195	12,568	10,710
Total water sales	2,963,223	2,868,978	3,026,076	2,866,383
REVENUE—				
Customer sales	$2,386,222	$2,204,967	$2,103,169	$1,566,730
Interdepartmental sales	2,580	2,721	5,970	3,585
Total water sales	$2,388,802	$2,207,688	$2,109,139	$1,570,315
Customers at year end	16,838	16,437	16,158	15,848

Source: PNM Annual Report, 1976.

continued

(1) Reclassified Against Expense.

(2) Certain customers were reclassified from commercial to industrial during 1975. The reclassification accounted for a change of 220 customers in both categories.

1972	1971	1970	1969	1968	1967	1966
706,973	648,626	583,136	532,200	486,468	443,916	420,891
985,431	885,782	792,376	732,807	659,836	617,209	565,752
653,761	618,695	552,118	524,180	479,883	444,907	416,594
123,568	116,202	107,598	97,762	89,835	86,790	85,532
2,469,733	2,269,305	2,035,228	1,886,949	1,716,022	1,592,822	1,488,769
114,333	106,000	98,026	91,890	86,765	80,322	78,864
2,584,066	2,375,305	2,133,254	1,978,839	1,802,787	1,673,144	1,567,633
$ 17,760	$ 15,295	$ 13,910	$ 12,861	$ 11,955	$ 11,135	$ 10,652
19,421	16,309	14,784	13,719	12,489	11,790	10,979
7,229	6,549	5,963	5,662	5,187	4,732	4,625
2,204	1,994	2,056	1,889	1,751	1,662	1,639
$ 46,614	$ 40,147	$ 36,713	$ 34,131	$ 31,382	$ 29,319	$ 27,895
937	857	778	659	557	550	597
$ 47,551	$ 41,004	$ 37,491	$ 34,790	$ 31,939	$ 29,869	$ 28,492
795	670	621	654	640	583	520
$ 48,346	$ 41,674	$ 38,112	$ 35,444	$ 32,579	$ 30,452	$ 29,012
136,515	127,911	120,865	115,595	112,765	110,501	108,845
15,754	14,775	13,908	13,395	13,084	12,776	12,588
303	308	300	290	296	303	319
221	205	201	199	187	184	187
152,793	143,199	135,274	129,479	126,332	123,764	121,939
3	3	3	2	2	2	3
152,796	143,202	135,277	129,481	126,334	123,766	121,942
542,000	540,700	540,700	437,400	334,000	334,000	334,000
491,700	458,700	400,600	372,300	347,800	328,500	316,300
24.47¢	23.55¢	23.04¢	24.48¢	24.26¢	24.03¢	24.00¢
10,841	10,870	11,058	11,552	11,550	11,263	11,199
2,781,854	2,563,745	2,564,580	2,397,078	2,356,690	2,253,347	2,145,483
3,638	1,707	1,782	1,609	1,132	1,261	1,630
2,785,492	2,565,452	2,566,362	2,398,687	2,357,822	2,254,608	2,147,113
$1,530,012	$1,434,685	$1,417,697	$1,209,617	$1,172,831	$1,144,096	$1,100,523
(1)	813	899	780	659	689	757
$1,530,012	$1,435,498	$1,418,596	$1,210,397	$1,173,490	$1,144,785	$1,101,280
15,454	15,024	14,495	14,216	14,092	13,811	13,679

APPENDIX 2 Functional area executives

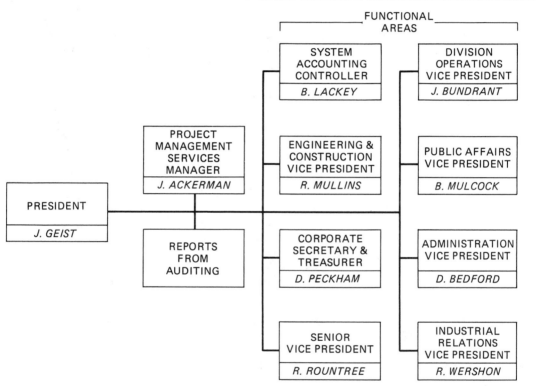

Source: PNM Records.

APPENDIX 3 Marketing goals and significant actions by plan element

Element	Goals	Actions
Public Relations	Level of customer support at 75% in 1980	Introduce Energy Efficient Home
Builder Program	Total Electric = 10% of new homes	Introduce Energy Efficient Home
Heat Pump	In 20% of new Total Electric Homes	Secure applications of State solar system income tax credit to Heat Pump
Heat Pump Maintenance	100% certification of new homes	Offer guaranteed maintenance; begin certification of dealers
Preferred Solar Home	5 homes built	Construct test homes
Design Liaison	25% of all new commercial construction as Total Electric	Initiate regular tours and seminars; host professionals to national schools
Electric Transportation	Initial trials of equipment	Conduct initial trials in cooperation with interested organizations and agencies
Lighting	1 MW/year	Expand program to include media advertising
Industrial Development	1 MW/year	Begin aggressive promotional campaign out-of-state
Mechanical Manuf. Reps.	25% of all new commercial construction as Total Electric; calls	Sponsor local seminar; develop Electric League
Electric Manuf. Reps.	25% of all new commercial construction as Total Electric; calls	Sponsor local seminars; develop Electric League
Load Management	Reduce peak by 5 MW	Establish systematic load management consulting program; introduce interruptable service rates
Residential Market Segmentation	Level of minority customer support at 65% by 1980	Evaluate success and make adjustments to program
Home Economics	(See Public Relations and Residential Market Segmentation)	Help with introduction of Energy Efficient Home; extend dealer service program to outlying Divisions
Retail Sales Support	Electric ranges at 75% of replacement market	Same as for 1976, adding freezers
Mobile Homes	Total Electric = 10% of new mobile homes	Increase emphasis in outlying Divisions
Irrigation	Complete conversion by 1980	Complete surveys; complete system designs
Pricing Objectives	(See Public Relations and Res. Market Segmentation)	Complete preparation of recommendations
Energy Efficient Home	25% of new home construction	Market introductory homes

Element	Goals	Actions
Wholesale Distribution	(See Builder Program)	Use as entree to develop cooperative advertising with manufacturers
Electric League	Establishment of League	Found League
EVAC Conversion	5 MW/year converted in 1980	Begin aggressive consulting effort
Electrical Contractors	calls	Promote membership in Electric League
Mechanical Contractors	calls	Secure cooperation in connection with dealer certification for Heat Pump Maintenance Program
Insulation	(See Builder Program and Energy Efficient Home)	Secure State Income Tax credit for adoption of increased insulation standards
Storage Heating Development	Install storage heating system in test home	Build local prototype and evaluate

Source: PNM Marketing Plan, October 1975.

DISCUSSION

1. Write a brief statement of the marketing objectives and strategy adopted by the PNM company in 1975. Evaluate whether the outlined program would be likely to accomplish those aims.

2. In what ways, if at all, did the abolition of the marketing department and assignment of its functions to other departments affect the implementation and control of the 1975 marketing plan?

3. As reorganized in 1975, how would the PNM conduct future strategic-marketing planning? After making this assessment, would you say that there should be a single marketing department embracing the remaining marketing functions or that the 1975 reassignment of them should be continued? Include in this assessment the matters of preparing, implementing, and controlling marketing plans.

Suggested Readings

PART ONE—INTRODUCTION

ALDERSON, W., and P. E. GREEN, *Planning and Problem Solving in Marketing.* Homewood, Ill.: Richard D. Irwin, 1964.

ANSOFF, H. I., R. P. DELBECK, and R. L. HAYES, *From Strategic Planning to Strategic Management.* New York: Wiley-Interscience, 1976.

BOYD, H. W., Jr., and J. -C. LARRECHE The Foundations of Marketing Strategy," in *Annual Review of Marketing,* ed. G. Zaltman and T. Bonoma, pp. 42–72. Chicago: American Marketing Association, 1978.

CHANG, Y. N., and F. CAMPO-FLORES, *Business Policy and Strategy.* Santa Monica, Calif.: Goodyear, 1980.

DAY, GEORGE, *Strategic Market Planning: The Pursuit of Competitive Advantage* (St. Paul, Minn.: West Publishing, 1984.

KERIN, R. A., and R. A. PETERSON, eds., *Perspectives on Strategic Marketing Management* (2nd ed.). Boston: Allyn & Bacon, 1983.

KOTLER, PHILIP, *Marketing Management (5th ed.).* Englewood Cliffs, N.J.: Prentice-Hall, 1984.

———, and K. K. COX, eds., *Marketing Management and Strategy: A Reader* (3rd ed.). Englewood Cliffs, N. J.: Prentice-Hall, 1984.

LORANGE, P., and R. F. VANCIL, *Strategic Planning Systems.* Englewood Cliffs, N.J.: Prentice-Hall, 1977.

LUCK, D. J., and A. E. PRELL, *Market Strategy.* Englewood Cliffs, N. J.: Prentice-Hall, 1968.

SCHENDEL, D., and C. HOFER, eds., *Strategic Management: A New View on Business Policy and Planning.* Boston: Little, Brown, 1979.

PART TWO—STRATEGIC DECISIONS
AND THEIR INTEGRATION

ABELL, D., *Defining the Business: The Starting Point of Strategic Planning.* Englewood Cliffs, N. J.: Prentice-Hall, 1980.

———, and D. S. Hammond, *Strategic Market Planning.* Englewood Cliffs. N.J.: Prentice-Hall, 1979.

ACKOFF, R., *A Concept of Corporate Planning.* New York: John Wiley, 1970.

ANDERSON, P. "Marketing, Strategic Planning, and the Theory of the Firm," *Journal of Marketing,* Spring 1982, pp. 15–20.

ANDREWS, K. R., *The Concept of Corporate Strategy* (rev. ed.). Homewood, Ill: Richard D. Irwin, 1980.

BIGGADIKE, E. R., "The Contribution of Marketing to Strategic Management," *Academy of Management Review,* October 1981, pp. 621–33.

Business Week, "The New Planning," December 19, 1978, pp. 62–68.

DAY, G. S., "Diagnosing the Product Portfolio," *Journal of Marketing,* April 1977, pp. 29–38.

———, "Strategic Market Analysis: Top-down and Bottom-up Approaches," a working paper. Cambridge, Mass.: Marketing Science Institute, 1980.

———, and R. WENSLEY, "Priorities for Research in Strategic Marketing," a working paper. Cambridge, Mass.: Marketing Science Institute, 1984.

HALL, W. K., "SBU's: Hot, New Topic in the Management of Diversification," *Business Horizons,* February 1978, pp. 17–25.

———, "Survival Strategies in a Hostile Environment," *Harvard Business Review,* September–October 1980, pp. 75–85.

HASPELAGH, P., "Portfolio Planning, Uses and Limits," *Harvard Business Review,* January–February 1982, pp. 58–74.

HEDLEY, B., "Strategy and the Business Portfolio," *Long Range Planning,* February 1977, pp. 9–15.

HOFER, C. W., and D. E. SCHENDEL, *Strategy Formulation: Analytical Concepts.* St. Paul, Minn.: West Publishing, 1981.

HOPKINS, D. S., and E. L. BAILEY, *The Chief Marketing Executive: A Profile.* New York: Conference Board, 1971.

HUSSEY, D. E., "Portfolio Analysis: Practical Experience with the Directional Policy Matrix," *Long Range Planning,* August 1978, pp. 2–8.

KIECHEL, W., II, "Oh Where, Oh Where Has My Little Dog Gone? Or My Cash Cow? Or My Star?" *Fortune,* November 2, 1981.

LINNEMAN, R. E., *Shirt-Sleeve Approach to Long-Range Planning for the Smaller, Growing Corporation.* Englewood Cliffs, N. J.: Prentice-Hall, 1980.

LORANGE, P., *Corporate Planning: An Executive Viewpoint.* Englewood Cliffs, N. J.: Prentice-Hall, 1980.

PORTER, M. E., *Competitive Strategy: Techniques for Analyzing Industries and Competition.* New York: Free Press, 1980.

Schoeffler, S., "Cross Sectional Study of Strategy, Structure and Performance: Aspects of the PIMS Program, in *Strategy + Structure = Performance*, ed. H. Thorielli. Bloomington: Indiana University Press, 1977.

——, Buzzell, R. D., and D. F. Heany, "Impact of Strategic Planning on Product Performance," *Harvard Business Review*, March–April 1974, pp. 137–45.

Tregoe, B. B., and J. W. Zimmermann, *Top Management Strategy*. New York: Simon & Schuster, 1981.

Wensley, R., "Strategic Marketing: Betas, Boxes or Basics," *Journal of Marketing*, Summer 1981, pp. 173–82.

——, "PIMS and BCG: New Horizons or False Dawns in Strategic Marketing?" *Strategic Management Journal*, October–December 1981, p. 2.

Wind, Y., and V. Mahajan, "Designing Product and Business Portfolios," *Harvard Business Review*, January–February 1981, pp. 155–65.

PART THREE—MARKETING STRATEGY AND PLANS

Abernathy, William J., and Kim B. Clark, and Alan M. Kantrow, "The New Industrial Competition," *Harvard Business Review*, September–October 1981, pp. 68–81.

Buzzell, Robert D., and Frederik D. Wiersema, "Successful Share-Building Strategies," *Harvard Business Review*, January–February 1981, pp. 135–144.

Cravens, David W., "Strategic Marketing's New Challenge," *Business Horizons*, March–April 1983, pp. 18–24.

Ford, David, and Chris Ryan, "Taking Technology to Market," *Harvard Business Review*, March–April 1981, pp. 117–126.

Frohman, Alan L., "Technology as a Competitive Weapon," *Harvard Business Review*, January–February 1982, pp. 97–104.

Gluck, Frederick W., and Stephen P. Kaufman, and A. Steven Walleck, "Strategic Management for Competitive Advantage," *Harvard Business Review*, July–August 1980, pp. 154–161.

Hall, William K., "Survival Strategies in a Hostile Environment," *Harvard Business Review*, September–October 1980, pp. 75–85.

Hamermesh, R. G., and M. J. Anderson, Jr., and J. E. Harris, "Strategies for Low Market Share Businesses," *Harvard Business Review*, May–June 1978, pp. 95–102.

Hughes, G. David, "Antitrust Caveats for the Marketing Planner," *Harvard Business Review*, March–April 1978, pp. 40–192.

Jelinek, Mariann, and Joel D. Golhau, "The Interface Between Strategy and Manufacturing Technology," *Columbia Journal of World Business*, (Spring 1983, pp. 26–36.

Kantrow, Alan M., "The Strategy-Technology Connection," *Harvard Business Review*, July–August 1980, pp. 6–21.

Kotler, Philip, and Ravi Singh, "Marketing Warfare in the 1980's," *The Journal of Business Strategy*, Vol. 1, No. 3 (Winter 1981), pp. 30–42.

LEONE, ROBERT A., and JOHN R. MEYER, "Capacity Strategies for the 1980's," *Harvard Business Review,* November–December 1980, pp. 133–140.

LEVITT, THEODORE, "Marketing When Things Change," *Harvard Business Review,* November–December 1977, pp. 107–113.

MORTON, MAXWELL R., "Technology and Strategy: Creating a Successful Partnership," *Business Horizons,* January–February 1983, pp. 44–48.

OLD, BRUCE S., "Corporate Directors Should Rethink Technology," *Harvard Business Review,* January–February 1982, pp. 6–14.

PORTER, MICHAEL E., "How Competitive Forces Shape Strategy," *Harvard Business Review,* March–April 1979, pp. 137–145.

RESNIK, ALAN J., and PETER B. B. TURNEY, and J. BARRY MASON, "Marketers Turn to 'Countersegmentation'," *Harvard Business Review,* September–October 1979, pp. 100–106.

RESNIK, ALAN J., and HAROLD E. SAND, and J. BARRY MASON, "Marketing Dilemma: Change in the 80's," *California Management Review,* Vol. XXIV, No. 1 (Fall 1981), pp. 49–57.

SHANKLIN, WILLIAM L., "Strategic Business Planning: Yesterday, Today, and Tomorrow," *Business Horizons,* October 1979, pp. 7–14.

STEINBERG, BRUCE, "The Mass Market Is Splitting Apart," *Fortune,* November 28, 1983, pp. 76–82.

WALTERS, KENNETH D., and R. JOSEPH MONSON, "State-Owned Business Abroad: New Competitive Threat," *Harvard Business Review,* March–April 1979, pp. 160–170.

WATSON, CRAIG, M., "Counter-Competition Abroad to Protect Home Markets," *Harvard Business Review,* January–February 1982, pp. 40–42.

WEBER, JOHN A., "Market Structure Profile Analysis and Strategic Growth Opportunities," *California Management Review,* Vol. XX, No. 1 (Fall 1977), pp. 34–46.

WEIGAND, ROBERT E., "Buying into Market Control," *Harvard Business Review,* November–December 1980, pp. 141–149.

WIND, YORAM, "Marketing and Corporate Strategy," *The Wharton Magazine,* Summer 1982, pp. 38–45.

WOO, CAROLYN Y., and ARNOLD C. COOPER, "The Surprising Case for Low Market Share," *Harvard Business Review,* November–December 1982, pp. 106–113.

PART FOUR—PRODUCT/MARKET UNIT STRATEGIES

ADAMEC, R. J. "How to Improve Your New Product Success Rate," *Management Review,* January 1981, pp. 39–42.

BIGGADIKE, R., *Entering New Markets: Strategies and Performance.* Cambridge, Mass.: Marketing Science Institute, 1977.

BUZZELL, R. D., and F. D. WIERSMAN, "Successful Share-Building Strategies," *Harvard Business Review,* January–February 1981, pp. 135–44.

BOOZ, ALLEN & HAMILTON, Inc., *New Products for the 1980s.* New York, 1982.

CALANTONE, R. J., and R. J. COOPER, "New Product Scenarios: Prospects for Success," *Journal of Marketing*, Spring 1981, pp. 48–61.

CRAWFORD, C. M., *New Product Management*. Homewood, Ill.: Richard D. Irwin, 1983.

DAY, G. S., "Product Life Cycles: Analysis and Application," *Journal of Marketing*, Fall 1981, pp. 66–67.

DHALLA, N., and S. YUSPEH, "Forget the Product Life Cycle Concept," *Harvard Business Review*, January–February 1976, pp. 102–12.

LUCK, D. J., *Product Policy and Strategy*. Englewood Cliffs, N. J.: Prentice-Hall, 1972.

PORTER, M. E., *Competitive Strategy: Techniques for Analyzing Industries and Competition*. New York: Free Press, 1980.

———, "Please Note Location of Nearest Exit: Exit Barriers and Planning," *California Management Review*, Winter 1976, pp. 24–33.

RINK, D. K., and J. E. SWAN, "Product Life Cycle Research: A Literature Review," *Journal of Marketing*, September 1978, pp. 219–42.

URBAN, G. L., and J. R. HAUSER, *Design and Marketing of New Products*. Englewood Cliffs, N. J.: Prentice-Hall, 1980.

YIP, G. S., "Gateways to Entry," *Harvard Business Review*, September–October 1982, pp. 82–86.

ZARECOR, W. D., "High Technology Product Planning," *Harvard Business Review*, January–February 1975, pp. 108–18.

PART FIVE—MARKETING MIX DECISIONS

ASSMUS, GERT, JOHN U. FARLEY, and DONALD R. LEHMANN, "How Advertising Affects Sales: Meta Analysis of Econometric Results," *Journal of Marketing Research*, Vol. XXI (February 1984), pp. 65–74.

AYAL, IGAL, "International Product Life Cycle: A Reassessment and Product Policy Implications," *Journal of Marketing*, Vol. 45, No. 4 (Fall 1981), pp. 91–96.

BECKENSTEIN, ALAN R., and H. LANDIS GABEL, "Experience Curve Pricing Strategy: The Next Target of Antitrust?" *Business Horizons*, September–October 1982, pp. 71–77.

BLAIR, EDWARD A., and E. LAIRD LANDON, Jr., "The Effects of Reference Prices in Retail Advertisements," *Journal of Marketing*, Vol. 45 (Spring 1981), pp. 61–69.

BLOCH, PETER H., and MARSHA L. RICHINS, "A Theoretical Model for the Study of Product Importance Perceptions," *Journal of Marketing*, Vol. 47, No. 3 (Summer 1983), pp. 69–81.

CABALLERO, MARJORIE J., and WILLIAM M. PRIDE, "Selected Effects of Salesperson Sex and Attractiveness in Direct Mail Advertisements," *Journal of Marketing*, Vol 48, No. 1 (Winter 1984), pp. 94–100.

CALANTONE, ROGER, and ROBERT G. COOPER, "New Product Scenarios: Prospects for Success," *Journal of Marketing*, Vol. 45, No. 2 (Spring 1981), pp. 48–60.

COHEN, ARTHUR I., and ANA LOUD JONES, "Brand Marketing in the New Retail Environment," *Howard Business Review*, (September–October 1978), pp. 141–148.

Cossé, Thomas J., and John E. Swan, "Strategic Marketing Planning by Product Managers—Room for Improvement?" *Journal of Marketing,* Vol. 47., No. 3 (Summer 1983), pp. 92–102.

Day, George, "The Product Life Cycle? Analysis and Applications Issues," *Journal of Marketing,* Vol. 45, No. 4 (Fall 1981), pp. 60–67.

Dickson, Peter R., "Distributor Portfolio Analysis and the Channel Dependence Matrix: New Techniques for Understanding and Managing the Channel," *Journal of Marketing,* Vol. 47, No. 3 (Summer 1983), pp. 35–44.

Dolan, Robert J., and Abel P. Jeuland, "Experience Curves and Dynamic Demand Models: Implications for Optimal Pricing Strategies," *Journal of Marketing,* Vol. 45, No. 1 (Winter 1981), pp. 52–62.

Dowling, Grahame R., "Information Content in U. S. and Australian Content in U. S. and Australian Television Advertising," *Journal of Marketing,* Vol. 44, No. 4 (Fall 1980), pp. 34–37.

Eliasberg, Jehoshua, and Donald A. Michie, "Multiple Business Goals Sets as Determinants of Marketing Channel Conflict: An Empirical Study," *Journal of Marketing Research,* Vol. XXI (February 1984), pp. 75–88.

Farris, Paul W., and Mark S. Albion, "The Impact of Advertising on the Price of Consumer Products," *Journal of Marketing,* Vol. 44, No. 3 (Summer 1980), pp. 17–35.

Frazier, Gary L., "On the Measurement of Interfirm Power in Channels of Distribution," *Journal of Marketing Research,* Vol. XX (May 1983), pp. 158–166.

Harrell, Stephen G., and Elmer D. Taylor, "Marketing the Product Life Cycle for Consumer Durables," *Journal of Marketing,* Vol. 45, No. 4 (Fall 1981), pp. 68–75.

Hayes, Robert H., and Steven C. Wheelwright, "Link Manufacturing Process and Product Life Cycles," *Harvard Business Review,* January–February 1979, pp. 133–140.

Hayes, Robert H., and Steven G. Wheelwright, "The Dynamics of Process-Product Life Cycles," *Harvard Business Review,* March–April 1979, pp. 127–136.

Heskett, James L., "Logistics-Essential to Strategy," *Harvard Business Review,* November–December 1977, pp. 85–96.

Johnson, Wesley, J., and Thomas V. Bonoma, "The Buying Center: Structure and Interaction Patterns," *Journal of Marketing,* Vol. 45, No. 3 (Summer 1981), pp. 143–156.

Lambert, Zarrel V., "Perceived Prices as Related to Odd and Even Price Endings," *Journal of Retailing,* Vol. 51, No. 3 (Fall 1975), pp. 13–78.

Lawton, Leigh, and A. Parasuraman, "The Impact of the Marketing Concept on New Product Planning," *Journal of Marketing,* Vol. 44, No. 1 (Winter 1980), pp. 19–25.

Midgley, David F., "Toward a Theory of the Product Life Cycle: Explaining Diversity," *Journal of Marketing,* Vol. 45, No. 4 (Fall 1981), pp. 109–115.

Monroe, Kent B., and Albert J. Della Bitta, "Models for Pricing Decisions," *Journal of Marketing Research,* Vol. XV (August 1978), pp. 413–428.

MOORE, TIMOTHY E., "Subliminal Advertising: What You See Is What You Get," *Journal of Marketing*, Vol. 46, No. 2 (Spring 1982), pp. 38–47.

NAGLE, THOMAS, "Pricing as Creative Marketing," *Business Horizons*, July–August 1983, pp. 14–19.

NARASIMHAN, CHAKRAVARTHI, and SUBRATA K. SEN, "New Product Models for Test Market Data," *Journal of Marketing*, Vol. 47, No. 1 (Winter 1983), pp. 11–24.

OXENFELDT, ALFRED R., "A Decision-Making Structure for Price Decisions," *Journal of Marketing*, Vol. 37 (January 1973), pp. 48–53.

RAO, ASHOK, "Quantity Discounts in Today's Markets," *Journal of Marketing*, Vol. 44 (Fall 1980), pp. 44–51.

ROEDDER, DEBORAH L., BRIAN STERNTHAL, and BOBBY J. CALDER, "Attitude-Behavior Consistency in Children's Responses to Television Advertising," *Journal of Marketing Research*, Vol. XX (November 1983), pp. 337–349.

ROTHSCHILD, MICHAEL L., and WILLIAM C. GAIDIS, "Behavioral Learning Theory: Its Relevance to Marketing and Promotions," *Journal of Marketing*, Vol. 45, No. 2 (Spring 1981), pp. 70–78.

SANDS, SAUL, and ROBERT J. POSCH, Jr., "A Checklist of Questions for Firms Considering a Vertical Territorial Distribution Plan," *Journal of Marketing*, Vol. 46, No. 3 (Summer 1982), pp. 38–43.

SCHUL, PATRICK L., WILLIAM M. PRIDE, and TAYLOR L. LITTLE, "The Impact of Channel Leadership Behavior on Intrachannel Conflict," *Journal of Marketing*, Vol. 47, No. 3 (Summer 1983), pp. 21–34.

SHAPIRO, BENSON P., "Making Money Thru Marketing," *Harvard Business Review*, (July-August 1979), pp. 135–142.

SHAPIRO, BENSON P., and BARBARA B. JACKSON, "Industrial Pricing to Meet Customer Needs," *Harvard Business Review*, November–December 1978, pp. 119–127.

SOLDOW, GARY F., and GLORIA PENN THOMAS, "Relational Communication: Form Versus Content in the Sales Interaction," *Journal of Marketing*, Vol. 48, No. 1 (Winter 1984), pp. 84–93.

SRIVASTAVA, RAJENDRA K., ROBERT P. LEONE, and ALLAN D. SHOCKER, "Market Structure Analysis: Hierarchical Clustering of Products Based on Substitution-in-use," *Journal of Marketing*, Vol. 45, No. 3 (Summer 1981), pp. 38–48.

STERN, LOUIS W., and TORGER REVE, "Distribution Channels as Political Economies: A Framework for Comparative Analysis," *Journal of Marketing*, Vol. 44, No. 3 (Summer 1980), pp. 52–64.

SWAN, JOHN E., and DAVID R. RINK, "Fitting Market Strategy to Varying Product Life Cycles," *Business Horizons*, January–February 1982, pp. 72–76.

SWAN, JOHN E., DAVID R. RINK, G. E. KISER, and WARREN S. MARTIN, "Industrial Buyer Image of the Saleswoman," *Journal of Marketing*, Vol. 48, No. 1 (Winter 1984), pp. 110–116.

TELLIS, GERALD J., and C. MERLE CRAWFORD, "An Evolutionary Approach to Product Growth Theory," *Journal of Marketing*, Vol. 45, No. 4 (Fall 1981), pp. 125–132.

THORELLI, HANS B., and STEPHEN C. BURNETT, "The Nature of Product

Life Cycles for Industrial Goods Businesses," *Journal of Marketing,* Vol. 45, No. 4 (Fall 1981), pp. 97–108.

VANDEN BERGH, BRUCE G., and LEONARD N. REID,   "Puffery and Magazine Ad Readership," *Journal of Marketing,* Vol. 44, No. 2 (Spring 1980), pp. 78–81.

WESTBROOK, ROBERT A.,   "A Rating Scale for Measuring Product/Service Satisfaction," *Journal of Marketing,* Vol. 44, No. 4 (Fall 1980), pp. 68–72.

PART SIX—APPLYING THE STRATEGIC PROCESS

BONOMA, T. V.,   *Note on Marketing Implementation.* Cambridge, Mass.: Harvard Business School, 1982.

HOPKINS, D. S.,   *The Marketing Plan.* New York: Conference Board, 1981.

HULBERT, J. M., and N. E. TOY,   "A Strategic Framework for Marketing Control," *Journal of Marketing,* April 1977, pp. 12–20.

KOTLER, P.,   "Marketing Mix Decisions for New Products," *Journal of Marketing Research,* February 1964, pp. 43–49.

LINNEMAN, R. E.,   *Shirt-Sleeve Approach to Long-Range Planning for the Smaller, Growing Corporation.* Englewood Cliffs, N. J.: Prentice-Hall, 1980.

PETERS, T., and R. WATERMAN, Jr.,   *In Search of Excellence: Lessons from America's Best-Run Companies.* New York: Harper & Row, 1982.

SHETH, J. N., and G. L. FRAZIER,   "A Margin-Return Model for Strategic Planning," *Journal of Marketing,* Spring 1983, pp. 100–109.

Name Index

Subject Index

"Cash Cow" product category, 76–78, 85, 86, 397
Cash flow:
  assessment of, 47–48, 124–30
  as objective, 344–45
Challengers, market, 227–29
Chief executive officer (CEO), 20–22, 469–70, 474
  leadership role of, 30–31
  (*See also* Corporate decisions)
Chief marketing executive (CME), 117, 152, 154–59
Clayton Act (1914), 266
Communicability of innovation, 311
Compatibility of innovation, 311
Competition, 221–52
  analysis of competitive positions, 227–30
  cases, 238–52
  competitive strategies, 231–36
  defined, 222–23
  as determinant of price, 393–94
  evaluation of competitive relationships, 223–27
  expansion decision and, 45–46
  function manager and, 161
  growth stage products and, 325
  introduction stage products and, 307
  maturity stage products and, 346–47
  product strategy and, 372–73
Competitive-parity promotion budget approach, 427
Competitive strategy, generic, 278, 280
Complexity of innovation, 311
Concentration, 40–42
Concept development, 285
Conglomeration, 41–43
Consumer goods marketing channels, 447–48
Consumer Goods Pricing Act (1975), 266–67
Consumer markets, 189
Consumer needs, 307–8
Contingency planning, 130, 507, 515–16
Control, 505–17
  cases, 519–24
  concepts, 505–6
  corrective action, 510–16
  criteria for, 508–10
  monitoring system, 507–8
  performance information system, 508
  purpose of, 506–7
  standards for, 508–10
Corporate decisions, 30–70
  business area definition, 32, 34–37
  cases, 52–70
  development stage strategies and, 274, 279
  leadership role of chief executive officer, 30–31
  objectives, 32–34
  in overall strategic planning process, 20–22
  process of, 31–32
  resource allocation, 32, 38–39, 47–48

sequence of, 153, 154
strategic programs, 32, 37–46
Corrective action, 510–16
Cost leadership strategy, 231–32, 234
Cost levels, maturity stage products and, 346
Coupons, 313
Creativity, 379
Credit, 260
Current assessment, 7–8
  at corporate level, 33
  price decisions, 398
  at product/market unit level, 165, 167
  at strategic business unit level, 118–19
Current planning gap, 7
Customer functions, product/market unit definition and, 114, 115
Customer power, 224

Data processing, 458
Decision-to-purchase stage of buyer decision process, 420
Decline stage strategies, 357–62
  growth/share matrix and, 76, 77
  objectives, 358
  price decisions, 361, 396, 397
  situation analysis, 359
  strategic needs, 359–60
  strategic options, 360–62
Delphi probes, 205, 257
Demand:
  maturity stage products and, 346, 347
  as strategic variable, 259
Demographic segmentation, 194–96
Demonstrations, 312–13
Dependability, 309
Development, expansion with, 43
Development stage strategies, 273–303
  cases, 298–303
  decision making, 290–95
  development decisions, 283–85
  feasibility and, 379–80
  implementation of, 290–95
  nature and scope of new products, 274–75
  new product categories, 275
  organization of, 275–78
  predevelopment decisions, 278–83
  price decisions, 395, 396
  relationship between other strategies and, 274
  strategic options, 284, 286–90
Diagnosis, 72, 507, 515–16
Differential advantages, 3, 11, 12, 378–79
  development stage products and, 293
  expansion decision and, 46
  growth stage products and, 322
  introduction stage products and, 309–10
Differentiation strategy, 232–35
Discount prices, 395

Distribution, 445–65
  case, 462–65
  concepts, 446–47
  in decline stage, 361
  in growth stage, 327–28
  in introduction stage, 313–14
  marketing channels (*see* Marketing
    channels)
  in maturity stage, 346
  performance evaluation, 459–60
  physical, 446, 449, 450, 457–59
  significance of, 446–47
  strategic decisions, 456–59
Distributor needs, 309
Diversification, 37, 41–42, 46
Divestment, 123
  in decline stage, 358, 360, 361
  in maturity stage, 348
Divisibility of innovation, 311
"Dog" product category, 76, 77, 86, 397

Ecological concerns, 262
Economic determinants of price, 392
Economic Indicators, 202
Economies of scale:
  maturity stage products and, 346
  promotion effectiveness and, 430
Economy, 258–61
Efficiency, 161, 348
Engineering, development stage products
  and, 276, 278
Environmental variables:
  competition (*see* Competition)
  economy, 258–61
  government, 263–67
  market decisions (*see* Market decisions)
  social forces, 261–63
  technology (*see* Technology)
Evaluation-of-alternatives stage of buyer
  decision process, 420
Evolution stage strategies (*see* Development
  stage strategies)
Exclusive representation, 314
Expansion:
  decision factors in, 45–46
  implementation methods, 43–45
  strategic business unit decisions on, 120
  strategies for, 39–43
Expectations, 8
Experience, pooled, 83–87, 89, 90, 127
Experience curve, 72–73
Experience curve pricing, 397–98

Federal regulatory agencies, 264–66
Federal Reserve Bulletin, 202
Federal Trade Commission Act (1914),
  266
Feedback, 506
Final development, 285

Finance, development stage products and,
  276, 278
Financial objectives, 158
Flanker products, 305–6
Followers, market, 227, 229
Forecasting:
  macroeconomic changes, 258, 260–61
  sales (*see* Sales forecasting)
  technological changes, 257–58
Forward integration, 40
Function managers, 152, 159–62
Future assessment, 10–12
  at corporate level, 33–34
  price decisions and, 398–99
Future planning gap, 9–10, 12, 14

Generic competitive strategies, 278, 280
Generic development strategies, 280–81
Geographic segmentation, 194
Goals (*see* Objectives)
Goodwill, retention of, 359–60
Government, 263–67
Growth rate, 73
Growth/share matrix method, 72–78, 88, 125,
  127
Growth stage strategies, 318–29
  growth/share matrix and, 76, 77
  objectives, 318–19
  price decisions, 326, 396
  situation analysis, 319–21
  strategic needs, 322
  strategic options, 322–28

Harvesting, 123
  in decline stage, 360, 361
  in maturity stage, 348

Idea generation, 285
Idea screening, 285
Image of product, 353–55, 417–18
Implementation, 502–5
Incremental costs, 16, 19
Index of Industrial Production, 202
Inducements to buy, 308, 312, 350
Industrial buyers, 448–49
Industrial product-marketing channels, 448–49
Industry structure, 36
Information about product, 308
Innovation, 305, 378–80
  adoption rate and, 311
  degree of, 306–7
  (*See also* Development stage strategies)
Integration of strategic decisions, 22–23
Integration strategy, 39–40
  (*See also* Analytical methods; Corporate
    decisions; Marketing function decisions;
    Strategic business units)
Intensive distribution, 314

Intro

Introduction has several aspects which ~~has~~ are relevent to this stage the first is objectives. This ~~is what~~ ~~Market~~ ~~and is~~ Is this product a New innovation or

COMPOSITE OF THE
4-STAGE PLANNING MODEL

PRESENTED IN CHAPTER 1

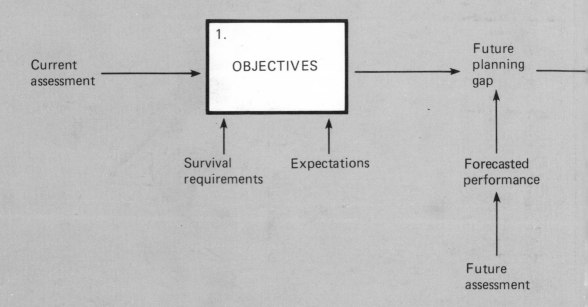